Supplements Designed to Aid Instructors and Students . . .

For Students

 Student website includes a rich variety of additional re... related to specific chapter content, web links that allow students to further explore global marketing issues and resources, ACE study questions for each chapter, and step-by-step guidance for completing a comprehensive Country Market Project Report.

 ***Wall Street Journal* subscription offer** available with this textbook. Students whose instructors have adopted *WSJ* with Gillespie/Jeannet/Hennessey will receive, shrink-wrapped with their book, a registration card for the 10-week print and online subscription to the *WSJ*. Students must fill out and return the registration card found in text to initiate the subscription privileges. The text package will also include a copy of the *Wall Street Journal Student Subscriber Handbook,* which explains how to use both print and online versions of the newspaper. The cost of the *WSJ* will be $13.50 in addition to the net cost of the core text. This is only sold as a package with new textbooks. *WSJ* subscriptions cannot be sold as a standalone item.

For Instructors

 Instructors Resource Manual with Test Bank contains suggestions on how to design a global marketing course, lecture outlines, student projects, answers to text questions, chapter outlines, and complete case teaching notes. The Test Bank portion includes true/false, multiple-choice, fill-in-the-blank, and essay questions, complete with answers.

 PowerPoint classroom presentation package (downloadable from web). This lecture tool includes over 25 slides per chapter combining clear, concise text and art to create a total presentation package.

 Instructor website provides Lecture Notes and PowerPoint slides, as well as additional classroom resources.

 Videos highlight global companies and correspond with the concepts and topics highlighted in the text. The video guide provides complete teaching notes to help prepare for each video and to provide in-class discussion ideas.

Appendix Cases

Web Site Highlights

Country Market Report

Suggested Readings

"Survival Tactics"

"Evolution of a Convenience Store Culture"

"Big Boy's Adventures in Thailand"

"Foreign Flavor"

"Looming Battle"

"Risky Returns"

"In India, Roads Become All the Rage"

"What GM's Daewoo Deal Says About Korea"

"Hard Profits"

"Turkish Conglomerate Prepares to Slim Down"

"What the Chinese Want"

"Mum's the Word: Mexico Isn't Free with
Information"

"As Brazil Booms"

"The Advantages of Marrying Local"

"Sainsbury Becomes Target"

"Mexico Goes Top-Flight"

"Increasingly, Rules of Global Economy Are Set
in Brussels"

"Harry Potter, Meet Ha-li Bo-te"

"Visions of Sugar Plums South of the Border"

"Motor Nation"

"From Trash to Treasure"

"Local Strategy Fizzles—Coke Hunts for Talent to
Re-establish Its Marketing Might"

"Can Esprit Be Hip Again?"

Hyperlinks

IMF (International Monetary Fund)

WTO (World Trade Organization)

NAFTA (North Atlantic Free Trade Association)

EU (European Union)

Export Promotion

Current Travel Warnings

U.S. Trade Sanctions and Embargoes

Public Citizen: Global Trade Watch

OPIC (Overseas Private Investment Corporation)

Government Tenders

Country Corruption Scores

Online Sources of Secondary Data

Safe Harbor

International Trade Fairs

U.S. Government

Japanese Government

Travel Information

Regional Groups

International Franchise Association

U.S. Federal Trade Commission

ISO (International Standards Organization)

ANSI (American National Standards Institute)

Anti-Counterfeiting

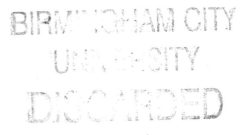

Global Marketing

AN INTERACTIVE APPROACH

Kate Gillespie
University of Texas at Austin

Jean-Pierre Jeannet
Babson College, Wellesley, Massachusetts
International Institute for Management Development (IMD)
Lausanne, Switzerland

H. David Hennessey
Babson College, Wellesley, Massachusetts
Ashridge Management College, Berkhamsted, United Kingdom

Houghton Mifflin Company   Boston   New York

Publisher: *Charles Hartford*
Editor in Chief: *George T. Hoffman*
Associate Sponsoring Editor: *Joanne Dauksewicz*
Senior Project Editor: *Kathryn Dinovo*
Senior Manufacturing Coordinator: *Marie Barnes*
Senior Marketing Manager: *Steven W. Mikels*

Cover photograph © by John Still/Photonica

Printed in the U.S.A.

Library of Congress Control Number: 2001131499

ISBN: 0-618-00508-0

123456789-VHP-07 06 05 04 03

Brief Contents

Contents

Part 3   *Developing Global Marketing Strategies 195*

8 *Global Marketing Strategies 196*

11 *Developing New Products for Global Markets 296*

Preface

Today, virtually every major firm must compete in a global marketplace. Buyers can comprise ordinary consumers or local businesses in international markets, multinational corporations, or foreign governments. Competitors can be local firms or global firms. Although some consumer needs and wants may be converging across national markets, and multilateral agreements seek to bring order to the international economic and legal environment, global marketers must still navigate among varied cultures where unexpected rules apply. Addressing this varied and increasingly competitive marketplace and developing strategies that are both efficient and effective are the tasks that face the global marketer.

Whether they oversee foreign markets or face international competitors at home, every undergraduate student who plans to enter marketing as a profession will need to understand and apply the essentials of global marketing. This text prepares them for that challenge.

▶ Why this New Book?

There are a number of global marketing texts on the market. Our approach differs from other books in several ways.

Targeting the Undergraduate Student. Other texts target both graduate and undergraduate students. By focusing on the undergraduate student we seek to better serve this segment. Our experience in teaching undergraduates has taught us a number of things. Students like clear writing that gets to the point. They want relevant real-life examples that bring to life theoretical concepts. They like pictures and appreciate humor. They enjoy discussing cases if the cases are rich but not too long. They appreciate pedagogical tools that help them learn efficiently. And they like to leave a marketing class with a set of hands-on skills and tools that look good to potential employers.

Current Coverage Across a Wide Variety of Topics. Our combined research and consulting experience allows us to speak with enthusiasm and conviction across the many areas covered by a global marketing text—such as global strategy, cross-cultural consumer behavior, and marketing organization as well as the effects government policy can have on international markets and global marketing. Our text combines recent academic research along with in-the-news corporate stories.

A Dual Focus: International Buyers and Global Competition. While most texts envisage global marketing as an understanding of international buyers, we envisage it as *competing* for those buyers. Immediately following our chapter on global markets we present the student with a chapter on global and local competitors. From then on we keep students focused on both buyers and competitors throughout the book.

A Global View Combined with a Strong Appreciation for Cultural Differences. Some global marketing texts downplay culture. Others make cultural differences their focus. Our approach is to recognize that cultural differences do exist and influence global marketing in a plethora of ways. To this end, we introduce the student early to cultural issues and ways of analyzing culture that are reinforced throughout the book. But we also present students with a global view of managing cultural differences that is both efficient and effective. For example, if you know you are going to sell a new product in 70 countries, why not take this into consideration when you first design the product? What is the best design that will allow for necessary adaptations with the least effort and cost?

Regional Balance. For a text to be a true guide to global marketing, it must present students with a regional balance. Most texts concentrate on the markets of the United States, Europe, and Japan. Some briefly discuss markets in Latin America or the Pacific Rim. Our book delivers a balance of developed and developing markets including insights into the often-overlooked markets of Africa and the Middle East. We also encourage students to think of competitors as hailing from all countries, including developing countries such as India, Korea, and Mexico.

Gender Representation. We have taken care to present examples of women as well as men in roles of global marketers. This is apparent in our end-of-chapter cases as well as the current vignettes in our *World Beat* insets.

An Interactive Approach. Because the field of global marketing changes so quickly, perhaps no subject is better suited to take advantage of Internet technology. Our website allows us to present updates to subjects without waiting years for another edition of the book. Students and instructors have access to current events as they unfold. Additionally, the Internet now offers a variety of respected sites that allow students to do research and formulate preliminary marketing plans. Our goal is to familiarize each student with the tools that are available to the global marketer.

▶ *Content and Organization of the Book*

Chapter 1 presents an introduction to global marketing. In this chapter we describe the development of global marketing and the importance of global marketing to both firms and the managers of the future. We explore the need for a global mindset and set forth the structure of the book.

Part 1 is entitled "Understanding the Global Marketing Environment." In this early section we investigate the key ways that the macro environment can affect global marketers. While the concepts may be macro, we constantly show how they apply to a variety of firms trying to succeed in a vibrant international marketplace. In Chapter 2, "The Global Economy," we present the student with basic theories of trade, explain how exchange rates work, explore issues of protectionism and trade restrictions, and conclude with a discussion of economic integration as a means for encouraging international marketing. In Chapter 3, "Cultural and Social Forces," we explore the impact on marketing of factors such as religion, family structure, education, and attitudes toward time. We describe the Hofstede measures of culture and present ratings for nearly 70 countries—ratings that can be used time and again when analyzing cultural underpinnings of marketing dilemmas later in the book. The chapter continues with a discussion of issues relating to language and communication such as the difference between high- and low-context cultures and the social acceptability (or not) of showing emotion. We conclude with insights into overcoming the language barriers and dealing with culture shock. In Chapter 4, "Political and Regulatory Climate," we begin by asking the question, "what do governments want?" We then explore the varied ways that both host and home countries can impact global marketers. We then describe how legal systems and attitudes toward rules vary around the world. We conclude by explaining the difference to the global marketer between the task of forecasting and managing regulatory change and the task of managing political risk, and offer concrete ideas on how to do both.

Part 2 concentrates on "Analyzing Global Opportunities." Beginning with Chapter 5, "Global Buyer Behavior," we introduce students to global concerns and cross-cultural aspects of consumer, business, and government markets, including a discussion of bribery and international contracts. Chapter 6, "Global Competitors," introduces students to issues of global firm versus global firm as well as global firm versus local firm. In particular, we present ways in which one global firm can successfully engage another as well as ways in which a local firm can respond to an encroaching global firm—including going global itself. We then explore cultural attitudes toward competition that can help explain why government regulation of corporate behavior varies around the world and why firms from different countries can be expected to behave differently. We describe how home country actions can affect the global competitiveness of their firms. Besides discussing firms from the developed world—the United States, Europe and Japan—we devote a separate section to better understanding firms from the emerging markets of the developing world. We conclude by examining the country-of-origin advantage (or sometimes disadvantage) that affects global competition. In Chapter 7, "Global Marketing Research," we present issues of research design and organization in a global setting and discuss the collection of secondary and primary data across cultures.

Part 3, "Developing Global Marketing Strategies," examines the key decisions of determining where and how to compete and how to enter foreign markets. In Chapter 8, "Global Marketing Strategies," we look at traditional patterns of how firms internationalize as well as the more recent phenomenon of born-global firms that enter foreign markets from their inception. We identify the pros and cons of geographic market choices such as targeting developed versus developing economies and explore the concept of lead and must-win markets. We then provide a format for country selection. We conclude with a discussion of multidomestic versus global or regional marketing strategies. In Chapter 9, "Global Market Entry Strategies," we cover the varied options of how to enter (and sometimes leave) a foreign market, including production and ownership decisions, portal or e-business entry options, and when to consider exiting markets.

Part 4, "Designing Global Marketing Programs," covers the global management of the marketing mix and the cross-cultural challenges involved in decisions concerning products, pricing, channels, and promotion. Chapter 10, "Global Product and Service Strategies," explores necessary and desirable product (including packaging and warranty) adaptations for international markets. We discuss branding decisions, including issues of brand protection. We then present the particular cross-cultural challenges of services marketing and explain the importance of managing a global product line. In Chapter 11, "Developing New Products for Global Markets," we examine a new paradigm—designing a product with multiple national markets in mind. We also explore the decision to design (rather than adapt) a product for an important foreign market. We identify different sources for new products—whether developed in-house or outsourced—and conclude with an examination of global roll-outs for new products. In Chapter 12, "Pricing for International and Global Markets," we examine how cost and market factors as well as environmental factors such as exchange rate movements and inflation can affect pricing in international markets. We then explore managerial issues such as determining transfer prices, quoting prices in foreign currencies, dealing with parallel imports, and deciding when and how to participate in countertrade arrangements.

Part 4 continues with Chapter 13, "Managing Global Distribution Channels." This chapter reviews global channels and logistics and introduces the potential differences that exist among local channels, with special emphasis on accessing and managing these channels. Recent trends are examined including the globalization of retail chains and the growth of direct marketing worldwide, as well as the peculiar challenges of smuggling and the increasing presence of organized crime in the global movement of consumer goods. Chapter 14, "Global Promotion Strategies," begins by exploring global selling and cross-cultural differences in local selling and sales-force management. It continues with a discussion of international sports sponsorship and public relations, as well as cross-cultural differences in sales promotions and managing word-of-mouth. Part 4 concludes with Chapter 15, "Managing Global Advertising," which explores issues of global versus local advertising as well as global media strategies and agency selection.

Chapter 16, "Organizing for Global Marketing," in Part 5 identifies the elements that will determine the most appropriate organization for a firm's global marketing and outlines the characteristics of various organizational options. The chapter examines issues of control as well and discusses the particular problem of conflict between headquarters and national subsidiaries. We conclude with a discussion of global marketing as a career.

▶ *Pedagogical Advantages*

Our book has incorporated several features to help undergraduate students learn about global marketing.

Chapter-Opening Stories. Each chapter begins with a short recap of a recent experience of a firm that illustrates key issues that the chapter will discuss. This helps students grasp right away the real-life relevance and importance of issues presented in the chapter.

Chapter Outlines and Learning Objectives. At the beginning of each chapter we present both a chapter outline and a list of clear learning objectives to help focus students on the understanding they can expect to take away from the chapter.

"World Beat" Boxed Inserts. Numerous, timely examples from well-known companies in Europe, Asia, and the Americas help students to further explore international and global issues.

Internet Icons. Throughout the text we draw the student's attention to readings, exercises, or hyperlinks provided on our website that have particular relevance to the subject under discussion.

Pictures and Two-Color Text and Graphics. We believe that engaging the student visually enhances the learning experience.

Short but Evocative End-of-Chapter Cases. We believe cases can be short but conceptually dense. We have included two such cases at the end of each chapter. These cases were written or chosen to work with the chapter content. The end-of-case questions often refer specifically to chapter content in order to test a student's ability to apply the chapter to the case.

Review and Discussion Questions. Also at the end of each chapter, we provide review questions that test a student's knowledge of the chapter content as well as separate discussion questions that challenge a student's creativity to stretch beyond the chapter.

Longer Cases for More In-Depth Analysis. We are aware that some instructors like to augment shorter cases with several longer ones, either throughout the course or at the end of a course. For these instructors, we have provided several longer cases that have been selected with undergraduates in mind.

An Internet-Based International Marketing Plan. This exercise presents students with an opportunity to apply concepts from the chapters in the book as well as introduces them to Internet sites that are useful to global marketers.

▶ *Complete Teaching Package*

A variety of ancillary materials are designed to assist the instructor in the classroom.

Instructor's Resource Manual with Test Bank. An instructor's manual prepared by Kate Gillespie, Liesl Riddle, and Vivek Padmanaban provides lecture outlines for each chapter, answers to end-of-chapter review questions, ideas pertaining to the discussion questions, and teaching notes for both the end-of-chapter cases and the longer cases presented at the end of the book. Suggestions for course syllabi are also provided. A test bank provides multiple choice and true/false questions for each chapter.

Instructor Website. This password-protected site provides Lecture Notes and PowerPoint slides for downloading, as well as additional classroom resources.

HM Testing. This electronic, Windows version of the Test Bank allows instructors to generate and change tests easily on the computer. The program will print an answer key for each version of the text. A call-in test service is also available.

Videos The video package highlights global companies and corresponds with the concepts and topics highlighted in the text. The video guide provides complete teaching notes to help prepare for each video and to provide in-class discussion ideas.

PowerPoint. This classroom presentation package (downloadable from the web) includes about 25 slides per chapter combining clear, concise text and art to create a total presentation package. Instructors who have access to PowerPoint can edit slides to customize them for their presentations. Slides can also be printed as lecture notes for class distribution.

Call-in Test Service. This service lets instructors select items from the Test Bank and call our toll-free faculty services number (800-733-1717) to order printed tests.

The student package includes:

Student Website. This especially rich resource for students includes additional readings related to specific chapter content, web links that allow students to further explore global marketing issues and resources, ACE study questions, and step-by-step guidance for completing a comprehensive Country Market Project.

***Wall Street Journal* Subscription Offer** available with this textbook. Students whose instructors have adopted *WSJ* with Gillespie/Jeannet/Hennessey will receive, shrink-wrapped with their book, a registration card for the 10-week print and online subscription to the *WSJ*. Students must fill out and return the registration card found in the text to initiate the subscription privileges. The text package will also include a copy of the *Wall Street Journal Student Subscriber Handbook,* which explains how to use both print and online versions of the newspaper. The cost of the *WSJ* will be $13.50 in addition to the net cost of the core text. This is only sold as a package with new textbooks. *WSJ* subscriptions cannot be sold as a stand-alone item.

▶ *Acknowledgments*

We would like to extend our heartfelt thanks to the dedicated professionals at Houghton Mifflin. We are particularly grateful to Joanne Dauksewicz and Kathryn Dinovo. We are also indebted to Merrill Peterson and Michele Ostovar of Matrix Productions, and Terri Wright of Terri Wright Design and Image Research. We very much appreciate the contributions of case studies from Anna Andriasova, Juliet Burdet-Taylor, William Carner, Jaeseok Jeong, Kamran Kashani, Martha Lanning, Michael Magers, Sam Perkins, Liesl Riddle, K. B. Saji, and Valerie VinCola. We are also thankful to Liesl Riddle for testing a number of our cases in her international marketing classes at The George Washington University.

We are also especially grateful to the following reviewers for their insights and guidance:

David Andrus	Kansas State University (KS)
Gloria Christian	Butler County Community College (KS)
Glen Johns	Cedar Crest College (PA)
Marilyn Liebrenz-Himes	The George Washington University (DC)
Michell Marette	Northern Virginia Community College (VA)
Michael Weinstein	Brooklyn College (NY)
Tevfic Dalgic	University of Texas, Dallas (TX)
Maria McConnell	Lorain County Community College (OH)
Theodore Jula	Stonehill College (MA)
Fred Tennant	Webster University (AR)
Steven Lysonski	Marquette University (WI)
Darrell Goudge	University of Central Oklahoma (OK)
Paul Herbig	Tri State University (IN)
Walter H. Beck, Sr.	Reinhardt College (GA)
Mark Mitchell	University of Southern California (CA)

Global Marketing

1 Introduction to Global Marketing

The Scope of Global marketing includes many business activities. Boeing, the world's largest commercial airline manufacturer, engages in global marketing when it sells its aircraft to airlines across the world. Likewise, Ford Motor Company, which operates automobile manufacturing plants in many countries, engages in global marketing, even though a major part of Ford's output is sold in the country where it is manufactured. Large retail chains, such as Kmart and Wal-Mart, search for new products abroad to sell in the United States. In doing so they practice another form of global marketing.

A whole range of service industries are involved in global marketing. Major advertising agencies, banks, investment bankers, accounting firms, consulting companies, hotel chains, airlines, and even law firms now market their services worldwide. Leading orchestras from Vienna, Berlin, New York, and Philadelphia command as much as $150,000 per concert. Booking performances all over

Chapter Outline

the world, they compete with new global entrants from St. Petersburg and Moscow.

This first chapter is intended to introduce you to the field of global marketing. Initially, we concentrate on the scope of global marketing. We examine the differences among domestic, international, and global types of marketing and explain why companies often have difficulty marketing abroad. We then move to explain why mastering global marketing skills can be valuable to your future career. A conceptual outline of the book concludes the chapter.

Learning Objectives

After studying this chapter, you should be able to

▶ Describe the development of global marketing.

▶ Explain the importance of global marketing.

▶ Describe the organization of this book in terms of competencies and decision areas.

▶ *The Development of Global Marketing*

The term **global marketing** has been in use only since the early 1980s. Before that decade, international marketing and multinational marketing were the terms used most often to describe international marketing activities. Global marketing is not just a new label for an old phenomenon, however. In fact, global marketing is a subcategory of international marketing. Before we explain global marketing in detail, let us first look at the historical development of international marketing as a field in order to gain a better understanding of the phases through which it has passed (see Figure 1.1.)

Domestic Marketing

Marketing that is aimed at a single market, the firm's domestic market, is known as **domestic marketing**. In domestic marketing, the firm faces only one set of competitive, economic, and market issues. It essentially deals with only one set of national customers, although the company may serve several segments in this one market.

Export Marketing

Export marketing covers marketing activities that are involved when a firm sells its products outside its domestic base of operation and when products are physically shipped from one country to another. The major challenges of export marketing are the selection of appropriate markets or countries through marketing research, the determination of appropriate product modifications to meet the demand requirements of export markets, and the development of export channels through which the company can market its products abroad. In export marketing the firm may concentrate mostly on product modifica-

Figure 1.1 *International and Global Marketing*

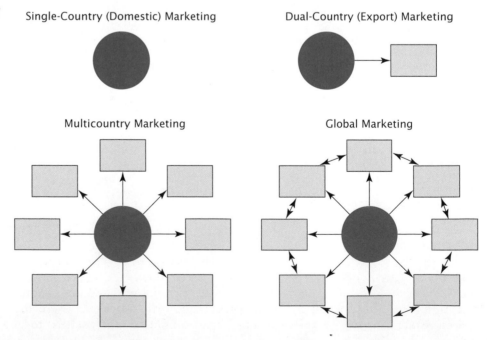

Single-Country (Domestic) Marketing

Dual-Country (Export) Marketing

Multicountry Marketing

Global Marketing

tions, running its export operations as a welcome and profitable by-product of its domestic strategy. Because the movement of goods across national borders is a major part of an exporting strategy, the skills required include knowledge of shipping and export documentation. Although export marketing probably represents the most traditional and least complicated form of nondomestic marketing, it remains an important feature for many firms.

International Marketing

A company that practices **international marketing** goes beyond exporting and becomes much more directly involved in the local marketing environment within a given country. The international firm is likely to have its own sales subsidiaries and will participate in and develop entire marketing strategies for foreign markets. At this point, the necessary adaptations to the firm's domestic marketing strategies become a main concern. Companies that are "going international" need to decide how to adjust an entire marketing strategy, including how they sell, advertise, and distribute products, in order to fit new market demands. Understanding different cultural, economic, and political environments becomes necessary for success for international markets. Typically, much of the field of international marketing has been devoted to making the environment understandable and helping managers navigate the differences.

Multinational Marketing

The focus on multinational marketing came as a result of the development of the **multinational corporation (MNC)**. These companies, characterized by extensive investments in assets abroad, operate in a number of foreign countries as though they were local companies. Multinationals traditionally pursue a **multidomestic strategy**, wherein the multinational firm competes by applying many different strategies, each one tailored to a particular local market. Often, multinational corporations attempt to appear "local" wherever they compete. The major challenge confronting the multinational marketer is to find the best possible adaptation of a complete marketing strategy to each individual country. This approach to international marketing leads to a maximum amount of localization and to a large variety of marketing strategies. Ironically, the traditional multidomestic strategies of multinational corporations failed to take advantage of the global reach of these firms. Lessons learned in one domestic market were often not applied elsewhere. Good ideas in product development or promotions were not always shared among national subsidiaries. Similarly, multinationals often failed to take advantage of their global size in negotiating with suppliers and distributors.

Pan-Regional Marketing

Given the diseconomies of scale that plague individualized marketing strategies, each tailored to a specific local environment, many companies have begun to emphasize strategies for larger regions. These regional strategies encompass a number of markets, such as pan-European strategies for Europe, and have come about as a result of regional economic and political integration. Such integration is also apparent in North America, where the United States, Canada, and Mexico have committed themselves to a

Headquartered on Lake Geneva, Swiss-based Nestlé is the world's largest foods company. Its products are sold in virtually every country.

far-reaching trade pact in the form of the North American Free Trade Agreement (NAFTA). Companies considering regional strategies seek synergies in marketing operations in one region with the aim of achieving increased efficiency. Many firms are presently working on such solutions, moving from many multidomestic strategies toward selected pan-regional strategies.

Global Marketing

Over the years, academics and international companies alike have become aware that opportunities for economies of scale and enhanced competitiveness are greater if firms can manage to integrate and create marketing strategies on a global scale. A **global marketing strategy** involves the creation of a single strategy for a product, service, or company for the entire global market. It encompasses many countries simultaneously and is aimed at leveraging the commonalities across many markets. Rather than tailoring a strategy perfectly to any individual market, a firm that pursues global marketing settles on a basic strategy that can be applied throughout the world market, all the while maintaining some flexibility to adapt to local market requirements where necessary. Such strategies are inspired by the fact that many markets appear increasingly similar in environmental and customer requirements. The management challenges are to design marketing strategies that work well across multiple markets, while remaining alert to the possible adaptations that may be advisable on a market-to-market basis.

Even though global marketers face the unique challenge of finding marketing strategies that fit many countries, the skills and concepts that have been critical since the earliest stages in the history of marketing remain important and continue to be needed. Firms that pursue global strategies must also be adept at international marketing because designing one global strategy requires a sound understanding of the cultural, economic, and political environment of many countries. Furthermore, few global marketing strategies can exist without some local tailoring, which is the hallmark of multinational marketing. Managing global marketing is the last in a series of skills that managers must acquire to be successful in the global marketplace.

▶ The Importance of Global Marketing

Global markets are expanding rapidly. The combined value of world exports (in the form of physical goods or merchandise) reached $6 trillion in 2001. For the period 1990–2000, world merchandise exports grew 4 percent or more in most years, exceeding world gross domestic product (GDP) growth. This indicates that the international aspect of the world economy has been growing more rapidly than the domestic segments, further contributing to the ever-increasing pace of globalization.[1]

Furthermore, international trade statistics do not reflect a substantial portion of international marketing operations. In particular, overseas sales of locally manufactured and locally sold products are not included in world trade figures. Consequently, the total volume of international marketing far exceeds the volume of total world trade. Sales of overseas subsidiaries for U.S. companies are estimated at three times the value of these companies' exports. Although no detailed statistics are available, this pattern suggests that the overall volume of international marketing amounts to a multiple of the world trade volume.

Why Companies Seek Global Markets

Companies become involved in international markets for a variety of reasons. Some firms simply respond to orders from abroad without making any organized efforts of their own. Most companies take a more active role. They often determine that it is to their advantage to pursue export business in order to realize increased sales and profits.

For some firms, the impetus to globalize results from a domestic competitive shock. General Electric Lighting (a division of GE) was the traditional market leader in the United States. Then Westinghouse, its largest U.S. competitor, sold its lighting division to Philips of the Netherlands. This introduced a strong foreign competitor into GE's own backyard. At the time, GE was not competing in Europe. To counter Philips's move into the U.S. market, GE Lighting bought Tungsram, a Hungarian lighting company. All this activity was followed by the acquisition of Thorn-EMI's lighting interest, a U.K.-based unit. In Asia, GE concluded a joint venture with Hitachi of Japan. This deal boosted GE's international sales from just 20 percent in 1988 to a projected 50 percent in 1996. In Europe alone, GE Lighting's share rose to 15 percent. In the space of just a few years, GE's lighting business changed from a predominantly domestic business into a global business.[2]

Some companies pursue growth in other countries when their domestic market has reached maturity. Coca-Cola, a market leader worldwide in the soft drink business, finds that on a per-capita basis, foreign consumers drink

Franchising is one of the many industries that derives a high proportion of its sales from overseas.

only a fraction of the cola that Americans drink. Coca Cola sees enormous growth potential in international markets, where it already sells 70 percent of its total volume outside North America. Some of Coke's largest growth rates in 2001 could be found in China, Africa, and the Middle East.[3]

Many firms launch their international marketing operations by following customers who move abroad. Major U.S. banks have opened branches in key financial centers around the world in order to serve their U.S. clients better. Similarly, advertising agencies in the United States have created networks to serve the interests of their multinational clients. When Japanese automobile manufacturers opened plants in the United States, many of their component suppliers followed and built operations nearby. Failing to accommodate these important clients could result in the loss not only of foreign sales but of domestic sales as well.

For some firms, however, the reason to become involved in global marketing has its roots in pure economics. Producers of television shows in Hollywood can spend $1.5 million to produce a single show for a typical series. United States networks pay only about $1 million to air a single show, and the series producers rely on international markets to cover the difference. Without the opportunity to market globally, they would not even be able to produce the shows for the U.S. market.

Why Study Global Marketing?

You have probably asked yourself why you should study global marketing. Each year U.S.-based international companies hire large numbers of marketing professionals. As these firms become increasingly globalized, competence in global marketing will become even more important in the future—and many marketing executives will be pursuing global marketing as a career. Other career opportunities exist with a large number of exporters, where job candidates will require international marketing skills. Furthermore, many university graduates are hired each year for the marketing efforts of foreign-based companies. These companies also seek international and global competence within their managerial ranks.

With the service sector becoming increasingly globalized, many graduates joining service industries find themselves confronted with international opportunities at early stages of their careers. Today, consulting engineers, bankers, brokers, public accountants, medical services executives, and e-commerce specialists all need global marketing skills to compete in a rapidly changing environment. Consequently, a solid understanding and appreciation of global marketing will benefit the careers of most business students, regardless of the field or industry they choose to enter.

A Need for Global Mindsets

The Swedish firm IKEA is today one of the world's largest furniture retailing chains. IKEA entered the important U.S. market in 1985. Sixteen years later, the company had grown the business to almost $500 million of sales in the United States and Canada, or about 14 percent share of market. Today the United States is IKEA's second largest market, accounting for 13 percent of corporate sales in 2001.[4] IKEA's success is largely attributable to a new concept that it introduced to the United States: setting up large stores where consumers could browse, buy, and take furniture home in disassembled form at the end of their visit.[5] IKEA is but one example of an international global competitor entering a previously "safe" market with new ideas, bringing global competition to the doorstep of strictly domestic companies.

Few firms can avoid the impact of global competition today. Foreign competition has made enormous inroads into the manufacture of apparel, textiles, shoes, electronic equipment, and steel. Although foreign competition for many consumer goods has been evident for years, inroads by foreign firms into the industrial and capital goods markets have been equally spectacular. Managing companies that compete with foreign firms requires a global mindset: an ability to judge the next move of foreign competitors by observing them abroad. Managers who possess this skill are better prepared to compete at home.

The need to become more competitive in a global economy will force many changes on the typical company. Firms will have to compete in global markets to defend their own domestic markets and to keep up with global competitors based in other countries. These firms will need an increasing cadre of managers who can adopt a global perspective. This requires not only a knowledge of other countries, economies, and cultures but also a clear understanding of how the global economy works. Managers with a global perspective will also have to integrate actions taken in one national market with actions in another national market. This means that global marketers will be required to use ideas and experiences from a number of other countries so that the best products can be marketed the most efficiently and effectively.

Assembling a trained cadre of professional global marketing executives is of particular concern to U.S.-based firms. The United States has typically lagged behind other countries in this area, simply because the U.S. market is so large that domestic problems tend to overshadow global marketing opportunities. As a result, most U.S. executives develop their careers largely in a domestic setting and have little direct exposure to foreign markets. Executives in foreign countries, in contrast, are more apt to have traveled abroad and tend to speak one or two foreign languages. Often their ability to understand global complexities is more developed than that of their U.S. counterparts. For this reason non-U.S. firms sometimes may have an edge in competing for global dominance.

Managers with a global perspective will need to deal with new strategies that were not part of the domestic or older international business scenes. These concepts, created and developed over the past 15 years, have been included in our text and will be presented on a chapter-by-chapter basis. As a result, the reader will come to appreciate that the term *global* is more than just a replacement for *international*. It is a combination of a new perspective on the world and a series of new strategic concepts that enhance the competitiveness of global marketing strategies. Mastering both this new outlook and these new concepts is vital for firms that aspire to be global players in their chosen industries or market segments.

▶ *Organization of This Book*

This text is structured around the basic requirements for making sound global marketing decisions. It takes into account the need to develop several types of competencies to analyze global marketing issues. The global marketer must be able to deal with decisions on various levels of complexity. We will discuss each of the dimensions of the global marketing task before we examine the outline for this text.

Competencies

To compete successfully in today's global marketplace, companies and their management must master certain areas. *Environmental competence* is needed to navigate the global economy. This area of expertise includes a knowledge of the dynamics of the world economy, of major national markets, and of political, social, and cultural environments. *Analytic competence* is necessary to pull together a vast array of information and data and to assemble relevant facts. *Strategic competence* helps executives focus on the strategic or long-term requirements of their firms, as opposed to short-term, opportunistic decisions. A global marketer must also possess *functional competence,* or a thorough background in all areas of marketing. Finally, *managerial competence* is the ability to implement programs and to organize effectively on a global scale.

Managers with domestic responsibility also need analytic, strategic, functional, and managerial competence. They may not need global competence. Consequently, we will concentrate on those areas that set global marketing executives apart from their domestic counterparts.

Decision Areas

Successful global marketing requires an ability to make decisions not typically faced by single-country firms. These decisions are related to environmental analysis, analysis of global opportunities, global marketing strategies, global marketing programs, and marketing management. Managers must continually assess foreign environments and perform *environmental analyses* relevant to their businesses. As a second step, managers must do *opportunity analyses* that tell them which products to pursue in which markets. Once opportunities have been identified, *global marketing strategies* are designed to direct the long-term efforts of the firm. The company will then design *global marketing programs* to determine the marketing mix. Finally, international marketing managers must *manage the global marketing effort,* a task that requires attention to organization and personnel.

Our five competence levels are closely related to the five major global marketing decision areas just described. Environmental competence is needed to perform an analysis of the global economic environment. Analytic competence is the basis for global opportunity analysis. Sound global marketing

Figure 1.2 *International Marketing Management*

COMPETENCE LEVEL   DECISION AREAS

COMPETENCE LEVEL	DECISION AREAS
Environmental Competence	**Understanding the Global Marketing Environment** CH 2 *The Global Economy* CH 3 *Cultural and Social Forces* CH 4 *Political and Regulatory Climate*
Analytic Competence	**Analyzing Global Opportunities** CH 5 *Global Buyer Behavior* CH 6 *Global Competitors* CH 7 *Global Marketing Research*
Strategic Competence	**Developing Global Marketing Strategies** CH 8 *Global Marketing Strategies* CH 9 *Global Market Entry Strategies*
Functional Competence	**Designing Global Marketing Programs** CH 10 *Developing Product Strategies* CH 11 *Developing Global Products* CH 12 *Pricing for Global Markets* CH 13 *Managing Global Channels* CH 14 *Global Promotion Strategies* CH 15 *Managing Global Advertising*
Managerial Competence	CH 16 *Organizing for Global Marketing*

strategies are based on strategic competence. To design global marketing programs requires functional competence. Finally, managerial competence is needed for managing a global marketing effort.

Chapter Organization

This text is organized around the flow of decisions, as depicted in Figure 1.2. The five decision areas are treated in several chapters that describe the respective competence levels most appropriate for each decision area.

Part 1, Chapters 2 through 4, is concerned with the global marketing environment. Special emphasis is placed on the economic, cultural, political, and legal environments that companies must navigate in order to be successful.

Part 2, Chapters 5 through 7, concentrates on global market opportunity analysis. Chapters in this section discuss global buyers, competitors, and the research methods that are necessary to apply in order to understand marketing opportunities globally.

Chapters 8 and 9, which make up Part 3, deal with strategic issues. Chapter 8 introduces elements of global marketing strategy. Chapter 9 describes the various modes of entry that companies employ when they decide to enter a foreign market.

Part 4, which comprises Chapters 10 through 15, aims at developing competence in designing global marketing programs consistent with a global strategy. The chapters in this section cover product strategies, product development, pricing, channel management, promotion, and advertising.

The text concludes with Part 5, which consists of Chapter 16. Here the emphasis is on building managerial competence in a global environment. Chapter 16 discusses how firms organize for effective global marketing and also explores career issues of concern to the global marketer.

At the end of each of Chapters 2 through 16, there are two short cases taken from real life. These cases will help you think concretely about global marketing and apply concepts from the chapter. At the end of the book, we have included several longer, capstone cases that will give you a chance to synthesize what you have learned across chapters.

▶ *Conclusions*

As a separate activity of business, global marketing is of great importance to nations, to individual companies, and to prospective managers. With markets and industries becoming increasingly globalized, most companies must become active participants in global marketing. The competitive positions of most companies, both abroad and in their domestic markets, rest on their ability to succeed in global markets. At the same time, the economies of entire countries depend on the global marketing skills of managers. The standard of living of many people will be governed by how well local industry performs in the global marketplace. These forces will place a premium on executive talent that is able to direct marketing operations from a global perspective. Clearly, many business professionals will need to understand the global dimension of the marketing function if they are to progress in their careers.

Although the need to develop a global competence may be clear, the circumstances that determine successful marketing practices for foreign markets are far less clear. The foreign marketing environment is characterized by a wide range of variables not typically encountered by domestic firms. This makes the job of global marketing extremely difficult. Despite the complexities involved, there are concepts and analytic tools that can help global marketers. By learning to use these concepts and tools, you can enhance your own global marketing competence. As a result, you will be able to contribute to the marketing operations of a wide range of firms, both domestic and foreign.

Review Questions

1. How and why does export marketing differ from international marketing?
2. How does global marketing differ from multinational marketing?
3. List the reasons why firms seek global markets.
4. Why do U.S.-based firms have a particular need for more marketers with global mindsets?

Questions for Discussion

1. How is global marketing as a field related to your future career? How would you expect to come into contact with global marketing activities?
2. What do you think are the essential skills of a successful "global marketer"?
3. Which important skills make up an effective "global mindset"?
4. List ten things that are important to you that you hope to be able to understand or accomplish after studying this book.

Notes

[1] *WTO Annual Report 2001* at www.wto.org.

[2] "Old World, New Investment," *Business Week*, October 7, 1996: 66–67.

[3] "Operations Review," *The Coca-Cola Company 2001 Annual Report*.

[4] "Facts and Figures" at www.ikea-usa.com.

[5] "Furnishing the World," *The Economist*, November 19, 1994: 79–80.

Part 1 *Understanding the Global Marketing Environment*

COMPETENCE LEVEL	DECISION AREAS
Environmental Competence	**Understanding the Global Marketing Environment** CH 2 *The Global Economy* CH 3 *Cultural and Social Forces* CH 4 *Political and Regulatory Climate*
Analytic Competence	**Analyzing Global Opportunities** CH 5 *Global Buyer Behavior* CH 6 *Global Competitors* CH 7 *Global Marketing Research*
Strategic Competence	**Developing Global Marketing Strategies** CH 8 *Global Marketing Strategies* CH 9 *Global Market Entry Strategies*
Functional Competence	**Designing Global Marketing Programs** CH 10 *Global Product and Service Strategies* CH 11 *Developing New Products for Global Markets* CH 12 *Pricing for International and Global Markets* CH 13 *Managing Global Distribution Channels* CH 14 *Global Promotion Strategies* CH 15 *Managing Global Advertising*
Managerial Competence	**Managing the Global Marketing Effort** CH 16 *Organizing for Global Marketing*

2 The Global Economy

When EuroDisney Opened outside Paris, French attendance at the theme park was disappointing. Some attributed low ticket sales to a cultural snub of this American icon. Others noted a particularly wet and cold season. Still others blamed the strength of the franc against the U.S. dollar. French consumers could buy—and spend—dollars at bargain prices. If the French wanted Disney, they could catch a plane to Florida's Disney World for not much more than they would pay for a weekend at EuroDisney.

The global economy constantly affects international marketing. Billions of dollars of goods and services are traded among nations each day. Currency exchange rates fluctuate, affecting sales and profits. Businesses establish operations and borrow funds in locations throughout the world. Banks lend and arbitrage currencies worldwide. When these transactions are interrupted or threatened, we can truly appreciate the scope and significance of the international economy.

This chapter introduces the important aspects of world trade and finance. We begin by explaining the concept of comparative advantage, the basis for international trade. Then we

Chapter Outline

explain the international system to monitor world trade, particularly the balance-of-payments measurement system. From this base, we describe the workings of the foreign exchange market and the causes of exchange rate movements. We discuss the international agencies that promote economic and monetary stability, as well as the strategies that countries use to protect their own economies. We conclude with a look at economic integration as a means of promoting trade.

Learning Objectives

After studying this chapter, you should be able to

▶ Distinguish among the basic theories of world trade: absolute advantage, comparative advantage, and competitive advantage.

▶ List and explain the principal parts of the balance-of-payments statement.

▶ Describe how and why exchange rates fluctuate.

▶ List and describe the major agencies that promote world trade, as well as those that promote economic and monetary stability.

▶ Describe common trade restrictions and explain their impact on international marketers.

▶ Compare the four different forms of economic integration.

▶ *International Trade: An Overview*

Few individuals in the world are totally self-sufficient. Why should they be? Restricting consumption to self-made goods lowers living standards by narrowing the range and reducing the quality of goods we consume. For this reason, few nations have economies independent from the rest of the world, and it would be difficult to find a national leader willing or able to impose such an economic hardship on a country.

International Dependence of Nations

Foreign goods are central to the living standards of all nations. But as Table 2.1 shows, countries vary widely in their reliance on foreign trade. Imports are less than 8 percent of the gross domestic product (GDP) of Japan, whereas Switzerland and Mexico have import-to-GDP ratios of 31 and 42 percent, respectively. Even in countries that seemingly do not have a great reliance on imports, such as the United States where imports are 15 percent of the GDP and exports are 9 percent, world trade in goods and services plays an important role. In addition, most of the U.S. Fortune 500 companies receive over 50 percent of their profits from overseas.

Peter Johnson, a student, is awakened in the morning by his Sony clock radio. After showering, he puts on an Italian-made jacket. At breakfast, he has a cup of Brazilian coffee, a bowl of cereal made from U.S.-grown wheat, and a Colombian banana. A quick glance at his Swiss watch shows him that he will have to hurry if he wants to be on time for his first class. He drives to campus in a Toyota, stopping on the way to fill the tank with gas refined from Saudi Arabian oil. Once in class, he rushes to take a seat with the other students, 30 percent of whom hold non-U.S. passports.

The figures given in Table 2.1 are useful for identifying the international dependence of nations, but they should be viewed as rough indicators only. In any widespread disruption of international trade, there is little doubt that the United States would be harmed much less than the Netherlands. Yet this is not to say a disruption of trade would not be harmful to both the United States and Japan, both of which have large domestic markets but depend heavily on world trade for growth.

So far, the focus has been on world trade for goods. Services also are an important and growing part of the world's economy and make up approximately 20 percent of the world's exports. Industries such as banking, telecommunications, insurance, construction, transportation, tourism, and consulting make up over half the national income of many rich economies. A country's **invisible exports** include services, transfers from workers abroad, and income earned on overseas investments. In volume, the top five countries in service exports are the United States, the United Kingdom, France, Germany, and Italy.

The Growth in World Trade

After its stock market crash of 1929, the United States turned its back on free trade. Fearing losses of jobs at home, this country tried to assist local industries by sharply increasing taxes on imports from other countries. Unfortunately, other countries retaliated with similar measures. In less than a year, world trade collapsed, sending the world into a global depression. Two hard-

Table 2.1 *Imports and Exports as a Percentage of GDP, 2000 Estimates (in billions of dollars)*

	GDP	IMPORTS	IMPORTS/GDP	EXPORTS	EXPORTS/GDP
Industrial Countries					
Australia	385.4	71.3	19%	63.9	17%
Canada	635.4	249.1	39	277.2	44
Japan	4620.0	379.5	8	479.3	10
Norway	157.1	33.8	22	58.1	37
Switzerland	263.2	82.5	31	80.5	31
United States	8241.4	1258.0	15	782.4	9
Developing Countries					
Brazil	781.5	58.6	7%	55.1	7%
China	1062.0	225.1	21	249.2	23
India	491.2	49.8	10	42.4	9
Mexico	431.2	182.6	42	66.4	39
Russia	434.7	44.2	10	105.2	24
Saudi Arabia	152.0	32.8	22	84.1	55
South Korea	465.6	160.5	34	172.6	37
India	382	59	16	44	12

Sources: Adapted from *WTO Report 2000*, the Economist Intelligence Unit (www.eiu.com), and the U.S. Embassy Riyadh, Key Economic Data.

The port of Singapore is a major entrepôt for products heading to and from Asia.

hit countries were Germany and Japan. Many believe that this severe economic downturn encouraged the militaristic regimes that precipitated World War II. After the war, the United States and other industrialized nations were eager for world trade to be promoted and to expand.

Their vision has certainly come to pass. World trade has increased over 16-fold since 1950, far outstripping the growth in world gross domestic product. This growth has been fueled by the continued opening of markets around the world. The Bretton Woods conference of world leaders in 1944 led to the establishment in 1950 of the General Agreement on Tariffs and Trade (GATT), which we will discuss in detail later. GATT, and subsequently the World Trade Organization (WTO), helped to reduce import tariffs from 40 percent in 1947 to an estimated 4 percent in 2000. The principle of free trade has led to the building of market interdependencies. As shown in Figure 2.1, international trade has grown much more rapidly than world GDP output, demonstrating that national economies are becoming much more closely linked and interdependent via their exports and imports. Foreign direct investment, another indication of global integration, increased over 100 percent in the 1990s.

▶ *The Basic Theories of World Trade: Absolute, Comparative, and Competitive Advantage*

Internationally traded goods and services are important to most countries, as shown in Table 2.1. Because jobs and standard of living seem to be so closely tied to these inflows and outflows, there is much debate about why a particular country finds its comparative advantages in certain goods and services and not in others.

The past 20 years have witnessed not only a dramatic rise in the volume of trade but also numerous changes in its patterns. Countries that once exported

Figure 2.1 *Growth of World Trade and GNP (1950 = 100)*

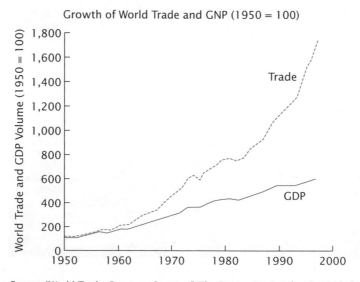

Source: "World Trade: Runaway Success," *The Economist*, October 3, 1998, Survey p. 4. © 1998 The Economist Newspaper Group, Inc. Reprinted with permission, further reproduction prohibited. www.economist.com

vast amounts of steel, such as the United States, are now net importers of the metal. Other nations, such as Japan, once known for producing inexpensive, handmade trinkets, now compete globally in high-tech products. What caused these changes in trade patterns? Why do countries that are able to produce virtually any product choose to specialize in certain goods? Where do international cost advantages originate? As the twenty-first century continues, will we still think of Indonesia and China as having the greatest advantage in handmade goods, or will they come to be like Japan and Taiwan are today?

The early work of Adam Smith provides the foundation for understanding trade today. Smith saw trade as a way to promote efficiency because it fostered competition, led to specialization, and resulted in economies of scale. Specialization supports the concept of absolute advantage—that is, sell to other countries the goods that utilize your special skills and resources, and buy the rest from those who have some other advantage. This theory of selling what you are best at producing is known as **absolute advantage**. But what if you have no advantages? Will all your manufacturers be driven out of business? David Ricardo, in his 1817 work *Principles of Political Economy*, offered his theory of **comparative advantage.** This theory maintains that it is still possible to produce profitably what one is best at producing, even if someone else is better. The following sections further develop the concepts of absolute and comparative advantage, the economic basis of free trade and hence of all global trade.

Absolute Advantage

Although many variables may be listed as the primary determinants of international trade, productivity differences rank high on the list. Take, for example, two countries—Vietnam and Germany. Suppose the average Vietnamese worker can produce either 400 machines or 1,600 tons of tomatoes in one year. Over the same time period, the average German worker can produce either 500 machines or 500 tons of tomatoes. (See example 1 in Table 2.2.) In this case, German workers can produce more machinery, *absolutely*, than Vietnamese workers can, whereas Vietnamese workers can produce more tomatoes, *absolutely*, than can their German counterparts.

Given these figures, Vietnam is the obvious low-cost producer of tomatoes and should export them to Germany. Similarly, Germany is the low-cost producer of machines and should export them to Vietnam.

Comparative Advantage

We should not conclude from the previous example that absolute differences in production capabilities are necessary for trade to occur. Consider the same two countries—Vietnam and Germany. Now assume that the average Vietnamese worker can produce either 200 machines or 800 tons of tomatoes each year, whereas the average German worker can produce either 500 machines or 1,000 tons of tomatoes (see example 2 in Table 2.2). Germany has an absolute advantage in both goods, and it appears that Vietnam will benefit from trade because it can buy from Germany cheaper goods than Vietnam can make for itself. Even here, however, the basis for mutually advantageous trade is present. The reason lies in the concept of comparative advantage.

Comparative advantage measures a product's cost of production not in monetary terms but in terms of the forgone opportunity to produce something else. It focuses on tradeoffs. To illustrate, the production of machines means that re-

Table 2.2 *Absolute versus Comparative Advantage: Worker Productivity Examples*

	VIETNAM	GERMANY
Example 1		
Yearly output per worker		
Machinery	400	500
Tomatoes	1,600 tons	500 tons
Absolute advantage	Tomatoes	Machinery
Example 2		
Yearly output per worker		
Machinery	200	500
Tomatoes	800 tons	1,000 tons
Opportunity costs of production	1 machine costs 4 tons tomatoes *or* 1 ton tomatoes costs 0.25 machine	1 machine costs 2 tons tomatoes *or* 1 ton tomatoes costs 0.50 machine
Absolute advantage	None	Tomatoes Machinery
Comparative advantage	Tomatoes	Machinery

sources cannot be devoted to the production of tomatoes. In Germany, the worker who produces 500 machines will not be able to grow 1,000 tons of tomatoes. The cost can be stated as follows: Each ton of tomatoes costs 0.5 machine, or 1 machine costs 2 tons of tomatoes. In Vietnam, producing 200 machines forces the sacrifice of 800 tons of tomatoes. Alternatively, this means that 1 ton of tomatoes costs 0.25 machine, or 1 machine costs 4 tons of tomatoes.

From this example, we see that even though Vietnam has an absolute disadvantage in both commodities, it still has a comparative advantage in tomatoes. For Vietnam the cost of producing 1 ton of tomatoes is 0.25 machine, whereas for Germany the cost is 0.5 machine. Similarly, even though Germany has an absolute advantage in both products, it has a comparative cost advantage only in machines. It costs Germany only 2 tons of tomatoes to produce a single machine, whereas in Vietnam the cost is 4 tons of tomatoes.

The last step in examining the concept of comparative advantage is to choose a mutually advantageous trading ratio and show how it can benefit both countries. Any trading ratio between 1 machine = 2 tons of tomatoes (Germany's domestic trading ratio) and 1 machine = 4 tons of tomatoes (Vietnam's domestic trading ratio) will benefit both nations (see Table 2.3). Suppose we choose 1 machine = 3 tons of tomatoes. Because Germany will be exporting machinery, it gains by getting 3 tons of tomatoes rather than the 2 tons it would have produced domestically. Likewise, because Vietnam will be exporting tomatoes, it gains because one machine can be imported for the sacrifice of only 3 tons of tomatoes, rather than the 4 tons it would have to sacrifice if it made the machine in Vietnam.

Our discussion of comparative advantage illustrates that relative rather than absolute differences in productivity can form a determining basis for international trade. Although the concept of comparative advantage provides a

Table 2.3 *Mutually Advantageous Trading Ratios*

TOMATOES	MACHINES
Germany, 1 ton tomatoes = 0.50 machine	Vietnam, 1 machine = 4 tons tomatoes
Germany, 1 machine = 2 tons tomatoes	Vietnam, 1 ton tomatoes = 0.20 machine

powerful tool for explaining the rationale for mutually advantageous trade, it gives little insight into the source of the differences in relative productivity. Specifically, why does a country find its comparative advantage in one good or service rather than in another? Is it by chance that the United States is a net exporter of aircraft, machinery, and chemicals but a net importer of steel, textiles, and consumer electronic products? Or can we find some systematic explanations for this pattern?

The notion of comparative advantage requires that nations make intensive use of those factors they possess in abundance—in particular, land, labor, natural resources, and capital. Thus Hungary, with its low labor cost of US$1 per hour, will export labor-intensive goods such as unsophisticated chest freezers and table linen, whereas Sweden, with its high-quality iron ore deposits, will export high-grade steel.

Competitive Advantage

Michael Porter argues that even though the theory of comparative advantage has appeal, it is limited by its traditional focus on land, labor, natural resources, and capital. His study of ten trading nations that account for 50 percent of world exports and one hundred industries resulted in a new and expanded theory.[1] This theory postulates that whether a country will have a significant impact on the competitive advantage of an industry depends on the following factors:

1. The elements of production
2. The nature of domestic demand
3. The presence of appropriate suppliers or related industries
4. The conditions in the country that govern how companies are created, organized, and managed, as well as the nature of domestic rivalry

Porter argues that strong local competition often benefits a national industry in the global marketplace. Firms in a competitive environment are forced to produce quality products efficiently. Demanding consumers in the home market and pressing local needs can also stimulate firms to solve problems and develop proprietary knowledge before foreign competitors do.

A good example of a country that enjoys a competitive advantage in digital products is South Korea. South Koreans are among the most "wired" people on earth. More than half of Korea's households have broadband service, and more than 60 percent of Koreans own cell phones. Seventy percent of share trades in the Korean securities market are done online. Korean companies can use entire urban populations in their home market as test markets for their latest digital ideas. This in turn gives these Korean companies an advantage when they want to export new products or know-how abroad.[2]

▶ *Balance of Payments*

Newspapers, magazines, and nightly TV news programs are filled with stories related to aspects of international business. Often, media coverage centers on the implications of a nation's trade deficit or surplus or on the economic consequences of an undervalued or overvalued currency. What are trade deficits? What factors will cause a currency's international value to change? The first step in answering these questions is to gain a clear understanding of the contents and meaning of a nation's balance of payments.

The **balance of payments** is an accounting record of the transactions between the residents of one country and the residents of the rest of the world over a given period of time. Transactions in which domestic residents either purchase assets (goods and services) from abroad or reduce foreign liabilities are considered **outflows of funds,** because payments abroad must be made. Similarly, transactions in which domestic residents either sell assets to foreign residents or increase their liabilities to foreigners are **inflows of funds,** because payments from abroad are received.

Listed in Table 2.4 are the principal parts of the balance-of-payments statement: the current account, the capital account, and the official transactions account. There are three items under the **current account.** The **goods category** states the monetary values of a nation's international transactions in physical goods. The **services category** shows the values of a wide variety of transactions, such as transportation services, consulting, travel, passenger fares, fees, royalties, rent, and investment income. Finally, **unilateral transfers** include all transactions for which there is no quid pro quo. Private remittances, personal gifts, philanthropic donations, relief, and aid are included within this account. Unilateral transfers have less impact on the U.S. market but are important to markets elsewhere. For example, remittances from workers abroad have fueled demand for consumer products in many developing countries such as Egypt, Mexico, and the Philippines.

Table 2.4 *Balance of Payments*

	USES OF FUNDS	SOURCES OF FUNDS
Current Account		
1. Goods	Imports	Exports
2. Services	Imports	Exports
3. Unilateral transfers	Paid abroad	From abroad
Capital Account		
1. Short-term investment	Made abroad	From abroad
2. Long-term investments	Made abroad	From abroad
a. Portfolio investment		
b. Direct investment		
Official Transactions Account		
Official reserve changes	Gained	Lost

The **capital account** is divided into two parts on the basis of time. **Short-term transactions** refer to maturities less than or equal to one year, and **long-term transactions** refer to maturities longer than one year. Purchases of treasury bills, certificates of deposit, foreign exchange, and commercial paper are typical short-term investments. Long-term investments are separated further into portfolio investments and direct investments.

In general, the purchaser of a **portfolio investment** holds no management control over the foreign investment. Debt securities such as notes and bonds are included under this heading. **Direct investments** are long-term ownership interests, such as business capital outlays in foreign subsidiaries and branches. Stock purchases are included as well, but only if such ownership entails substantial control over the foreign company. Countries differ in the percentage of total outstanding stock an individual must hold in order for an investment to be considered a direct investment in the balance-of-payment statements. These values range from 10 percent to 25 percent.

Because it is recorded in double-entry bookkeeping form, the balance of payments as a whole must always have its inflows (sources of funds) equal its outflows (uses of funds). Therefore, the concept of a deficit or surplus refers only to selected parts of the entire statement. A deficit occurs when the particular outflows (uses of funds) exceed the particular inflows (sources of funds). A surplus occurs when the inflows considered exceed the corresponding outflows. In this sense, a nation's surplus or deficit is similar to that of individuals or businesses. If we spend more than we earn, we are in a deficit position. If we earn more than we spend, we are running a surplus.

The most widely used measure of a nation's international payments position is the statement of balance on current account. It shows whether a nation is living within or beyond its means. Because this statement includes unilateral transfers, deficits (in the absence of government intervention) must be financed by international borrowing or by selling foreign investments. Therefore, the measure is considered to be a reflection of a nation's financial claims on other countries.

▶ *Exchange Rates*

The purchase of a foreign good or service can be thought of as involving two sequential transactions: the purchase of the foreign currency, followed by the purchase of the foreign item itself. If the cost of buying either the foreign currency or the foreign item rises, the price to the importer increases. A ratio that measures the value of one currency in terms of another currency is called an **exchange rate.** An exchange rate makes it possible to compare domestic and foreign prices.

When a currency rises in value against another currency, it is said to **appreciate.** When it falls in value, it is said to **depreciate.** Therefore, a change in the value of the U.S. dollar exchange rate from 0.50 British pound to 0.65 British pound is an appreciation of the dollar and a depreciation of the pound. The dollar now buys more pounds, whereas a greater number of pounds must be spent to purchase 1 dollar.

The strength of a domestic currency against the currency of the country's trading partners can have a negative effect on exporters. Recreational

World Beat 2.1 *Ecuador Dollarizes*

The Andean nation of Ecuador was a mess. It had defaulted on its public debt, banks had collapsed, and a president had been overthrown. Real wages were declining and 56 percent of Ecuadorians earned less than $42 a month. Two years later, however, Ecuador's economy was on a rebound with a growth rate of 5.4 percent—the highest in Latin America.

Joyce de Ginatta, a grandmother of twelve, had pushed to have the local currency, the sucre, replaced by the U.S. dollar. Ms. de Ginatta had been an importer of toilets and sinks from American Standard but saw her products become too expensive as the dollar gained 300 percent against the sucre from 1991 to 1997. Tired of dealing with a national currency that was always losing value against the dollar, she sold her business and began her relentless media campaign to be done with the sucre once and for all. She arranged news conferences and held public forums.

But things kept getting worse for the sucre. It was battered by low prices for oil, a major export for Ecuador, as well as by shrimp disease that hit another key export. A financial crisis in Asia discouraged foreign investors from putting money in any developing country. By June 1999, the sucre was selling for 12,000 to the dollar. On January 9, 2000, newly elected President Mahuad shocked both Ecuadorians and the United States by announcing that the dollar would replace the sucre.

President Mahuad was ousted 2 weeks after taking office by a military-backed coup, but his successor continued with dollarization. On March 13, 2000, a fixed exchange rate was set (25,000 sucres to the dollar), and the government proceeded to remove 98 percent of the old national currency from circulation.

But was dollarization the cause of Ecuador's economic improvement? Part of the improvement could be attributed to a rise in oil prices. Oil export earnings jumped 63 percent in 2000. Also, 400,000 Ecuadorians working abroad helped the economy by sending home remittances. These remittances had become the country's second largest source of foreign exchange earnings. Analysts also warned that dollarization robbed Ecuador of any flexibility in monetary or foreign exchange policy that could help buffer the country from external shocks such as a decline in oil prices. Most important, a dollarized economy requires a constant source of dollars, and this means exports and fiscal responsibility.

Sources: Stephen Wisnefski, "One Year After, Jury Still Out on Ecuador Dollarization," *Dow Jones International News*, March 14, 2001; Marc Lifsher, "As Argentina Teeters, the Ecuadorean Success Story Looms," *Wall Street Journal*, November 29, 2001, p. A14; and "Mixed Blessings," *Economist.com*, posted January 24, 2002.

Equipment Inc., for example, sells outdoor clothing in Japan via catalogue and the Internet. The yen price of its $375 North Face mountaineering jacket went from 42,000 yen to 55,000 yen in less than a year simply because of a depreciation of the yen against the dollar.[3]

The Foreign Exchange Market

Foreign exchange transactions are handled on an over-the-counter market, largely by phone or e-mail. Private and commercial customers as well as banks, brokers, and central banks conduct millions of transactions on this worldwide market daily.

As Figure 2.2 shows, the foreign exchange market has a hierarchical structure. Private customers deal mainly with banks in the retail market, and banks stand ready either to buy or to sell foreign exchange as long as a free

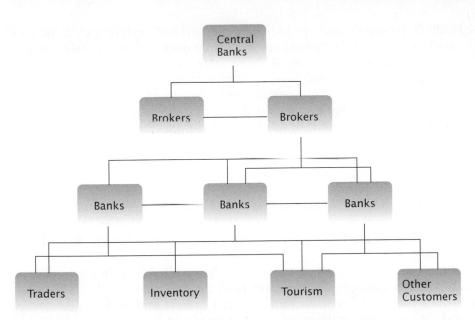

Figure 2.2 *Structure of the Foreign Exchange Market*

and active market for the currency exists. Banks that have foreign exchange departments trade with private commercial customers on the retail market, but they also deal with other banks (domestic or foreign) and brokers on the wholesale market. Generally, these wholesale transactions are for amounts of $US1 million dollars or more. Not all banks participate directly in the foreign exchange market. Smaller banks may handle customers' business through correspondent banks.

Central banks play a key role in the foreign exchange markets because they are the ultimate controllers of domestic money supplies. When they enter the market to influence the exchange rate directly, they deal mainly with brokers and large money market banks. Their trading is done not to make a profit but to attain some macroeconomic goal such as altering the exchange rate value, reducing inflation, or changing domestic interest rates. In general, even if central banks do not intervene in the foreign exchange markets, their actions influence exchange rate values because large increases in a nation's money supply increase its inflation rate and lower the international value of its currency.

Causes of Exchange Rate Movements

Exchange rates are among the most closely watched and politically sensitive economic variables. Regardless of which way the rates move, some groups are hurt and other groups are helped. When a currency's value rises, domestic businesses find it more difficult to compete internationally, and the domestic unemployment rate may rise. For example, the weakening yen against the dollar in 1998 caused Ford to realize less profit on every car it made in the United States and sold in Japan. In response, Ford considered expanding production in Japan. When the value of a currency falls, foreign goods become more expensive, the cost of living increases, and domestically produced goods become cheaper to foreign buyers. What are the causes of these exchange rate movements, and to what extent can governments influence them?

Most major currencies are **freely floating.** Their exchange rates are determined by the forces of supply and demand. Consumers in different countries can affect the supply and demand for these national currencies. An increase in a nation's GDP gives consumers in that country the wherewithal to purchase more goods and services. Because many of the newly purchased goods are likely to be foreign, increases in GDP will raise the demand for foreign products and therefore raise the demand for foreign currencies.

Similarly, a relatively high inflation rate can shift consumer demand and weaken a currency. If the U.S. inflation rate exceeds that of Japan, then U.S. goods will become progressively more expensive than Japanese goods. Consequently, U.S. consumers will begin to demand more Japanese goods, thereby increasing the supply of dollars to the foreign exchange market while increasing the demand for Japanese yen. For the same reason, Japanese consumers will reduce their demand for dollars (that is, reduce their supply of yen) as they purchase fewer U.S. goods. Therefore, inflation in the United States will cause the international value of the dollar to fall and the value of other currencies to rise.

Supply and demand for currencies are also affected by investors and speculators. If, for example, Japanese interest rates were greater than U.S. interest rates (adjusted for such things as risk, taxes, and maturity), then investors would have an incentive to sell dollars and purchase yen in order to place their funds where they earned the highest return—in Japan. Speculators buy and sell currencies in anticipation of changing future values. If there were a widespread expectation that the Japanese yen would rise in value relative to the dollar, speculators would try to purchase yen now (that is, sell dollars) in anticipation of that change.

Finally, governments affect foreign exchange markets in a variety of ways. Because governments exercise strong and direct controls over domestic money supplies, their activities affect inflation rates and interest rates, which, in turn, affect the exchange rates of their currencies. Perhaps the most pronounced impact governments have is as buyers and sellers in foreign exchange markets. Suppose the United States and Japan agreed to lower the dollar's value relative to the yen. For this to occur, dollars would have to be supplied—and yen demanded—in the foreign exchange markets. For the United States, this would mean putting upward pressure on the domestic money supply as newly created dollars were exchanged for circulating Japanese yen. For Japan, this type of intervention would mean putting downward pressure on its money supply as dollar reserves were used to take yen off the market.

Intuitively, citizens may be proud of a strong national currency. It can, however, present challenges to international marketers and particularly to firms that export products manufactured in their home country. In 2002 the U.S. dollar reached a 16-year high against most foreign currencies, pushing up the cost of American-made products in foreign markets. This forced U.S. manufacturers to find creative ways to compete overseas as well as to protect their own home market from foreign competitors that enjoyed a cost advantage. Automatic Feed Company of Ohio embarked on its most extensive product redesign in its 52-year history trying to offset the cost advantage of its foreign competitors. Angell Manufacturing Company established its first manufacturing operation outside the United States in order to supply less expensive car parts to clients in Germany. Other companies discovered that they needed to invest in more salespeople and market research in order to deliver better value to customers.[4]

READ MORE ABOUT IT:
Check out "Survival Tactics"
under *Supplemental Readings*
on our website.

Market Limitations

The foreign exchange market described here is not applicable to all currencies. Small, less developed countries often have currencies that attract little global demand. No effective international markets develop for these **soft currencies.** Also, until recently, most foreign exchange rates in developing countries were set by the government. This is still true in many countries today.

Nonetheless, these currencies are not immune to the forces of supply and demand. Governments cannot indefinitely prop up weakening currencies if there is little demand for them because of such factors as low levels of export earnings or low levels of inward bound foreign investment. An attempt to postpone the inevitable can lead to sudden large devaluations in developing countries instead of more gradual ones. By 2002, Venezuela was experiencing depressed export earnings because of continued low prices on oil, its major export. The Venezuelan bolivar plunged 19 percent against the U.S. dollar on February 13 when the Venezuelan government relinquished its six-year-old system to keep the bolivar steady with the dollar. Analysts projected that the bolivar could eventually lose 60 percent of its value before it reached market equilibrium.[5]

▶ *International Agencies for Promoting Economic and Monetary Stability*

Stability in the international economy is a prerequisite for worldwide peace and prosperity. It was for this reason that at the end of World War II, representatives from several countries met at Bretton Woods, New Hampshire, and formed both the International Monetary Fund and the World Bank (the International Bank for Reconstruction and Development). With headquarters in Washington, DC, these two agencies continue to play major roles on the international scene.

International Monetary Fund (IMF)

The core mission of the International Monetary Fund (IMF) is to help stabilize an increasingly global economy. The IMF's original goals were to promote orderly and stable foreign exchange markets, restore free convertibility among the currencies of member nations, reduce international impediments to trade, and provide assistance to countries that experienced temporary balance-of-payments deficits.

Over the years, the IMF has shifted its focus from exchange rate relations among industrialized countries to the prevention of economic instability in developing countries and countries from the former Eastern European bloc. The Mexican economic crisis in 1994 prompted an unprecedented bailout of $47 billion and launched the recent trend of providing rescue packages to major economies in the developing world. For example in 1998 and 1999, the IMF led a $17.2 billion rescue for Thailand, a $42 billion package for Indonesia, and a $41.5 billion deal for Brazil. South Korea got a whopping $58.4 billion when it was on the verge of bankruptcy.[6] In 2001, the IMF approved a $19 billion rescue package for Turkey. These rescue packages

The World Bank in Washington, DC is one of several institutions that support economic development and world trade.

Want to know more about the IMF? Check out the link on our website.

stabilize the respective economies and avoid total economic collapse of the countries involved.

To qualify for assistance, the Fund may require that countries take drastic economic steps, such as reducing tariff barriers, privatizing state-owned enterprises, curbing domestic inflation, and cutting government expenditures. Although many nations have resented such intervention, banks worldwide have used the IMF as a screening device for their private loans to many developing countries. If countries qualify for IMF loans, they are considered for private credit.

World Bank

The World Bank (International Bank for Reconstruction and Development) acts as an intermediary between the private capital markets and the developing nations. It makes long-term loans (usually 15 or 25 years) carrying rates that reflect prevailing market conditions. By virtue of its AAA credit rating, the bank is able to borrow private funds at relatively low market rates and pass the savings along to the developing nations. However, because it must borrow to obtain capital and is not funded by members' contributions, the World Bank must raise lending rates when its costs (that is, market interest rates) rise. Table 2.5 lists typical projects that the World Bank finances.

Table 2.5 *Selected World Bank Projects*

COUNTRY	PROJECT
Albania	Agricultural Services
Azerbaijan	Highway Project
Bangladesh	Legal and Judicial Capacity Building
Bulgaria	Child Welfare Reform
Cambodia	Flood Emergency Rehabilitation
China	Jianxi Highway Project
Colombia	Conservation in the Andes Region
Croatia	Court and Bankruptcy Administration
Ethiopia	Distance Learning Project
India	Powergrid System Development
Indonesia	Library Development
Kenya	Regional Trade Facilitation Project
Mexico	Methane Capture and Landfill Demonstration
Morocco	Information Infrastructure Sector Development
Nigeria	Privatization Technical Assistance Credit
Pakistan	On-Farm Water Management
Peru	Biodiversity Conservation
Poland	Krakow Energy Efficiency Project
Senegal	Long-Term Water Supply
Russia	Education Restructuring Support
Ukraine	Municipal Water and Wastewater
West Bank/Gaza	Education Action Project
Republic of Yemen	Rural Access Improvement

Source: World Bank Projects 2001 at www.worldbank.org.

When private funds were pouring into developing economies, some critics questioned the future role of the World Bank. However, a pan-Asian economic crisis caused the flow of private funds to developing countries to drop by more than $100 billion in 1998. The World Bank has expanded its role from mostly loans to partial guarantees of government bonds for investment projects. In Thailand, the World Bank partially guaranteed the Electricity Generating Authority of Thailand. The guarantee attracted investors and spawned interest in similar programs in South Korea and the Philippines. In addition, the bank is encouraging governments to improve financial supervision and reduce red tape.

Group of Seven

The world's leading industrial nations have established a Group of Seven, which meets regularly to discuss the world economy. Finance ministers and central bank governors from the United States, Japan, Germany, France, Britain, Italy, and Canada make up this group, which is often referred to as the G7. The members work together informally to help stabilize the world economy and reduce extreme disruptions. For example, the G7 met in June 1999 and developed proposals to reduce the debt of thirty-three impoverished nations, mostly in Africa, by 70 percent. When Russian President Boris Yeltsin joined the meeting for one day (when Russia joins the talks, the group calls itself the G8), the G8 agreed to rebuild the Balkans, including Serbia if it demonstrated a full commitment to economic and democratic reforms.

European Monetary System

In the early 1970s, a group of European countries established the European Joint Float agreement. The values of the currencies were fixed against one another in a narrow range of plus or minus 2.25 percent. This early system was later replaced by the European Monetary System (EMS), which included the fifteen members of the European Union (EU). The EMS included measures to force member countries to regulate their economies so that their currencies stayed within 2.25 percent of the central rates. For example, a country could be required to increase or lower interest rates to stay in line with the other currencies.

Beginning in January 1999, the new European Union single currency, the euro, replaced eleven national currencies in Europe. These countries used national currencies for notes and coins until 2002, when the euro replaced the national currencies for these applications as well. The European Central Bank (ECB) has complete control over the euro and is obliged to maintain price stability and avoid inflation or deflation. Supporters of the euro think it will reduce transaction costs and foreign exchange risk within Europe and provide a strong viable currency alternative to the dollar.

The change to the euro was not easy, however. One study showed that a vending machine in France that dispensed coffee for two French francs could not charge the equivalent in euros. The conversion rate turned out to be .3049. The coffee could be repriced at .30 euro, causing the vendor to lose 1.5 percent of gross revenue. Alternatively, the vending machine could be expensively reconfigured to dribble out slightly less coffee.[7]

▶ *Protectionism and Trade Restrictions*

It is a fact of life that like virtually all changes, free trade creates both beneficiaries and victims. By increasing competition, free trade lowers the price of imported goods and raises the overseas demand for efficiently produced domestic goods. In these newly stimulated export industries, sales will increase, profits will rise, and stock prices will climb. Clearly, consumers of the imported good and producers of the exported good benefit from these new conditions. However, it is equally clear that other groups are harmed. Domestic producers of the import-competing goods are one of the most visible of such groups. They experience noticeable declines in market share, falling profits, and deteriorating stock prices.

Herein lies the major reason for protectionist legislation. The victims of free trade are highly visible and their losses quantifiable. Governments use protectionism as a means of lessening the harm done to these easily identified groups. Conversely, the individuals who are helped by free trade tend to be dispersed throughout the nation rather than concentrated in a specific region.

Protectionist legislation tends to take the form of tariffs, quotas, or qualitative trade restrictions. This section describes these barriers and their economic effects.

Tariffs

Tariffs are taxes on goods moving across an economic or political boundary. They can be imposed on imports, exports, or goods in transit through a country on their way to some other destination. In the United States, **export tariffs** are constitutionally prohibited, but in other parts of the world they are quite common. Of course, the most common type of tariff is the **import tariff**, and it is on this tariff that we focus our attention.

Import tariffs have a dual economic effect. First, they tend to raise the price of imported goods and thereby protect domestic industries from foreign competition. Second, they generate tax revenues for the governments imposing them. Regardless of what the goals are, tariffs may not be the most direct or effective means of attaining them. For example, foreign sellers may lower their prices to offset any tariff increase. The net effect is for the consumer-paid price to differ only slightly, if at all, from the price before the tariff was imposed. Consequently, the nation has greater tariff revenues but little additional protection for the domestic producers.

When tariffs do raise the price of an imported good, consumers are put at a disadvantage, whereas the import-competing industries are helped. However, tariffs can have wider implications. The U.S. Department of Commerce revoked its high duty on advanced flat screens used on laptop computers. Although the duty helped some small U.S. screen manufacturers, it hurt computer companies such as Apple, Compaq, and IBM. These companies argued that the high duty inflated the cost of their products, undermined their ability to compete abroad, and would force them to shift production to other countries.

Quotas

Quotas are physical limits on the *amount* of goods that can be imported into a country. Unlike tariffs, which restrict trade by directly increasing prices, quotas increase prices by directly restricting trade. Naturally, to have such an effect, imports must be restricted to levels below the free-trade level.

For domestic producers, quotas are a much surer means of protection. Once the limit has been reached, imports cease to enter the domestic market, regardless of whether foreign exporters lower their prices. Consumers have the most to lose with the imposition of quotas. Not only are their product choices limited and the prices increased, but the goods that foreign exporters choose to ship often carry the highest profit margins. Restrictions on imported automobiles, for instance, result in the import of more luxury models with high-cost accessories. Because foreign producers are restricted in the number of cars they can sell, they seek the highest margin per car.

Orderly Marketing Arrangements and Voluntary Export Restrictions

An **orderly marketing arrangement** or **voluntary export restriction** is an agreement between countries to share markets by limiting foreign export sales. Usually, these arrangements have a set duration and provide for some annual increase in foreign sales to the domestic market. The euphemistic terms are intended to give the impression of fairness. After all, who can be against anything that is orderly or voluntary?

Scratch the surface of these so-called negotiated settlements, however, and a different image appears. First, the negotiations are initiated by the importing country with the implicit threat that unless concessions are made, stronger unilateral sanctions will be imposed. They are really neither orderly nor voluntary. They are quotas in the guise of negotiated agreements. The U.S. Commerce Department reached an agreement whereby Russia would voluntarily limit its steel imports into the United States to 750,000 tons per year, compared to 3,500,000 tons in 1998. If Russia had not agreed to the limits, the Commerce Department was prepared to announce duties of 71 to 218 percent on Russian steel.[8]

The Omnibus Trade and Competitiveness Act of 1988 gave presidents of the United States the right to negotiate orderly marketing arrangements and set countervailing duties to deal with the problems of trade deficits, protected markets, and dumping. The use of these voluntary export restraints (VERs) has spread to textiles, clothing, steel, cars, shoes, machinery, and consumer electronics. There are approximately three hundred VERs worldwide, most protecting the United States and Europe. Over fifty agreements affect exports from Japan, and another thirty-five affect South Korea.

A study conducted by the Institute for International Economics in Washington revealed that import restrictions, tariffs, and voluntary restraints in Europe cost the European consumer dearly. For example, banana import restrictions cost European consumers $2.0 billion, or 55 cents per kilo; beef tariffs, local subsidies, and bans on hormone-treated beef cost consumers $14.6 billion, or $1.60 per kilo. The total costs of protection in Europe on fruits, cars, steel, textiles, video recorders, beef, milk, cheese, telecoms, airlines, and more is estimated to be $43 billion. Research by the Institute for International Economics suggests that these restrictions save approximately 200,000 jobs in Europe at a cost of $215,000 per job saved, or enough to buy each lucky worker a new Rolls Royce each year![9]

Formal and Administrative Nontariff Trade Barriers

The final category of trade restrictions is perhaps the most problematic and certainly the least quantifiable. **Nontariff barriers** include a wide range of charges, requirements, and restrictions such as surcharges at border crossings, licensing regulations, performance requirements, government subsidies, health and safety regulations, packaging and labeling regulations, and size and weight requirements. Not all of these barriers are discriminatory and protectionist. Restrictions dealing with public health and safety are certainly legitimate, but the line between social well-being and protection is a fine one.

At what point do consular fees, import restrictions, packaging regulations, performance requirements, licensing rules, and government procurement procedures discriminate against foreign producers? Is a French tax on automobile horsepower targeted against powerful U.S. cars, or is it simply a tax on inefficiency and pollution? Are U.S. automobile safety standards unfair to German, Japanese, and other foreign car manufacturers? Does a French ban on advertising bourbon and Scotch (but not cognac) serve the public's best interest?

Sometimes, nontariff barriers can have considerable impact on foreign competition. For decades, West German authorities forbade the sale of beer in Germany unless it was brewed from barley malt, hops, yeast, and water. If any other additives were used—a common practice elsewhere—German authorities denied foreign brewers the right to label their products as beer. The law was eventually struck down by the European Court of Justice.

General Agreement on Tariffs and Trade (GATT)

Because of the harmful effects of protectionism, which were most painfully felt during the Great Depression of the 1930s, twenty-three nations banded together in 1947 to form the General Agreement on Tariffs and Trade (GATT). Over its life, GATT has been a major forum for the liberalization and promotion of nondiscriminatory international trade between participating nations.

The principles of a world economy embodied in the articles of GATT are reciprocity, nondiscrimination, and transparency. The idea of **reciprocity** is simple. If one country lowers its tariffs against another's exports, then it should expect the other country to do the same. **Nondiscrimination** means that one country should not give one member or group of members preferential treatment over other members of the group. This principle is embodied in the **most favored nation (MFN) status.** MFN does not mean that one country is *most* favored, but rather that it receives no less favorable treatment than any other. **Transparency** refers to the GATT policy that nations make any trade restrictions overt, such as replacing nontariff barriers with tariffs. Through these principles, trade restrictions have been effectively reduced.

Although its most notable gains have been in considerably reducing tariff and quota barriers on many goods, GATT has also helped to simplify and homogenize trade documentation procedures, discourage government subsidies, and curtail dumping (that is, selling abroad at a cost lower than the cost of production).

The Uruguay Round of GATT talks, which lasted seven years, was finally completed in late 1993. This agreement covered several controversial areas, such as patents and national protection of agriculture and the textile and clothing industry.

World Trade Organization (WTO)

The final act of GATT was to replace itself with the World Trade Organization in 1996. The WTO continues to pursue reductions in tariffs on manufactured goods as well as liberalization of trade in agriculture and services. With 144 member countries in 2002 and with 31 more having observer status, the WTO will be the global watchdog for free trade. Even China became part of the WTO in 2001 after 14 years of negotiations concerning its vast semiplanned economy, with its formidable array of import quotas, trade licenses, and import inspections. But entry into the WTO has its price. In 2002, Russia was ambivalent about joining the WTO. The government wanted to keep high tariffs to protect its domestic car and aircraft manufacturers from foreign competition. Many Russian business leaders strongly opposed swift entry because they believed that the inflow of cheap imports would destroy the country's manufacturing base.[10]

The major advantage that the WTO offers over GATT involves the resolution of disputes. Under GATT, any member could veto the outcome of a panel ruling on a dispute. WTO panels are stricter. They must report their decisions in nine months and can be overturned only by consensus. Countries that break the rules must pay compensation, mend their ways, or face trade sanctions.

The use of quotas and voluntary export restrictions is declining with the strengthening of the WTO and with increased compliance by its member countries. In its first 3 years, the WTO dealt with 132 complaints. The WTO has not been used by the big countries solely to control the smaller ones, as some feared. Costa Rica, for example, asked the WTO to rule against American barriers to its export of men's underwear. It won the case, and the United States was forced to change its import rules.

Increasingly, the WTO may become an arena wherein one country can challenge the values of another. In 2002, the United States was strongly considering filing a suit against the European Union for blocking the import of U.S. bioengineered seeds. United States corn growers alone were losing over $200 million a year as a result of the EU action. The Europeans, however, were standing firm, refusing to allow imports of what many consumers in Europe considered "Frankenstein food."[11] Similarly, a forum in China convened to discuss the trade issues involving its culture industry, including the effect that WTO policies could have on cultural exchange and censorship in China. Taiwan, for example, has a strong modern dance culture that is accepting of nudity on stage. Mainland Chinese authorities consider this pornographic. Did joining the WTO mean that China could no longer ban performing arts that it considered offensive?[12]

The WTO's current concerns focus on four challenges. First, the WTO continues to push for liberalization of trade, especially in the areas of agriculture and services. Information technology is another item on the liberalization agenda for the WTO, because the United States wants reduced tariffs on computers, semiconductors, and software.

A second challenge facing the WTO comprises the "new issues" of trade policy on foreign investment, competition policy, and labor standards. Although most countries want foreign investment, developing countries such as India, Malaysia, and Tanzania still want to set the terms of entry for foreigners. The United States and Europe insist on some core labor standards, such as trade union freedom and a ban on child labor. Many countries are in favor of labor standards, but the developing countries argue that low labor costs are the basis of most of their exports.

The third issue facing the WTO is the spread of regional trading agreements. The WTO acknowledges eighty regional agreements. Given the seven years it took to resolve many of the issues in the Uruguay Round of trade talks, many governments seem to be favoring regional agreements to establish some collective trade power. These regional groups tend to favor regional trade over global trade, so the WTO will need to address potential conflicts between regional and global needs.[13]

The final issue facing the WTO is how to handle an increasingly global and organized opposition to its agenda. Some parties believe that the WTO favors developed countries seeking to sell to developing countries and not vice versa. The United States, Japan, and Europe continue to maintain some of their highest tariffs on foodstuffs, textiles, and clothing, all major exports from the developing world. For example, Swaziland and the Sudan face 174 percent tariffs on their peanut exports to the United States. Developing countries also claim that food safety standards imposed by developed countries are often discriminatory. Thailand has sued Australia for requiring chicken parts to be precooked at such a high temperature that it renders the product inedible. Agricultural subsidies in the developed world also undermine the ability of developed countries to compete in the global marketplace. The European

Demonstrations against the
WTO turned violent in Seattle.

Union alone spent $300 billion in 2000 on agricultural subsidies that allowed
European agricultural exports to be sold abroad below production costs.[14]

In December 1999, groups representing organized labor, human rights,
and environmental interests confronted the WTO in what has come to be
known as the Battle of Seattle. The WTO had convened in the American city
for a new round of negotiations to reduce trade barriers. Thirty thousand
protesters from around the world, angered by what they believed was a failure of the WTO to properly address their concerns, blocked traffic and in a
few cases engaged in vandalism and violence. The police responded with tear
gas and rubber bullets. The 2001 meeting of the WTO was subsequently
scheduled in the Arab Gulf state of Qatar, described by a U.S. State Department report as a country that "severely limits freedom of assembly and prohibits workers from organizing unions."[15]

**Want to know more about the
WTO? Check out the WTO link
on our website.**

▶ *Economic Integration as a Means of Promoting Trade*

For years, public policymakers, economists, and academics have argued over
the linkage between economic freedom and economic growth. Through a
study of 102 countries over 20 years, economists James Gwartney, Robert
Lawson, and Walter Block classified countries on the basis of concrete measures of economic liberty and compared these ratings with GDP per person
and GDP growth per person. Countries with high levels of economic freedom,
such as Hong Kong, Singapore, New Zealand, the United States, and Switzerland, had a GDP of $16,000 per person and GDP growth per person of over

3 percent per year, whereas countries with low levels of economic freedom, such as Zaire, Algeria, Iran, Syria, Haiti, and Romania, had a GDP of less than $2,000 per person and GDP growth per person of 11 percent per year.[16]

There is little argument that free trade bestows net gains on trading nations—especially in the long run. The problem is that with so many entrenched vested interest groups, it is difficult to update existing trading rules. As a partial step in the trade liberalization process, groups of countries have begun to move toward limited forms of economic integration. There are more than eighty regional agreements between countries granting preferential access to each other's markets. Nearly all members of the WTO belong to at least one regional pact. Table 2.6 lists examples of such agreements.

Table 2.6 *Regional Integration Agreements*

AGREEMENT	COUNTRIES	FOUNDING DATE	COMBINED GDP (IN BILLIONS US$)	AGREEMENT TYPE
NAFTA (North *American Free-Trade Agreement*)	Canada, U.S., Mexico	1994	$10,015.0	free-trade area
EU *(European Union)*	Austria, Belgium, Denmark, Finland, France, Germany, Greece, Ireland, Italy, Luxembourg, Netherlands, Portugal, Spain, Sweden, United Kingdom	1951	$7,753.0	common market
LAIA *(Latin American Integration Association)*	Argentina, Bolivia, Brazil, Chile, Colombia, Ecuador, Mexico, Paraguay, Peru, Uruguay, Venezuela, Cuba	1980	$3,117.7	free-trade area
AFTA *(Asian Free-Trade Area)*	Brunei, Laos, Cambodia, Indonesia, Malaysia, Burma, Philippines, Singapore, Thailand, Vietnam	1992	$1,759.3	free-trade area
Mercosur	Argentina, Brazil, Paraguay, Uruguay	1991	$1,457.4	customs union
Andean Pact	Bolivia, Colombia, Peru, Ecuador, Venezuela	1969	$643.1	free-trade area
CIS *(Commonwealth of Independent States)*	Armenia, Azerbaijan, Belarus, Georgia, Kazakhstan, Kyrgyztan, Moldova, Russia, Tajikistan, Turkmenistan, Ukraine, Uzbekistan	1999	$337.9	free-trade area
GCC *(Gulf Cooperation Council)*	Bahrain, Kuwait, Oman, Qatar, Saudi Arabia, the United Arab Emirates	1981	$308.5	free-trade area
EFTA *(European Free-Trade Area)*	Iceland, Liechtenstein, Norway, Switzerland	1960	$307.5	free-trade area
CACM *(Central American Common Market)*	Costa Rica, El Salvador, Guatemala, Honduras, Nicaragua	1960	$113.2	common market

Although the degree of economic integration can vary considerably from one organization to another, four major types of integration can be identified: free-trade areas, customs unions, common markets, and monetary unions.

Free-Trade Areas

The simplest form of integration is a free-trade area. The most famous is the North American Free Trade Association (NAFTA), which includes the United States, Canada, and Mexico. Within a **free-trade area,** nations agree to drop trade barriers among themselves, but each nation is permitted to maintain independent trade relations with countries outside the group. There is little attempt at this level to coordinate such things as domestic tax rates, environmental regulations, and commercial codes. Generally such areas do not permit resources (that is, labor and capital) to flow freely across national borders. Moreover, because each country has autonomy over its money supply, exchange rates can fluctuate relative to both member and nonmember countries.

Free-trade areas have been less successful among developing countries. A case in point is the Asian Free Trade Area (AFTA). AFTA was envisaged to create a regional free-trade zone by slashing tariffs. However, the actual free trade that ensued has fallen far short of the rhetoric. For example, Malaysia refused to remove protective tariffs for its auto industry. Furthermore, the association's member countries represent widely disparate development levels, political institutions, and economic philosophies. Some countries are democracies, others military dictatorships. In 2002 Cambodia, Vietnam, and Laos were not even members of the World Trade Organization and tended to view trade liberalization with suspicion.[17]

Want to know more about NAFTA? Check out the NAFTA links on our website.

Customs Unions

Customs unions, a more advanced form of economic integration, possess the characteristics of a free-trade area but with the added feature of a common external tariff/trade barrier for the member nations. Individual countries relinquish the right to set trade agreements outside the group independently. Instead, a supranational policymaking committee makes these decisions.

Common Markets

The third level of economic integration is a **common market**. This arrangement has all the characteristics of a customs union, but the organization also encourages the free flow of resources (labor and capital) among the member nations. For example, if jobs are plentiful in Germany but scarce in Italy, workers can move from Italy to Germany without having to worry about severe immigration restrictions. In a common market, there is usually an attempt to coordinate tax codes, social welfare systems, and other legislation that influences resource allocation. Finally, although each nation still has the right to print and coin its own money, exchange rates among nations often are fixed or are permitted to fluctuate only within a narrow range. The most notable example of a common market is the European Union. The EU has been an active organization for trade liberalization and continues to increase its membership size.

Want to know more about the EU? Check out the link on our website.

World Beat 2.2   *Taking Them to Court*

When a Mississippi jury slapped a $500 million judgment on Loewen Group, a Canadian funeral home chain, in 1995 for breaching a contract with a hometown rival, the company quickly settled the case for $129 million but then decided to appeal. Instead of going to a U.S. court, however, the Canadians took their case to an obscure three-judge panel that stands distinctly apart from the U.S. legal system and whose decisions cannot be appealed.

Thanks to some fine print in the 1994 North American Free Trade Agreement, the case of *Loewen Group* v. *U.S.* is just one of two dozen wending their way through a little-known and highly secretive process. The panels, using arbitration procedures established by the World Bank, are supposed to ensure that governments in the United States, Mexico, and Canada would pay compensation to any foreign investor whose property they might seize. U.S. business groups originally demanded the investor-protection mechanism, noting that the Mexican government had a history of nationalizing its oil, electricity, and banking industries, including many U.S. assets.

But even some of NAFTA's strongest supporters say that clever and creative lawyers in all three countries are rapidly expanding the anti-expropriation clause in unanticipated ways. "The question in a lot of these pending cases is, will the panels produce a pattern of decisions that the negotiators never envisioned?" says Charles E. Roh, Jr., deputy chief U.S. negotiator for NAFTA.

In one case, a NAFTA panel issued an interpretation of the Mexican constitution, thereby exercising authority that NAFTA negotiators hadn't intended to give the panel. In the dispute, a California waste disposal company, Metalclad Corporation, was awarded $16.7 million by a NAFTA tribunal after the governor of the state of San Luis Potosi and a town council refused to honor the company's permit to open a toxic-waste site. The company had asked for $90 million in damages, insisting that the state and local governments had overstepped their authority.

Although such panels may favor U.S. businesses abroad, foreign plaintiffs enjoy the same privileges in the United States, sometimes giving them protections against regulations far exceeding those that domestic companies enjoy in their own courts. What's more, states and municipalities have warned that their ability to govern is being compromised by "a new set of foreign investor rights."

No laws can be overturned by the panel, but the critics charge that the cost of defending against a NAFTA lawsuit may run so high that it could still deter agencies from imposing strict regulations on foreign companies. They point to a decision by Canada not to restrict cigarette marketing after Ottawa was threatened with a NAFTA case by U.S. tobacco companies.

Source: Paul Magnusson, "The Highest Court You've Never Heard Of," *Business Week*, April 1, 2002: 76–77.

READ MORE ABOUT IT:
Check out "Fox's Dream: A North American Common Market" under *Supplemental Readings* on our website.

When Vicente Fox was elected president of Mexico in 2000, he called for expanding NAFTA into a common market. He admitted, however, that this would be a long-term project that would gradually evolve over 20 to 40 years. As an initial step, however, he wanted the United States to accept more Mexican labor, expanding its temporary-worker program so that 300,000 or more Mexicans a year could be legally employed in the United States.[18]

Monetary Unions

The highest form of economic integration is a monetary union. A monetary union is a common market in which member countries no longer regulate their own currencies. Rather, member-country currencies are replaced by a common currency regulated by a supranational central bank. With the passage of the Maastricht Treaty by EU members, the European Monetary System became the first monetary union in January 1999.

▶ *The Global Economy*

The global economy is in a state of transition from a set of strong national economies to a set of interlinked trading groups. This transition has accelerated over the past few years with the collapse of communism, the coalescing of the European trading nations into a single market, and the expansion of membership in the WTO. In much of the developing world, trade and investment liberalization has accelerated. As companies globalize, we will see microchips designed in California, sent to Scotland to be fabricated, shipped to the Far East to be tested and assembled, and returned to the United States to be sold.[19]

The investment by Europeans, Japanese, and Americans in one another's economies is unprecedented. U.S. companies create and sell over $80 billion per year in goods and services in Japan. Foreign direct investment into emerging economies has soared and is estimated to be $145 billion in 2000. China is one of the largest beneficiaries, having received $20 billion in 1998.[20] The physical shipment of goods is increasingly being supplemented by local manufacturing as global companies complement trade with foreign investment. Foreign direct investment is coming predominantly from industrial countries, especially the United States, Japan, Germany, France, and the United Kingdom, with approximately 60 percent of the funds going to developed economies.

There is no doubt that the world is moving toward a single global economy. Of course, there are major difficulties on the horizon, such as the development of a market-based economy in Eastern Europe, a reduction of hostilities and the establishment of political stability in the Middle East and parts of Eastern Europe, and stabilization and growth in the former Soviet Union. The global marketer needs to be familiar with the interdependencies that make up the world economy in order to understand how a drop in the U.S. discount rate will affect business in Stockholm or how Britain's joining the European Monetary System will affect sales in London.

Information technology, telecommunications, and the Internet have made worldwide information on prices, products, and profits available globally and instantaneously. With markets more transparent, buyers, sellers, and investors can access better opportunities, lowering costs and ensuring that resources are allocated to their most efficient use. As change accelerates, successful companies will be able to anticipate trends or respond to them quickly. Less successful companies will miss the changes going on around them and wake up one day to a different marketplace governed by new rules.

▶ *Conclusions*

We learn from the study of economics that changes in rules or in financial circumstances help some groups and hurt others. Therefore, it is important to understand that politicians, special-interest groups, and the media have

PUT THIS CHAPTER TO USE:
Check out *Country Market Report* on our website.

particular points of view. Exchange rate movements, tariffs, quotas, and customs unions can be viewed as alternative ways to achieve economic goals. The issue is not whether a change will take place but rather *which* change will provide the most benefit to the greatest number at the least cost.

This chapter describes the fundamentals of international trade and finance. An understanding of the fundamentals will enable you to comprehend the technical issues raised by the media and to formulate your own views. It is particularly important to understand how actions or events in one part of the world can impact a business in another part of the world.

Review Questions

1. Explain the difference between absolute advantage and comparative advantage.
2. List and describe the principal parts of the balance-of-payments statement.
3. What are freely floating currencies? Which factors affect their exchange rates?
4. What is the main focus of the IMF today?
5. Explain the differences among tariffs, quotas, and nontariff barriers.
6. Describe five major issues facing the WTO today.
7. What is the difference between a free-trade area and a common market?

Questions for Discussion

1. Suppose that Brazil can produce, with an equal amount of resources, either 100 units of steel or 10 computers. At the same time, Germany can produce either 150 units of steel or 10 computers. Explain which nation has a comparative advantage in the production of computers. Choose a mutually advantageous trading ratio and explain why this ratio increases the welfare of both nations.
2. Why would a government want to place export tariffs on products leaving its country? What problems could export tariffs cause?
3. Do you agree with the protestors who claim that the WTO has excessive power over national governments? Will free trade widen the gap between rich and poor? Why or why not?
4. Should the WTO force Europe to accept bioengineered seeds from the United States? Should the WTO force China to accept nudity on stage?
5. What makes regional integration more difficult for developing countries?

For Further Reading

Barshefsky, Charlene. "Trade Policy for a Networked World." *Foreign Affairs* March/April 2001: 134–146.

Bulmer-Thomas, Victor, ed. *Regional Integration in Latin America and the Caribbean.* Washington, DC: The Brookings Institution Press, 2001.

Fairbanks, Michael, and Stace Lindsay. *Plowing the Sea: Nurturing the Hidden Sources of Growth in the Developing World.* Boston: Harvard Business School Press, 1997.

Pomfret, Richard. "Reintegration of Formerly Centrally Planned Economies into the Global Trading System." *ASEAN Economic Bulletin* 18, 1 (April 2001): 35–47.

Porter, Michael E. *The Competitive Advantage of Nations.* New York: Free Press, 1998.

Case 2.1 *Banana Wars*

For nearly a decade, the European Union (EU) and the United States have been engaged in a heated trade dispute over bananas.

In 1993, the European Union (EU) introduced new tariffs and quotas that discriminated in favor of bananas grown in former European colonies and dependencies located in the Caribbean and Africa. The new rules were favorable to the European-based banana companies, whose production was heavily located in these preferred regions. However, the new rules were disadvantageous to the U.S.-based companies, such as Chiquita and Dole, that owned banana plantations in Latin America.

Dole responded to the crisis by shifting more banana production to West Africa. Over the next few years, Dole's market share in European bananas actually increased. Chiquita, however, asked the U.S. government to bring a complaint against the EU under GATT. The United States won two subsequent suits, but the EU used its veto power under GATT to avoid compliance. These veto rights were rescinded under the WTO in 1995.

The WTO then ruled on the case again in favor of the United States, calling Europe's quota system blatantly discriminatory. This time the United States was allowed to employ sanctions against the EU if it failed to comply. The EU proceeded to make what most observers believed to be cosmetic, ineffectual changes to its banana importation rules. In retaliation, the United States announced that it would levy 100 percent tariffs on seventeen categories of European goods, including printed cards, cashmere clothing, coral jewelry, and chandeliers.

EU officials objected, claiming that the United States was not authorized to determine whether the EU's actions were insufficient and thus was required to take the case back to the WTO. The U.S. government believed this was a delaying tactic that the EU could employ again and again. The WTO supported the U.S. position and approved the retaliatory actions.

In Europe, the U.S. sanctions were called "silly" and a "return to the Middle Ages." Many EU manufacturers were angry that they were made to suffer over a trade issue that did not concern them. For example, thousands of jobs were at risk in the Belgian biscuit industry, where some companies exported 20 percent of their production to the United States. The sanctions also threatened Asian investors in Europe such as the British battery subsidiary of the Japanese Yuasa Corporation, which had only recently developed export sales to the United States. Now that effort would be for nothing. Only products from Denmark and the Netherlands escaped sanctions because these countries had lobbied the EU for compliance with the banana decision.

Some questioned why the United States was pursuing the banana case so vehemently. After all, no jobs were at risk in the United States. Still, Chiquita's lobbying efforts paid off. The head of Chiquita, Carl H. Lindner, was a major donor to both the Republican and Democratic parties in the United States. A lobbyist for Greek feta cheese was less successful in his efforts to keep feta off the sanction list, despite his argument that the pain would be borne by Greek Americans, for whom feta was a dietary staple.

The United States insisted that the issue at stake in the banana wars was nothing less than the credibility of the WTO. Europe could not flaunt a WTO decision. Ironically, the U.S. trade representative had angered Europeans five years earlier by stating that WTO membership would not obligate America to obey its rules. The United States could defy WTO rules and accept retaliation from an injured party. After all, few countries would wish to initiate a trade war with the United States. Despite this rhetoric, the United States had complied with WTO rulings against it, such as one concerning U.S. restrictions affecting the import of oil from Brazil and Venezuela.

The United States was not alone in its attempts to receive redress for losses in the EU banana market. The WTO arbitration panel allowed Ecuador to impose over $200 million in sanctions, an amount equivalent to its banana exports shut out of EU markets. However, Ecuador annually imported products worth only $62 million from the EU, and these imports were mainly medicines. In May 2000, the WTO authorized Ecuador to impose punitive tariffs on service providers and copyrighted material, including compact discs, from the EU. The EU trade ambassador announced that the EU would monitor Ecuador's penalties and challenge them if they were excessive.

Questions

1. Who are the winners and the losers in the banana wars?
2. Is the U.S. response silly?
3. What potential threats to the WTO are illustrated by the banana wars?

Sources: Michael M. Weinstein, "The Banana War between the United States and Europe Is More Than a Trivial Trade Spat," *New York Times*, December 24, 1998, p. 2; Helen Coopers, "Curdish War," *Wall Street Journal*, March 1, 1999, p. A1; Brian Kenety, "Trade: Banana Producers Fear Tariff Solution to EU-US Trade War," *Inter Press Service*, March 16, 2000; and Elizabeth Olsen, "WTO Allows Ecuador to Impose Tariffs on EU in Banana Dispute," *International Herald Tribune*, p. 13.

Case 2.2   *Trouble in Mercosur*

Since its inception, Mercosur had become Latin America's most successful integration agreement. Among its members were Latin America's largest economy, Brazil (GDP = US$1,035 billion), and its third largest economy, Argentina (GDP = US$374 billion). From 1991 to 1998, trade between Brazil and Argentina increased 500 percent to $15 billion. However, in 1999 Mercosur trade volume fell 20 percent. Argentina and Brazil were both experiencing recessions and disagreed on which foreign exchange policy to follow. This disagreement threatened the future of Mercosur.

Argentina's Convertibility Plan pegged its peso to the U.S. dollar and banned the printing of unbacked currency. By restricting its money supply and curbing government spending, Argentina reduced inflation from 5,000 percent in 1989 to 1 percent by the year 2000. Through the early and mid-1990s, Argentina experienced an economic boom attributed to its trade liberalization, monetary and foreign exchange stability, and the privatization of previously state-owned companies.

Similarly, Brazil's Real Plan initially pegged the Brazilian real to the U.S. dollar. Inflation fell from 2,500 percent in 1993 to 2.5 percent in 1998. Trade and investment liberalization encouraged investment in Brazil, but pent-up demand for capital and consumer goods caused the country's merchandise balance to drop from a surplus of US$10.5 billion in 1994 to a deficit of US$6.3 billion in 1998. The Asian financial crisis in mid-1997 caused foreign investors to worry about the future of other developing countries. Foreign capital fled Brazil, and the country's balance of payments (BOP) deteriorated. A recession in 1998, augmented by the failure of the Brazilian Congress to pass key spending reforms, further eroded investor confidence in the country. Brazil's foreign exchange reserves continued to dwindle. The government responded by announcing a change to the free float of the real in January 1999. The real plummeted against the dollar and consequently plummeted against the Argentine peso.

Still, the Argentine government remained committed to foreign exchange stability. Argentina even began discussing with the U.S. Treasury the possibility of formally dollarizing its economy. The idea was feasible. Panama had adopted the U.S. dollar as its currency in 1904. Already over half of the bank deposits and loans in Argentina were in dollars. Automated teller machines dispensed both pesos and dollars. The U.S. Federal Reserve shipped tons of dollar-denominated bills overseas every year. Nearly two-thirds of the almost $500 billion in U.S. currency circulated outside the United States.

Nonetheless, dollarization would be practically irreversible. Argentina would give up control over its money supply to the U.S. Federal Reserve. Critics argued that the U.S. Federal Reserve set policy to assist the U.S. economy, which had little in common with the Argentine economy. Even talking about dollarization would undermine confidence in the peso. Others noted that the alternative of allowing the peso to float freely like the real would be likely to erode confidence even more, resulting in a devaluation of the peso.

Nonetheless, costs of doing business in Brazil were soon 30 percent below those in Argentina. Argentina saw its trade surplus with Brazil disappear. The placing of quotas on certain products imported from Brazil, the first quotas in Mercosur history, had alarmed Brazil, which was investigating legal means to have them lifted. Many Argentine companies and multinational corporations, such as Philips Electronics NV and Goodyear Tire and Rubber Company, had shifted production from Argentina to Brazil. Argentina claimed to have lost 250,000 jobs since the devaluation in Brazil. Unemployed workers marched with signs saying "Made in Brazil-No!" The state governor of Buenos Aires summed up the anti-Brazilian feeling: "The Brazilians are like bad neighbors that come into our house to steal the furniture."

In December 2001, the Argentine government temporarily set limits on the amount of money that Argentines could withdraw from banks or transfer abroad. In the previous year, 20 percent of bank deposits in the country had been converted by their owners into dollars and moved to overseas accounts. Banks were concerned about how long dollar reserves would last in the country at the rate of one peso to one dollar. Rumors of a possible devaluation of the peso were rife by early 2002. But devaluation remained problematic. Many debts and contracts in Argentina were denominated in dollars. A devaluation of the peso would increase the cost in pesos of meeting those dollar obligations. This situation in turn could cause a banking crisis.

Questions

1. What foreign exchange regime should Argentina adopt: dollarization, a freely floating peso, the status quo, or another? Why?
2. Which foreign exchange regime would you prefer to see in Argentina if you were a U.S. exporter of heavy machinery? A European exporter of cosmetics? A Brazilian exporter of automobiles? Why?
3. What problems related to regional integration agreements are illustrated in this case?

Sources: David Wessel and Craig Torres, "Passing the Buck," *Wall Street Journal*, January 18, 1999, p. A1; Craig Torres and Matt Moffet, "Neighbor-Bashing," *Wall Street Journal*, May 2, 2000, p. A1; U.S. Department of State, *FY 2000 Country Commercial Guides: Argentina and Brazil;* and Michelle Wallin, "Analysts Warn That a Free-Floating Peso Is Only Part of the Fix That Argentina Needs," *Wall Street Journal*, February 8, 2002, p. A16.

Notes

[1]Michael E. Porter, *The Competitive Advantage of Nations* (New York: Macmillan, 1990), pp. 69–175.

[2]Moon Ihlwan, "A Nation of Digital Guinea Pigs," *Business Week*, February 4, 2002: 50.

[3]Khanh T. L. Tran, "Falling Yen Creates Painful Dilemma for U.S. Marketers in Japan," *Wall Street Journal*, June 30, 1998, p. A13.

[4]Timothy Aeppel, "Survival Tactics," *Wall Street Journal*, January 22, 2002, p. A1.

[5]Marc Lifsher, "Bolivar Takes a Dive on Day 1 of Free Float," *Wall Street Journal*, February 14, 2002, p. A14.

[6]Michael Phillips, "A Look at How the Global Finance Crisis Began and How It Spread," *Wall Street Journal*, April 4, 1999, p. R4.

[7]Thomas T. Semon, "Euro Currency's Ripple Effects Are Far, Wide," *Marketing News*, February 18, 2002: 7.

[8]Helene Cooper, "Russia Agrees to Limit Steel Shipments," *Wall Street Journal*, February 23, 1999, p. A8.

[9]"Trade: Europe's Burden," *The Economist*, May 22, 1999: 12.

[10]Guy Chazan, "Trade Negotiator Says Russia Will Compromise in WTO Bid," *Wall Street Journal*, March 19, 2002, p. A15.

[11]Neil King, Jr., "U.S. Courts African Allies for Brewing Biotech-Food Fight," *Wall Street Journal*, February 20, 2002, p. A24.

[12]Ken Smith, "Eye on Beijing: Can China Liberalize Its Culture Industry?" *Wall Street Journal*, March 28, 2002, p. A18.

[13]"World Trade: All Free Traders Now," *The Economist*, December 7, 1996: 21–23.

[14]William Drozdiak, "Poor Nations May Not Buy Trade Talks," *Washington Post*, May 15, 2001.

[15]Paul Blustein, "A Quiet Round in Qatar?" *Washington Post*, January 30, 2001.

[16]"Economic Freedom: Of Liberty and Prosperity," *The Economist*, January 13, 1996: 21–23.

[17]Andrew Marshall, "Southeast Asia Talks Free Trade, But Progress Slow," Reuters English News Service, April 5, 2002.

[18]Geri Smith and Paul Magnusson, "Fox's Dream," *Business Week*, August 14, 2000: 56.

[19]William Van Dusen Wishard, "The 21st Century Economy," *Futurist*, May–June 1987: 23.

[20]"Uncertain Prospects," *The Economist*, April 24, 1999: 23.

3 Cultural and Social Forces

McDonald's Operates in over a hundred countries and is the world's largest user of beef. The U.S.-based fast-food chain was drawn to India with its population of 1,000 million, even though the majority of Indians were Hindus and did not eat beef. At the McDonald's in Delhi a sign reads, "No beef or beef products sold at this restaurant." Pork is also omitted to avoid offending India's Muslims. Food on the menu is strictly divided into vegetarian and nonvegetarian lines. Even the mayonnaise has no egg in it. Despite the cultural sensitivity shown by many fast-food chains that have established themselves in India, many Indians consider these foreign-based businesses to be an assault on their culture. Kentucky Fried Chicken found its restaurant in the city of Bangalore under siege from farmers and anti-globalization protesters. A mob vandalized the restaurant, and KFC abandoned the Indian market.[1]

In Chapter 1 we saw that the complexities of international marketing are partially caused

Chapter Outline

by societal and cultural forces. In Chapter 3 we describe some of these cultural and societal influences in more detail. However, because it is not possible to list all of them—or even to describe the major cultures of the world—only some of the more critical forces are highlighted. Figure 3.1 shows the components of culture that are de-scribed in this chapter. Rather than identifying all the cultural or societal factors that might affect international marketers, we concentrate on analytic processes that marketers can use to identify and monitor any of the numerous cultural influences they will encounter around the globe.

Learning Objectives

After studying this chapter, you should be able to

▶ Define what *culture* is and demonstrate how various components of culture affect marketing.

▶ Explain how different world religions affect marketing.

▶ Describe how family structure can vary and explain its impact on marketing.

▶ Illustrate ways in which the educational system of a country can affect marketers.

▶ Differentiate between monochronic and polychronic cultures and explain the three temporal orientations.

▶ List and describe Hofstede's four dimensions of culture.

▶ Explain why language can be important in gaining true understanding of a culture.

▶ Identify ways of adapting to cultural differences.

Figure 3.1 *Cultural Analysis*

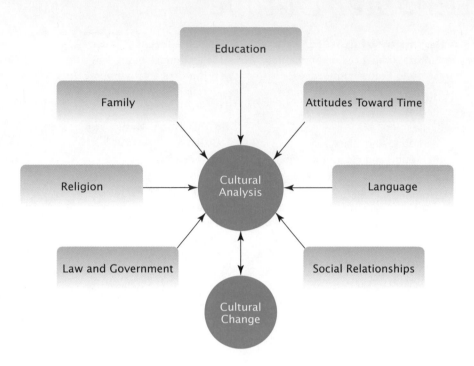

▶ *A Definition of Culture*

Anthropology is the study of human behavior. Cultural anthropology examines all learned human behaviors, including social, linguistic, and family behaviors. **Culture** encompasses the entire heritage of a society transmitted orally, via literature, or in any other form. It includes all traditions, morals, habits, religion, art, and language. Children born anywhere in the world have the same essential needs for food, shelter, and clothing. But as they mature, children experience desires for nonessential things. *How these wants develop* and *what relative importance the individual assigns to them* are based on messages from families and peers. This socialization process reflects each person's culture.

The role and influence of culture in modern society are evolving as more and more economies become interlinked. Samuel Huntington identifies the cultures of the world as Western (the United States, Western Europe, Australia), Orthodox (the former Soviet republics, Central Europe), Confucian (China, Southeast Asia), Islamic (the Middle East), Buddhist (Thailand), Hindu (India), Latin American, African, and Japanese.[2] He argues that conflict in the post-cold-war era will occur between the major cultures of the world rather than between nations. Francis Fukuyama disagrees that cultural differences will necessarily be the source of conflict. Instead, he foresees that increasing interaction between cultures will lead to cross-stimulation and creative change.[3] In any case, understanding cultures helps marketers avoid costly mistakes in the marketplace today.

Cultural Influences on Marketing

The function of marketing is to earn profits from the satisfaction of human wants and needs. In order to understand and influence consumers' wants

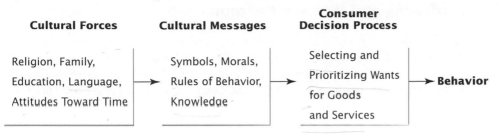

Figure 3.2 *Cultural Influences on Buyer Behavior*

and needs, we must understand their culture. Cultural understanding is also necessary when international marketers interact with foreign competitors, distributors, suppliers, and government officials.

Figure 3.2 is a diagram of how culture affects human behavior. As the figure shows, culture is embedded in such elements of the society as religion, language, history, and education. These aspects of the society send direct and indirect messages to consumers regarding the selection of goods and services. The culture we live in answers such questions as the following: Is tea or coffee the preferred drink? Is black or white worn at a funeral? What type of food is eaten for breakfast?

Isolating Cultural Influences

One of the most difficult tasks for global marketers is assessing the cultural influences that affect their operations. In the actual marketplace, several factors are always working simultaneously, and it is extremely difficult to isolate any one factor. Frequently, cultural differences have been held accountable for any noticeable differences among countries. But do these differences result from underlying religious beliefs, from the prevailing social structure, or simply from different sets of laws? In this chapter we will examine the cultural influences of religion, the family, education, attitudes toward time, social interactions, and language. The cultural factors of government and law will be discussed in Chapter 4.

▶ *Religion*

Many businesspeople ignore the influence religion may have on the marketing environment. Religion can have a profound impact on societies. It helps determine attitudes toward social structure and economic development. Its traditions and rules may dictate what goods and services are purchased, when they are purchased, and by whom. For example, the Shinto religion encourages the Japanese people to cultivate a strong patriotic attitude, which may in part account for Japan's excellent economic performance. Alcoholic beverages are banned in Saudi Arabia on religious principles, and El Al, the national airline of Israel, does not fly on Saturday, the Jewish Sabbath. It is beyond the scope of this text to give a complete description of all world religions and their implications for marketing. By briefly examining several of the world's major religions, however, we can illustrate their potential impact.

Marketing and Western Religions

Historically, the religious tradition in the United States, based on Christianity and Judaism, emphasizes hard work, thrift, and a simple lifestyle. These religious values have certainly evolved over time; many of our modern marketing activities would not exist if these older values had persisted. Thrift, for instance, presumes that a person will save hard-earned wages and use these savings for purchases later on. Today, Americans take full advantage of the ample credit facilities that are available to them. The credit card is such a vital part of the American lifestyle that saving before buying seems archaic. Most Americans feel no guilt in driving a big SUV or generously heating a large house.

Christmas is one Christian tradition that remains an important event for many consumer goods industries in all Christian countries. Retailers have their largest sales around that time. However, Christmas is a good illustration of the substantial differences that still exist among even predominantly Christian societies. A large U.S.-based retailer of consumer electronics discovered these differences the hard way when it opened its first retail outlet in the Netherlands. The company planned the opening to coincide with the start of the Christmas selling season and bought advertising space accordingly for late November and December, as retailers do in the United States. The results proved less than satisfactory. Major gift giving in Holland takes place not around December 25, Christmas Day, but on St. Nicholas Day, December 6. Therefore, the opening of the company's retail operation was late and missed the major buying season.

The **kosher** diets of Orthodox Jews present certain marketers with both challenges and opportunities. For example, eating pork is forbidden, and meat and milk may not be eaten together. Many processed foods containing meat products have come under increased scrutiny. These include cereals, such as Kellogg's Frosted Mini Wheats, that are traditionally eaten with milk.[4]

The rigorously Orthodox make up about 12 percent of Israel's 4.7 million Jews, but their numbers are growing more rapidly than those of the rest of the population. As a result, Israeli food manufacturers have expanded their lines of strictly kosher products and have employed packaging and advertising in keeping with the more traditional sensitivities of Israel's Orthodox communities. Elite, a chocolate manufacturer, ran a contest for Orthodox children in which chocolate wrappers could be exchanged for cards showing prominent rabbis or religious teachers. The company also offered lottery prizes, including a trip abroad to tombs of revered Jewish sages. Coca-Cola ran a separate line of advertisements aimed at Orthodox consumers in Israel. These ads depicted Coke drinkers in conservative dress instead of the scantily clad young people used in advertisements aimed at the Israeli public in general.[5]

Recently, U.S. manufacturers and Israeli exporters have been battling over the U.S. market for matzo, the unleavened bread eaten during the Jewish holiday of Passover. Symbolic of the bread baked during the exodus of the Hebrew slaves from Egypt, matzo is now a $90 million market in the United States. The U.S. manufacturers were not worried when the Israelis entered the market in the early 1990s, offering matzo at much lower prices than the American competitors. They believed that consumers bought matzo on the basis of tradition and were unlikely to switch to the new Israeli brands that competed on price. By 2001, however, Israeli matzo had captured 35–40 percent of the U.S. market.[6]

Marketing and Islam

Islam is the religion of nearly 20 percent of the world's population. It is an important cultural force not only in the Middle East but in Asia and Africa as well. In fact, some of the world's largest Muslim populations live in China, Indonesia, and Malaysia.

The prophet Mohammed established Islam in Mecca, located in modern-day Saudi Arabia, in the year 610. By the time of the prophet's death in 632, the holy book of Islam, the **Koran,** had been completely revealed. Muslims believe it contains God's own words. The Koran was supplemented by the **Hadith** and the **Sunna,** which contain the reported words and actions of the prophet Mohammed. These works are the primary sources of guidance for all Muslims on all aspects of life.

Islam affects marketers in a number of ways. (See Table 3.1.) For example, Islam prohibits the paying or collecting of interest. In most Muslim countries, commercial banks must compete with Islamic banks, which do not offer savings accounts that pay interest. Although these accounts are not attractive to all, many devout Muslims prefer to keep their money in these banks. Islamic banks have also developed a unique product to compete with interest-bearing accounts at other banks. The profit-loss account allows customers to invest their savings in businesses that the bank preselects. Annual profits from the businesses are distributed into the shareholders' accounts.

Islam also prescribes a number of rules concerning food consumption and personal cleanliness. Greater awareness of these Islamic traditions can create new business opportunities. For example, Kohilal is a small business

Islam is influential in many Asian markets such as Malaysia.

Table 3.1 *Marketing in an Islamic Framework*

ELEMENTS	IMPLICATIONS FOR MARKETING
Fundamental Islamic Concepts	
A. *Unity*—Concept of centrality, oneness of God, harmony in life.	Product standardization, mass media techniques, central balance, unity in advertising copy and layout, strong brand loyalties, a smaller evoked size set, loyalty to company, opportunities for brand extension strategies.
B. *Legitimacy*—Fair dealings, reasonable level of profits.	Less formal product warranties, need for institutional advertising and/or advocacy advertising, especially by foreign firms, and a switch from a profit-maximizing to a profit-satisficing strategy.
C. *Zakat*—2.5 percent per annum compulsory tax binding on all classified as "not poor."	Use of "excessive" profits, if any, for charitable acts; corporate donations for charity, institutional advertising.
D. *Usury*—Cannot charge interest on loans. A general interpretation of this law defines "excessive interest" charged on loans as not permissible.	Avoid direct use of credit as a marketing tool; establish a consumer policy of paying cash for low-value products; for high-value products, offer discounts for cash payments and raise prices of products on an installment basis; sometimes possible to conduct interest transactions between local/foreign firms in other non-Islamic countries; banks in some Islamic countries take equity in financing ventures, sharing resultant profits (and losses).
E. *Supremacy of human life*—Compared with other forms of life, objects, human life is of supreme importance.	Pet food and/or products less important; avoid use of statues, busts—interpreted as forms of idolatry; symbols in advertising and/or promotion should reflect high human values; use floral designs and artwork in advertising as representation of aesthetic values.
F. *Community*—All Muslims should strive to achieve universal brotherhood—with allegiance to the "one God." One way of expressing community is the required pilgrimage to Mecca for all Muslims at least once in their lifetime, if able to do so.	Formation of an Islamic economic community—development of an "Islamic consumer" served with Islamic-oriented products and services ("kosher" meat packages, gifts exchanged at Muslim festivals, and so forth); development of community services—need for marketing of nonprofit organizations and skills.
G. *Equality of peoples*	Participative communication systems; roles and authority structures may be rigidly defined, but accessibility at any level relatively easy.
H. *Abstinence*—During the month of Ramadan, Muslims are required to fast without food or drink from the first streak of dawn to sunset—a reminder to those who are more fortunate to be kind to the less fortunate and as an exercise in self-control.	Products that are nutritious, cool, and digested easily can be formulated for Sehr and Iftar (beginning and end of the fast).
Consumption of alcohol and pork is forbidden; so is gambling.	Opportunities for developing nonalcoholic items and beverages (for example, soft drinks, ice cream, milk shakes, fruit juices) and nonchance social games, such as Scrabble; food products should use vegetable or beef shortening.

catering to traditional Muslims in Malaysia. The company markets, among other items, a soap made of palm oil that is free of animal fats. Its products contain no forbidden ingredients such as pork products and alcohol and are thus **halal** (acceptable under Islamic teaching).

The world market for Muslim halal food is estimated at $80 billion, and even fast-food companies such as McDonald's and Kentucky Fried Chicken have obtained halal certificates to serve the Muslim market. In Malaysia a government agency certifies that products are halal. Products must be free of

ELEMENTS	IMPLICATIONS FOR MARKETING
I. *Environmentalism*—The universe created by God was pure. Consequently, the land, air, and water should be held as sacred elements.	Anticipate environmental, antipollution acts; opportunities for companies involved in maintaining a clean environment; easier acceptance of pollution control devices in the community (for example, recent efforts in Turkey have been well received by the local communities).
J. *Worship*—Five times a day; timing of prayers varies.	Need to take into account the variability and shift in prayer timings in planning sales calls, work schedules, business hours, customer traffic, and so forth.

Islamic Culture	
A. *Obligation to family and tribal traditions*	Importance of respected members in the family or tribe as opinion leaders; word-of-mouth communication, customer referrals may be critical; social or clan allegiances, affiliations, and associations may be possible surrogates for reference groups; advertising home-oriented products stressing family roles may be highly effective—for example, electronic games.
B. *Obligations toward parents are sacred*	The image of functional products should be enhanced with advertisements that stress parental advice or approval; even with children's products, there should be less emphasis on children as decision makers.
C. *Obligation to extend hospitality to both insiders and outsiders*	Product designs that are symbols of hospitality, outwardly open in expression; rate of new product acceptance may be accelerated and eased by appeals based on community.
D. *Obligation to conform to codes of sexual conduct and social interaction*—These may include the following:	
1. Modest dress for women in public.	More colorful clothing and accessories are worn by women at home, so promotion of products for use in private homes could be more intimate—such audiences could be reached effectively through women's magazines; avoid use of immodest exposure and sexual implications in public settings.
2. Separation of male and female audiences (in some cases).	Access to female consumers can often be gained only through women as selling agents, salespersons, catalogues, home demonstrations, and women's specialty shops.
E. *Obligations to religious occasions*—For example, two major religious observances are celebrated—Eid-ul-Fitr, Eid-ul-Adha.	Tied to purchase of new shoes, clothing, and sweets and preparation of food items for family reunions, Muslim gatherings. There has been a practice of giving money in place of gifts. Increasingly, however, a shift is taking place to more gift giving; because of lunar calendar, dates are not fixed.

Source: Mushtaq Luqmani, Zahir A. Quraeshi, and Linda Delene, "Marketing in Islamic Countries: A Viewpoint," *MSU Business Topics*, Summer 1980: 20–21. Reprinted by permission.

forbidden foods, and production facilities must meet standards of cleanliness and proper storage. Every product sold by Nestlé Malaysia is certified halal. Even Singapore, where only 14 percent of the 3 million population is Muslim, has established its own halal certification body. Indonesia has a Muslim population of nearly 200 million. In response to consumer demand, the Indonesian government also established halal certification. When it was discovered that the Japanese food company Ajinomoto was using a pork-based enzyme in its halal seasoning products in Indonesia, the company had to pull tons of product off the shelves. The company not only faced possible legal action but also suffered a loss of consumer trust.[7]

Coca-Cola also targeted the Muslim market when it developed an advertisement to be played during Ramadan (the month in which Muslims fast from dawn to dusk). Developed by McCann-Erickson Malaysia, the commercial included a small boy and his mother going with gifts to an orphanage, the mother with a rug and basket of food, the boy with his cherished bottle of Coca-Cola. After sunset the little boy leaves his house to go back to the orphanage to break fast and share the Coca-Cola with his new friends. The ad ends with the slogan "Always in good spirit. Always Coca-Cola." This advertisement, which appealed to religious sentiment across national boundaries, was scheduled to air in twenty countries.[8]

Marketing and Eastern Religions

Asia is a major market today for many international firms, and global marketers must take into account the possible impact of the Eastern religious and philosophical traditions of Hinduism, Buddhism, Confucianism, and Shintoism.

Hinduism and Buddhism are the two largest Eastern religions. Hinduism is professed by about 450 million people, most of whom live in India, where Hindus constitute nearly 85 percent of the population. Hindu theology varies among believers but is generally polytheistic, with different groups showing a preference for one or several gods. Hinduism includes a doctrine of rebirth into conditions determined by a person's prior life. A person can be reborn as a human, an animal, or a celestial being. Hinduism also encompasses a hereditary caste system that requires Hindus to marry within their own caste. Many Hindus are vegetarian, and eating beef is particularly taboo. Buddhism also began in India but rejected many of Hinduism's hierarchical structures. Today it is influential predominantly in East and Southeast Asia.

In India, Hyundai respects local beliefs when it launches new car models on auspicious days selected from the Hindu calendar.[9] A Seattle-based company showed far less sensitivity when it launched a line of toilet seats. The Sacred Seat Collection depicted images of Hindu gods such as Ganesh, the elephant god of learning. Several Indian politicians joined members of the large U.S. Hindu population in condemning the company.[10]

Confucianism is not a religion, but its founder Confucius is regarded as the greatest of China's sages and his impact is still greatly felt. Confucius taught respect for one's parents and for education, values common among Chinese today. Confucius' name has also proved valuable to marketers in China. Kong Demao, age eighty, is one of the two surviving members of the seventy-seventh generation of the family of Confucius. Since the early 1990s, she had been the nominal chair of three distillers in the Qufu region of China, the ancestral home of Confucius. When all three distillers took the Confucius family name for their products in the mid-1980s, sales soared. In the 1990s, two of the distillers went to court over who really owned the name. Although the case remained unsettled, all three distillers decided it would be wise to contact Kong and pay a stipend for the use of her name. She has also been named "Lifetime Honorary President" of the Confucius International Travel Agency.[11]

Japan has been heavily influenced both by Buddhism from Korea and by Confucianism from China. In the late nineteenth century, Japan's earlier Shinto religion was revived as the patriotic symbol of Japan, the emperor being exalted as the descendent of the sun goddess. Shinto rituals were performed at state occasions. State Shinto was abolished after World War II, but popular cults persist. When the first Starbucks abroad opened in Tokyo, Shinto priests offered prayers at the opening ceremony.[12] One enterprising tour group brings foreign tourists to Japan to view Shinto processions during October, a festival month in a number of Japanese cities.[13]

Global marketers require a keen awareness of how religion can influence business. They need to search actively for influences that may not be readily apparent. Showing respect for local religious traditions is an important part of cultural sensitivity.

▶ *The Family*

The role of the family varies greatly among cultures, as do the roles that the various family members play. Across cultures, we find differences in family size, in the employment of women, and in many other factors of interest to marketers. Companies familiar with family interactions in Western society cannot assume that they will find the same patterns elsewhere.

In the United States, there has been a trend toward the dissolution of the traditional nuclear family. With people marrying later and divorcing more often, the "typical" family of father, mother, and children living in one dwelling has become far less common than in the past. More recently, a similar trend in Western Europe has resulted in an increase in the number of households even in countries where the overall population is decreasing. This outcome has in turn increased demand for many consumer durables, such as washing machines and ovens, whose sales correlate with number of households rather than with population. Also, an increasing number of women are working outside the home (see Table 3.2), a situation that boosts demand for frozen dinners and child care centers.

Marketers should not expect to find the same type of family structure in all countries. In many societies, particularly in Asia and Latin America, the role of the male as head of the household remains pronounced. Some cultures still encourage the bearing of male rather than female children. In most cultures, 105 boys are born for every 100 girls, but in China the figure for boys is 118.5 and in South Korea, 116. In some areas of South Korea, boy births outnumber girls 125 to 100, indicating that female fetuses may be being aborted.[14] This male dominance coincides with a lower rate of participation by women in the labor force outside the home. This situation results in a lower average family income. The number of children per family also varies substantially by country or culture. In many Eastern European countries and in Germany, one child per family is fast becoming the rule, whereas families in many developing countries are still large by Western standards.

Extended Families

So far we have discussed only the nuclear family. However, for many cultures, the extended family—including grandparents, in-laws, aunts, uncles, and so on—is of considerable importance. In the United States, older parents usually live alone, whether in individually owned housing, in multiple housing for the elderly, or in nursing homes (for those who can no longer care for

Table 3.2 *Family Statistics of Selected Countries (in percentages)*

COUNTRY	POPULATION GROWTH RATES[a]	FEMALE POPULATION IN LABOR FORCE[b]
Australia	1.3	44
Austria	0.4	40
Belgium	0.2	41
Brazil	1.7	35
Canada	1.1	46
Chile	1.6	33
China	1.3	45
Denmark	0.2	46
Finland	0.4	48
France	0.4	45
Germany	0.2	42
Greece	0.5	38
Hungary	−0.3	45
India	2.0	32
Indonesia	1.8	41
Ireland	0.5	34
Italy	0.1	38
Japan	0.4	41
Malaysia	2.6	38
Mexico	1.9	33
Netherlands	0.6	40
New Zealand	1.1	45
Norway	0.5	46
Pakistan	2.6	28
Portugal	0.1	44
Singapore	2.6	39
South Africa	2.2	38
Spain	0.3	37
Sweden	0.3	48
Switzerland	0.6	40
Thailand	1.3	46
Turkey	1.9	37
United Kingdom	0.3	44
United States	1.1	46
Venezuela	2.4	35

[a]Average annual population growth rate between 1980 and 1999
[b]Percentage of total labor force, 1999
Sources: 2001 World Development Indicators, World Bank Group (www.worldbank.org).

themselves). In countries with lower income levels and in rural areas, the extended family still plays a major role, further increasing the size of the average household. In China, 67 percent of parents with children live with one of their children, and 80 percent of parents have contact with their children at least once a week.[15]

Extended families or clans play an important role among overseas Chinese as well. Driven by poverty and political upheaval, waves of families fled China

World Beat 3.1 *Who'll Clean the House?*

Housecleaners, common in the United States, are just starting to gain popularity in Japan. For decades, housecleaning was considered one of the central missions of Japanese housewives, and even those with money to burn wouldn't dream of handing off such a critical job to strangers. But now, with traditional industries declining in a decade-long economic slump, more Japanese are eager to overturn stereotypes as they search for new livelihoods.

Housecleaning has inspired one of the biggest, and unlikeliest, of gold rushes. Stodgy companies such as Tokyo Electric Power Company and Nishi-Nippon Railroad Company are launching housecleaning businesses. The Japan Housecleaning Organization, a volunteer group with 60 members, offers a 10-day training course for novices, mainly middle-aged men who have lost their corporate jobs. In a sign of the times, housecleaners got their own section in the yellow pages, under the English word "housecleaning," which is preferred over the common Japanese word "soji."

Cleaning entrepreneurs say they are encouraged by some sweeping social changes. More women are working these days, which leaves them with more discretionary income and less time for housework. More elderly Japanese are living apart from their children and require help around the house.

But the industry faces some hurdles. Because Japan keeps out immigrants and labor costs remain high, it's difficult to offer housecleaning as an everyday service. Many companies are attempting to pitch housecleaning as a specialized service that only well-paid professionals can provide. At the high end is Duskin Company, a franchise operator and a pioneer in Japan's housecleaning market. Duskin, which has a licensing agreement with the ServiceMaster unit of Aramark Corporation of the United States, charges 15,000 yen ($113) to clean a single toilet bowl and a minimum of $420 to do spring cleaning of a two-bedroom apartment. Hasegawa Enterprise Inc. offers its services à la carte. It charges 9,800 yen ($73) per kitchen exhaust fan. The company recently offered a half-price sale on weekdays, explaining that at such a bargain, housewives who felt guilty about goofing off could keep the outsourcing secret from their husbands.

Source: Yumiko Ono, "Japan's Distress Prompts an Odd Career Transition," *Wall Street Journal*, April 1, 2002, p. B1.

to other countries in Asia during the past two hundred years. They developed dense networks of thrifty, self-reliant communities united by their Chinese ethnicity. These Chinese communities have flourished in both commerce and industry. For example, ethnic Chinese make up 1 percent of the population and 20 percent of the economy in Vietnam, 1 percent and 40 percent in the Philippines, 4 percent and 50 percent in Indonesia, and 32 percent and 60 percent in Malaysia.[16] Ironically, the Chinese homeland has followed a one-child policy during the past generation in an attempt to curb its population growth. This policy is having an immediate impact on the younger generation's ability to form the traditional Chinese family business. Young entrepreneurs in China report that they establish business relationships with fellow students from high school or university instead of with siblings and cousins.

Beyond the Family

Most societies appreciate and promote a strong family unit. However, Francis Fukuyama argues that a culture can suffer from too great an emphasis on family values. Some cultures, such as that of southern Italy, emphasize nuclear family relationships to the exclusion of all others. It has been said that adults are not persons in Southern Italy; they're only parents. In this **low-trust society,** trust is extended only to immediate family members.[17]

Yet business relationships depend on trust. Even with contracts and law courts, businesses could not survive if managers spent all their time in litigation. If trust is not extended beyond the family, business dealings must stay within the family. This practice stymies the growth of modern large-scale enterprises and impedes development. For this reason, southern Italy remains one of the poorest regions in Western Europe. Most of the developing world qualifies as relatively low-trust, according to Fukuyama's paradigm. Comparatively few large corporations in the private sector evolved outside North America, Europe, and Japan. Those that did retained their family ties much longer than firms in developed countries.

Germany, Japan, and the United States are all very different in many aspects of culture. However, Fukuyama notes that these three countries are **high-trust societies.** They all share a history of voluntary associations—civic, religious, and business—that extend beyond the family. This history of associating with non–family members to accomplish common goals taught people that they could trust others who were not blood relations. This experience paved the way for large, publicly owned corporations to emerge, because family businesses could feel secure in raising money outside the family and stockholders could eventually trust their investments in the hands of professional managers. Marketers who compete in high-trust countries usually must contend with these large corporate competitors. However, the history of associations can also be exploited by savvy marketers. Marketers of credit cards in Japan discovered that consumers took quickly to credit cards cobranded with associations and clubs, because the typical Japanese was proud to belong to civic groups.

► *Education*

Education shapes people's outlooks, desires, and motivations. To the extent that educational systems differ among countries, we can expect differences among consumers. However, education not only affects potential consumers; it also shapes potential employees for foreign companies and for the business community at large.

Levels of Participation

In the United States, compulsory education ends at age sixteen. Virtually all students who obtain a high school diploma stay in school until age eighteen. In high school, about 25 percent take vocational training courses. After high school, students either attend college or find a job. About half of all high school graduates go on to some type of college.

This pattern is not shared by all countries. Many students in Europe go to school only until age sixteen. Then they join an apprenticeship program. This is particularly the case in Germany, where formal apprenticeship programs exist for about 450 job categories. These programs are under tight government supervision and typically last three years. They include on-the-job training, with one day a week of full-time school. About 70 percent of young Germans enter such a program after compulsory full-time education.[18] During the first year, they can expect to earn about 25 percent of the wages earned by fully trained craftspeople in their field. Only about 30 percent of young Germans finish university schooling. In Great Britain, the majority of young people take a job directly in industry and receive only informal on-the-job training. In a study of frontline employees in German, Japanese, and U.S. companies, the U.S. employees received the least training once employed.[19]

Even with similar levels of participation in secondary education, attitudes toward the quantity and quality of education can differ. For example, Japanese high school students attend class more days than students in the United States, where the school year is only 180 days long. Because students in other countries also spend a higher percentage of their school day on core academic subjects, the differences in hours spent on mathematics, science, and history are great: 1,460 total hours for high school students in the United States, 3,170 in Japan, 3,280 in France, and 3,528 in Germany.[20] It is not surprising that among twenty-one countries studied, U.S. high school seniors ranked near the bottom in these fields, behind all their European counterparts and 6 percent below the international average.[21]

A study of reading comprehension in eight countries, conducted by the Organization for Economic Cooperation and Development (OECD), found that the United States outperformed only Poland. One out of five Americans surveyed did not understand the directions on an aspirin bottle. Why, then, is the United States economy so productive? A study by McKinsey Consulting found that differences in basic skills were not a large factor in productivity. Management talent, labor rules, and regulatory environment were more important—all areas in which the United States does well.[22] The OECD study also found a definite link between the percentage of students staying in school beyond the minimum leaving age and a country's economic well-being. Countries such as Japan, Holland, Germany, Austria, and the United States get a high return on their educational expenses because so many young people stay in school, in either traditional or vocational schools. Portugal, Spain, Britain, and New Zealand get a poor return on their educational expenses because so few young people continue their education. On average, each additional year of formal schooling results in a return of anywhere from 5 to15 percent per year in additional earnings.[23]

Impact on Consumers and Employees

The extent and quality of education in a society affect marketing on two levels: the consumer level and the employee level. In societies where the average level of participation in the educational process is low, one typically finds a low level of literacy. Basic literacy levels can vary widely across countries (see Table 3.3). This variation in reading ability not only affects the earning potential of consumers, and thus the level of consumption, but also determines the communication options for marketing programs, as we will see in Chapters 14 and 15. Another concern is how much young people earn. In countries such as Germany, where many of its youth have considerable earnings by age twenty, the value and potential of the youth market is quite different from those in the United States, where a substantial number of young people do not enter the job market until age twenty-one or twenty-two.

Table 3.3 *Adult Illiteracy Rates for Selected Countries (in percentages)*

COUNTRY	MALE	FEMALE
Algeria	23	44
Argentina	3	3
Armenia	1	3
Bangladesh	48	71
Bolivia	8	21
Brazil	15	15
Bulgaria	1	2
Cambodia	41	79
Cameroon	19	31
Chile	4	5
China	9	25
Egypt	34	57
Ethiopia	57	68
Greece	2	4
Hungary	1	1
India	32	56
Iran	17	31
Israel	2	6
Italy	1	2
Morocco	39	65
Peru	6	15
Poland	<1	<1
Russia	<1	<1
Saudi Arabia	17	34
South Africa	14	16
Spain	2	3
Turkey	7	24
Vietnam	5	9

Source: "Education Outcomes," *World Development Indicators 2001*, pp. 94–96 (www.worldbank.org).

The educational system also affects employee skills and executive talent. In the United States, the sales organizations of many large companies are staffed strictly with university graduates. In many other countries, sales as a profession has a lower status and attracts fewer university graduates. The typical career path of an American executive involves a 4-year college program and, in many cases, a master's degree in business administration (MBA) program. This format for executive education is less common in other countries, despite the fact that MBA programs have proliferated around the world in the past 20 years. For example, large corporations in Korea hire fewer MBAs than their American counterparts, but they import top management educators to teach in their in-house executive programs.

Thus different countries have substantially different ideas about education in general and about management education in particular. Traditional European education emphasizes the mastery of a subject through knowledge acquisition. In contrast, the U.S. approach emphasizes analytic ability and an understanding of concepts. Students passing through the two educational systems probably develop different thinking patterns and attitudes. It requires a considerable amount of cultural sensitivity for an international manager to understand these differences and to make the best use of the human resources that are available.

▶ *Attitudes Toward Time*

In Poland, decisions are usually made quickly. In Kazakhstan, canceling a meeting at the last minute is common, whereas punctuality is strictly observed in Romania.[24] These are all examples of behaviors that reflect cultural attitudes toward time. In the United States, time is seen as having economic value. It is a commodity to be planned for and used wisely. Schedules are set and appointment times are interpreted precisely. If a meeting is scheduled at 3:00 p.m., participants are expected to arrive at 3:00 p.m. In many other countries, such as Costa Rica and Saudi Arabia, meetings rarely begin on time. An American arriving at a meeting in Saudi Arabia can wait quite a while for others to show up. Faced with this phenomenon, the American is likely to be annoyed. Time is being wasted!

Monochronic versus Polychronic Cultures and Temporal Orientation

The United States is basically a **monochronic** culture. Activities are undertaken one at a time. People respect schedules and agendas. In **polychronic** cultures, expectations are different.[25] At any one time, a manager is expected to be managing multiple tasks. Schedules and agendas must bend to the needs of people, and interruptions are not the exception but the rule. It is not unusual for a high-ranking Indian manager to stop work to listen to an employee's family problems. In Brazil, it would be impolite to abruptly cut off a conversation with one group in order to attend a prearranged meeting with another group. Salespeople from monochronic cultures who travel to polychronic cultures should expect to be kept waiting and should not interpret their clients' tardiness as lack of interest or disrespect.

Temporal orientations also vary by culture. Some cultures, such as Mexico and Brazil, are oriented to the present: Life is enjoyed for the moment. One Mexican ceramics manufacturer noted that as soon as his employees made enough money for the week, they stopped coming to work. The United States is a future-oriented culture, where efforts are focused more on working to achieve a future goal. European and Middle Eastern cultures are more oriented to the past, placing a greater emphasis on historical achievements and relationships. When Israel and Egypt signed a peace treaty 25 years ago, it ended a war that had been going on for nearly 30 years. The U.S. government, which had assisted in the peace process, expected business relations to blossom between the two countries. Today, Israeli firms have barely begun to penetrate the Egyptian market. Egyptians—consumers, distributors, potential partners, and government officials—are still highly aware of the 30 years of war that preceded the peace.

In many countries such as Turkey, the traditional and the modern coexist—presenting marketers with both challenges and opportunities.

READ MORE ABOUT IT:
Check out "Less Work, More Shopping?" under *Supplemental Readings* on our website.

Work and Leisure Time

Different societies have different views about the amounts of time it is appropriate to spend at work and in leisure pursuits. In most economically developed countries, leisure has become a major aspect of life. In such countries, the development of the leisure industries is an indication that play and relaxation can be as intensely consumed as any other products.

Society significantly influences work and leisure through statutory vacation allowances and public holidays. As shown in Figure 3.3, European statutes require companies to give employees 25–30 days of vacation annually, whereas many workers in the United States, Japan, Mexico, and the Philippines enjoy only 5–10 vacation days. These differences result in lower working hours per year in Europe than in the United States, Japan, and Mexico.

These differences in the use of leisure time reflect, to some degree, differences in attitudes toward work (see Table 3.4). An OECD study found that in Germany, the United Kingdom, and Japan, working hours declined over a period of about 20 years, whereas in the United States, working hours increased.[26] Management concepts such as performance-related pay, reengineering, and outsourcing also support longer working hours in the United States. Nonetheless, a study by Robert Half International found that two-thirds of U.S. workers would like shorter hours even if the cutback meant lower wages.[27]

**Statutory Vacation Allowances
(number of public holidays in parentheses)**

Figure 3.3 *Statutory Vacation Allowances*

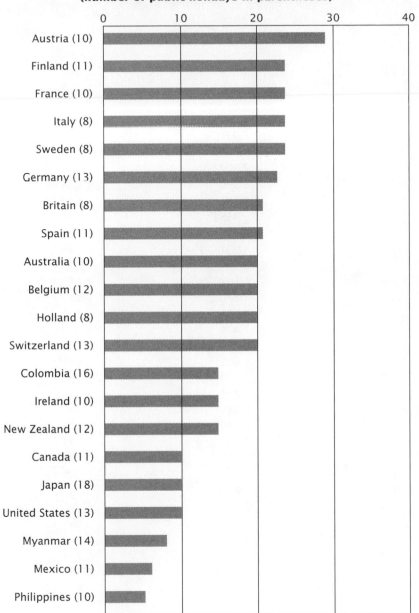

Source: "Time Out: Statutory Holiday Allowances, Working Days," *The Economist,* December 23, 1995.
Copyright © 1995 The Economist Newspaper Group, Inc.

Table 3.4 *Values of Selected Countries*

COUNTRY	AVERAGE NUMBER OF WORKING HOURS PER YEAR[a]	EXTENT TO WHICH VALUES OF SOCIETY SUPPORT COMPETITIVENESS[b]	MANAGERS' SENSE OF ENTREPRENEURSHIP[c]
Australia	1,749	7.814	6.282
Austria	1,699	7.520	6.560
Belgium	1,712	6.424	6.657
Brazil	1,931	6.786	6.357
Canada	1,891	7.561	6.707
Chile	2,244	6.857	6.704
China	1,983	7.407	5.934
Denmark	1,687	6.394	5.606
Finland	1,723	8.272	6.914
France	1,587	5.355	5.370
Germany	1,688	6.805	5.870
Greece	1,780	5.902	6.146
Hong Kong	2,181	8.195	7.429
Hungary	1,988	6.121	6.667
India	2,097	5.116	4.782
Indonesia	2,065	5.000	5.000
Ireland	1,798	7.429	6.929
Italy	1,732	5.410	6.154
Japan	1,864	5.615	3.941
Korea	2,073	7.324	5.803
Malaysia	2,217	6.225	5.350
Mexico	2,150	5.481	4.883
Netherlands	1,686	7.389	6.917
New Zealand	1,873	5.887	6.038
Norway	1,730	6.237	5.187
Philippines	2,164	4.921	5.302
Portugal	1,738	5.778	5.333
Singapore	1,988	8.507	5.970
South Africa	1,929	5.065	5.065
Spain	1,724	7.072	5.797
Sweden	1,860	6.879	6.727
Switzerland	1,855	7.386	6.598
Taiwan	2,176	7.443	6.861
Thailand	2,092	5.815	4.892
Turkey	2,074	6.464	6.607
United Kingdom	1,833	6.381	5.229
United States	1,918	8.380	7.107
Venezuela	1,956	3.840	4.615

[a]Average number of working hours per year.

[b]Where 0 equals "do not support competitiveness" and 10 equals "supports competitiveness." Average reported from 4,160 executives from 47 countries.

[c]Where 0 equals "a lack of entrepreneurship" and 10 equals "a sense of entrepreneurship." Average reported from 4,160 executives from 47 countries.

Source: The World Competitiveness Report 2001 (Lausanne: IMD, 2001), pp. 453, 470, and 514.

▶ *The Hofstede Measures of Culture*

Geert Hofstede developed a four-dimensional framework by which to measure several key attributes of cultures. This framework emerged as a result of his research on IBM employees and has since attracted considerable interest among business scholars.[28] The research involved over 116,000 questionnaires and incorporated seventy-two different national subsidiaries, twenty languages, and thirty-eight occupations. Hofstede's insights can be very useful to international marketers. The four dimensions are power distance, individualism, masculinity, and uncertainty avoidance. The scores for sixty-nine countries and regions are listed in Table 3.5. Although Hofstede's four dimensions do not, of course, fully describe national cultures, they are a useful place to begin.

Table 3.5 *Values of Hofstede's Cultural Dimensions for 69 Countries or Regions*

COUNTRY/REGION	POWER DISTANCE	INDIVIDUALISM	MASCULINITY	UNCERTAINTY AVOIDANCE
Arabic countries[1]	80	38	53	68
Argentina	49	46	56	86
Australia	36	90	61	51
Austria	11	55	79	70
Bangladesh	80	20	55	60
Belgium	65	75	54	94
Brazil	69	38	49	76
Bulgaria	70	30	40	85
Canada	39	80	52	48
Chile	63	23	28	86
China	80	20	66	30
Colombia	67	13	64	80
Costa Rica	35	15	21	86
Czech Republic	57	58	57	74
Denmark	18	74	16	23
East African region[2]	64	27	41	52
Ecuador	78	8	63	67
Estonia	40	60	30	60
Finland	33	63	26	59
France	68	71	43	86
Germany	35	67	66	65
Greece	60	35	57	112
Guatemala	95	6	37	101
Hong Kong	68	25	57	29
Hungary	46	80	88	82
India	77	48	56	40
Indonesia	78	14	46	48
Iran	58	41	43	59
Ireland	28	70	68	35
Israel	13	54	47	81
Italy	50	76	70	75

Table 3.5 *Values of Hofstede's Cultural Dimensions for 69 Countries or Regions* Continued

COUNTRY/REGION	POWER DISTANCE	INDIVIDUALISM	MASCULINITY	UNCERTAINTY AVOIDANCE
Jamaica	45	39	68	13
Japan	54	46	95	92
Luxembourg	40	60	50	70
Malaysia	104	26	50	36
Malta	56	59	47	96
Mexico	81	30	69	82
Morocco	70	46	53	68
Netherlands	38	80	14	53
New Zealand	22	79	58	49
Norway	31	69	8	50
Pakistan	55	14	50	70
Panama	95	11	44	86
Peru	64	16	42	87
Philippines	94	32	64	44
Poland	68	60	64	93
Portugal	63	27	31	104
Romania	90	30	42	90
Russia	93	39	36	95
Salvador	66	19	40	94
Singapore	74	20	48	8
Slovakia	104	52	110	51
South Africa	49	65	63	49
South Korea	60	18	39	85
Spain	57	51	42	86
Surinam	85	47	37	92
Sweden	31	71	5	29
Switzerland	34	68	70	58
Taiwan	58	17	45	69
Thailand	64	20	34	64
Trinidad	47	16	58	55
Turkey	66	37	45	85
United Kingdom	35	89	66	35
United States	40	91	62	46
Uruguay	61	36	38	100
Venezuela	81	12	73	76
Vietnam	70	20	40	30
West African region[3]	77	20	46	54
Yugoslavia	76	27	21	88

[1]Egypt, Iraq, Kuwait, Lebanon, Libya, Saudi Arabia, and United Arab Emirates.

[2]Ethiopia, Kenya, Tanzania, and Zambia.

[3]Ghana, Nigeria, and Sierra Leone.

Source: Geert Hofstede, *Cultures and Organizations: Software of the Mind* (New York: McGraw-Hill, 1991), pp. 53, 68, 84, and 113 and Geert Hofstede, *Culture's Consequences* (Thousand Oaks, California: Sage Publications, 2001), p. 502.

Power Distance

Power distance is the extent to which the less powerful members within a society accept that power is distributed unevenly. Geert Hofstede tells the story of a clash of cultures between the high-power-distance culture of France and the low-power-distance culture of Sweden:

> The nobles of Sweden in 1809 deposed King Gustav IV, whom they considered incompetent, and surprisingly invited Jean Baptiste Bernadotte, a French general who had served under their enemy Napoleon, to become King of Sweden. Bernadotte accepted and he became King Charles XVI; his descendents occupy the Swedish throne to this day. When the new king was installed, he addressed the Swedish Parliament in their language. His broken Swedish amused the Swedes, and they roared with laughter. The Frenchman who had become king was so upset that he never tried to speak Swedish again.[29]

As a French general, Bernadotte was used to deference from those below him in the hierarchy. Members of Parliament would never laugh at a king in France or criticize him to his face. Even today, France has a high-power-distance score compared to other Western European countries. Nearly all the top jobs in the French public and private sectors are held by graduates of two elite institutions—the École Nationale d'Administration and the École Polytechnique.

Beginning in the family, children in high-power-distance cultures are expected to be obedient to their parents. Respect for parents and elders is considered a virtue. In low-power-distance countries, children learn to say no at a young age and are encouraged to attain personal independence from the family. In these societies, subordinates are less dependent on their bosses and are more comfortable approaching their bosses and contradicting them.

Individualism-Collectivism

Hofstede's second dimension of culture is the **individualism-collectivism** dimension. The United States rates very high on individualism. However, most of the world is far more collectivist. In collectivist societies, the good of the group prevails over the good of the individual. From birth, individuals are integrated into strong, cohesive groups. They are identified in terms of their group allegiance and their group role.

The collectivist world view tends to divide people into in-groups and out-groups. In other words, people do not simply choose which in-group to join. Often one has to be born into an in-group, such as a family, an ethnic group, or a nationality. Collectivist societies tend to be more suspicious of outsiders, whereas individualistic societies are more welcoming of them. For example, only one of an individual's parents needs to be an American for the individual to qualify as an American citizen. Furthermore, one can be an American citizen simply by virtue of having been born in the United States, even of foreign parents. And if one does not qualify by birth, immigration is a possibility. Each year tens of thousands of immigrants request and are granted American citizenship. More collectivist societies, on the other hand, do not bestow citizenship so freely. For one to qualify as an Egyptian citizen, both of one's parents should be Egyptian, and naturalization is virtually unknown in this country.

Individuals in collectivist societies are more dependent on their group and more loyal to it than members of individualistic societies. Group members are expected to take care of each other. In turn, they tend to follow group norms and to avoid deviating from the group in opinions or behavior. This group cohesiveness may transfer to groups joined later in life, such as friends from high school and college or corporate colleagues.

Outsiders may come to be trusted in collectivist societies, but only after they have invested much time and effort. Many firms relate a common experience in Saudi Arabia: A manager is sent to Saudi Arabia to establish business relations. After a long time, the potential Saudi client agrees to do business with the firm, but only if the manager who originally established the relationship stays and manages the relationship. In other words, the trusted outsider must be a person, not a firm.[30]

Masculinity-Femininity

Hofstede's third dimension of culture is **masculinity-femininity.** This was (not surprisingly) the only dimension identified in the IBM study in which male and female respondents' scores were significantly different. Nonetheless, some countries were rated more masculine overall, including their women, and some more feminine overall, including their men. Masculinity is associated with assertiveness. Femininity is associated with modesty and nurturing. Masculine societies value ambition, competitiveness, and high earnings. Feminine societies are concerned with public welfare. For example, the percentage of GNP that a state allocates for aid to poor countries does not correlate with wealth but does correlate with femininity.

In Denmark, a feminine country, students tend to prepare a résumé that underplays their achievements. Interviewers know that they must ask leading questions to elicit an account of these achievements in the interview. Students in more masculine societies such as the United States tend to construct their résumés to broadcast any achievements. In this regard, Hofstede noted that Americans look like braggarts to Danes and that Danes look like suckers to Americans.

Uncertainty Avoidance

Uncertainty avoidance is the state of being uneasy or worried about what may happen in the future. It is not the same as being averse to risk. People who are risk averse are afraid that something specific might happen—for example, that an inflated stock market might crash or that they might fail their final exams because they haven't studied hard. People who are uncertainty-avoidant are *anxious in general*. Exams always make them anxious, even if they have studied hard and have done well in the past. The future is uncertain for all of us. Typical persons from low-uncertainty-avoidance societies accept this fact and are confident that they can deal with whatever might arise. In other words, they are comfortable "rolling with the punches." Typical persons from high-uncertainty-avoidance societies try to control and minimize future uncertainty. They have a tendency to work hard or at least to feel more comfortable if they are busy doing something.

Uncertainty-avoidant cultures don't like ambiguity. Events should be clearly understandable and as predictable as possible. Teachers in these cultures are expected always to have the answers. In low-uncertainty-avoidance cultures, on the other hand, teachers are allowed to say, "I don't know." High-uncertainty-avoidance cultures have an emotional need for formal and informal rules. Low-uncertainty-avoidance cultures dislike rules. What rules they do employ, however, are generally more respected than are the many rules of uncertainty-avoidant cultures.

High-uncertainty-avoidance cultures tend to think that what is different is potentially dangerous. This fear may make such cultures less innovative than low-uncertainty-avoidance cultures, because radically new ideas are suspect to them. However, they can prove outstanding at implementing the ideas of others. As Hofstede noted, Britain (a low-uncertainty-avoidance culture) has produced more Nobel Prize winners than Japan (a high-uncertainty-avoidance culture), but Japan has brought more new products to the world market.[31]

Uses and Limitations of the Hofstede Measures

The Hofstede measures are an excellent way to identify quickly those areas where significant cultural differences exist. Americans dealing with distributors in Guatemala must remember that their agents come from a very different culture. Guatemala scores much higher on power distance and uncertainty avoidance. It is a very collectivist society, whereas the United States is a very individualistic one. If we send a young American manager to negotiate terms with Guatemalan distributors, our American manager must be careful to show proper respect and deference to any older distributors. Our manager should expect the distributors to ask for clear and detailed contracts. In turn, our manager should take care that the distributors belong to the right in-group. For example, do their group ties allow them to reach the right retailers and to access preferential financing? Have the potential distributors conformed to group norms, and have they established themselves as trustworthy within their group?

We must remember that all these scores are relative. Depending on the reference point, Japan can appear collectivist or individualistic. American culture is more individualistic than Japanese culture, but Japanese culture is more individualistic than South Korean culture. When a multinational company sends American managers to deal with Japanese customers, these managers must adjust to a more collectivist culture. When the multinational sends South Korean managers to deal with the same Japanese customers, they must adjust to a more individualistic culture.

The Hofstede measures have a number of limitations. Not all countries were included in the original IBM study. Because IBM had no subsidiaries in Russia or Eastern Europe in the late 1970s, with the exception of Yugoslavia we have no original scores for these markets. Luckily, new studies have added to the list. Still, for reasons of sample size, some countries in both Africa and the Middle East were grouped together despite probable cultural differences between them. We must also keep in mind that ethnic groups and regional populations within a country can vary significantly from the national average. Finally, the Hofstede measures should not be used for stereotyping people. They do present us with central tendencies or averages for a culture, but they cannot be used to describe any one person who might come from that culture. Some individual Swedes will behave in a more "masculine" manner than some Japanese, even though Sweden as a whole is a feminine culture and Japan as a whole is a masculine one.

Finally, although the Hofstede measures are useful for identifying cultural differences and suggesting potential cross-cultural problems that international marketers may face, they do not capture or elucidate all aspects of a culture. Britain and the United States appear nearly similar across all the Hofstede measures. Still, they differ in many aspects of culture. For example, Britain exhibits greater class-consciousness than is found in the United States, and the United States scores higher on religiosity, as exhibited, for example, in church attendance. We cannot hope to capture a complete culture in four numeric measures. They are a great place to start, but they are only a start.

Cultural Change

How quickly does culture change? Are the Hofstede measures valid after 25 years? Will they be valid 25 years from now? Culture does change, but most writers on culture agree that it changes very slowly. In the 1920s, the Ottoman Empire that ruled Turkey was ousted in a military uprising. A new charismatic leader, Ataturk, attempted in various ways to distance Turkey from its culture of the past and force Turks to adopt more European ways. A major assault was made on collectivism. Voluntary organizations such as political parties and business associations were required by law to be open to all. Ethnic affiliations that had played a major role in the politics of the Ottoman Empire were discouraged under Ataturk. Citizens were socialized to think of themselves simply as Turks. Physical emblems of religious affiliations, such as the veil worn by Muslim women and the fez worn by Muslim men, were outlawed. Eighty years later, much has changed in Turkey, and Ataturk enjoys hero status among nearly all Turks. Yet his attempt to defeat collectivism has failed. Modern Turkey struggles with the Kurdish ethnic question in the east, Islamic political parties win elections, and Turkey scores only 37 on Hofstede's individualism measure.

It is true that most developing countries rate high on power distance and collectivism (see Figure 3.4.) This fact has led some to conclude that as economies develop, all societies will someday converge in a single, modern culture. Americans in particular tend to believe that this modern culture will resemble American culture. The opening of U.S.-style convenience stores in Japan, along with the introduction of late-night television programming, is credited with accelerating changes in Japanese eating patterns. The easy access to prepared food at these convenience stores is even associated with a decrease in the demand for rice in Japan.[32]

Still, it is important to remember that cultures in the world today vary greatly. With global media, Internet connection, and human migration, virtually all cultures are affected by other cultures. All societies are evolving. In a hundred years, Indonesia will undergo cultural change, but it won't become America. In a hundred years, America will undergo cultural change as well. Marketing managers from all nations will continue to deal with the cultural differences that make all nations unique.

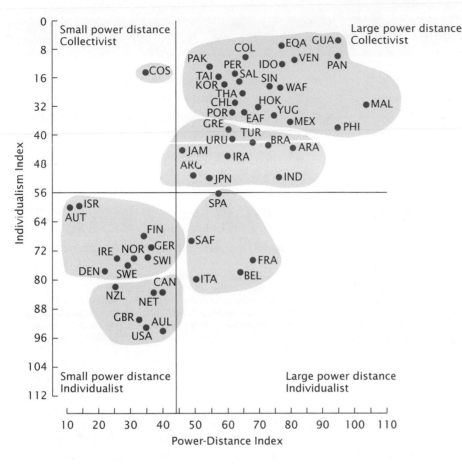

Figure 3.4 *The Positions of 50 Countries and 3 Regions on Power-Distance and Individualism–Collectivism Dimensions*[a]

a. ARA, Arabic-speaking countries (Egypt, Iraq, Kuwait, Lebanon, Libya, Saudi Arabia, United Arab Emirates); ARG, Argentina; AUL, Australia; AUT, Austria; BEL, Belgium; BRA, Brazil; CAN, Canada; CHL, Chile; COL, Colombia; COS, Costa Rica; DEN, Denmark; EAF, East Africa (Ethiopia, Kenya, Tanzania, Zambia); EQA, Ecuador; FIN, Finland; FRA, France; GBR, Great Britain; GER, Germany F.R.; GRE, Greece; GUA, Guatemala; HOK, Hong Kong; IDO, Indonesia; IND, India; IRA, Iran; IRE, Ireland (Republic of); ISR, Israel; ITA, Italy; JAM, Jamaica; JPN, Japan; KOR, South Korea; MAL, Malaysia, MEX, Mexico; NET, Netherlands; NOR, Norway; NZL, New Zealand; PAK, Pakistan; PAN, Panama; PER, Peru; PHI, Philippines; POR, Portugal; SAF, South Africa; SAL, Salvador; SIN, Singapore; SPA, Spain; SWE, Sweden; SWI, Switzerland; TAI, Taiwan; THA, Thailand; TUR, Turkey; URU, Uruguay; USA, United States; VEN, Venezuela; WAF, West Africa (Ghana, Nigeria, Sierra Leone); YUG, Yugoslavia.

Source: Geert Hofstede, *Cultures and Organizations,* (New York: McGraw-Hill, 1991), pp. 23, 51, 83, and 111. Reprinted with permission of the McGraw-Hill Companies.

► *Language and Communication*

Knowing the language of a society can become the key to understanding its culture. Language is not merely a collection of words or terms. Language expresses the thinking pattern of a culture—and to some extent even forms the thinking itself. Linguists have found that cultures with more primitive languages or a limited range of expression are more likely to be limited in their thought patterns. Many languages cannot accommodate modern technological or business concepts, forcing the cultural elite to work in a different language.

World Beat 3.2 *Cinema Sensitivities*

In 2002, Walt Disney Studios, the newest addition to EuroDisney, opened outside Paris. The $530 million venture spreads over 50 acres with a lay-out modeled after an old Hollywood studio com-plex complete with palm trees and a 1940s Holly-wood Boulevard. Starlets pose for cameras and producers recruit visitors as actors. A studio tram tour offers a behind-the-scene view of movies, including a special-effects show based on the film *Armageddon*.

But Disney is careful to pay homage to European cul-ture and filmmaking traditions. One show celebrating the history of animation depicts Disney characters speaking in six different languages. Another documen-tary reminds visitors of the European roots of Disney's animated classics. Cinderella weeps in French and Pinoc-chio cries for help in Italian. A stunt show features cars and motorcycles racing through a village modeled after the French resort town of St. Tropez. The park also promotes the history of European film because French camera makers helped invent the motion picture in the late 1890s. Street musicians play tunes from *La Dolce Vita*, and visitors can pose for pictures outside a shop called "The Umbrellas of Cher-bourg" after a 1974 French musical classic. *Les Enfants de Paradis*, a French film from the 1940s, is a staple for CineMagique, the park's retrospective film attraction.

Sources: Paulo Prada and Bruce Orwall, "A Certain 'Je Ne Sais Quoi' at Disney's New Park," *Wall Street Journal*, March 12, 2002, p. B1; Angela Doland, "EuroDisney Opens New Cinema Theme Park Outside Paris," *Associated Press Newswires*, March 15, 2002; and Richard Verrier, "Disney Looking for Boost in Paris Entertainment," *Los Angeles Times*, March 15, 2002, p.C1.

The French are particularly sensitive about their language as an embodi-ment of their culture and seek to protect it from outside influence. The French government has proposed legal action to limit further incursions by other languages, especially by English. For example, *le airbag* is called *"coussin gonflable de protection"* and *fast food* is *"restauration rapide."* France persuaded the European Community that 40 percent of TV programming should be produced domestically. Cinema tickets in France are taxed and the funds used to support the French film industry as protection against the U.S. film industry, which has come to dominate the European film market.

Forms of Address

The English language has one form of address: All persons are addressed with the pronoun *you*. This is not the case in many other languages. The Ger-manic, Romance, and Slavic languages always have two forms of address, the personal and the formal. Japanese has three forms. A Japanese person will use a different form of address with a superior, a colleague, or a subordi-nate, and there are different forms for male and female in many expressions. These differences in language represent different ways of interacting. En-glish, particularly as it is spoken in the United States, is much less formal than Japanese. Americans often address their bosses and customers by their first names. In Japan this practice could be considered rude. Consequently, knowing the Japanese language gives a foreigner a better understanding of cultural mores regarding social status and authority.

The Context of Language

When an American executive says "Yes" in a negotiation, this usually means "Yes, I accept the terms." However, *yes* in Asian countries can have a variety of meanings. It can mean that your hearers recognize that you are talking to them but not necessarily that they understand what you are saying. It can mean that they understood you but disagree with you. It can mean that they understand your proposal and will consult with others about it. Or, finally, it can indicate total agreement.

The simple term *yes* is a good example of how some languages can be affected by social milieu or context. In **low-context cultures** such as the United States, communication is explicit and words tend to retain their meaning in all situations. In **high-context** Asian **cultures,** meanings are more implicit. The meanings of words change depending on who is speaking to whom, where that person is speaking, and under what circumstances. These subtleties make communication all the more difficult for persons who were not born and raised in those cultures.[33]

Before beginning a conversation or a negotiation, the parties involved need to take part in preliminary chats in order to place one another in the correct social context. For example, do both parties come from the same social background, or is one an outsider? Do both negotiators possess the status required to make a final decision on their own, or will they need to consult with others? In high-context cultures, these questions would never be asked or answered directly. Instead, people are socialized to pick up on the right cues, such as where someone went to school or how long that person has been employed with his or her company. "Placing each other" helps negotiators determine how they will interact and interpret each other's statements.

Body Language

As important as understanding a verbal foreign language is, it is only part of the challenge. The use of nonverbal communications, or **body language,** is also important. Body language includes such elements as touching, making arm and hand gestures, and keeping the proper distance between speakers. Mexicans happily come within 16–18 inches of a stranger for a business discussion. For Latins, Arabs, and Africans, proximity is a sign of confidence. Asians, Nordics, Anglo-Saxons, and Germanic people consider space within 1 yard or meter as personal space. When a Mexican moves closer than this to an English person, the English person feels invaded and steps back, giving the Mexican the incorrect message that he or she does not want to do business.[34] The appropriateness of eye contact varies with culture as well. Americans consider making eye contact while speaking a sign of trustworthiness. Many Asian cultures, such as that of Korea, can consider it a sign of disrespect.

Showing Emotion

Another way in which cultures vary in their communication style is the degree to which they exhibit emotion. In **affective cultures,** such as Italy, the United States, and Arab countries, speakers are allowed—even expected—to express emotions more than in nonaffective or **neutral cultures,** such as China, Korea, and Japan. If upset or even excited, a speaker is allowed to speak

Students at a Japanese smiling school

louder and gesticulate. This is not to say that Americans and Italians feel emotions more strongly than Koreans but merely that Koreans are expected not to *show* emotions. Persons from affective cultures can unnerve those from neutral cultures with their displays of emotion. On the other hand, persons from neutral cultures can appear inscrutable to those from affective cultures.

Despite their nonaffective culture, Japanese marketers are reconsidering the power of a smile. Some retail and service businesses are sending employees to newly opened smile schools that consider "importing joviality" to be their corporate mission. Yoshihiko Kadokawa, author of *A Laughing Face*, believes that smiling at customers increases sales and boosts employee morale. However, teachers at Japan's smile schools concede that smiling excessively is still controversial in Japan, where it is thought to reflect suicidal tendencies, especially among males.[35]

▶ *Overcoming the Language Barrier*

International marketing communications are heavily affected by the existence of different languages. Advertising has to be adjusted to each language, and personal contacts are made difficult by the language barrier. To overcome this language barrier, businesspeople all over the world have relied on three approaches: the translation of written material, the use of interpreters, and the acquisition of foreign-language skills.

Translating and Translators

Translations are needed for a wide range of documents, including sales literature, catalogues, advertisements, and contracts. Some companies send all correspondence through a translation firm. For a company that does not have a local subsidiary in a foreign market, competent translation agencies are available in most countries. The largest translation staff in the world belongs to the European Union, which has 1,500 people translating 1.2 million pages of text per year into its three working languages: English, French, and German. EU bureaucrats also use machine translation to provide rough translations used for e-mail and other less official communications.

Traveling with executives and attending meetings, personal translators can perform a very useful function when a complete language barrier exists. They are best used for a limited time only. Realistically, they cannot overcome long-term communication problems. When one is traveling in Asia, it is tempting to use senior subsidiary managers, who are usually bilingual, as translators. However, this pratice should be avoided. Translators are considered low-level staff members in Asia, and senior managers who employed them in this manner would be looked down on.

Translation Problems

Both translation services and translators work by translating one language into another. In certain situations, however, it is almost impossible to translate a given meaning accurately and fully into a second language. When the original idea, or thought, is not part of the second culture, for example, the translation may be meaningless. When China first liberalized its economy after years of strict communism, Chinese translators had difficulty translating basic English business terms such as *profit* and *loss*, because these concepts were unknown in the communist-planned economy.

Translation problems abound with the use of brand names in various markets. Brand names can be particularly affected by language, because they are not normally translated but are merely transliterated. Consequently, a company may get into trouble using a product name in a foreign country, even though its advertising message is properly translated. Coca-Cola's launch in China was complicated by the fact that, when spoken aloud, its brand name sounds like "bite the wax tadpole" in Chinese.

Today, global companies tend to choose product names carefully and test them in advance to ensure that the meaning in all major languages is neutral and positive. They also make sure that the name can be easily pronounced. Language differences may have caused many blunders, but careful translations have now reduced the number of international marketing mistakes. Still, the language barrier remains, and companies that make a conscientious effort to overcome this barrier frequently achieve better results than those that do not.

Which Language to Learn?

One can draw two major conclusions about the impact of language on international marketing. First, a firm must adjust its communication program and design communications to include the languages used by its customers. Second, the firm must be aware that a foreign language may reflect different thinking patterns or indicate varying motivations on the part of prospective clients and partners. To the extent that such differences occur, the simple mechanical translation of messages will not suffice. Multinational firms require marketing managers with foreign-language abilities.

Still, managers cannot be expected to speak all languages. Global marketers are increasingly united by the use of English as a global business language. English has the advantage of being a noncontextual language that many consider relatively easy to learn. Its influence in international commerce was established first by the British Empire and later by the influence of the United States and U.S. multinational firms. According to a study by the OECD in Paris, 78 percent of all websites and 91 percent of secure websites are in English.[36]

The widespread use of English has even allowed U.S. firms to outsource customer service tasks to call centers based in India. These centers tap into a large pool of English-speaking labor to answer calls from U.S. consumers concerning anything from late credit card payments to problems with software. Indian service personnel call themselves by American names—Barbara, not Bhavana—and learn to speak with an American accent. Customers on the line have no idea they're talking to someone on the other side of the world.[37]

Matsushita, the world's largest seller of consumer electronics, issued a controversial directive in 2000: Managers must pass an English-competency test in order to be promoted. Other Japanese companies that have tied promotions to the ability to speak English include Toyota, NEC, Hitachi, Komatsu, and IBM Japan. In 2000, only students in Afghanistan, Laos, and Cambodia scored lower on English standardized tests than did students in Japan, despite a heavy emphasis on English in Japanese schools. Matsushita believes that its company's mentality has remained monocultural and monolingual even though half its revenues and half its employees are non-Japanese. It hopes to globalize the mindset of managers by requiring them to think occasionally in a foreign language.[38]

Although English has become the language of commerce and electronic communications, a marketing manager's personal relationships will often benefit from the manager's having achieved language skill in a customer's native tongue. Cultural empathy is best developed by learning a foreign language, and learning any language will help develop cultural sensitivity. By learning even one foreign language, a student can gain a better appreciation of all different cultures.

► *Adapting to Cultural Differences*

Some companies make special efforts to adapt their products or services to various cultural environments. Even when a firm tries hard to understand the culture of a new market, however, it is easy to make mistakes. When Disney, the U.S-based entertainment giant, decided to open a theme park in Europe, it had almost no direct overseas experience. Tokyo Disneyland had proved successful, but it had been developed and run by a local Japanese partner. When EuroDisney opened in France, management had already incorporated changes in its successful models from California and Florida. To accommodate the cooler, damper climate in France, more indoor attractions were developed and more covered walkways were installed. Multilingual telephone operators and guides were hired to assist visitors from different European countries. Kennels were built for the many French families who would never think of going on vacation without the family dog. Estimates of restaurant traffic took into consideration the fact that Europeans like to linger over their food and are far less tolerant of standing in lines than Americans.

Still, for the first year of operations, EuroDisney refused to sell alcohol on its premises because this practice clashed with its American idea of family entertainment. The management also refused to cut prices during off-season months, despite a time-honored European tradition of doing this at vacation destinations. The first year of operation was disappointing. Disney then bowed to cultural realities and adopted wine, beer, and differentiated prices. Adapting to European culture paid off. By 2002, EuroDisney was Europe's top tourist attraction—even more popular than the Eiffel Tower.[39]

As the story of EuroDisney illustrates, the influence of culture is particularly important for food products. However, quite a few food firms have overcome cultural barriers. One such celebrated case is McDonald's, the U.S. fast-food franchise operator. Sixty percent of McDonald's sales and all of its top ten restaurants, measured in terms of sales and profits, are now overseas. Leading stores are in Moscow, Paris, and Rome, hardly markets where one would expect the typical U.S.-style hamburgers to do well. In general, McDonald's restaurants overseas have sales about 25 percent higher than the average U.S. outlet. In fact, one of the company's stores in Poland holds the world record for first-day sales, having served 33,000 customers on its opening day.[40]

Still, there are some countries where the McDonald's hamburger menu does not do well. In Japan, McDonald's had to substantially adapt its original U.S.-style menu. It introduced McChao, a Chinese fried rice dish. This dish proved to be a good idea in a country where 90 percent of the population eats rice daily. The results were astounding. Sales climbed 30 percent after the McChao was introduced. McDonald's continues to innovate in Japan with the Teriyaki McBurger and Chicken Tatsuta.[41]

Similar adjustments were made by Domino's Pizza, one of the many pizza franchises active in Japan. The types of pizza favored by Japanese consumers are quite different from those favored in the United States. Although Domino's advertises its pizza as "from the U.S.A.," it offers such toppings as teriyaki gourmet, consisting of Japanese-style grilled chicken, spinach, onion, and corn. In addition, Domino's offers squid and tuna toppings, as well as corn salad.[42]

When Big Boy, a U.S.-based hamburger chain, opened in Bangkok, the franchisee in Thailand also discovered that he needed to make adaptations to the menu to suit Thai tastes. However, those were not the only cultural surprises. Many Thai consumers were at a loss about what to make of the chain's giant statue of a boy in checkered overalls. Some Thais left bowls of rice and incense at the feet of the statue as though it were a religious icon. Other Thais said the statue spooked them. In addition, the restaurant employees would not eat on shifts but insisted on eating together, all at the same time.[43]

READ MORE ABOUT IT: Check out "Big Boy's Adventures in Thailand" under *Supplemental Readings* on our website.

Culture Shock

Interbrew, the Belgian brewing giant, entered the Korean market by purchasing 50 percent of Korea's Oriental Brewing Company. Both sides experienced a degree of culture shock when managers from Belgium and the United States arrived in Korea. The Western managers insisted that the staff speak their minds. The Korean managers, on the other hand, were used to a hierarchical relationship based on respect and unswerving loyalty to the boss. Still, after a bumpy start, the blend of two cultures turned out to be a good thing for the company.[44]

Marketing managers who enter different cultures must learn to cope with a vast array of new cultural cues and expectations as well as to identify

READ MORE ABOUT IT: Check out "Foreign Flavor" under *Supplemental Readings* on our website.

which old ones no longer work. Often they experience stress and tension as a result. This effect is commonly called **culture shock**. The authors of *Managing Cultural Differences* offer the following ten tips to deflate the stress and tension of cultural shock:

▶ Be culturally prepared.
▶ Be aware of local communication complexities.
▶ Mix with the host nationals.
▶ Be creative and experimental.
▶ Be culturally sensitive.
▶ Recognize complexities in host cultures.
▶ See yourself as a culture bearer.
▶ Be patient, understanding, and accepting of yourself and your hosts.
▶ Be realistic in your expectations.
▶ Accept the challenge of intercultural experiences.

▶ *Conclusions*

How do cultural considerations affect your marketing plans? Continue with your *Country Market Report* on our website.

In this chapter, we explored a small sample of the wide variety of cultural and social influences that can affect international marketing operations.

It is essential for international marketers to avoid cultural bias in dealing with business operations in more than one culture. As the president of a large industrial company in Osaka, Japan, once noted, our cultures are 80 percent identical and 20 percent different. The successful businessperson is the one who can identify the differences and deal with them. Of course, this is a very difficult task, and few executives ever reach the stage where they can claim to be completely sensitive to cultural differences.

Review Questions

1. Explain the difference between innate wants and needs and culturally derived wants and needs.
2. Note three ways in which religion can affect marketing. Give examples.
3. Why is Europe a growth market for consumer durables?
4. What is the difference between a high-trust and a low-trust society?
5. Note three ways in which differences in national educational systems can affect marketing.
6. Contrast monochronic and polychronic cultures.
7. List and explain the three temporal orientations.
8. List and explain Hofstede's four dimensions of culture.
9. Contrast high-context and low-context cultures.
10. Why has English become the language of world business?

Questions for Discussion

1. How might the educational systems of the United States, England, and Germany affect the marketing of banking services to young adults aged sixteen to twenty-two?
2. You have been asked to attend a meeting with Belgian, Turkish, and Japanese colleagues to develop a global plan for a new aftershave. Using the Hofstede scores for these countries, discuss

the challenges you would face in the meeting. Assume your native culture.

3. What effects might the Internet have on cultural differences?

4. Why do you think food is such a culturally sensitive product?

5. When a firm enters a new market, how can managers "learn" the culture?

For Further Reading

Bradley, T. L. "Cultural Dimensions of Russia: Implications for International Companies in a Changing Economy." *Thunderbird International Business Review* 41, 1 (January/February 1999): 49–98.

Fukuyama, Francis. *Trust: The Social Virtues and the Creation of Prosperity*. New York: Diane, 2000.

Hofstede, Geert. *Culture's Consequences*. Thousand Oaks, CA: Sage, 2001.

Iyer, Gopalkrishnan. "Cultures and Societies in a Changing World." *Journal of Global Marketing* 9, 3 (1996): 95–96.

Usunier, Jean Claude. *Marketing Across Cultures.* (London: Prentice-Hall), 2000.

| Case 3.1 | *Banning Barbie* |

The Institute for Intellectual Development of Children and Young Adults has declared Barbie a cultural threat to Iran. The tall, blonde, blue-eyed doll represents the American woman who never wants to get old or pregnant. She wears make-up and indecent clothes. She drinks champagne in the company of boyfriend doll Ken. To replace Barbie, the Institute has designed Sara. Sara has darker skin, and black hair, and she wears the traditional floor-length chador.

Since its Islamic Revolution over 20 years ago, Iran has been particularly wary of Western influences. In the mid-1990s, a Coca-Cola factory was shut down for "promoting American culture." A call to ban Barbie is not popular with all Iranians, however. Toy-store owners think Barbie is about business, not culture, and many moderate Iranians oppose attempts to protect national culture by force and prohibitions.

In the Arab world at large, Barbie remains the most popular doll among affluent consumers, but she is about to face new competition. The proposed Leila doll will attempt to give Arab girls a feeling of pride in belonging to their own culture. Leila will have black eyes and hair and will look about ten years old. Her wardrobe options will include Western outfits as well as traditional dresses from the various Arab regions, such as Egypt, Syria, and the Gulf states.

Both Sara and Leila will have brother dolls, not boyfriend dolls. The idea of having a boyfriend is a concept not acceptable to most Middle Eastern families. Sara's brother Dara is dressed in the coat and turban of a Muslim cleric or mullah. Arab children have suggested grandparent dolls for Leila.

The Arab League has sponsored feasibility studies to interest private-sector investors in producing Leila and her family. However, both Leila and Sara will enjoy government subsidies. Currently, 90 percent of toys in the Middle East are imported. High tariffs on imported raw materials have made it cheaper to import toys than to produce them locally. Sara and Leila will sell at about $10, whereas Barbie commands between $30 and $150 in the capital cities of Cairo and Tehran.

Discussion Questions

1. Why is Barbie popular in the Middle East?
2. Should Muslim countries ban Barbie? Why or why not?
3. Should local producers receive subsidies for making Sara and Leila? Why or why not?

Sources: Hasan Mrove, "Arabs to Make Their Own Decently Dressed, Dark Haired, Dark Eyed Barbies," *Deutsche Presse-Agentur*, June 16, 1999; "Toy Shop Owners in Tehren Dismiss Barbie Threat," *Deutsche Presse-Agentur*, October 23, 1996; and "Iran's Sara Challenges Barbie Doll," *Toronto Star*, October 28, 1996, p. A2.

Case 3.2   *Sacred Work, Sacred Leisure*

Unlike their counterparts in many countries, employers in the United States are not required by law to provide paid vacations for their employees. In fact, American culture in general appears suspicious of leisure. Some attribute this to the Protestant work ethic. Many Americans fill their free time with intellectually or physically demanding hobbies or *volunteer work*. Even on vacation, Americans stay in touch with the workplace via their cellular phones and laptop computers.

Europeans, on the other hand, hold leisure in high regard. A new French law in 2000 gave France the shortest work week in Europe. Companies with more than twenty employees are required to cut work hours from 39 to 35 per week. Besides creating more leisure time for workers, this move is expected to help ease unemployment. In Germany, however, longer work weeks may soon be the norm. To Germans, prosperity once meant less work and more leisure time. However, a low birth rate has resulted in fewer workers supporting more and more retired Germans in the generous state pension system. Germans in the workforce may soon have to work longer hours to support the retirees.

The restful German Sunday is also under attack. Sunday is designated "a day for spiritual reflection" in the German constitution. This custom results in a ban on Sunday shopping. Since the reunification of Germany in 1990, former East Germans who grew up in a largely atheistic society have waged war on Sunday closings. East German cities routinely exploit loopholes in the law to allow stores to stay open; one loophole that is commonly invoked allows sales to tourists. Department stores in Berlin now welcome tens of thousands of Sunday shoppers, using the argument that their products could be of interest to tourists. Union leaders, bent on protecting leisure time for their members, have joined churches in denouncing this trend.

If Germans may soon work longer hours, Japanese may soon work less. Japanese workers take an average of only 9 vacation days a year. However, many have been reconsidering the value of leisure since their prime minister suffered a stroke brought on by overwork. Japan has seen a sharp increase in suicides and *karoshi*, or death caused by overwork. The Secretary-General of Japan's ruling party made longer vacations a campaign pledge. Japan has also introduced "Happy Mondays," creating longer weekends by switching certain public holidays from Saturdays to Mondays. The government hopes that more holidays will deliver the added bonus of encouraging Japanese to spend more money in pursuit of leisure and thus boost the economy.

Discussion Questions

1. What cultural factors influence a society's attitudes toward work and leisure?
2. How can different attitudes toward leisure affect the marketing of products?

Sources: William Drozdiak, "German Shoppers Seek to Bring Down Another Wall," *Gazette* (Montreal), p. B3; Andrew McCathie, "A Revolution Takes Hold in German Retailing," *Deutsche Presse-Agentur*, July 20, 1999; and "A Great Time to Work," *The Economist*, August 6, 1999.

Notes

[1]"Give Me a Big Mac But Hold the Beef," *Guardian*, December 28, 2000.

[2]"Cultural Explanations: The Man in the Baghdad Café," *The Economist*, November 9, 1996: 23–26.

[3]Francis Fukuyama, *Trust: The Social Virtues and the Creation of Prosperity* (New York: Free Press, 1996), p. 6.

[4]Michael Arndt, "Where's the Beef? Everywhere," *Business Week*, June 4, 2001: 14.

[5]Joel Greenberg, "Who in Israel Loves the Orthodox? Their Grocers," *New York Times*, October 17, 1997.

[6]Barry Shlachter, "A Matzo Monopoly No More," *Houston Chronicle*, April 8, 2001.

[7]Shahidan Shafie and Osman Mohamed, "'Halal'—The Case of the Malaysian Muslim Consumers' Quest for Peace of Mind," *Proceedings of the American Marketing Association*, Winter 2002: 118.

[8]Kang Siew Li, "Coca-Cola's Global Ramadhan Commercial," *Business Times*, *The New York Straits Times Press*, January 14, 1998, p. 17.

[9]Henry Sender, "Foreign Car Makers Make Mark in India," *Asian Wall Street Journal*, August 22, 2000, p. 1.

[10]"U.S. Company Criticized for Misusing Images of Indian Hindu Deities," *BBC Monitoring*, November 18, 2000.

[11]John Pomfret, "80-Year-Old Cashes In on Famous Name," *Seattle Times*, August 25, 1998, p. A13.

[12]"Trouble Brewing," *Newsweek*, July 19, 1999.

[13]Karin Esterhammer, "Fall Festivals Fill Japan's Streets with Pageantry," *Los Angeles Times*, June 10, 2001, p. L6.

[14]Sheryl Wu Dunn, "Korean Women Still Feel Demands to Bear a Son," *New York Times International*, January 14, 1997, p. A3.

[15]Fuq-in Bian, John R. Logan, and Yanjie Bian, "Intergenerational Relations in Urban China," *Demography*, February 1998: 119–122.

[16]Simon Saulkin, "Chinese Walls," *Management Today*, September 1996: 62–68.

[17]Francis Fukuyama, *Trust*, pp. 62 and 98.

[18]"Teaching Business How to Train," *Business Week/Reinvesting America*, 1992, p. 90.

[19]Paul Osterman, "Reforming Employment and Training Programs," *USA Today*, January 1,1999, p. 20.

[20]"U.S. Pupils Short on Basics, Study Finds," *International Herald Tribune*, May 6, 1994, p.3.

[21]"Math, Physics Scores in U.S. Come Up Short," *Pittsburgh Post-Gazette*, February 25, 1998, p. A1.

[22]"Baffled: Reading Comprehension," *The Economist*, December 9, 1995: 27.

[23]Joop Hartog, "Behind the Veil of Human Capital," *OECD Observer*, January 1999: 38.

[24]Scheherazade Daneshkhu, "Poor Communication and Bureaucracy Make Eastern Europe Frustrating," *Financial Times*, September 9, 1996: 12.

[25]Edward T. Hall, *The Dance of Life* (New York: Anchor Press), p. 12.

[26]"Why Is Jack a Dull Boy?" *The Economist*, January 5, 1996: 112.

[27]"Business: Undue Diligence," *The Economist*, August 24, 1996: 47–48.

[28]K. Sivakumar and Cheryl Nakata, "The Stampede Towards Hofstede's Framework: Avoiding the Sample Design Pit in Cross-Cultural Research," *Journal of International Business Studies* 32, 3 (Third Quarter 2001): 555.

[29]Geert Hofstede, *Culture and Organizations: Software of the Mind* (New York: McGraw Hill, 1991), p. 23.

[30]Ibid., p. 50.

[31]Ibid., p. 123.

[32]Kaoru Sakuraba, "Evolution of a Convenience Store Culture," *Nikkei Weekly*, April 26, 1999, p. 19.

[33]Jean-Claude Usunier, *Marketing Across Cultures*, pp. 416–420.

[34]Judith Bowman, "Before Going Overseas, Be Ready: Know the Protocol," *Mass High Tech*, April 26, 1999: 31.

[35]Valerie Reitman, "Japanese Workers Take Classes on the Grim Art of Grinning," *Los Angeles Times*, April 8, 1999, p. E4.

[36]"English and Electronic Commerce: The Default Language," *The Economist*, May 15, 1999: 67.

[37]"It's Barbara Calling," *The Economist*, April 29, 2000.

[38]Kevin Voigt, "Japanese Firms Want English Competency," *Wall Street Journal*, June 11, 2001, p. B7.

[39]Paula Prada and Bruce Orwall, "A Certain 'Je Ne Sais Quoi' at Disney's New Park," *Wall Street Journal*, March 12, 2002, p. B1.

[40]"Big Mac's Counter Attack," *The Economist*, November 13, 1993: 71.

[41]Elizabeth Brent, "Japan's Deep Recession Spells Big Changes for Branches of U.S. Brands," *Nation's Restaurant News*, February 15, 1999: 1–5.

[42]Phillip R. Harris and Robert T. Moran, *Managing Cultural Differences*, 2nd ed. (Houston: Gulf, 1987), pp. 212–215.

[43]Robert Frank, "Big Boy's Adventures in Thailand," *Wall Street Journal*, April 12, 2000, p. B1.

[44]Michael Schuman, "Foreign Flavor," *Wall Street Journal*, July 24, 2000, p. A1.

4

Political and Regulatory Climate

Oil-Rich Venezuela

was once considered an attractive Latin American market. However, when Venezuelans elected Lieutenant Colonel Hugo Chavez president, he threatened to default on Venezuela's foreign debt and to reassert government control over much of the economy. The new president overhauled the country's constitution and judiciary, centralizing more power in the presidency.

The response of foreign businesses was immediate. The next year foreign investment fell 40 percent. Eli Lilly and Honda were among the multinational firms that closed operations in Venezuela.[1] Across the globe, Exxon found itself embroiled in a guerilla war between separatists and the Indonesian government. After sustaining 28 attacks in only one month, Exxon shut down a natural gas plant when it came under mortar fire.[2]

This chapter identifies the political forces that influence global marketing operations. These forces include both the host and home governments of international firms. Governments both support and restrict business as they seek to achieve a variety of goals from self-preservation to protecting their nation's cultural identity. Inter-

Chapter Outline

national marketers must also be aware of special-interest groups that exert pressure on governments with respect to an increasing number of issues from environmental concerns to human rights.

Dealing simultaneously with several political and regulatory systems makes the job of the international marketing executive a complex one. These factors often precipitate problems that increase the level of risk in the international marketplace. Global companies have learned to cope with such complexities by developing strategies that address the more predictable regulatory changes and the less predictable political risks. These strategies are explained at the end of the chapter.

Learning Objectives

After studying this chapter, you should be able to

▶ List and explain the political motivations behind government actions that promote or restrict international marketing.

▶ Identify pressure groups that affect international marketing.

▶ Discuss specific government actions salient to international marketing, such as boycotts and takeovers.

▶ List and compare the four basic legal traditions that marketers encounter worldwide.

▶ Cite examples illustrating how national laws can vary and change.

▶ Differentiate between the steps involved in managing political risk and those involved in planning for regulatory change.

► *Host Country Political Climate*

The rapidly changing nature of the international political scene is evident to anyone who regularly reads, listens to, or watches the various news media. Political upheavals and changes in government policy occur daily and can have an enormous impact on international business. For the executive, this means constant adjustments to exploit new opportunities and minimize losses.

Besides the international company, the principal players in the political arena are the host country governments and the home country governments. Sometimes transnational bodies or agencies such as the EU or the WTO can be involved. Within a national market, the interactions of all these groups result in a political climate that may positively or negatively affect the operations of an international business. The difficulty for the international company stems from the firm being subject to all these forces at the same time. The situation is further complicated by the fact that companies maintain operations in many countries and hence must simultaneously manage many sets of political relationships.

In this section of the chapter, we discuss the political climate of host countries. Any country that contains an operational unit (marketing, sales, manufacturing, finance, or research and development) of an international company can be defined as a **host country**. International companies deal with many different host countries, each with its own political climate. These political climates are largely determined by the motivations and actions of host country governments and local interest groups.

Political Motivations

Businesses operate in a country at the discretion of its government, which can encourage or discourage foreign businesses through a variety of measures. The host government plays the principal role in host countries in initiating and implementing policies regarding the operation, conduct, and ownership of businesses. Today about 175 nations have been accepted as full members at the United Nations, a figure that gives some indication of the large number of independent countries that exist at this time. Although each government may give the impression of acting as a single and homogeneous force, governments in most countries represent a collection of various, and at times conflicting, interests. Governments are sharply influenced by the prevailing political philosophy, local pressure groups, and the government's own self-interest. All of these factors lead to government actions that international companies must recognize and actively incorporate into their marketing strategies. Of prime importance is the marketer's ability to understand the rationale behind government actions.

To understand how government decisions are made, and how business and government are related in a particular country, it is helpful to examine the prevailing political structure. Is it a democracy, a dictatorship, or a monarchy? One way to classify governments is by the degree of representation of the populace in government. Democratic or parliamentary governments hold regular elections so that government policies better reflect the will of the people. Over the past decade, the world has seen a considerable shift toward democratic government. This was most apparent in Eastern Europe, where communist governments were swept away in the 1989 political upheaval. However, changes in Latin America have been equally significant. In the early 1980s, true democracies existed in only a few countries, Venezuela and Costa Rica among them. Now, most military dictatorships in that region have been supplanted, and democratic governments hold sway in nearly all Latin American countries.

Whether in a democracy or in a dictatorship, governmental behavior makes sense only if there is a rational basis for the leaders' actions and decisions. As many political scientists have pointed out, these actions usually flow from the government's interpretation of its own self-interest. This self-interest, often called national interest, may be expected to differ from nation to nation, but it typically includes the following goals:

1. **Self-preservation**. This is the primary goal of any entity, including states and governments.
2. **Security**. To the greatest extent possible, each government seeks to maximize its opportunity for continued existence and to minimize threats from the outside.
3. **Prosperity**. Improved living conditions for the country's citizens are an important and constant concern for any government. Even dictatorships base their claim to legitimacy in part on their ability to deliver enhanced prosperity.
4. **Prestige**. Most governments or countries seek this either as an end in itself or as a means of reaching other objectives.
5. **Ideology**. Governments frequently protect or promote an ideology in combination with other goals.
6. **Cultural identity**. Governments often intervene to protect the country's cultural identity.[3]

The goals cited above are frequently the source of government actions either encouraging or limiting the business activities of international companies. (See Table 4.1.) Many executives erroneously believe that such limiting

Table 4.1 *Host Government Goal and Policy Actions*

ACTION	GOAL					
	SELF-PRESERVATION	SECURITY	PROSPERITY	PRESTIGE	IDEOLOGY	CULTURAL IDENTITY
"Buy Local"	X	X	X			
Nontariff Barriers	X		X			
Subsidies	X		X	X		
Operating Restrictions	X	X				X
Local Content			X			
Ownership Conditions		X			X	X
Boycotts					X	
Takeovers	X	X	X		X	

X = Likelihood of using given action to accomplish that goal.

actions occur largely in developing countries. On the contrary, there are many examples of restrictive government actions in the most developed countries. Such restrictive behavior most often occurs when a government perceives the attainment of its own goals to be threatened by the activities or existence of a body beyond its total control, namely the foreign subsidiary of a multinational company.

National Sovereignty and the Goal of Self-Preservation

A country's self-preservation is most threatened when its national sovereignty is at stake. **Sovereignty** is the complete control exercised within a given geographic area, including the ability to pass laws and regulations and the power to enforce them. Governments or countries frequently view the existence of sovereignty as critical to achieving the goal of self-preservation. Although sovereignty may be threatened by a number of factors, it is the relationship between a government's attempt to protect its sovereignty and a company's efforts to achieve its own goals that are of primary interest to us.

Subsidiaries or branch offices of international companies can be controlled or influenced by decisions made at headquarters, beyond the physical or legal control of the host government. Therefore, foreign companies are frequently viewed as a threat to the host country's national sovereignty. (It is important to recognize in this context that *perceptions* on the part of host countries are typically more important than actual facts.)

Many countries limit foreign ownership of newspapers, television, and radio stations for reasons of preserving national sovereignty. Countries fear that if a foreign company controlled these media, it could influence public opinion and limit national sovereignty. The Australian-born Rupert Murdoch controls 70 percent of the major newspapers in Australia. He traded his Australian passport for an American passport to evade ownership restrictions when he decided to expand into media in the United States. As a result, Kerry Packer, owner of Australia's largest magazine-publishing company and television network, tried to convince the Australian prime minister that Murdoch was now a foreigner and should be required to reduce his media holdings in Australia.[4]

Many attempts at restricting foreign firms are now discouraged under agreements established by the World Trade Organization (WTO). Still, these agreements exclude a number of sensitive areas. One such area is the airline industry, where governments remain heavily involved in setting policy, restricting access to airspace, and limiting landing rights. It is therefore not surprising that the takeoff and landing slots at any European airport are dominated by the major domestic airline. For example, Alitalia has 70 percent of the slots in Rome, Lufthansa has 60 percent in Frankfurt, SAS 55 percent in Copenhagen, KLM 50 percent in Amsterdam, Air France 45 percent in Paris, and British Airlines has 40 percent at London's Heathrow airport.[5]

The Need for National Security

It is natural for a government to try to protect its country's borders from outside forces. The military typically becomes a country's principal tool to prevent outside interference. Consequently, many concerns about national security involve a country's armed forces or related agencies. Other areas sensitive to national security are aspects of a country's infrastructure, its essential resources, utilities, and the supply of crucial raw materials, particularly oil. To ensure their security, some host governments strive for greater control of these sensitive areas and resist any influence that foreign firms may gain over such industries.

Examples of such government influence abound. The U.S. government, for one, does not typically purchase military material from foreign-controlled firms, even if they have subsidiaries in the United States. The U.S. government's involvement with the licensing of telecommunications scrambling devices is another example of its sensitivity concerning national security. As scrambling devices for communications become more readily available and more widespread, the U.S. government wants users to deposit the respective codes with a national security agency. The U.S. government, through its National Security Agency (NSA), has always been able to listen in on international communications. The extensive use of modern scrambling devices would make such access impossible. As a result, the government proposed the use of a standard computer chip, "Clipper," developed by the NSA, containing communications in a mathematically unbreakable code. The code would be deposited with the courts and would allow the U.S. government, with proper authorization, to listen in on communications. Even more restrictive is a government attempt to use existing U.S. laws to force installation of such a chip in all computers shipped from the United States.[6]

The protection of national security interests such as defense and telecommunications through regulations requiring local sourcing is declining. This trend has been influenced by two factors. First, it is not economical for each country to have its own defense and telecommunications industry. The high cost of research and development means that in many cases, the small local defense supplier will have inferior technologies. Second, the European Union has agreed to open up public spending to all EU companies. This opening of European public spending has caused many U.S. and Japanese firms to form alliances with European partners in order to pursue these markets.

Fostering National Prosperity

Another key goal for governments is to ensure the material prosperity of their citizens. In fact, a major opposition party in Macedonia calls itself the Party for Democratic Prosperity.[7] Prosperity is usually expressed in national income or gross national product (GNP), and comparisons between countries are frequently made in terms of per-capita income or GNP per capita. (Comparisons are also made on the basis of GNP adjusted by purchasing-power parity to reflect comparable standards of living.) However prosperity is measured, most governments strive to provide full employment and an increasing standard of living. Part of this goal is to enact an economic policy that will stimulate the economic output of businesses active within their borders. International companies that set up production facilities in a host country can assume an important role, because they can add to a host country's GNP and thus enhance its income.

Many host governments also try to improve the nation's prosperity by increasing its exports. Particularly in Europe, heads of governments often engage in state visits to encourage major export transactions. Political observers often note that both the French president and the German chancellor

How does the United States promote exports? How does Turkey? Check out the export promotion links on our website.

spend a substantial amount of their state visits on business and trade affairs, more so than is typically the case for the president of the United States. Attracting international companies with a high export potential to set up operations in their countries is of critical interest to host governments. Frequently, such companies can expect special treatment or subsidies, especially from governments in developing countries. For example, Egypt offered attractive tax holidays to foreign investors who undertook export-oriented projects, and Mexico exempted foreign investors from local-partner requirements if their projects were totally for export.

In many countries, regional or local governments can also influence decisions that affect international firms. When BMW and Daimler-Benz were seeking a U.S. location for their assembly plants, the relevant governments were not the national one but state governments. Various local governments lobbied intensively for the plant. Alabama, the winning state for the Daimler-Benz plant, had to offer a $253 million commitment in infrastructure improvements to attract the project. A year earlier, the government of South Carolina committed $150 million to attract the BMW plant.[8]

Enhancing Prestige

When Olusegun Obasanjo was elected president of Nigeria, he inherited a decision to host the 2003 All-Africa Games. Nigeria had recently rescheduled its foreign debt. By hosting the games, the Nigerian government had accrued building costs for a new stadium that exceeded $340 million, twice what the government planned to spend on health care for one year.[9]

The pursuit of prestige has many faces. Whereas the governments of some countries choose to support team sports or host international events to enhance national prestige, other governments choose to influence the business climate for the same reason. Having a national airline may give rise to national prestige for a developing country. Other countries may support industries that achieve leadership in certain technologies, such as telecommunications, electronics, robotics, or aerospace.

A host government trying to enhance its country's prestige will frequently encourage local or national companies at the expense of a foreign company. In 1991, the U.S. secretary of the interior raised a number of objections to the Japanese ownership of the concessions in Yosemite National Park. Although the concessions were not a strategic business, the idea of part of Yosemite being in foreign hands challenged the nation's sense of prestige.[10] However, U. S. sensitivity to foreign investors appeared to have diminished by 2001, with the Japanese owning much of Hollywood entertainment companies, the Germans buying Chrysler and Random House, and the British purchasing New England Electric and Amoco.

Promoting Ideology

For nearly 50 years North and South Korea have been technically at war. In the 1950s, North Korea was the richer and more industrialized of the two Koreas. North Korea pursued the ideology of *juche*, or self-reliance.[11] Today it is South Korea that is by far the wealthier and more industrialized country.

Governments often attempt to promote ideology. In doing so, they affect business in a variety of ways. Throughout most of the twentieth century, communist governments disallowed private enterprise. Trade with noncommunist Western countries was strongly discouraged. Like North Korea, the Soviet Union paid a high price for its desire to be free of the capitalist world. Rather than taking advantage of licensing technology that was developed in the West, the Soviets followed the more expensive route of attempting to develop their own parallel technologies.

In the 1950s and 1960s, many developing countries adopted the ideology of nonalignment. In practice, this meant strengthening trade and business ties with China and the Soviet Union in order to be less dependent on Europe and the United States. Egypt under President Nasser was a leader in this movement. When President Sadat succeeded Nasser, he sought to diminish his country's growing dependence on the Soviet Union. He sought to establish a closer relationship with the United States and personally met with CEOs from Fortune 500 companies to ask them to invest in Egypt.

For seven decades the PRI party ruled Mexico until Vicente Fox of the National Action Party (PAN) took office as president on December 2, 2000. The PRI had instituted many restrictions on multinational firms. President Fox, a former CEO of Coca-Cola in Mexico, aligned himself with a more liberal and outward-looking economic ideology that encouraged free trade. His party proved especially popular among younger and more urban Mexicans.

The role that ideology plays in communist China seems ambiguous from the point of view of foreign firms doing business there today. China reopened trade and investment relations with the West in the early 1970s. In the past 30 years, the country has undergone significant market liberalization. General Motors and Starbucks operate with and alongside China's traditional state-owned industries. Some state-owned enterprises have been privatized. In other words, they have been sold, wholly or in part, to private owners.

Many foreign businesses target the Chinese market despite the government's adherence to communism.

Chinese firms must now generate profits or face the specter of new bankruptcy laws. Still the Chinese government insists that these changes do not compromise communist ideology.

Protecting Cultural Identity

With the global village becoming a reality, one of the major effects on countries is in the area of culture. Governments can sometimes resist what they believe to be a foreign assault on their culture. For example, both Iran and Venezuela have at one time attempted to outlaw foreign brand names, requiring international marketers to establish names for their products in Persian and Spanish, respectively.

Whereas most countries once were able to determine broadcast policy on their own, control over broadcasting, and therefore culture, is now perceived to be in the hands of a few large, mostly U.S. firms. These firms are most visible in entertainment, the production and distribution of movies, TV programs, videos, and music recordings. Even more important have been the roles of TV companies through the use of satellite transmission. As we saw in Chapter 3, this massive invasion of foreign cultural products has prompted a negative reaction among certain European governments. Led by the French, they have resisted an effort to open up European markets to more foreign movies and TV programs. Recently, the Internet has become an even greater challenge. China bans access to a number of websites, ranging from those carrying foreign news reports to those displaying sexually explicit pictures. Cuba and Iran also restrict access to certain foreign websites.[12]

Host Country Pressure Groups

When the Chinese government prepared to sell stock in a newly formed subsidiary of its mammoth state-owned oil company, it targeted large investors and public pension funds in the United States. However, it met with opposition from several quarters. The AFL-CIO, a major labor interest group, persuaded many key investors to issue statements that they would not participate in the sale. Religious and conservative groups complained that the Chinese parent firm was involved in the Sudan, a country condemned by the United Nations for allowing slavery and alleged to be supporting terrorists. Environmental groups feared that U.S. investment dollars would support environmentally damaging oil projects in Tibet.[13]

As this case illustrates, host country governments are not the only forces able to influence the political climate and affect the operations of foreign companies. Other groups have a stake in the treatment of companies and in political and economic decisions that indirectly affect foreign businesses. In most instances, they cannot act unilaterally. Thus they try to pressure either the host government or the foreign businesses to conform to their views. Such pressure groups exist in most countries and may be made up of either ad hoc groups or established associations. Political parties are common pressure groups, although they frequently cannot exert much influence outside the government. Parties generally associated with a nationalist point of view frequently advocate the adoption of policies restricting foreign companies.

Environmental groups have had a major influence on consumers around the world, raising concerns about nuclear energy, oil transportation, waste disposal, rain forest destruction, fishing techniques, and global warming. Environmental groups forced McDonald's to replace styrofoam packing with cardboard. Even though McDonald's internal market research revealed that environmental issues have neither a positive nor a negative impact on sales, they agreed to work with the Environmental Defense Fund, an environmental pressure group, to reduce unnecessary and harmful waste.[14]

Some of the most potent pressure groups are found within the local business community itself. These include local industry associations and occasionally local unions. When local companies are threatened by foreign competition, they frequently petition the government to help by placing restrictions on the foreign competitors. In China local newsprint factories were being hurt by cheap newsprint from the United States, Canada, and South Korea. In response, the Chinese government assessed a 55–78 percent tax on U.S., Canadian, and South Korean newsprint.[15] In the wake of the terrorist attacks of September 11, 2001, Pakistan became a potentially critical U.S. ally in the Afghan war. The Pakistani government consequently asked the United States to reduce tariffs on textiles from Pakistan. However, officials at the American Textile Manufacturing Institute moved immediately to stop any possible cuts in tariffs that could hurt U.S. textile firms.[16]

READ MORE ABOUT IT:
Check out *Looming Battle* on
our website.

▶ *Host Government Actions*

Governments promulgate laws and take actions in a variety of ways to advance their agendas. In Chapter 2 we reviewed a number of government actions that affect a firm's ability to transfer products across borders. Many government actions, such as those affecting exchange rates, can indirectly affect international markets. Other actions can have a more direct impact on a firm's ability to access a foreign market and operate successfully. Some of these actions are discussed below.

Government Subsidies

Government subsidies represent free gifts that host governments dispense in the hope that the overall benefits to the economy will far exceed such grants. They are popular instruments used to attract foreign investment. Governments are especially inclined to use direct or indirect subsidies to encourage firms that will be major exporters. Exporters bring multiple benefits, providing employment and increasing national revenue through export sales.

An example of a direct subsidy is a government's paying $1 for each pair of shoes to help a local producer compete more effectively in foreign markets. WTO agreements outlaw direct export subsidies but usually do not prohibit indirect subsidies. An indirect subsidy is the result of a subsidy on a component of the exported product. For example, a government may provide a subsidy on the canvas used to manufacture tents that are then exported.

Subsidies can also be used by governments to increase the international competitiveness of local firms and to create or protect jobs. In most countries, subsidies amount to between 2 and 3.5 percent of the value of industrial output. The rate of subsidy in the United States is estimated to be 0.5 percent, whereas it is 1.0 percent in Japan. In Europe, subsidies range from 0.9 percent of industrial output in Britain to 3.1 percent in Germany, 5.3 in Italy, and a high of 5.6 percent in Greece.[17] The European Union has tightened its policy on state aid to industry. However, European governments continue to support manufacturing industries, especially the automobile industry.

Ownership Restrictions

Host governments sometimes pursue the policy of requiring that local nationals become part owners of foreign subsidiaries operating within their borders. These governments believe that this guarantees that multinationals will contribute to the local economy. Restrictions can range from an outright prohibition of full foreign ownership to selective policies aimed at key industries.

India has used ownership conditions extensively. India's Foreign Exchange Regulation Act of 1973 stipulated that foreign ownership could not exceed 40 percent. International Business Machines Corporation (IBM) decided to leave rather than give up majority control over its subsidiary. Coca-Cola also decided to leave rather than share its secret formula with Indian partners.

However, changes in the government have brought a softening of India's stance, and the country is again tentatively courting firms. In 1988, Coke began negotiations to return to India without revealing its cola formula, and the reintroduction of Coca-Cola in the Indian market took place in 1994. Ironically, a major force of liberalization has been the Bharatiya Janata Party (BJP), which was elected in 1998 on a platform of protectionism, threatening to throw out foreign companies. Once in power, the BJP continued to open up markets to outsiders, and it is expected to continue reforms mandated by the WTO. In some industries, such as ports and toll roads, the Indian government is now allowing 100 percent foreign ownership.[18]

In many ways, the Indian case reflects the patterns of many countries. The 1960s and 1970s saw a tightening of the control over foreign ownership. More recently, the trend has been toward investment liberalization. Most countries now recognize that foreign investment provides significant benefits to the nation, such as employment, technology, and marketing know-how. This new trend has brought the elimination of many prior restrictions, such as those related to ownership.

Operating Conditions

Governments establish and enforce many regulations that establish the framework in which businesses operate. Host countries control firms in the areas of product design and packaging, pricing, advertising, sales promotion, and distribution. Some of these restrictions, and strategies to deal with them, are included in later chapters that deal directly with marketing mix. Where such operating restrictions apply to all firms, domestic and international, the competitive threat is lessened. However, companies may still find restrictions a problem when the way they have to operate varies from that to which they are accustomed.

Where operating restrictions apply to foreign or international firms only, the result will be a lessening of competitiveness, and companies should seriously consider these constraints before entering a market. One such restriction involves work permits or visas for foreign managers or technicians whom multinational firms may wish to employ in their various national subsidiaries.

Any citizen of an EU country is free to work in any other EU country, but visa constraints remain an operational hindrance in most of the world.

Some host governments impose local content requirements on products or services sold in their countries. For product-based companies, local-content laws mean that some part of the manufacturing must be done in the host country. Such restrictions are often applied to encourage the use of local suppliers. Local-content requirements also appear in regional agreements such as NAFTA and MERCOSUR to ensure that products granted exemption from tariffs are indeed primarily produced in the region.

Sometimes operating conditions are affected by what governments fail to do. Kidnappings for ransom have risen in Latin America, especially in Colombia, which saw 4,000 kidnappings in 1995; there were 800 in Brazil and Mexico, and 200 in Ecuador, that same year. Senior business executives and political officials are the most common targets of these kidnappings.[19] Mexico City has become particularly notorious for kidnappings, and foreign companies can find it difficult to recruit expatriate managers for their Mexico City operations. In any case, operating costs may increase in these countries as a result of the need to provide employees with heightened security.

What countries are the most dangerous and why? Check out *Current Travel Warnings* on our website.

Boycotts of Firms

Government boycotts can be directed at companies of certain origin or companies that have engaged in transactions with political enemies. Boycotts tend to shut some companies completely out of a given market. One of the most publicized boycott campaigns was the 50-year boycott waged by Arab countries against firms that engaged in business activity with Israel. The boycott was administered by the Arab League. Ford Motor Company was one U.S. company placed on the Arab boycott list when it supplied an Israeli car assembler with flat-packed cars for local assembly. Xerox was placed on the list after financing a documentary on Israel, and the Coca-Cola Company was added to the boycott list for having licensed an Israeli bottler.

The Arab boycott became less relevant with the changing political situation in the Middle East. The last major fighting between Israel and the Arab states took place in 1973, and since then Egypt has signed a peace treaty with Israel. By the early 1990s, many Arab countries only selectively enforced the boycott. After the Iraq conflict and Desert Storm, many more countries abandoned it. Coca-Cola returned to the Arab soft-drinks market in 1994. Coke's sales grew at a rate of 25 percent per year, and Coco-Cola attained a 33 percent share of the Arab Gulf's $1.2 billion market.[20] However, an Arab summit held in Beirut in 2002, called in response to renewed Israeli-Palestinian fighting, discussed the possible reactivation of the Arab boycott.[21]

Takeovers

No action a host government can take is more dramatic than a takeover. Broadly defined, **takeovers** are any host-government initiated actions that result in a loss of ownership or direct control by the foreign company. There are several types of takeovers.[22] **Expropriation** is a formal, or legal, seizure of an operation with or without the payment of compensation. Even when

World Beat 4.1   *Is the Arab Boycott Dead?*

Even if Arab governments fail to enforce the formal boycott of Israel and firms sympathetic to Israel, this doesn't stop Arab consumers from organizing grass-roots boycotts. American firms are often targets because of perceived U.S. support of Israel. These impromptu consumer boycotts have been a way for Arab consumers, many living under nondemocratic regimes, to vent their frustration with the slow progress of peace negotiations between Israel and the Palestinians.

In the United Arab Emirates, supporters of a boycott distributed a list of American brands and firms to avoid. In Egypt, boycott victims included the perennial targets McDonald's and Coca-Cola. But even Pepsi—a longtime favorite in the Arab World from the days of the Arab boycott against Coke—failed to escape unscathed. A chain message circulated among Egyptian high school students claimed that Pepsi stood for Pay Every Penny to Support Israel and called for a ban on the soft drink. Fliers were distributed asking consumers to stop eating at Pizza Hut and to reject American products such as Gillette razors, Nike shoes, and Marlboro cigarettes.

Americana Foods—an Egyptian company that owns franchises for Pizza Hut, KFC, Baskin-Robbins, Hardee's, TGI Friday's, and Subway—saw its sales plunge 30 percent. Procter & Gamble's top-selling detergent, Ariel, saw sales collapse, partly because the brand shares its name with Ariel Sharon, the leader of Israel's Likud Party. Even U.K.-based Sainsbury's saw its supermarkets in Cairo subject to violent attacks as a consequence of the firm's alleged connections with Israel.

McDonald's responded to the situation with leaflets stressing its local Egyptian ownership of outlets and its employment of 2,000 Egyptians. Sales soon recovered. Outlets of A&W, Chili's, and Radio Shack displayed Palestinian flags. Coca-Cola sponsored Egypt's most popular soccer team as well as the Palestinian national soccer team. Sainsbury's took to playing Koranic music in its supermarket aisles and published an advertisement signed by 4,800 Egyptian employees stating that the company did not support Israel.

Sources: "Cairene Shoppers' Intifada," *The Economist*, November 4, 2000; Simon Bowers, "Protests Force Sainsbury Out of Egypt," *Guardian*, April 10, 2001; and James Cox, "Firms Say Arab Boycott Sinking," *USA Today*, June 4, 2001, p. B05.

compensation is paid, there are often concerns about the adequacy of the amount, the timeliness of the payment, and the form of payment. **Confiscation** is expropriation without any compensation. The term **domestication** is used to describe the limiting of certain economic activities to local citizens. This can involve a takeover by compensated expropriation, confiscation, or forced sale. Governments may also domesticate an industry by merely requiring the transfer of partial ownership to nationals or by requiring that nationals be promoted to higher levels of management. If an international company cannot or will not meet these requirements, however, it may be forced to sell its operations in that country.

At one time, studies suggested that takeovers were becoming more frequent and were a major threat to companies operating abroad. A study conducted in 1975 found that 170 foreign takeovers of U.S. subsidiaries occurred between 1946 and 1973. Comparing these findings with the total of 23,282 U.S. subsidiaries operating outside the United States yielded a takeover rate of about six percent.[23] These statistics were supported by a broader survey of all countries, conducted by the United Nations, in which 875 takeovers were identified for the 1960–1974 period.[24] Ten countries had accounted for two-thirds of all takeovers, and fifty countries registered none at all. Nationalization of international firms peaked in the mid-1970s, when up to thirty countries were involved each year, affecting as many as eighty firms.

By 1985, expropriations had virtually ceased. In fact, since the mid-1970s a reverse trend has emerged. In renewed attempts to encourage foreign investment, countries such as Algeria, Egypt, and Tanzania have considered returning companies to prior foreign owners, or at least allowing these former owners to repurchase them. The British bank Barclays International returned to Egypt, where it had been expropriated 15 years earlier. Like many oil-exporting countries, Saudi Arabia nationalized its energy sector in the 1970s, but it began to reopen the sector in 1999. In 2001 Saudi Arabia named Exxon, the world's largest publicly owned oil company, as operator of a major natural-gas project requiring an investment of $15 billion.[25]

▶ *Home Country Political Forces*

Managers of international companies need to be concerned not only about political developments abroad. Many developments that take place at home have a great impact on what a company can do internationally. Political developments in a company's home country tend to affect either the role of the company in general or, more often, some particular aspects of its operations abroad. Consequently, restrictions can be placed on companies not only by host countries but by home countries as well. Therefore, an astute international marketer must be able to monitor political developments both at home and abroad. This section of the chapter explores home country policies and actions directed at international companies.

Home Country Actions

Home countries are essentially guided by the same six interests described earlier in this chapter: self-preservation, national security, prosperity, prestige, ideology, and cultural identity. In general, a home government wishes to have its country's international companies accept its national priorities. As a result, home governments at times look toward international companies to help them achieve political goals.

In the past, home country governments have tried to prevent companies from doing business overseas on ideological, political, or national security grounds. In the extreme, this can result in an embargo on trade with a certain country. The U.S. embargo on trade with Cuba dates back to 1962, following the assumption of power of Fidel Castro. For nearly 40 years, U.S. businesses could not trade with Cuba, and many restrictions still apply today. Another long-running trade embargo imposed by the U.S. government involved Vietnam. Imposed in 1975, this embargo was lifted in 1994. On the other hand, the United States, an ally of Israel, passed legislation forbidding U.S. firms from complying with the Arab boycott. The U.S. government did not want U.S.-based multinational firms to comply with someone else's embargo. Such unilateral restrictions, those imposed by one country only, put businesses from that country at a competitive disadvantage and thus are often fought by business interests. For example, during the embargo against Vietnam, U.S. companies were forbidden to participate in a market of 70 million consumers, while firms from other nations were free to enter.

Because of this risk to the competitiveness of their businesses, governments prefer to take multilateral actions together with many other countries. Such actions may arise from a group of nations or, increasingly, from the United Nations. The trade embargo by the international community against South Africa was one of the first such actions. As a result of consumer group pressures, many companies had already left South Africa to protest its apartheid regime. However, the embargo affected a wider group of firms in the late 1980s when it was imposed by most countries. When the political situation in South Africa changed and apartheid was abolished, the United States, together with other nations, lifted the embargo in July 1991. The United States has since been the largest foreign investor in South Africa, some of the largest firms being Dow Chemical, Ford, General Motors, Coca-Cola, Hyatt, and EDS.[26]

Other multilateral actions by the international community are the trade sanctions enforced by the United Nations against Iraq as a result of the Gulf War in 1991. The most recent multinational embargo is one against Serbia. Although this embargo was partially lifted in October 2000, Serbia's access to international funds is still contingent on its continued transition to democracy.

Home Country Pressure Groups

The kinds of pressures that international companies are subject to in their home countries are frequently different from the types of pressures brought to bear on them abroad. International companies have had to deal with special-interest groups abroad for a long time. The types of special-interest groups found domestically have come into existence only recently. Such groups are usually well organized and tend to get extensive media coverage. They have succeeded in catching many companies unprepared. These groups aim to garner support in order to pressure home governments to sponsor regulations favorable to their point of view. They also have managed to place companies directly in the line of fire.

International companies come under attack for two major reasons: (1) for their choice of markets and (2) for their methods of doing business. A constant source of controversy involves international companies' business practices in three areas: product strategies, promotion practices, and pricing policies. Product strategies include, for example, the decision to market potentially unsafe products such as pesticides. Promotional practices include the way products are advertised or pushed through distribution channels. Pricing policies include the possible charging of higher prices in one market than in another.

The infant formula controversy of the early 1980s involved participants from many countries and serves as a good example of the type of pressure that international companies sometimes face. Infant formula was being sold all over the world as a substitute for or supplement to breast-feeding. Although even the producers of infant formula agreed that breast-feeding was superior to bottle feeding, changes that had started to take place in Western society decades before had caused infant breast-feeding to decline. Following World War II, several companies had expanded their infant formula production into developing countries, where birth rates were much higher than in the West. Companies that had intended their products to be helpful found

For the latest information on unilateral U.S. actions, check out *U.S. Trade Sanctions and Embargoes* on our website.

themselves embroiled in controversy. Critics blasted the product as unsafe under Third World conditions. Because the formula had to be mixed with water, they maintained, poor sanitary conditions and contaminated water in developing countries led to many infant deaths. Poor mothers could also water down the formula to such an extent that babies were malnourished. As a result, these critics urged an immediate stop to all promotional activities related to infant formula, such as the distribution of free samples.

The Nestlé Company, as one of the leading infant formula manufacturers, became the target of a boycott by consumer action groups in the United States and elsewhere. Under the leadership of INFACT, the Infant Formula Action Coalition, a consumer boycott of all Nestlé products was organized to force the company to change its marketing practices. Constant public pressure resulted in the development of a code sponsored by the World Health Organization (WHO) that primarily covers the methods used to market infant formula. Under the code, producers and distributors may not give away any free samples. They must avoid contact with consumers and are forbidden to do any promotion geared toward the general public. The code is subject to voluntary participation by WHO member governments.

Boycotts can have very visible effects. A boycott against tuna caught in nets that also trap and kill dolphins caused Heinz, owner of Star-Kist, to switch to dolphin-safe tuna. Other manufacturers quickly followed suit. Recently Massachusetts passed a state law denying state contracts to companies that did business in Myanmar (formerly Burma) because of that country's brutal dictatorship. Apple, Motorola, and Hewlett-Packard all cited the Massachusetts law when pulling out of Myanmar. A U.S. District Court judge subsequently ruled that the Massachusetts law interferes with the federal government's right to set foreign policy, and the dispute will probably be appealed to the U.S. Supreme Court.[27]

Global marketers must continue to be on the lookout for relevant actions on the part of home country special-interest groups. Pressure groups with specific interests, such as animal protection groups, environmentalists, and other such focused organizations, are likely to be of even greater importance in the future.

What causes are global rights activists pursuing now? Check out the *Public Citizen: Global Trade Watch* home page on our website.

▶ *International and Global Legal Forces*

In many ways, the legal framework of a nation reflects a particular political philosophy or ideology. Just as each country has its own political climate, so the legal system changes from country to country. Internationally active companies must understand and operate within these various legal systems. Most legal systems of the world are based on one of four traditions: common law, civil law, Islamic law, or socialist law.

Common law is derived from English law found in the United Kingdom, the United States, Canada, and other countries previously part of the British Commonwealth. Common law acknowledges the preeminence of social norms. Law arises from what society acknowledges as right and from what has commonly been done and accepted. Laws passed in such countries are frequently interpreted in the courtroom, where a jury consisting of citizens often determines the outcome of a case. Lawyers in these countries are as likely to look to prior case decisions as to the law itself in order to argue their own cases.

Civil, or code, law is based on the Roman tradition of the preeminence of written laws. It is found in most European countries and in countries influenced by European colonialism, such as countries in Latin America. In these countries, laws may be more encompassing as well as precise. Judges play a far more important role in the civil-law system than under common law, whereas juries usually play a lesser role. A traditional difference between civil-law countries and common-law countries has been the way they have viewed trademark protection. The first to officially register a trademark in civil-law countries owns the trademark. However, in common-law countries, someone who actually used the trademark before another registered it could successfully challenge the registration.

Islamic law is derived from the Koran as well as from other Islamic traditions. Islamic law dominates family law in most Muslim countries, but its application to business situations varies greatly from country to country. To begin with, there are four major schools of Islamic law, and countries differ as to which they follow. Furthermore, not all Muslim countries apply Islamic law to commercial transactions. Some do, of course. Saudi Arabia forbids the collection of interest on loans. An importer cannot go to a bank and pay interest to borrow money to import automobiles from overseas. However, an importer can borrow money and pay interest in many Muslim countries. In fact, during the nineteenth and twentieth centuries, most Muslim countries adopted their commercial laws from one or more European countries. Because of this, business law in the Middle East often falls under the civil-law tradition.

Socialist law arose from the Marxist ideological system established in China, Russia, and other former Eastern bloc countries during the twentieth century. Under Marxist rule, economic power was often centralized, and market economies were virtually unknown. Business laws as we know them were absent or underdeveloped. For example, Chinese citizens have only recently been allowed to bring lawsuits against foreign companies or Chinese government ministries. This has inspired activists in China to consider suing tobacco companies for targeting young people.[28]

As many socialist countries liberalize their economies, they are often forced to look outside for quick fixes for their lack of legal sophistication. For example, Russia turned to the United States and law professors in Houston to help develop laws pertaining to petroleum. When Russia joined the WTO, it agreed to adopt new laws concerning trademarks and patents. Unfortunately, many observers note that Russia today has difficulty enforcing these laws effectively. Even the judges have little experience with the new legislation.

China faces similar problems. The Chinese legal system has inspired little confidence from foreign investors. However, when China joined the WTO, the government began training judges to administer the new trade regulations. Legal teams were organized to ensure that city and provincial governments adhered to the new policies.[29]

Attitudes Toward Rules

Egypt experiences 44 traffic deaths per 100 million kilometers of driving. This compares to 20 deaths in Turkey and only 1.1 in the United States. To try to decrease traffic fatalities, the Egyptian government began the new millennium by instituting tough new speeding and seat belt laws, complete with hefty fines. Seat belt sales soared at first and then precipitously declined. One auto parts dealer who once sold 250 seat belts a day saw his sales fall to only 2 or 3 a day. A year later, Egypt's fatality statistics remained the same. Many Egyptians had chosen to buy cheap seat belts that could fool the police but didn't really work. Furthermore, the police were deluged with complaints when they gave out tickets. Because the seat belts didn't work, why should the driver be fined for not buckling up? One Egyptian summed up the public's skepticism, "I think those laws are just so the government can make our lives more miserable than they already are. They want to imitate the West in everything."[30]

Jean-Claude Usunier notes that rules and laws can be established that are respected and implemented quite explicitly. On the other hand, there may be a discrepancy between rules and what people actually do. He suggests that attitudes toward rules are affected by two basic criteria—the level of power distance in a society and whether a society has a positive or a negative human nature orientation (HNO). **HNO-positive societies** assume people can be trusted to obey the rules, whereas **HNO-negative societies** assume just the opposite. The United States is an HNO-positive society with low power distance. This results in pragmatic rules that most people respect and obey. In countries such as Italy and France, HNO is also positive but power distance is high. Ordinary people view themselves as being better than their rulers. As a result, many feel that laws can be challenged to a certain degree. In Germany and Switzerland, power distance is low but HNO is negative. Laws are made democratically, but society still does not trust people to obey them. To ensure compliance, rules must be applied strictly and with very explicit sanctions. In many developing countries, power distance is high and HNO is negative. Rules may often be strict, formal, and even unrealistic. In this atmosphere there is often a high discrepancy between the law and what people actually do or what is even enforced by the authorities.[31] Societies such as these can be especially confusing to international marketers who come from countries such as the United States.

Legal Evolution

China's trade ministry was called in to resolve a dispute in 2001 between China's state postal system and foreign freight forwarders such as FedEx, DHL Worldwide Express, and United Parcel Service over the right to deliver mail in China. The state post office claimed that by law it had the exclusive right to deliver mail. The companies claimed that an order by the State Council, China's cabinet, granted them an exception to the law. In the meantime, the postal service had reportedly inspected and confiscated documents at branches of the freight forwarders and set up roadblocks to intercept their deliveries in some areas.[32]

China is not the only country where international marketers face ambiguous or evolving laws. In addition to dealing with many different national laws, managers must constantly contend with changes. As the global marketplace becomes ever more interconnected, legal changes appear all the more regularly.

One area of law that has seen considerable evolution worldwide is product liability law. Regulations concerning product liability were first introduced in the United States. If a product is sold in a defective condition such that it becomes unreasonably dangerous to use, then both the manufacturer and the distributor can be held accountable under U.S. law. For a long time, product liability laws in Europe were lax by U.S. standards, but they have been expanded in the past 20 years. Still there are differences that result from the different legal and social systems. In the EU, trials are decided by judges, not common jurors, and the extensive welfare system automatically absorbs many of the medical costs that are subject to litigation in the United States. Traditionally, product liability suits seldom posed problems for international marketers in developing countries. However, when accidents attributable to Firestone tires on Ford Explorers occurred, plaintiffs appeared in Saudi Arabia and Venezuela as well as in the United States. Today global publicity surrounding product crises no doubt prompts more consumers in more countries to seek redress for problems.

A second area of law that varies from country to country involves bankruptcy. In Germany and Japan, bankruptcies are often handled by banks behind closed doors. The emphasis is on protecting the company and helping it reestablish itself. Also, creditor preference varies by country. For example, Swiss law gives preference to Swiss creditors.

As with product liability, attitudes toward bankruptcy and regulations pertaining to it have not remained static. In China, bankruptcies were unheard of under the communist system until China drafted its first bankruptcy code in 1988. One proponent of the new law noted that nobody understood it and everybody was scared of it. A major case in 1998 involving a trust and investment corporation revealed that many vagaries in the law still existed. Creditors settled out of court and experienced huge losses. Nonetheless, the number of bankruptcies in China soared in 2000.[33]

In the United Kingdom, Canada, and France, the laws governing bankruptcy favor creditors. When a firm enters bankruptcy, an administrator is appointed. The administrator's job is to recover the creditors' money. In the United States, bankruptcy tends to protect the business from its creditors. Under Chapter 11, the management prepares a reorganization plan that is voted on by the creditors. However, the huge number of new-economy bankruptcies is causing the United States to reconsider its relatively lenient policies. Many who rose with the dot.com boom went under with its demise. In 2001, many Americans were hurrying to file for bankruptcy under Chapter 11 before the U.S. Congress made it more difficult to do so. In the future, many more Americans will face instead Chapter 13, which will require them to repay their debt.[34]

Today the regulation of transactions in cyberspace is critical to the future of electronic commerce. In Geneva in 1998, all WTO members made a political commitment to maintain a duty-free cyberspace.[35] However, many other issues concerning the governance of the Internet have not been resolved, and it even remains unclear which country can claim territorial jurisdiction in this inherently international medium. What will be the future of Internet taxation, privacy safeguards, and censorship? The complexity of the technology, as well as its rapid change, challenge traditional ideas of regulation.[36]

In the following chapters, we will be discussing other national and international laws that affect the management of products, pricing, distribution, and promotion. In many cases these laws are also evolving. Regional associations, especially the European Union, are increasingly setting supranational laws that affect marketing within their member states. Attempts are also under way to set global standards of legal protection, such as in the area of patents and trademarks. In the future, this may help simplify the job of the international marketer.

Some moves to internationalize laws, however, are opposed by multinational firms. In summer 2001, the Hague Conference on International Private Law was considering a global treaty for enforcement of legal judgments. This agreement would require U.S. courts to enforce judgments by foreign courts in exchange for similar treatment abroad for U.S. judgments. Internet providers were among the many U.S. firms that opposed the treaty. E-commerce businesses were especially concerned that the treaty would subject them to a plethora of lawsuits by allowing consumers to sue businesses under local law wherever their websites were accessible.[37] For the time being, however, national laws still prevail in the vast majority of cases, and even global standards, when established, will be administered through local legal systems.

► *Forecasting and Managing Regulatory Change*

International marketers must understand the different political and regulatory climates in which they operate. This is a challenging job in itself because of the many national markets involved. They must also be prepared to deal with changes in those environments. These changes can be moderate or drastic, and they can be more or less predictable. The more moderate and predictable changes we call **regulatory change**. The more drastic and unpredictable changes we call political risk. We will discuss political risk in the next section. Regulatory change encompasses many government actions, such as changes in tax rates, the introduction of price controls, and the revision of labeling requirements. Although less dramatic than the upheavals associated with political risk, regulatory changes are very common. International marketers lose far more money to regulatory change than to political risk.

James Austin suggests four strategic options for a company to consider when faced with regulatory change:

1. **Alter**. The company can bargain to get the government to alter its policy or actions.
2. **Avoid**. The company can make strategic moves that bypass the impact of a government's action.
3. **Accede**. The company can adjust its operations to comply with a government requirement.
4. **Ally**. The company can attempt to avoid some risks of government actions by seeking strategic alliances.[38]

As Figure 4.1 shows, a company is more likely to try to alter a policy when the policy significantly affects its operations and the firm's bargaining power is high. If a policy is not very threatening and the firm's power is relatively low, the firm is more likely to accede.

Motorola discovered after it had designed and test-marketed a new pager in Japan that the pager did not meet new industry standards. These standards were developed by Motorola's Japanese competitors and enforced by the Japanese government. Instead of redesigning its pager, Motorola first attempted to convince the Japanese government to alter its policy and allow the Motorola design to go to market. Redesigning the pager would prove

FIGURE 4.1 *Strategic Approaches to Regulatory Change*

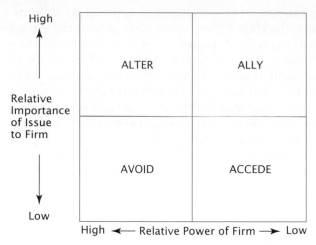

Source: James E. Austin, *Managing in Developing Countries* (New York: The Free Press, 1990), p. 167.

costly, and Motorola believed its bargaining power was high, especially if the U.S. government would back it in its appeal.[39]

By contrast, Pepsi used the two strategies associated with low bargaining power—accede and ally—when negotiating to enter the Indian market. At the time, India had strict foreign-exchange regulations that would stop Pepsi from taking profits out of the country. Pepsi believed that any attempt to convince the Indian government to alter this policy on its behalf would prove futile. The firm also expected to reinvest all Indian profits in the local market for the foreseeable future. Therefore, Pepsi acceded to the government policy. This accession allowed the firm to save time on lengthy negotiations and enter a potentially lucrative market sooner. Also, Pepsi tried unsuccessfully for several years to enter the Indian market as a wholly owned subsidiary. Finally, the company found a powerful local partner in the Indian beverage industry with whom to enter into a joint venture. The joint venture was quickly approved.

Other companies find that they can avoid regulations by making relatively minor changes in their marketing mix. For example, Clearasil could sell its product in Japanese supermarkets if it did not explicitly promote the product as an acne medicine. Otherwise, it was restricted to selling through pharmacies. For years Brazil's price control board allowed firms to set any price they wanted on newly introduced products. Current products or improved versions of current products, however, were subjected to a tedious and unpredictable appeal process before any increase in price was authorized. As a result, companies such as Gillette were inclined to introduce an improved product, such as a better razor blade, as a totally new product rather than as an improved version of an existing line.

Whatever strategy a firm chooses to employ in the face of regulatory change, it is useful to be able to predict whether and when such change will occur. Nothing is certain, but most regulatory change affecting international marketers should not come as a total surprise. Many government actions have economic bases. By understanding the issues covered in Chapter 2, an international marketer can identify probable government responses to prevailing conditions. For example, if export earnings are depressed in a developing country and if foreign investment is low, the government may be forced to devalue the currency. No one may be able to predict what day this will occur, but contingency plans should be in place for when it does occur.

It is also very important that the international marketer listen for signals from the government or influential parties. For months before Egypt disallowed additional foreign investment in packaged foods, local business leaders could be heard in the local media calling for such restrictions. When foreign investors first returned to China, the Chinese government warned them concerning repatriation of profits. They were told that their ability to remove profits from China would be somehow contingent on their export sales. Many firms paid no attention to this warning and later discovered that they did not qualify to repatriate profits. Some even admitted that they thought China had been joking about the possible restriction.

Firms can find themselves caught in embarrassing situations if they fail to heed signals. On the other hand, if they take signals seriously, they can formulate plans for different contingencies. How should the firm respond to a currency devaluation, an increased tax, or new restrictions on advertising? Contingency planning enables marketing managers to avoid crises and to make deliberate and careful decisions about what strategy it will be appropriate to employ in the face of regulatory change.

▶ *Managing Political Risk*

Recently, the U.S. Securities and Exchange Commission (SEC) announced new disclosure rules for firms seeking to sell securities in the United States. Firms must now disclose their activities in countries subject to American government sanctions, such as Cuba, Iraq, and the Sudan. The SEC requires firms to disclose anything that could make their offering risky or speculative. In the past, this included environmental risks and impending lawsuits. Now it includes political risks as well.[40]

The presence of political risk means that a foreign company can lose part or all of its investment, market, or earnings in another country as a result of political actions on the part of a host government, the firm's home government, or pressure groups. As we have noted, the political climate of a country is hardly ever static. Sometimes, a firm is faced with sudden and radical changes in the political climate of a host country.

Political risk is the possibility that an unexpected and drastic change due to political forces will result in adverse circumstances for business operations. Sudden changes of power, especially when the new leadership is committed to a leftist economic and political philosophy, have led to hostile political climates and takeovers. Such changes in government can happen as a result of unexpected coup d'états or revolutions. However, as occurred in Venezuela, it can sometimes result from a democratic election.

The fall of the Iranian shah in 1979 is a vivid example of a sudden change that caught many companies by surprise. Unlike communist revolutions earlier in the century, Iran's revolution was centered on Islam. Still, anti-American sentiment resulted in the taking hostage of U.S. citizens at the American Embassy in Tehran. President Jimmy Carter retaliated by seizing Iranian assets under U.S. jurisdiction and ordered all U.S. companies to cease doing business with Iran. The impact on U.S. business alone involved around 4,000 firms whose claims against Iran were eventually settled by the International Tribunal at the Hague. One of the largest settlements outside the petroleum industry was $49.8 million paid to the tobacco company R. J. Reynolds.[41] And not only U.S. companies sustained damage. Many companies operating from Europe and Japan were forced, as a result of the revolution, to shut down either all or parts of their operations. The subsequent war between Iran and Iraq further limited the attractiveness of the Iranian market and inflicted additional losses on remaining foreign investors.

The Iranian experience taught international marketers an important lesson pertaining to political risk. For many years, firms believed political risk applied only to capital investments in foreign countries. After all, expensive manufacturing plants could be seized. Surprisingly, the Reynolds case involved damage not to brick and mortar but to unpaid accounts receivable for cigarettes exported to Iran. In fact many companies that were simply exporting to Iran found themselves the victims of political risk. So did firms that were licensing their technology or brand names to local Iranian manufacturers. In many cases, the new government forbade importers and licensees from making payments to foreign businesses. However a firm chooses to enter a market, political risk may be a concern.

Political events, such as the detention in Britain of the former president of Chile, can ignite anti-foreign sentiment and in turn threaten international markets.

What can companies do? Internationally active companies have reacted on two fronts. First, they have started to perfect their own intelligence systems to avoid being caught unaware when changes disrupt operations. Second, they have developed several risk-reducing strategies that help limit their exposure, or the losses they would sustain, should a sudden change occur. The following sections will concentrate on these two solutions.

Political Risk Assessment

The business disruption in Iran inspired many companies to establish systems to systematically analyze political risk. To establish an effective political risk assessment (PRA) system, a company has to decide first on the objectives of the system. Another aspect concerns the internal organization, or the assignment of responsibility within the company. Finally, some agreement has to be reached on how the analysis is to be done.

Objectives of Political Risk Assessment

Companies everywhere would like to know about impending government instabilities in order to avoid making new investments in those countries. Even more important is the monitoring of existing operations and their political environment. Particularly with existing operations, knowing in advance about potential changes in the political climate is of little value unless such advance knowledge can also be used for future action. As a result, political risk assessment is slowly moving from predicting events to developing strategies that help companies cope with changes. But first, political risk assessment has to deal with the potential political changes. Many questions must be answered: Should we enter a particular country? Should we stay in a particular country? What can we do with our operations in market X, given that development Y can occur? In undertaking political risk assessment, companies are well advised to look for answers to six key questions:

1. How stable is the host country's political system?
2. How strong is the host government's commitment to specific rules of the game, such as ownership or contractual rights, given its ideology and power position?
3. How long is the government likely to remain in power?
4. If the present government is succeeded by another, how will the specific rules of the game change?
5. What would be the effects on our business of any expected changes in the specific rules of the game?
6. In light of those effects, what decisions and actions should we take now?

Organization and Analysis

One survey of large U.S.-based international firms found that over half the firms had internal groups reviewing the political climate of both newly proposed and current operations. In companies that did not have formalized

World Beat 4.2 *Staying Put in Indonesia*

When the Indonesian economy collapsed 4 years ago, a common perception was that the multinationals would simply flee. In fact, nothing could have been further from the truth. Management consultants estimate that fewer than 300 of the 3,000 foreign companies in Indonesia have withdrawn since 1998, when the fall of President Suharto unleashed race riots, bombings, religious massacres, secessionist revolts, labor strikes, and a 90 percent depreciation of the rupiah. Against all expectations, manufacturers of everything from Energizer batteries to Nike running shoes to L'Oreal cosmetics have dug in their heels, determined to stay the course.

The calculus is simple: Indonesia boasts among the lowest costs in the world, a big domestic market, and proximity to the rest of Asia. As a result, some companies are not merely sticking around, they are expanding. Coca-Cola plans to open a new bottling plant. Renault has announced a joint venture with Suzuki assembler Indomobil to assemble and distribute several Renault models. All told, over the past 3 years, the government has approved $26.2 billion in new foreign investment.

For its part, L'Oreal of France has given up on cracking the domestic market and has switched to an export strategy. Indonesians could barely afford the company's products before the crisis, let alone nowadays. Therefore, 70 percent of the cosmetics produced at L'Oreal's Jakarta plant now head overseas to Malaysia, Singapore, Thailand, Hong Kong, Taiwan, and China.

Of course, not all companies are immune to Indonesia's political unrest. Nike Inc., for example, has a full-time labor relations manager at its Jakarta headquarters. Her job is to prevent disruption of the company's operations. For example, Indonesian workers launched a series of strikes to demand a hike in the minimum wage. Mindful that local factories produce 32 percent of the footwear it sells worldwide, Nike dispatched its labor relations monitor to determine whether the production lines were in danger of being halted. It turned out to be a false alarm.

Source: Michael Shari, "Staying Put," *Business Week*, September 17, 2001: 18.

systems for political risk assessment, top executives tended to obtain firsthand information through foreign travel and talking with other businesspeople.[42]

Rather than rely on a centralized corporate staff, some companies prefer to delegate political risk assessment responsibility to executives or analysts located in a particular geographic region. Exxon and Xerox both use their subsidiary and regional managers as a major source of information. Other firms employ distinguished foreign-policy advisers. Bechtel, the large California-based engineering company, made use of the services of Richard Helms, a former CIA director and U.S. ambassador to Iran. Henry Kissinger, a former U.S. secretary of state, has advised Merck, Goldman Sachs, and the Chase Manhattan Bank. General Motors and Caterpillar have also maintained outside advisory panels.[43]

Several public or semipublic sources exist that regularly monitor political risk. The Economist Intelligence Unit (EIU), a sister company of the *Economist,* monitors some eighty countries on the basis of twenty-seven economic and political factors. These factors include debt, current account position, economic policy, and political stability. The rating of 100 is used to denote highest risk. For example, in one quarter Russia was the riskiest country, with an index of 80, followed by Mexico, Venezuela, Argentina, Brazil,

Turkey, and China.[44] Another index produced by Lehman brothers and Eurasia Group ranked Hungary and Poland among the most stable emerging economies.[45] Euromoney publishes country risk ratings, including political risk evaluations. The results of these ratings are displayed in Table 4.2.

Usually firms use several approaches and sources to assess political risk. For example, Motorola used consultants to evaluate the investment risk for a facility in a Southeast Asian country. A business information service reported on how other businesses were responding to the political climate. Another consultant analyzed the project's financial risks, and an academic analyzed risks relating to operating costs.[46]

What companies do with their assessment depends on the data they collect. Political risk assessment can help the firms stay out of risky countries. However, go/no-go decisions can be difficult to make. Risk analysis is not fortune telling. No one can predict with certainty when the next revolution or war will take place. Like Iran in the late 1970s, some politically risky countries possess very attractive markets. Therefore, political risk analysis is only one of the activities that must be undertaken in the course of deciding whether or not to enter or stay in a foreign market. Many companies, such as Exxon, integrate their political assessments into their overall financial assessments of projects. In cases where Exxon expects higher political risk, the company may add anywhere from 1 to 5 percent to its required return on investment.[47] In this manner the company balances political risk against market attractiveness.

▶ *Risk Reduction Strategies*

Political risk assessment not only aids firms in market entry and exit decisions but can also alert them to the necessity of risk-reducing strategies. Such strategies can enable companies to enter or stay in riskier markets. A classic way to deal with politically risky countries is to seek higher and faster returns on investment. During the 1990s, the average return on foreign direct investment in Africa was higher than that for any other region of the world, according to an UNCTAD study. This was partially because firms invested in projects that promised quick returns.[48] Many companies have also experimented with different ownership and financing arrangements. Others utilize political risk insurance to reduce potential losses.

READ MORE ABOUT IT:
Check out *Business in Difficult Places* on our website.

Local Partners

Relying on local partners who have excellent contacts among the host country's governing elite is a strategy that has been used effectively by many companies. This may range from placing local nationals on the boards of foreign subsidiaries to accepting a substantial capital participation from local investors. For example, General Motors joined forces with Shanghai Automotive Industry Corporation, a state-owned firm, in a 50-50 joint venture to make Buicks, minivans, and compact cars in China.

However, the use of local partners may not decrease the chance of expropriation, and such partners can become liabilities if governments change. General Motors entered into a joint venture in Iran with a partner closely connected with the shah. After the revolution ousted the shah, GM's partner's

Table 4.2 *Political Risk Rankings (2000)*

COUNTRY	POLITICAL RISK	COUNTRY	POLITICAL RISK
Switzerland	10.0	Qatar	6.2
United States	10.0	Macau	6.2
United Kingdom	9.9	Mexico	6.0
Luxembourg	9.8	South Africa	5.9
Netherlands	9.8	Barbados	5.8
France	9.8	Mauritius	5.7
Germany	9.8	Uruguay	5.7
Canada	9.7	New Caledonia	5.7
Austria	9.6	Egypt	5.6
Finland	9.6	Morocco	5.6
Sweden	9.6	Thailand	5.6
Norway	9.5	India	5.5
Denmark	9.5	Estonia	5.4
Japan	9.5	Philippines	5.3
Belgium	9.4	Latvia	5.2
Ireland	9.4	Botswana	5.1
Singapore	9.3	Argentina	5.0
Australia	9.2	Trinidad & Tobago	5.0
Italy	9.1	Turkey	4.9
Portugal	9.1	Costa Rica	4.9
Spain	9.0	Lithuania	4.8
New Zealand	9.0	Namibia	4.6
Taiwan	8.4	Panama	4.4
Iceland	8.1	Slovak Republic	4.4
Greece	8.0	Brazil	4.4
Bermuda	7.6	El Salvador	4.3
Malta	7.6	Colombia	4.3
Kuwait	7.4	Croatia	4.1
United Arab Emirates	7.2	Jordan	4.1
Cyprus	7.1	Fiji	3.9
Hong Kong	7.1	Ghana	3.9
Israel	7.0	Venezuela	3.9
Chile	7.0	Belize	3.9
Korea, South	6.9	Peru	3.8
Slovenia	6.7	Dominican Republic	3.7
Brunei	6.7	Guatemala	3.6
Bahamas	6.7	Sri Lanka	3.6
Saudi Arabia	6.7	Iran	3.6
Czech Republic	6.7	Swaziland	3.6
Hungary	6.6	Maldives	3.6
Poland	6.5	Lebanon	3.5
Malaysia	6.5	Paraguay	3.5
Bahrain	6.4	Libya	3.5
Oman	6.3	Papua New Guinea	3.4
Tunisia	6.3	St. Lucia	3.4
China	6.3	Bulgaria	3.3

COUNTRY	POLITICAL RISK	COUNTRY	POLITICAL RISK
Kazakhstan	3.3	Russia	1.9
Kenya	3.3	Mongolia	1.9
Vietnam	3.2	Moldova	1.9
Jamaica	3.2	Central African Republic	1.9
Azerbaijan	3.2	Antigua & Barbuda	1.9
St. Vincent & the Grenadines	3.2	Madagascar	1.8
Vanuata	3.2	Guinea	1.8
Bolivia	3.1	Mozambique	1.8
Romania	3.0	Uzbekistan	1.8
Bangladesh	2.9	FYR Macedonia	1.7
Algeria	2.9	Niger	1.7
Cape Verde	2.9	Turkmenistan	1.7
Indonesia	2.9	Ukraine	1.7
Syria	2.8	Benin	1.6
Uganda	2.8	Armenia	1.6
Malawi	2.8	Maurutania	1.4
Tonga	2.8	Laos	1.4
Solomon Islands	2.8	Guinea-Bissau	1.4
Samoa	2.8	Somalia	1.4
Seychelles	2.7	Belarus	1.3
Lesotho	2.7	Albania	1.3
Gambia	2.7	Ecuador	1.3
Nigeria	2.7	Bhutan	1.3
Cameroon	2.7	Nicaragua	1.3
Surinam	2.7	Myanmar	1.3
Honduras	2.6	Cuba	1.3
Guyana	2.6	Cambodia	1.2
Senegal	2.5	Haiti	1.2
Gabon	2.5	Chad	1.1
Tanzania	2.5	Liberia	1.0
Grenada	2.5	Djibouti	1.0
Zimbabwe	2.4	Iraq	1.0
Pakistan	2.4	Equatorial Guinea	0.9
Mali	2.3	Angola	0.9
Burkina Faso	2.3	Congo	0.9
Zambia	2.3	Tajikistan	0.7
Sao Tome & Principe	2.3	Korea, North	0.7
Kyrgyz Republic	2.2	Congo, Dem. Republic	0.7
Cote d'Ivoire	2.2	Rwanda	0.6
Dominica	2.2	Sudan	0.6
Yemen	2.1	Georgia	0.5
Ethiopia	2.0	Sierra Leone	0.5
Nepal	1.9	Yugoslavia	0.3
Togo	1.9	Afghanistan	0.0

Source: "Commodity Prices Boost Emerging Markets," Euromoney, March 10, 2000, pp. 106 and 112; and author's calculations.

shares were expropriated. GM then found itself in partnership with the new Islamic government.

Minimizing Assets at Risk

If a market is politically risky, international marketers may try to minimize assets that are at risk. For example, R.J. Reynolds could have refused to extend credit to its cigarette importer in Iran. Instead of accumulating accounts receivable that were at risk, the firm could have demanded payment before shipment. However, as we have mentioned before, some politically risky countries can be attractive markets. This was the case in Iran in the mid-1970s, when many foreign firms were vying for Iranian markets. In light of such intense competition, few companies could afford to be heavy-handed with their Iranian customers.

Another way to minimize assets at risk is to borrow locally. Financing local operations from indigenous banks and maintaining a high level of local accounts payable minimize assets at risk. These actions also maximize the negative effect on the local economy if adverse political actions are taken. Typically, host governments are reluctant to cause problems for their local financial institutions. Local borrowing is not always possible because restrictions may be imposed on foreign companies that might otherwise crowd local companies out of the credit markets. However, projects located in developing countries can sometimes qualify for loans from the World Bank. Pioneer, a major global firm in hybrid seeds, was offered such financing when it considered investing in Ethiopia. These arrangements not only reduce the capital at risk but also lend multilateral support for the venture.

Finally, larger multinational firms may attempt to diversify their assets and markets across many countries as a way to manage political risk. If losses are realized in one market, their impact does not prove devastating to the company as a whole. Of course, this is more difficult to do if a company is small. Several smaller U.S. firms faced bankruptcy as a result of losses ensuing from the Iranian Revolution.

Political Risk Insurance

As a final recourse, international companies can often purchase insurance to cover their political risk. With the political developments in Iran and Nicaragua occurring in rapid succession and the assassinations of President Park of Korea and President Sadat of Egypt all taking place between 1979 and 1981, many companies began to change their attitudes on risk insurance. Political risk insurance can be costly but can offset large potential losses. For example, as a result of the U.N. Security Council's worldwide embargo on Iraq, companies stood to collect $100–200 million from private insurers and billions from government-owned insurers.[49]

For more information on OPIC, check out its home page on our website.

Companies based in the United States can utilize the Overseas Private Investment Corporation (OPIC). OPIC was formed in 1969 by the U.S. government to facilitate the participation of private U.S. firms in the development of less developed countries. Since the Islamic Revolution in Iran, OPIC has covered exporters as well as foreign investors. OPIC offers project financing and political risk insurance in one hundred developing countries. The agency covers losses caused by currency inconvertibility, expropriation, and bellicose actions such as war and revolution. Selected projects utilizing OPIC are listed in Table 4.3.

Table 4.3 Selected OPIC Projects

COUNTRY/ TERRITORY	COMPANY	PROJECT DESCRIPTION	AMOUNT IN U.S. DOLLARS
Angola	American Commodity Associates, LLC	Food Production Facility	40,000,000 Insurance 22,600,000 Finance
Argentina	Citibank, N.A.	Financial Services	55,000,000 Insurance
	U.S. Capital Markets Investors	Water and Sewage Services	150,000,000 Insurance
	U.S. Capital Markets Investors	Residential Mortgage Securitization Services	200,000,000 Insurance
Armenia	A.K. Development, LLC	Hotel	18,000,000 Finance
Bangladesh	El Paso Energy International Company	Power Generation	65,000,000 Insurance
Bolivia	Enron Corporation	Gas Pipeline	85,817,000 Finance
Brazil	EAES Corporation	Power Generation	115,000,000 Finance
	Citibank, N.A.	Financial Services	52,108,000 Insurance
	El Camino Resources De America Latina, Inc.	Leasing Services	1,444,892 Insurance
	Golden Managers Acceptance Corporation	Restaurant Franchising	67,000,000 Insurance
Colombia	Citibank, N.A.	Financial Services	58,937,500 Insurance
	Sector Resources Ltd./Sector Capital	Mining	12,950,000 Insurance
Gaza	Enron Corporation	Power Generation	22,500,000 Insurance
Ghana	Phyto-Riker Pharmaceuticals Ltd.	Pharmaceuticals	24,611,461 Insurance 12,500,000 Finance
India	Enron Corporation/Nations Bank, N.A.	Power Generation	60,000,000 Finance 31,770,000 Insurance
Indonesia	John Hancock Mutual Life Insurance Company	Group Pension and Life Insurance	22,820,000 Insurance
Jordan	Raytheon Infrastructure Inc., Wisconsin Central International, Inc.	Railway Upgrade and Expansion	6,000,000 Insurance 51,583,000 Finance
Kenya	D&D Products, Inc.	Performance bond for Lake Victoria environmental cleanup	1,408,572 Insurance
Lebanon	Elie Naim	Hotel	8,000,000 Finance
Pakistan	Align Technology, Inc.	Data Processing and Graphic Design	3,500,000 Insurance
Panama	Colite Outdoor LLC	Advertising Services	1,008,000 Insurance
Peru	Citibank, N.A.	Financial Services	62,000,000 Insurance
Philippines	Counterpart International, Inc.	Environmental Development Facility	750,000 Finance
Russia	International Scientific Products Corporation	Optical Components Manufacturing	250,000 Finance
	Leap Wireless International, Inc./Qualcomm Inc.	Telecommunications Services	200,000,000 Finance
	Russian Dairy Farms Inc.	Dairy Operation	250,000 Insurance
Turkey	U.S. Capital Markets Investors	Soft Drink Bottling	150,000,000 Insurance
	U.S. Capital Markets Investors/ Ford	Vehicle Assembly	200,000,000 Insurance
Vietnam	V-TRAC Holdings Ltd.	Equipment	2,281,723 Finance
Venezuela	Bank of America NT & SA	Salt Production	40,000,000 Insurance
	U.S. Capital Markets Investors	Expansion and Upgrade of Power Facilities	200,000,000 Insurance
Zambia	Seaboard Corporation	Flour Mill	43,740,049 Insurance

Source: www.opic.gov

▶ *Conclusions*

In this chapter, we have outlined major political and regulatory issues facing international companies. Our approach was not to identify and list all possible government actions that may have an impact on international marketing. Instead, we have provided a background to make it easier to understand these actions and the motivations behind them. It is up to executives with international responsibility to devise strategies and systems for dealing with these challenges posed by governments.

What is important is to recognize that companies can forecast and manage regulatory change. They can also adopt risk reduction strategies to compensate for some of the more unpredictable political risks. For effective international marketing management, executives must be forward-looking, must anticipate potentially adverse or even positive changes in the environment, and must not merely wait until changes occur. To accomplish this, systematic monitoring procedures that encompass both political and regulatory developments must be implemented.

The past several years have brought enormous political changes to the world, changes that are affecting global marketing operations of international firms. These changes have resulted in the opening of many previously closed markets. Even so, substantial political and regulatory risks remain in many countries. Regulatory and political risk management will continue to play a large role in international marketing, allowing firms not only to avoid disasters but also to take advantage of opportunities.

How do political issues affect your marketing plans? Continue with your *Country Market Report* on our website.

Review Questions

1. List and describe the six political motivations behind government actions.
2. Why is a boycott potentially more dangerous to a firm than other government actions such as subsidies and ownership restrictions?
3. Give an example of how home country pressure groups have affected an international marketer.
4. Describe the four basic legal traditions.
5. What factors affect a society's attitudes toward rules?
6. Explain the difference between regulatory change and political risk.
7. List and describe the four strategic options for handling regulatory change.
8. Explain the three steps involved in establishing an effective political risk assessment system.
9. List and describe the three common political risk reduction strategies.

Questions for Discussion

1. The construction industry in Japan has traditionally been dominated by the domestic suppliers. Few foreign construction companies have won projects in Japan. What aspects of Japan's political forces may have influenced this local control over the Japanese construction market? What political or regulatory forces may lead to the opening of this market for foreign firms?
2. Do ownership restrictions such as local-partner requirements always ensure that multinational firms will contribute more to the local economy than they would otherwise?

3. What are the different methods a company can use to obtain and/or develop political risk assessment information? What do you think are the strengths and weaknesses of each?

4. John Deere has decided to enter the tractor market in Central America. What strategies could it use to reduce the possible effects of political risk?

5. Choose a cause promoted by Public Citizen's Global Trade Watch. Do you agree with the cause? Why or why not? What firms are or could be involved in the controversy?

For Further Reading

Bremer, L. Paul. "Doing Business in a Dangerous World." *Harvard Business Review*, Harvard Business School Publishing, Reprint F0204C, 2002.

Brouthers, K. D., L.E. Brouthers, and G. Nakos. "Entering Central and Eastern Europe: Risk and Cultural Barriers." *Thunderbird International Business Review* 40, 5 (September–October 1998): 482–505.

Henriksen, Thomas H. "The Rise and Decline of Rogue States." *Journal of International Affairs* 54, 2 (Spring 2001): 349–373.

Kobrin, Stephen J. "Territoriality and the Governance of Cyberspace." *Journal of International Business Studies* 32, 4 (Fourth Quarter 2001): 687–704.

Rodman, Kenneth A. *Sanctions Beyond Borders: Multinational Corporations and U.S. Economic Statecraft.* Lanham: Rowman & Littlefeld, 2001.

| Case 4.1 | *Cuba: Re-entering the World* |

In the 1950s, the economy of Cuba was dominated by Spanish landowning families and U.S. corporations. A communist revolution led by Fidel Castro resulted in thousands of confiscations of foreign and local properties. These confiscations included factories, plantations, mines, and real estate. The United States government responded to the confiscations by placing an embargo on Cuba in 1962. The embargo disallowed U.S. exports to or imports from Cuba. In addition, U.S. foreign investment in Cuba was forbidden. Castro originally offered to pay claimants with money from sugar sales to the United States, but the U.S. government refused to negotiate with the dictator. Today the United States recognizes nearly 6,000 claims against Cuba, totaling nearly $7 billion in today's prices.

For years Cuba remained a satellite of the Soviet Union. Virtually all its trade was with Russia or the Soviet bloc. With the dissolution of the Soviet Union in the early 1990s, Cuba was left one of the few remaining communist states in the world. It lost its traditional trading partners and found itself financially destitute. Though wary of capitalism, the island nation began tentatively to encourage foreign investment in the mid-1990s. Investments, primarily from Canada and the European Union, quickly grew to several hundred in number.

The United States, never having lifted its embargo on Cuba, was quick to respond. In March 1996, the Helms-Burton law was passed allowing U.S. citizens to sue foreign companies that used property that had been previously confiscated by the Cuban government. In addition, the U.S. government would deny visas to corporate officers of such companies. Some foreign companies quickly complied by checking for claims against their new Cuban investments. Many more ignored the U.S. threat. President Clinton eventually waived the right to sue under the Helms-Burton law in response to an EU initiative to ask for a WTO ruling against the American law.

In October 2000, after nearly 40 years, the United States partially lifted its embargo against Cuba. Supported by a politically powerful farm lobby, the embargo was amended to allow sales of agricultural products and medicine to Cuba. Still the Cuban government remains wary of closer economic ties with the United States. Although the Cuban economy has improved since the early 1990s, the country remains a tightly controlled society with 11 million people living at subsistence level.

Cuba has once again suggested that it is ready to meet its claims obligations under international law, but it is unclear where Cuba would find the money. Cuba has stated that it plans to seek redress from the United States for the economic cost inflicted by the U.S. embargo, a cost estimated at $60 billion. Another option could be the sale of government-owned properties. Some suggest that after the death of Castro, who is now in his seventies, the U.S. government should offer Cuba a bailout plan to welcome the nation back into the fold. In the meantime, a Miami financier proposes pooling corporate and personal claims against Cuba into a fund that would issue shares to claim holders. These shares would then be speculatively bought and sold.

Discussion Questions:

1. List the various issues covered in Chapter 4 that are illustrated by this case.
2. Should claim holders be compensated? If so, *who* should pay? Why?
3. If you were considering investing in the proposed claims fund, what discount rate would you apply? In other words, how many cents on the dollar do you think these claims are worth? Why?

Sources: Christopher Marquis, "Helms-Burton Puts Squeeze on Cuba's Sugar," *Record*, November 28, 1996, p. A10; James Cox and Christina Pino-Marino, "Awaiting a Return to the Good Life in Cuba," *Financial Post*, March 30, 1999, p. C16; and Christopher Marquis, "Despite U.S. Restrictions Against Cuba, Door Opens Wider for Visits by Americans," *New York Times*, June 19, 2000, p. A10.

Case 4.2 *Coke Under Fire*

For over two years, Coca-Cola struggled to acquire the soda brands of Cadbury Schweppes, which included Dr Pepper and 7-Up. The proposed purchase originally encompassed all of Cadbury Schweppes's international markets except those in the United States, France, and South Africa. A successful purchase would increase Coca-Cola's market share in soda in over 150 countries. For example, Coca-Cola's share in Canada was expected to rise from 39.4 percent to 49.1 percent. In Mexico, its share would rise from 68.4 percent to 72.6 percent.

Not everyone was pleased with the proposed purchase. Pepsi, Coke's major rival, sent letters to legislators in Canada asking the Canadian government to disallow the purchase of the Canadian operations, maintaining that it would result in weaker competition, higher prices, and the loss of 300 jobs in Pepsi's Canadian operations. Smaller independent bottlers joined Pepsi in opposition. Canada's Federal Competition Bureau agreed to undertake a costly investigation that resulted in Coke canceling its plans in Canada. In the meantime, Australia, Belgium, and Mexico rejected the purchase. A number of European countries and the Chilean government also put it under review. As a result, Coke scaled back on its attempts to buy the brands in Europe. Instead, South Africa was added to the deal.

The Cadbury Schweppes purchase is not the only encounter Coke has had with competition regulators in Europe and elsewhere. In May 2000, the offices of Coca-Cola Enterprises were raided in London and Brussels. EU regulators were seeking incriminating documents related to Coke's allegedly having given German, Austrian, and Danish supermarkets illegal incentives to stock fewer rival products. A similar investigation the year before in Italy had resulted in a $16 million fine being levied on the company. If found guilty in the broader EU case, the company could be fined as much as $14.4 billion.

Doug Daft, the new head of Coca-Cola, visited Europe and personally met with top anti-trust officials at the EU and various European countries. He wanted to present Coke's case personally and to achieve a better understanding of the concerns of the officials. He stated that Coke was committed to playing by the house rules wherever they did business. However, what Coke called aggressive yet honest competition, Europe viewed as abrasive, domineering, and unacceptable American behavior.

Meanwhile, problems were cropping up back in the home market as well. A jury in Daingerfield, Texas, found the company guilty of breaking Texas antitrust laws and assessed a $15.6 million fine. Coke was accused of demanding exclusive advertising, displays, and vending machines from retailers. In addition, a U.S. Federal Trade Commission report concluded that acquisitions of other soft-drink brands by industry leaders resulted in higher prices to American consumers.

Discussion Questions:

1. Why do you think some countries disallowed the Cadbury Schweppes acquisition whereas others did not?
2. Given Mr. Daft's statement that Coca-Cola is committed to playing by the rules, why is the firm in trouble in so many countries?
3. What advice would you give Coca-Cola concerning their handling of government relations?

Sources: Betsy McKay, "New Formula," *Wall Street Journal*, June 23, 2000, p. A1; Eric Beauchesne, "Pepsi Challenge Builds Against Coke Merger," *Ottawa Citizen*, July 13, 2000; Betty Liu, "Coke Abandons Cadbury Plans," *Financial Times*, July 27, p. 21; and Constance L. Hays, "How Coke Pushed Rivals off the Shelf," *New York Times*, August 6, 2000, Section 3, p. 1.

Notes

[1] Kerry A. Dolan, "Dancing with Chavez," *Forbes*, November 13, 2000: 72.

[2] Carl Mortished, "Ethnic Violence Threatens World Energy Security," *Times of London*, April 2, 2001, p. 4M20.

[3] Vern Terpstra and Kenneth David, *The Cultural Environment of International Business*, 3rd ed. (Cincinnati: Southwestern, 1992), p. 203.

[4] "Australian Media: Let Battle Commence," *The Economist*, April 26, 1997: 60–63.

[5] "Let the Market Take Off," *The Economist*, January 18, 1997: 74.

[6] "Cyberspace Under Lock and Key," *New York Times*, February 13, 1994, p. E3.

[7] "Macedonia to Form a Unity Government," *New York Times*, May 11, 2001, p. 14.

[8] Peter S. Canellos, "German Auto Plant Revs up in Alabama," *Boston Globe*, June 30, 1997, p. A1.

[9] "Bill, Borrow, and Embezzle," *The Economist*, February 17, 2001.

[10] "That Tough New Line on Foreign Investment Is Only a Mirage," *Business Week*, January 21, 1991: 43.

[11] "About Face," *The Economist*, December 9, 2000.

[12] "U.S. Hackers to Release Software to Bypass Government Block," *AFX News Limited*, December 6, 2000.

[13] Aaron Berstein, "Pouring Oil on the Flames," *Business Week*, April 3, 2000: 108.

[14] Holman W. Jenkins, Jr., "How to Save McDonald's," *Wall Street Journal Europe*, March 19, 1998, p. 12.

[15] "China Starts New Antidumping Tax on Newsprint," *Dow Jones News Service*, June 3, 1999.

[16] Helene Cooper, "Looming Battle," *Wall Street Journal*, October 29, 2001, p. A1.

[17] "Subsidies to Industry," *The Economist*, April 10, 1999: 105.

[18] "India Opens Trade Doors," *International Business Asia*, January 18, 1999: 4.

[19] James Brook, "Kidnappings Soar in Latin America, Threatening Region's Stability" *New York Times*, April 7, 1995, p. A8.

[20] "Coke Opens Saudi Plant in Cola War," Agence France-Presse, May 5, 1999, p.1.

[21] "Damascus Regional Boycott Office to Hold Meeting," *BBC Monitoring*, April 1, 2002.

[22] Richard D. Robinson, *International Business Management* (New York: Dryden, 1973), p. 374.

[23] Robert G. Hawkins, Norman Mintz, and Michael Provissiero, "Government Takeovers of U.S. Foreign Affiliates," *Journal of International Business Studies*, Spring 1976: 3–16.

[24] Ibid.

[25] Bhushan Bahree, "Exxon, Shell Poised to Win Saudi Deals," *Wall Street Journal*, June 1, 2001, p. A11.

[26] Christopher Ogden, "Special Report South Africa, Less Aid More Trade," *Time*, May 24, 1999: 57.

[27] "U.S. Court Hears Appeal of Massachusetts' Burma Law," *Dow Jones News Service*, May 4, 1999.

[28] Leslie Chang, "Chinese Lawyers Plan to Take On Big Tobacco," *Wall Street Journal*, May 16, 2001, p. A17.

[29] Peter Wonacott, "As WTO Entry Looms, China Rushes to Adjust Legal System," *Wall Street Journal*, November 9, 2001, p. A13.

[30] Susan Postlewaite, "A Crackdown on Madcap Drivers," *Business Week International Editions*, April 30, 2001: 5.

[31] Jean-Claude Usunier, *Marketing Across Cultures* (New York: Prentice-Hall, 2000), pp. 83–85.

[32] Craig S. Smith, "A Roiling Battle over Express Mail Service," *New York Times*, May 10, 2001, p.1.

[33] "Of Laws and Men," *The Economist*, April 7, 2001.

[34] Michelle Conlin, "Bankruptcy on Internet Time," *Business Week*, June 4, 2001: 72.

[35] Charlene Barshefsky, "Trade Policy for a Networked World," *Foreign Affairs*, March/April 2001: 141.

[36]Stephen J. Kobrin, "Territoriality and the Governance of Cyberspace," *Journal of International Business Studies*. 32, 4 (Fourth Quarter 2001): 687–704.

[37]"Telecom, Web Firms Want Cautious Moves on Global Legal Pact," *Wall Street Journal*, June 6, 2001, p. A28.

[38]James E. Austin, *Managing in Developing Countries*. (New York: The Free Press, 1990), p. 166.

[39]David B.Yoffie and John J. Coleman, "Motorola and Japan," Harvard Business School Case # 9-388-056.

[40]"A Long Arm for Securities Law," *The Economist*, May 19, 2001.

[41]"Slow Progress on Iran Claims," *New York Times*, November 14, 1984, pp. D1, D5.

[42]Stephen J. Kobrin et al., "The Assessment and Evaluation of Noneconomic Environments by American Firms: A Preliminary Report," *Journal of International Business Studies*, Spring–Summer 1980: 32–47.

[43]"The Multinationals Get Smarter About Political Risks," *Fortune*, March 24, 1980, p. 87.

[44]"Risk Ratings," *The Economist*, December 7, 1996: 98.

[45]*The Economist*, February 16, 2002.

[46]"How MNCs Are Aligning Country-Risk Assessment with Bottom-Line Concerns," *Business International Weekly Report to Managers of Worldwide Organizations*, June 1, 1987: 169–170.

[47]"The Multinationals Get Smarter About Policital Risks," *Fortune*, March 24, 1980, p. 88.

[48]"Business in Difficult Places," *The Economist*, May 20, 2000.

[49]"Political Risk Insurers Fear Crisis Escalation," *Business Insurance*, 24, 33a (1990): 1

Part 2 *Analyzing Global Opportunities*

COMPETENCE LEVEL	DECISION AREAS
Environmental Competence	**Understanding the Global Marketing Environment** **CH 2** *The Global Economy* **CH 3** *Cultural and Social Forces* **CH 4** *Political and Regulatory Climate*
Analytic Competence	**Analyzing Global Opportunities** **CH 5** *Global Buyer Behavior* **CH 6** *Global Competitors* **CH 7** *Global Marketing Research*
Strategic Competence	**Developing Global Marketing Strategies** **CH 8** *Global Marketing Strategies* **CH 9** *Global Market Entry Strategies*
Functional Competence	**Designing Global Marketing Programs** **CH 10** *Global Product and Service Strategies* **CH 11** *Developing New Products for Global Markets* **CH 12** *Pricing for International and Global Markets* **CH 13** *Managing Global Distribution Channels* **CH 14** *Global Promotion Strategies* **CH 15** *Managing Global Advertising*
Managerial Competence	**Managing the Global Marketing Effort** **CH 16** *Organizing for Global Marketing*

5 Global Buyer Behavior

Since the Signing of NAFTA, many U.S.-based companies have eyed Mexico's market with great interest. Thanks in part to the rising purchasing power of women, Mary Kay, a Dallas-based manufacturer of cosmetics, has watched Mexico become one of its top foreign markets. Wal-Mart has become Mexico's number-one retailer. But for latecomer Starbuck's, Mexico presented an enigma. Mexico was the fifth largest producer of coffee in the world, yet Mexicans barely drank coffee. The average Mexican consumed less than 2 pounds of coffee a year, compared to the 10 pounds consumed by the average American and the 26 pounds consumed by the average Swede. Could Starbuck's create a greater demand for coffee among Mexican consumers? Could its upscale coffee shop format offer a product that was attractive to customers in a developing country?[1]

To begin to develop an effective strategy for global markets, a firm must first consider buy-

Chapter Outline

ers. Buyers can be consumers, businesses, or governments.

In this chapter we explore issues that arise when targeting these different categories of buyers in global markets. We address factors that make each category similar—and yet different—across cultures. Consumer markets may exhibit global segments whose needs and behaviors are relatively uniform across cultures. Business-to-business markets can produce global buyers with unique demands. Government buyers often have multiple agendas. Still, national differences affect all these buyers, making the job of addressing their wants and needs all the more challenging for the global marketer.

Learning Objectives

After studying this chapter, you should be able to

▶ List the factors that influence consumers' abilities to buy and explain how these affect various national markets.

▶ Describe Maslow's hierarchy-of-needs model and apply it to consumers in different cultures.

▶ Give examples of how consumer behavior is similar across cultures and examples of how it may differ from one culture to another.

▶ Explain why business-to-business markets vary in buyer needs and behavior from one country to another.

▶ List the special qualities of national and multinational global buyers.

▶ Describe the five "screens" a foreign firm must pass through to win a government contract.

▶ Explain the role of bribery in international contracts.

▶ *Understanding Buyers*

All buyers go through much the same process in selecting a product or service for purchase. But even though the process may be similar from country to country, the final purchase decisions will vary because of differences in economic and cultural environments. International buyers can differ in terms of who actually makes the decision to buy, what they buy, why they buy, how they buy, when they buy, and where they buy.

To assume that buyers in different countries engage in exactly the same buying processes and apply exactly the same selection criteria can be disastrous. When launching disposable diapers worldwide, Procter & Gamble established a global marketing team in Cincinnati, believing that babies' diaper needs would be the same around the globe. They later found out that whereas mothers in most countries are concerned about keeping their babies' bottoms dry, Japanese mothers had different needs. In Japan, babies are changed so frequently that thick, ultra-absorbent diapers were not necessary and could be replaced by thin diapers that take up less space in the small Japanese home.[2]

In every marketing situation, it is important to understand potential buyers and the process they use to select one product over another. Most elements of a marketing program are designed to influence the buyer to choose one product over competitors' products. In the case of each type of buyer—consumer, business, and government—the marketer must be able to identify who the buyers are and how they make a purchase decision. For example, in automobile purchases in Italy, who usually makes the decision, the husband or the wife? When a Japanese company purchases a computer system, which employees are involved? When a young man in Germany decides to open a savings account, what information sources does he use to select a bank?

▶ *The Consumer Market*

Consumers around the world have many similar needs. There is even some evidence that global consumption patterns are converging. The traditionally wine-drinking French are drinking more beer, and beer-drinking Germans are drinking more wine. Japan, traditionally a fish-eating country, is consuming more beef. One study even suggested that the Swiss prefer French cheese to their traditional Swiss varieties.[3]

All people must eat, drink, and be sheltered from the elements. Once these basic needs are met, consumers then seek to improve their standard of living with a more comfortable environment, more leisure time, and increased social status. Still, consumption patterns vary greatly from one country to another, because consumers vary widely in their ability and motivation to buy. For example, consumption patterns for wine still vary tremendously from country to country. In France, the average annual consumption is 73 liters (19 gallons) per person, compared with 1.6 liters in Japan and 8 liters in the United States. The high consumption of wine in Europe relative to that in the United States is offset by the high U.S. consumption of soft drinks. The average American drinks five times as many soft drinks as a French consumer, three times as many as an Italian, and two and one-half times as many as a

FIGURE 5.1 *Alcohol Consumption for Selected Countries (in liters per person, 1998)*

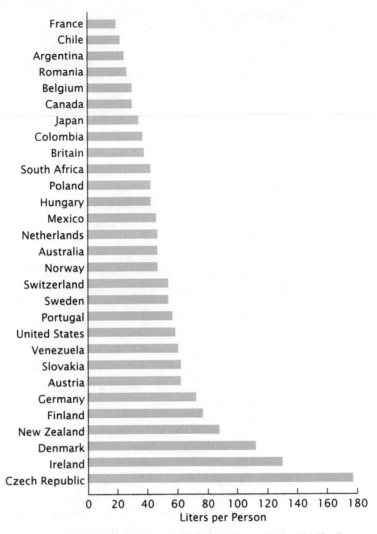

Source: *The Economist*, November 28, 1998: 108. Copyright © 1998 The Economist Newspaper Group, Inc. Reprinted by permission. Further reproduction prohibited.

German.[4] Similarly, Figure 5.1 depicts the vast differences exhibited in beer consumption at the national level.

Basic needs and the desire for an improved standard of living are universal throughout the world, but unfortunately, not everyone can achieve these objectives. The economic, political, and social structure of the country in which they live affects the ability of consumers to fulfill their needs and the methods they use to do so. To understand a consumer market, we must examine the following three aspects:

1. *The consumer's ability to buy*
2. *Consumer needs*
3. *Consumer behavior*

Ability to Buy

To purchase a product, a consumer must have the ability to buy. The medium of exchange in most societies is currency. The ability to buy a product is affected by the amount of wealth a country possesses. A country accumulates wealth by the production and sale of goods within the country and the sale of goods to other countries (exports). The inflows of money from the latter are offset by the outflows of money to pay for necessary imports.

A very important indicator of total consumer potential is **gross national income (GNI)** because it reflects the generation of wealth in a country, which is an indicator of market size. The GNI per capita expresses this value per person, so it is a crude indicator of potential per consumer. GNI and **per-capita income (PCI)** can vary significantly from country to country. With a PCI of $34,210 in Japan and $26,780 in Sweden, one can expect the demand for automobiles to be greater in those countries than in Niger or India, with a PCI below $460.[5] One of the main reasons why Starbuck's was attracted to Mexico was its increasing income per capita. Despite some cultural differences among markets, Starbuck's noticed a strong correlation between PCI and coffee consumption.

It is important to note, however, that PCI statistics have an inherent flaw that can undermine their comparability across all markets. The International Monetary Fund (IMF) recognizes that converting income denominated in local currencies into dollars at market rates can underestimate the true purchasing power of consumers in poor countries relative to those in rich countries. Because of this, the IMF suggests using statistics pertaining to **purchasing-power parity,** which take into account national differences in product prices. For example, assessed in terms of purchasing-power parity, India's buying power increases from a PCI of $460 to one of $2,390. Table 5.1 shows purchasing-power parity for selected developed and developing countries.

Distribution of wealth also has implications for market potential. The government has a major influence on the distribution of wealth in a national market. A government may take a large share of the wealth through taxes or ownership of industries. The government also sets policies and laws to regulate the distribution of wealth. For example, a graduated income tax with a 60 to 90 percent tax on high levels of income and no taxes on low levels of income will help to distribute the income more evenly. The revenue that remains in the private sector will be distributed among workers, managers, and owners of the industries. Low wages and unemployment will tend to increase the size of the lower-income class. Concentration of business ownership in a few families will decrease the size of the upper class.

Income distribution across the population of a country can distort the market potential in a country. For example, if a few people possess nearly all the wealth and the remainder are poor, there will be few people in the middle. As a result, many products that depend on a middle-class market may fare poorly. For example, in Belgium the top 10 percent of the population accounts for about 20 percent of the nation's income and consumption. In Armenia, this same group garners over 35 percent of income. In Bolivia, Colombia, and Guatemala, the top 10 percent accounts for about 46 percent of the nation's income.[6]

Surprisingly, lower-income segments of the population can be attractive markets for consumer goods. In many developing countries, the buying power of the poor may be underrepresented in official statistics. Much of the

Table 5.1 *Per Capita Income at Market Exchange Rates and Purchasing-Power Parity in Selected Countries, 2000*

	MARKET EXCHANGE RATES	PURCHASING POWER PARITY
Argentina	$7,440	$12,090
Brazil	3,570	7,320
Chile	4,600	9,110
Egypt	1,490	3,690
Ethiopia	100	660
Germany	25,050	25,010
Hungary	4,740	12,060
India	460	2,390
Indonesia	570	2,840
Iran	1,630	5,900
Japan	34,210	26,460
Kazakhstan	1,190	5,490
Kenya	360	1,010
Korea, Rep.	8,910	17,340
Mexico	5,080	8,810
Paraguay	1,450	4,460
Philippines	1,040	4,220
Poland	4,200	9,030
Romania	1,670	6,380
Russian Federation	1,660	8,030
Sweden	26,780	23,770
Switzerland	38,120	30,350
Turkey	3,090	7,030
United Arab Emirates	18,060	19,430
United States	34,260	34,260
Vietnam	390	2,030

Source: 2001 World Development Indicator Database, World Bank.

income earned by the poor in these countries is never reported to the authorities. Thus they are said to participate in the **informal sector** of the economy. Informal sectors can be very large. Peru's informal sector accounts for 27 percent of the nation's GNP, including 42 percent of construction, 45 percent of transportation, and 16 percent of manufacturing.[7] Furthermore, the relatively high cost of real estate in urban centers keeps many of the poor locked in slums. Any increase in their disposable income is spent not on relocating but on purchasing more up-scale consumer products. For example, mothers in poor neighborhoods of Calcutta, India, often buy the most expensive brand of milk for their children.

Consumer Needs

Money is spent to fulfill basic human needs. Abraham **Maslow's hierarchy of needs** divides human needs into four levels and proposes that humans will satisfy lower-level needs before seeking to satisfy higher-level needs. The

Shoppers buy Christmas decorations at a street market in Warsaw, Poland. Such markets are often part of the world's large informal economy.

World Beat 5.1 *In the Grip of Status*

They have long, elegant straps or funky square metal handles. They come in canvas, cotton, or luxuriously heavy paper, in seemingly every hue and pattern. Perhaps nowhere on earth does the lowly shopping bag rise above its utilitarian functionality more than in Tokyo, where it is not only a moving advertisement but also an essential fashion accessory and status symbol.

Shopping bags in the United States are toted around the mall briefly, tossed in the trunk, and then relegated to a closet or tossed in the trash; they have a far higher-minded purpose—and a far greater lifespan—in Japan. In this mass-transit-geared society, customers may carry the bag around for hours and then "wear" the bag five or ten times thereafter—in effect serving as mini-billboards.

In-the-know Western designers catering to the lucrative Japanese market generally use thicker, more expensive paper than they do in the United States. They also make the straps more elegant and more durable, ensuring that the bag can stand up to the snow in northern Sapporo, the heat in southern Okinawa, and the rain that pelts down on the entire country in early summer. Just as

Japanese consumers often buy a car first and foremost for its exterior finish, products here are definitely judged by their cover.

In fact, getting the bag is sometimes the main objective of a purchase. Young women sometimes shell out the equivalent of $50 to $100 for Chanel makeup just to get the prestigious bag—a bargain, considering that buying a piece of apparel from Chanel can set a customer back hundreds. The lust for the paper labels has created a second-hand market on the Internet: One site sells Egoiste bags, which are all the rage with high school girls.

Brand image is everything in Japan. "Here there's not much difference between rich and poor," says shopping-bag maker Yasuo Tanaka, referring to Japan's largely middle-class society. "Everybody is more or less the same. So we have to make something to distinguish ourselves from others." Even the post office has its own shopping bag, in a rich, laminated green made at a cost of 80 cents per bag.

Source: Valerie Reitman, "In the Grip of Status," *Los Angeles Times,* June 12, 2001, p. E1.

lowest level of needs is physiological needs. These include the need for safety, food, and shelter. The second level encompasses the social needs of friendship and love. The third level consists of the need to receive respect from others, and the highest level of needs is related to self-actualization or developing one's personality. Figure 5.2 illustrates how the consumption patterns within different countries illustrate Maslow's theory. The figure shows that the structure of consumption for each country varies depending on the income per capita. A developing country, such as China, spends over 50 percent of the national income on food, whereas consumers in developed countries, such as France and the United States, spend less than 20 percent on food.

Although it is possible to generalize about the order of consumer purchases on the basis of Maslow's hierarchy of needs, there is some debate about its cross-cultural applicability. Hindu cultures emphasize self-actualization before materialism. In developing countries, consumers may deprive themselves of food in order to buy refrigerators to establish their social status and fulfill their need for esteem.[8] Consumers from more individualistic countries such as the United States may attach less importance to purchases related to belonging to a group and more importance to hobby-related products that may enhance self-actualization.

In Japan, on the other hand, great attention and expense are devoted to ritual gift giving even among business associates, and Japanese children are socially obliged to hold lavish funerals for their parents. Signs of status continue to be important to Japanese consumers. Despite nearly a decade of poor economic performance in Japan, Japanese shoppers are still attracted to European luxury goods. They purchase about 40 percent of the world's high-quality leather goods and account for over half of all sales of such companies

FIGURE 5.2 *Consumer Expenditure Patterns of Selected Countries (percentage of total spending)*

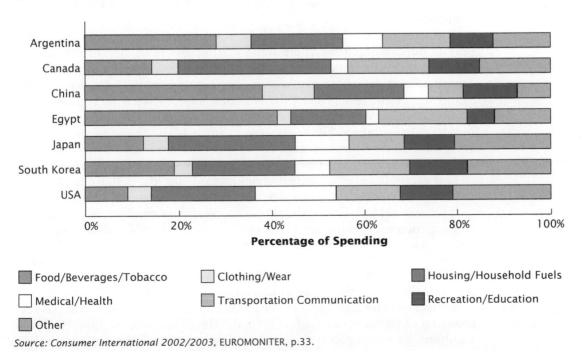

Source: Consumer International 2002/2003, EUROMONITER, p.33.

as Gucci and Louis Vuitton. Christian Dior attributes a quarter of its worldwide sales to the Japanese and has recently added seven stores in Japan.[9]

Consumer Behavior

The ability to buy is influenced by a variety of economic elements, which are much easier to identify and quantify than elements related to consumers' motivations to buy. As we noted earlier, all consumers exhibit some similarities as members of the human race. However, buyer behavior is not uniform among all humans. Buyer behavior is learned, primarily from the culture, and so it differs from one culture to another.

A good example of similarities and differences in buyer behavior across cultures is consumer attitudes toward color. A study of consumers in eight countries revealed that some universal color preferences do exist. Blue was either the first or the second favorite color in every country, and there was no difference in liking in respect to black, green, red, or white. However, there were differences in preferences for brown, gold, orange, purple, and yellow. Black and red signify happiness to the Chinese and are commonly chosen for wedding invitations. In India, Hindus consider orange the most sacred color. The color purple is associated with expensive products in Japan, China, and South Korea but with inexpensive products in the United States.[10] This last finding has possible implications for product design and packaging of luxury products that are marketed cross-culturally.

As we discussed in Chapter 3, culture consists of widely shared norms or patterns of behavior within a large group of people. These norms can directly affect product usage. For example, it may prove difficult to sell insurance in some Muslim countries because religious leaders consider buying insurance gambling, which is prohibited under Islam.[11] Mothers in Brazil believe that only they can properly prepare foods for their babies and therefore are reluctant to buy processed foods. This cultural norm in Brazil caused difficulty for Gerber, despite the fact that its products sold well in other Latin American countries.[12]

The structure of the family and the roles assigned to each member also play an important part in determining what products are purchased and how the decision to purchase is made. Table 5.2 shows the results of a study that examined and compared decision-making roles in families from the United States and Venezuela. Nine products and services were picked, and each family surveyed was asked to identify which member made the decision to purchase the product. The overriding contrast between the two samples involved the role of the husband. More joint decisions regarding major purchases were made in the United States than in Venezuela. In all purchase decisions except those involving groceries and savings, the Venezuelan husband made more decisions than the U.S. husband.

International marketers should be aware that variations in family purchasing roles exist in foreign markets as a result of social and cultural differences. Marketing strategy may need to change to take into account the respective roles of family members. For example, a U.S. manufacturer of appliances or furniture may find it advisable to incorporate the husband into a Venezuelan marketing strategy to a larger extent than in the United States.

Social class can also affect buyer motivation and behavior. Social class is a grouping of consumers based on income, education, and occupation. Within a culture, consumers in the same social class tend to have similar purchase

Table 5.2 *Mean Number of Purchase Decisions by Product Type*

PRODUCT	UNITED STATES	VENEZUELA	PRODUCT	UNITED STATES	VENEZUELA
Groceries			Vacations		
Husband	.23	.23	Husband	1.00	1.51
Joint	.60	.69	Joint	3.68	3.18
Wife	3.20	3.08	Wife	.40	.41
Furniture			Savings		
Husband	.41	1.16	Husband	1.00	1.07
Joint	3.41	2.71	Joint	1.61	1.60
Wife	2.23	2.16	Wife	.44	.34
Major appliances			Housing		
Husband	.98	1.97	Husband	.34	.87
Joint	3.21	2.10	Joint	2.47	1.82
Wife	.85	.93	Wife	.34	.39
Life insurance			Doctor		
Husband	2.65	3.38	Husband	.03	.10
Joint	1.23	.55	Joint	.35	.42
Wife	.15	.05	Wife	.62	.49
Automobiles					
Husband	2.59	4.16			
Joint	3.06	1.42			
Wife	.41	.40			

Source: Robert T. Green and Isabella Cunningham, "Family Purchasing Roles in Two Countries," *Journal of International Business Studies*, Spring–Summer 1980, p. 95. Reprinted by permission.

patterns. Even across cultures this may be the case, especially among young, affluent professionals. A study of MBA students representing 38 nationalities revealed cross-cultural similarities in how these students evaluated product quality. The students were young, affluent, mobile, well-educated, and fluent in English. Across nationalities and cultural groups, all rated brand names the highest as a cue to product quality. Similarly, all rated retailer reputation the lowest and placed price between the other two cues. The importance of physical appearance of the product did vary some among cultures, however.[13] Still, findings such as these have motivated some global marketers to think in terms of **global segments,** transnational consumer segments based on age, social class, and lifestyle rather than on national culture.

▶ *Business Markets*

It is commonly said that business buyers around the world are much more predictable and similar than consumers in their purchasing behavior. They are thought to be more influenced by the economic considerations of cost and product performance and less affected by social and cultural factors. After all, a purchasing agent in Japan who is buying specialty steel for his company will attempt to get the best possible product at the lowest cost, which is similar to how a purchasing agent in the United States or Germany would act.

In fact, business-to-business marketing in the global arena is considerably influenced by variations across cultures. Take for instance the offer of a personal gift to a prospective buyer. Small gifts are often given at first meetings in Japan. Similarly, such gifts are customarily exchanged with Chinese buyers as a way of saying, "I hope this friendship will last." In Latin America, Europe, and the Arab world, however, offering a gift at first meeting is usually considered inappropriate and may even be construed as a bribe.[14]

A number of cross-cultural differences can be observed in buyer motivation and behavior. Because business markets often encompass longer-term relationships between customer and supplier, cultural attitudes toward social relationships are especially important. Sales are often subject to negotiations, and negotiating encompasses many aspects of culture. In addition to dealing with cross-cultural differences, international marketers increasingly find themselves selling to multinational firms, whose buyer behavior presents its own challenges.

The Business Buyer's Needs

Industrial products, such as machinery, intermediate goods, and raw materials, are sold to businesses for use in a manufacturing process to produce other goods. If the objective of the manufacturer is to maximize profit, the critical buying criterion will reflect the performance of the product purchased relative to its cost. This **cost–performance criterion** is a key consideration for industrial buyers, along with such other buying criteria as the service and dependability of the selling company.

Similar considerations arise in other business-to-business sales transactions. A study of how international companies chose foreign exchange suppliers revealed that price was an important factor in both the selection of a supplier and the volume of business allotted to a supplier. Also, large suppliers were generally preferred over smaller suppliers. Nonetheless, account management and service quality could outweigh price, and customers favored suppliers from their home markets.[15]

Large-scale projects such as this pipeline in Russia present opportunities to a number of global contractors and suppliers.

Because the cost–performance criterion is often critical, the economic situation in the purchasing country affects the decision process. This is particularly true for the purchase of new machinery. When buying machinery, a firm must weigh the advantages of adopting a capital-intensive technology against those of adopting a labor-intensive technology. Labor costs play a key role in this decision. Countries with a surplus of labor normally have lower labor costs because supply exceeds demand. These lower pay rates weigh heavily in favor of a labor-intensive method of manufacture. Therefore, these countries will be less apt to purchase sophisticated automatic machinery; the same job can be done with the cheaper labor.

As Figure 5.3 shows, wage levels vary from country to country. Selling an industrial robot that replaces three workers in the manufacture of a product

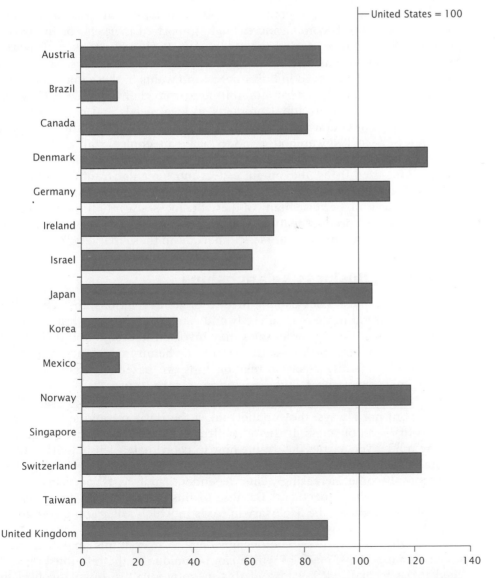

FIGURE 5.3 *Index of Manufacturing Labor Costs per Worker-Hour for Selected Countries*

Note: United States = 100.
Source: United States Department of Labor, Bureau of Labor and Statistics, September 2002.

can be more easily justified in Norway or Germany, where average labor costs are 20 percent more than in the United States, than in Britain, where labor costs are less than 80 percent of the U.S. labor rate. Developed countries with a high labor rate are prime targets for automated manufacturing equipment. Companies that want to export to developing countries where labor is cheaper must be aware that labor-saving measures may not be appreciated or readily applied. For example, the Chinese government encourages the import of labor-intensive technology that can effectively utilize its vast population.

Of course, there are exceptions to this rule. When international banks expanded into the Arab Gulf, they were faced with a decision concerning the level of technology for teller services. In other developing countries, the banks employed older, labor- and paper-intensive technology. However, labor in the Gulf was scarce and expensive as a consequence of the region's sudden oil wealth and its small population. In light of this, many banks chose to purchase the latest technology available from the United States.

The newly industrialized countries of Asia, such as South Korea, Taiwan, and Singapore, are becoming increasingly important markets for industrial products. For example, during the 1990s, Asia-Pacific overtook both North America and Europe as the major market for new elevator sales. Still, some differences can be observed in buyer needs and wants in these markets. Business buyers look for long-term commitment from their suppliers. They expect to see foreign firms adapt products to local needs and commit themselves to frequent contact with the buyer. A global competitor should expect to keep a well-stocked warehouse and to locate a technical staff and sales office in the local market. Because many of the industrial buyers in this region are medium-sized firms, they might expect more regular training to be provided over the life of the business relationship. Price can be a critical factor in the sales as well, because many of these businesses work on tight margins. Similarly, special product features that might appeal to buyers in more industrially developed markets are less important in these markets.[16]

Developing Business Relationships

Business-to-business sales usually involve ongoing relationships. The seller and buyer communicate more directly and establish a relationship that continues over time. For example, sales may involve the design and delivery of customized products, or after-sale service may be an important component of the product. These business relationships are based on mutual understanding, past experiences, and expectations for the future.

Building such a relationship involves a social exchange process. One firm (usually, but not always, the supplier) takes the initiative and suggests that the two firms do business. If the other firm responds, commitments gradually are made. The parties determine how to coordinate their activities, trust is established, and a commitment to a continued relationship arises. The firms may become increasingly interdependent, such as by agreeing to develop a new product together.[17] Because of this close working relationship, cultural sensitivity will be necessary in cases in which seller and buyer come from different cultures.

Although these business relationships have an overall informal character, specific transactions, many of which can be unique to the relationship, will need to be formalized. Because of this, negotiations are often involved in business-to-business sales. Negotiations encompass not only specifics concerning price and financing terms but also such issues as product design, training, and after-sale service.

Cross-cultural negotiations are a particular challenge to global marketers. To begin with, marketers may face the translation problems that we discussed in Chapter 3. Furthermore, whereas some cultures enter negotiations with a win-win attitude, other cultures envisage negotiations as a zero-sum game wherein one side is pitted against the other. Americans can be especially nonplussed when they find themselves negotiating with Russians. Russian negotiators often begin with unreasonable requests in order to test their American counterparts and see how tough they really are. Russian negotiators can surprise Americans with emotional outbursts and anti-Western tirades. Russians also take advantage of Americans' sense of urgency and desire to use time effectively. They may ask the same question repeatedly, feign boredom, and even appear to fall asleep during negotiations![18]

Perhaps some of the toughest cross-cultural negotiations took place after China reopened to world trade. Many foreign firms were interested in the potential of the Chinese market. Americans wanted to negotiate clear, legal contracts with Chinese clients and partners. The Chinese, on the other hand, interpreted this approach as betraying a lack of trust on the part of Americans. They sought to establish close relationships with foreign firms based on mutual loyalty. To them a contract was far less important than these relationships. For their part, Americans found the Chinese passive in their demeanor and as irreverent of time as the Russians. Many Chinese would appear at the negotiating table, and American negotiators found it difficult to figure out who had real authority to agree to terms. Cross-cultural negotiations frustrated many Americans and discouraged, or at least delayed, their entry into this huge market. In the meantime, competitors from Japan and Asia's overseas Chinese community found the negotiations less culturally harrowing. As a result, many entered the Chinese market more rapidly.

Because negotiations involve many aspects of culture—social relationships, attitudes toward power, perceptions of time, and of course language—they must be undertaken with the greatest cultural sensitivity. In most business-to-business sales, negotiations do not end with the first purchase decision. They permeate the continuing relationship between global marketer and buyer. For this reason, global marketers must never assume that marketing industrial products or services remains the same worldwide.

Marketing to Global Buyers

Global buyers present marketers with new challenges. There are two kinds of global buyers: national global buyers and multinational global buyers.[19] **National global buyers** search the world for products that are used in a single country or market. Their job has been far easier since the introduction of the Internet. **Multinational global buyers** similarly search the world for products but use those products throughout their global operations. Such buyers are commonly multinational firms, but they also include organizations such as the World Health Organization. Because both national and multinational global buyers are relatively sophisticated about suppliers and prices, competition for their business tends to be intense.

Multinational global buyers in particular may represent large accounts. They use their market power to command better service and even lower prices. Finding cost-effective inputs is increasingly crucial for most multinational firms, because they too are often under pressure to deliver good products at a low price. Centralized purchasing is one way in which MNCs attempt to keep costs down. Many Fortune 500 companies have recognized this strategic importance of purchasing and have elevated purchasing managers to the vice-president level within their organizations. Firms that sell to multinational global buyers often give them special attention. Practicing what is called **global account management,** they assign special account executives and service teams to these valuable but demanding global buyers. We will discuss this further in Chapter 14.

▶ *Government Markets*

A large number of international business transactions involve governments. For example, 80 percent of all international trade in agricultural products is handled by governments. The U.S. government buys more goods and services than any other government, business, industry, or organization in the world.[20] Selling to governments can be both time-consuming and frustrating. However, governments are large purchasers, and selling to them can yield enormous returns.

The size of government purchases depends on the economic or political orientation of the country. In highly developed, free-market countries, the government plays less of a role than in other markets. The amount of govern-

Fluor Corporation is one of the world's largest engineering, procurement, and construction organizations. It maintains offices in 25 countries across six continents.

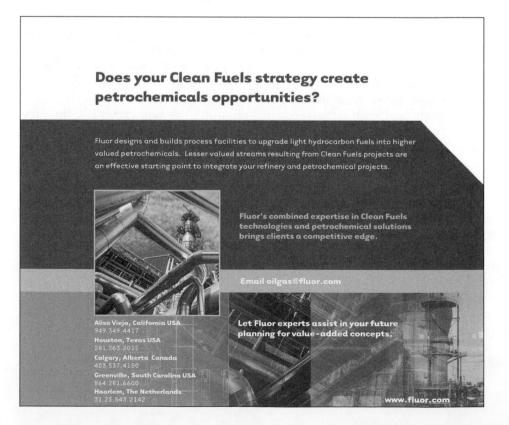

ment purchases is also a function of state-owned operations. For example, in the United States the only government-owned operation is the postal system, whereas in India the government owns not only the postal system but also much of the telecommunications, electric, gas, oil, coal, railway, airline, and shipbuilding industries.

The Buying Process

Governmental buying processes tend to be highly bureaucratic. In order to sell to the U.S. Department of Defense, a firm has to get on a bidding list for each branch of the armed forces. These bidding lists are issued on an annual basis. A firm that is unable to get on the list must wait a full year to try again. Similarly, negotiating with foreign governments can be a very long and formal process.

As we saw in Chapter 4, governments pursue several different agendas, which often complicate government purchasing. For example, a government might wish to promote its local industry as well as decrease its trade deficit. For these reasons, governments often discriminate against foreign suppliers and give preference to local suppliers. In some sophisticated industries such as aerospace, there may be no viable local competitor in many countries. Then the government might ask potential foreign suppliers to subcontract simpler project inputs to local firms. Alternatively, Saudi Arabia asks foreign winners of major government contracts to invest some of their profits in local Saudi industries.

Global marketers pursuing government sales in high-tech fields may also run afoul of the national agendas of their home countries. The threat of compromising national security has prompted governments, especially that of the United States, to institute restrictions on the overseas sale of certain technologies, such as nuclear plants, computers, telecommunications, and military weapons.

Government procurement processes vary from country to country. In Belgium, 90 percent of all public contracts are awarded to the lowest bidder. The remaining 10 percent are granted through "invitation to tender," with factors other than price coming into play. These other factors may include the company's financial viability, technical competence, and after-sale service. Central government supplies, excluding data processing and telecommunications, must be bought through the Central Supplies Office. Regional, local, and quasi-governmental bodies, such as Sabena Airlines, purchase supplies independently.

Here are several recommendations to companies that wish to sell to the Belgian government:

▶ *Manufacture in Belgium.* Preference is given to a local supplier if other things are equal.
▶ *Develop a European image.* A strong EU image has given an advantage to companies such as Siemens and Philips.
▶ *Use the appropriate language.* Although both Flemish and French are officially accepted, ask which is preferred in the department that is receiving the bid.
▶ *Emphasize the recruitment of labor following the winning of a contract.* Companies are favored if they will employ Belgian citizens.
▶ *When new technology is involved, get in at the beginning.* It is often difficult and expensive for the government to change to a different technology at a later date.

▶ *Whenever possible, use local contractors.* The Belgian government likes a bidder to use as many local contractors as possible.[21]

Government Contracts in Developing Countries[22]

Figure 5.4 depicts the various "screens" that global marketers must pass through to secure large government contracts in developing countries. A foreign firm must first address the **eligibility screen.** In order to make the bidding process efficient and manageable, governments seek to weed out firms that are not serious or are too small to handle the contract. For example, Saudi Arabia may ask bidders on a contract to submit a $100,000 fee with their bid or to provide a bond for 1 percent of the tender value. Alternatively, governments may simply restrict the bidding to several well-known international firms that are invited to bid on a particular project. This approach is common in the defense and civil aviation industries.

If the project is complicated or represents a new task for the purchasing government, outside consultants may be employed to design the project and oversee its implementation. For example, Bechtel, a large U.S. engineering firm, could be hired as a consultant for complex construction projects. As a result, Bechtel's designs are more likely to follow U.S. industry standards, and this gives U.S. firms a competitive advantage when bidding on the contract.

After passing the eligibility screen, the foreign firm encounters the **procedural screen**. At this point, numerous bureaucratic procedures must be followed and numerous forms properly filled out. And this can be all the more difficult because the process may not be overt. The firm may need to take special care to discover who is actually in charge and to understand exactly what needs to be done. Hiring local consultants who have experience with the process is often a good idea.

The firm must then meet the **linkage screen**. It must address and implement the various government requirements related to assisting local businesses. This can include finding local suppliers to outsource a portion of the contract. Alternatively, it might involve finding a local partner with whom to establish a joint venture.

After passing through these three screens, the firm must still face the **competitive screen**. Passing this screen not only involves bidding a competitive price; the firm's reputation, its past experience in developing countries, and its cultural sensitivity are also important. Because large projects can take several years to negotiate and many years to implement, the firm must exhibit an ability to be flexible as situations evolve and change.

Firms may even be asked to help finance the project they bid on. A good example of how governments seek creative financing from firms involves India's highway improvement plans. The World Bank estimates that India's annual highway spending will soon quadruple to $4 billion a year, making India very attractive to international road-building firms. But how India will finance road construction remains uncertain. One Indian state is looking for builders that will agree to operate the roads as private concerns before turning them over to the state. In lieu of direct payment from the government, the builders can collect tolls for 10 years.[23]

For current examples of available government contracts, check out the *Government Tenders* links on our website.

Figure 5.4 *Marketing to Governments in Developing Countries*

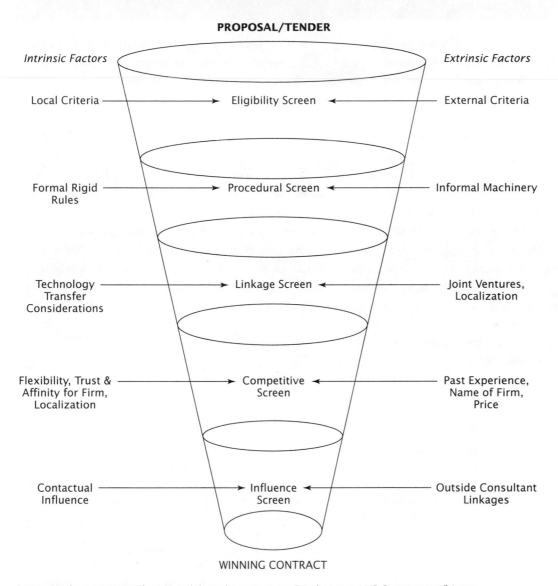

PROPOSAL/TENDER

Intrinsic Factors   *Extrinsic Factors*

Local Criteria → Eligibility Screen ← External Criteria

Formal Rigid Rules → Procedural Screen ← Informal Machinery

Technology Transfer Considerations → Linkage Screen ← Joint Ventures, Localization

Flexibility, Trust & Affinity for Firm, Localization → Competitive Screen ← Past Experience, Name of Firm, Price

Contactual Influence → Influence Screen ← Outside Consultant Linkages

WINNING CONTRACT

Source: Mushtaq Luqman; Ghazi M. Habib, and Sami Kassem, "Marketing to LDC Governments," *International Marketing Review,* Spring 1988: 59.

The final hurdle, the **influence screen,** requires a firm to identify the ultimate decision makers and to be sure it meets their needs. For example, selling radar to the Taiwanese may involve high officers in the air force who are pursuing a defense agenda. However, the ministry of industry may be involved as well. It may be pursuing an agenda of technology transfer and local outsourcing. The firm must be sure to address all these concerns. Managing this process is challenging for global marketers, but winning a large and attractive contract can make it all worthwhile.

READ MORE ABOUT IT:
Check out *In India, Roads Become All The Rage* on our website.

World Beat 5.2 *Cleaning Up Russia*

President Vladimir Putin is serious about cleaning up Russia. He realizes that the entrepreneurial sector can never achieve its potential without a full-scale battle against corruption. What's more, Putin wants closer ties to the West—an initiative that has prompted Putin to cooperate with the United States in the fight against terrorism. But Putin knows that foreign investment will not pour in without a major improvement in corporate governance.

Accordingly, Putin is leading the Kremlin's biggest crackdown on corruption since the Soviet Union's collapse. A high-profile probe of suspect bureaucrats is making headlines. But a second, less-sensational effort is the heart of this campaign: the drive to limit the myriad opportunities for bribery and pilferage that plague business and government.

A new package of reforms aims to cut down on court-room bribes by increasing judges' woeful salaries fivefold. The new law also bans the intervention of state prosecutors in private litigation between contending business parties. The Kremlin wants to rein in other bureaucrats too. New rules demanded by Putin sharply restrict the discounts that railroad regulators can give shippers. These discounts often reward customers who cough up the biggest bribes. Another law reduces the number of business activities that require a license from 2,000 to 100. Fewer licenses mean fewer chances for a bureaucrat to get his palm greased.

The cost of such graft is huge. A cleanup could attract an additional $10 billion annually in foreign direct investment, figures Pricewaterhouse-Coopers. Only $5 billion a year trickles in now.

Source: Paul Starobin and Catherine Belton, "Cleanup Time," *Business Week*, January 14, 2002: 46–47.

Bribery and Government Markets

Bribery is the giving of something of value to an individual in a position of trust to influence their judgment or behavior. Bribes can be offered to purchasing agents or other decision makers within companies to induce them to favor one supplier over another. Most bribery scandals in international marketing, however, involve government contracts. Government employees are in a particular position of trust because they are hired to work for the public good. If a government is awarding an aerospace contract, the government employees responsible for choosing the supplier should consider the value of the supplier to the country as a whole. If a key decision maker influences the decision for his or her personal gain, then public trust is betrayed. Bribes offered to win contracts are most common in industries where contracts are large and where few public employees are involved in the award decision.

Bribery is more endemic in less developed countries. A recent study confirmed that a country's GNP per capita is the best barometer of the level of government bribery (corruption) in that country. The same study also showed that bribery is more prevalent in countries that score higher on the Hofstede power-distance dimension.[24] Table 5.3 lists ratings by country on an index of perceived corruption.

Virtually all countries outlaw the bribing of their own government officials. In the late 1970s, the United States went a step further and outlawed the bribing of foreign officials. Until then, American firms that bribed foreign officials were not prosecuted under U.S. law. Ironically, U.S. law did

Table 5.3 *Corruption Perceptions Index, 2001*

COUNTRY RANK	COUNTRY	2001 CPI SCORE[a]
1	Finland	9.9
2	Denmark	9.5
3	New Zealand	9.4
4	Iceland	9.2
5	Singapore	9.2
6	Sweden	9.0
7	Canada	8.9
8	Netherlands	8.8
9	Luxembourg	8.7
10	Norway	8.6
11	Australia	8.5
12	Switzerland	8.4
13	United Kingdom	8.3
14	Hong Kong	7.9
15	Austria	7.8
16	Israel	7.6
	USA	7.6
18	Chile	7.5
	Ireland	7.5
20	Germany	7.4
21	Japan	7.1
22	Spain	7.0
23	France	6.7
24	Belgium	6.6
25	Portugal	6.3
26	Botswana	6.0
27	Taiwan	5.9
28	Estonia	5.6
29	Italy	5.5
30	Namibia	5.4
31	Hungary	5.3
	Trinidad and Tobago	5.3
	Tunisia	5.3
34	Slovenia	5.2
35	Uruguay	5.1
36	Malaysia	5.0
37	Jordan	4.9
38	Lithuania	4.8
	South Africa	4.8
40	Costa Rica	4.5
	Mauritius	4.5
42	Greece	4.2
	South Korea	4.2
44	Peru	4.1
	Poland	4.1
46	Brazil	4.0

[a]10 = highly clean and 0 = highly corrupt

Table 5.3 *Corruption Perceptions Index, 2001* (Continued)

COUNTRY RANK	COUNTRY	2001 CPI SCORE[a]
47	Bulgaria	3.9
	Croatia	3.9
	Czech Republic	3.9
50	Colombia	3.8
51	Mexico	3.7
	Panama	3.7
	Slovak Republic	3.7
54	Egypt	3.6
	El Salvador	3.6
	Turkey	3.6
57	Argentina	3.5
	China	3.5
59	Ghana	3.4
	Latvia	3.4
61	Malawi	3.2
	Thailand	3.2
63	Dominican Republic	3.1
	Moldova	3.1
65	Guatemala	2.9
	Philippines	2.9
	Senegal	2.9
	Zimbabwe	2.9
69	Romania	2.8
	Venezuela	2.8
71	Honduras	2.7
	India	2.7
	Kazakhstan	2.7
	Uzbekistan	2.7
75	Vietnam	2.6
	Zambia	2.6
77	Cote d'Ivoire	2.4
	Nicaragua	2.4
79	Ecuador	2.3
	Pakistan	2.3
	Russia	2.3
82	Tanzania	2.2
83	Ukraine	2.1
84	Azerbaijan	2.0
	Bolivia	2.0
	Cameroon	2.0
	Kenya	2.0
88	Indonesia	1.9
	Uganda	1.9
90	Nigeria	1.0
91	Bangladesh	0.4

Source: Transparency International *www.transparency.org*

disallow claiming foreign bribes as tax deductions. This resulted in many multinationals keeping records of these bribes for their tax accountants. When government investigators were searching for illegal contributions to President Nixon's reelection fund, they discovered many such entries in company books.

The American public was dismayed. Despite heavy business lobbying against its passage, the **U.S. Foreign Corrupt Practices Act (FCPA)** was passed in 1977. This law forbids U.S. citizens to bribe foreign government employees and politicians. U.S. citizens are also forbidden to pay money to agents or other individuals who in turn pass money on to government employees. They are required to report any bribery occurring within their organizations and must not cover it up. The firm itself is required to keep good records. If audited, it must be able to account for all payments overseas. Fines are assessed for noncompliance. More important, perhaps, the managers involved face jail sentences. In one case prosecuted under the law, Lockheed Martin Corporation was accused of paying $1 million to an Egyptian parliamentarian. The company was fined $25 million, and two company executives were jailed.[25]

U.S. firms are allowed to make expediting payments, however. **Expediting payments** are small sums paid to civil servants to do their jobs. For example, if office computers were sitting at customs and not being processed, an expediting payment might speed up the paperwork. Two multinational companies, Unilever and BP Amoco, admitted in parliamentary hearings in London that their managers did make facilitating payments in developing countries. The counsel for Unilever said that although these payments were not encouraged, they were tolerated as long as they were small and were used to expedite something that would have happened eventually anyway. The general auditor of BP Amoco said the payments were made to avoid delays and not to gain an unfair advantage over competitors.[26] However, some firms have refused to participate in facilitating payments. Procter & Gamble refused to do so when entering Brazil, despite the prevalence of such payments there. One P&G manager recalls that government employees soon learned not even to ask the firm for such payments.

Many U.S. businesses feared that the U.S. FCPA would put them at a competitive disadvantage overseas, especially in emerging markets, because other competitor nations had not adopted a similar law. The law was no doubt a handicap in some cases, but overall it does not appear to have undermined U.S. exports to bribe-prone countries. The law may have helped U.S. managers in one respect: It has kept them out of jail overseas. A study of bribery scandals in the Middle East over a period of nearly 20 years revealed no American having been imprisoned for bribing a government official. This was in contrast to the experiences of Asians and Europeans.[27]

In 1997, 34 nations signed an antibribery pact. These included the 29 members of the Organization for Economic Cooperation and Development (OECD), as well as Argentina, Brazil, Chile, Bulgaria, and Slovakia. Under the agreement, the member countries agreed to propose to their parliaments national laws designed to combat overseas bribery.[28] Table 5.4 ranks 19 leading exporting countries in terms of perceptions of their propensity to bribe senior government officials.

Check out our website for the latest country corruption scores.

Table 5.4 *Bribe Payers Index 1999*

RANK	COUNTRY	SCORE[a]	OECD CONVENTION[b]
1	Sweden	8.3	Ratified
2	Australia	8.1	Ratified
2	Canada	8.1	Ratified
4	Austria	7.8	Ratified
5	Switzerland	7.7	Signed but not Ratified
6	Netherlands	7.4	Signed but not Ratified
7	United Kingdom	7.2	Ratified
8	Belgium	6.8	Ratified
9	Germany	6.2	Ratified
9	United States	6.2	Ratified
11	Singapore	5.7	Not Signed
12	Spain	5.3	Signed but not Ratified
13	France	5.2	Signed but not Ratified
14	Japan	5.1	Ratified
15	Malaysia	3.9	Not Signed
16	Italy	3.7	Signed but not Ratified
17	Taiwan	3.5	Not Signed
18	South Korea	3.4	Ratified
19	China	3.1	Not Signed

[a]0 = very high level of bribery and 10 = negligible bribery
[b]Posted October 26, 1999

Source: Transparency International *www.transparency.org* October 26, 1999

▶ *Conclusions*

Which buyers will you target? Continue with your *Country Market Report* on our website.

In this chapter we have introduced some basic issues of buyer behavior across cultures. We have shown that buyers in various national markets can exhibit similar needs, wants, and even behaviors. In many ways, however, buyers differ from one culture to another. This is true whether the buyer is a consumer, a business, or a government. The challenge to the global marketer is to understand when it is possible to exploit similar needs and behaviors and when it is important to adapt to different buyer conditions. In addition, we observe that many buyers increasingly search the world for products. This intensifies competition and makes it all the more imperative that global marketers understand their markets and address the needs of their buyers.

Review Questions

1. How does the distribution of wealth in a country affect market potential there?

2. How does the informal sector affect purchasing power in developing countries?

3. How is Maslow's hierarchy of needs limited in its cross-cultural application?

4. Contrast the effects of the cost–performance criterion and those of cultural differences on global business-to-business marketing.

5. Explain the difference between a national global buyer and a multinational global buyer.

6. What is global account management?

7. Describe the five screens a foreign firm must pass through in order to win a contract in a developing country.

8. What is allowed and disallowed under the U.S. Foreign Corrupt Practices Act?

Questions for Discussion

1. What critical factors influence a consumer's ability to purchase a product such as a stereo system?
2. Given the data on family decision making in the United States and Venezuela that appears in Table 5.2, how will the marketing of automobiles be different in the two countries?
3. Will the buying process be more similar from country to country for deodorant or delivery vans? Why?

4. If you were selling a product such as a nuclear power plant that is purchased mostly by governments, how would you prepare to sell to Belgium, Egypt, and Mexico? What means would you use to understand the government buying process in each of these countries?
5. Why do you think that the U.S. Foreign Corrupt Practices Act allows expediting payments? Why are these payments seen as less reprehensible than other forms of bribery?

For Further Reading

Armstrong, Robert W., and Siew Min Yee. "Do Chinese Trust Chinese? A Study of Chinese Buyers and Sellers in Malaysia." *Journal of International Marketing* 9, 2 (2001): 63–86.

Craig, C. Samuel, and Susan P. Douglas. "Responding to the Challenges of Global Markets: Change, Complexity, Completion and Conscience." *Columbia Journal of World Business*, Winter 1996: 6–18.

Cui, Geng, and Qiming Liu. "Emerging Market Segments in a Transitional Economy: A Study of Urban Consumers in China." *Journal of International Marketing* 9, 1 (2001): 84–106.

Russow, Lloyd C., and Andrew Solocha. "A Review of the Screening Process Within the Context of the Global Assessment Process." *Journal of Global Marketing* 7, 1 (1993): 65–85.

Case 5.1	*What Teens Want*

Increasingly, consumer product companies and retailers are targeting teens. In the United States, the teen and preteen market comprises about 60 million consumers. Their online purchases alone total $1.5 billion each year. Some teen-specific sites, such as Delias.com, have proved successful. Delias sells clothes that appeal to teens while providing chat rooms and links to other teen sites. Two of the most popular teen sites are Amazon.com and Gap.com. Wal-Mart.com is also popular, despite the fact that it does nothing in particular to attract teens to its site. Teens like it for its good prices.

Marketers in Europe also are trying to understand the teen market better. European teens were once seen as being closer to their parents and more irreverent than American teens. They also watched television less and were more influenced by European music trends. However, a recent study of German teens—thought to be indicative of most Europeans—showed the teens spending their leisure time watching television, talking on the phone, and listening to music, in that order. At the top of the shopping list for buyers ten to seventeen years old was a computer, preferably one connected to the Internet. Other favored products were video recorders, televisions, and mobile phones. Already, 62 percent of this age group owned a television, and 32 percent owned a video recorder.

But does a global teen segment exist? Clinique, a division of the cosmetics company Estée Lauder, has begun a multinational survey to determine what teens find "cool." The results so far from the United

States and the United Kingdom have revealed no clearly targetable differences. Mothers and daughters appeared surprisingly similar in what they wanted in cosmetics and fragrances, although teens seemed to appreciate advertising geared to them. Teens also shopped for upscale fragrances at mass markets where prices were cheaper.

Whether it is possible to extrapolate teen consumer behavior from the developed to the developing world is even more problematic. At a United Nations convention on youth, one girl from Bangladesh described her 15-year-old sister as pregnant and working in a textile factory all day. To her, luxury products and the Internet had little meaning. However, a study of homeless street kids in Brazil revealed that the desire to own global brands was a major impetus for their leaving home for life on the streets. Those who were able to find work would usually spend their first earnings on a pair of Reebok or Nike shoes.

Discussion Questions

1. Would it be useful for global marketers to think of teens as a global segment? Why or why not?
2. Suggest ways in which teen consumer behavior is likely to differ between developed and developing countries.
3. Why do you think street kids in Brazil are attracted to global brand names?

Sources: Mario Osava, Children—Brazil: Street Kids Are Caught Up by Consumer Fever," Inter Press Service, December 9, 1999; "Teens Want—and Get—Attention," Responsive Database Services, June 14, 1999, p. 94; "Television and Telephoning Among Top Ten Adolescent Leisure Pursuits," *Deutsche Presse-Agentur*, May 11, 2000; Anne-Beatrice Clasmann, "Young People in Developing Nations Seek More Responsibility," *Deutsche Presse-Agentur*, February 26, 2000; and Nicole Grasse, "For Teens Dubbed Generation Y, Online Shopping Is as Common as a Can of Coke," Responsive Database Services, May 2000, p. 52.

Case 5.2   *Questionable Payments*

Scenario 1: Thomas Karel is a Swiss national who works as the export manager for a major U.S. producer of machinery and software systems for petroleum exploration. His company is bidding on a $25 million contract that could produce $5 million in profit for his firm. The potential customer is the state-owned oil company in a Latin American country. Thomas has recently heard from his company's agent in that country. The agent suggests that he can "nail down" the contract if Thomas will give him $1 million to pass on to an influential cabinet member in charge of awarding the contract. The competition, a French multinational firm, is also bidding on the contract. *What should Thomas do?*

Scenario 2: David Yang has been sent to a country in Southeast Asia to negotiate the possible sale of a large-scale traffic control system to be adopted across the country. The contract involves not only traffic lights but also their installation and servicing, as well as computer software to monitor traffic flows. Another American in the country has suggested to David that he retain the public relations firm owned by the wife of the country's prime minister. The prime minister is not directly involved with the negotiations for the traffic control system. *What should David do?*

Scenario 3: Michael Avila is the general manager of a subsidiary in the Middle East of an American shipping company. His company specializes in moving the household belongings of expatriates working for multinational companies. Michael is about to authorize the monthly slush fund for payments to customs officials to expedite the movement of his clients' goods through customs when he catches sight of an article in the local newspaper. The government has announced a crackdown on corruption. *What should Michael do?*

Scenario 4: Ana Weiss is the new general manager of DeluxDye in Taiwan. DeluxDye produces high-quality industrial paints and dyes that are used in the manufacture of such products as toys and housewares. Compared to competitors' products, DeluxDye products are relatively expensive to purchase. However, they save costs over the long run. Their higher quality ensures more consistent color and performance and less manufacturing down time. The money customers save can more than make up for the higher initial price of the product.

Corporate guidelines, established in the United States, forbid the paying of any bribes, however small. In Taiwan, Ana's sales force is complaining that their inability to offer "tea money" is discouraging sales growth in the market. Tea money consists of small cash payments or gifts, such as tickets to rock concerts or sports events. These payments are often given to lower-level employees who act as gatekeepers to the higher-level manager—often the head of one of Taiwan's many family-owned manufacturing firms—who in turn makes the buying decision. DeluxDye believes its products are superior to those of its competitors and insists that its sales forces around the world promote the product on its merits alone. Bribery is immoral, and it casts doubts on the integrity of the briber. *What should Ana do?*

Discussion Questions

1. Explain and defend a course of action for each of the managers above.
2. When considering questionable payments, should marketers emphasize ethical concerns, legal considerations, or making the sale? Explain your answer.

Notes

[1]Brendan M. Case, "Latin Flavor Brewing," *Dallas Morning News*, March 26, 2002, p.1D.

[2]Brian Dumaine, "P&G Rewrites the Rules of Marketing," *Fortune*, November 6, 1989: 48.

[3]Sara Calian, "Swiss Cheese Now a Mature Market in Switzerland," *Wall Street Journal*, March 3, 1996, p. A1.

[4]*Beverage Industry Annual Manual* (Cleveland: Harcourt, 1987), p. 16.

[5]*World Bank Atlas* 2001 (Washington, DC: World Bank, 2001).

[6]"Distribution of Income or consumption," *2001 World Development Indicators* (Washington, DC: World Bank), p. 70.

[7]James E. Austin, *Managing in Developing Countries* (New York: The Free Press, 1990), p. 135.

[8]Jean-Claude Usunier, *Marketing Across Cultures* (New York: Prentice-Hall, 2000), p. 104.

[9]Deborah Ball, "Despite Downturn, Japanese Are Still Having Fits for Luxury Goods," *Wall Street Journal*, April 24, 2001, p. B1.

[10]Thomas J. Madden, Kelly Hewlett, and Martin S. Roth, "Managing Images in Different Cultures: A Cross-National Study of Color Meaning and Preferences," *Journal of International Marketing* 8, 4 (2000): 90–107.

[11]D. E. Allen, "Anthropological Insights into Consumer Behavior," *European Journal of Marketing* 5 (Summer 1971): 54.

[12]Ann Helmings, "Culture Shocks," *Advertising Age*, May 17, 1982: M-9.

[13]Niraj Dawar and Philip Parker, "Marketing Universals: Consumers' Use of Brand Name, Price, Physical Appearance, and Retailer Reputation as Signals of Product Quality," *Journal of Marketing* 58, 2 (April 1994): 81–95.

[14]The Parker Pen Company, *Do's and Taboos Around the World.* (Elmsford, NY: The Benjamin Company, 1985).

[15]Douglas Bowman, John U. Farley, and David C. Schmittlein, "Cross-National Empirical Generalization in Business Services Buyer Behavior," *Journal of International Business Studies* 31, 4 (2000): 667–685.

[16]Lawrence H. Wortzel, "Marketing to Firms in Developing Asian Countries," *Industrial Marketing Management*. 12(1983): 113–123.

[17]Desirée Blankenburg Holm, Kent Eriksson, and Jan Johanson, "Business Networks and Cooperation in International Business Relationships," *Journal of International Business Studies* 27 (1996): 1033–1053.

[18]James K. Sebenius, Rebecca Green, and Randall Fine, "Doing Business in Russia: Negotiating in the Wild East," Harvard Business School, Note #9-899-048 1999, pp. 6–7.

[19]George S. Yip, *Total Global Strategy* (Englewood Cliffs, NJ: Prentice-Hall, 1995), pp. 32–33.

[20]*Selling to the Government Markets*: *Local, State, Federal* (Cleveland: Government Product News, 1975), p. 2.

[21]The information in this section has been drawn from *Business International*, "How to Sell to Belgium's Public Sector," Business Europe, October 2, 1981, pp. 314–315.

[22]Mushtaq Luqmani, Ghazi M. Habib, and Sami Kassem, "Marketing to LDC Governments," *International Marketing Review*, Spring 1988: 56–67.

[23]Daniel Pearl, "In India, Roads Become All the Rage," *Wall Street Journal*, January 3, 2001, p. A10.

[24]Bryan W. Husted, "Wealth, Culture, and Corruption," *Journal of International Business Studies* 30, 2 (1999): 339–359.

[25]Kate Gillespie, "Middle East Response to the U.S. Foreign Corrupt Practices Act," *California Management Review* 29, 4 (1987): 9–30.

[26]"Two Companies Admit Payments to Officials," *New York Times*, January 11, 2001, p. CP 10.

[27]Kate Gillespie, "Middle East Response to the U.S. Foreign Corrupt Practices Act," *California Management Review* 29, 4 (1987): 9–30.

[28]"Thirty-four Nations Sign Anti-Bribery Agreement at OECD," *Dow Jones Newswire*, December 17, 1997.

6 Global Competitors

Procter & Gamble largely created the market for shampoo in China. Prior to 1990, most Chinese washed their hair with bar soap. Slick Western-style commercials launched P&G's Head and Shoulders brand, and its success encouraged other multinationals to develop the Chinese market further. These multinationals included Japan's Kao Corporation, France's L'Oreal, and Anglo-Dutch Unilever, as well as U.S.-based Colgate-Palmolive and Bristol-Myers Squibb. Throughout most of the 1990s, big global brands such as Coke and Head and Shoulders killed local brands in China. In 1999, local competitors held only one-third of the market in shampoo. But by 2001, Chinese brands had recaptured two-thirds of the shampoo market and had strongly reasserted themselves in other consumer nondurables such as soap, laundry detergent, and skin moisturizer. A state-owned company even produced one of China's largest-selling toothpastes.

Local brands competed mainly on price but were learning to develop other selling points as well. One Chinese shampoo, Olive, successfully advertised that it made black hair glossier, an attribute that appealed to local consumers. Procter & Gamble took note and introduced a new shampoo that included traditional medicinal elements to add sheen to black hair. The general manager of P&G's shampoo business summed up the new environment: "These days new local brands are always coming at you. And we take them very seriously, whereas five years ago all eyes were on the other multinationals."[1]

Chapter Outline

To begin to develop an effective strategy for global markets, a firm must consider not only buyers but competitors as well. Understanding global buyers is only half the job. Global marketers must compete for those buyers. Potential competitors include both global competitors and local competitors. Each presents unique challenges. Furthermore, the national origin and cultural heritage of firms can determine their organization, their sources of competitive advantage, and the tactics they employ to compete.

In this chapter we address issues of global competition. We begin by noting ways in which competitors can engage each other globally and citing examples of international rivalries—global firm versus global firm, and local firm versus global firm. We explore why cultures developed different attitudes toward competition and look at differences among competitors from different parts of the world. The chapter concludes by examining how buyers respond to firms from different countries.

Learning Objectives

After studying this chapter, you should be able to

▶ Describe ways in which one global competitor can address another.

▶ List and explain four basic strategic options that local firms can employ in the face of competition from multinational firms.

▶ Explain how attitudes toward competition have evolved differently in different cultures, and cite examples from both developed and developing countries.

▶ Note examples of how home governments can still support the global competitiveness of their firms despite the trend toward trade liberalization.

▶ Discuss the major competitors from developing countries—state-owned enterprises and business groups—and explain how they differ from multinational companies.

▶ Describe how a firm's country of origin can help or hurt it in the global marketplace.

145

▶ *The Globalization of Competition*

In order to be successful in global markets, firms must not only understand their potential buyers but also learn to compete effectively against other firms from many different countries. International firms have both advantages and disadvantages when they encounter local competition in foreign markets. Multinational corporations may be larger than local firms and may have better access to sources of finance. They may enjoy greater experience worldwide in product development and marketing. This experience can be brought to play in the new market. However, local competitors may better understand the local culture and hence operate more effectively not only in addressing consumer needs but in dealing with local distributors and governments as well. Today many local competitors, even those in less developed markets, have built up popular brands that a foreign newcomer can find difficult to dislodge.

Global Firm versus Global Firm

Some industries are becoming increasingly global. In these industries, the same global competitors hold significant global market share and face each other in virtually every key market. Major global competitors such as Kodak and Fuji Film consider each other carefully on a worldwide basis. They watch each other's moves in various markets around the world in order to respond to, or even preempt, any actions that will give the competitor a market advantage. Unilever, a European-based firm, and Procter & Gamble of the United States clash in many markets, particularly in laundry products. The two firms compete with each other in most world markets, and action in one market easily spills over into others. Observers have described this competitive action as "The Great Soap Wars."

George Yip suggests several ways in which one global competitor can address another.[2]

- ▶ **Cross-Country Subsidization** Using profits from one country in which a business operates to subsidize competitive actions in another country. Bic was one of the first companies to do this effectively. Bic used profits made in France to attack competitor Scripto's pen business in Britain. Then Bic used profits made in Europe to attack Scripto in its U.S. home market. Because Scripto's national subsidiaries were largely independent of each other, the firm didn't see Bic coming.
- ▶ **Counterparry** Defending against a competitive attack in one country by counterattacking in another country. Fuji successfully entered the United States and gained 25 percent of the film market. Kodak counterattacked in Japan, exerting great efforts to strike back at Fuji in its home market.
- ▶ **Globally Coordinated Moves** Mounting a coordinated assault in which competitive moves are made in different countries. For example, some multinational firms now choose global rollouts for products. By introducing new products in all major national markets simultaneously, a firm ensures that its global competitors have no time to learn from one market in order to respond in another.
- ▶ **Targeting of Global Competitors** Identifying actual and potential global competitors and selecting an overall posture—attack, avoidance, cooperation, or acquisition. We will have more to say about cooperating with potential competitors in Chapter 9.

One of the longest-running battles in global competition has been the fight for market dominance between Coca-Cola and PepsiCo, the world's largest soft-drink companies. Traditionally, the two firms have been relatively close in the U.S. market, but Coca-Cola has long been the leader in international markets. Because international markets grow much more rapidly than the domestic market, the global advantage continues to shift in favor of Coca-Cola. Coca-Cola, with its Coke brand, outsells Pepsi in nine of the world's ten largest markets. Pepsi leads only in the Middle East and is within striking distance only in Canada. In terms of worldwide market share, Coke leads Pepsi by 46 to 21 percent, better than a 2-to-1 margin.[3]

This battle for global market share is an ongoing one that erupts simultaneously on several fronts. Some of the most dramatic action has taken place in Latin America. Coke struck at Pepsi in Venezuela, the only market in Latin America where Pepsi led Coke by a substantial margin (76 percent share versus 13 percent) thanks to long-standing ties with a local bottler. In a bold play for share, Coke negotiated with Pepsi's Venezuelan bottler to acquire a controlling interest in that company. The day after the deal was announced, the Venezuelan bottler switched to bottling Coke, and Pepsi lost its distribution literally overnight.[4] It took Pepsi 30 months and a combined investment of more than $500 million to reestablish itself in the country.[5]

Soon thereafter, Pepsi scored against Coke in Argentina. When Coke landed a deal to sponsor the Argentine national soccer team, Pepsi signed an agreement to sponsor the annual soccer championship series on an exclusive basis—calling it "Torneo de Pepsi"—and secured exclusive promotional opportunities throughout the season on key games.[6]

Another arena, and potentially the largest prize, is Asia. While the mature U.S. market grows slowly, Coke and Pepsi have set their sights on major growth markets, such as China, India, and Indonesia, that are home to almost half the world's population. In India, Pepsi attempted to preempt Coke. Coca-Cola had previously relinquished its position in the Indian market when the Indian government passed a law that would require the company to share its secret cola formula with local partners. Although the law was later repealed, Coke delayed returning to India while rival Pepsi made India a priority market. When Coke returned in 1993, it found Pepsi well established in the market. In the race for local dominance, Coke acquired a leading local soft-drink firm, Parle, with some fifty-four bottling plants. Coke has rapidly built up its Indian operations. It has already overtaken Pepsi in this large market, partially because of Parle's local brands such as the lemon drink Limca.

As can be expected in true global competition, Coke and Pepsi square off in all important markets. Both firms coordinate their strategies across markets, leverage knowledge and experience gained in many national markets, and employ vast global resources as they battle for global market share.

Global Firm versus Local Firm

Local firms can compete effectively against much larger international companies if they act wisely. Ramlösa, the leading Swedish bottler of mineral water, competed effectively against Perrier of France, probably the most successful marketer of mineral water worldwide. Ramlösa sold its mineral water primarily in Sweden, with some minor export business to neighboring Norway and Finland. Ramlösa executives had watched Perrier invade market after market in Europe and finally dominate the premium segment for mineral water worldwide.[7]

When Perrier attacked in Denmark, Ramlösa executives realized that it would not be long before Perrier would invade their market also. In Sweden, Ramlösa enjoyed a market share of close to 100 percent, and it was feared that an aggressive new entrant like Perrier might lower Ramlösa's share considerably. Having studied Perrier's strategy in other European markets, the firm searched for a solution. Because Perrier entered markets by creating a premium positioning for their product, Ramlösa decided to preempt Perrier by launching its own premium brand of mineral water. The company invested in expensive packaging and bottles, advertised to obtain a premium image, and increased the price by almost 50 percent, even though the mineral water of the premium brand was identical to that sold under its regular label.

When Perrier finally entered the Swedish market, it followed its proven strategy of aiming to capture the premium segment. However, with Ramlösa already strong in the premium segment, Perrier was forced to enter with an ultra-premium positioning. This resulted in such a high price that Perrier gained very little market share. By anticipating Perrier's arrival and correctly predicting its competitor's strategy, Ramlösa was able to prevent Perrier from cashing in on the approach that had been so successful elsewhere.

Strategies for Local Firms

Although global firms have superior resources, they often become inflexible after several successful market entries and tend to stay with standard approaches when flexibility is needed. In general, the global firm's strongest local competitors are those who watch global firms carefully and learn from their moves in other countries. With some global firms, it is several years before a product is introduced in all markets, and local competitors in some markets can take advantage of such advance notice by building defenses or launching a preemptive attack on the same segment.

Niraj Dawar and Tony Frost suggest four successful strategies for smaller local firms that suddenly find themselves competing with more powerful multinationals. Depending on the type of industry they are in, local firms can choose to be defenders, extenders, contenders, or dodgers. In industries where customization to local markets remains a competitive asset, defender and extender strategies can be successful. Other industries, such as telecommunications and automobiles, are by nature more global—buyer needs vary relatively little from one market to another, and both economies of scale in production and high research and development (R&D) costs favor enterprises with global reach and vast resources. In such global industries, local firms must consider contender or dodger strategies. [8]

Defender Strategy A defender strategy focuses on leveraging local assets in market segments where multinational firms may be weak. Local assets often include knowledge of local tastes and customs, as well as good relationships with local distributors and suppliers. A good example of a defender strategy is the trend in Turkey for restaurants to bring back regional cuisines to compete with multinational fast-food chains. Ibrahim Tatlises, a Turkish pop music and television star, successfully created a fast-food chain based on lahmacun, a thin pizza-like dough with meat and spices.[9]

Spanish-speaking media have moved north into the U.S. market.

Extender Strategy Sometimes local firms find that the assets that worked well for a defender strategy can also work in certain foreign markets. Extenders focus on expanding into foreign markets similar to their own, using successful practices and competencies that they have already developed in their home market. Televisa, Mexico's largest media company, has extended to become one of the world's largest producers of Spanish-language soap operas.[10] Its impact is felt in the United States as well as in Latin America. In some local markets, such as Los Angeles and Houston, Spanish-language Univision is the most-watched network.[11]

Contender Strategy Competing in more global industries can be difficult for smaller local firms faced with established global competitors. Yet some have succeeded by upgrading their capabilities to take on the multinational companies. This usually means expanding their resources to invest in the necessary R&D expenditures and larger-scale production that these industries can demand. Many privately held local companies find that they need to go public to raise more money through a stock offering. Because their resources may still be limited compared to those of entrenched multinational firms, contenders may seek out niches that are underserved by their competitors. Arcelik is a top competitor in the Turkish market for appliances such as refrigerators, washing machines, and dishwashers. At home Arcelik enjoys a renowned brand name and vast distribution. It modernized its production facilities and then successfully entered the British market by targeting consumers who wanted small, tabletop refrigerators, a segment that U.S. and European competitors ignored.[12]

Dodger Strategy If local firms in more global industries lack the resources or managerial vision to become contenders, they can find themselves edged out even in their home market by multinational firms offering better and cheaper products. In order to survive, a local firm can avoid, or dodge, competition by finding a way to cooperate with its more powerful competitors. It can focus on being a locally oriented link in the value chain, becoming, for instance, a contract manufacturer or local distributor for a multinational firm. Many dodgers just sell out to a multinational firm that wishes to acquire them. Many such acquisitions have occurred in Europe and the United States as well as in developing countries.

European e-tailers originally were confident that they could compete with U.S. rivals because of their better understanding of European markets. However, the Americans proved to have far greater financial resources. U.S. e-tailers such as Amazon.com and eBay were able to transfer cutting-edge technology quickly to the European markets. By late 2000, many European competitors had collapsed. Others were rushing to merge or sell out.[13]

Car manufacturer Daewoo holds about 12 percent of the South Korean automobile market and once aspired to become a global competitor, investing in emerging markets such as India, Romania, and Iran. However, the firm soon ran up $47 billion in liabilities. When the company was on the verge of collapse, its chairman fled the country. In 2002, General Motors reached an agreement with Daewoo's creditors to purchase the firm's assets, giving GM a greater participation in the attractive Korean car market, as well as a production base for serving the rest of Asia.[14]

READ MORE ABOUT IT:
Check out *What GM's Daewoo Deal Says About Korea* on our website.

▶ *Cultural Attitudes Toward Competition*

Table 6.1 lists the top 100 companies in the world and their nations of origin.

Not surprisingly, understanding and responding appropriately to competitors is much more difficult if competitors come from different countries and cultures. Cultures vary in their attitudes toward competition and in their histories of industrial development. These attitudes affect the rules of the competitive game—both written and unwritten—in societies. Understanding these attitudes and histories can help marketers better understand both local competitors in host markets and global competitors that come from different home markets.

Table 6.1 *The Top 100 Global Companies*

RANK	COMPANY NAME	COUNTRY	REVENUES ($ MILLIONS)
1	General Motors	U.S.	176,558.0
2	Wal-Mart Stores	U.S.	166,809.0
3	Exxon Mobil	U.S.	163,881.0
4	Ford Motor	U.S.	162,558.0
5	Daimler-Chrysler	Germany	159,985.7
6	Mitsui	Japan	118,555.2
7	Mitsubishi	Japan	117,765.6
8	Toyota Motor	Japan	115,670.9
9	General Electric	U.S.	111,630.0
10	Itochu	Japan	109,068.9
11	Royal Dutch/Shell Group	Netherlands	105,366.0
12	Sumitomo	Japan	95,701.6

Table 6.1 *The Top 100 Global Companies*

RANK	COMPANY NAME	COUNTRY	REVENUES ($ MILLIONS)
13	Nippon Telegraph & Telephone	Japan	93,591.7
14	Marubeni	Japan	91,807.4
15	AXA	France	87,645.7
16	Intl. Business Machines	U.S.	87,548.0
17	BP Amoco	England	83,566.0
18	Citigroup	U.S.	82,005.0
19	Volkswagen	Germany	80,072.7
20	Nippon Life Insurance	Japan	78,515.1
21	Siemens	Germany	75,337.0
22	Allianz	Germany	74,178.2
23	Hitachi	Japan	71,858.5
24	Matsushita Electric Industrial	Japan	65,555.6
25	Nissho Iwai	Japan	65,393.2
26	U.S. Postal Service	U.S.	62,726.0
27	ING Group	Netherlands	62,492.4
28	AT&T	U.S.	62,391.0
29	Philip Morris	U.S.	61,751.0
30	Sony	Japan	60,052.7
31	Deutsche Bank	Germany	58,585.1
32	Boeing	U.S.	57,993.0
33	Dai-ichi Mutual Life Insurance	Japan	55,104.7
34	Honda Motor	Japan	54,773.5
35	Assicurazioni Generali	Italy	53,723.2
36	Nissan Motor	Japan	53,679.9
37	E. ON	Germany	52,227.7
38	Toshiba	Japan	51,634.9
39	Bank of America Corp.	U.S.	51,392.0
40	Fiat	Italy	51,331.7
41	Nestlé	Switzerland	49,694.1
42	SBC Communications	U.S.	49,489.0
43	Credit Suisse	Switzerland	49,362.0
44	Hewlett-Packard	U.S.	48,253.0
45	Fujitsu	Japan	47,195.9
46	Metro	Germany	46,663.6
47	Sumitomo Life Insurance	Japan	46,445.1
48	Tokyo Electric Power	Japan	45,727.7
49	Kroger	U.S.	45,351.6
50	Total Fina Elf	France	44,990.3
51	NEC	Japan	44,828.0
52	State Farm Insurance Cos.	U.S.	44,637.2
53	Vivendi	France	44,397.8
54	Unilever	England	43,679.9
55	Fortis	Belgium	43,660.2
56	Prudential	England	42,220.3
57	CGNU	England	41,974.4

Table 6.1   *The Top 100 Global Companies* (Continued)

RANK	COMPANY NAME	COUNTRY	REVENUES ($ MILLIONS)
58	Sinopec	China	41,883.1
59	Sears Roebuck	U.S.	41,071.0
60	American International Group	U.S.	40,656.1
61	Peugot	France	40,327.9
62	Enron	U.S.	40,112.0
63	Renault	France	40,098.6
64	BNP Paribas	France	40,098.6
65	Zurich Financial Services	Switzerland	39,962.0
66	Carrefour	France	39,855.7
67	TIAA-CREF	U.S.	39,410.2
68	HSBC Holdings	England	39,348.1
69	ABN AMRO Holding	Netherlands	38,820.7
70	Compaq Computer	U.S.	38,525.0
71	Home Depot	U.S.	38,434.0
72	Munich Re Group	Germany	38,400.4
73	RWE Group	Germany	38,357.5
74	Lucent Technologies	U.S.	38,303.0
75	Procter & Gamble	U.S.	38,125.0
76	Elf Aquitaine	France	37,918.3
77	Deutsche Telekom	Germany	37,835.1
78	Albertson's	U.S.	37,478.1
79	WorldCom	U.S.	37,120.0
80	McKesson HBOC	U.S.	37,100.5
81	Fannie Mae	U.S.	36,968.6
82	BMW	Germany	36,695.9
83	State Power Corporation	China	36,076.1
84	Kmart	U.S.	35,925.0
85	Koninklijke Ahold	Netherlands	35,798.1
86	Texaco	U.S.	35,690.0
87	Merrill Lynch	U.S.	34,879.0
88	Electricite de France	France	34,146.6
89	ENI	Italy	34,091.0
90	Meiji Life Insurance	Japan	33,966.6
91	Morgan Stanley Dean Witter	U.S.	33,928.0
92	Mitsubishi Electric	Japan	33,896.2
93	Chase Manhattan Corp.	U.S.	33,710.0
94	Target	U.S.	33,702.0
95	Suez Lyonnaise des Eaux	France	33,559.7
96	Royal Phillips Electronics	Netherlands	33,556.6
97	Verizon Communications	France	33,174.0
98	Credit Agricole	U.S.	32,923.5
99	Thyssen Krupp	Germany	32,798.0
100	Merck	U.S.	32,714.0

Source: Rank of companies and their revenues from http://www.fortune.com/fortune/global500.

Is competition good or bad? Most Americans would agree that competition is good. It encourages new ideas and keeps prices down. However, this is not a universal attitude. In the late nineteenth and early twentieth centuries, the United States established antitrust laws to discourage monopolies and encourage competition. Shortly before, Americans watched powerful firms cut prices to drive competitors out of the market. Afterwards, these firms or trusts took advantage of their monopolist positions to raise prices to consumers. Newspapers roused citizens across the country, and the U.S. government received a mandate to trust-bust. Even years later, General Motors was forced to operate divisions as separate firms to help dissipate its strong market power in the United States. Other countries have experienced different histories relating to competition and have therefore developed different attitudes toward it.

Competition in Europe

For many years, European governments allowed their firms to engage in cartel behavior that was outlawed in the United States. Even as late as the 1970s, European airlines met openly to discuss and later establish the mutual dropping of first-class services on trans-European flights. In fact, Europe rarely enforced antitrust laws until the 1980s. Recently, however, the EU has surprised many with a new vigilance in enforcing antitrust laws.

Although Europe imported much of its antitrust law from the United States, it has evolved differently. In the United States the laws aim to protect consumers from monopolists. In the EU they exist to guarantee fairness among competitors in the unified market. For example, under U.S. law, if a merger helps enable two companies to offer a broad portfolio of related products, this is seen as creating efficiencies that could in turn benefit consumers. In the EU, however, this would be seen as having the potential of blocking competitors out of the market. Consequently, the EU objected in 1997 to a merger between two EU firms, Grand Metropolitan and Guinness, that would have created the world's largest liquor company. The EU feared that the new firm, by combining their portfolios of products from champagne to whisky, could pressure distributors to shut out competitors. In 2001 the EU also blocked a merger under their jurisdiction of General Electric and Honeywell International, two U.S.-based multinationals in the aerospace industry.[15]

Competition in Japan

In the last three decades, Japanese markets have experienced more intense competition than markets in the United States and Europe. While IBM enjoyed dominance in the computer mainframe market in the United States, four major competitors—Fujitsu, Hitachi, NEC, and IBM Japan—fought for market share in Japan. In fact, four to eight strong contenders can be found in virtually every industry. Japanese firms are rarely seen to leave mature industries through acquisition, bankruptcy, or voluntary exit.[16]

Largely contributing to this phenomenon are the **horizontal keiretsus.** *Keiretsu* means "order or system." In Japan six large industrial groups, or keiretsus, have evolved, and each keiretsu is involved in nearly all major industries. Group companies are technically independent and publicly owned. However, they are loosely coordinated by minority cross-shareholdings and personal relationships. A major player in these groups is the keiretsu bank. Group companies and especially the group bank will help members out in times of trouble. When Mazda faced bankruptcy, the Sumitomo Bank provided the car company with generous financing and encouraged employees of group companies to buy Mazdas. Banks retain shares of group companies despite low returns and have been effective in preventing takeovers by competitors.[17]

For decades Japanese managers never worried about stock prices, and postwar Japan never experienced a hostile takeover of a major business. Despite increased competition, weak companies were not forced out of the Japanese market. However, the poor economic environment in Japan during the late 1990s began to show cracks in the system. The Japanese government made it clear that it would allow banks to fail, which caused Japanese banks to be more wary about propping up group companies. Sony, one of Japan's most efficient companies, reported a mere 5.5 percent return on equity in 2001. This compares to 15 percent for most U.S. technology companies. In an effort to improve performance, Sony has begun to pull out of less attractive businesses and has made plans to dispose of 15 plants by 2003.[18] In fact, Japan is experiencing one of the biggest transfers of corporate ownership in 50 years, with many U.S. companies now buying into Japanese firms.[19]

Competition in Emerging Markets

Developing countries have traditionally been wary of competition. In the mid-twentieth century, many of these countries were still dependent on commodities and were attempting to industrialize rapidly. However, the moneyed segments of society preferred to keep to the businesses they knew best—agriculture, commerce, and the military. The few who ventured into industry and were successful discovered that others quickly followed them into the same business. Soon there were far too many competitors vying for market share in a small market. New ventures failed. As a consequence, potential industrialists became even harder to find. In order to encourage local investment in industry and the building of factories, governments often limited foreign competition by raising tariffs or imposing quotas on imports. In addition, many governments licensed local production. For example, the Iranian government refused to issue further licenses for new factories once producers could establish that they were capable of supplying the entire Iranian market.

More recently, most developing countries, as well as the transitional economies of the former Soviet bloc, have embraced market liberalization. **Market liberalization** is the encouraging of competition where prior monopolies or strict entry controls previously existed. It takes a variety of forms. Production licensing is often relinquished and import controls relaxed. Host governments may further competition by encouraging multinational corporations to invest in their markets. India liberalized its market and encouraged foreign investment by granting multinational firms freer access to foreign exchange, the right to hold majority equity stakes in their Indian investments, and permission to use foreign brand names where these were previously not permitted. Other countries, such as Egypt, courted foreign investors with tax holidays for up to ten years.

There are several reasons for this change in attitude toward competition in the emerging world. Some of the pressure to liberalize markets is external. Many countries in the emerging world have joined the WTO and needed to remove barriers to imports in order to comply with WTO regulations. For example, India dismantled the last of its major import quotas in April 2001 in response to a ruling from the WTO. Until then, manufacturers of consumer goods faced virtually no import competition in India.[20] Other countries are under pressure to liberalize from bilateral partners such as the United States.

Much of the pressure to liberalize is internal, however. After 50 years of protection, local competitors have often failed to delivery quality products for reasonable prices. Part of this failure is due to conditions outside their control, such as limited financing available for businesses in developing countries. Still, consumers in the emerging world, along with their governments, have begun to think that protecting infant industries contributes to their failure ever to grow up. A study of 3,000 Indian firms revealed that productivity grew more slowly in the 1990s than in the 1980s.[21] Furthermore, many governments are setting their sights on competing in export markets. Allowing more competition in the national market forces local companies to be more globally competitive. Multinational corporations in particular, with their higher technology, more extensive financial resources, and global market know-how, are expected to help fuel export expansion.

As developing countries liberalize their markets, governments are also cracking down on what they deem to be improper competitive behavior. Many actions that have been accepted for many years are now outlawed. In Mexico, a new antitrust commission acts as both judge and jury on complaints of anticompetitive behavior brought against firms. The commission has the authority to investigate allegations and impose fines. It can block any corporate acquisition in Mexico and can prevent the creation of a private monopoly in cases where the government decides to sell prior state-owned monopolies to the private sector.[22]

In 2002, Mexico's antitrust commission found Coca-Cola and its bottlers guilty of abusing their dominant position in Coke's largest market outside the United States. Needless to say, Pepsi initiated the investigation. Coke had a 72 percent share of the Mexican carbonated soft-drinks market and most of its sales came from small mom-and-pop stores located across the country. Coke was ordered by the commission to stop using its exclusivity agreements that forbade the small retailers from carrying competitors' products. Pepsi has similar agreements with its retailers in Mexico. But the ruling doesn't apply to Pepsi, because Pepsi doesn't occupy the dominant position in the market.[23]

▶ *Home Country Actions and Global Competitiveness*

In Chapter 4 we discussed how the home governments of firms can affect these firms' international marketing—in particular, how home governments might possibly harm their firms and in so doing create political risk. However, most home governments are eager for their firms to prove competitive in the global marketplace, and many seek out specific ways to improve the competitiveness of their firms. The WTO discourages direct government subsidies to firms and restricts, in most cases, the ability of member states to protect home markets with quotas and high tariffs. Still, there are many other government policies that can affect global competitiveness. Governments can offer export assistance in the form of export promotion organizations that help educate local firms about foreign markets. Home governments may also assist in negotiations for major contracts with foreign governments. And governments can pursue economic and competition policies at home that enhance the ability of their firms to compete in foreign markets. These policies can include tax rates, labor laws, and the extent to which home governments tolerate monopolistic or oligopolistic behavior in the home market.

The heads of state of the European Union met in Barcelona in 2002 and determined that Europe should try to become the world's most competitive economy in the coming decade. The Barcelona summit resolved to liberalize labor markets by lowering labor taxes and reducing benefits to the unemployed. It also took steps to deregulate energy markets, giving businesses the freedom to choose their gas and electricity suppliers by 2004. It was hoped that these measures would decrease the costs of European-based businesses, allowing them to compete more effectively internationally.[24]

One ongoing controversy concerning home government policy and competitiveness involves the cement industry. Mexico's Cemex grew from a regional player in 1990 to the world's third largest cement supplier and the leading brand in the United States by 2002. U.S. rivals accuse Cemex of using its dominance in Mexico to finance its expansion overseas unfairly and to cut prices in the U.S. market. Cemex's position in the Mexican market, where it holds a 60 percent share of the market, allows it to charge unusually high prices. Profits in Mexico are an extraordinary 46 percent before taxes—nearly double what they are in the more competitive U.S. market. Such profits at home enable Cemex to buy competitors abroad as well as to decrease prices in foreign markets. In 1999, an investigation by Mexico's competition commission found Cemex innocent of monopolistic behavior. Unsatisfied with the commission's decision, the U.S. government continues to impose antidumping duties on cement imported from Mexico. In some years, these have amounted to more than 100 percent for Cemex.[25]

READ MORE ABOUT IT:
Check out *Hard Profits* on our website.

▶ *Competitors from Emerging Markets*

Until recently, most global strategists focused on the multinational companies from the United States, Europe, and Japan. But as we saw in the cases of Procter & Gamble in China and Arcelik in Britain, multinational companies increasingly find themselves competing with firms from developing countries. Table 6.2 lists the largest firms from the emerging markets. Major firms in developing countries are usually quite different from those in the United States. Large firms that have evolved locally in emerging markets are usually one of two types—state-owned enterprises and business groups. With the trend toward market liberalization, both face strong challenges at home from foreign multinationals. Nonetheless, these local firms can still prove quite competitive both in their own national markets and, increasingly, in global markets. Furthermore, new entrepreneurial ventures from developing countries are evolving and targeting overseas markets.

State-Owned Enterprises

State-owned enterprises (SOEs) sometimes appear in the developed world, especially Europe, but their scope and impact have been significantly greater in developing countries. In the second half of the twentieth century, many governments in developing countries were trying to end their dependence on commodity exports by rapidly industrializing their economies. Often the

Table 6.2 *The Top 50 Emerging Market Companies*

RANK 2001	2000	NAME	COUNTRY	MARKET VALUE IN U.S. $ MILLIONS
1	1	China Mobile (Hong Kong)	China	90,167
2	2	Taiwan Semiconductor Mfg.	Taiwan	30,861
3	7	Petrobras	Brazil	29,449
4	3	Samsung Electronics	Korea	28,984
5	4	Telefonos de Mexico (Telmex)	Mexico	25,223
6	9	Anglo American	South Africa	23,698
7	12	Gazprom	Russia	22,608
8	NR	China Unicom	China	20,520
9	5	United Microelectronics	Taiwan	17,596
10	NR	Chunghwa Telecom	Taiwan	17,360
11	6	SK Telecom	Korea	15,276
12	NR	America Movil	Mexico	14,997
13	8	Korea Telecom	Korea	13,892
14	13	Checkpoint Software Tech.	Israel	12,572
15	10	Korea Electric Power (Kepco)	Korea	12,142
16	73	Grupo Financiero Banamex-Accival	Mexico	12,069
17	31	Wal-Mart de Mexico	Mexico	11,738
18	66	Anglo American Platinum	South Africa	11,358
19	20	Lukoil Holding	Russia	10,616
20	32	Banco Itaú	Brazil	9,304
21	29	Vale do Rio Doce	Brazil	9,294
22	15	Hindustan Lever	India	9,236
23	38	Reliance Industries	India	8,809
24	47	Grupo Modelo	Mexico	8,666
25	NR	Companhia de Bebidas das Americas	Brazil	8,590
26	128	Grupo Financiero BBVA Bancomer	Mexico	8,324
27	30	Wipro	India	8,300
28	NR	CNOOC	China	8,162
29	26	Hon Hai Precision Industry Co.	Taiwan	8,143
30	62	Cemex	Mexico	8,102
31	39	Surgutneftegaz	Russia	7,910
32	45	Old Mutual	South Africa	7,877
33	17	Asustek Computer	Taiwan	7,627
34	53	Teva Pharmaceutical Industries	Israel	7,495
35	27	Telekomunikacja Polska	Poland	7,282
36	NR	CITIC Pacific	China	6,842
37	34	Electrobrás	Brazil	6,692
38	11	Türkiye İş Bankasi	Turkey	6,674
39	18	Tenaga Nasional Berhad (TNB)	Malaysia	6,662
40	44	Pohang Iron and Steel (POSCO)	Korea	6,644
41	97	Sasol	South Africa	6,537
42	54	Banco Bradesco	Brazil	6,506
43	19	Telekom Malaysia	Malaysia	6,457
44	36	Grupo Televisa	Mexico	6,457
45	14	Cathay Life Insurance	Taiwan	6,434
46	56	Dimension Data Holdings	South Africa	6,093
47	74	Standard Bank Investment	South Africa	5,914
48	190	Empresa Brasileira de Aeronautica	Brazil	5,858
49	28	Malayan Banking	Malaysia	5,854
50	70	Firstrand	South Africa	5,768

Source: Business Week July 9, 2001

private sector failed to meet government expectations in this regard. Most shied away from investing in factories and production, areas they knew little about. To meet their goals, governments increasingly fell back on doing the job themselves and established state-owned enterprises that operated not only in the manufacturing sector but sometimes in wholesaling and retailing as well. For example, SOEs in Egypt came to account for 25 percent of non-agricultural employment in the country.

Being state-owned gave firms certain competitive advantages over firms in the private sector, but some disadvantages were also involved. State-owned firms received priority access to financing that was scarce in the developing world. They were protected from bankruptcy, and they often were granted monopoly positions in their home markets. These advantages were offset by the many ancillary agendas they were forced to accept. Sri Lanka's state-owned timber company was expected to sell timber below market prices to subsidize housing in the country. Egyptian college graduates were guaranteed jobs in SOEs, and the Venezuelan government could commandeer the earnings of its state-owned oil company to help with a fiscal shortfall.

In the 1980s and 1990s many SOEs in developing countries, as well as those in the former Soviet Union and Eastern Europe, underwent privatization. **Privatization** occurs when state-owned enterprises or their assets are sold to private firms or individuals. Rather than investing the money necessary to re-vamp these enterprises, governments choose to sell them. Part of the impetus to do so involves a change in ideology. Many governments have lost faith in continued government-led industrialization. Privatizations have swept through more than 100 countries and have involved over 75,000 SOEs. In many cases, multinational corporations have purchased these firms. For example, Philip Morris, the U.S.-based food and tobacco company, was able to acquire a stake in Czechia's Tabak, previously the Czech monopolist in tobacco.

In a number of cases, however, privatizations have not proceeded smoothly. The privatization of India's 240 state-owned enterprises has been repeatedly sidetracked. In 2001, all major bidders for Air India withdrew from its privatization attempt, afraid that the Indian government would not allow the painful employment cuts that would be necessary to make the airline profitable. Singapore Airline, a potential buyer, allegedly withdrew because of political opposition to the privatization. But in 2002, India's stalled privatization campaign was given added impetus by the sale of two of the country's most promising SOEs—a gasoline retailer and India's only international phone service.[26]

The global impact of state-owned enterprises in the oil industry continues despite the trend toward privatization. The state-owned oil companies of Kuwait and Venezuela have ventured out of their countries and have invested in Europe and the United States. The Kuwaiti company purchased refinery capacity in Europe as well as an extensive network of retail outlets from former Gulf Oil. Both of these state-owned enterprises are considered serious global competitors.

Although the era of state-owned enterprises is waning, their importance in the Chinese market is still largely intact. In 2002, private express shipping companies, including U.S.-based FedEx, UPS, and DHL, were facing a deadline to turn over most of their Chinese business to the government's China Post. Private carriers were directed not to deliver letters or packages under 1.1 pounds and not to charge prices below those of China Post. In addition, they could not deliver any mail to private homes or to offices of the Chinese government. The industry estimated that the new restrictions could amount to a loss

World Beat 6.1 *Start-Up versus SOE*

Mark Davies wants to make serious money and help Africa join the twenty-first century at the same time. The only catch: His plan may be illegal.

Mr. Davies, a Welsh-born American and a dot.com millionaire, is the founder of BusyInternet, which provides Internet access to Ghanaians. By any standard, the company is already a tremendous African success story. Started with $1.7 million from Mr. Davies and local financiers, BusyInternet has positive cash flow after only 7 months in business. But Mr. Davies has bigger ideas: Internet phone calls, which the Ghanaian government currently doesn't permit.

Another entrepreneur, Nanayaa T. Owusu-Prempeh, was making good money by facilitating the flow of incoming international voice-over-Internet calls into the local phone system. In 2000, a police SWAT team swept into her offices and ripped out the satellite dish, computers, fax machine, tables, and everything else. Her entire staff was jailed for 3 days.

The government of Ghana is concerned about the impact that Internet calls would have on existing phone services such as Ghana Telecom. Like governments in other sub-Saharan countries, Ghana has a vested interest in protecting the revenue of the state telephone company. It hasn't ruled out Internet calls but is taking its time to study the matter. In the meantime, risk takers plunge ahead and dare the government to stop them. And the unlucky among them end up in jail.

Source: Michael M. Philips, "On Ghana's Tech Frontier," *Wall Street Journal*, May 22, 2002, p. B1.

---

of 60 percent of the Chinese market just as business was soaring. Industry executives claimed that the order violated commitments China made when it entered the World Trade Organization the previous December. The Chinese government maintained the action was legal and noted that China Post had to deliver mail to all locations in China, including places where it could not make a profit. Private companies were under no such obligation. China also invoked an antiterrorism rationale for the move. The government needed to ensure that all deliveries were subjected to screening for anthrax and other poisons.[27]

Business Groups

In the private sector of developing countries, business groups have emerged as the major competitors. Business groups differ from large corporations in developed countries in several key ways. Business groups have been exclusively or almost exclusively concentrated in their home markets. Most striking is their diversity. Business groups participate in many industries. It would not be uncommon to find a business group involved in steel, insurance, packaged goods, automobile distribution, and textiles. For example, Arcelik White Goods is part of the larger Koc Group in Turkey. This group participates in industries as diverse as consumer goods, energy, mining, finance, and construction. Group businesses are often interlinked, with group companies owning partial shares of each other. The true bond, however, is not one of equity ownership but is a fiduciary bond or bond of trust. It is the culture of businesses in the group to work for the good of the whole. Managers often move between these companies, and personal bonds are forged. In the difficult business environments of developing countries, all eventually benefit from mutual aid.[28]

Similar to Japanese keiretsus, most groups have a financial core—a business with access to cash to finance the other businesses. This is commonly a bank or an insurance company. In the case of Arab Contractors in Egypt, it was the parent company's own extensive retirement fund. This financial core proved a key competitive advantage in an environment where financing was scarce. Because these groups evolved in highly controlled economies, another competitive advantage was their adroit handling of government relations. For example, the Tata Group established India's first steel mill and attempted to address seriously the industrial policy goals of India. Dynastic marriages between business group families and politically connected families were not uncommon. The son of the head of Arab Contractors married the daughter of Egyptian president Anwar Sadat.

Like virtually all firms in developing countries, business groups began as family-owned enterprises, and today the original families still play an important role in most cases. However, as these firms expanded, more professional management was introduced. Other changes have swept through business groups as well. Perhaps the most important of these has been the new competition that business groups face from multinational corporations. Many more multinational corporations have entered emerging markets in the wake of trade and investment liberalization. With the lifting of protectionist policies that once protected local firms by excluding imports and even discouraging foreign investment, multinationals now threaten business groups with new technology, quality products at competitive prices, global brands, and strong financial resources. They also compete for the best management talent in the country, something that was once the domain of the business groups. Also, as governments loosen their hold over their economies, the groups' competitive advantage in managing government relations has become less important.

In response to these new threats, many business groups are rethinking the strategies that have served them well in the past. Some argue that the diversity of the past should be abandoned. Instead, the firm should restructure itself around its strongest business or businesses and expand these into foreign markets. In other words, business groups are considering becoming more like multinational firms. Of the 80 companies that make up the Tata Group, 11 account for 85 percent of the revenue and 90 percent of the profit. The group is considering cutting out low-margin businesses such as cement and abandoning toiletries, where Tata's market share has lagged behind competitors.[29] Anticipating an alignment with Europe and a subsequent loss of protection for local industries, Turkey's business groups have also been adapting to changing times. One of the largest of these groups, Haci Omer Sabanci Holding, is streamlining its activities by focusing on core areas such as energy, the Internet, and telecommunications, while planning to sell its interest in areas such as textiles and plastics. The Turkish group, like many groups in Latin America, is also actively seeking out foreign multinational firms as joint venture partners.[30]

Even so, some still argue that it is premature to expect that business groups will disband in developing countries. The political and economic environments in these countries remain tumultuous, and the strategic value of rendering mutual assistance and forming strong government ties is as real today as before. Whatever their future, business groups currently represent the strongest local competition in many developing countries.

READ MORE ABOUT IT:
Check out *Turkish Conglomerate Prepares to Slim Down* on our website.

New Global Players

Recently, firms from developing countries have appeared as major regional and even global competitors in a number of industries. These firms increasingly challenge the established positions of multinationals from the United States, Europe, and Japan. Some, like Arcelik White Goods, are outstanding units of older, restructuring business groups. Others are firms that have been established more recently. Acer, the Taiwanese computer giant, was founded in 1976 and rose to a strong position in the Asian consumer PC market.[31] Hikma Pharmaceuticals was established in Jordan in 1977 and carved out a niche for itself as a respected producer of generic drugs with operations in the United States, Europe, and several developing countries. A number of firms, such as Mexico's Cemex and South African Breweries, have used a strong cash flow from their dominant position in one of the larger emerging markets to fund the purchase of established companies abroad. This has helped catapult such companies into positions among the top-ranked global competitors of their industries. The success of these companies requires a rethinking of the impact that competitors from the emerging world may have on global markets in the future.

▶ The Country-of-Origin Advantage

Does an international company enjoy a market advantage—or disadvantage—because of the reputation of its home market? When Arcelik White Goods entered the European market, the firm was concerned that its home country, Turkey, would diminish its brand in the eyes of European consumers. Consumer response to the country of origin of products has been studied for 30 years. The findings are mixed, but certain trends can be observed. Although certain biases persist, consumers seem to change their minds over time, reflecting a dynamic environment for global competition.

Country of origin denotes the country with which a firm is associated—typically its home country. For example, IBM is associated with the United States and Sony with Japan. Several studies have concluded that consumers usually favor products from developed countries over those from less developed countries. The reputation of some countries appears to enhance the credibility of competitors in product groups for which the country is well known, such as wines and perfumes for France, video recorders for South Korea, and Persian carpets for Iran. Often the positive or negative effect of country of origin, as well as its ability to affect consumers' perceptions, is product-specific. Russian automobiles may evoke a negative image in the minds of consumers, but Russian vodka may evoke a positive response.[32] In a few cases, country of origin can connote more general product attributes. Germany is known for engineering quality and Italy for design.[33] The country-of-origin effect is a significant one; a positive country-of-origin effect can help certain global competitors, and even a strong global brand can have difficulty overcoming a negative country-of-origin bias.[34]

A country-of-origin bias is not limited to consumer markets. It has been observed among industrial buyers as well. Buyers of industrial products in South Korea rated Japanese, German, and American suppliers higher than suppliers from their own country.[35] Another study revealed that U.S. buyers

World Beat 6.2 *Dracula: Made in Romania?*

It's a creepy morning high in the Transylvanian mountains. Mist hovers over the long grass. Giant limbs of ancient oaks creak in the wind. Crows circle overhead. Werewolves, blood-sucking vampires, and legions of the undead have all emerged from the fog of these Transylvanian forests. But this latest creature, emerging from the haze of Transylvania's modern-day industrial pollution, may be the spookiest yet: Dracula Park.

"We'll have Draculas who will walk, speak, fly, land," says Dan Matei-Agathon, Romania's tourism minister. He offers a set of fangs, along with his business card, to a visitor in his Bucharest office. "But don't get the wrong idea," he adds. "This won't be Disneyland."

Certainly not; a German company that runs a Cowboys and Indians theme park in Bavaria is in on construction. "We know the border between interesting and ridiculous," assures the ministry's man in charge of the project.

Thus there will be an interesting Dracula golf course. There will be an interesting Dracula food court that serves fare from the Middle Ages. There will be a bizarre bazaar, where all Draculabilia from around the world will be on sale, from Dracula chess pieces and Dracula salt and pepper shakers to Dracula vodka (clear, not red) and Dracula baseball bats. There will be interesting amusements: One would-be vendor has proposed drawing visitors' portraits using the subjects' own blood.

Getting a bite out of the Dracula action has become a national obsession for Romania. "There's big money in Dracula all over the world—except in Romania," says Mr. Agathon. He shows off a Dracula watch. It's made in Switzerland. "See," he says, "I'm still wondering what Switzerland's connection to Dracula is."

For ages, Romania refused to acknowledge officially the vampire Dracula of novelist Bram Stoker and Hollywood's Bela Lugosi. Instead, they venerated the historical Dracula, Vlad Tepes, as a heroic count who fought off hordes of foreign invaders and brought law and order to this realm of southeastern Europe. Yes, "Vlad the Impaler" accomplished this by skewering his foes on stakes, "but he never sucked blood," the local mayor hastens to add. "That's silly."

Still, the mayor says, "This myth, his legend, we must use." He envisions 3,000 new jobs and a million visitors coming to this walled medieval fortress, home of Dracula. "If people believe this vampire comes from Transylvania, and this is his home, then why shouldn't we profit?"

But no sooner had they settled on a name than a letter arrived from Universal Studios in California. It informed the Romanians that Universal holds worldwide rights to the character Count Dracula as portrayed in seven films, including the legendary 1930s film with Bela Lugosi. This was news to Mr. Agathon. Discussions between the two sides continue.

Source: Roger Thurow, "The Vampire Strikes Back," *Wall Street Journal*, October 30, 2001, p. A1.

were more willing to purchase from established industrialized countries than from newly industrialized ones, with the exception of Mexico. However, buyers were more ready to buy from foreign suppliers if they established warehouses or sales offices in the United States.[36] Also, industrial buyers who were experienced with suppliers from Latin America rated these countries higher than buyers who had had no such business dealings.[37]

The issue of country of origin is further complicated in the case of multinational companies that produce products in various countries. Which matters most to consumers—the home country associated with the brand or the country where the product is actually manufactured or assembled? Research on this question is inconclusive, though it leans toward favoring the country

In spite of estranged relations between Iran and the United States, the appeal for American products persists in Iran. On a billboard in Tehran, a local candy manufacturer mimics American soft drink Coke.

of manufacture. For example, a study of Nigerian consumers of high-technology products revealed that where a product was produced was considered more important than the company name or brand of the product.[38]

Buyer attitudes toward certain countries can change rapidly, and this has important implications for global competitors. Both Japan and South Korea saw their products rise in esteem over a short period of time.[39] By the late 1990s, Japanese products were scoring higher than U.S. or German products in some countries, including Saudi Arabia.[40] By 2001, South Korean companies were strengthening their positions in the global cell phone market. Samsung placed sixth in global market share and had made strong inroads into the U.S. market, where it was adding product features and raising prices. The prestigious U.S. publication *Consumer Reports* rated Samsung's SCH-3500 web-surfing model as number one. Despite heavy competition from European and American firms such as Nokia and Motorola, Samsung aims to rise to at least number three globally. According to its marketing director, Park San Ji, "the full-fledged war will soon begin."[41]

Buyer biases—both at the consumer and business levels—continue to play a role in product perception, and this can help or hurt an international firm. However, country-of-origin considerations are only part of the consumer decision-making process, and over time a country-of-origin effect can lessen or even disappear. Global marketers must be aware of country-of-origin implications but remain alert to possible changes.

▶ *Conclusions*

This chapter has introduced some basic issues of global competition. We have explored ways by which global competitors engage each other and strategies that local firms employ to survive in an increasingly global marketplace.

WHAT COMPETITIVE ENVIRONMENT WILL YOU ENCOUNTER?
Continue with your *Country Market Report* on our website.

We also saw that the cultural challenge in the global marketplace is not limited to buyers. The rules of the competitive game will vary from country to country. Both local and global competitors may possess strengths and weaknesses that reflect to some extent the environment and history of their home countries. Strategic global marketers must not only target appropriate buyers worldwide but also understand and successfully engage the competition that exists for those buyers.

Review Questions

1. List and explain four key ways in which one global competitor can address another.
2. Explain each of the following strategies: defender, extender, contender, and dodger.
3. Compare and contrast U.S. and European attitudes toward competition.
4. How have keiretsus affected competition in Japan?
5. Why were many developing countries afraid that there could be too much competition in a market? What actions did they take to decrease competition?
6. What are the possible competitive advantages and disadvantages of being a state-owned enterprise?
7. How do business groups differ from big corporations in the United States?
8. List instances of positive and negative country-of-origin effect.

Questions for Discussion

1. What advantages might a Japanese competitor have in the Japanese market over an American firm attempting to enter that market?
2. What do you think governments should be allowed to do to help their home firms be more globally competitive? What do you think constitutes unfair assistance?
3. Are business groups doomed?
4. Nearly all studies of the country-of-origin effect focus on how buyers evaluate products and on their intention to purchase products. How might the country-of-origin effect manifest itself in other situations?

For Further Reading

Bartlett, Christopher A., and Sumantra Ghoshal. "Going Global: Lessons from Late Movers." *Harvard Business Review*, March–April 2000: 132–142.

Dawar, Niraj, and Tony Frost. "Competing with Giants: Survival Strategies for Local Companies in Emerging Markets." *Harvard Business Review*, March–April 1999: 119–129.

Guliz Ger. "Localizing in the Global Village: Local Firms Competing in Global Markets." *California Management Review* 41, 4 (Summer 1999): 64–83.

Jaffe, Eugene D., and Israel D. Nebenzahl. *National Image and Competitive Advantage: The Theory and Practice of Country-of-Origin Effect*. Copenhagen: Copenhagen Business School Press, 2001.

Tezuka, Hiroyuki. "Success as the Source of Failure? Competition and Cooperation in the Japanese Economy." *Sloan Management Review*, Winter 1997: 83–93.

Williamson, Peter J. "Asia's New Competitive Game." *Harvard Business Review*, September–October 1997: 55–67.

| Case 6.1 | *Buzzing Around McDonald's* |

Jollibee is the dominant fast-food restaurant chain in the Philippines, with over 60 percent share of the market. A 2001 survey revealed that 69 percent of Filipino respondents visited Jollibee most often, compared with only 16 percent for McDonald's. Jollibee's founder, Tony Tan, is ethnically Chinese. His family immigrated from China, and his father worked as a cook in a Chinese temple. Mr. Tan was just getting started with Jollibee when McDonald's entered the market in 1981. His friends suggested that he apply for a McDonald's franchise. Mr. Tan declined.

Instead, Mr. Tan went on to develop his own chain that offers unique Filipino food, such as spaghetti with meat sauce topped with smoked fish, deep-fried pork skin, bean curd, sliced boiled eggs, and spring onions. In keeping with local tastes that appreciate food with lots of sugar and salt, Jollibee hamburgers are especially sweet. Beef is served with honey and rice, and of course there are mango shakes. Jollibee is recognized by its bee icon, which symbolizes the Filipino spirit of lightheartedness and happiness as well as representing a busy worker. Besides its flagship Jollibee restaurants, Jollibee Foods Corporation (JFC) also owns a chain of Chinese restaurants, Chowking, in the Philippines. But the importance of this chain is relatively low compared to JFC. Only 2 percent of Filipino respondents replied that Chowking was their most visited restaurant.

A poll of Asian business leaders conducted by *Asian Business Magazine* rated Jollibee number one in Asia in terms of growth potential and contribution to society, number two in honesty and ethics, number three in long-term vision, and number four in financial soundness. In total, Jollibee received the highest ranking of all firms in the consumer category—ahead of major multinationals such as Coca-Cola, Nestlé, and Procter & Gamble. Another poll, this one conducted by *Far Eastern Economic Review*, ranked Jollibee the highest on its leading-companies indicator, ahead of Toyota Motor of Japan and Singapore Airlines.

Like most other fast-food chains in the Philippines, Jollibee buys most of its food inputs from overseas. Imports tend to be cheaper and of better quality than food products available locally. In 2002, the company announced that it would build a $32 million food-processing plant and logistics and distribution center in the Philippines with the incentive of a 4-year tax holiday from the government of the Philippines. The center would serve both local and international operations. Keeping costs low is essential to a company already working on low margins. With a recession continuing into 2002, Jollibee refused to raise prices in the Philippines, opting instead to try to increase revenues through expansion. Mr. Tan announced that he would like to see JFC open at least 15 stores in every major market around the world. To finance expansion, the company has gone public, raising money by selling shares on the stock market.

Jollibee had already begun its overseas expansion in 1987 with a restaurant in Brunei, a small, oil-rich country with a relatively large Filipino migrant worker population. JFC moved on to enter other Asian and Middle East markets such as Indonesia, Kuwait, Malaysia, Guam, and New Guinea. In 1998, the company opened its first restaurant in the United States in a location near San Francisco. Soon five more locations were opened in California, in areas with high Filipino populations where brand awareness of Jollibee was already high. For example, the clientele at the restaurant in the San Francisco Bay area is about evenly split between ethnic Filipinos and others. All the U.S. restaurants exceeded expectations. However, an attempt to open a Jollibee restaurant in China proved less successful. The restaurant was eventually closed.

Discussion Questions

1. What strategies did Jollibee follow—or consider following—during its evolution: dodger, defender, extender, and/or contender? Explain your answer.
2. Which strategy do you think is most appropriate for Jollibee? Why?
3. Why do you think Jollibee was successful in the United States but not in China?

Sources: "Jolly News for Jollibee," *Borneo Bulletin*, January 11, 2002; Rosemarie Francisco, "Jollibee Food Stays Cheap," *Reuters English News Service*, May 5, 2002; "Philippines' Jollibee Foods to Build $31.9 MLN Processing Plant," *Asia Pulse*, May 1, 2002; "Jollibee's Sweet Filipino Burger Chain Seeking Fast-Food Niche," *Houston Chronicle*, July 14, 2000; Doris C. Dumlao, "Jollibee Eyes Foreign Markets," *Philippine Daily Inquirer*, July 2, 2001, p.1; and "Face Value," *The Economist*, March 2, 2002: 62.

At the beginning of the twenty-first century, U.S. defense companies held about 44 percent of the world armaments market. Nonetheless, the market was shrinking and becoming more competitive. U.S. defense purchases were down as a result of the dissolution of the Soviet Union. Low oil prices had reduced the ability of major Middle Eastern clients to purchase arms, and the Asian economic crisis had caused other major clients such as Taiwan to cut back orders. There had been few large deals in the industry for several years. U.S.-based Lockheed Martin Corporation could boast of a major contract with the United Arab Emirates (UAE), but negotiations had been tortuous.

The UAE first considered major defense purchases shortly after its neighbor Kuwait was invaded by Iraq in 1990. It proceeded to buy Mirage jets from France and invited companies from France, Sweden, Russia, and the United States to bid on an order of expensive advanced fighter planes. In 1996, the competitors were narrowed down to Lockheed and France's Dassault Aviation S.A. In an attempt to remain in the bidding, another U.S. firm, McDonnell Douglas, had offered steep price cuts but to no avail. Two years later, the UAE announced its final decision in favor of Lockheed. Still, details of the contract remained unresolved, and negotiations began that lasted two more years. At one time, Lockheed became so discouraged that its negotiators were called home. The U.S. government intervened and brought the two sides back together.

Like virtually all defense firms worldwide, Lockheed needed permission from its home government to make sales to foreign governments. Accordingly, the U.S. government closely monitored and even joined in the sales negotiations. U.S. firms could not sell to embargoed countries such as Libya and Iraq. Certain technologies could not even be sold to friendly countries. Yet the U.S. government under the Clinton administration played the most proactive role in assisting U.S. defense firms of any administration in 20 years. Both President Clinton and Vice-President Gore became personally involved in promoting the Lockheed sale.

The UAE finally agreed to purchase Lockheed's Desert Falcon planes. To clinch the deal, Lockheed made concessions that would have seemed outlandish 20 years earlier. The company agreed to supply state-of-the-art technology and to put up a $2 billion bond to safeguard against technological failure. It also signed on to an "off-set" agreement of $160 million to help the UAE expand its state-owned petroleum sector. Off-set agreements had become increasingly a part of arms deals. Defense contractors found themselves agreeing to reinvest part of their earnings in the client country, participating in projects such as building hotels and factories, or, in the case of Korea, helping to upgrade the electronics industry.

As Lockheed relaxed with the Desert Falcon contract in hand, across the globe the Russian government was hosting Ural Expo Arms 2000. Fifty foreign delegations were in attendance to view the 800 exhibits. The Expo was designed to highlight Russian defense suppliers and to help increase overseas sales. Russia's world market share was fluctuating between 2 and 4 percent, and the Russian government was eager to increase exports to generate foreign exchange. Long-time clients such as India and China appeared to show some preference for the Russians. Potential clients agreed that Russian products possessed certain advantages, such as simplicity of use, reliability, and low cost. However, Russian servicing was unreliable, and spare parts could be hard to get. The Russian bureaucracy moved very slowly in approving export licenses, and Russian firms rarely became involved in off-set agreements. Furthermore, there were so many intermediaries involved in Russian defense sales that the Russian companies themselves saw only a fraction of the profits. Still, Russian President Putin vowed to increase armament purchases at home and to support Russia's defense industry abroad.

Discussion Questions

1. How is the global arms market similar to other government markets? How does it differ?
2. How can home governments help and hurt firms competing in this market?
3. What qualities are necessary for a firm to compete in this market? Why are Russian companies relatively weak competitors?

Sources: Tim Weiner, "Russia and France Gain on U.S. Lead in Arms Sales, Report Says," *New York Times*, August 4, 1998; Anne Marie Squeo and Daniel Pearl, "The Big Sell," *Wall Street Journal*, April 20, 2000, p. A1; and Guy Chazan, "Russia's Defense Industry Launches Bid to Boost Sales," *Wall Street Journal*, July 14, 2000, p. A10.

Notes

[1]Michael Flagg, "Enjoy Shinier Hair! Chinese Brands Arrive," *Wall Street Journal*, May 24, 2001, p. A17.

[2]George S. Yip, *Total Global Strategy* (New York: Prentice-Hall, 2002), pp. 171–175.

[3]*Carbonated Soft Drink Industry*, Brokerage Report: Solomon Smith Barney, March 4, 2002.

[4]"How Coke Is Kicking Pepsi's Can," *Fortune*, October 28, 1996: 70–84.

[5]"PepsiCo's Venezuelan Joint Venture Inaugurates $32 Million Plant," *Financial Times*, May 27, 1999, p. 19.

[6]"PepsiCo Secures $8 Million Argentine Soccer Deal," *Financial Times*, March 4, 1997, p. 19.

[7]Jean-Pierre Jeannet. *Competitive Marketing Strategies in a European Context*, Lausanne: IMD, 1987.

[8]Niraj Dawar and Tony Frost, "Competing with Giants," *Harvard Business Review*, March-April 1999: 119–129.

[9]Guliz Ger, "Localizing in the Global Village: Local Firms Competing in Global Markets," *California Management Review* 41, 4 (Summer 1999): 64–83.

[10]"Competing with Giants," p. 124.

[11]Jaime Mejia and Gabriel Sama, "Media Players Say 'Si' to Latino Magazines," *Wall Street Journal*, May 15, 2002, p. B4.

[12]*Koc Holding: Arcelik White Goods*, Harvard Business School, #9-598-033, 1997.

[13]William Echikson, Carol Matlack, and David Vannier, "American E-Tailers Take Europe by Storm," *Business Week*, August 7, 2000: 54.

[14]Hae Won Choi, "What GM's Daewoo Deal Says About Korea," *Wall Street Journal*, April 24, 2002, p. A19.

[15]Dan Carney and William Echikson, "Europe: A Different Take on Anti Trust," *Business Week*, June 25, 2001, p.40.

[16]Hiroyuki Tezuka, "Success as the Source of Failure? Competition and Cooperation in the Japanese Economy." *Sloan Management Review* (Winter 1997): 83–93.

[17]Ibid.

[18]Peter Landers, "Foreign Aid," *Wall Street Journal*, June 14, 2001, p. A1.

[19]Phred Dvorak, Robert A. Guth, Jason Singer and Todd Zaun, "Loose Ends," *Wall Street Journal*, March 2, 2001, p. A1.

[20]"Knights in Tarnished Armour: India's Big Business," *The Economist*, June 2, 2001.

[21]Ibid.

[22] David Luhnow, "Striking Back Against Empires," *Wall Street Journal*, October 1, 2001, p. R9.

[23] Betsy McKay and David Luhnow, "Mexico Finds Coke and Its Bottlers Guilty of Abusing Dominant Position in Market," *Wall Street Journal*, March 8, 2002, p. B3.

[24] Gary S. Becker, "Is Europe Starting to Play by U.S. Rules?" *Business Week*, April 22, 2002: 24.

[25]Peter Fritsch, "Hard Profits," *Wall Street Journal*, April 22, 2002, p. A1.

[26]Eric Bellman, "After Delays, India Sells Stakes in Two Big Firms," *Wall Street Journal*, February 6, 2002, p. A12.

[27]Josh Gerstein, "Chinese Law Delivers Shipping Controversy," *USA Today*, April 5, 2002, p. B8.

[28]James E. Austin, *Managing in Developing Countries* (New York: The Free Press, 1990), pp. 127–129.

[29]"Reinventing Tata," *The Economist*, February 17, 2001.

[30]James M. Dorsey, "Turkish Conglomerate Prepares to Slim Down," *Wall Street Journal*, August 14, 2000, p. A14.

[31]Bruce Einhorn, Stuart Young, and David Rocks, "Another About-Face at Acer," *Business Week*, April 24, 2000.

[32]Eugene D. Jaffe and Israel D. Nebenzahl, *National Image and Competitive Advantage* (Copenhagen: Copenhagen Business School Press, 2001), p. 53.

[33]Saeed Samiee, "Customer Evaluation of Products in a Global Market," *Journal of International Business Studies* 25, 3 (1994): 579–604.

[34]David K. Tse and Gerald J. Gorn, "An Experiment on the Salience of Country-of-Origin in an Era of Global Brands," *Journal of International Marketing* 1, 1 (1995): 57–76.

[35]Dae Ryun Chang and Ik-Tae Rim, "A Study on the Rating of Import Sources for Industrial Products in a Newly Industrialized Country: The Case of South Korea," *Journal of Business Research* 32 (1995): 31–39.

[36]Hans B. Thorelli and Aleksandra Glowaka, "Willingness of American Industrial Buyers to Source Internationally," *Journal of Business Research* 32 (1995): 21–30.

[37]Massoud M. Saghafi, Fanis Varvoglis, and Tomas Vega, "Why U.S. Firms Don't Buy from Latin American Companies," *Industrial Marketing Management* 20 (1991): 207–213.

[38]Chike Okechuku and Vincent Oneyemah, "Nigerian Consumer Attitudes Toward Foreign and Domestic Products," *Journal of International Business Studies* 30, 3 (1999): 611–622.

[39]Michael A. Kamins and Akira Nagashima, "Perceptions of Products Made in Japan versus Those Made in the United States Among Japanese and American Executives: A Longitudinal Perspective," *Asia Pacific Journal of Management* 12, 1 (1995): 49–68; and Inder Khera, "A Broadening Base of U.S. Consumer Acceptance of Korean Products" in Kenneth D. Bahn and M. Joseph Sirsy (eds.), *World Marketing Congress* (Blacksburg, VA: Academy of Marketing Science, 1986), pp. 136–141.

[40]Shahid N. Bhuian, "Saudi Consumer Attitudes Towards European, U.S. and Japanese Products and Marketing Practices," *European Journal of Marketing* 31, 7 (1997): 467–486.

[41]Moon Ihlwan, "Dialing for Dominance," *Business Week*, June 11, 2001, p. 66E2.

7 Global Marketing Research

Spanish Retailer Zara takes only 4 or 5 weeks to design a new fashion collection, compared to the 6 months it takes such major competitors as the Gap Inc., Italy's Benetton SpA, and Sweden's Hennes and Mauritz AB. Zara's designers frequent fashion shows and talk to customers. One designer remarks, "We're like sponges. We soak up information about fashion trends from all over the world." The firm sent out new khaki skirts during the night to some of its 449 stores worldwide. From their desks at headquarters, Zara managers can check real-time sales on computers to see where the skirts are selling. They keep in constant contact with store managers in order to spot and react to trends quickly. After selling well in Asia earlier in the year, camouflage motifs are now popular in France and Lebanon. But stripes outsell camouflage in Spain. Long plaid skirts are big in Kuwait.[1]

In the previous chapters, we introduced a variety of global consumers, competitors, and national environments. Our purpose in Chapter 7 is to elaborate further on methods for

CHAPTER OUTLINE

collecting appropriate data to understand potential markets better. Our emphasis is managerial rather than technical. Throughout the chapter, we focus on how companies can obtain useful and accurate information that will help them make more informed strategic decisions, such as decisions related to market choice and to the marketing mix that will be discussed in later chapters. This chapter begins by examining the scope and challenges of international research. We then describe the research process with particular emphasis on data collection. The chapter continues with an overview of analytic techniques and concludes with a discussion of global information systems.

LEARNING OBJECTIVES

After studying this chapter, you should be able to

▶ List and describe the four steps involved in the research process.

▶ Differentiate between the challenges posed by secondary data collection and those posed by primary data collection.

▶ Note cultural differences in marketing research, and explain ways in which market researchers can adjust to them.

▶ Describe problems related to comparability of studies undertaken in different national markets.

▶ Compare analytic techniques—demand analysis and analysis by inference—and explain their value to global marketers.

▶ Note ways to monitor global competitors.

▶ List and describe the components of an environmental review.

▶ Explain the requirements for a global marketing information system.

▶ *The Scope of Global Marketing Research*

Global marketing research is meant to provide adequate data and cogent analysis for effective decision making on a global scale. The analytic research techniques practiced by domestic businesses can be applied to international marketing projects. The key difference is in the complexity of assignments because of the additional variables that international researchers must take into account. Global marketers have to judge the comparability of their data across a number of markets and are frequently faced with making decisions based on the basis of limited data. Because of this, the researcher must approach the research task with flexibility, resourcefulness, and ingenuity.

Traditionally, marketing research has been charged with the following three broad areas of responsibility:

1. **Market studies.** One of the tasks that researchers most frequently face is to determine the size of a market and the needs of potential customers.
2. **Competitive studies.** Another important task for the international marketing researcher is to provide insights about competitors, both domestic and foreign.
3. **Environmental studies.** Given the added environmental complexity of global marketing, managers need timely input on various national environments—particularly the economic, political, and legal contexts of potential markets.

Global marketing research is used to make both strategic and tactical decisions. Strategic decisions include deciding what markets to enter, how to enter them (exporting, licensing, joint venture), and where to locate production facilities. Tactical decisions are decisions about the specific marketing mix to be used in a country. Decisions about advertising, sales promotions, and sales forces all require data derived from testing in the local market. The type of information required is often the same as that required in domestic marketing research, but the process is made more complex by the variety of cultures and environments. Table 7.1 shows the various types of tactical marketing decisions needed and the kinds of research used to collect the necessary data.

The complexity of the international marketplace, the extreme differences that exist from country to country, and the company's frequent lack of familiarity with foreign markets accentuate the importance of international marketing research. Before making market entry, product positioning, or marketing mix decisions, a marketer must have accurate information about the market size, customer needs, competition, and relevant government regulations. Marketing research provides the information the firm needs to avoid the costly mistakes of poor strategies or lost opportunities.

Marketing research can guide product development for a foreign market. On the strength of a research study conducted in the United States, one U.S. firm introduced a new cake mix in England. Believing that homemakers wanted to feel that they participated in the preparation of the cake, the U.S. marketers devised a mix that required homemakers to add an egg. Given its success in the U.S. market, the marketers confidently introduced the product in England. The product failed, however, because the British did not like the

Table 7.1 *International Marketing Decisions Requiring Marketing Research*

MARKETING MIX DECISION	TYPE OF RESEARCH
Product policy	Focus groups and qualitative research to generate ideas for new products
	Survey research to evaluate new product ideas
	Concept testing, test marketing
	Product benefit and attitude research
	Product formulation and feature testing
Pricing	Price sensitivity studies
Distribution	Survey of shopping patterns and behavior
	Consumer attitudes toward different store types
	Survey of distributor attitudes and policies
Advertising	Advertising pretesting
Advertising post-testing, recall scores	Surveys of media habits
Sales promotion	Surveys of response to alternative types of promotion
Sales force	Tests of alternative sales presentations

Source: Susan P. Douglas and C. Samuel Craig, International Marketing Research, © 1983, p. 32. Reprinted by permission of Prentice-Hall, Inc., Englewood Cliffs, New Jersey.

fancy American cakes. They preferred cakes that were tough and spongy and could accompany afternoon tea. The ploy of having homemakers add an egg to the mix did not eliminate basic differences in taste and style.[2]

Whirlpool's market research helped speed its entry into the European microwave market. Although less than one-third of European households owned microwave ovens, research suggested that European consumers would buy a microwave that performed like a conventional oven. Whirlpool introduced a model that incorporated a broiler coil for top browning and a unique dish that sizzled the underside of the food. This new product, the Crisp, became Europe's best-selling microwave.[3]

Companies also use research to position a product better in foreign markets. PepsiCo's research found that the youth market in Europe was ready for a new cola that did not contain sugar. However, Pepsi also found that the youth market, especially males, was adverse to a diet soda. Therefore, the soft-drink giant launched Pepsi Max not as a diet soda but as a trendy, cool, sugar-free cola. The TV campaign showed Pepsi Max drinkers "Living Life to the Max," performing death-defying stunts.[4]

▶ *Challenges in Planning International Research*

After determining what key variables to investigate, international marketers still face a number of challenges. Whereas domestic research is limited to one country, international research includes many. The research design is more complex because the researcher defining the possible target market must choose which countries or segments to research. This initial step in the research process is further complicated by limited secondary information. Even if the appropriate secondary information exists, it may be difficult to locate and acquire. Thus researchers are forced either to spend considerable resources finding such data or to accept the limited secondary data that are available. In many countries, the cost of collecting primary data is substantially higher than in the domestic market. This is particularly the case for developing countries. Consequently, researchers have to accept tradeoffs between the need for more accurate data and the limited resources available to accomplish the tasks.

The comparison of research results from one national study to another is hindered by the general difficulty of establishing comparability and equivalence among various research data. Definitions of homemakers, socioeconomic status, incomes, and customers vary widely in Europe.[5] Educational levels can be used to determine socioeconomic status, but educational systems vary widely from country to country, making comparisons very crude. Information about marital status and head of household vary from country to country. Ireland, for example, recognizes only the categories single, married, and widowed, whereas Latin American countries often include cohabitation in their marital categories. These differences from country to country can make even the simplest demographic comparisons between markets challenging.[6]

▶ *The Research Process*

Although conducting marketing research internationally adds to the complexity of the research task, the basic approach remains the same for domestic and international assignments. Either type of research is a four-step process:

1. Problem definition and development of research objectives
2. Determination of the sources of information
3. Collection and analysis of the data from primary and secondary sources
4. Analysis of the data and presentation of the results

These four steps may be the same for both international and domestic research, but problems in implementation may occur because of cultural and economic differences from country to country.

Problem Definition and Development of Research Objectives

In any market research project, the most important tasks are to define the problem and, subsequently, to determine what information is needed. This process can take weeks or months. It eventually determines the choice of methodologies, the types of people to survey, and the appropriate time frame in which to conduct the research.

Marketing problems may differ between countries or cultures. This may reflect differences in socioeconomic conditions, levels of economic development, cultural forces, or the competitive market structure. For example, bicycles in a developed country may be competing with other recreational goods, such as skis, baseball gloves, and exercise equipment. In a developing country, however, they provide basic transportation and hence compete with small cars, mopeds, and scooters. A global firm could fail to understand why growth in bicycles was declining in Malaysia if it asked questions only about the consumer's purchase and use of other recreational products.

Data Collection

For each assignment, researchers may choose to base their analyses on **primary data** (data collected specifically for this assignment), **secondary data** (previously collected and available data), or a combination of both secondary and primary sources. Because costs tend to be higher for research based on primary data, researchers usually exhaust secondary data first. Often called

---

World Beat 7.1 *Middle East Research*

Marketing research professionals working in Middle Eastern nations with predominantly Muslim populations say that the area's already limited acceptance of Western marketing research methods was not undermined by the terrorist attacks in September 2001 and their military aftermath—but neither is there any reason to expect tremendous growth in the region.

According to an industry newsletter, the international marketing research industry's total research revenues derived from studies done in Muslim nations amount to no more than about $25 million annually, a tiny slice of the $4.3 billion in non-U.S. research revenues posted by the 25 largest international marketing research firms alone. The most significant new trend in the research industry—the Internet interview—is not even an option in the Middle East because of the small number of consumers with home Internet service.

In the Middle East, one distinct social boundary exists between men and women in nearly all endeavors, including, for example, most research focus groups. In conservative Saudi Arabia, where strict interpretation of Islam demands segregation of the sexes, mixed-gender groups are flatly prohibited. But even in more liberal Muslim nations such as Egypt, mixed-gender groups are usually not recommended. Muslim women often defer to men, letting males dominate the conversation, which skews the results of a focus group. Segregation still is the best way to get Muslim women to open up. Yet the idea of females caught on tape and possibly observed by strangers also conflicts with cultural norms.

In rural areas of Saudi Arabia, mail is delivered not to homes or P.O. boxes, but only to businesses, so researchers can't use the postal system for consumer recruitment. Mall intercept is not common or widely understood by consumers, and this makes it difficult to approach strangers in Middle Eastern shopping malls. Western researchers are left to recruit via word of mouth (so-called snowballing). Typically, they partner with a local research company or use other local contacts willing to inquire among their own social circles for participants. But although a native can better explain the project's concept and more effectively recruit fellow citizens, each "seed contact" can be allowed to generate only a small number of referrals, lest the information be collected from within too narrow a circle of acquaintances. A few weeks of recruitment field work in the United Kingdom could translate into many more weeks for the same study in a Muslim country. As a result, research projects typically take much longer to complete in Muslim countries.

Source: Steve Jarvis, "Western-Style Research in the Middle East," *Marketing News,* April 29, 2002: 37–38.

desk research or library research, this approach depends on the availability and reliability of material. Secondary sources may include government publications, trade journals, and data from international agencies or service establishments such as banks, ad agencies, and marketing research companies.

▶ *Collecting Secondary Data*

For any marketing research problem, the location and analysis of secondary data should be a first step. Although secondary data are not available for all variables, data can often be obtained from public and private sources at a fraction of the cost of obtaining primary data. Increasingly, these sources are disseminating or selling their data over the Internet.

Sources of Secondary Data

A good approach to locating secondary sources is to ask yourself who would know about most sources of information on a specific market. For example, if you wanted to locate secondary information on fibers used for tires in Europe, you might consider asking the editor of a trade magazine on the tire industry or the executive director of the tire manufacturing association or the company librarian for Akzo, a Dutch company that manufactures fibers. Also, most business libraries have some type of directory of secondary information. Some online data sources are Datastream International (Dun & Bradstreet), Textline (Reuters Limited), DunsPrint (Dun & Bradstreet), Harvest Marketing Research (Harvest Information Services), and ABI/Inform.

It would be impractical to list all the sources of secondary data that are available on international markets, but they include web search engines,

Check out our website for ideas and links to online sources of secondary data.

A census taker collects information in Delhi, India.

banks, consulates, embassies, foreign chambers of commerce, libraries with foreign information sections, foreign magazines, public accounting firms, security brokers, and state development offices in foreign countries. Marketers can also "eavesdrop" on the Internet. Every day customers comment online concerning products and services. By monitoring chat rooms, newsgroups, and listservs, marketers can analyze comments to learn what their customers and their competitors are thinking.[7]

Problems with Secondary Data

There are problems associated with the use of secondary data. They include (1) the fact that not all the necessary data may be available, (2) uncertainty about the accuracy of the data, (3) the lack of comparability of the data, and (4) the questionable timeliness of some data. In some cases, no data have been collected. For example, many countries have little data on the number of retailers, wholesalers, and distributors. In Ethiopia and Chad, no population statistics were available for many years.

The quality of government statistics is definitely variable. For example, Germany reported that industrial production was up by 0.5 percent in July 1993 but later revised this figure, reporting that production actually declined by 0.5 percent, an error of 100 percent in the opposite direction. An *Economist* survey of twenty international statisticians rated the quality of statistics from thirteen developed countries on the criteria of objectivity, reliability, methodology, and timeliness. The leading countries were Canada, Australia, Holland, and France; the worst were Belgium, Spain, and Italy.[8]

Although a substantial body of data exists from the most advanced industrial nations, secondary data are less likely to be available for developing countries. Not every country publishes a census, and some published data are not considered reliable. In Nigeria, for example, population size is of such political sensitivity that published census data are generally believed to be highly suspect. A study by the International Labor Organization found actual unemployment to be 10.4 million people in Russia, compared with the official figure of 1.7 million people unemployed![9] According to a report by the U.S. Foreign Commercial Service in Beijing, Chinese government statistics are often riddled with *shuifen* or "water content." China has begun to crack down on fraudulent statistics, however, using new laws to discipline local officials who exaggerate their successes. Still, data reliability remains a problem in many developing countries. For this reason, companies sometimes have to proceed with the collection of primary data in developing countries at a much earlier stage than in the most industrialized nations.

The entry of private-sector data collectors into major emerging markets may help ameliorate the shortcomings of government statistics. Since the late 1990s, the Gallup Organization has collected data on the Chinese. Gallup interviewers poll 4,000 randomly selected respondents from both rural and urban China. Questions cover a wide range of topics: How much money do you make? What do you buy? What are your dreams? The results of these surveys are compiled in Gallup publications of consumer attitudes and lifestyles in modern China.[10]

Another problem is that secondary data may not be directly comparable from country to country. The population statistics in the United States are

READ MORE ABOUT IT:
Check out *What the Chinese Want* on our website.

collected every 10 years, whereas population statistics in Bolivia are collected every 25 years. Also, countries may calculate the same statistic but do so in different ways. Gross domestic product (GDP) is the value of all goods and services produced in a country and is often used in place of GNP. GDP per capita is a common measure of market size, suggesting the economic wealth of a country per person. As we noted in Chapter 5, the International Monetary Fund (IMF) has decided that the normal practice of converting expressions of GDP in local currencies into dollars at market exchange rates understates the true size of developing economies relative to rich ones. Therefore, the IMF has decided to use purchasing-power parity, which takes into account differences in prices among nations.

Finally, age of the data is a constant problem. Population statistics are usually between 2 and 5 years old at best. Industrial production statistics can be from 1 to 2 years old. With different markets exhibiting different growth rates, it may be unwise to use older data to make decisions among markets. Market surveys previously undertaken by governments or private research firms are seldom as timely as a marketing manager truly needs.

▶ *Collecting Primary Data*

Often, in addition to secondary data or when secondary data are not available or usable, the marketer will need to collect primary data. Researchers can design studies to collect primary data that will meet the information requirements for making a specific marketing decision. Primary sources frequently reveal data that are simply not available from secondary sources. For example, Siar Research International undertook a survey on shaving habits and discovered that over 50 percent of Kazakhstan men shave every day, whereas most Azerbaijan men shave only once a week.[11]

For the global marketer, collecting primary data involves developing a research instrument, selecting a sample, collecting the data, and (often) comparing results across cultures.

Developing a Research Instrument

The process of developing a research instrument such as a survey questionnaire or a focus group protocol must often be done with multiple markets in mind, and every effort should be made to capture the appropriate environmental variables. Even research aimed at a single market might be compared, at a later date, with the results of research in another country.

Another challenge of instrument design involves translation from one language to another. Accurate translation equivalence is important, first to ensure that the respondents understand the question and second to ensure that the researcher understands the response. **Back translation** is commonly used. That is, first the questionnaire is translated from the home language into the language of the country where it will be used; this is done by a bilingual speaker who is a native speaker of the foreign country. Next a bilingual person who is a native speaker of the home language translates this version back into the home language. This translation is then compared to the original wording. Another translation technique is **parallel translation,** in which two or more translators translate the questionnaire. The results are compared, and any differences are discussed and resolved.

Idiomatic expressions and colloquialisms are often translated incorrectly. To avoid these translation errors, experts suggest the technique of back translation in the local dialect, so that *ji xuan ji*, which means "computers" to Chinese and Taiwanese, does not become "calculators" to Singaporeans or Malaysians through mistranslation.[12] Even within the same city, differences in social class can result in different idioms. In one study of the adoption of new products, interviewers in Mexico City were selected from among the same social class as respondents.[13]

Even with the best of translations, research can suffer if a concept is not readily understood. For example, Western researchers discovered that the Vietnamese tend to be very literal in their understanding of ideas. If a company asks for an opinion on a new package design concept, Vietnamese consumers may say they never saw it before, so it can't be done. Researchers must instead explain that the new packaging is available in other countries and then ask what consumers think of it.[14]

Selecting a Sample

After developing the instrument and translating it into the appropriate language, the researcher must determine the appropriate sample design. What population is under investigation? Is it housewives between twenty and forty years old or manufacturing directors at textile plants? Researchers prefer using a probability sample in order to have greater assurance that sample results can be extrapolated to the population under investigation. In order to have a probability sample, potential respondents must be randomly selected from frames, or lists, of the population. In many countries such lists are difficult to find.

In many developing countries, the existing infrastructure and the lack of available data or information substantially interfere with attempts to use probability samples. Sampling of larger populations requires the availability of detailed census data, called census tracts, or neighborhood maps from which probability samples can be drawn. Even where such data are available, they are often out of date. Some market researchers use telephone directories. However, in Mexico the telephone directory may not correspond with those who currently possess the phone numbers. Further difficulties arise from inadequate transportation, which may prevent field workers from reaching selected census tracts in some areas of the country. Sampling is particularly difficult in countries where several languages are spoken, because carrying out a nationwide survey under such conditions is impractical.

Collecting the Data

The next task of the international market researcher is to collect the data. An immediate problem may involve the researcher's own employees. In developing countries, data collectors may be poorly paid and are often paid by the response. This can lead to collectors simply filling out questionnaires themselves. Some of the safeguards against this in developed countries cannot be easily replicated in developing ones. To ensure quality, supervisors can call back respondents on a random basis to confirm their responses. Alternatively, supervisors can randomly listen in on telephone interviews. However, phone interviews are rare in developing countries, and collectors must often intercept respondents on the streets. This can make it more difficult for supervisors to check responses.

Data can be collected by mail, by telephone, electronically, or face-to-face. The technique will vary by country. For example, in the United States, telephone interviews are common. As shown in Table 7.2, face-to-face interviews at home or work may be very popular in Switzerland and the United Kingdom, whereas interviews in shopping areas are popular in France and the Netherlands. Telephone interviewing dominates Swedish data collection.[15]

The use of the Internet for research varies greatly across countries. In 2000, the overall research markets in the United States and Europe were both large: $7.1 billion and $5.9 billion, respectively. However, the Internet segment accounted for 3.7 percent of the U.S. market but for only 0.7 percent of the European market. Although Internet penetration in Northern Europe equals or exceeds that of the United States, in Southern Europe—Spain, Portugal, Italy, and Greece—Internet penetration is low. Furthermore, many Europeans harbor concerns over the protection of data on the Internet. This has resulted in strict laws that affect how data over the Internet are collected and used.[16]

Data collection and privacy concerns being raised in the European Union (EU) may affect marketing research globally. The EU Data Privacy Directive that went into effect in November 1998 requires unambiguous consent from a person for each use of her or his personal data.[17] This could seriously limit the use of telephone interviews that include questions related to health problems, political beliefs, sex habits, and so on. All fifteen EU nations have data privacy legislation and a government privacy commission to enforce the EU policy. This legislation stipulates that data cannot be sent to a country that is not a member of the EU unless that country has an adequate level of privacy protection. The U.S. Department of Commerce has worked with EU officials to develop the Safe Harbor framework. This framework provides a streamlined way for individual U.S. firms to comply with the European standards and thus continue to receive data from Europe.

A major issue in primary research, of course, is the willingness of the potential respondent to participate in the study. For example, in many cultures a man will consider it inappropriate to discuss his shaving habits with anyone, especially with a female interviewer. Respondents in the Netherlands or Germany are notoriously reluctant to divulge information about their personal financial habits. The Dutch are more willing to discuss sex than money.[18]

For more on Safe Harbor, including how to apply and who has applied, check out the *Safe Harbor* link on our website.

Table 7.2 *Comparison of European Data Collection Methods*

	FRANCE	THE NETHERLANDS	SWEDEN	SWITZERLAND	U.K.
Mail	4%	33%	23%	8%	9%
Telephone	15	18	44	21	16
Central location/streets	52	37	—	—	—
Home/work	—	—	8	44	54
Groups	13	—	5	6	11
Depth interviews	12	12	2	8	—
Secondary	4	—	4	8	—

Source: Emanual H. Demby, "ESOMAR Urges Changes in Reporting Demographics, Issues Worldwide Report," *Marketing News,* January 8, 1990: 24. Reprinted by permission of the American Marketing Association.

In Japan, consumers will generally not respond to telephone interviews. Only 5 percent of interviews are done by telephone, compared with 30 percent in business offices, 20 percent by mail, 19 percent in the surveyor's office, 14 percent in focus groups, and the rest in other ways.[19] Although personal interviews are expensive and time-consuming, the Japanese preference for face-to-face contact suggests that personal interviews yield better information than data collected by mail or telephone. In fact, Japanese managers are skeptical about Western-style marketing research. Senior and middle managers often go into the field and speak directly with consumers and distributors. This technique of collecting "soft data," though less rigorous than large-scale consumer studies, gives the manager a real feel for the market and the consumers.[20]

Developing countries can present additional problems to market researchers, including poor infrastructure, lower literacy levels, and disinclination

READ MORE ABOUT IT: Check out "Mum's the Word: Mexico Isn't Free with Information" under *Supplemental Readings* on our website.

World Beat 7.2 *Checking Out Real Life*

The maker of Tide laundry detergent, Pampers diapers, and Crest toothpaste plans to send video cameras into about 80 households around the world, hoping to capture, on tape, life's daily routines and procedures in all their boring glory.

Procter & Gamble thinks this exercise in voyeurism will yield a mountain of priceless insights into consumer behavior that more traditional methods—focus groups, interviews, home visits—may have missed. People, it seems, tend to have selective memories when talking to a market researcher. They might say, for example, that they brush their teeth every morning or indulge in just a few potato chips at a time when in fact they often forget to brush and usually eat the whole bag.

Videotape, P&G hopes, will help it get at the whole truth. Initially, the study will follow families in the U.K., Italy, Germany, and China. After a subject family agrees to participate, one or two ethnographer-filmmakers will arrive at the home when the alarm clock rings in the morning and stay until bedtime, usually for a 4-day stretch.

There are ground rules. If friends come over, the subjects must inform them that they are being filmed. The subjects and filmmakers agree on boundaries ahead of time: Most bedroom and bathroom activities aren't taped. A P&G spokeswoman says, "Personal bathing and going to the bathroom" and "any kind of romantic thing that goes on" are off-limits for the camera.

In a recent test of the program, P&G marketers huddled around a laptop computer in a Cincinnati conference room to watch a mother make breakfast for her baby in a tidy kitchen in Thailand. She rests her baby on a hip with one arm and stirs a pot of noodles with her other hand. Then she brings baby and bowl to a table, sits the baby on her lap, and feeds him while he grabs for the spoon. Occasionally she looks over his head at a television set droning the morning news. The P&G managers note several things: She has only one hand to cook with. She isn't using a high chair. There aren't any toys strewn across the floor. P&G is trying to come up with products that solve problems that shoppers didn't even know they had. The behaviors that consumers don't talk about—such as multitasking while feeding a baby—could inspire product and package design in ways that give the company a real edge over rivals.

One-third of the world's population buys P&G products, a proportion far below the astounding 98 percent of U.S. households that have them. P&G is hoping to learn about the lifestyles and local habits of young couples, families with children, and empty-nesters in other countries. Such understanding is critical for a company whose major growth opportunities are overseas.

Source: Emily Nelson, "P&G Checks Out Real Life," *Wall Street Journal*, May 17, 2001, p. B1.

to share information with strangers. In Mexico, respondents prefer shorter questionnaires and may be less forthcoming if interviewed at home than they would be if intercepted on the street. This is particularly true regarding information about personal income, because respondents may believe that the researchers are the tax authorities in disguise.[21] Convincing business buyers to participate in research studies is also difficult in many developing countries. Potential respondents are often concerned that the information they provide will be released to competitors or to the authorities.

Alternatives to Surveys

When surveys prove difficult to administer, another technique that can be used for collecting marketing research data is focus groups. The focus group can also be used at an early stage in the development of a new product concept to gain valuable insights from potential consumers. The researcher assembles a set of six to twelve carefully selected respondents to discuss a product. The research company assembles the participants and leads the discussion; this avoids the bias that the active presence of a company representative might introduce. Of course, the discussion leader must speak in the mother tongue of the participants. Representatives of the company can observe the focus group via video or audio taping, through a one-way mirror, or by sitting in the room. Focus groups are subject to cross-cultural challenges of their own. In some Muslim countries, it can be difficult to find women who will agree to participate. In other countries, such as Japan, it may be difficult to get participants to criticize a potential product.[22] However, experienced focus group companies can be resourceful at using questioning techniques and interpreting body language to get the full value from this research approach.

Communist Vietnam has only recently opened to Western businesses, yet marketing researchers find that the Vietnamese are enthusiastic about joining focus groups. Participation rates can range between 35 and 50 percent.

Customers test perfumes in Paris, France. Just observing how consumers shop can provide global marketers with valuable insights.

As in China, however, the government of Vietnam restricts what can be asked in these groups and bans topics it considers too sensitive.[23]

Finally, observation can be a powerful research tool, especially in developing countries where other techniques may be taboo or difficult to administer. In Cuba, where administering questionnaires on the street is strictly forbidden, foreign marketers can explore how Cubans behave by unobtrusively watching them shop. However, this approach should be used with caution. Unless a researcher is very familiar with the culture, observations can prove difficult to interpret and can lead to wrong research conclusions.[24]

▶ *Comparing Studies Across Cultures*

The researcher must deal with problems of comparability if a study is undertaken in more than one country. Were the samples similar in all markets? A study comparing software adoption among small-business owners in Brazil with that among managers in large U.S. corporations may identify differences based more on firm size than on nationality.

Were the concepts and measures understood in the same way? Some cultures express themselves comfortably in extremes, whereas responses in other cultures hover more centrally, making it difficult to determine whether consumers in that country are indeed more neutral about products or whether these tepid responses are an artifact of culture. When interpreting surveys in particular, researchers should be concerned with **scalar equivalence**. What does it mean to rate a product "7" or "8" on a scale from 1 to 10? In Latin America an "8" would indicate lack of enthusiasm, whereas in Asia it would be a very good score.[25]

Another issue that affects comparability is **courtesy bias**. Courtesy bias arises when respondents attempt to guess what answer the interviewer wants to hear and reply accordingly. For example, a taste test could result in respondents saying they liked the product even if they didn't. The level of courtesy bias varies among cultures. It can be a particular problem in Mexico as well as in many Middle Eastern and Asian countries.

▶ *Analytic Techniques*

Once the appropriate secondary and/or primary data have been collected, a variety of analytic techniques can be applied. Although these techniques may be used in domestic marketing research, they are often modified to deal with the complexities of international markets.

Demand Analysis

Demand for products or services can be measured at two levels: aggregate demand, for an entire market or country, and company demand, as represented by actual sales. The former is generally termed market potential, whereas the latter is referred to as sales potential. A very useful perspective developed by Richard Robinson views both market potential and sales potential as part of a filtering process. According to Robinson, demand or potential demand can be measured at six successive levels, the last and final level representing actual sales by the firm.[26] The six levels of demand he cites are as follows:

Potential Need The researcher has to pose the question "Is there a potential need, either now or in the future?" Potential need for a product or service is primarily determined by the demographic and physical characteristics of a country. Its determinants are a country's population, climate, geography, natural resources, land use, life expectancy, and other factors that are part of the physical environment. The potential need could be realized only if all consumers in a country used a product to the fullest extent, regardless of social, cultural, or economic barriers.

Felt Need Even though a potential need as defined above may exist, there is no reason to assume that everyone in a market actually feels a need for the product or service under investigation. Different lifestyles mean that some consumers may not feel a need for a product. For instance, a farmer in a developing country who drives his produce to a local market in an animal-drawn cart potentially has a use for a pickup truck. Yet he may not feel the need for one. Thus, felt need is substantially influenced by the cultural and social environment, including the amount of exposure consumers or buyers have to modern communications. The key task for the researcher is to evaluate the extent to which the potential need is culturally and socially appropriate among the target customers.

Potential Demand The felt need represents the aggregate desire of a target population to purchase a product. However, lack of sufficient income may prevent some customers from actually purchasing the product or service. The result is the potential demand, or the total amount of the product or service that the market would be ready to absorb. Economic variables preventing the realization of sales are generally beyond the control of any individual company. For example, the average income per household may seem to indicate a large demand for washing machines, but the distribution of income may be skewed in such a way that 10 percent of the population has 90 percent of the wealth. To determine whether potential demand is blocked, a firm must look at income distribution data.

Effective Demand Even though potential demand exists, regulatory factors may prevent prospective customers from being able to satisfy their demand. Such constraints include regulations on imports, tariffs, and foreign exchange; specific regulations on product standards with respect to safety, health, and pollution; legal aspects such as patents, copyrights, and trademarks; fiscal controls such as taxes, subsidies, and/or rationing and allocations; economic regulations, including price controls and wage controls; and political factors, including restrictions on buying foreign goods, the role of the government enterprises, and the power of the government to impose and enforce controls.

Any of these factors can cause the potential demand to be reduced to a lower level—in other words, to effective demand. Therefore, marketing research needs to uncover the extent to which regulatory factors are present and to determine what actions a firm might take to avoid some of the impact on demand.

Market Demand The extent to which effective demand can be realized depends substantially on the marketing infrastructure available to competing firms in a country. The degree to which a country's transportation system has been developed is important, as is its efficiency in terms of cost to users. Additional services that marketers use regularly are storage facilities, banking facilities (particularly for consumer credit), available wholesale and retail structure, and advertising infrastructure. The absence of a fully developed marketing infrastructure will cause market demand to be substantially lower than effective demand. Marketing research will determine the effectiveness of the present marketing system and reveal the presence of any inhibiting factors.

Sales Potential The actual sales volume that a company will realize in any country is essentially determined by its competitive offering vis-à-vis other firms who also compete for a share of the same market. The resulting market share is determined by the number of competitors and the relative effectiveness of the company's marketing mix. In determining sales potential, the researcher must assess whether the company can meet the competition in terms of product quality and features, price, distribution, and promotion. This assessment should yield an estimate of the company's market share and, consequently, its sales potential.

Analysis by Inference

As we have noted, data available from secondary sources are frequently of an aggregate nature and fail to satisfy the specific information needs of a firm. A company must often assess market size on the basis of very limited data on foreign markets. In such cases, market assessment by inference is a possibility. This technique uses available facts about related products or other foreign markets as a basis for inferring the necessary information for the market under analysis. Market assessment by inference is a low-cost activity that should take place before a company engages in the collection of any primary data, which can be quite costly. Inferences can be made on the basis of related products, relative market size, and analysis of demand patterns.

Related Products Few products are consumed or used "in a vacuum"—that is, without any ties to prior purchases or to products in use. If actual consumption statistics are not available for a product category, proxy variables can prove useful. A **proxy variable** is a related product that indicates demand for the product under study. Relationships exist, for example, between replacement tires and automobiles on the road and between electricity consumption and the use of appliances. In some situations, it may be possible to obtain data on related products and their uses as a basis for inferring usage of the product to be marketed. From experience in other, similar markets, the analyst is able to apply usage ratios that can provide for low-cost estimates. For example, the analyst can determine the number of replacement tires needed per automobile on the road.

Relative Market Size Quite frequently, if data on market size are available for other countries, this information can be used to derive estimates for the particular country under investigation. For example, say that market size is known for the United States and that estimates are required for Canada, a country with a reasonably comparable economic system and consumption patterns. Statistics for the United States can be scaled down, by the relative size of GNP, population, or other factors, to about one-tenth of U.S. figures. Similar relationships exist in Europe, where the known market size of one country can provide a basis for inferences about a related country. Of course, the results are not exact, but they provide a basis for further analysis.

Electricity consumption can be used as an indicator of demand for electrical appliances in developing countries.

Analysis of Demand Patterns By analyzing industrial growth patterns for various countries, researchers can gain insights into the relationship of consumption patterns to industrial growth. Relationships can be plotted between GDP per capita and the percentage of total manufacturing production accounted for by major industries. During earlier growth stages with corresponding low per-capita incomes, manufacturing tends to center on necessities such as food, beverages, textiles, and light manufacturing. With growing incomes, the role of these industries tends to decline, and heavy industry assumes greater importance. By analyzing such manufacturing patterns, it is possible to make forecasts for various product groups for countries at lower income levels, because they often repeat the growth patterns of more developed economies.

Similar trends can be observed for a country's import composition. With increasing industrialization, countries develop similar patterns modified only by each country's natural resources. Energy-poor countries must import increasing quantities of energy as industrialization proceeds, whereas energy-rich countries can embark on an industrialization path without significant energy imports. Industrialized countries import relatively more food products and industrial materials than manufactured goods, which are more important for the less industrialized countries. Understanding these relationships can help the analyst determine future trends for a country's economy and may help determine future market potential and sales prospects.

▶ *Studying the Competition*

Results in the marketplace do not depend solely on researching buyer characteristics and meeting buyer needs. To a considerable extent, success in the marketplace is influenced by a firm's understanding of and response to its competition. Keeping track of a firm's competitors is an important international research function. Kodak learned through competitive intelligence that Fuji was planning a new camera for the U.S. market. Kodak launched a competing model just one day before Fuji. Motorola discovered, through one of its intelligence staff who was fluent in Japanese, that the Japanese electronics firms planned to build new semiconductor plants in Europe. Motorola changed its strategy to build market share in Europe before the new capacity was built. This type of intelligence can be critical to a firm.[27]

Companies competing on an international level have to be particularly careful to monitor all major competitors. Because some of the competing firms are likely to be located abroad, this creates additional difficulties in keeping abreast of the latest developments. Many companies fail to spot competitors until it is too late. When Honda first entered the U.S. motorcycle industry in 1959, the British and U.S. motorcycle firms that dominated the industry paid little attention. Honda's entry with a 50-cc bike posed little threat to the macho bikes of Harley Davidson and Triumph. But 30 years later, 80 percent of the bikes are Japanese, and they compete from 50 cc to 1,400 cc. Similarly, while the Swiss were making increasingly more complex mechanized watches, Casio launched basic digital watches that sold at half the price of cheap mechanical watches. Only with the launch of the fashionable electronic Swatch watch were the Swiss able to regain some of their lost market.

First, a company must determine who its competitors are. The domestic market will certainly provide some input here. However, it is important to include any foreign company that either presently is a competitor or may become one in the future. The monitoring should not be restricted to activity in the competitors' domestic market but, rather, should include competitors' moves anywhere in the world. Many foreign firms first innovate in their home markets, expanding abroad only when the initial debugging of the product has been completed. Therefore, a U.S. firm would lose valuable time if it began monitoring a Japanese competitor's activities only upon that competitor's entry into the U.S. market. Any monitoring system needs to be structured in such a way as to ensure that competitors' actions will be spotted wherever they occur first. Komatsu, Caterpillar's major competitor worldwide in the earth-moving industry, subscribed to the *Journal Star*, the major daily newspaper in Caterpillar's hometown, Peoria, Illinois. Also important are the actions taken by competitors in their foreign subsidiaries. These actions may signal future moves elsewhere in a company's global network of subsidiaries.

Table 7.3 lists the types of information a company may wish to collect on its competitors. Aside from general business statistics, a competitor's profitability may shed some light on its capacity to pursue new business in the future. Learning about others' marketing operations may enable a company to assess, among other things, the market share to be gained in any given market. Whenever major actions are planned, it is extremely helpful to anticipate the reactions of competitive firms and include them in the company's contingency planning. Of course, monitoring a competitor's new products or expansion programs may give early hints of future competitive threats.

Analysis that focuses solely on studying the products of key competitors can often miss the real strength of the competitor. To understand an industry and where it is headed over the next 5 years, it is important to study the core competencies in the industry. For example, Chaparral Steel, a profitable U.S. steel maker, sends its managers and engineers to visit competitors, customers, and suppliers' factories to identify the trends and skills that will lead steel

Table 7.3 *Monitoring Competition: Facts to Be Collected*

Overall Company Statistics
Sales and market share profits
Balance sheet
Capital expenditures
Number of employees
Production capacity
Research and development capability

Marketing Operations
Types of products (quality, performance, features)
Service and/or warranty granted
Prices and pricing strategy
Advertising strategy and budgets
Size and type of sales force
Distribution system (includes entry strategy)
Delivery schedules (also spare parts)
Sales territory (geographic)

Future Intentions
New product developments
Current test markets
Scheduled plant capacity expansions
Planned capital expenditures
Planned entry into new markets/countries

Competitive Behavior
Pricing behavior
Reaction to competitive moves, past and expected

making in the future. Chaparral also visits university research departments to spot new competencies that may offer an opportunity or pose a threat.[28]

There are numerous ways to monitor competitors' activities. Thorough study of trade or industry journals is a starting point. Also, frequent visits can be made to major trade fairs where competitors exhibit their products. At one such fair in Texas, Caterpillar engineers were seen measuring Komatsu equipment.[29] Other important information can be gathered from foreign subsidiaries located in the home markets of major competitors. The Italian office equipment manufacturer Olivetti assigned a major intelligence function to its U.S. subsidiary because of that unit's direct access to competitive products in the U.S. marketplace. A different approach was adopted by the Japanese pharmaceutical company Esei, which opened a liaison office in Switzerland, home base to several of the world's leading pharmaceutical companies.

Some secondary sources are available that describe the competitive nature of a marketplace. The *Findex Directory* publishes a listing of the most readily available research reports. These reports tend to concentrate on North America and Europe, but some reports can be obtained on Japan, the Middle East, and South America. Such research reports usually cost between $500 and $5,000, with the average fee being about $1,200. In some cases, there may be no research report covering a specific country or product category, or it may be too expensive.

Check out our *International Trade Fairs* link on our website.

▲ Two Burmese monks walk past a billboard advertising Apple Macintosh computers in Myanmar. The appeal of a low price is appropriate in this Asian country where only about one person in a thousand owns a personal computer.

► Global marketing or culture shock? A veiled woman sits by an advertisement for a U.S. film in Morocco. For Hollywood, overseas sales are critical to the success of a film. But many countries, including France, consider Hollywood films a threat to their national culture.

◄ Beneath a billboard advertising American cosmetics, retired Russian army officers join a march in Moscow marking the anniversary of the Bolshevik Revolution. When Russia opened to the West in the early 1990s, foreign products became the rage. Today, global marketers face more ambivalent attitudes in this market. Some report a backlash against Western brands, with Russian consumers supporting a call to "Buy Russian." Others find that their products are just too expensive for the Russian market. But many global firms such as General Motors believe the potential payoff of a large Russian market is worth the difficulties of operating in Russia today.

▲ From Coca-Cola in Poland to Pepsi in Cambodia, these two global firms compete around the globe. Their vast distribution networks bring soft drinks to virtually every market of the world—whether urban or rural. In Africa, Coke volunteered its distribution system to carry AIDS information to villages across the continent. But in Latin America, Pepsi and Coke have become embroiled in distribution wars. Coke bought the majority share in Pepsi's Venezuelan bottler, causing Pepsi to lose its distribution in that country virtually overnight. In Mexico, Pepsi initiated a successful antitrust suit against Coke. The complaint: Coke used its dominant market position to forbid small retailers from carrying Pepsi.

▲ An Egyptian girl drinks a bottle of Coca-Cola in downtown Cairo, Egypt. Shortly before, the country's top religious authority concluded that the Coke logo represented no threat to Islam. A Muslim Internet site started the rumor that the Coke logo, if read upside down and reflected in the mirror, was insulting to Islam because it read "No Mohammed, no Mecca" in Arabic script. Mohammed is the prophet of Islam, and Mecca is its holiest city.

Problems in the Middle East are nothing new for Coke. After the firm entered the Israeli market, it was banned for decades from entering Arab markets as a result of the Arab Boycott. Today, the Arab Boycott is far less enforced than it used to be by governments in the region. But a new challenge has emerged in its place—grass-roots consumer boycotts of Western brands.

▲ Mickey Mouse is popular in China—maybe too popular. Disney is one of the many companies that contend with counterfeit products in the Chinese market. Counterfeit products have become a major challenge for global marketers in many countries. In Bulgaria, Microsoft responded to pirated software by slashing prices. In Malaysia, the firm set up a toll-free number and offered substantial rewards for evidence against companies using pirated software. But Microsoft lost the first piracy case that it brought in the Chinese courts, causing many to worry that eradicating counterfeits in China will be more difficult than first supposed.

▲ Adapting to cultural preferences often pays off for global marketers. A McDonald's employee in Hong Kong points to a picture of the fast-food chain's new rice meals. News that the U.S. fast-food giant had begun to sell local-style dishes worried many local restaurant owners. And it's no wonder. When McDonald's began to sell rice meals in Japan, sales jumped 30 percent in one year.

▲ A man cooks fresh tortillas at an outside restaurant in Mexico. Despite the encroachment of multinational giants such as McDonald's, local competition still thrives in many markets. One Filipino entrepreneur dismissed the idea of becoming a McDonald's franchisee and instead opened his own chain of fast-food restaurants. Today, the Jollibee chain is one of Asia's most esteemed firms with restaurants as far away as Kuwait and California.

◀ In many developing countries, consumers still shop at traditional markets such as this one in Rajasthan, India. But traditional retailers increasingly face global competition from firms such as Wal-Mart.

▶ A customer walks past a poster advertising money exchange at a bank in Seoul, South Korea. When the Korean won surged in value against the U.S. dollar, American products became less expensive and more appealing to Korean consumers. But Korean products became more expensive in the U.S. marketplace. Not surprisingly, currency fluctuations are a major concern to global marketers.

▲ A Dairy Queen in Bahrain offers a half price Deluxe Double Cheeseburger as a special Ramadan promotion. During the month of Ramadan, observant Muslims abstain from eating or drinking between sunrise and sunset as part of a spiritual fast. Consequently, restaurants in Bahrain are closed dawn to dusk. Increasingly, global food companies that market in Muslim countries—the largest of which are in Asia, not the Middle East—are adapting to Islamic prescriptions on food consumption. For example, the consumption of pork products or alcohol is forbidden. Every product sold by Nestlé Malaysia is certified halal, or acceptable under Islamic teaching. McDonald's and KFC have also obtained halal certificates to serve the Muslim market.

▶ *Environmental Review*

Frequently it becomes necessary to study the international environment beyond the customary monitoring function that most international executives perform. Of particular interest are the economic, physical, sociocultural, and political environments. Studies focusing on a country are frequently undertaken when a major decision regarding that country has to be made. This could include a move to enter the country or an effort to increase significantly the firm's presence in that market through large new investments.

In any assessment of the economic environment, the primary focus is on the **economic activity** in target countries. Major economic indicators are GNP growth, interest levels, industrial output, employment levels, and the monetary policy of the country under investigation.

Because the **physical environment** tends to be the most stable aspect of the foreign marketing environment, such studies are frequently made for major market entry decisions or when the introduction of a new product requires a special analysis of that particular aspect of the environment. Included within the physical environment are population and related statistics on growth, age composition, birthrates, and life expectancy, as well as data on the physical infrastructure, climate, and geography of a country.

Of particular interest is the **sociocultural environment,** which we discussed in some detail in Chapter 3. The salient factors include social classes, family life, role expectations of the sexes, religion, education, language, customs, and traditions. The primary interest of these variables to the international company is their potential effect on the sale of its products. Because the sociocultural environment is also unlikely to change over the short run and because changes that do occur tend to be of a more gradual nature, such studies are most likely to be ordered when a major marketing decision in the local market is contemplated. As a company gains experience in any given country, its staff and local organization accumulate considerable data on the social and cultural situation, and this store of information can be tapped whenever needed. Therefore, a full study of these environmental variables is most useful when the company does not already have a base in that country and its relevant experience is limited.

Frequently, management investigates the **regulatory environment** of a given country because those influences can substantially affect marketing operations anywhere. Today, regulatory influences can originate with both national and supranational organizations. National bodies tend to influence the marketing scene within the borders of one country only, whereas supranational agencies have a reach beyond any individual country. National regulations may include particular rulings affecting all businesses, such as product liability laws, or may be targeted at individual industries. In the United States, industry-specific regulations include those established by such regulatory agencies such as the U.S. Food and Drug Administration (FDA) and the U.S. Department of Commerce. Examples of supranational regulations are those issued by the European Union with respect to business within the member nations and the nonbinding code of conduct for international companies drawn up by the United Nations' Center for Transnational Corporations.

Regulatory trends can be of great importance to international companies. Consequently, a company must monitor the regulatory environment. For example, it is generally accepted by most observers that U.S. safety and emissions control regulations for passenger automobiles are the world's most stringent. Recognizing this fact, the French company Peugeot has maintained a small beachhead in the U.S. market, in spite of an insignificant sales volume, primarily to gain the experience of engineering cars under these stringent conditions. The company believes that it will be able to apply this experience elsewhere, as other countries adopt similar regulations. In addition, firms may find it useful to keep informed about the latest regulations governing their industry in other countries, even if they do not conduct any business there. Policies in one country often spread to others. This is particularly true within regional blocs. And on an even larger scale, the trade and investment policies of a country have been shown to be influenced by the country's trading partners and competitors.[30]

▶ *Developing a Global Information System*

Companies that already have become global marketers, as well as those that plan to do so, must look at the world marketplace to identify global opportunities. The forces that affect an industry must also be analyzed to determine the firm's competitiveness. To evaluate the full range of opportunities requires a global perspective for market research. Researchers must provide more than data on strictly local factors within each country. All firms that market their products in overseas markets require information that makes it possible to perform analysis across several countries or markets. However, leaving each local subsidiary or market to develop its own database will not result in an integrated marketing information system (MIS). Instead, authority to develop a centrally managed MIS must be assigned to a central location, and market reports need to be sent directly to the firm's chief international marketing officer.

Coca-Cola has joined forces with its bottling partners around the world to share information and best practices. In a planned 7-year roll-out, Coca-Cola plans to boost revenue by sharing sales information and communicating more effectively with partners. The new system will upgrade and expand data warehouses, decision support systems, and a worldwide Intranet to improve communications.[31]

A principal requirement for a worldwide MIS is a standardized set of data collected from each market or country. The actual data collection can be left to a firm's local units, but they must proceed according to central and uniform specifications. By assessing client needs on a worldwide basis, the company ensures that products and services are designed with all buyers in mind. This avoids the traditional pattern of initially designing products for the company's home market and looking at export or foreign opportunities only once a product has been designed.

Outsourcing Research

The global firm can either attempt to collect and analyze all data itself or outsource some of its marketing research by utilizing marketing research companies. Today all major national markets have local marketing research firms that can assist the international marketer. The early marketing research industry in China was strongly supported by Procter & Gamble—in fact, some believe that it wouldn't have survived without P&G.[32]

Furthermore, the demand for quality multicountry research has spurred the marketing research industry to expand beyond traditional national boundaries and become increasingly global. Many larger firms have been acquiring smaller firms to expand their global abilities. For example, in 1990 ACNielsen offered services in only 25 countries. Five years later it had expanded to 100.[33] More recently, Nielsen introduced its first pan-European research service, called Quartz, which provides simulated market tests based on consumer reactions in five European countries. Twenty-five multinationals, including Nestlé, Procter & Gamble, and BSN, quickly signed up for the service.[34] Table 7.4 lists the top research companies in the U.S. market, along with the importance of their non-U.S. business.

Table 7.4 *Global Reach of Top U.S. Research Organizations*

RANK 2001	ORGANIZATION	WEBSITE	U.S. RESEARCH REVENUES ($, IN MILLIONS)	WORLDWIDE RESEARCH REVENUES ($ MILLIONS)	PERCENT NON-U.S. REVENUES
1	VNU Inc.	www.vnu.com	1,300.0	2,400.0	45.8
2	IMS Health Inc.	imshealth.com	469.0	1,171.0	60.0
3	Information Resources Inc.	www.infores.com	420.3	555.9	24.4
4	The Kantar Group	www.kantargroup.com	299.1	962.3	68.9
5	Westat Inc.	www.westat.com	285.8	285.8	–
6	Arbitron Inc.	arbitron.com	219.6	227.5	3.5
7	NOP World US	www.nopworld.com	206.6	224.1	7.8
8	NFO WorldGroup	www.nfow.com	163.0	452.9	64.0
9	Market Facts Inc.	marketfacts.com	156.2	189.7	17.7
10	Taylor Nelson Sofres USA	www.tnsofres.com	150.5	166.9	9.8
11	Maritz Research	www.maritzresearch.com	127.1	181.7	30.0
12	Ipsos	www.ipsos.com	112.9	204.3	44.7
13	J.D. Power Associates	jdpa.com	109.3	128.0	14.6
14	Opinion Research Corp.	www.opinionresearch.com	91.4	133.6	31.6
15	The NPD Group	npd.com	88.7	101.7	12.8
16	Jupiter Media Metrix Inc.	jmm.com	68.6	85.8	20.0
17	Harris Interactive Inc.	www.harrisinteractive.com	64.9	75.4	13.9
18	Abt Associates Inc.	abtassociates.com	53.4	62.8	15.0
19	C&R Research Services Inc.	www.crresearch.com	43.6	43.6	–
20	Wirthlin Worldwide	www.wirthlin.com	39.6	46.8	15.4
21	Lieberman Research Worldwide	lrwonline.com	38.8	43.1	10.0
22	Burke Inc.	www.burke.com	34.3	45.5	24.6
23	MORPACE International Inc.	www.morpace.com	32.4	48.3	32.9
24	Market Strategies Inc.	marketstrategies.com	30.2	31.7	4.7
25	GfK Custom Research Inc.	www.customresearch.com	28.9	29.8	3.0
26	ICR / Int'l Communications Research	icrsurvey.com	28.5	28.8	1.0
27	M/A/R/C Research	www.marcresearch.com	24.0	24.5	2.0
28	Elrick & Lavidge Marketing Research	elrickandlavidge.com	22.9	22.9	–
29	RDA Group Inc.	rdagroup.com	22.4	26.0	13.8
30	Lieberman Research Group	liebermanresearch.com	21.8	22.3	2.2

Source: Marketing News, June 10, 2002: H4.

► *Conclusions*

It's time to consider the sources for your own research. What are their strengths and weaknesses? What are some possible sources and costs for some customized primary research? Continue with *Country Market Report* on our website.

In this chapter, we discussed some major challenges and difficulties that companies encounter in securing data necessary for international marketing. Major difficulties include the lack of basic data on many markets and the likelihood that research methods will have to be adapted to local environments. A final goal of global marketing research is to provide managers with a uniform database covering all the firm's present and potential markets. This will allow for cross-country comparisons and analysis, as well as the incorporation of worldwide consumer needs into the initial product design process. Given the difficulties in data collection, achieving this international comparability of data is indeed a challenge for even the most experienced professionals.

Still, the world has changed greatly in the past 25 years. At that time, market information around the world was sparse and unreliable, especially in developing and undeveloped countries. Now, through the efforts of governments, transnational organizations, and global marketing research companies, information is available for virtually every market in the world, from Canada and Mexico to Uzbekistan and Mongolia. As a revolutionary communications tool, the Internet is also pushing research horizons. Today global marketers can use more widely available information to make better market decisions and devise more effective marketing strategies.

Review Questions

1. List problems related to the collection and use of secondary data internationally.

2. Explain the processes of back translation and parallel translation.

3. List problems related to the design and implementation of primary data collection internationally.

4. Compare and contrast demand analysis and analysis by inference.

5. List ways in which Kodak might monitor Fuji Film. Why is such surveillance important?

6. When and why does a firm usually undertake an environmental review? What are the four key components of such a review?

7. List the requirements for a global marketing information system.

Questions for Discussion

1. Why is it so difficult to do marketing research in multicountry settings?

2. What are the challenges of using a marketing research questionnaire that is developed in the United States but will be used in Japan and Mexico as well?

3. If you were estimating the demand for vacuum cleaners, what type of inference analysis would you use? Give a specific example.

4. Note various ways in which the Internet could assist international marketing researchers.

For Further Reading

Craig, C. Samuel, and Susan P. Douglas. *International Marketing Research: Concepts and Methods*. New York: Wiley, 1999.

Helgeson, Neil. "Research Isn't Linear When Done Globally." *Marketing News*, July 19, 1999: 13.

Lee, Barton, Soumya Saklini, and David Tatterson. "Research: Growing in Guangzhou." *Marketing News*, June 10, 2002: 12–13.

Mundorf, Norbert, Rudy Roy Dholakia, Nikhilesh Dholakia, and Stuart Westin. "German and American Consumer Orientations to Information Technologies: Implications for Marketing and Public Policy." *Journal of International Consumer Marketing* 8, 3 (1996): 125–143.

Murphy, H. Lee. "Japanese Keeping Fewer Secrets from U.S. Firms." *Marketing News*, June 21, 1999: 4–6.

Case 7.1	*Surveying the Turkish Clothing Industry*

Gretchen Renner had escaped to the serenity of a small tea garden overlooking the Bosporus Sea, which separates the European and Asian sides of Istanbul. As she sipped a glass of strong tea, she fought the urge to abandon her thesis research project and return to the United States.

Before arriving in Istanbul, Gretchen had been excited about the project. She had designed a survey to measure Turkish clothing firm owners' use and satisfaction with the services offered by the Textile Association of Istanbul (TAI). This association offers marketing, export-counseling, and educational services designed to encourage producers to pursue export opportunities.

Two months before Gretchen had come to Turkey, a Turkish friend had told her that she must apply for a research visa from the Turkish government. Foreigners planning to conduct research projects in Turkey must possess a government-approved research visa to display to government officials and potential research participants. Foreigners conducting research projects without a research visa in Turkey risk arrest and deportation. Gretchen was surprised that the research visa application had to be completed prior to her arrival in Turkey. She waited four months to receive the visa, inconveniently postponing her trip.

Once in Turkey, Gretchen sought a list of Turkish clothing firm owners from which she could draw a representative sample for her survey. Although TAI was supportive of Gretchen's project, it hesitated to share its membership list. Gretchen spent months developing relationships with key officials at TAI, conducting interviews, and collecting information. TAI officials readily shared information about the organization's history, structure, and services. Yet each time she asked about the list, she was denied access. Some of Gretchen's contacts claimed that releasing such information compromised the firms' privacy. Others maintained that no precedent existed for releasing the list to a non-TAI employee. Additionally, several of her close contacts explained to her that she could not have the list because she was not Turkish. Finally, with no explanation, TAI supplied the list of names.

Problems then emerged during survey pretesting. The questionnaire was administered via the telephone by interviewers employed by *İtimat*, a well-known Istanbul market research firm. During this pretesting, Gretchen and her interviewers discovered that it was difficult to circumvent gatekeepers, such as secretaries and receptionists, to interview Turkish clothing firm owners.

Hoping to increase response rates, Gretchen sent potential respondents a presurvey fax introducing herself, explaining the survey's objectives, and noting the involvement of *İtimat*. But respondents voiced concerns about the fax. Most complained that no high-level *İtimat* executive had signed the fax; it had been signed only by Gretchen and an *İtimat* interview supervisor. Others were suspicious of Gretchen's authenticity. They remembered Turkish media reports that several Europeans recently had posed as academic researchers to expose child labor practices in Turkish clothing factories. Because of Gretchen's German name and the unfamiliar name of her university, many suspected that Gretchen was actually an industrial spy.

Even when Gretchen or the interviewers gained access to firm owners, few agreed to participate in the survey. One scoffed, "If you really valued my opinion, you would make an appointment and discuss this with me in person. I am a very busy person. I don't have time to talk on the phone about such things."

Face-to-face interviews, however, would be more time-consuming than telephone interviews. First, it would take time to get past the gatekeepers to make appointments with potential respondents. Second, because the firms were widely dispersed and Istanbul is a very large and traffic-congested city, Gretchen and her team of four *İtimat* interviewers could complete only 10 surveys a day. Gretchen needed to complete 300 surveys. Gretchen's research funding was dwindling, and she had to return home in 6 weeks.

Looking toward the Asian side of Istanbul, Gretchen wondered how she could successfully complete her research project in the remaining time.

Discussion Questions

1. What cultural factors might contribute to the obstacles Gretchen encountered while attempting to execute the survey? How might Hofstede's dimensions of culture explain Gretchen's difficulties?

2. Why do you think Gretchen finally received the list of Turkish clothing exporters from TAI? If TAI had not supplied the list, where else could Gretchen have looked to find a suitable list?

3. How should Gretchen proceed with the survey? Do you think the benefits of the face-to-face option outweigh the costs? Or could changes be made to the telephone survey to increase response rates? Are there other research options that Gretchen should consider instead?

Source: Prepared by Liesl Riddle. Used by permission.

Case 7.2   *Selector's European Dilemma*

Ken Barbarino, CEO of Selector Inc., was ecstatic. The president of Big Burger, one of Selector's largest clients, had arranged for Ken to meet with the vice-president of Big Burger's European operations. "Selector is going global," Ken smiled to himself.

Selector was a market research firm that provided market analyses to restaurant and retail chains. Selector's products helped clients select optimal geographic locations for successful chain expansion.

Although Big Burger was an international restaurant chain, currently Big Burger utilized Selector's services only for its U.S. operations. Specifically, Selector provided Big Burger's real estate team with trade-area profiles for prospective Big Burger locations. Because Big Burger was a quick-service hamburger restaurant, most of its customers were drawn from the homes and businesses within a 2-mile radius around each location. Selector's trade-area profiles provided Big Burger with an overview of the individuals, households, and businesses within a potential location's trade area.

By purchasing and amalgamating databases from a large number of data vendors, Selector had amassed a broad warehouse of U.S. demographic, business, and consumer behavior data, and the reports were extremely detailed. For example, Selector's trade-area profile described proximal households according to their composition, annual income, type of residence, and commute time to work. It also reported the number of area households that dined at a quick-serve hamburger restaurant last year as well as the total dollars these households spent at quick-serve hamburger restaurants during that year. Selector's trade-area profiles also included a count of the total number of businesses and employees in the 2-mile radius, as well as the percent of businesses and employees within each 2-digit standard industry code (SIC) and a list of all quick-serve hamburger restaurants within a 5-mile radius and their gross unit sales. These trade-area profiles enabled Big Burger's real estate team to determine whether there was enough demand in the trade area to support a successful Big Burger location.

Ken waltzed into the office of Selector's research director, Katrina Walsh. "Guess what? Big Burger is sending us overseas!" he exclaimed. Ken told Katrina that the president of Big Burger had asked Selector to provide trade-area profiles for their prospective European locations. The president had arranged for Ken to meet with Big Burger's vice president of European operations in 2 weeks to demonstrate the trade-area profiles that could be used to assess potential European Big Burger locations. Big Burger had provided Ken with the addresses of seven potential sites (two in London, one in Madrid, and four in Berlin) so that Selector could create examples of their trade-area profiles for these sites. Katrina was excited about the international project and assured Ken she would acquire the European data that was needed to generate the trade-area profiles.

Katrina contacted Selector's data vendors—the companies that sold the various databases that Selector had compiled in its broad data warehouse—and inquired about purchasing European demographic, business, and consumer behavior data. She quickly learned that acquiring the data at a small, precise level of geography would be a greater challenge than she had anticipated.

In the United States, the U.S. Census Bureau aggregates the data it collects into a set of standard hierarchical geographic units (see Table 1). To protect individual privacy, data are released at the Zip+4 level and higher. The standardization of the Census Bureau's geographic order and the degree of detail within the Zip+4 level enable companies like Selector to extract precise data for a geographic area, such as a 2-mile radius around a particular location, because the Census Bureau units are typically small enough to fit within that area.

However, as Katrina learned from her data vendors, European countries were geographically organized in a different way. All members of the European Union were organized according to the Nomenclature of Territorial Units for Statistics (NUTS) devised by the Statistical Office of the European Communities (Eurostat) in 1988. There were several design challenges associated with the NUTS program because the countries possessed divergent geographic organizational systems and were reluctant to abandon their existing geographic hierarchies. Five NUTS levels were created. The geographic data of most EU countries are divided into NUTS Levels 1–3. Some countries further divide their geographic data into NUTS Levels 4 and 5.

Ideally, Eurostat would have liked to standardize units by either territorial size or population size. It proved difficult to do either. For example, the largest geographic unit, NUTS Level 1, includes British government office regions, German *länder*, and Finish *ahvenanmaa*. But the southeast government office region of England possesses over 17 million inhabitants, whereas the Finish *ahvenanmaa*, Åhland, includes only 25,000 people. These disparities also exist at lower levels of geography. Greater London, Berlin, and the Spanish provinces of Madrid and Barcelona—all NUTS Level 3 geographies—comprise populations exceeding 3 million people, whereas several NUTS Level 3 regions in Germany, Belgium, Austria, Finland, and Greece include fewer than 50,000 people. The NUTS levels also differed greatly in territorial size. For example, some Level 5 geographies could be as small as 50 square meters, and others could comprise an entire town.

Katrina also discovered that it would be challenging to acquire data for a 2-mile radius around a specific address in Europe. NUTS data—even those at Levels 4 and 5—were for areas much larger than the 2-mile radius that Big Burger was interested in. Even a simple analysis of the NUTS level that a prospective site resided in would not be comparable across national boundaries within the European Union. Furthermore, although she could identify data vendors that could provide demographic and "firmographic" data, such as the total population, the number of households, household composition, marital status, the sex and age distribution of the population, and the number of businesses and employees, she could not locate a data vendor that offered the more important consumer behavior data. Estimating quick-serve hamburger dollar demand would be extremely difficult—if not impossible—without a measure of the total dollars spent on quick-serve hamburger restaurants and the number of households dining at quick-serve hamburger restaurants last year. It was also

Table 1 *U.S. Statistical Territorial Units: Lowest Five Geographies Available from the U.S. Census*

STATISTICAL UNIT	TOTAL NUMBER	APPROXIMATE NUMBER OF HOUSEHOLDS
Metropolitan standard unit	316	30,245
Zip code	41,940	3,167
Census tract	62,276	1,551
Block group	229,466	420
Zip+4	28,000,000	10

unclear whether Katrina would be able to acquire a reliable database of quick-serve restaurant competitors and their unit sales, because most of the existing European restaurant databases were old and out-of-date.

With 10 days left to go before Ken's meeting with Big Burger, Katrina wondered how she would generate trade-area profiles for Big Burger's seven European prospective locations.

Discussion Questions

1. What assumptions have Ken and Katrina made in their response to Big Burger's request for European trade-area data?
2. How—if at all—can Katrina utilize the available European data?
3. What should be included on the trade-area profiles for Big Burger's seven European locations?

Source: Prepared by Liesl Riddle. Used with permission.

Notes

[1]Carlta Vitzthum, "Just-in-Time Fashion," *Wall Street Journal*, May 23, 2001, p. B1.

[2]David A. Ricks, *Blunders in International Business*, 3rd ed. (New York: Blackwell, 1999), pp.130–136.

[3]"How to Listen to Consumers," *Fortune*, January 11, 1993: 77.

[4]Juliana Koranteng, "Tracking What's Trendy, Hot Before It's Old News," *Advertising Age International*, May 1996: 130.

[5]Tom Lester, "Common Markets," *Marketing*, November 9, 1989: 41.

[6]Donald B. Pittenger, "Gathering Foreign Demographics Is No Easy Task," *Marketing News*, January 8, 1991: 23.

[7]Pierre Berthon, Leyland Pitt, Constantine S. Katsikeas, and Jean Paul Berthon, "Virtual Services Go International," *Journal of International Marketing* 7, 3 (1999): 98.

[8]C. Samuel Craig and Susan P. Douglas, *International Marketing Research: Concepts and Methods* (New York: Wiley, 1999), pp.16–19

[9]"Russia's Unemployment Rate Rises Year-on-Year," *Interfax News Agency*, June 21, 1999, p. 1.

[10]Brian Palmer, "What the Chinese Want," *Fortune*, October 11, 1999.

[11]"Sharp as a Razor in Central Asia," *The Economist*, June 5, 1993: 36.

[12]Kevin Reagan, "In Asia, Think Globally, Communicate Locally," *Marketing News*, July 19, 1999: 12–14.

[13]J. Brad McBride and Kate Gillespie, "Consumer Innovativeness Among Street Vendors in Mexico City," *Latin American Business Review* 1, 3 (2000): 71–94.

[14]Dana James, "Back to Vietnam," *Marketing News*, May 13, 2002: 1, 13–14.

[15]Emanual H. Demby, "ESOMAR Urges Changes in Reporting Demographics, Issues Worldwide Report," *Marketing News*, January 8, 1990: 24.

[16]David Jamieson, "Online Research Gets Fewer Euro Cheers," *Marketing News*, January 21, 2002: 15.

[17]James Heckman, "Marketers Waiting, Will See on EU Privacy," *Marketing News*, June 7, 1999: 4.

[18]Robin Cobb, "Marketing Shares," *Marketing*, February 22, 1990: 44.

[19]H. Lee Murphy, "Japanese Keeping Fewer Secrets from U.S. Firms," *Marketing News*, June 21, 1999: 4.

[20]Johny K. Johansson and Ikujiro Nonaka, "Market Research the Japanese Way," *Harvard Business Review*, May–June 1987: 16–22.

[21]J. Brad McBride and Kate Gillespie, "Consumer Innovativeness Among Street Vendors in Mexico City."

[22]Catherine Bond, "Market Research—Spy in a Corner," *Marketing*, August 17, 1989: 35.

[23]Dana James, "Back to Vietnam," *Marketing News*, May 13, 2002.

[24]Elizabeth Robles, "In Cuba, the Usual MR Methods Don't Work," *Marketing News*, June 10, 2002: 12.

[25]Jennifer Mitchell, "Reaching Across Borders," *Marketing News*, May 10, 1999: 19.

[26]Richard D. Robinson, *Internationalization of Business*, 2nd ed. (Chicago: Dryden Press, 1984), p. 36.

[27]"High Price of Industrial Espionage," Times of London, June 5, 1999, p. 31.

[28]C. K. Prahalad and Gary Hamel, "The Core Competence of the Corporation," *Harvard Business Review*, May–June 1990: 79–91.

[29]Ibid.

[30]Balaji R. Koka, John E. Prescott, and Ravindranath Madhavan, "Contagion Influence on Trade and Investment Policy: A Network Perspective," *Journal of International Business Studies*, 30, 1 (1999): 127–148.

[31]Bob Violino, "Extended Enterprise: Coca-Cola Is Linking Its IT System with Those of Worldwide Bottling Partners As It Strives to Stay One Step Ahead of the Competition," *Information Week*, March 22, 1999: 46–54.

[32]Barton Lee, Soumya Saklini, and David Tatterson, "Research: Growing in Guangzhou," *Marketing News*, June 10, 2002: 12–13.

[33]"Market Research Data Wars," *The Economist*, July 22, 1995: 60–61.

[34]"ACNielsen and Catalina Develop Powerful New Loyalty Marketing Approach," *P. R. Newswire*, June 4, 1999.

Part 3 *Developing Global Marketing Strategies*

COMPETENCE LEVEL	DECISION AREAS
Environmental Competence	**Understanding the Global Marketing Environment** CH 2 *The Global Economy* CH 3 *Cultural and Social Forces* CH 4 *Political and Regulatory Climate*
Analytic Competence	**Analyzing Global Opportunities** CH 5 *Global Buyer Behavior* CH 6 *Global Competitors* CH 7 *Global Marketing Research*
Strategic Competence	**Developing Global Marketing Strategies** CH 8 *Global Marketing Strategies* CH 9 *Global Market Entry Strategies*
Functional Competence	**Designing Global Marketing Programs** CH 10 *Global Product and Service Strategies* CH 11 *Developing New Products for Global Markets* CH 12 *Pricing for International and Global Markets* CH 13 *Managing Global Distribution Channels* CH 14 *Global Promotion Strategies* CH 15 *Managing Global Advertising*
Managerial Competence	**Managing the Global Marketing Effort** CH 16 *Organizing for Global Marketing*

8 Global Marketing Strategies

Kraft Is the Largest packaged-foods company in North America. In the United States, it has dominated grocery store shelves for years, with such famous brands as Jell-O, Kool-Aid, Life Savers, Oreo cookies, and Philadelphia Cream Cheese. However, Kraft is stuck in a slow-growth industry in the United States. Despite careful cost cutting and imaginative marketing, sales dropped 16 percent between 1994 and 2001. These numbers are all the more worrisome because U.S. sales account for 73 percent of total firm sales. This percentage stands in striking contrast to Heinz, where U.S. sales account for only 56 percent of total sales. Furthermore, Kraft's strongest overseas market is Western Europe, a market that is nearly saturated as well. Kraft now plans to expand into emerging markets. Unfortunately, major global competitors such as Unilever and Nestlé entered these markets much earlier. Also, Kraft's strongest products—convenience foods—don't sell as well in developing countries where consumers have less disposable income. In contrast, Unilever offers such basics as fortified rice in India.[1]

In this chapter, we introduce three key issues that companies face as they develop global marketing strategies. First, companies such as Kraft must consider internationalization. Internationalization patterns range from opportunistic, or

Chapter Outline

unplanned, responses to overseas opportunities to carefully constructed expansion. Firms must determine whether going international is merely an option or a necessity for survival in the global marketplace. Second, firms must select an appropriate course for market expansion. Entering new foreign markets can be expensive and can place heavy demands on management time. Firms must decide which regions and specifically which foreign markets will receive priority. Finally, firms must pursue an appropriate global marketing strategy. Once a firm is internationalized, it must determine what is the best manner in which to manage its various national subsidiaries in light of its customers and its competitors. How much coordination is necessary? How much standardization is desirable? The chapter ends with an introduction to different marketing strategies that international marketers can employ.

Learning Objectives

After studying this chapter, you should be able to:

▶ List and describe the five reasons why firms internationalize.

▶ Differentiate between born-global firms and other companies.

▶ Cite the advantages and disadvantages of targeting developed countries rather than developing ones.

▶ Define "lead markets" and "must-win" markets.

▶ List and describe the filters used for screening national markets.

▶ Identify the four major criteria for choosing overseas markets.

▶ Explain the pros and cons of choosing markets on the basis of market similarity.

▶ Differentiate among multidomestic strategies, regional strategies, and various global strategies.

► *Internationalizing Marketing Operations*

Internationalization is the term we use for a firm's expansion from its domestic market into foreign markets. Whether to internationalize is a strategic decision that will fundamentally affect any firm, including its operations and its management. Today, most large companies operate outside their home markets. Nonetheless, it is still useful for these companies to consider their motivations for continued international expansion. For many smaller companies, the decision to internationalize remains an important and difficult one. There can be several possible motives behind a company's decision to begin to compete in foreign markets. These motives range from the opportunistic to the strategic.

Opportunistic Expansion

Many companies, particularly those in the United States, promote their products in trade journals or on the Internet to their U.S. customers. These media are also read by foreign business executives or distributors, who place orders that are initially unsolicited. Such foreign transactions are usually more complicated and more involved than a routine shipment to a domestic customer. Therefore, the firm must decide whether to respond to these unsolicited orders. Some companies adopt an aggressive policy and begin to pursue these foreign customers actively. Many have built sizable foreign businesses by first responding to orders and then adopting a more proactive approach later. Most large, internationally active companies began their internationalization in this opportunistic manner.

Pursuing Potential Abroad

Some firms maximize their domestic market and then deliberately reach out for more potential abroad. This is particularly true of firms, such as Anheuser-Busch, that began internationalizing more recently. With a 45 percent market share in the United States, Anheuser-Busch dominates its home beer market. A latecomer to international expansion, the company remained domestic until 1982. Now Anheuser-Busch has become active in a number of major international markets, including Japan and China, and is trying to build a global brand for Budweiser. Still, international sales are only about 7 percent of total corporate sales as the firm continues to pursue its potential abroad.[2]

A need to diversify beyond a single country can also motivate a firm to internationalize. This is a less of a factor for U.S.-based companies than for firms in smaller home markets. For example, Saint-Gobain, a large French company founded by King Louis XIV some 330 years ago, has a long-standing tradition in glass and building materials. For years it followed a strategy designed to help the firm break out of its France-only position. Acquiring large companies in the same field in Germany and the United Kingdom, the company was able to expand international sales until French sales were only 25 percent of corporate sales. The acquisition of Norton Company and Carborundum significantly strengthened Saint-Gobain's position in the U.S. market. The company now ranks as the number-one worldwide producer for several business lines, including flat glass, insulation, ductile iron pipes, major industrial ceramics, and abrasives. About two-thirds of its 120,000 employees currently work outside France.[3]

Following its customers abroad, DHL delivers in Afghanistan.

Following Customers Abroad

For a company whose business is concentrated on a few large customers, the decision to internationalize is usually made when one of its key customers moves abroad to pursue international opportunities. Many of the major U.S. automobile component suppliers have established operating plants abroad to supply their customers in foreign locations. PPG Industries, a major supplier of car body paints, originally did little overseas business other than licensing its technology to other foreign paint makers. In the early 1980s, however, the company followed its major customers abroad and began to service them directly in Europe and elsewhere. The company then began to sell to non-U.S. car companies as well and achieved the leading position in supplying paints to car manufacturers worldwide.[4]

The service sector has seen similar expansions triggered by client moves overseas. The establishment of international networks of major U.S. professional accounting and consulting firms, such as Deloitte Touche Tohmatsu, was motivated by a desire to service key domestic clients overseas. Now Deloitte has 28,000 employees and professionals in its U.S. operation and another 54,000 spread over some 130 countries' operations.[5] Similarly, express shipper DHL probably became the first Western firm to re-enter war-torn Afghanistan in 2002. Its rationale: The U.S. military was one of its biggest customers.[6]

Exploiting Different Market Growth Rates

Market growth rates are subject to wide variations among countries. A company based in a low-growth country may suffer a competitive disadvantage and may want to expand into faster-growing countries to take advantage of growth opportunities. The area of the Pacific Rim (which includes Japan, South Korea, Taiwan, China, Hong Kong, Thailand, Singapore, Malaysia, and Indonesia) experienced above-average economic growth rates in the early 1990s. This prompted many international firms to invest heavily in that region. For example, the chemicals industry in Asia experienced above-average growth rates, ranging between 12 percent for China and 7–9 percent for several other Asian Pacific Rim markets. This enormous growth soon made the non-Japanese Asian chemicals market the largest in the world, surpassing those in the United States, Europe, and Japan.[7] Although the region suffered from a substantial economic recession in 1998, many of its economies have rebounded and are rapidly making up the lost ground.

On the other hand, the U.S. market is currently the target market of many Japanese pharmaceutical companies that have been late in moving out of their home market. For years, these firms concentrated solely on Japan, the world's second largest pharmaceutical market. Recent growth in the Japanese market has been relatively flat, partly because of a crackdown on high pharmaceutical prices by the Japanese government's national health insurance company. However, the U.S. market continues to climb and is now nearly four times the size of the Japanese market.[8]

When the market for a firm's product becomes mature, a company can open new opportunities by entering foreign markets where the product may not be very well known. Among U.S. firms following this strategy are many packaged-goods marketers, such as Philip Morris, Coca-Cola, and PepsiCo. They often target markets where the per-capita consumption of their products is still relatively low. With economic expansion and the resulting improvement in personal incomes in these new markets, these companies can experience substantial growth over time—even though operations in the United States show little growth.

For example, one report showed Coca-Cola selling 189 twelve-ounce servings per person annually in the United States, whereas its international average was only 37 servings. This number varied widely: 215 in Iceland, 173 in Mexico, 111 in West Germany, 61 in the United Kingdom, 35 in Japan, and 26 in France. China trailed with 0.3 serving per capita. When consumption in China reaches the levels of other Asian countries, such as Australia, Coca-Cola of China will become as large as the entire Coca-Cola Company is today.[9]

Globalizing for Defensive Reasons

Sometimes companies are not particularly interested in pursuing new growth or potential abroad but decide to enter the international business arena for purely defensive reasons. When a domestic company sees its markets invaded by foreign firms, that company may react by entering the foreign competitor's home market in return. As a result, the company can learn valuable information about the competitor that will help in its operations at home. The company can also slow down a competitor by denying it some of the cash flow from its profitable domestic operation—cash that could otherwise be invested in expansion abroad.

Many U.S. companies opened operations in Japan to be closer to their most important competitors. Major companies such as Xerox and IBM use their local subsidiaries in Japan to learn new ways to compete with the major Japanese firms in their field. Similarly, Kao, the Japanese packaged-goods giant, opened an office in Cincinnati to be close to the headquarters of Procter & Gamble.

Cemex is the largest cement producer in the Western Hemisphere and the third largest worldwide. The Mexican company began its drive to internationalize by expanding across its border into the United States. Cemex then acquired two large cement plants in Spain, taking the company into Europe. Cemex's entry into international markets occurred partly in response to the invasion of its market by Holderbank, a Swiss-based company and the world's largest cement producer. Cemex has since expanded its international operations into about 20 countries and now generates half of its income abroad.[10]

Born Globals

Most large global corporations have followed a similar sequence of internationalization. Typically, these companies develop their domestic markets and then tentatively enter international markets, usually by exporting. As their international sales grow, these companies gradually establish marketing and production operations in many foreign markets. This traditional pattern seems to be followed by most firms. However, some newer firms are jumping into global markets without going through the various stages of development. Such firms are termed **born global**.

Born-global firms recognize from the beginning that their customers and competition are international. This is particularly true of many high-tech start-up companies. Logitech, the maker of computer input devices, is one such company. Logitech's market coverage and its marketing strategy were

---

World Beat 8.1 *Born Global in Israel—or Not?*

Mergers, acquisitions, and other corporate transactions take more time, work, and money in Israel than in the United States. In addition, mergers and spin-offs trigger taxes in Israel, which deters companies from reorganizing activities. The capital-gains tax for private companies is 50 percent, compared with 25 percent in the United States. Increasingly, Israel's stodgy corporate regulations and heavy corporate taxation are proving to be a serious burden on its businesses and are prompting a growing number of Israeli companies to establish themselves as U.S. corporations with Israeli subsidiaries.

Haim Chasman, an American who moved to Israel 8 years ago when the high-tech boom was just starting, founded GlobalCommerceZone Inc. in Jerusalem. A year later he moved back to Chicago to set up its headquarters and focus on corporate development for the company, which handles transactions for international postal shipment on the Internet. Another American,

David Teten, immigrated to Israel and started GoldNames Inc. Thirty immigrants from 20 countries joined the company in its first year. But even Mr. Teten says that the host of corporate regulations gives him "every incentive to go back" to the United States.

It is difficult to assess exactly how much money Israel is losing as a result of the departure of such companies. But the trend threatens to have serious implications for the Israeli economy, because fewer Israeli-based companies would mean fewer jobs, lower tax revenues, and less interest on the part of the global business community in investing in Israel. Already, the partners who manage Neurone Ventures advise nearly every high-technology start-up they fund to go West, particularly to the United States, where corporate taxation won't leave them down and out as it will in Israel.

Source: Tamar Hausman, "Managing Change," *Wall Street Journal Europe,* June 27, 2000, p. 30.

global virtually from its inception. The company not only opened sales offices rapidly throughout the world but also established factories in China, Taiwan, the United States, Switzerland, and Ireland.[11] As a result Logitech has become the world's leading PC mouse maker, having attained a global market share of 50 percent.[12]

▶ *Geographic Market Choices*

Once a company commits itself to extending its business internationally, management is confronted with the task of setting a geographic or regional emphasis. At any one time, a company may decide to emphasize the developed nations of Europe, Japan, and North America. Alternatively, it may prefer to pursue less developed countries in Latin America, in Africa, in Asia, or in the former Soviet bloc. Others might decide to enter lead or must-win markets. Management must direct business development in such a way that its particular geographic choices are congruent with the company's overall objectives.

Targeting Developed Economies

Developed economies account for a disproportionately large share of world gross national product (GNP) and thus tend to attract many companies. Ten developed countries (the United States, Canada, the United Kingdom, Germany, France, the Netherlands, Sweden, Switzerland, Japan, and Australia) account for 50 percent of the world's international trade, 70 percent of its inward investment, and 90 percent of its foreign direct investment. As a result, companies that see themselves as world-class marketers cannot afford to neglect these pivotal markets.[13] Firms with technology-intensive products have especially concentrated their activities in the developed world. Although competition from both international firms and local companies is usually more intense in these markets, doing business in developed countries is generally preferred over doing business in developing nations. This is primarily because the business environment is more predictable and the trade and investment climate is more favorable.

Developed countries are located in North America (the United States and Canada), Western Europe, and Asia (Japan, Australia, and New Zealand). Although some global firms such as IBM operate in all of these countries, many others may be represented in only one or two areas. U.S. multinational companies established strong business bases in Europe very early in their development but only more recently in Japan. Japanese firms tend to start their overseas operations in the United States and Canada and then move to Europe.

Kenichi Ohmae first articulated the importance of developing a competitive position in the major developed markets. Ohmae maintained that for most industries, it was important to compete effectively in all three parts of the **triad** of the United States, Europe, and Japan. The three areas of this strategic triad account for about 80 percent of sales for many industries. In these cases, the position of competitors in triad markets can determine the outcome of the global competitive battle. Companies need to be strong in at least two areas and at least to be represented in the third. Real global competitors are advised to have strong positions in all three areas.[14]

Because of the importance of the triad countries in international trade, global companies go to great lengths to balance their presence such that their sales begin to mirror the relative size of the three regions. A company underrepresented in one area or another will undertake considerable investment, often in the form of acquisitions, to balance its triad portfolio. Alcatel, a leading European manufacturer of telecommunications equipment, realized that 50 percent of the global opportunity for its market was located in the United States. In response, the company began a major investment drive into the LAN switching business (local area networks), acquiring Xylan Corporation and Assured Access Technology, two California-based firms.[15]

Many firms now think of the third leg of the triad as the Asia Pacific region rather than just Japan. Most European and U.S. global firms, traditionally weak in Asia, have made considerable efforts to balance their market positions. In a survey among managers of international firms, investment in the Asian region was given great importance, ranking equal to investment in their home countries and ahead of any other region. Whirlpool of the United States, the world's largest white-goods company, set up a regional headquarters for Asia in Singapore. The company indicated that with its past investments in Europe and Latin America, the remaining missing piece was Asia, where unit sales are expected to outpace those in both Europe and North America. Whirlpool entered into several joint ventures in Asia and acquired controlling interest in four appliance companies in China and two in India.[16]

Targeting Developing Markets

Developing markets differ substantially from developed economies in terms of both geographic region and level of economic development. Markets in Latin America, Africa, the Middle East, and some parts of Asia are characterized by a higher degree of risk than markets in developed countries. Because of the less stable economic climates in those areas, a company's operation can be expected to be subject to greater uncertainty and fluctuation. Furthermore, the frequently changing political situations in developing countries often affect operating results negatively. As a result, some markets that have experienced high growth for some years may suddenly experience drastic reductions in growth. Even so, a recent study suggests that the average market value of multinational firms with operations in developing countries is significantly higher than that of multinationals that are not present in such countries.[17]

In many situations, the higher risks in these markets are compensated for by higher returns, largely because competition is often less intense in developing markets. Hyundai, the largest of Korea's major car manufacturers, has expanded by acquiring or building car plants in Turkey, India, Egypt, Botswana, and Eastern Europe. Hyundai was particularly attracted to these markets by the lack of intense competition there.[18]

Market growth in developing countries can sometimes be higher than in the triad, often as a result of higher population growth. Furthermore, middle-class consumers are appearing in markets once seen as consisting of a small elite and a large impoverished underclass. India now boasts the world's largest middle-class market in absolute numbers. Consequently, companies need to balance the opportunity for future growth in the developing nations with the existence of higher risk.

When Unilever faced lower growth in its traditional markets of Europe and the United States, the company moved aggressively into emerging markets where growth averaged 5 percent or more in most of its core business categories. Unilever recently declared five geographic areas as top targets: Central and Eastern Europe, Latin America, India, and Southeast Asia. In China alone, Unilever has invested $800 million. Although that enormous country still accounts for only a small portion of Unilever's sales, the potential in China is viewed as huge. The company plans to obtain half of its global sales from developing countries in the near future.[19]

The past experience of international firms doing business in developing countries has not always been positive. Trade restrictions often forced companies to build local factories in order to access the local market. Many firms believed that such an investment was not justified, given the market size and the perceived risk of the venture. However, with the present trend toward global trade liberalization, many formerly closed countries have opened their borders to imports. This has encouraged many more firms to consider emerging markets.

It cannot be denied, however, that many risks exist for international marketers, whether they produce in emerging markets or only export to them. Many firms that were excited about Mexico were seriously hurt by Mexico's economic crisis in the early 1990s. More recently, Whirlpool saw its results severely affected by the economic situation in Brazil. Currency devaluation in that country resulted in a substantial net loss in the company's income. Whirlpool's sales in Brazil, measured in U.S. dollars, declined by $200 million as a result of the devaluation.[20]

Expanding in Eastern Europe and Russia

The economic liberalization of the countries in the former Soviet bloc opened a large new market for many international firms. This market typically represents about 15 percent of the worldwide demand in a given industry. Many companies consider these countries as offering long-term potential but little profit opportunity in the near term. Unlike other less developed countries, these transitional economies lack a recent history of free enterprise or commercial law. Most still suffer under poorly performing economies. However, a number of firms have moved to take advantage of opportunities in areas where they once were prohibited from doing business.

The first wave of investments into Eastern Europe was led by companies marketing industrial and construction equipment, such as Otis Elevator. In Poland, where Otis has been operating since 1975, the company has captured a market share of 30 percent. Otis was attracted to the Polish market because most of Poland's 60,000 operating elevators were old, and the replacement and service markets looked promising.[21] Companies marketing consumer goods tended to enter the region later. Procter & Gamble has set up regional centers for each of its product lines, making the Czech Republic its center for detergents and Hungary its center for personal-care products.

The behavior of international car manufacturers demonstrates an aggressive approach to Eastern Europe. Initially low auto sales levels were followed by substantial growth as the income levels of Eastern European populations improved. In Poland, automobile sales jumped 20 percent in one year. In Hungary they jumped 40 percent in one year. Low labor costs, at rates only a fraction of what they are in Western Europe, attracted international firms to build cars in Eastern Europe (see Table 8.1). Many firms set up assembly plants and car component factories or acquired local firms.[22]

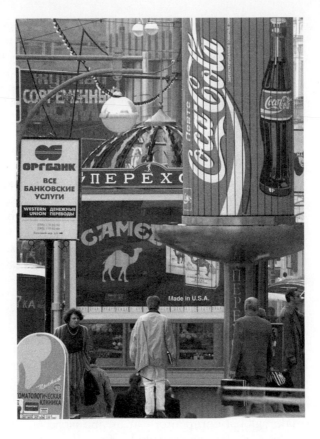

U.S. brands make inroads into Russia.

Table 8.1 *Operations of Automobile Firms in Eastern Europe*

COMPANY NAME	COUNTRY	TYPE OF OPERATION	INVESTMENT[a]
GM/Opel	Poland	Car assembly	DM 30 mio
		New car plant	DM 500 mio
	Hungary	New engine & car plant	DM 1.0 bio
	East Germany	New car plant	DM 1.0 bio
Ford Motor	Poland	Car & van assembly	DM 54 mio
Volkswagen	Poland	Car & van assembly	DM 54 mio
	Hungary	New Audi engine & car plant	DM 1.0 bio
	Slovakia	Assembly & gearbox plant	DM 215 mio
	Czech Republic	Skoda acquisition (70% stake), new car plant & models	DM 3.7 bio
	Eastern Germany	2 plants, new engine & cars	DM 3.2 bio
Fiat	Poland	FSM (78% stake) new plant & models	DM 1.8 bio
Suzuki	Hungary	New car plant (80% stake)	na
Daewoo	Poland	Acquisitions of FS Lublin & FSO, new plants & models	DM 1.34 bio

[a]Some investments staged over several years into 2000–2002 period.

Source: Financial Times, February 13, 1997: 11. Reprinted by permission.

Few companies can match Germany's Volkswagen in its expansion into Eastern Europe. Aside from establishing assembly plants, new-car plants, and engine plants, the company also invested in a range of new models through its stake in Skoda, the leading Czech company with a long tradition in the automotive industry. Skoda became VW's low-budget brand throughout Europe and VW's answer to cheaper imports from Asia. Skoda's latest model, Felicia, was engineered largely in the Czech Republic and is doing very well in many European markets.

The Russian market has proved to be more problematic than most markets in Eastern Europe. Liberalization has been slower, and markets have often been plagued by a lack of regulation and by the presence of organized crime. Procter & Gamble began its Russian operations in August 1991 in St. Petersburg. The company slowly introduced a line of products while expanding its geographic reach. Still the company estimates that only 10 to 15 percent of the Russian population can afford Western consumer goods.[23] Cadbury opened its first chocolate plant in Russia in 1997. By 2001, its Russian operations had yet to totally recover from the 1998 devaluation of the Russian ruble.[24] General Motors began producing Chevrolet Blazers in Russia in 1997. However, bureaucratic impediments and political uncertainties have made most global automotive companies cautious of the Russian market, despite its long-term potential.[25]

Targeting Lead Markets

It is sometimes important to have a market presence in **lead markets**. Lead markets are usually major research sites as well as the home markets of major global competitors in an industry. As Figure 8.1 shows, the United States is no longer the only lead market in many key industries. In electronics and semiconductor manufacturing, Japan has captured the lead in a number of segments. This loss of leadership to Japan and other countries has become pronounced in several areas of the electronics industry.

In a demonstration of the dynamic nature of lead markets, U.S. semiconductor firms were able to reverse this trend. In 1988 the U.S. market share amounted to 43 percent, compared to 48 percent for Japanese firms. By 1994 the relative strength was 48 percent for the United States versus 36 percent for Japanese producers. Much of this success was credited to the formation of Sematech, a consortium that was founded in 1987 and links eleven of the largest U.S.-based chip manufacturers. Matching the U.S. government's investment of $690 million, the consortium was also able to improve the position of semiconductor equipment makers, whose share rebounded to just above 50 percent from a low of 45 percent in 1990. As the United States reemerged as the lead market in chip manufacturing, U.S.-based firms benefited from being exposed to new developments and better practices.[26]

It is essential for globally competing firms to monitor lead markets in their industries or, better yet, to build up some relevant market presence in those markets. Toray Industries, a leading Japanese company in a number of plastic and textile industries, runs its artificial-leather affiliate, Alcantara, from Italy. Although Japanese firms have tended to shy away from Italy as a market for investment, Alcantara's success can be attributed largely to the design of its leather products. Toray's management considers Italy the world leader in design, and Italy is a recognized lead market for high-end textiles and clothing.[27]

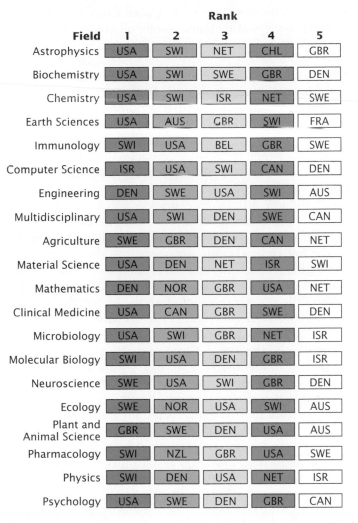

Rank

Field	1	2	3	4	5
Astrophysics	USA	SWI	NET	CHL	GBR
Biochemistry	USA	SWI	SWE	GBR	DEN
Chemistry	USA	SWI	ISR	NET	SWE
Earth Sciences	USA	AUS	GBR	SWI	FRA
Immunology	SWI	USA	BEL	GBR	SWE
Computer Science	ISR	USA	SWI	CAN	DEN
Engineering	DEN	SWE	USA	SWI	AUS
Multidisciplinary	USA	SWI	DEN	SWE	CAN
Agriculture	SWE	GBR	DEN	CAN	NET
Material Science	USA	DEN	NET	ISR	SWI
Mathematics	DEN	NOR	GBR	USA	NET
Clinical Medicine	USA	CAN	GBR	SWE	DEN
Microbiology	USA	SWI	GBR	NET	ISR
Molecular Biology	SWI	USA	DEN	GBR	ISR
Neuroscience	SWE	USA	SWI	GBR	DEN
Ecology	SWE	NOR	USA	SWI	AUS
Plant and Animal Science	GBR	SWE	DEN	USA	AUS
Pharmacology	SWI	NZL	GBR	USA	SWE
Physics	SWI	DEN	USA	NET	ISR
Psychology	USA	SWE	DEN	GBR	CAN

AUS = Australia
BEL = Belgium
CAN = Canada
CHL = Chile
DEN = Denmark
FRA = France
GER = Germany
GBR = Great Britain
ISR = Israel
NET = Netherlands
NZL = New Zealand
NOR = Norway
SWE = Sweden
SWI = Switzerland
USA = United States

Figure 8.1 *Nations That Lead in Research*

Source: Table from *Tages Anzeiger* (Zurich, Switzerland), February 11, 1997: 6. Reprinted by permission.

Taiwan provides a good example of how newly industrializing countries can become lead markets by wresting competitive positions away from developed nations. Taiwanese electronics companies have become world leaders in several important product categories. Elitegroup and First International are the world's largest independent manufacturers of printed circuit boards. GVC, another Taiwanese company, has risen to the leading position as modem producer, surpassing Hayes of the United States. Taiwan, through agreements with many Western chip manufacturers, has reached the number-four position worldwide in the semiconductor industry and the number-three position in the computer industry.[28] In certain industries, international firms must be present in Taiwan if they intend to keep abreast of changes.

"Must-Win" Markets

As global marketers eye the array of countries available, they soon become aware that not all countries are of equal importance on the path to global leadership. Markets that are defined as crucial to global market leadership, markets that can determine the global winners among all competitors, markets that companies can ill afford to avoid or neglect—such markets are **must-win markets.**

The starting point for analyzing which markets are must-win markets is the relevant global chessboard that best depicts the industry in question. Not all industries show the same countries as must-win markets. Typically, absolute size is an important criterion for market selection. In the past, the United States has been the largest single market for many industries, thus becoming a decisive piece in global competitive struggles. The larger developed countries often qualify as must-win markets because of their relative wealth and purchasing power. However, many developing countries qualify as well. Coke considered India a problematic market and had withdrawn from India, but as soon as Pepsi invested there, Coke committed itself to re-entering India. Coke was afraid it could lose its permanent global position to Pepsi if Pepsi captured the Indian market unopposed.

With the rapid rise of China and its ongoing industrialization, China is increasingly assuming must-win status thanks to the sheer size of this market of 1.2 billion people. With China now represented on the global chessboard, sales in many categories of consumer goods areas are growing rapidly. Procter & Gamble's annual Chinese sales had grown to $1 billion by 1999.[29] As the second largest beer market in the world, China has attracted as many as 60 foreign brewers. Carlsberg of Denmark, a brewer with a large international business, predicts that China will be the world's largest beer market in the near future, usurping that distinction from the United States. Carlsbad entered into a major joint venture in Shanghai, eventually investing as much as $1 billion in the country.[30] Similarly, McDonald's views China as one of its biggest single opportunities. The fast-food company expects its presence in China to double every year until it reaches 600 restaurants in early 2003.[31] With an installed base of 11 million PCs and 2.1 million Internet users, China is also an attractive market for any IT-related company.[32]

Competing in must-win markets takes vigilance. Citibank considers Brazil a must-win market where it has long been a favorite bank among the Brazilian elite. However, in the late 1990s, Citibank was distracted by a merger with Travelers Group and failed to pursue the Brazilian market aggressively just as other foreign banks were rapidly making headway through acquisitions. Because of this, Citibank dropped to fourteenth place in the market.[33]

Competing for a must-win market also has its risks. Compaq, the U.S. PC maker, has experienced considerable growth in sales in China. However, it has had great difficulty collecting accounts receivable from its independent dealers and distributors. Microsoft also faces problems in China and is fighting pirated software by adjusting its local price and initiating legal action.[34] If a market is in the must-win category, however, companies will have to find ways to overcome such difficulties. Unlike other markets, must-win markets cannot be avoided, because global market leadership is at stake.

READ MORE ABOUT IT:
Check out "As Brazil Booms" under *Supplemental Readings* on our website.

▶ Country Selection

After determining what type of foreign markets it wishes to pursue, the firm must choose which countries in particular to target. There are more than 200 countries and territories, but very few firms compete in all of these. Adding another country to a company's portfolio requires additional investment in management time and effort, as well as in capital. Each additional country also represents a new business risk. It takes time to build up business in a country where the firm has not previously been represented, and profits may not be realized until much later on. Consequently, companies need to perform a careful analysis before they decide to move ahead.

The Screening Process

The assessment of country markets usually begins with gathering relevant information on each country and screening out the less desirable countries. A model for selecting foreign markets is shown in Figure 8.2.

The model includes a series of filters to screen out countries. The overwhelming number of market opportunities makes it necessary to break the selection process down into a series of steps. Although a firm does not want to miss a potential opportunity, it cannot conduct extensive marketing research studies in every country of the world. The screening process is used to identify good prospects. Two common errors that companies make in screening countries are (1) ignoring countries that offer good potential for the company's products and (2) spending too much time investigating countries that are poor prospects. The firm should be able to focus quickly on a few of the most promising market opportunities by using published secondary sources available online or in most business libraries.[35]

The first stage of the selection process is to use macrovariables to discriminate between countries that represent basic opportunities and those that either offer little or no opportunity or involve excessive risk. **Macrovariables** describe the total market in terms of economic, social, geographic, and political information. The variables that are included reflect the potential market size and the market's acceptance of the product or similar products. The second stage of the screening process focuses on microlevel considerations such as competitors, ease of entry, cost of entry, and profit potential. The focus of the screening process switches from total market size to profitability. The final stage of the screening process is an evaluation and rank-ordering of the potential target countries on the basis of corporate resources, objectives, and strategies. Lead markets and must-win markets receive extra consideration.

Criteria for Selecting Target Countries

The process of selecting target countries through the screening process requires that the companies decide what criteria to use to differentiate desirable countries from less desirable countries. Research on international investment decisions has shown that the four critical factors affecting market selection are market size and growth, political conditions, competition, and market similarity.[36] In this section, we explain each of these factors and their uses in the market selection process.

Market Size and Growth The greater the potential demand for a product in a country, the more attractive that market will be to a company. Measures of market size and growth can be made on both a macro and a micro basis. On a macro basis, it may be determined that the country needs a minimum set of potential resources to be worth further consideration. The macroindicators of market potential and growth are generally used in the first stage of

Figure 8.2 *A Model for Selecting Foreign Markets*

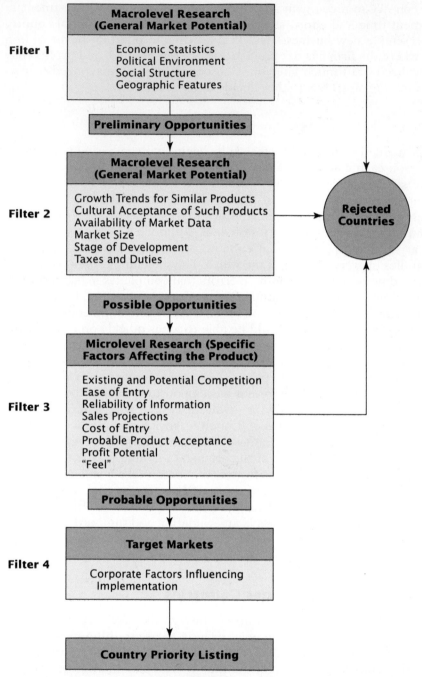

Source: R. Wayne Walvoord, "Export Market Research," Global Trade Magazine, May 1980: 83. Reprinted by permission.

the screening process, because the data are readily available and can be used to eliminate quickly those countries with little or no potential demand. Table 8.2 summarizes the potential macroindicators of market size.

A variety of readily available statistics can serve as macroindicators of market size. A company that sells microwave ovens may decide not to consider

Table 8.2 *Macroindicators of Market Size*

Geographic Indicators
Size of country, in terms of geographic area
Climatic conditions
Topographical characteristics
Demographic Characteristics
Total population
Population growth rate
Age distribution of the population
Degree of population density
Economic Characteristics
Total gross national product
Per-capita gross national product
Per-capita income (also income growth rate)
Personal or household disposable income
Income distribution

any country with a personal disposable income per household of less than $10,000 a year. The rationale for this criterion is that if the average household has less than $10,000, the potential market for a luxury item such as a microwave oven will not be great. However, a single statistic can sometimes be deceptive. For example, a country may have an average household income of $8,000, but there may still be a million households with an income of over $10,000. These million households will be potential buyers of microwaves.

Because the macroindicators of market size are general and crude, they do not necessarily indicate a perceived need for the product. For example, a country such as Iraq may have the population and income to suggest a large potential market for razors, but the male consumers, many of whom are Muslims and wear beards, may not feel a need for the product. In the next stage of the screening process, it is recommended that microindicators of market potential be used. Microindicators usually indicate actual consumption of a company's product or a similar product, therefore signaling a perceived need. Table 8.3 lists several examples of microindicators of market size.

Table 8.3 *Microindicators of Market Size*

Radios	Hotel beds
Televisions	Telephones
Cinema seats	Tourist arrivals
Scientists and engineers	Passenger cars
Hospitals	Civil airline passengers
Hospital beds	Steel production
Physicians	Rice production
Alcohol consumption	Number of farms
Coffee consumption	Land under cultivation
Gasoline consumption	Electricity consumption

These microindicators can be used to estimate market size further. The number of households with televisions indicates the potential market size for televisions if every household purchased a new television. Depending on the life of the average television in use, one can estimate the annual demand. As we noted in Chapter 7, consumption figures for similar or substitute products can be used as proxy variables if actual consumption statistics are not available for a certain product category. For example, if a firm is trying to measure the potential market size and receptivity for a palm-held communicator, it might chose as a proxy variable the number of telephone lines per person, the number of personal computers per person, or cellular telephone usage. Similarly, in determining the market size for surgical sutures, marketers might use the number of hospital beds or the number of doctors as a proxy variable. The number of farms might indicate the potential demand for tractors, just as the number of cars is likely to indicate the number of tires needed.

Political Conditions The influence of the host country's political environment was described in detail in Chapter 4. Although political risk tends to be more subjective than the quantitative indicators of market size, it is equally important. Any company can be hurt by political risk, which can result in anything from limitations on the number of foreign company officials and on the amount of profits paid to the parent company, to refusal to issue a business license. For example, the invasion of Kuwait in 1990 resulted in millions of dollars of U.S. assets being exposed to risk. Though less radical than invasions, industrial disputes such as strikes can be a major disruption to business. The incidence of such events varies greatly from country to country. The most "strike-prone" among the developed countries are Greece, Norway, and Canada.[37] Table 8.4 shows some indicators of political risk that may be used in country selection.

Competition The number, size, and quality of the competition in a particular country affect a firm's ability to enter and compete profitably. In general, it is more difficult to determine the competitive structure of foreign countries than to determine the market size or political risk. Because of the difficulty of obtaining information, competitive analysis is usually done in the last stages of the screening process, when a small number of countries are being considered.

Another reliable source of information is the U.S. government. The U.S. Department of Commerce and the State Department (or their equivalents in other countries) may be able to provide information on the competitive situation. Also, in nearly every country, embassies employ commercial attachés

Table 8.4 *Indicators of Political Risk*

Probability of nationalization	Percentage of the voters who are communist
Bureaucratic delays	
Number of expropriations	Restrictions on capital movement
Number of riots or assassinations	Government intervention
Political executions	Limits on foreign ownership
Number of socialist seats in the legislature	Soldier/civilian ratio

World Beat 8.2 *Landing Rights*

As the world's airlines grounded planes and slashed staff amid the industry's worst crisis in years, Air France announced that it would begin to fly to Kinshasa, the ravaged capital of the Congo. Kinshasa is one of the world's poorest cities, so unsafe for arriving crews that they are shuttled elsewhere for overnight stays. Taxiing down the scarred tarmac feels like driving over railroad ties. Managers charge extra to turn on the runway lights at night, and departing passengers can encounter several layers of bribes before boarding.

But serving Kinshasa also is lucrative, for there is little competition and the airport is used by a reliable stream of business travelers willing to pay high fares for access to the Congo's mineral wealth. There are destinations like that across most of Africa, where flights can yield twice as much revenue per passenger as flights of similar length to the United States. Air France, which flies to more African cities than any non-African airline, recently increased the number of seats it offers to Africa by almost 70 percent over last year, while it cut flights to North America. Even as airlines struggle with losses, Africa is helping Air France stay profitable.

As in many West African markets, Air France planes land in Kinshasa with their high-end seats filled by diamond dealers, gold traders, and petroleum executives paying as much as $6,000 as their round-trip fare. Aid workers and locals shuttling to and from Europe fill economy class, usually paying more than $1,000 for the carrier's cheapest round-trip ticket from Paris to Kinshasa.

France's colonial history and the recent bankruptcies of several Air France rivals—Belgium's Sabena, Swissair, and Air Afrique—have helped the French airline mine Africa for exclusive markets. Air France has an edge in its old African empire—which includes Cameroon, Chad, Gabon, Guinea, Ivory Coast, Mali, Senegal, and other countries—thanks to linguistic, economic, and cultural ties. This advantage extends even to a few markets such as Kinshasa, capital of the former Belgian Congo, where French is an official language and Paris has long wielded political influence. Colonial ties have long been a boon to Europe's former imperial powers. Today, air routes to Africa still reflect how Europeans carved up the continent in the 1880s.

Source: Daniel Michaels, "Landing Rights," *Wall Street Journal*, April 30, 2002, p. A1.

---

whose main function is to assist home companies entering that foreign marketplace. Embassies of the foreign country that is being investigated may also be able to help marketers in their analysis. For example, a firm that is investigating the competition among companies that sell farm implements in Spain can contact the Spanish embassy in Washington, DC, and secure a list of manufacturers of farm implements in Spain. In developing countries, U.S. AID (United States Agency for International Development) can be a very good source of information.

Other sources of information on competition vary widely, depending on the size of the country and the product. Many of the larger countries have chambers of commerce or other in-country organizations that may be able to assist potential investors. For example, if a firm is investigating the Japanese market for electronic measuring devices, the following groups could help it determine the competitive structure of the market in Japan:

▸ U.S. Chamber of Commerce in Japan
▸ Japan External Trade Organization (JETRO)

business.college.hmco.com

Check out the U.S. Government links on our website.

Check out the Japanese links on our website.

Check out the travel information links on our website.

▶ American Electronics Association in Japan
▶ Japan Electronic Industry Development Association
▶ Electronic Industries Association of Japan
▶ Japan Electronic Measuring Instrument Manufacturers Association

The final (and usually the most expensive) way to assess the market is to go to the country and interview potential customers to determine the size and strength of the competition. A trip to a potential market is always required before a final decision is made, and it should not be overlooked as an important part of the screening process. If those who are making the visit are well prepared in advance, several days in a country talking to distributors, large buyers, and trade officials can be extremely valuable in assessing the competitiveness of the market and the potential profitability of entering it.

Market Similarity Strong evidence exists that market similarity can be used for country selection. A study of 954 product introductions by 57 U.S. firms found a significant correlation between market selection and market similarity.[38] As shown in Table 8.5, the selection of foreign markets followed market similarity very closely.

The concept of market similarity is simple. Managers believe that their success in the home market is more easily transferable to markets similar to the one in which they already compete. This idea is sometimes called **psychic distance**. Therefore, when a company decides to enter foreign markets,

Table 8.5 *Correlation of Similarity and Position in the Entry Sequence*

	SIMILARITY TO THE UNITED STATES	POSITION IN INVESTMENT SEQUENCE
Canada	1	2
Australia	2	3
United Kingdom	3	1
West Germany	4	6
France	5	4
Belgium	6	10
Italy	7	9
Japan	8	5
Netherlands	9	12
Argentina	10	15
Mexico	11	8
Spain	12	13
India	13	16
Brazil	14	7
South Africa	15	14
Philippines	16	17
South Korea	17	18
Colombia	18	11

Source: Reprinted by permission of the publisher from "Market Similarity and Market Selection: Implications for International Market Strategy," by William H. Davidson, *Journal of Business Research* 11, 4: 446. Copyright 1983 by Elsevier Science Publishing Co., Inc.

it will first tend to enter markets that are psychically close or most similar to its home market. For example, a U.S. firm usually enters Canada, Australia, and the United Kingdom before entering less similar markets such as Spain, South Korea, and India. The premise behind the selection of similar markets is the desire of a company to minimize risk in the face of uncertainty. Entering a market that has the same language, a similar distribution system, and similar customers is less difficult than entering a market in which all these variables are different.

There are two dangers of choosing markets on the basis of similarity. First, the benefits of similarity need to be balanced against the market size. Australia may be similar to the United States but may have relatively little demand compared to China or Indonesia. Second, sometimes firms can overestimate the degree of similarity between markets. When Canadian retail chains entered the United States, managers assumed that the United States was just like Canada only bigger. They believed that the retail concepts that worked in Canada would work in the United States. Instead, U.S. consumers proved very different from Canadian consumers. They demanded more service, shopped harder for bargains, and were far less loyal to national chains than were their Canadian counterparts. In addition, competition proved far more intense in the United States. As a result, familiarity bred carelessness, and the chains struggled to survive in what proved to be a very alien market.[39]

Listing Selection Criteria

A good way to screen countries is to develop a set of criteria that serve as minimum standards that a country must meet in order to move through the stages of the screening process. The minimum cut-off number for each criterion will be established by management. As one moves through the screening process, the selection criteria become more specific. The screening process that could be used by a manufacturer of kidney dialysis equipment is depicted in Table 8.6.

Table 8.6 *Screening Process Example: Targeting Countries for Kidney Dialysis Equipment*

FILTER NUMBER	TYPE OF SCREENING	SPECIFIC CRITERIA
1	Macrolevel research	GDP over $15 billion
		GDP per capita over $1,500
2	General market factors related to the product	Fewer than 200 people per hospital bed
		Fewer than 1,000 people per doctor
		Government expenditures over $100 million for health care
		Government expenditures over $20 per capita for health care
3	Microlevel factors specific to the product	Kidney-related deaths over 1,000
		Patient use of dialysis equipment—over 40 percent annual growth in treated population
4	Final screening of target markets	Numbers of competitors
		Political stability

The analysis begins by looking at gross national products. Introduction of dialysis equipment in a new market requires a significant support function, including salespeople, service people, replacement parts inventory, and an ensured continuous supply of dialysate fluid, needles, tubing, and so on. Some countries lack the technical infrastructure to support such high-level technology. Therefore, management may decide to consider only countries that have a minimum size of $15 billion GNP, a criterion that excludes many of the developing economies of the world from consideration.

The selection process continues by examining the concentration of medical services in the remaining countries. Hemodialysis is a sophisticated procedure that requires medical personnel with advanced training. In order for a country to support advanced medical equipment, it requires a high level of medical specialization. Higher levels of medical concentration allow doctors the luxury of specializing in a field such as nephrology (the study of kidneys). Management may determine that a population of less than 1,000 per doctor and a population of less than 200 per hospital bed indicate that medical personnel will be able to achieve the level of specialization needed to support a hemodialysis program.

Public health expenditures reflect the government's contribution to the medical care of its citizens—a factor of obvious importance in hemodialysis. Management may believe that countries that do not invest substantially in the health care of their populations generally are not interested in making an even more substantial investment in a hemodialysis program. Thus countries that do not have a minimum of $20 in public health expenditure per capita or $100 million in total expenditures for health care would be eliminated from consideration.

Then management may decide that there are two microlevel factors to consider: the number of kidney-related deaths and the growth rate of the treated patient population. The number of deaths due to kidney failure is a good indicator of the number of people in each country who could have used dialysis equipment. The company will be interested only in countries with a minimum of 1,000 deaths per year due to kidney-related causes. Analysis of the growth rate of the population requiring kidney treatment demonstrates a growth in potential demand.

Finally, management must consider political risk and competition. Newly opened markets with the greatest growth potential may be the best targets for a new supplier of dialysis equipment, because competition is not so entrenched as is it would be in a mature market. Alternatively, management may decide to enter a lead market where a major competitor is strong in order to monitor technology development and possibly block that competitor. It is the weighting of these microlevel factors that will determine the primary target market.

Grouping International Markets

A final consideration in selecting national markets is the option of entering a group of countries in a single geographic region, be they the developed countries of Western Europe or the less developed countries in South America or the Middle East. It is often necessary to group countries together so that they can be considered as a single market or as a group of similar markets. Two principles that often drive the need for larger market groupings are critical

The parliament of the European Union convenes in Brussels.

mass and economies of scale. **Critical mass,** a term used in physics and military strategy, embodies the idea that a certain minimum amount of effort is necessary before any impact will be achieved. **Economies of scale** is a term used in production situations; it means that greater levels of production result in lower costs per unit, which obviously increases profitability.

The costs of marketing products within a group of countries are lower than the costs of marketing products to the same number of disparate countries for four reasons. First, the potential volume to be sold in a group of countries is sufficient to support a full marketing effort. Second, geographic proximity makes it easy to travel from one country to another, often in 2 hours or less. Third, the barriers to entry are often the same in countries within an economic group—for example, the European Union. Finally, in pursuing countries with similar markets, a company gains leverage with marketing programs.

There is some debate over the long-term role of market groups. The European Union has become a strong group with a single currency, but many economic groups may become subordinate to the role of the WTO. Also, given the broad membership of the WTO and its strong enforcement powers, the regional market group will generally need to conform to the rules and practices of the WTO when dealing with all other WTO countries.

It is also important to remember that just being neighbors isn't enough to make countries into a viable market group. Take, for example, the countries in the Caucasus region. Armenia and Azerbaijan are technically at war. Turkey blockades Armenia in sympathy with Azerbaijan. Relations between Georgia and Armenia remain strained, as do relations between Iran and Azerbaijan. Travel and shipping among the countries are poor as well. Roads are bad, and the easiest flight connections in the region are all via Moscow or Istanbul.[40] Clearly these countries do not present themselves as a likely group to the global marketer.

business.college.hmco.com

Which countries belong to which regional groups? Check out Regional Groups on our website.

▶ *Selecting a Global Marketing Strategy*

After a firm has internationalized and selected the foreign markets it wishes to enter, it must determine how it will direct its marketing function across its various geographic locations. This decision must focus both on the customers it serves and on the competition it faces. A firm may choose to take a hands-off approach to its foreign operations. On the other hand, it might wish to pursue global integration or even standardization. **Integration** is the coordination of various country strategies and the subordination of these separate strategies to one global framework. **Standardization** refers specifically to the similarity that some companies want to achieve across many markets with respect to their marketing strategies and marketing mix.

Multidomestic Marketing Strategies

We explore organization issues in more detail in Chapter 16. However, some general principles of how multidomestic firms are organized should be noted at this point, because organizational structure often provides a good picture of a firm's global strategy. Many international firms operate as multidomestic firms with their businesses organized around country markets. Although some key strategic decisions with respect to products and technology are made at the central or head office, the details of implementing marketing strategies are left largely to local subsidiaries. Each subsidiary represents a separate business that must be run profitably. At the extreme, this leads to an organization that runs many different businesses in a number of countries—hence the term **multidomestic.**

Multidomestic strategies are most appropriate in industries that are themselves multidomestic in nature. There is little need for central direction if buyers vary greatly from country to country or where competition is usually local. Local managers are better able to make decisions because they are close to the local consumers, distributors, and competitors. Similarly, there is less incentive to standardize products if the production of the product doesn't lend itself to economies of scale.

A large number of U.S. firms listed by *Fortune* magazine in its Fortune 500 list have traditionally operated multidomestically. This includes such well-known firms as General Motors, Ford, IBM, Gillette, General Electric, and Kodak, as well as such major service businesses as Citibank and Chase, two of the largest U.S.-based financial services organizations. These firms generate a large percentage of their sales and profits from overseas business.

Nestlé, the world's largest food company, is represented in most markets of the world, including its operating companies such as Carnation, Rowntree, and Buitoni. Nestlé traditionally practiced a decentralized approach to management. Local operating managers were thought to be much more in tune with local markets and were therefore given the freedom to develop marketing strategies tailored to local needs. In the foods business, where considerable differences exist among countries' cultures, consumer habits, and competitive environments, decentralization was judged by management to be imperative.[41] Still, like many other companies pursuing a multidomestic strategy, Nestlé has begun to move toward a more centralized management structure, reorganizing around major business lines.

Global Marketing Strategies

Ever more industries are becoming globalized. Buyers are becoming more similar, cost savings can be reaped from standardization, and the activity of global competitors demands more centralized surveillance. Consequently, firms respond with more centralized strategies that are either globally or regionally focused.

In the early phases of development, global marketing strategies were assumed to be of one type only. Global strategies were associated with totally integrating market strategies across the globe. As marketers gained more experience, many other types of global marketing strategies were devised. Some of these are much less complicated and expose a smaller aspect of a marketing strategy to the need for integration. In this section, we explore various generic types of global marketing strategies and review the conditions under which they may best succeed. Figure 8.3 depicts the level of integration involved in such options.

Global Product Category Strategy Possibly the oldest and least integrated type of global marketing strategy is the pursuit of the global category. Firms pursuing this strategy compete in the same category country after country. Nonetheless, they will consider targeting different segments in each category or tailoring the product, advertising, and branding according to local market requirements. In short, they leverage knowledge across markets without pursuing standardization. This strategy works best when there are significant differences across markets and when few global segments are present.

Procter & Gamble has employed this strategy for several of its product categories, including disposable baby diapers. Senior executives at headquarters coordinate and share information across one category on a global basis. Recently, P&G decided to structure its entire organization around seven product categories with global responsibility. Its competitor, Unilever, is also focusing its business on some fourteen main categories.[42]

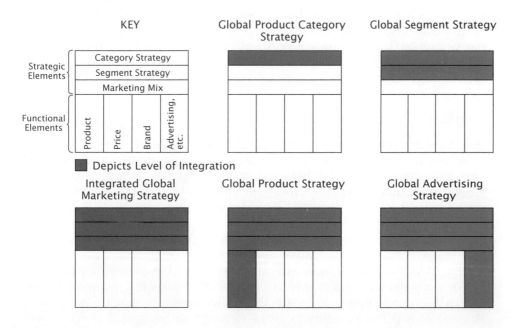

Figure 8.3 *Levels of Integration for Global Marketing Strategies*

Global Segment Strategy A company that decides to target the same segment in many countries is following a global segment strategy. The company may develop an understanding of a particular customer base and leverage that experience around the world. In both consumer and industrial markets, significant knowledge is accumulated when a company gains in-depth understanding of a niche or segment. A pure global segment strategy even allows for different products, brands, or advertising, although some standardization is expected.

Segment strategies are relatively new to global marketing, but industrial firms in particular have begun to adopt them. ICI Nobel Explosives, a world leader in mining explosives, has adopted global segmentation strategies for both deep mining and surface mining. ICI coordinates its national activities by segments and leverages products, experience, and sales activities around the world. Among financial services firms, several companies have adopted global segment strategies. Citibank runs several segment strategies for different categories of private banking clients. Deloitte Touche Tohmatsu, a leading professional services firm, has adopted global strategies for several key client segments, such as for the financial services industry and telecommunications.

Global Marketing Mix Strategies Global marketing mix strategies go further than either product category strategies or segment strategies and pursue global integration along all or some marketing mix elements such as pricing, distribution, communications, or product. If all elements are involved, we call this a **fully integrated global marketing strategy**. However, firms can pursue partially integrated strategies that allow them to customize some but not all aspects of their marketing mix. Two common **partially integrated global marketing strategies** are global product strategies and global advertising strategies. Pursuing a **global product strategy** implies that a company has largely integrated its product offering. Although the product may not need to be completely standardized worldwide, key aspects or modules may in fact be standardized. Global product strategies require that the conditions of product use, expected features, and required product functions be largely identical from one market to the next so that few variations or changes are needed. Companies that implement a global product strategy can leverage product development costs and take advantage of economies of scale in production. Similarly, **a global advertising strategy** entails the use of similar themes if not the same actual advertisements worldwide, and the firm is likely to employ an international advertising agency to help implement its global plan.

Regional Strategies

Regional strategies are marketing strategies deployed across a number of countries in close proximity. As we noted earlier, grouping countries by region can often help achieve both critical mass and economies of scale. Regional marketing strategies focusing on Europe, Asia, or Latin America represent a halfway point between multidomestic and truly global strategies. Typically, regional marketing strategies revolve around the three large trading blocs of North America (the United States, Canada, and Mexico), Europe, and the Asia Pacific area (Japan and the Pacific Rim countries). A global strategy, by contrast, would include all the regions in the strategic triad.

For example, we speak of a North American strategy if a company has integrated its marketing strategy for the United States, Canada, and Mexico. Passage of NAFTA caused many firms to adopt an integrated North American strategy by merging the operations of the three signatory countries. The process that companies go through to determine what regional strategy is appropriate across, say, ten Asian markets is identical to the analysis a company would apply to determine the best global marketing strategy across its top twenty global markets.

Pan-European Strategies Pan-European marketing strategies have received considerable attention because of the European integration into a single European market. As a result, many companies have begun to integrate their marketing strategies across Europe, striving for pan-European brands, pan-European products, and pan-European advertising strategies.

In a 1992 study, some 80 percent of consumer-goods companies expressed an interest in pursuing a pan-European strategy. Yet only a fourth of these companies had begun the process of integration, and less than 6 percent of them believed their pan-European marketing integration had been completed.[43] Since that time, many more firms have begun to integrate their European marketing operations.

Lever, a European company active in the detergent field, began to switch its strategy in the mid-1980s after Procter & Gamble from the United States adopted pan-European strategies. Lever appointed European brand managers and started coordinating many of its policies. To avoid alienating consumers who may still require local differences, Lever has implemented this process step by step. Most brands still retain some local variations, but the company continues to strive for more uniform and standardized products across most of its European markets.[44]

Pan-Asian Strategies Much has been written about pan-European strategies, which deal with countries that are relatively similar. The opposite is true of pan-Asian strategies. Differences across the various Asian markets are much greater, and much less is known about pan-Asian or even pan-Pacific strategies.

Among the major companies building pan-Asian strategies are the large automotive manufacturers. Toyota, with its strong position in Japan, has been building its market position in other Asian countries by tying together a string of operations. The company is aggressively enhancing plant capacity in various Asian countries, closely followed by Honda. Both companies are also building distinct car models for the Asian market. Honda launched its City model as its first low-priced "Asia car." The City catapulted Honda into market leadership in Thailand, the largest single car market in Southeast Asia. Similarly, Toyota expects its Soluna model to be the basis for its market penetration in many Asian countries. Both models take advantage of the low-cost labor pool in Asia and do not require costly components imported from other parts of the world.

▶ *Conclusions*

Any company that wishes to engage in global marketing operations must make a number of very important strategic decisions. At the outset, the company must commit itself to some level of internationalization. Increasingly, firms are finding that an international presence must be pursued for competitive reasons. It is a necessity, not simply an option. Once committed, the company needs to decide where to go, both in terms of geographic regions and specific countries.

How strategic is your market choice? Continue with your *Country Market Report* **on our website.**

In the past, many firms competed in many local markets and attempted to meet those local markets' requirements as best they could. Although some firms still approach their international marketing effort this way, an increasing number are taking a regional or global view of their marketplace.

Globalization of many industries is a fact today. Some companies have no choice but to become more integrated. Once key competitors in their industries are globalized, other firms must follow. This necessitates a rethinking of the strategic choices and inevitably leads to new priorities. Globalization is not simply a new term for something that has existed all along. It is a new competitive game requiring companies to coordinate better and probably to standardize some if not all of their marketing mix. For many companies, survival as well as success depends on how well they learn this new game.

Review Questions

1. List five reasons why firms internationalize.
2. What is the triad and why is it important to global marketers?
3. What are the pros and cons of targeting developing countries or transnational economies?
4. What is a lead market?
5. Compare and contrast a global product category strategy and a global segment strategy.
6. Compare and contrast global strategies and regional strategies.

Questions for Discussion

1. What advantages might a Korean-based company such as Hyundai have entering markets in developing countries?
2. Discuss the pros and cons of targeting Eastern Europe and Russia by packaged-goods manufacturers.
3. What could be the advantages and disadvantages of being a born-global firm?
4. Unlike firms early in their internationalization, MNCs do not appear to favor entering new markets that are similar to their home markets over entering those that are dissimilar. Why do you think that is?
5. Compare and contrast the global product category strategy and the global segment strategy.

For Further Reading

Bartlett, Christopher A., and Sumantra Ghoshal. "Going Global: Lessons from Late Movers." *Harvard Business Review*, March–April 2000: 132–142.

Craig, C. Samuel, and Susan P. Douglas. "Configural Advantage in Global Markets." *Journal of International Marketing* 8, 1 (2000): 6–26.

Ellis, Paul. "Social Ties and Foreign Market Entry." *Journal of International Business Studies* 31, 1 (Third Quarter 2000): 443–469.

Ganesh, Jaishankar. "Converging Trends Within the European Union: Insights from an Analysis of Diffusion Patterns." *Journal of International Marketing* 6, 4 (1998): 32–48.

Oviatt, Benjamin M., and Patricia Phillips McDougall. "Global Start-ups: Entrepreneurs on a Worldwide Stage." *Academy of Management Executive* 9, 2 (May 1995): 30–43.

Pantzalis, Christos. "Does Location Matter? An Empirical Analysis of Geographic Scope and MNC Market Valuation." *Journal of International Business Studies* 32, 1 (First Quarter 2001): 133–155.

Yip, George S. *Total Global Strategy*. Upper Saddle River, NJ: Prentice-Hall, 2003.

Case 8.1 | *Gillette Targets Emerging Markets*

As it entered the twenty-first century, Gillette faced a difficult choice. Should it continue targeting emerging markets or not? Its strategy to move aggressively into markets in the developing world and the former Soviet bloc had been hailed as a success only a few years before. Recent poor earnings, however, had management considering whether this choice had been a wise one.

The Boston-based firm was founded in 1895 and is still best known for its original products, razors and razor blades. By the end of the twentieth century, Gillette had grown into a global corporation that marketed its products in 200 countries and employed 44,000 people worldwide. About 1.2 billion people use Gillette products every day. Its sales are about equally distributed among the United States (30 percent), Western Europe (35 percent), and the rest of the world (35 percent).

As markets matured in developing countries, Gillette sought growth through product diversification, moving into lines such as home permanents, disposable lighters, ballpoint pens, and batteries. In the mid-1990s, Gillette targeted several key emerging markets for growth. Among them were Russia, China, India, and Poland. Russia was already a success story. Gillette had formed a Russian joint venture in St. Petersburg, and within 3 years Russia had become Gillette's third largest blade market.

Gillette's move into the Czech Republic had prospered as well, and in 1995 Gillette bought Astra, a privately owned local razor blade company. Astra gave Gillette expanded brand presence in the Czech market. Astra's relatively strong position in export markets in East Europe, Africa, and Southeast Asia proved a boon to Gillette in those markets as well. Just as in other markets in the developing world, 70 percent of East European blade consumers used the older, lower-tech double-edge blade. (In more developed markets, consumers appreciated product innovation, and the shaving market had moved to more high-tech systems such as Gillette's Sensor.)

Then in 1998 disaster struck. A financial crisis that began in Thailand in 1997 quickly spread across Asia. Many wary investors responded by pulling money out of other emerging markets as well, depressing economies across the globe. Bad economies meant slower sales for Gillette, especially in Asia, Russia, and Latin America. In Russia, wholesalers could not afford to buy Gillette products. Consequently, these products disappeared from retail stores, and Gillette's Russian sales plummeted 80 percent in a single month. Gillette found it could not meet its projected annual profit growth of 15–20 percent. The price of Gillette shares tumbled 36 percent in 6 months. To save money, Gillette planned to close 14 factories and lay off 10 percent of its workforce.

Despite its recent bad experience in developing countries and in the former Soviet bloc, Gillette was still moving ahead with plant expansion plans in Russia and Argentina that would total $64 million. Some even suggested that this was a good time to expand in the emerging markets by buying up smaller competitors that had been hurt even worse by the crises. Meanwhile, back in the developed world, another large global consumer-products firm, Unilever, announced that it would be entering the razor market.

Discussion Questions

1. Why do companies such as Gillette target emerging markets? Do you agree with this strategy?
2. What are the dangers to Gillette of targeting emerging markets?
3. Why would local, privately owned companies like Astra want to sell out to companies like Gillette? Why are such companies attractive acquisitions to multinational firms?
4. What global strategy would you suggest for a company such as Gillette? Explain your choice.

Sources: Claire Oldfield, "Unilever Goes for a Cut of Razor Market," *Sunday Times*, September 10, 2000; Mark Maremont, "Gillette Won't Meet Profit-Growth Goal While Emerging Markets Face Turmoil," *Wall Street Journal*, September 30, 1998; Mary Kelleher, "Latin America's Pain Starts to Hurt Banks, Consumer Product Firms," *Toronto Star*, September 19, 1998, p. C4; "Gillette Acquires Leading Czech Blade and Razor Company," *Business Wire*, October 16, 1996; and Alex Pham, "Russian Mayor Seeks to Lure Business," *Boston Globe*, February 21, 1995, p. 53.

Case 8.2   *Indian Food Goes Global*

Mr. R. Krishnan, president of South Indian Foods Limited (SIFL), was deep in thought in his office at corporate headquarters in Coimbatore, India. Eleven years earlier he had founded SIFL with the help of his wife, Maya. Now, after returning from a week-long business trip to the United States, Mr. Krishnan was pondering the future of his company. Should SIFL enter foreign markets? If so, which ones?

SIFL began as a company selling only three items but had quickly expanded to a dozen products. It produced and marketed batters, pastes, and flours that formed the ingredients of traditional South Indian cooking. For example, its Maami's Tamarind Mix consisted of mustard, ground nuts, asafetida, curry leaves, coriander powder, and dried chilies fried in oil and then combined with tamarind extract, salt, turmeric, and vinegar. The mix was next bottled and vacuum-sealed to preserve the traditional homemade flavor and aroma of tamarind mix.

The company began to market its products in and around Coimbatore. Soon, however, new production units were established in Bangalore and Madras to serve the whole South Indian market. Then three more manufacturing units were established in the states of Maharashtra, Andhra Pradesh, and West Bengal. SIFL estimated that its share of market varied between 19 and 27 percent across its product categories in the territories where it competed. Recently, new competitors had entered the market. Their market shares were slightly lower than those of SIFL. In response to increased competition, however, SIFL attempted to avoid adding new product lines that might have to compete head-on with aggressive competitors.

SIFL attributed part of its success to its promotional efforts. It used advertising campaigns in local radio and newspapers. Handbills, printed in the local language of the different Indian states, were distributed in newspapers in selected cities. The company also offered sample packets of its batter products. All these efforts had helped make Maami's a household name in South India.

When Mr. Krishnan raised the question of international expansion at an emergency board meeting, there was great enthusiasm but little agreement. Some of the managers' comments were as follows:

Krishnan Why can't we think of going international? Our strategy did very well in the Indian market. With our state-of-the-art production facilities and marketing expertise, I believe we could easily create a niche overseas.

Sunder We have to be optimistic about the U.S. market. As you know, the Indian population there is large enough to absorb our product. Our market research also reveals that our dishes are even favored by native Americans.

Shankar I accept your views, but we are forgetting the fact that in the U.S. market we have to compete with powerful packaged-food companies.

Krishnan What about Asia? In South Asia, the raw materials necessary for making our products are readily available.

Maya I do not think targeting all of Asia is a viable option. Although the Chinese and Japanese are accustomed to rice, most of these Asian countries are culturally different from India. Why not the United Kingdom? It has a considerable South Indian population.

Dinakar Why not set up production facilities in the United States or the United Kingdom? I believe production overseas would be a better choice than exporting to these markets.

Discussion Questions

1. What are SIFL's motivations for expanding abroad?
2. What are the advantages of targeting Indian populations residing in foreign countries? What problems might arise?
3. Should SIFL pursue a global category strategy or a global segment strategy? Explain your answer.
4. To what degree should SIFL standardize its marketing mix—product, price, distribution, and promotion? Explain your answer.
5. What are the pros and cons of entering the United States first? The United Kingdom? Neighboring Asian markets?
6. Is there any advantage or disadvantage to this product being "Made in India"?
7. SIFL will face competitors such as Kraft in the United States. What overall posture should SIFL adopt in relation to these strong competitors—attack, avoid, or cooperate? How might U.S. competitors respond to SIFL's entry into the market?

8. To investigate the competitive environment for these products in your country, visit a local grocery store or supermarket. What Indian foods or food products are sold there? Do they appear to be targeted at ethnic communities or at a wider segment? What firms make these products? What insights could your visit give SIFL?

This case is based on *South_Indian_Foods_Limited _(A)_* by K. B. Saji. Used by permission.

Notes

[1]Julie Forster and Becky Gaylord, "Can Kraft Be a Big Cheese Abroad as Well?" *Business Week,* June 4, 2001: 63–67.

[2]"This Bud's for Them: Anheuser-Busch Takes Closer Aim at Foreign Markets," *New York Times,* June 23, 1999, p. C1.

[3] "Compagnie de St.-Gobain," *Industry Week,* June 7, 1999: 38.

[4]Jean-Pierre, Jeannet, "The World Paint Industry" (1992), case (Lausanne: IMD International, 1993).

[5]Deloitte & Touche Secure E-Business Practice to Globalize" *PR Newswire,* July 2, 1999.

[6]Michael Zielenziger, "DHL Worldwide Express Starts Service in Kabul, Afghanistan," *San Jose Mercury News,* April 6, 2002.

[7]"Bayer Plans Investments in Asia Through 2010," *Chemical Market Reporter,* February 22, 1999: 28.

[8]Peter Landers, "U.S. Is Tonic for Japan's Top Pharmaceuticals," *Wall Street Journal,* May 21, 2002, p. B6.

[9]Richard Seet and David Yoffie, "Internationalizing the Cola Wars (A): The Battle for China and Asian Markets," Harvard Business School, Case 9-795-186, 1995.

[10]Mexico's Cemex Wins Bet on Acquisitions," *Wall Street Journal,* April 30, 1998, p. A14.

[11]Vijay Jolly, "Logitech International (A)," case (Lausanne: IMD International, 1991).

[12]"PC Mouse Maker Logitech Still No. 1," *Taiwan Economic News,* June 8, 1999.

[13]"Subramanian Rangan: Seven Myths to Ponder Before Going Global," *Financial Times,* Mastering Strategy, Part 10, November 29, 1999, p. 2.

[14]Kenichi Ohmae, *Triad Power: The Coming Shape of Global Competition* (New York: Free Press, 1985).

[15]"Alcatel Open to More Acquisitions," *Business World,* March 25, 1999.

[16]"Asia Challenges Whirlpool Technology," *Research Technology Management,* September 1, 1998: 4.

[17]Christos Pantzalis, "Does Location Matter? An Empirical Analysis of Geographic Scope and MNC Market Valuation," *Journal of International Business Studies* 32, 1 (First Quarter 2001): 133–155.

[18]"Fast Drive Out of the Shadows," *Financial Times,* June 17, 1996: 17.

[19]"China: Unilever Seeks Market in China," *China Daily,* June 21, 1999, p. 5.

[20]"Whirlpool Says Net Fell by 65 Percent on Impact of Brazil Devaluation," *Wall Street Journal,* April 16, 1999, p. B2.

[21]"Otis Signs $5 Million Contract with TPSA," *Polish Press Agency,* June 9, 1999.

[22]"Into the East at Full Throttle," *Financial Times,* February 13, 1997: 11.

[23]"The Frugal Felicia Proves to Be a Firm Favourite," *Western Morning News* (Devon, U.K.), July 7, 1999.

[24]Sarah Ellison, "Cadbury Schweppes Works to Tempt More Sweet Tooths," *Wall Street Journal,* April 24, 2001, p. B4.

[25]"Russia's Vast Potential Drawing U.S. Auto Makers," *Tribune Business News* (Detroit Free Press), August 18, 1998.

[26]"A Declaration of Chip Independence," *New York Times,* October 6, 1994, p. D1.

[27]"Manager's Hands-Off Tactics Right Touch for Italian Unit," *Nikkei Weekly,* February 3, 1997: 17.

[28]"Acer's Semiconductor Unit Weighs Market Listing as Picture Brightens," *Dow Jones Business News,* January 20, 1999.

[29]"Procter & Gamble Warns on Soft Sales in China," *Asian Wall Street Journal,* October 1, 1999, p. 4.

[30]"Carlsberg A/S," *Food and Drink Weekly,* October 26, 1998.

[31]"Chinese Market Offers Big Expansion for Big Mac," *Financial Times,* February 20, 1995: 4.

[32]"China: Gates Launches Venus Project as Cheap Alternatives to PCs," *China Daily,* March 14, 1999.

[33]Pamela Druckerman, "As Brazil Booms, Citibank Is Racing to Catch Up," *Wall Street Journal,* September 11, 2000, p. A30.

[34]"PC Producers Find China to Be a Chaotic Market," *Asian Wall Street Journal,* April 9, 1996, p. 1.

[35]See C. Samuel Craig and Susan P. Douglas, *International Marketing Research* (New York: Wiley, 1999), pp. 306–325, for a detailed listing of secondary sources of information.

[36]William H. Davidson, "Market Similarity and Market Selection: Implications for International Market Strategy," *Journal of Business Research,* December 1983: 439–456.

[37]"Greece is OECD's Most Strike Prone Nation," *Financial Times,* April 9, 1998: 7.

[38]Davidson, "Market Similarity and Market Selection."

[39]Shawna O'Grady and Henry L. Lane, "The Psychic Distance Paradox," *Journal of International Business Studies* 27, 2 (Second Quarter 1996): 319, 324–325.

[40]"The Caucasus, a Region Where Worlds Collide," *The Economist,* August 19, 2000.

[41]Helmut Maucher, "Global Strategies of Nestle," *European Management Journal* 7, 1(1989): 92–96.

[42]P&G Moves Forward with Reorganization," *Chemical Market Reporter,* February 1, 1999: 12.

[43]"Who Favors Branding with Euro Approach?" *Advertising Age International,* May 25, 1992: 1–16.

[44]"In Pursuit of the Elusive Euroconsumer," *Wall Street Journal,* April 23, 1992, p. B1.

9 Global Market Entry Strategies

Even the Arts are going global. Russia's Bolshoi Ballet has actively sought overseas expansion since the collapse of the Soviet Union left the world-famous dance troupe strapped for funds. The Guggenheim art museum in New York, concerned with its limited endowment, has also expanded into foreign markets. But what is the best way for ballet companies and art museums to enter foreign markets? Traditionally, they exported their product by taking their dancers or art exhibits on tour. Today other market entry options are being employed. The Bolshoi has licensed its name to schools in Brazil and Tokyo and recently announced a similar move into Australia. The Guggenheim has established subsidiary branches in Bilbao, Venice, and Berlin and plans to open another in Rio de Janeiro.[1] Even the Vatican is considering ways to enter world markets by licensing the images from its repository of manuscripts, prints, coins, and art work to interested companies in the fields of collectibles, giftware, apparel, and décor.[2]

Any enterprise, whether a for-profit company or a not-for-profit museum, that pursues a global strategy must determine the type of presence it expects

Chapter Outline

Learning Objectives

After studying this chapter, you should be able to:

▶ Differentiate among market entry options—indirect exporting, direct exporting, licensing, franchising, contract manufacturing, assembly, and full-scale integrated manufacturing—and note the conditions under which each is an appropriate strategy.

▶ Explain the role of export management companies, export agents, and export consortiums.

▶ Note the ways in which the Internet has affected the international entry strategies employed by firms.

▶ List the pros and cons of establishing wholly owned subsidiaries and the pros and cons of establishing joint ventures.

▶ Compare and contrast technology-based, production-based, and distribution-based strategic alliances.

▶ Explain when entering a market by acquisition is desirable.

▶ Define entry strategy configuration, bundling, and unbundling, and explain their significance to market entry strategies.

▶ Explain why market exit—and possibly re-entry—strategies might be necessary.

to maintain in every market where it competes. A company may choose to export to the new market, or it may decide to produce locally. It may prefer full ownership of a local operation, or it may seek partners. Once a commitment has been made, changes can be difficult and costly. Therefore, it is important to approach these decisions with the utmost care. Not only is the financial return to the company at stake, but the extent to which the company can implement its global marketing strategy also depends on these decisions. In this chapter, we concentrate on the major entry strategies by explaining each alternative in detail and citing relevant company experiences. An overview of possible entry strategies appears in Figure 9.1.

► *Exporting as an Entry Strategy*

Exporting to a foreign market is a strategy that many companies follow for at least some of their markets. Few countries offer a large enough market to justify local production. Exporting allows a company to manufacture its products for several markets centrally and thus achieve economies of scale. When this occurs, a firm can realize more profits, lower its prices, or sometimes do both. In addition, both transportation costs and government tariffs have fallen considerably in the past 25 years. These conditions make exporting all the more cost-effective.

A firm has two basic options for carrying out its export operations. Markets can be contacted through an intermediary located in the exporter's home country—an approach called **indirect exporting**. Alternatively, markets can be reached directly or through an intermediary located in the foreign market—an approach termed **direct exporting**.

Indirect Exporting

Several types of intermediaries located in the domestic market are ready to assist a manufacturer in contacting international markets or buyers. A major advantage of using a domestic intermediary lies in its knowledge of foreign market conditions. Particularly for companies with little or no experience in

Figure 9.1
Market Entry Strategies

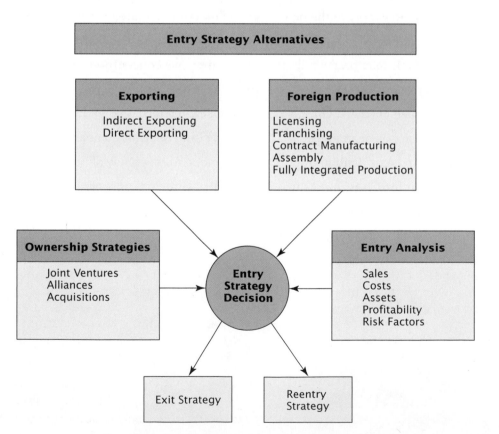

exporting, the use of a domestic intermediary provides the exporter with readily available expertise.

Export Management Company An export management company (EMC) is a firm that handles all aspects of export operations under a contractual agreement. The EMC normally takes responsibility for the marketing research, patent protection, channel credit, and shipping and logistics, as well as for the actual marketing of products in a foreign market or markets. An EMC can operate either as a merchant that takes title to the products or as an agent that does not take title but provides services for a fee or commission. The population of EMCs is estimated to be 1,200 firms in the United States; they represent some 10,000 manufacturers and account for 10 percent of manufactured exports.

Arrangements between an EMC and a manufacturer will vary, depending on the services offered and the volume expected. The advantages of an EMC include the following: (1) Little or no investment is required to enter the international marketplace. (2) No in-house personnel are required. (3) The EMC offers an established network of sales offices as well as international marketing and distribution knowledge. The main disadvantage is that the manufacturer gives up direct control of the international sales and marketing effort. Also, if the product has a long purchase cycle and requires a large amount of market development and education, the EMC may not expend the necessary effort to penetrate a new market.

Export Agents Export agents are individuals or firms that also assist manufacturers in exporting goods. They are similar to EMCs, except that they tend to provide more limited services and to focus on one country or one part of the world. Export agents understand all the requirements for moving goods through international channels, but they do not provide all the services that an EMC provides. These agents focus more on the sale and handling of goods. The advantage of using an export agent is that the manufacturer does not need to have an export manager to handle all the documentation and shipping tasks. The main disadvantage is the export agent's limited market coverage. To cover different parts of the world, a firm would need the services of numerous export agents.

Direct Exporting

A company engages in direct exporting when it exports directly to customers or solely through intermediaries located in foreign markets. In other words, no domestic intermediary is involved. In direct exporting, an exporter must deal with a large number of foreign contacts, possibly one or more for each country the company enters. A direct exporting operation requires more expertise, management time, and financial resources than does indirect exporting, but it gives the company a greater degree of control over its distribution channels.

Independent Distributor versus Marketing Subsidiary To handle the marketing of its products within its target market, the company must choose between relying solely on local independent distributors and establishing its own marketing subsidiary. In making this choice, the company must consider costs, control, and legal restrictions.

An independent distributor earns a margin on the selling price of the products. Although using an independent distributor entails no direct cost to the exporter, the margin the distributor earns represents an opportunity that is lost to the exporter. By switching to a sales subsidiary to carry out the distributor's tasks, the exporter can keep the margin previously paid to the distributor. For example, say a manufacturer of electronic machinery exports products priced at $7,500 each (at the factory in Boston). With airfreight, tariffs, and taxes added, the product's landed costs amount to $9,000. An independent distributor will have to price the products at $13,500 to earn a desired gross margin of 33 ⅓ percent, or $4,500 per machine.

Alternatively, the exporter can set up a wholly owned marketing subsidiary, in this case consisting of a manager, a sales manager, several sales agents, clerical staff, a warehousing operation, and the rental of both an office and a warehouse location. If the total estimated cost of these arrangements is $450,000 annually, the firm can break even at sales of 100 machines.

With increasing volume, the incentive to start a marketing subsidiary grows. On the other hand, if the anticipated sales volume is small, using the independent distributor will be more efficient because sales are channeled through a distributor who is maintaining the necessary staff for several product lines. For example, Sega, the Japanese video game company, had to close its marketing subsidiaries in Austria, Belgium, and the Netherlands when sales slumped in Europe. In those countries, as in many other European markets, Sega decided to market through independent local agents, serving only the United Kingdom, France, Germany, and Spain through company-owned marketing subsidiaries.[3]

World Beat 9.1 *Women Leap into Foreign Markets*

When it comes to exporting, female entrepreneurs don't tiptoe tentatively into foreign markets. They prefer to make the leap quickly, according to a study by Equinox Management Consultants, which provides insights into Canada's estimated 10,000 to 26,000 export businesses owned by women.

Thirty percent of 254 female business owners in a Canadian survey said they began exporting as soon as they launched their businesses. And 55 percent of respondents made their first foreign sale within 2 years of starting their companies. Many respondents reported achieving profitability shortly after jumping into the global marketplace. Fifty-seven percent said exporting became profitable within 1 year, whereas 22 percent of businesses said it took more than 5 years.

Contrary to the overall profile of businesses owned by women—a profile that is highly service-oriented—these exporters are primarily product-based firms. Seventy-six percent are manufacturing products that range from crafts to chemicals, and only 22 percent are peddling services. The rest are retailers or wholesalers.

The United States proved to be the largest trading partner, where 72 percent of exporters are conducting business. Sixty percent are making sales in Asia, 58 percent in Europe, and 30 percent in Central and South America.

Source: Dawn Walton, "Women Leap into Foreign Markets," *The Globe and Mail*, March 9, 1999, p. B10.

Research has also shown that firms marketing products that require the development of special skills or special working relationships with customers tend to have their own marketing subsidiaries.[4] This way the company may better control the delivery of after-sale service. If the firm has definite ideas about the correct way to price and promote its products, it may wish to establish a marketing subsidiary as well. The subsidiary could then implement the full strategy for the marketing mix, such as setting prices, developing advertising programs, and choosing media.

Still, a commitment to a marketing subsidiary should not be made without careful evaluation of all the costs involved. The operation of a subsidiary adds a new dimension to a company's international marketing operation. It requires a financial commitment in a foreign country, primarily for the financing of accounts receivable and inventory. Also, the operation of a marketing subsidiary entails a number of general administrative expenses that are essentially fixed in nature.

When General Motors decided to export its Saturn car to Japan, it opted to open its own marketing subsidiary. With the eventual goal of selling 30,000 vehicles annually, the company sidestepped Yanase, the Japanese importer that handled its Opel cars.[5] However, Saturn could find only about 10 dealerships to carry its cars. As a result, it sold only 1,400 units in its first 16 months of operations in Japan.[6] Going it alone in a difficult market turned out to be much more difficult than Saturn had anticipated.

Firms may also face government restrictions on the use of wholly owned marketing subsidiaries. Although these constraints are declining with trade liberalization, they persist in some developing countries such as Saudi Arabia. Exporters to Saudi Arabia have traditionally been required to use Saudi agents or establish a marketing subsidiary with a Saudi partner.

Cooperating for Export Companies that compete against each other in their domestic market may sometimes unite to address export markets. Brazil's Ministry of Development, Industry and Foreign Trade promotes such **export consortiums** wherein companies unite to share the logistical and promotion costs of entering foreign markets. Brazil's two largest frozen meat processors have formed a consortium in order to target Russia and selected countries in Africa, the Middle East, and the Caribbean. These markets currently account for less than 3 percent of the exports of either firm. However, they expect their consortium, BRF Trading Company, to sell about $150 million in these markets in the first year of operation. It is very unlikely that Brazilian antitrust law would allow such cooperation in the domestic market, but governments often encourage it in export markets.[7]

Export cooperation can also occur among small and medium-sized enterprises (SMEs). One study of exporter SMEs in the Jutland peninsula of Denmark revealed that 83 percent cooperated with other firms in the same industrial sector. For example, a manufacturer of windmills exported to California purchased the motors from another local SME. Firms in the textile and clothing sector mounted mutual exhibits at trade fairs. Manufacturers of wooden furniture might contribute different products—a desk, chair, or bookshelf—to a commonly marketed export suite. The success of these smaller ventures in competitive export markets can be attributed in part to sort of this cooperation.[8]

Exporting and the Internet The Internet has greatly increased the ability of firms to export directly. The impact has been felt by small and medium-sized firms (SMEs) as well as larger multinationals. In 1987, SMEs accounted for about one-quarter of total U.S. exports. By 2001 this figure had risen to about one-third. The Internet can be credited with supporting this trend. SMEs can take advantage of virtual trade missions, video conferencing, and online ordering. They can reach markets with daily communication and advertising without the need to send full-time salespeople into the field or to employ traditional export management companies.[9]

Exporters on the Internet can face language problems, and the fulfillment side of e-exporting remains a challenge as well. Companies face various cross-border issues involved with completing a sale, such as shipping the product, collecting funds, and providing after-sale service to customers all over the world. New export management consultants have arisen to help with a number of these problems. One such company, Next Linx, was founded by Rajiv Uppal, an Indian-born engineer working in the United States. Uppal realized that new e-exporters still needed to know that their product would be hit with an education tax in Pakistan or that the same product would be subject to state tariffs as well as a national tariff in Brazil. Exporters of wine to the European Union would face the EU's 132 different categories of wine, each with its own tariff schedule. The Next Linx system was designed to calculate import duties, taxes, and shipping costs. It determines whether a customer's product needs an export license and whether the importer is located in an embargoed country. It then prints all relevant shipment documentation at a cost of as little as $10 per order. A number of competitors have entered this market as well. A key to competitiveness is the ability of any online export consultant to stay alert to the constant regulatory and logistics changes that affect its customers.[10]

▶ *Foreign Production as an Entry Strategy*

Licensing

With licensing, a company assigns the right to a copyright or patent (which protect a product, technology, or process) and/or a trademark (which protects a product name) to another company for a fee or royalty. Proprietary information, or trade secrets not protected by patents, can also be licensed. Using licensing as a method of market entry, a company can gain market presence without making an equity investment. The foreign company, or licensee, gains the right to exploit the patent or trademark commercially on either an exclusive (the sole right to sell in a certain geographic region) or a nonexclusive basis.

Sometimes the licensee initiates the contract. Infopro, the largest information-technology media group in Taiwan, specializes in publishing Chinese-language editions of American publications under license. It recently entered a licensing agreement with the Harvard Business School to produce a Chinese version of the prestigious management journal *Harvard Business Review*. The new *Infopro Harvard Business Review* is designed to have about 70 percent of its content translated from the original American text, supplemented with locally researched articles on business and management techniques.[11]

Licenses are signed for a variety of time periods. Depending on the investment needed to enter the market, the foreign licensee may insist on a longer licensing period to recover the initial investment. Typically, the licensee makes all the necessary capital investments (machinery, inventory, etc.) and markets the products in the assigned sales territories, which may consist of one or several countries. Licensing agreements are subject to negotiation and tend to vary considerably from company to company and from industry to industry.

Reasons for Licensing Licensing can be very attractive for some companies; an example is Everlast Worldwide Inc. Since 1910 Everlast has been the preeminent brand in the world of boxing equipment. Its products have been used for training and professional fights by leading figures in the sport. Everlast's licensed products generate over $200 million in retail sales each year, prompting the company to create a new management position: *senior vice-president of global licensing.*[12]

Companies use licensing for many reasons. A company may not have the knowledge or the time to engage more actively in international marketing. If so, it can still realize income from foreign markets by using licensees. Licensing may also be employed for less attractive foreign markets, allowing the firm's scarce managerial resources to be concentrated on more lucrative markets. The market potential of the target country may be too small to support a new manufacturing or marketing operation. A licensee may have the option of adding the licensed product to an ongoing operation, thereby reducing the need for a large investment in new fixed assets. Finally, some smaller companies with a product in high demand may not be able to satisfy demand unless licenses are granted to other companies with sufficient manufacturing capacity.[13]

In some countries where the political or economic situation appears uncertain, a licensing agreement may avoid the potential risk associated with investing in fixed facilities. Both commercial and political risks are absorbed by the licensee. In other countries, governments favor the granting of licenses to independent local manufacturers as a means of building up a local industry. In such cases, a foreign manufacturer may prefer to team up with a capable licensee despite a large market size, because other forms of entry may not be possible.

Licensing can also help global firms enter difficult markets. International paint firms, with operations in both Europe and North America, have often had difficulty penetrating the Japanese market. As a result, many have signed licensing agreements with Japanese firms. PPG of the United States licensed Nippon Paint to produce its line of automotive paints. In other markets, however, PPG decided to stay away from licensing.[14]

Licensing can also be a way of entering many markets quickly. The French pharmaceutical company Sanofi used licensing especially effectively to accelerate its internationalization. A recent entrant into the drug business in 1997, the company soon realized that it could do only a limited number of research projects if it had to bring its new products from lab to trial and eventual market entry. Sanofi therefore decided to engage in active licensing, letting other pharmaceutical companies market its newly discovered drugs. In the case of Plavix, a drug that reduces the risk of blood clots in heart patients, Sanofi licensed Bristol-Myers Squibb to produce and market the drug in the United States. With this strategy, Sanofi quickly advanced to twenty-fifth place in the pharmaceutical industry and achieved sales of $3.5 billion.[15]

Disadvantages of Licensing A major disadvantage of licensing is the company's substantial dependence on the local licensee to produce revenues and thus royalties. **Royalties** are usually paid as a percentage of sales volume. Once a license is granted, royalties are paid only if the licensee is capable of performing an effective marketing job. Because the local company's marketing skills may be less developed, revenues from licensing may suffer accordingly. Although there is a great variation from one industry to another, licensing fees in general are substantially lower than the profits that can be made through exporting or local manufacturing. Depending on the product, licensing fees may range anywhere between 1 percent and 20 percent of sales, 3 to 5 percent being more typical for industrial products.

Ironically, if a local licensee is too successful, an international firm may reconsider the wisdom of licensing. More direct participation in a successful market can reap higher rewards in profits than mere licensing fees. Such a situation arose between Mexico's Televisa and Los Angeles–based Univision. Televisa is the world's largest producer of Spanish-language television programming. Univision is the leader in the rapidly growing U.S. Hispanic media market. Hispanics account for 12 percent of the U.S. population, and Univision has captured 80 percent of Hispanic television viewers. Under a licensing agreement dating from the early 1990s, Univision received the right of first refusal on Televisa's programming. Most of Univision's programming is from Televisa, but the Mexican company receives only 9 percent of Univision's advertising revenue. In 2001, Televisa proposed a partial merger with its U.S. licensee, because U.S. law forbids foreign entities to own more than 25 percent of a U.S. broadcaster. Although Univision was not enthusiastic about the idea, Televisa threatened to look for new partners if its offer was not considered.[16]

Some licensing contracts include provisions for the licenser to increase its participation if it eventually wishes to do so. Hutchinson Whampoa Ltd. of Hong Kong announced that it was forming a new company that would license Priceline's patented bidding system to allow consumers to purchase tickets online. The service would be targeted at Hong Kong, Singapore, and Taiwan, with a later roll-out to other Asian countries. As part of the arrangement, Priceline would be given the option of eventually buying up to 50 percent of the new company.[17]

Another potential disadvantage of licensing is the uncertainty of product quality. A foreign company's image may suffer if a local licensee markets a product of substandard quality. For this reason, firms often seek licensees based on their production knowledge and reputation for quality. For example, U.S.-based Miller Brewing Company recently decided to expand into the French and Dutch markets using a Dutch licensee. The licensee is responsible for the production and marketing of Miller's largest international brand, Miller's Genuine Draft. It is essential that the licensee maintain Miller's quality standards in these important markets. Therefore, Miller selected a licensee well known as a quality brewer.[18] Even when a quality licensee is located, however, ensuring uniform quality requires the licenser to provide additional resources that may reduce the profitability of the licensing activity.

Licensing will also require a certain commitment of management time and resources. Licensees may need to be trained. Appropriate records must be kept, and licenser audits must be conducted. Serious consideration must be given to problems that could arise. In case of disagreements between licenser and licensee, there must be provisions for dispute resolution. In the context of which national law will the contract be interpreted? How and in which country will arbitration take place? What are the conditions for termination of the licensing contract?

The possibility of nurturing a potential competitor is viewed by many companies as a final disadvantage of licensing. Licenses are usually limited to a specific time period. Licensees will use the same technology independently after the license has expired and will, therefore, turn into a competitor. This is less of a concern if the licensed technology changes quickly or if a valuable copyrighted brand name is involved. Of course, firms must be careful that they—and not their licensee—hold the copyright to their brand in each national market.

Franchising

Franchising is a special form of licensing in which the franchiser makes a total marketing program available, including the brand name, logo, products, and method of operation. Usually, the franchise agreement is more comprehensive than a regular licensing agreement, inasmuch as the total operation of the franchisee is prescribed.

According to the International Franchise Association, there are about 15,000 franchising companies worldwide. The Internet has had a profound impact on the industry and has helped fuel its recent growth. Franchisers use websites to communicate with current franchisees as well as to recruit new ones. Dot.com companies have also joined the ranks of franchisers.[19]

Numerous companies that successfully exploited franchising in their home market are exploiting opportunities abroad. Among these companies are McDonald's, Kentucky Fried Chicken (KFC), Burger King, and other U.S. fast-food chains with operations in Latin America, Asia, Europe, and the Middle East. About 80 percent of all McDonald's restaurants are franchised, and the firm operates about 24,500 stores in 116 countries.[20] Service companies such as Holiday Inn, Hertz, and Manpower have also successfully used franchising to enter foreign markets.

The United States is home to the greatest number of franchisers. As of 2001, there were 2,200 franchise systems in operation in the United States, compared to 890 in Japan, 450 in Australia, and 268 in Malaysia. Franchising accounts for about 40 percent of retail sales in the United States, compared to about 5 percent in Malaysia.[21] In China the percentage drops to only 2 percent.[22]

However, growth rates for franchising are higher in many non-U.S. markets. In recent years, the market in the United States has only grown 5 to 10 percent, compared to about 15 percent in Europe and 20 to 25 percent in Latin America.[23]

In 1997 there were only 30 franchising operations in Venezuela and 300 retail outlets. These figures grew to 1,900 franchising operations and 18,000 retail outlets by 2001, making Venezuela the third largest franchise country in Latin America, after Brazil and Mexico. Poor economic conditions in the country probably contributed to the industry's growth as many laid-off professionals became franchisees. Many even became franchisers themselves, including an economics professor who began a franchise chain of coconut drink kiosks. Such local chains have begun to challenge the dominance of the multinational franchisers. In 1997, 70 percent of franchisers operating in Venezuela were foreign. By 2001 only 45 percent were foreign.[24]

In fact, franchisers of many national origins have entered international markets. Singapore-based Informatics Holdings Inc. franchises computer training schools in Asia. Interbrew franchises its Belgium Beer Café. The Japanese company Yohinoy D&C has opened 91 stores in California that sell gydun, a seasoned beef and rice dish. Even an Egyptian college student who began exporting hookahs, Egypt's traditional water pipes, to the United States has recently branched into franchising. He supplies 50 accounts with a complete hookah system for a water pipe café, including equipment, staff training, and management advice.[25]

Many franchisees worldwide are individual entrepreneurs. In some countries, companies or wealthy individuals buy **master franchises** that give them exclusive rights to a whole city or even a whole country. Master franchisees have traditionally been sophisticated partners of established multinational franchise chains. With its rapid global growth, however, the franchising industry has been hit with numerous complaints and has even been plagued by fraud in the past few years. One individual on the Internet actually claimed his government had privatized its Consumer Protection Agency, for which he was selling local franchises.[26] As a result of the surge in complaints, many countries are tightening their franchising laws to help protect franchisees.

The International Franchise Association gives tips on how to avoid franchising pitfalls. The U.S. Federal Trade Commission's website lists complaints against franchisers. Check out these and other franchise links on our website.

Local Manufacturing

Another widely practiced form of market entry is the local manufacturing of a company's products. Many companies find it advantageous to manufacture in the host market instead of supplying that market with products made elsewhere. Sometimes local production represents a greater commitment to a market. Numerous factors, such as local costs, market size, tariffs, labor laws, and political considerations, may affect a choice to manufacture locally. The actual type of local production depends on the arrangements made. It may be contract manufacturing, assembly, or fully integrated production.

Contract Manufacturing Under contract manufacturing, a company arranges to have its products manufactured by an independent local company on a contractual basis. The local manufacturer's responsibility is restricted to production. The local producer manufactures in accordance with orders from the international firm. The products are then turned over to the international company, which assumes the marketing responsibility for sales, promotion, and distribution. In a way, the international company "rents" the production capacity of the local firm to avoid establishing its own plant and to circumvent barriers that prevent the import of its products.

Typically, contract manufacturing is chosen for countries with a low-volume market potential combined with high tariff protection. In such situations, local production appears advantageous to avoid high tariffs, but the local market does not support the volume necessary to justify the building of a single plant. These conditions tend to exist in the smaller countries of Central America, Africa, and Asia. Contract manufacturing is also employed where the production technology involved is widely available. Otherwise, contract manufacturers would not have the necessary know-how. If research and development and/or marketing are of crucial importance in the success of the product, then contract manufacturing can be an attractive option, especially when excess capacity in an industry makes manufacturing the least profitable part of the product's value chain. However, contract manufacturing is viable only when an appropriate local manufacturer can be located.

Assembly By moving to an assembly operation, the international firm locates a portion of the manufacturing process in the foreign country. Typically, assembly consists only of the last stages of manufacturing and depends on a ready supply of components or manufactured parts to be shipped in from another country. (In the chemical and pharmaceutical industry, this latter stage is referred to as **compounding**.) Assembly usually involves the heavy use of labor rather than extensive investment in capital outlays or equipment. Sometimes host governments force firms to establish assembly operations either by banning the import of fully assembled products or by charging excessive tariffs on them.

Motor vehicle manufacturers have made extensive use of assembly operations in numerous countries. General Motors has maintained major integrated production units only in the United States, Germany, the United Kingdom, Brazil, and Australia. In many other countries, disassembled vehicles arrive at assembly operations that produce the final product on the spot.

The opening of the Vietnam market in 1991 led to a series of car assembly operations. Carmakers have signed twelve assembly operations agreements, most of them on a joint venture basis. Many of the world's leading auto manufacturers are represented, such as Daewoo of Korea; Mitsubishi, Daihatsu, Toyota, and Isuzu of Japan; and Ford and Chrysler of the United States. With annual demand estimated at only 35,000 new units per year, it will be some time before the market is large enough to support full-scale manufacturing operations for most car companies.[27]

Full-Scale Integrated Production Establishing a fully integrated local production unit is the greatest commitment a company can make for a foreign market. Building a plant involves a substantial capital outlay. Companies do so only where demand appears ensured. International companies can have any number of reasons for establishing factories in foreign countries. These reasons are related primarily to market demand or cost considerations. Often, the main reason is to take advantage of lower costs in a country, thus providing a better basis for competing with local firms or other foreign companies already present. Also, high transportation costs and tariffs may make imported goods noncompetitive.

Establishing Local Operations to Gain or Defend Market Position Some companies build a plant to gain new business and customers. Local production can represent a strong commitment to a market and is often the only way to convince clients to switch suppliers. This is of particular importance in industrial markets, where service and reliability of supply are main factors in the choice of product or supplier. In some developing countries, establishing local operations may be the only way to enter a local market, although this requirement is becoming more rare with the spread of trade liberalization and the impact of the World Trade Organization.

At other times, companies establish production abroad to protect markets already built through exporting. Such markets can be threatened by protectionist government policies or by relative changes in currency exchange rates. In the late 1980s, the surge in market share of imported Japanese cars prompted the United States to threaten Japan with import quotas if it didn't place voluntary restrictions on car exports to the United States. Also, the Japanese yen had begun to appreciate against the dollar, making Japanese imports more expensive. In response to these threats, Japanese car manufacturers began to build factories in the United States to protect their market share. In 1982, Honda became the first Japanese car manufacturer to set up production in the United States. By 1993, Japanese car manufacturers produced more cars in the United States than they exported there from Japan. Japan's major producers are Toyota, Honda, Nissan, Mitsubishi, Mazda, and Suzuki.

Following an established customer can also be a reason for setting up plants abroad. In many industries, important suppliers want to nurture a relationship by establishing plants near customer locations. When customers build new plants elsewhere, suppliers move too. The automobile industry, with its intricate network of hundreds of component suppliers feeding into the assembly plants, is a good example of how companies follow customers. As Japanese car manufacturers built plants in the United States and Canada, their Japanese suppliers built some 400 component plants in these two countries as well.[28]

Shifting Production Abroad to Save Costs Firms can shift production abroad to save costs in order to be competitive in the host market. When Mercedes-Benz was looking at new opportunities in the automotive market, the company targeted the luxury sports utility vehicle segment. In the United States, its major market, the company was suffering a 30 percent cost disadvantage against major Japanese and U.S. competitors in this segment. Despite the fact that the company had never before produced cars outside Germany, Mercedes-Benz decided to locate a new factory to produce such vehicles in the United States, where total labor, components, and shipping costs were among the lowest in the developed world.[29]

Some products may be too costly to transport long distances, and this makes them poor candidates for export. Fresh orange juice is one such product. Brazil is currently the top producer of orange juice in the world, whereas the United States consumes 40 percent of all orange juice. The U.S. market has a strong demand for fresh, not-from-concentrate orange juice that sells for higher prices. This fresh product is particularly costly to ship because it consists mainly of water.[30] During the 1990s, Brazilian orange juice firms bought land to develop orange groves in Florida. By 2001, multinationals with Brazilian ties accounted for about half of Florida's orange juice industry.[31]

Sometimes, international firms with plants in Taiwan, Malaysia, Thailand, and other foreign countries may have little intention of penetrating these markets with the help of their new factories. Instead, they locate abroad to take advantage of favorable conditions that reduce the manufacturing costs of products that are sold elsewhere. This strategy has been employed by many U.S. companies in the electronics industry and has more recently been adopted by Japanese and European firms as well. Morinaga, Japan's leading dairy company, built a new powdered-milk plant in China not so much to enter the Chinese market as to establish a low-cost base from which to capture share in other Asian markets. Such decisions of a sourcing or production nature are not necessarily tied to a company's market entry strategy but may have important implications for its global competitiveness.

Manufacturing and Intrafirm Licensing Although international licensing arrangements were originally designed as an alternative for firms manufacturing abroad, today they are sometimes used in conjunction with a firm's own manufacturing operations. A firm may license its trademark or technology to its own manufacturing subsidiary if taxes on royalties are less than taxes on repatriated profits. Such an arrangement might also be employed when a subsidiary is not wholly owned but, rather, shared with a local partner. A licensing contract with its own joint venture can give an international firm a greater and more guaranteed payback on its contribution to the venture.

▶ *Ownership Strategies*

As we have noted, companies investing in foreign markets also face ownership decisions. Do they want to establish a wholly owned subsidiary or a joint venture? Alternatively, they may decide to explore longer-term contractual relationships, or alliances.

Wholly Owned Subsidiaries

Wholly owned subsidiaries are operations in a host country that are fully owned by a foreign parent firm. They can involve marketing, assembly, or full-scale integrated production operations. Firms must have the necessary capital investment and must be committed to devoting the management time necessary to establish and run an overseas operation on their own. There are, of course, advantages to this entry option. The firm has a free hand to establish the strategy for the subsidiary. It is also able to keep all the profits of the subsidiary and need not share them with partners. For these reasons, national markets that are more strategically important may be good candidates for a wholly owned subsidiary. Such a subsidiary can also be more easily integrated into a global network. For example, a parent can allot the U.S. export market to its wholly owned subsidiary in Taiwan. If relative production and transportation costs change, however, the firm can take the U.S. market away from the Taiwanese subsidiary and give that market to its wholly owned Mexican subsidiary. There would be no local Taiwanese partner to oppose this move.

If firms do not have the resources to invest in a wholly owned subsidiary, or if host government restrictions disallow them, companies can consider entering a market with a joint venture or other alliance partner.

Joint Ventures

Under a joint venture arrangement, the foreign company invites an outside partner to share stock ownership in the new unit. Traditionally, the other partner has been a local firm or individual located in the host market. The particular equity participation of the partners may vary, with some companies accepting either a minority or a majority position. In most cases, international firms prefer wholly owned subsidiaries for reasons of control; once a joint venture partner secures part of the operation, the international firm can no longer function independently. This sometimes leads to inefficiencies and disputes over responsibility for the venture. If an international firm has strictly defined operating procedures for budgeting, planning, manufacturing, and marketing, getting the joint venture to accept the same methods of operation may be difficult. Problems may also arise when the partner wants to maximize dividend payout instead of reinvestment, or when the capital of the venture has to be increased and one side is unable to raise the required funds. Experience has shown that joint ventures can be successful if the partners share the same goals and if one partner accepts primary responsibility for operational matters.

Reasons for Entering into Joint Ventures Despite the potential for problems, joint ventures are common because they offer important advantages to the foreign firm. Sometimes the partner is an important customer who is willing to contract for a portion of the new unit's output in return for an equity participation. In markets where host governments disallow wholly owned investments, joint ventures with a local partner may be the only alternative. For example, the Vietnamese government has steered a number of multinational companies into joint ventures with local partners, many of whom do not provide capital contributions equal to their equity shares in these ventures.[32]

If a firm is trying to enter many foreign markets quickly, joint ventures may help leverage scarce capital and managerial resources. By bringing in a partner, the company can share the business and political risks for a new venture. Furthermore, the partner may have important skills or contacts of value to the international firm. In some cases, the partner may provide local manufacturing or excellent government or distribution contacts. Even in e-marketing, an international joint venture partner can sometimes be advisable. German-based e-financialdepot.com Inc. signed a joint venture with EqTechnologies Inc. (EQTI) to launch its financial services—such as marketing and trading technologies and online mortgages and insurances services—in the Middle East and Africa. EQTI, a management consulting firm, focuses on taking successful U.S. and European high-tech and Internet companies into Africa and the Middle East. It was chosen for its excellent connections in the region.[33]

Many international firms have entered Japan via joint ventures. During the 1960s and 1970s, the Japanese market was viewed as a difficult environment, much different from other industrialized markets. Government regulations tightly controlled equity participation in ventures. When McDonald's entered Japan in 1971, it did so in a joint venture with Fujita & Company, a trading company owned by private Japanese businessman Den Fujita. Fujita was adept at locating real estate and obtaining government permits for new outlets. He also insisted on some practices that differed from the typical U.S. approach of McDonald's, such as opening the first store in the fashionable Ginza shopping district rather than going to a suburban location.[34] The chain grew enormously; just 27 years after its entry into the market, McDonald's has 2,400 restaurants operating in Japan, with sales of more than $3 billion. Each year the chain adds 400 to 500 new restaurants.[35]

Gillette, the U.S. razor blade manufacturer, has extensive experience with joint ventures in China. In the early 1980s, the company formed its first, small joint venture, called Shenmei Daily Use Products, with Chinese authorities in a province northeast of Beijing. Then a second joint venture was formed with the Shanghai Razor Blade Factory, and Gillette obtained 70 percent ownership and management control.[36] The Shanghai plant evolved into Asia's largest blade plant. Gillette's joint venture now controls 80 percent of China's $51 million razor blade market.[37]

With the liberalization of industry and trade in Eastern Europe and Russia over the past few years, many international firms have pursued joint ventures in those countries. Originally, Western firms were not allowed to own any stock, capital, or real estate. Restrictions on foreign investments have now been lifted in many countries, and foreign firms are allowed to start new companies with full ownership. However, because of the difficulties of operating in these markets, many foreign firms continue to prefer joint ventures with local partners. For example, Gillette established a joint venture with Leninets, a Russian consumer products company. Gillette built a $60 million plant and holds a 65 percent stake in the operation. [38]

Of course, in order to enter into a joint venture, an international firm must find an available partner. Table 9.1 gives some indication why local partners seek to establish joint ventures with international firms. A survey of Mexican companies identified access to technology and association with recognized international brands as the two most often cited reasons why local firms sought U.S. partners. In liberalizing markets such as Mexico, some

Table 9.1 *What Motivates Mexican Firms to Seek U.S. Partners?*

MOTIVATION	PERCENTAGE OF RESPONDENTS
Access to technology	71
Access to recognized brand	56
Product/service knowledge of partner	47
Access to products and services	40
Supplier access	33
Access to new products/market areas	27
Short-term credit	24
Access to raw materials	22
Customer access	22
Reduce costs	22
Block competitors	20
Capital access	18
Access to marketing infrastructure	16
Geographic market access	16
Reduce risks	13
Co-opt competitor	13
Geographic market knowledge of partner	13
Access to long-term credit	11

Source: Kate Gillespie and Hildy J. Teegen, "Market Liberalization and International Alliance Formation: The Mexican Paradigm," *Columbia Journal of World Business* (Winter 1995): 63.

firms seek international ties to become more competitive and thus block new competitors from entering their previously protected markets. Others go so far as to try to co-opt potential competitors by directly partnering with them.

Joint Venture Divorce: A Constant Danger Not all joint ventures are successful or fulfill their partners' expectations. Various studies have placed the instability rates of joint ventures at between 25 and 75 percent.[39] In most cases, the ventures are either liquidated or taken over by one of the original partners.[40]

There are a number of reasons for ending a joint venture. Sometimes the regulations that force foreign firms to take local partners are rescinded. When China first opened to foreign investment, foreign firms were required to partner with Chinese enterprises. Recently China has begun considering wholly owned foreign investments. This has caused many foreign partners to seek exclusive ownership of their Chinese joint ventures. When joint ventures are used to enter many international markets relatively cheaply and quickly, a parent firm may wish later to increase its stake in the venture or even reclaim full control when financial resources are more readily available. Starbucks began its international expansion in 1996 and estimates that it will operate in 1,500 overseas locations by 2003. In some markets, Starbucks stores operate under joint venture agreements in which the company holds about 20 percent. The company plans eventually to increase this stake to at least 50 percent.[41]

Sometimes the choice of partner turns out to be less than ideal. Cristal, a U.K.-based food hygiene consultancy, advises hotels, food processing plants, and restaurants around the world. Joint ventures have played an important part in the firm's international expansion. In Egypt, however, Cristal chose a well-established partner with expertise in engineering rather than in tourism. Trying to learn the tourism industry and the food hygiene industry in a short time proved overwhelming. Cristal had to buy back shares from the partner and take over management of the venture.[42]

At times, problems can arise between parents over the strategic direction of the joint venture. Brasil Telecom is a joint venture between Telecom Italia and Opportunity, a local Brazilian investment company. Despite being one of Brazil's largest fixed-line telecommunications companies, Brasil Telecom found itself headed for arbitration in London when its two parents became deadlocked over expansion options. The Italian parent wanted to move quickly into mobile telephone operations. Opportunity wanted the joint venture to pursue what it thought were more profitable businesses, such as acting as an Internet service provider. The relationship between the parent companies became increasingly hostile, and both wished to take full control of the joint venture.[43]

In some cases, however, joint venture divorce can be amiable. Teijin of Japan dissolved its joint venture with U.S.-based Molecular Simulations (MSI), a major global player in computerized chemistry. The negotiated settlement specified that Teijin would receive $10 million from Pharma-copeia, the company that had since acquired MSI. Teijin was willing to sell its share in the joint venture because it had already accomplished its objective—gaining adequate expertise in computerized chemistry through the venture.[44]

Even when one parent agrees to sell its stake in the venture, buying out partners can be expensive. Glaxo, the large U.K.-based pharmaceutical company, entered Japan via a joint venture in 1994. Until recently, a local partner

World Beat 9.2 *Flying Solo Overseas*

You would think that in this age of globalization, international joint ventures would multiply like mushrooms after a spring rain. Partnering with local business, after all, would seem like a good way for a company to get a foothold in a foreign market.

In reality, the past two decades have seen a decreased reliance on international joint ventures by U.S. multinationals, according to a study by Mihir A. Desai and C. Fritz Foley of Harvard University and James R. Hines, Jr., of the University of Michigan. In 1997, the latest year for which data are available, joint ventures made up only 20 percent of U.S. multinationals' foreign affiliates. That's down from 29 percent in 1982, a drop that probably reflects both a decline in the number of new joint ventures and a tendency to shut down existing ones. At the same time, a record 80 percent of all affiliates were wholly owned.

Moreover, the trend continues today, report the authors, who draw that conclusion on the basis of their conversations with managers. The problem is that globe-spanning multinational corporations and their local partners have different interests. For one thing, the multinationals want to move production to the countries where demand is growing, whereas their joint venture partners want to keep the factories at home running at full capacity. Also, the multinationals may want their affiliates to offer discounts to other subsidiaries of the same company, whereas the local partners want to maximize profits at home. As a result, companies increasingly prefer to buy their foreign affiliates outright rather than dealing with the hassle of coordinating with a partner.

Source: Margaret Popper, "Flying Solo Overseas," *Business Week*, May 20, 2002, p. 28.

in Japan was considered necessary for an international company in the medical field, because Japan's health culture is unique. (Among other things, Japanese doctors both prescribe and sell drugs.) However, Glaxo was dissatisfied with its performance in Japan, the world's second largest pharmaceuticals market. Its market share amounted to only 2 percent, compared to 5 percent worldwide. Glaxo decided to assume full control and bought back the other half of its joint venture for almost $600 million.[45]

It is always wise to have a "prenuptial agreement." Yet a surprising number of joint venture agreements fail to acknowledge the possibility of joint venture dissolution. In 1999 AT&T and British Telecom formed a joint venture, Concert, to serve large multinational business customers. A former AT&T executive involved in the negotiations claims that the absence of an exit agreement was deliberate. It was intended to make sure both companies remained committed to the partnership. Two years later, however, the venture was losing $210 million a quarter and was judged a failure by both parents. Without an exit agreement, there was no simple way to determine how Concert's assets—including 75,000 kilometers of fiber optic cable—would be divided.[46]

Strategic Alliances

A more recent phenomenon is the development of a range of strategic alliances. Alliances encompass any relationship between firms that exceeds a simple sales transaction but stops short of a full-scale merger. Thus the traditional joint venture between an MNC and a local company is a form of alliance. So is a contract manufacturing or licensing agreement. However, the term **strategic alliance** is commonly used to denote an alliance involving two or more global firms in which each partner brings a particular skill or resource—usually, they are complementary. By joining forces, each firm expects to profit from the other's experience. Typically, strategic alliances involve technology development, production, or distribution.

Technology-Based Alliances A survey conducted by the Maastricht Economic Research Institute reviewed 4,182 technology-based alliances. Most of these alliances were in the biotechnology and information technology industries. The most commonly cited reasons for entering these alliances were access to markets, exploitation of complementary technology, and a need to reduce the time it takes to bring an innovation to market.[47]

One of the companies most experienced with technological alliances is Toshiba, a major Japanese electronics company. The company's first technological tie-ups go back to the beginning of this century, when it contracted to make lightbulb filaments for U.S.-based General Electric. The company has since engaged in alliances with many leading international companies, among them United Technologies, Apple Computer, Sun Microsystems, Motorola, and National Semiconductor (all of the United States), as well as European firms Olivetti, Siemens, Rhône-Poulenc, Ericsson, and SGS-Thomson.[48]

More recently, Toshiba concluded a wide-ranging alliance with U.S.-based Carrier, a leader in air-conditioning equipment. Both Toshiba and Carrier placed their respective Japanese units into the alliance, forming a new company owned 60 percent by Toshiba. Carrier will access Toshiba's leading technology related to lighter-weight air-conditioning equipment, and Toshiba will access Carrier's technology in heavier systems.[49] A similar technology alliance between Carrier and IBM resulted in the first web-enabled air conditioners. By accessing a website via a computer or Internet-enabled cell phone, customers are able to adjust remotely the temperature on their home air conditioners. A pilot program for the new system was initiated in Italy, Greece, and Britain in 2001.[50]

Production-Based Alliances A large number of production-based alliances have been formed, particularly in the automobile industry. These alliances fall into two groups. First, there is the search for efficiency through component linkages that may include engines or other key components of a car. Second, companies have begun to share entire car models, either by developing them together or by producing them jointly. With development costs of a new-car-model generation now surpassing $2 billion, U.S. automobile manufacturers have been very active in creating global alliances with partners, primarily in Japan. Ford's major Japanese partner is Mazda, of which Ford owns a 25 percent equity share. The two firms have collaborated intensively, creating more than ten projects over the years.

Alliances have also been known to run into trouble when their respective partners changed strategic direction. Volvo of Sweden and Renault of France entered a far-reaching production alliance in 1990. The two companies agreed to a series of interlocking deals linking each other's truck and bus divisions. Separately, Renault bought 25 percent of Volvo's car operation and another 10 percent of Volvo Corporation. In return, Volvo acquired 20 percent of Renault with an option to purchase another 5 percent later on.

In 1993, both Volvo and Renault came to the conclusion that a full-scale merger was necessary. What had begun as a venture of equals (50:50) was to turn into a 65:35 deal, with Renault of France holding the majority of shares. Because Renault was a state-controlled company, this presented certain difficulties. Volvo was rapidly improving its profitability, whereas Renault was sliding into a period of poor financial results. In the end, the deal did not go through because of resistance by Volvo shareholders and senior managers.[51] Following abandonment of the full merger, the two companies decided to unravel their existing cross-shareholdings, and many of the anticipated joint projects were shelved. Volvo was later acquired by Ford. This shows that even two originally willing partners can have difficulties sustaining an alliance.

Distribution-Based Alliances Alliances with a special emphasis on distribution are becoming increasingly common. General Mills, a U.S.-based company marketing breakfast cereals, had long been number two in the United States, with some 27 percent market share, compared to Kellogg's 40 to 45 percent share. With no effective position outside the United States, the company entered into a global alliance with Nestlé of Switzerland. Forming Cereal Partners Worldwide (CPW), owned equally by the two companies, General Mills gained access to the local distribution and marketing skills of Nestlé in Europe, the Far East, and Latin America. In return, General Mills provided product technology and the experience it had acquired competing against Kellogg's. CPW was formed as a full business unit with responsibility for the entire world except the United States. Its market share outside the United States has reached almost 20 percent.[52]

Distribution alliances are also part of international express mail. The U.S. Postal Service approved a plan to form an alliance with DHL Worldwide Express to jointly offer two-day service between selected U.S. cities and Europe. The post office could expect major improvements in its service to Europe for relatively little investment. In exchange, DHL received access to part of the post office's network of retail customer counters and had an opportunity to boost its brand in the U.S. market.[53]

The Future of Alliances Although many older alliances were spawned by technology exchange and were contracted among manufacturing companies, some of the most innovative arrangements are signed by service firms. Many of these, however, have proved to be short-lived in a never-ending rearrangement between the world's leading players. This is particularly true of large telecommunications carriers. One alliance was WorldPartner, which included AT&T, the Japanese KDD, Singapore Telecom, and Unisource of Europe, itself a combination of several European firms. The alliance served about 700 international clients, including MasterCard and Whirlpool, in 35 countries. However, the alliance was effectively dissolved as a result of AT&T's move to link up with British Telecommunications, which prompted KDD to look for other overseas partners.[54]

No less active in forming and breaking international alliances are airlines. Delta joined Sabena, Austrian Airlines, and Swissair in an alliance termed Atlantic Excellence. However, when Delta saw more opportunity to anchor its European business in Paris with Air France, it abandoned its other partners. Then Swissair quickly signed an agreement with American Airlines and sold its stake in Delta. Austrian Airlines saw its future with Lufthansa and left the alliance as well.[55] Some 200 international airlines are or have been members of at least one alliance. These alliances allow airlines to offer fuller services and more extensive routes, as well as providing cost savings to the participating firms. Lufthansa estimated that its alliance with United Airlines saved it more than $270 million in a single year.[56]

Strategic alliances have typically been the domain of large companies, but SMEs are increasingly being encouraged to look for partnering opportunities. The Productivity and Standards Board of Singapore united with the U.S. Chamber of Commerce to launch UspartnerSingapore, a business-matching initiative to bring together Singapore and U.S. small and medium-sized enterprises. The project focuses on firms in the information technology, telecommunications, life sciences, franchise, and business services industries. Besides employing the Internet to match companies, the program offers market research and potential funding. The program aims at establishing at least 40 successful alliances.[57]

Although many alliances have been forged in a large number of industries worldwide, it is not yet clear whether these alliances will actually become successful business ventures. Experience suggests that alliances with two equal partners are more difficult to manage than those with a dominant partner. Furthermore, many observers question the value of entering alliances with technological competitors. The challenge in making an alliance work lies in the creation of multiple layers of connections, or webs, that reach across the partner organizations. Eventually, this will result in the creation of new organizations out of the cooperating parts of the partners. In that sense, alliances may very well be just an intermediate stage until a new company can be formed or until the dominant partner assumes control.[58]

Entering Markets Through Mergers and Acquisitions

International firms have always made acquisitions. However, the need to enter markets more quickly has made the acquisition route extremely attractive. This trend has probably been aided by the opening of many financial markets, making the acquisition of publicly traded companies much easier. Even unfriendly takeovers in foreign markets are now becoming increasingly common. The result: During the 1990s alone, cross-border mergers and acquisitions increased fivefold.[59]

By purchasing an established business, the firm eliminates the need to build manufacturing and distribution capabilities from scratch. Buying an established brand gives the firm immediate market presence and market share. Reckitt & Coleman of the United Kingdom competed in household cleaners in the United States but was a weak rival to Procter & Gamble. The British company jumped at the chance to buy L&F Household from Eastman Kodak. The acquisition comprised several U.S. brands, including Lysol, and contributed $775 million in immediate sales. Reckitt & Coleman considered the acquisition both faster and cheaper than building the same business on their own.[60]

Acquisition is also an attractive strategy when a market is already dominated by established brands and saturated with competitors. New entrants would find such a market difficult to break into, and the addition of a totally new player might make the market even more competitive and unprofitable for all. In some extreme cases, the government might allow entry only by acquisition in order to protect a depressed industry from new entrants. Such was the case with the Egyptian banking industry in 2001, when the government would allow international banks only to buy existing Egyptian banks and refused to grant them licenses to start new businesses.[61]

Because they are often late movers into international markets, firms from developing countries frequently opt for acquisitions as a route to enter markets, including more mature markets such as the United States. Mexico's Bimbo is a bakery with a virtual monopoly at home. It expanded into the United States with the purchase of Texas-based Mrs. Baird's Bakeries for $300 million in 1998. In 2002 it paid an additional $610 million for the Western U.S. division of Canada's George Weston Ltd., purchasing five bakeries and the rights to sell Oroweat, Thomas' English Muffins, Entenmann's, and Boboli brands everywhere except in Canada and east of the Mississippi. The purchase elevated Bimbo to third largest bakery worldwide with sales of near $4 billion.[62] Similarly, South African Breweries PCL became the third largest brewery as a result of acquisitions. In 2002 it was negotiating to purchase Miller Brewing Company of the United States. The Miller deal would make South African Breweries number two worldwide, behind Anheuser-Busch and ahead of Heineken.[63]

Sometimes an international firm may choose—or settle for—a partial acquisition. In many ways, such an acquisition can resemble an alliance with equity ownership involved. For example, General Motors currently owns 49 percent of Japanese truck maker Isuzu Motors Ltd. GM had largely abandoned trying to sell cars on its own in Japan and instead bought stakes in three domestic automakers, including 20 percent stakes in Suzuki Motor Corporation and Fuji Heavy Industries Ltd., the maker of Subaru vehicles. Isuzu is particularly hoping that the new owners will help the firm reduce costs by tapping into GM's global purchasing network for cheaper parts. Also, Isuzu plans to sell its trucks in GM dealerships and to offer more GM vehicles in Isuzu showrooms.[64]

Nevertheless, acquisitions present certain challenges. Attractive firms may not be available for purchase or may be available only at inflated prices that detract from profit potential. Acquisitions can also be difficult to make work. One study indicated that among 89 American firms acquired over the 1977–1990 period, most failed to achieve their targets for their foreign buyers. U.S. companies fared equally poorly; Ford's acquisition of Jaguar of the United Kingdom, for example, is hopelessly far from recouping the company's original investment of $2.5 billion.[65]

▶ *Portal or e-Business Entry Strategies*

The technological revolution of the Internet, with its wide range of connected and networked computers, has given rise to the virtual entry strategy. Employing electronic means, primarily through the use of web pages, e-mail, file transfer, and related communications tools, firms have begun to enter markets without establishing a physical presence in the host country. A company that establishes a server on the Internet and opens up a web page can be contacted from anywhere in the world. Table 9.2 rates the websites of the top twenty-five global brands. Consumers and industrial buyers who use modern Internet browsers can search for products, services, or companies and, in many instances, can make purchases online.

The number of global Internet users has passed 145 million by some counts. Business-to-consumer volume in e-commerce was expected to grow

Table 9.2 *The Top 25 Global Brands' Websites*

BRAND	WEBSITE	SCORE
IBM	www.ibm.com	81.8
Intel	www.intel.com	80.3
Microsoft	www.microsoft.com	76.5
Nokia	www.nokia.com	75.9
Disney	www.disneygo.com	75.0
Mercedes	www.mercedes.com	71.2
Kodak	www.kodak.com	70.8
Compaq	www.compaq.com	70.5
Sony	www.sony.com	70.0
McDonald's	www.mcdonalds.com	68.0
Heinz	www.heinz.com	67.8
Coca-Cola	www.coca-cola.com	67.7
BMW	www.bmw.com	66.9
Hewlett-Packard	www.hp.com	65.7
Cisco Systems	www.cisco.com	65.6
American Express	www.americanexpress.com	65.4
Ford	www.ford.com	62.2
General Electric	www.ge.com	61.6
AT&T	www.att.com	61.6
Nescafé	www.nescafe.com	59.5
Toyota	www.toyota.com	58.8
Honda	www.honda.com	54.6
Gillette	www.gillette.com	53.0
Citibank	www.citibank.com	51.3
Marlboro	No site found	——

Note: BrandNet tested websites for the top 25 global brands on the basis of the Intesbrand/Citibank top 60 international brand league table (July 2000). The overall evaluation is based on how local websites translate the core global online proposition, content, and services. This is the first survey of global brands. Sites will be reevaluated on a regular basis.
Source: "The Top 25 Global Brand Websites," *Marketing Week*, November 2, 2000: 40.

to $400 billion in 2002, and business-to-business trade to $1.3 trillion by 2003. Cisco, a U.S.-based Internet equipment supplier, believes that by 2010 some 25 percent of all retail transactions will be Internet-based.[66] Whatever the forecasts, most experts agree that the opportunities for Internet-based commerce are huge.

Although it is difficult to guess how much actual trading is done with international customers at all Internet sites, the trend is clear when one looks at some major Internet companies. Amazon.com, the leading Internet retailer, early established a presence overseas. After establishing a website in the United States, it opened a second one in Britain (Amazon.co.uk) by acquiring Bookpages, an existing U.K. Internet book retailer. In Germany the company purchased Telebuch to establish Amazon.de. Both international websites are patterned after the U.S. one. The German site is entirely in German, and the merchandise inventory is specific to the different markets.[67] Each of these operations has its own fulfillment operation that packages and ships from local stocks. A customer can always order from the United States, but international customers who do so must pay the extra charges for shipment and delivery.

U.S. portal sites, such as AOL, are also engaged in expanding internationally. AOL has tended to engage in joint ventures in overseas markets. In Europe, AOL established a venture in 1995 with Bertelsmann, a leading German media company. Its Japan operation was established in 1997 with Mitsui, a Japanese trading house, and Nhihon Keizai Shimbun, a publisher. Although clearly dominant in the United States, AOL has encountered stiff

Amazon.com's German website is patterned after its U.S. site.

local competition. Brazil, with its 6.8 million Internet users, is one of the world's most important markets. AOL had to battle established local providers in Brazil, some supported by foreign venture capital.

E-commerce is expanding rapidly through Asia. China, Australia, South Korea, Taiwan, and Hong Kong are the main user markets. Forecasts vary widely, but one source estimates that Chinese Internet users will grow to 80 million in a few years as access to PCs and to the Net expands.[68] In India, where the creation of commercial software has become a major export industry, the leading portal service, Satyam Infoway, has acquired a smaller company with a search engine that provides access to Indian sports, culture, and food recipes, something of great value to the many Indians living overseas. All the main players in this market are local and provide local content. Currently, India, with its small population of 500,000 Internet subscribers, is still too small for a large number of players.[69]

A third group of major Internet players with global ambitions is made up of service providers, such as Schwab and Merrill Lynch with their online trading.[70] Financial services firms, however, encounter legal restrictions and need to obtain regulatory approval for offering their services to any given country. On the other hand, it is difficult for governments to police the access. Financial services firms will probably have to provide special access, or qualifying service, to local customers before they can sign on. Given the low cost of the Internet, it is very likely that many more established firms will use the Internet as the first point of contact for countries where they do not yet have a major base.

Would-be Internet-based global marketers still face many challenges. One of the biggest is language. One research company estimated that within 3 years, 60 percent of the world's Internet users and 40 percent of its e-commerce revenue would be from outside the United States, mostly from non-English-speaking areas. Although many people are able to surf the Net in English, they still prefer to do transactions in their local language.[71]

▶ *Entry Strategy Configuration*

This chapter has been dedicated to explaining the various entry strategies available to international and global firms. In reality, however, most entry strategies consist of a combination of different formats. We refer to the process of deciding on the best possible entry strategy mix as **entry strategy configuration**.

Rarely do companies employ a single entry mode per country. A company may open up a subsidiary that produces some products locally and imports others to round out its product line. The same foreign subsidiary may even export to other foreign subsidiaries. In many cases, companies have bundled such entry forms into a single legal unit, in effect layering several entry strategy options on top of each other.

Bundling of entry strategies is the process of providing just one legal unit in a given country or market. In other words, the foreign company sets up a single company in one country and uses that company as a legal umbrella for all its entry activities. However, such strategies have become less typical—particularly in larger markets. Many firms have begun to unbundle their operations.

When a company **unbundles**, it essentially divides its operations in a country into different companies. The local manufacturing plant may be incorporated separately from the sales subsidiary. When this occurs, companies may select different ownership strategies, for instance allowing a joint venture in one operation while retaining full ownership in another part. Such unbundling becomes possible in the larger markets, such as the United States, Germany, and Japan. It also enables the firm to run several companies or product lines in parallel. ICI, the large U.K. chemicals company, operates several subsidiaries in the United States that report to different product line companies back in the United Kingdom and are independently operated. Global firms that grant such independence to their product divisions will find that each division will need to develop its own entry strategy for key markets.

▶ Exit Strategies

Circumstances may make companies want to leave a country or market. Failure to achieve marketing objectives may be the reason, or there may be political, economic, or legal reasons for a company to want to dissolve or sell an operation. International companies have to be aware of the high costs attached to the liquidation of foreign operations; substantial amounts of severance pay may have to be dispensed to employees, and any loss of credibility in other markets can hurt the company's future prospects.

Consolidation Sometimes an international firm may need to consolidate its operations. This may mean a consolidation of factories from many to fewer such plants. Production consolidation, when not combined with an actual market withdrawal, is not really what we are concerned with here. Rather, our concern is a company's actually abandoning its plan to serve a certain market or country.

Market consolidation often occurs when an international firm acquires more debt than it can handle. To service the debt, poorly performing markets must be abandoned. Even successful operations may be sold to raise cash. In the 1970s, several U.S.-based multinational firms had to revamp their international operations. Chrysler sold its European operations in the United Kingdom and France to European car manufacturers, mainly Peugeot, and concentrated on the U.S. market. More recently, Avon Products sold 60 percent of its successful Japanese company for about $400 million. It had previously, in 1987, sold 40 percent of its Japanese company to the public. Avon had started its Japanese subsidiary 20 years before, and sales had reached sales of $285 million.[72] Nonetheless, the sale was necessitated by the need to reduce Avon's debt in the United States.

Consolidation can also be an option if a firm fails to establish itself in a particularly competitive market. In 2002, Yahoo announced that it would suspend its auction sites in five European markets—the U.K., Ireland, France, Germany, and Spain. Yahoo found itself a distant third in these markets. Auctions have proved to be well suited to the Internet, but sellers and buyers tend to gravitate to the largest sites, leading to natural monopolies in online auction markets. Ebay, the auction leader in the United States and most of Europe, agreed to pay exiting Yahoo to promote eBay's European auction sites through banner ads and text links.[73]

Political Considerations Changing government regulations can at times pose problems that induce some companies to leave a country. India is a case in point. There, the government adopted in 1973 its Exchange Regulation Act that required most foreign companies to divest themselves of 60 percent ownership in each of their subsidiaries by the end of 1977. Companies that manufactured substantially for export and those whose operations used advanced technology were exempted. Because IBM's Indian operation did little exporting and sold mostly older computer models, the computer manufacturer was asked to sell 60 percent of its equity to Indian citizens. In light of the new requirements, Coca-Cola eventually chose to leave the Indian market in 1977.

Political risk can also motivate firms to leave a market. Sainsbury is a U.K.-based supermarket chain that employs 100,000 people worldwide. It entered the Egyptian market in 1999 by purchasing 80 percent interest in a state-owned retailer. The subsidiary posted a $15 million operating loss for the first half of 2000, partly as a result of problems with goods clearing customs and difficulty in obtaining building permits. These losses were exacerbated by an organized campaign against the company orchestrated by anti-Israel protesters who generally targeted Western companies operating in Egypt.[74] In 2002, Sainsbury announced that it would pull out of Egypt, selling its stake to its Egyptian partner and incurring a loss of $140–175 million.[75]

Exit strategies can also be the result of negative reactions in a firm's home market. When the policy of apartheid that then existed in South Africa was being widely challenged on moral grounds, many multinational corporations exited that country by abandoning or selling their local subsidiaries. In 1984, some 325 U.S. companies were maintaining operations in South Africa. Two years later, this number had decreased to 265. Some of the U.S. firms that left were Coca-Cola, General Motors, IBM, Motorola, and General Electric. Many European firms also withdrew from that country, among them Alfa-Romeo of Italy, Barclays Bank of the United Kingdom, and Renault of France .[76]

READ MORE ABOUT IT:
Check out "Sainsbury Becomes Target" under *Supplementary Readings* on our website.

Private security officers stand guard outside a KFC restaurant in Rawalpindi, Pakistan, after the United States led attacks on neighboring Afghanistan. As icons of American culture, U.S.-based fast-food chains are often targets of politically motivated mobs. One such mob burned a KFC restaurant in Karachi, Pakistan. Mob violence in India encouraged KFC to leave that market.

Re-entry Options Several of the markets left by international firms over the past decades have become attractive again, and some companies have reversed their exit decisions and entered those markets a second time. For example, since July 1991, when the ban on investing in South Africa was lifted, a number of firms have returned. Among them is Honeywell, a manufacturer of industrial controls equipment. The company returned by repurchasing the industrial distributor it had sold to local interests in 1985.[77]

In India, the government relaxed earlier restrictive ownership legislation as part of its overall policy of economic liberalization in August 1991. Coca-Cola re-entered India in 1993 to counter the first-time entry of rival PepsiCo. General Motors returned to India after a much longer absence. After producing cars in India from 1928 to 1953, GM left because of poor economic prospects. After a time, however, it developed licensing agreements with Hindustan Motors. This later evolved into the announcement of a full-scale 50:50 venture to produce GM models jointly in India again.[78] More recently, DHL Worldwide Express returned to Afghanistan after exiting 15 years earlier when market prospects looked bleak.[79]

▶ *Conclusions*

Market entry strategies can have a profound impact on a firm's global strategy. They determine the number of foreign markets a firm can enter and the speed at which a firm can internationalize. They affect the profits the firm will make in each national market and the risk it will assume. They can even obligate a firm to local partners, thus constraining its power to act solely in its global self-interest.

Given the implications of the market entry decision, surprisingly few multinationals appear to recognize its strategic importance. A study of 228 U.S. manufacturing firms revealed that only 34 percent approached market entry options using any strategic rules.[80] Another study of 105 firms in four European countries found that only 36 percent of managers even reviewed alternative entry options.[81] Franklin Root suggests that managers often employ the "naïve rule" for entry mode selection—they simply utilize the same strategy worldwide, ignoring differences among national markets.[82]

Choosing the best entry strategy is complex and involves many considerations. The relative importance of these considerations varies by industry and by the strategic goals of each firm. It also varies according to the strategic importance of each national market. Table 9.3 presents some key considerations and their impact on the potential appropriateness of different entry options. Clearly, no one option is ideal under all conditions.

For example, speed of market entry may be an important consideration in some cases. If a firm is in an industry where products face high development costs, it will want to sell in many countries. If it is not already present in many markets, it will need to expand rapidly in order to keep up with global competitors. This is all the more true if products have a short life cycle, as is the case with many high-technology products. Often the need to be in many markets quickly requires a firm to take partners, because it simply doesn't have enough money or managerial talent to take on the task itself. Licensing, joint venturing, or entering distribution alliances becomes attractive.

Table 9.3 *Appropriateness of Market Entry Strategies*

STRATEGIC CONSIDERATION	MODE OF ENTRY					
	Indirect Exporting	Direct Exporting- Marketing Subsidiary	Licensing	Wholly Owned Production	Joint Venture	Acquisition
Speed of entry	High	High	High	Low	Low	High
Ease of exit	High	Moderate	Moderate	Low	Low	Low
Rapidly changing technologies	Low	High	High	Moderate	Moderate	Moderate
Resource demands	Low	Moderate	Moderate	High	High	High
Profit potential	Low	High	Low	High	Moderate	Moderate
Competitive intensity of market	Low	Moderate	Moderate	Moderate	Moderate	High
Integration into global network	Low	High	Low	High	Low	Moderate
Strategically important country	Low	High	Low	High	Moderate	Moderate
Unimportant market	High	Low	Moderate	Low	Low	Low
Cultural distance	High	Low	Moderate	Low	Moderate	Low
Congruence with host government's goals	Low	Low	Moderate	High	High	Moderate

In all cases, managers must decide how many resources they can and want to commit to a market. Resources include investments necessary for increasing or relocating manufacturing, as well as investments related to product research and development and to the implementation of marketing strategy. Exporting or licensing might require no new capital investment or very little incremental investment to increase current production. Wholly owned manufacturing facilities require significant capital investments. Joint ventures and other alliances can cut capital costs in research and development, manufacturing, and distribution. Another important resource is management time. Direct exporting may not require additional capital investment but will require a greater commitment of management time than indirect exporting. Joint ventures and alliances can help ease the demands on this critical resource.

Other concerns include profitability and flexibility. Will exporting to a market produce higher returns than producing there? Economies of scale in global or regional production may or may not offset the costs of transportation and tariffs. Licensing and joint ventures require that profits be shared. If the political environment or the business prospects of a country are uncertain, the flexibility involved with an entry strategy becomes a consideration. How quickly and at what cost can the firm expand in the market or retreat from it? Redirecting exports is easier than closing a plant. Partnership or licensing agreements can limit future actions both within the market and globally.

Firms must also consider different entry strategies for different countries. Establishing a sales subsidiary may be the best alternative for entering some countries, whereas joint ventures may be necessary to enter others. Firms should allot their greatest efforts and resources to the most strategic global markets. They should always consider how an entry strategy will later affect their ability to integrate operations in that country into the global whole.

Firms must balance the advantages and disadvantages of different entry strategies. Even when a firm is clear about its strategic goals, rarely does an entry option present no drawbacks whatsoever. Also, governments may disallow the ideal market entry choice, forcing a company to fall back on a less desirable option or to avoid the market altogether. Compromises must often be made. Marketers should expect to manage a variety of entry strategies, and still other types of entry strategies may be devised in the future, presenting international marketers with new opportunities and challenges.

What could be an appropriate entry strategy for your target market? Continue with your *Country Market Report* on our website.

Review Questions

1. What are the advantages and disadvantages of using an export management company?

2. Why are marketing subsidiaries desirable for many exporters?

3. List at least three ways in which the Internet has affected market entry strategies.

4. Compare and contrast licensing and integrated production as market entry strategies.

5. Explain the concept of entry strategy configuration and the strategies of bundling or unbundling entry strategies.

6. Under what circumstances is market entry by acquisition advisable?

Questions for Discussion

1. Why might entry strategies differ for companies entering the United States, those entering China, and those entering Costa Rica?

2. How might the entry strategy of a born-global firm (see Chapter 7) differ from that of a mature multinational company?

3. Why would licensing sometimes be appropriate—and sometimes inappropriate—for a strategically important country?

4. Is there such a thing as a "no-fault" joint venture divorce? Or is joint venture dissolution always the result of some sort of failure?

5. If a company exits a market and then wishes to return 10 years later, what peculiar challenges might it face?

For Further Reading

Alon, Ilon, and Moshe Banai. "Franchising Opportunities and Threats in Russia." *Journal of International Marketing* 8, 3 (2000): 104–119.

Root, Franklin R. *Entry Strategies for International Markets*. Rev. and exp. ed. Lexington, MA: Lexington Books, D.C. Heath, 1994.

Westland, J. Christopher, and Theodore H.K. Clark. *Global Electronic Commerce*. Cambridge, MA: M.I.T. Press, 2000.

Yan, Aimin, and Yadong Luo. *International Joint Ventures: Theory and Practice*. Armonk, NY: M.E. Sharpe, 2001.

Yoshino, Michael Y., and U. Srinivasu Rangan. *Strategic Alliances*. Cambridge, MA: Harvard Business School Press, 1995.

Case 9.1   *Unhappy Marriage*

In 1993 Anheuser-Busch purchased 17.7 percent of Grupo Modelo for $477 million, with an option of increasing its shares to 50.2 percent. At the time of the purchase, Anheuser held 45 percent of the U.S. beer market. Modelo was the world's tenth largest beer producer. It held 50 percent of the Mexican beer market and exported to 124 countries in every continent of the world. However, with the passing of NAFTA, Mexico's 20 percent tariffs on imported beer were to be phased out. Modelo feared that U.S. breweries would invade its market. Anheuser viewed its stake in Modelo as a profitable acquisition of brands such as Corona, as well as a way to increase Anheuser's distribution network in Mexico quickly.

Anheuser told its U.S. distributors that they would soon have access to a major imported beer. Distributors assumed this meant Corona, which was fast growing in popularity in the United States. However, in late 1996, management at Modelo renewed the firm's 10-year contract with its existing U.S. distributors, dashing Anheuser's hopes of gaining Modelo brands for its own U.S. distribution system. In December 1996, Anheuser announced that it would exercise its option to increase its stake in Modelo.

A 6-month dispute over price ensued, and the parties settled for $605 million. In June 1997, Anheuser opted to increase its stake to the full 50.2 percent. Discussions became so contentious that the two parties went into international arbitration, and the price was eventually set at $556 million. By 1998 the price of Anheuser's stake in Modelo, as valued on the Mexican stock exchange, was twice what it had paid for the stock. However, its 50.2 percent stake in Modelo did not give Anheuser a controlling share of board votes. It held only 10 of the 21 seats on the board of directors.

Despite trade liberalization, Modelo's brands increased their share of the Mexican market to 55 percent by 1998. In the United States, where beer imports accounted for 14 percent of the market, Corona has pulled ahead of Heineken to become the best-selling import. Corona was enjoying 40 percent growth per year in the United States and had already become the tenth-best-selling beer in that market. It was particularly successful among college students and consumers in their twenties. Anheuser's major brand, Budweiser, found itself competing against Corona. Anheuser began a campaign to disparage the freshness of Corona. It distributed display cards to thousands of bars and restaurants, noting that Corona didn't put the manufacturing date on its bottles. Anheuser also introduced three Corona clones—Azteca, Tequiza, and Rio Cristal—all produced in the United States.

Discussion Questions

1. Why did Anheuser purchase its stake in Grupo Modelo?
2. Why was Grupo Modelo willing to sell the stake?
3. What went wrong? Why?
4. What lessons about choosing international partners can be learned from this case?

Sources: "U.S. Brewers Forge Partnerships with Two Largest Mexican Beer Producers," *SourceMex*, March 31, 1993; Rekha Balu and Jonathan Friedland, "Anheuser-Busch Paying $556 Million, Raises Stake in Brewer Grupo Modelo," *Wall Street Journal*, September 11, 1998, p. B8; and Jonathan Friedland and Rekha Balu, "Head to Head," *Wall Street Journal*, October 1998, p. A1.

Case 9.2   *Déjà Vu?*

In 1990, Coca-Cola, the world's largest soft-drinks company, and Nestlé, the world's largest packaged-foods company, announced that they were forming a joint venture to develop and market ready-to-drink coffee and tea products. Each would contribute $50 million to the new venture. Nestlé possessed well-known trademarks in coffee and tea. It sold iced coffee in Europe and had recently test-marketed a mocha cooler in the United States. Still, it was not very active in the ready-to-drink category overall. For its part, Coke offered a global distribution system for soft drinks.

The newly formed company, Coca-Cola Nestlé Refreshment, had its headquarters in Tampa, Florida. (Coca-Cola was headquartered in Atlanta, Georgia, and Nestlé in Vevey, Switzerland.) The only market excluded from the venture was Japan, where Coke already had a position in ready-to-drink coffee. Nestlé came to the venture with prior experience with an alliance partner. It distributed General Mills cereals through its international distribution system. Coke, on the other hand, had no such alliance experience. In 1992 the venture launched its first product, Nestea Iced Tea, a single-serve tea drink. In the following two and a half years, more than a dozen tea and coffee drinks were developed.

In 1994 the two companies announced that they were dissolving the equity joint venture and were closing the Tampa office. Some believed the venture had moved too slowly and had been beaten to the market by an alliance between Pepsi and Lipton. Under new terms, Coke received a 100-year license to use the Nestea trademark anywhere in the world and would pay Nestlé an undisclosed royalty for Nestea sales. Nestlé would continue to try to sell Nescafé products through the Coke distribution system.

During the 1990s, Nestlé embarked on an aggressive acquisition strategy. By 2001 it slowed down this activity to concentrate more on the 7,000 brands it already had. Coca-Cola continued in the 1990s to dominate in worldwide soda sales but saw Pepsi dramatically expand its noncarbonated lines. To help its ailing juice business, Coca-Cola entered a joint venture in 1996 with France's Groupe Danon

to expand the distribution of Minute Maid refrigerated orange juice in supermarkets throughout Europe and Latin America.

In 2001 Coke and Nestlé announced that they were resurrecting their earlier alliance and renaming the venture Beverage Partners Worldwide. The new headquarters were to be located in Zurich, Switzerland, and the revived venture would operate in 40 countries. Nestlé would develop the products, and Coke would distribute them. However, Coke would contribute the teas it developed for the Chinese market, along with its line of Planet Java coffees. Nestlé would add its Belte tea line. This time around, the parents envisioned that the venture would operate with the "speed and culture of a start-up company."

Discussion Questions

1. Why were Coca-Cola and Nestlé interested in forming a joint venture in 1990?
2. What do you think went wrong the first time?
3. What might be different in 2001? Do you think this resurrected venture may work better? Why or why not?

Sources: Michael J. McCarthy, "Coke, Nestle Get Together Over Coffee," *Wall Street Journal*, November 30, 1990, p. B1; Laurie M. Grossman, "Coca-Cola, Nestle are Ending Venture in Tea and Coffee But Plan Other Ties," *Wall Street Journal*, August 30, 1994, p. B3; and Marcel Michelson, "Nestle, Coca-Cola Boost Health Drinks Venture," *Reuters English News Service*, January 30, 2001.

Notes

[1]Carolyn Webb, "The Fine Art of Franchising," *The Age*, May 8, 2001: 1.

[2]"1451 International Launches the Vatican Library Collection Licensing Program," *Businesswire*, February 12, 2001.

[3]"Sega to Scale Down European Sales Operations," *Financial Times*, February 28, 1996: 1.

[4]Erin Anderson and Anne T. Coughlan, "International Market Entry and Expansion in Independent or Integrated Channels of Distribution," *Journal of Marketing*, January 1987: 71-82.

[5]"GM Revving Up for Big Push into Japan," *Nikkei Weekly*, August 21, 1995, p. 1.

[6]"How Does GM's Saturn Sell Cars in Japan? Very Slowly," *Wall Street Journal*, August 25, 1998, p. B1.

[7]Amy Guthrie, "Brazil's Top Poultry Producers Target Export Markets," *Dow Jones Newswires*, May 9, 2001.

[8]Niles Hansen, Kate Gillespie, and Esra Gencturk, "SMEs and

Export Involvement: Market Responsiveness, Technology and Alliances," *Journal of Global Marketing* 7, 4 (1994): 7–27.

[9]S. Mitra Kalita, "Going Global," *Newsday*, March 19, 2001, p. C18.

[10]Chandrani Ghosh, "E-Trade Routes Planning to Do Global Business on the Web? Next Linx Will Ease the Way," *Forbes*, August 7, 2000: 108.

[11]"Harvard Business School Publishing and New York Times Syndicate Announce Harvard Business Review to Be Published in Mandarin Chinese," *Businesswire*, July 17, 2001.

[12]"Everlast Worldwide Inc. Announces New Head of Global Licensing," *PR Newswire*, October 25, 2000.

[13]"Licensing May Be the Quickest Route to Foreign Markets," *Wall Street Journal*, September 14, 1990, p. B2.

[14]"The Pace of Change Slows," *Financial Times*, March 27, 1991, Sect. III, p. 1 (Survey, World Paints and Coatings).

[15]"French Drug Maker Reaps Profits with Offbeat Strategy," *Wall Street Journal*, November 14, 1996, p. B4

[16]David Luhnow, "Mexico's Televisa Wants New Univision Deal," *Wall Street Journal*, February 21, 2001, p. A18.

[17]Nick Wingfield, "Priceline.com Plans Asia Partnership with Hutchinson," *Wall Street Journal*, January 26, 2000, p. A19.

[18]Tom Daykin, "Miller Gets Deal with Dutch Firm," *Milwaukee Journal Sentinel*, July 11, 2001, p. 3D.

[19]Judith Rehak, "Franchising the World: Services and Internet Fuel of Global Boom," *International Herald Tribune*, October 14, 2000, p. 20.

[20]www.mcdonalds.com

[21]Vasantha Ganesan, "Malaysia Has Potential to Be Franchise Hub in Next Ten Years," *Business Times (Malaysia)*, June 8, 2001.

[22]Dai Yan, "Bright Future for Franchising," *China Daily*, November 18, 2000.

[23]Rehak, "Franchising the World."

[24]Christina Hoag, "Franchise Fever Hits Venezuela," *Houston Chronicle*, July 10, 2001, p. 1.

[25]"Happy Hookahs," *The Economist*, May 5, 2001.

[26]Rehak, "Franchising the World."

[27]"Ford Vietnam Targets Bigger Automobile Market Slide," *Saigon Times Daily*, July 2, 1999.

[28]"Successful Transplants," *Financial Times*, March 27, 1991: 2 (Survey, Automotive Components).

[29]"Why Mercedes Is Alabama Bound," *Business Week*, October 11, 1993: 138

[30]Doreen Hemlock, "Florida, Brazil Compete in Citrus Industry," *Knight Ridder Tribune Business News*, July 11, 2001.

[31]Andrew Meadows, "Florida Citrus Processors Concentrate on Brazilian Juice Invasion," *Knight Ridder Tribune Business News*, June 9, 2001.

[32]Dana James, "Back to Vietnam," *Marketing News*, May 13, 2002: 13.

[33]"e-financialdepot.com Signs New International Joint Venture for Entry into Africa and Middle East," *News Wire*, April 4, 2001.

[34]"Den Fujita, Japan's Mr. Joint-Venture," *New York Times*, March 22, 1992, Sect. 3, p. 1.

[35]"McDonald's Co. Japan Ltd," *Nation's Restaurant News*, January 1, 1998: 112.

[36]"Many Chinese Make Light Work of Razor Sales Targets," *Financial Times*, June 14, 1993.

[37]"The Next CEO's Key Asset: A Worn Passport," *Business Week*, January 19, 1998: 76.

[38]"Gillette Forms Soviet Link to Make Shavers," *Financial Times*, March 5, 1991: 26.

[39]Aimin Yan and Yadong Luo, *International Joint Ventures* (Armonk, NY: M.E. Sharpe, 2001), p. 223.

[40]J. Peter Killing, "How to Make a Global Joint Venture Work," *Harvard Business Review*, May–June 1982: 121.

[41]Jennifer Ordonez, "Starbucks to Start Major Expansion Overseas," *Wall Street Journal*, October 27, 2000, p. B10.

[42]"The Advantages of Marrying Local," *Financial Times*, December 21, 2000: 16.

[43]Raymond Colitt, "Telecom Italia Hits Brazil Block," *Financial Times*, FT.com, July 16, 2001.

[44]Aimin Yan and Yadong Luo, *International Joint Ventures: Theory and Practice* (Armonk, NY: M.E. Sharpe), p. 281.

[45]"Glaxo to Buy Out Partner in Japan for $594 Million," *Financial Times*, November 22, 1996: 15.

[46]"Alliance Tips for a Beautiful Relationship," *Financial Times-FT.com*, July 11, 2001.

[47]"Holding Hands," *The Economist*, March 27, 1993: 14 (Survey of Multinationals).

[48]"How Toshiba Makes Alliances Work," *Fortune*, October 4, 1993, p. 116.

[49]"Carrier and Toshiba Make It Official, Form a Strategic Alliance," *Business Wire*, April 1, 1999.

[50]William M. Bulkeley, "IBM, Carrier to Unveil Joint Internet Venture in Air Conditioning," *Wall Street Journal*, April 9, 2001, p. B6.

[51]"Driven by the Need to Survive," *Financial Times*, September 3, 1993: 17; "Hard Slog to Make the Marriage Work," *Financial Times*, September 7, 1993: 19; "Why Volvo Kissed Renault Goodbye," *Business Week*, December 20, 1993: 54.

[52]"Is the Cereal Bowl Half Full or Half Empty?" *Star-Tribune (Minneapolis-St. Paul)*, August 16, 1998, p. 1D.

[53]Douglas A. Blackmon, "Postal Service, DHL to Form an Alliance," *Wall Street Journal*, March 2, 1999, p. A6.

[54]*Deutsche Presse Agentur*, November 10, 1999.

[55]"Delta, Air France Play Global Partnership Catch Up" *Airline Financial News*, June 28, 1999.

[56]"Aviation Alliances—Whom Do They Benefit the Most?" *Deutsche Presse-Agentur*, July 1, 1999.

[57]Eugene Low, "S'pore, US in Business Matching Initiative," *Business Times (Singapore)*, November 15, 2000.

[58]George Taucher, "Beyond Alliances," *IMEDE Perspective for Managers*, no. 1 (Lausanne: IMEDE, 1988).

[59]David Wessel, "Cross-Border Mergers Soared Last Year," *Wall Street Journal*, September 19, 2000, p. A18.

[60]"Cleaning Up Its Act to Fight the Giants," *Financial Times*, September 27, 1994: 17.

[61]Mahmoud Kassem, "Banks Seek Takeover Targets in Egypt," *Wall Street Journal Europe*, July 11, 2001.

[62]Geri Smith, "Can Bimbo Cook in the U.S.?" *Business Week*, March 4, 2002: 32.

[63]John Koppisch, Gerry Khermouch, and Kerry Capell, "It's Miller Time in Johannesburg," *Business Week*, April 22, 2002: 52.

[64]Todd Zaun, "Japan's Isuzu Will Cut Jobs, Close Factory," *Wall Street Journal*, May 29, 2001, p. A14.

[65]"The World Is Not Always Your Oyster," *Business Week*, October 30, 1995: 132.

[66]"E-Commerce to Take Retailing to Another Realm," *South China Morning Post*, July 10, 1999, p. 2.

[67]"Internet Retailing: A New Leaf," *The Economist*, October 23, 1999: 72.

[68]"China's Online Date with Destiny," *Financial Times*, December 18, 1999: 8.

[69]"Portals in a Storm as Contest in India Heats Up," *Financial Times*, December 10, 1999: 22.

[70]"Joining Crowd, Merrill To Offer On-Line Trades," *Herald Tribune International*, June 3, 1999, p. 13.

[71]"Idiom App Speaks Your Language," *Computer World*, May 31, 1999: 66.

[72]"Saying Sayonara Is Such Sweet Sorrow," *Business Week*, March 12, 1990: 52; "Avon Agrees to Sell Rest of Japanese Unit," *New York Times*, February 22, 1991, p. D5.

[73]Nick Wingfield and Mylene Mangalindan, "Yahoo Agrees to Cede Most Auction in Europe to eBay," *Wall Street Journal Europe*, May 24, 2002, p. A5.

[74]William A. Orme, "A Grocer Amid Mideast Outrage," *New York Times*, January 25, 2001, p.C1.

[75]"Sainsbury's to Pull Out of Egypt," *Jerusalem Post Daily*, April 10, 2001, p. 10.

[76]"South Africa: Time to Stay—or Go?" *Fortune*, August 4, 1986: 45; "If Coke Has Its Way, Blacks Will Soon Own 'The Real Thing,'" *Business Week*, March 27, 1987: 56; "High Risks and Low Returns," *Financial Times*, November 25, 1986: 10.

[77]"Honeywell's Route Back to South Africa Market," *New York Times*, January 31, 1994, p. D1.

[78]"Indian Venture for 20,000 Cars a Year," *Financial Times*, May 12, 1994: 15.

[79]"DHL Resumes Afghanistan Service," *Jakarta Post*, March 20, 2002, p. 12.

[80]Kwon, Yung-Chul and Michael Y. Hu, "Comparative Analysis of Export-Oriented and Foreign Production-Oriented Firms' Foreign Market Entry Decisions," *Management International Review* 35, 4 (1995): 325–336.

[81]Frank Bradley and Michael Gannon, "Does the Firm's Technology and Marketing Profile Affect Foreign Market Entry?" *Journal of International Marketing* 8, 4 (2000): 12–36.

[82]Franklin Root, *Entry Strategies for International Markets* (Lexington, MA: Lexington Books, D.C. Heath, 1994).

Part 4 *Designing Global Marketing Programs*

COMPETENCE LEVEL   **DECISION AREAS**

Environmental Competence

Understanding the Global Marketing Environment
CH 2   *The Global Economy*
CH 3   *Cultural and Social Forces*
CH 4   *Political and Regulatory Climate*

Analytic Competence

Analyzing Global Opportunities
CH 5   *Global Buyer Behavior*
CH 6   *Global Competitors*
CH 7   *Global Marketing Research*

Strategic Competence

Developing Global Marketing Strategies
CH 8   *Global Marketing Strategies*
CH 9   *Global Market Entry Strategies*

Functional Competence

Designing Global Marketing Programs
CH 10   *Global Product and Service Strategies*
CH 11   *Developing New Products for Global Markets*
CH 12   *Pricing for International and Global Markets*
CH 13   *Managing Global Distribution Channels*
CH 14   *Global Promotion Strategies*
CH 15   *Managing Global Advertising*

Managerial Competence

Managing the Global Marketing Effort
CH 16   *Organizing for Global Marketing*

10

Global Product and Service Strategies

Even Internet Firms that only virtually enter international markets must consider the possible need to alter their products for many new environments. Simply translating the text of a website may not be enough. Do people read from right to left or from left to right, from top to bottom or from bottom to top? What colors and shapes do they like? The answers to these questions will strongly influence the graphical layouts of the site and its use of icons.[1] What standards—governmental or societal—could affect the content of the site? U.S. internet firms routinely alter the content of their sites in Asia, self-censoring to avoid offending local governments, especially those in China, Singapore, and Malaysia, which have clamped down on Internet access. In 2001 Yahoo carried a story of doctors harvesting organs from executed prisoners in China. The story appeared in the "world news" section of Yahoo's website in the United States and other parts of the world—but not in China.[2]

This chapter and the following chapter examine issues pertaining to the adaptation of products and services to global markets. In this chapter we begin by exploring the many environmental factors that can prevent the marketing of uniform or standardized products

Chapter Outline

across a multitude of markets. We discuss the various implications of selecting brand names for international markets. International firms are concerned not only with determining appropriate brand names but also with protecting those names against preemption and counterfeiting. Subsequent sections focus on packaging and labeling, the marketing of services on a global scale, and the management of support services. The chapter concludes with a discussion of product line management. In the next chapter, Chapter 11, we continue with a discussion of strategies for introducing products into foreign markets—strategies that emphasize standardization and those that emphasize adaptation—as well as examining issues of developing global products.

Learning Objectives

After studying this chapter, you should be able to:

► List the advantages of product standardization and product adaptation.

► Differentiate between mandatory and discretionary product adaptations.

► Explain the concepts of global product standards and generic management system standards.

► Compare the advantages and disadvantages of using global brand names and using single-country brand names.

► Differentiate between a global brand name and a global brand strategy.

► Define private branding and explain why it is used by some international firms.

► Differentiate among trademark preemption, counterfeiting, and product piracy, and suggest ways in which firms can seek to minimize each of these.

► Describe ways in which marketing services internationally differs from the international marketing of physical products.

► Explain why product lines can vary from country to country.

▶ *Product Design in a Global Environment*

One of the principal questions in global marketing is whether a firm's products can be sold in their present form or whether they need to be adapted to foreign market requirements. Standardizing products across markets has certain advantages. Economies of scale in manufacturing may be realized. If products have high development costs and short life cycles, as is the case for many high-technology products, they may need to enter global markets very rapidly. In other words, firms must sell high volumes in many markets in order to recoup their investment before the product becomes obsolete. Adapting such a product to different national markets may simply take too long. Furthermore, if buyers themselves are international firms, they may prefer a standardized product that is available worldwide.

Nonetheless, in many cases products do need to be adapted for different national markets. The benefits of adaptation are compared with those of standardization in Table 10.1. Many adaptations are **discretionary**. Firms may choose to make certain adaptations or not to do so. In some cases, however, adaptations are **mandatory**. They are necessary for the product to be sold in a local market. Some mandatory adaptations are responses to differing physical realities. For example, consumer electronics must be adapted to work with different voltages, alternating currents, and electric plug designs, each of which varies from country to country. Many mandatory adaptations are made to adhere to national legal requirements. In November 2000, a French court required Yahoo to block French users from accessing Nazi memorabilia on its U.S.-based website, thereby setting a precedent and suggesting that web companies operating on the global Internet could be required to conform to standards of individual countries. The judge gave Yahoo 3 months to comply with the ruling by installing a key-word-based filtering system to block French citizens from viewing Yahoo sites where Nazi items were being sold—or else be subject to fines of more than 1,000,000 francs ($12,940) a day.[3]

Table 10.1 *Benefits of Product Standardization and of Product Adaptation*

Benefits of Standardization

Lower costs of manufacturing may be achieved through economies of scale.

Lower input costs may be achieved through volume purchasing.

Cost savings may be achieved by eliminating efforts—market research, design and engineering—to adapt products.

Fast global product roll-outs are possible because no time is needed to make product adaptations.

International customers may prefer the same product available worldwide.

Standardized products may enhance consumer perceptions of a global brand.

Benefits of Adaptation

Mandatory adaptations allow products to be sold in otherwise closed markets.

Products can be sold for use in different climates and with different infrastructures.

Modified products may perform better under different use conditions.

Product costs may be decreased by varying local inputs.

Product costs may be decreased by eliminating unnecessary product features.

Greater sales may be attained by better meeting industry norms or cultural preferences.

Sometimes discretionary adaptations can become mandatory. Originally, Microsoft declined to translate its software into Icelandic, a language spoken by only 270,000 people. Customers in Iceland were apparently able to manage without it. However, when Iceland's government demanded that Microsoft translate its program, the firm agreed rather than face leaving the market.[4]

Selecting the most desirable product features for each market is an involved decision for global marketers. The approach taken should include a thorough review of a number of factors that could determine both discretionary and mandatory adaptations. These include climatic, infrastructure, and use conditions; performance and quality standards; and cultural preferences.

Climatic, Infrastructure, and Use Conditions

International marketers often adapt products to conform to physical realities such as regional variations in climate and infrastructure. Air conditioners in Saudi Arabia must be able to operate under conditions that are hotter and dustier than those in most U.S. locations. Paint must be adapted to various climatic conditions, such as heat, cold, moisture, and wind. Automobile manufacturers must consider which side of the street cars are driven on—the left or the right—and adjust the steering wheel accordingly. For instance, drivers in Britain and Japan drive on the left. Marketers of packaged foods must consider the distribution infrastructure of the country. How long will the product be in the distribution channels? Are warehouses air-conditioned and trucks refrigerated? Most chocolate is easily damaged if not kept cool. One worldwide manufacturer of industrial abrasives even had to adjust products to differing availability of raw materials. It responded by varying the raw-materials input from one country to another, while maintaining exacting performance standards.

Products may also need to be adapted to different use conditions in various markets. Procter & Gamble was forced to adapt the formulation of its Cheer laundry detergent to accommodate different use conditions in the Japanese market. Cheer was initially promoted as an all-temperature detergent. However, many Japanese consumers washed their clothes in cold tap water or used leftover bath water. The Japanese also liked to add fabric softeners that decreased the suds produced by detergent. Procter & Gamble reformulated Cheer to work more effectively in cold water with fabric softeners added and changed its positioning to superior cleaning in cold water. The brand is now one of the company's best-selling products in Japan.[5]

In some local markets, customers may even expect a product to perform a function different from the one for which it was originally intended. One U.S. exporter of gardening tools found that its battery-operated trimmers were used by the Japanese as lawn mowers on their small lawns. As a result, the batteries and motors did not last as long as they would have under the intended use. Because of the different function desired by Japanese customers, a design change was eventually required.

Adapting to Performance and Quality Standards

Manufacturers typically design products to meet domestic performance standards. Such standards do not always apply in other countries, and product changes are required in some circumstances. Some companies go to great

World Beat 10.1 *Rolling Over*

At the Detroit auto show, Volvo showcased its first sport utility vehicle against a novel backdrop—a video screen showing a test vehicle repeatedly rolling over. The message: Our roof doesn't crush. A few yards away, the Swedish automaker's corporate parent, Ford Motor Company, emphasized the more traditional appeal of its trucks and SUVs—size, style and power.

The messages conveyed by the displays reflect sharp differences between how U.S. auto companies and their corporate partners in Europe approach one of the most contentious issues in auto safety today: roof strength. While the Europeans build roofs to withstand being dropped upside down or flipped off a moving dolly, their U.S. counterparts are fighting to keep in place a less rigorous federal test that hasn't been changed in 30 years. The disparity has caught the attention of the National Highway Traffic Safety Administration (NHTSA), which is weighing whether to beef up its roof-strength test to take better account of the lethal forces in a rollover accident.

U.S. automakers say their roofs match the Europeans' in safety. But relying on videos and data from crash tests that they commissioned in the 1980s, the U.S. car-makers also insist that injuries occur as the vehicle flips, when occupants dive headfirst into the roof, before it crushes. The NHTSA test, developed by General Motors in the late 1960s, applies on support pillars a downward force that the agency itself says "is not representative of dynamic roof crush" in the real world. But most strikingly, the NHTSA standard calls for vehicles to be tested with their windshields. The significance? Vehicle roofs lose between 10 percent and 40 percent of their structural strength without the windshield. And in a rollover, safety advocates point out, the windshield frequently breaks when the roof first hits the ground.

Europe has no roof-strength standards, but all three of the U.S. automakers' affiliates—GM's Saab, Ford's Volvo, and DaimlerChrysler's Mercedes-Benz—choose to subject their vehicles to tougher roof tests because they say the benefits are clear. At Saab, vehicles under development are rammed at 43 miles per hour into a tightly wrapped bundle of electrical cable to simulate hitting a moose, a not uncommon occurrence in Sweden.

Source: Milo Geyelin and Jeffrey Ball, "How Rugged Is Your Car's Roof?" *Wall Street Journal*, March 4, 2002, p. B1.

---

lengths to meet different quality standards in foreign markets. The experience of BMW, the German automaker exporting to Japan, serves as an excellent example of the extra efforts frequently involved. BMW found that its customers in Japan expected the very finest quality. Typically, cars shipped to Japan had to be completely repainted. Even very small mistakes were not tolerated by customers. When service was required, the car was picked up at the customer's home and returned when the work was completed.

The necessity to increase product quality or performance for a foreign market tends, if the need exists, to be readily apparent. Opportunities for product simplification are frequently less obvious to the firm. Products designed in highly developed countries often exceed the performance needed in developing countries. Customers in these markets may prefer products of greater simplicity, not only to save costs but also to ensure better service over the products' lifetime. Companies have been criticized for selling excess performance where simpler products will do. Several imported video-cassette recorders experienced low sales in China because they offered functions many consumers did not use. Such products were shunned by the value-conscious Chinese.[6] Ready to fill this market gap are companies from less developed countries whose present levels of technology are more in line with consumer needs. For example, local Egyptian firms that produce consumer products invest very little in elaborate features or attractive packaging in order to deliver products at very low prices.

Of course, manufacturers from developing countries can face the opposite challenge when attempting to sell overseas. They must increase the performance of their products to meet the standards of industrialized countries. Producing quality products that are competitive on export markets has become something of a national obsession in Mexico. Major companies such as the Alfa business group and Cemex have joined forces with universities to establish programs to supply Mexican industry with top-flight engineers. And the effort has paid off. Fifteen years after the country joined NAFTA in 1994, Mexico's exports had more than doubled.[7]

READ MORE ABOUT IT:
Check out "Mexico Goes Top-Flight" under *Supplemental Readings* on our website.

Global Standards A lack of international standards is readily apparent in the movie industry. The ultra-grisly movie *Hannibal* grossed more than $230 million worldwide, but its scenes of cannibalism and dismemberment caused an outcry in Italy, where its rating suggested it was appropriate for all audiences. In the United States, no one under 17 was supposed to be admitted without an adult, but children as young as 8 were seen entering with their parents. In Western Europe, viewers had to be at least 15—with or without accompanying adults. But in Portugal and Uruguay they only had to be 12 years old.[8]

Many countries have organizations that set voluntary standards for products and business practices. Groups such as the Canadian Standards Association and the British Standards Institute (BSI) formulate standards for product design and testing. If producers adhere to these standards, buyers are assured of the stated level of product quality.[9]

The unification of Europe has forced Europeans to recognize the need for multicountry standards. In areas where a European standard has been developed, manufacturers who meet the standard are allowed to include the European Union Certification Symbol, CE. Firms both in and out of the European Union are eligible to use the CE symbol, but they must be able to demonstrate their compliance with the standards.[10]

The U.S. standard-setting process is much more fragmented than Europe's. In the United States, there are over 450 different standard-setting groups, loosely coordinated by the American National Standards Institute (ANSI). After a standard is set by one of the 450 groups, ANSI certifies that it is an "American National Standard," of which there are over 11,000 on the books.[11]

Incompatible national standards both help and hinder global competitors. Incompatible technologies in the mobile phone industry mean that it is very difficult for a single make of handset to compete worldwide. As of 2001, the United States used four cellular technologies, which made it expensive for firms to make cell phones for every network operator. Japan had its own mobile network technology that was different from the U.S. technologies. This protected Japanese competitors at home by making it difficult for foreign firms to enter the Japanese market. On the other hand, the lack of technologies overseas that were compatible with Japanese standards handicapped Japanese competitors abroad.[12]

Given the growth in international commerce, there are benefits to having international standards for items such as credit cards, screw threads, car tires, paper sizes, and speed codes for 35 mm film. And country-to-country differences become immediately obvious when you try to plug in your hair dryer in various countries. Although national standards institutes ensure consistency within countries, an international agency is necessary to coordinate across countries.

The International Standards Organization (ISO), located in Geneva, was founded in 1947 to coordinate the setting of global standards. The ISO is a nongovernment organization, a federation of national standards bodies from some 140 countries. Each member of the ISO is the firm "most representative of standardization in its country"; only one such member is allowed per country. Most standards set by the ISO are highly specific, such as standards for film speed codes or formats for telephone and banking cards. ISO standards for components of freight containers have made it possible for shipping costs around the world to be lowered substantially.[13]

To set an international standard, representatives from various countries meet and attempt to agree on a common standard. Sometimes they adopt the standard set by a particular country. For example, the British standard for quality assurance (BS5750) was adopted internationally as ISO 9000 in 1987. This standard was revolutionary in that it was a **generic management system standard**. As the first such international standard, ISO 9000 ensured that an organization could consistently deliver a product or service that satisfied the customer's requirements because the company followed a state-of-the art management system. In other words, the company possessed quality management. ISO 9000 can be applied to any organization, large or small, whatever its product or service. ISO 14000 is a similar generic management system standard that is primarily concerned with environmental management. Companies that meet this standard must show that they do minimal damage to the environment.

Sometimes product standards are not voluntary but regulated by law. In these cases, adaptation to standards is mandatory, not discretionary. Most often these mandatory standards involve product quality and safety, hygiene, and environmental concerns. Meeting these standards can add costs to the product but may be necessary for the firm to access or remain in important markets. To meet EU-imposed noise standards, Murray Ohio Manufacturing, a manufacturer of lawn mowers, incurred significant increases in production costs. To reduce noise, Murray had to slow down the blade speed, which in turn necessitated changes to the exhaust and bagging systems. In spite of the increased costs, Murray made these changes because the EU was a large and growing market that it could not afford to ignore.[14]

In fact, many believe that Europe has come to dominate the creation of international standards through its influence at the ISO and its proactive stance toward setting mandatory standards. Already the standards established by the European Commission have become effective standards for firms in Asia and Latin America that aspire to export to Europe. EU standards concerning consumer safety are generally tougher than their U.S. counterparts—forcing U.S. companies to take note and conform. In 2002 the Illinois Department of Agriculture asked local farmers not to plant a corn developed by the Monsanto Company because it wasn't approved in the European Union. California-based Mattel has reformulated the plastic it uses in its Barbie dolls and other toys to adhere to recently established EU standards.[15]

Visit the ISO and the ANSI links on our website.

READ MORE ABOUT IT: Check out "Increasingly, Rules of Global Economy Are Set in Brussels" under *Supplemental Readings* on our website.

Adapting Products to Cultural Preferences

Cultural adaptations are usually discretionary adaptations. Yet understanding cultural preferences and adapting products accordingly can be extremely important to success in local markets. To the extent that fashion and tastes differ by country, companies often change their styling. Color, for example, should reflect the aesthetic values of each country.[16] For Japan, red and white have happy associations, whereas black and white indicates mourning. Green is an unpopular color in Malaysia, where it is associated with the jungle and illness. Textile manufacturers in the United States who have started to expand their export businesses have consciously used color to suit local needs. For example, the Lowenstein Corporation has successfully used brighter colors for fabrics exported to Africa.

The scent and sounds of a product may also have to be changed from one country to another. S.C. Johnson & Son encountered resistance to its Lemon Pledge furniture polish among older consumers in Japan. Careful market research revealed that the polish smelled similar to a latrine disinfectant used widely in Japan in the 1940s. Sales rose sharply after the scent was adjusted.[17] Word processing engineers had to change programs destined for Japan that "pinged" when users tried to do something that was not possible. Japanese office workers complained that they were mortified that co-workers could hear when they made mistakes. The "ping" was deleted.[18]

As we noted in Chapter 3, food is one of the most culturally distinct product areas. Pizza is a Western product not introduced in Japan until 1986 by Domino's. The original cheese and pepperoni topping was quickly adapted to suit Japanese tastes. Today, a variety of ingredients are available for pizza in Japan, including curry, squid, spinach, corn, tuna, teriyaki, barbecued beef, burdock root, shrimp, seaweed, apple, and rice.[19] Of course, adaptation is not always necessary. Kentucky Fried Chicken is doing very well in Pakistan, where chicken is the preferred meat. The menu is not substantially different from that offered elsewhere.[20]

Even factual knowledge is not immune to a little cultural tweaking. Microsoft's online encyclopedia, Encarta, lists the height of Europe's highest mountain, Mont Blanc, as 4,808 meters (15,770 feet) in its French version. In the Dutch version this height is listed as 4,807 meters. The Italians believe the correct height to be 4,810 meters, so that's what the Italian version says.[21]

Product Size and Dimensions

Even when other design features require no modification, product size and dimensions may need adaptation. Product size can be affected by physical surroundings and available space. In many countries, limited living space necessitates home appliances that are substantially smaller than those found in a country such as the United States, where people live in larger dwellings. Recently, U.S.-made major appliances have been imported into Japan by discount chains. Although the volume is still small by international standards, certain wealthier Japanese consumers favor these large appliances. However, some customers have had to return them after purchase because they could not get the refrigerators through their apartment doors.

The different physical characteristics of consumers can also influence product design. Domino's Pizza found that one size pizza did not fit all appetites worldwide.[22] Swiss watch manufacturers learned over the years to

The typical Japanese home is smaller than its U.S. counterpart, creating a demand for smaller appliances.

adapt their watchbands to different wrist sizes. For example, Japanese have smaller wrists than Americans. A leading Italian shoe manufacturer had a similar experience exporting shoes to the United States. Research revealed that feet were not the same in every country. Americans were found to have longer toes than Italians and smaller insteps.[23] The company learned that Americans have thicker ankles and narrower, flatter feet. To produce a properly fitting shoe, the Italian company decided to make appropriate changes in its design to achieve the necessary comfort for U.S. customers.

In many countries, customers have come to expect certain products in certain sizes, and international firms are forced to adapt to meet these expectations. Sometimes product dimensions must be changed to conform to national standards set by law. Chrysler found it necessary to make numerous changes to its Jeep to be successful in Japan. The owner's manual had to be revised to include bigger diagrams and cartoons, and under-hood wiring was adjusted to meet Japanese standards.[24]

In markets where many potential consumers have little disposable income, packaged-goods manufacturers often determine that smaller sizes are necessary to offer the customer an accessible product. In India, Unilever has repackaged its products in small portions to make them more affordable. Similarly, in 2002, Coca-Cola launched its powdered soft drink concentrate Sunfill in single-serving packets in India to attract consumers who could not afford to buy more expensive products.[25]

One important factor, particularly for U.S. firms, is whether to select a metric or a nonmetric scale for the sale of their products abroad. With Europe and Japan operating on the metric standard, the United States is one of the few remaining major nonmetric markets. The firm must often go beyond a single translation of nonmetric into metric sizes (or vice versa) to help consumers understand the design of its products. In some cases, companies may be required to change the physical sizes of their products to conform to legal standards based on the metric scale.

▶ *Branding Decisions*

Brands provide a name or symbol that gives a product credibility and helps the consumer identify the product. A brand that consumers know and trust helps them make choices faster and more easily.[26] A globally recognized brand name can be a huge asset even when a firm enters new markets. For example, when McDonald's opened its doors in Johannesburg, South Africa, thousands of people stood in line. When Coke entered Poland, its red and white delivery trucks drew applause at traffic lights.[27]

Interbrand ranks the top global brands each year (see Tables 10.2 and 10.3). All brands must be global in nature—at least 20 percent of brand revenues must be derived outside the firm's domestic market. Interbrand determines what percentage of total firm revenues can be attributed to a global brand and projects its net earnings. It then deducts a charge for the cost of owning the tangible assets related to the brand and thus captures the value of intangible factors such as patents, customer lists, and brand. When the values of the other intangibles are calculated and deducted, the value of the brand remains.

The top global brands are dominated by U.S. brands, followed by European brands. Although a number of Japanese companies, including Toyota, Panasonic, and Sony, have built strong global brands, few other Asian companies have achieved such status. Acer Corporation, the Taiwanese PC maker, has begun to build a global brand, followed by LG, formerly known as Lucky–Gold Star, the Korean electronics company. Samsung, the South Korean electronics manufacturing company, retained Vogt-Wein of Westport, Connecticut, to build its global brand image to cover VCRs, satellite dishes, personal computers, and cameras.[28] It ranked thirty-fourth among global brands in 2002.

Table 10.2 *Top 100 Global Brands*

RANK	2002 BRAND VALUE ($ BILLIONS)	2001 BRAND VALUE ($ BILLIONS)	PERCENT CHANGE	COUNTRY OF OWNERSHIP
1. Coca-Cola	69.64	68.95	+1%	U.S.
2. Microsoft	64.09	65.07	−2	U.S.
3. IBM	51.19	52.75	−3	U.S.
4. GE	41.31	42.40	−3	U.S.
5. Intel	30.86	34.67	−11	U.S.
6. Nokia	29.97	35.04	−14	Finland
7. Disney	29.26	32.59	−10	U.S.
8. McDonald's	26.38	25.29	+4	U.S.
9. Marlboro	24.15	22.05	+10	U.S.
10. Mercedes	21.01	21.73	−3	Germany
11. Ford	20.40	30.09	−32	U.S.
12. Toyota	19.45	18.58	+5	Japan
13. Citibank	18.07	19.01	−5	U.S.
14. Hewlett-Packard	16.78	17.98	−7	U.S.
15. American Express	16.29	16.92	−4	U.S.
16. Cisco Systems	16.22	17.21	−6	U.S.

Table 10.2 *Top 100 Global Brands* (Continued)

RANK	2002 BRAND VALUE ($ BILLIONS)	2001 BRAND VALUE ($ BILLIONS)	PERCENT CHANGE	COUNTRY OF OWNERSHIP
17. AT&T	16.06	22.83	−30	U.S.
18. Honda	15.06	14.64	+3	Japan
19. Gillette	14.96	15.30	−2	U.S.
20. BMW	14.43	13.86	+4	Germany
21. Sony	13.90	15.01	−7	Japan
22. Nescafé	12.84	13.25	−3	Switzerland
23. Oracle	11.51	12.22	−6	U.S.
24. Budweiser	11.35	10.84	+5	U.S.
25. Merrill Lynch	11.23	15.02	−25	U.S.
26. Morgan Stanley	11.20	N/A	N/A	U.S.
27. Compaq	9.80	12.35	−21	U.S.
28. Pfizer	9.77	8.95	+9	U.S.
29. J.P. Morgan	9.69	N/A	N/A	U.S.
30. Kodak	9.67	10.80	−10	U.S.
31. Dell	9.24	8.27	+12	U.S.
32. Nintendo	9.22	9.46	−3	Japan
33. Merck	9.14	9.67	−6	U.S.
34. Samsung	8.31	6.37	+30	S. Korea
35. Nike	7.72	7.59	+2	U.S.
36. Gap	7.41	8.75	−15	U.S.
37. Heinz	7.35	7.06	+4	U.S.
38. Volkswagen	7.21	7.34	−2	Germany
39. Goldman Sachs	7.19	7.87	−9	U.S.
40. Kellogg's	7.19	7.01	+3	U.S.
41. Louis Vuitton	7.05	7.05	0	France
42. Sap	6.78	6.31	+7	Germany
43. Canon	6.72	6.68	+2	Japan
44. Ikea	6.55	6.01	+9	Sweden
45. Pepsi	6.39	6.21	+3	U.S.
46. Harley-Davidson	6.27	5.53	+13	U.S.
47. MTV	6.08	6.60	−8	U.S.
48. Pizza Hut	6.05	6.00	+1	U.S.
49. KFC	5.35	5.26	+2	U.S.
50. Apple	5.32	5.46	−3	U.S.
51. Xerox	5.31	6.02	−12	U.S.
52. Gucci	5.30	5.37	−1	Italy
53. Accenture	5.18	N/A	N/A	U.S.
54. L'oréal	5.08	N/A	N/A	France
55. Kleenex	5.04	5.09	−1	U.S.
56. Sun	4.78	5.15	−7	U.S.
57. Wrigley's	4.75	4.53	+5	U.S.
58. Reuters	4.61	5.24	−12	Britain
59. Colgate	4.60	4.57	+1	U.S.

Table 10.2 *Top 100 Global Brands* (Continued)

RANK	2002 BRAND VALUE ($ BILLIONS)	2001 BRAND VALUE ($ BILLIONS)	PERCENT CHANGE	COUNTRY OF OWNERSHIP
60. Philips	4.56	4.90	−7	Netherlands
61. Nestlé	4.43	N/A	N/A	Switzerland
62. Avon	4.40	4.37	+1	U.S.
63. AOL	4.33	4.50	−4	U.S.
64. Chanel	4.27	4.27	0	France
65. Kraft	4.08	4.03	+1	U.S.
66. Danone	4.05	N/A	N/A	France
67. Yahoo!	3.86	4.38	−12	U.S.
68. Adidas	3.69	3.66	+1	Germany
69. Rolex	3.69	3.70	0	Switzerland
70. Time	3.68	3.72	−1	U.S.
71. Ericsson	3.59	7.07	−49	Sweden
72. Tiffany	3.48	3.48	0	U.S.
73. Levi's	3.34	3.75	−8	U.S.
74. Motorola	3.42	3.77	−9	U.S.
75. Duracell	3.41	4.14	−18	U.S.
76. BP	3.39	3.24	+4	Britain
77. Hertz	3.36	3.62	−7	U.S.
78. Bacardi	3.34	3.20	+4	Bermuda
79. Caterpillar	3.22	N/A	N/A	U.S.
80. Amazon.com	3.18	3.13	+1	U.S.
81. Panasonic	3.14	3.50	−10	Japan
82. Boeing	2.97	4.06	−27	U.S.
83. Shell	2.81	2.84	−1	Brit./Neth.
84. Smirnoff	2.72	2.59	+5	Britain
85. Johnson & Johnson	2.51	N/A	N/A	U.S.
86. Prada	2.49	N/A	N/A	Italy
87. Moet & Chandon	2.45	2.47	−1	France
88. Heineken	2.40	2.27	+6	Netherlands
89. Mobil	2.36	2.41	−2	U.S.
90. Burger King	2.16	2.43	−11	U.S.
91. Nivea	2.06	1.78	+16	Germany
92. Wall Street Journal	1.96	2.18	−10	U.S.
93. Starbuck's	1.96	1.76	+12	U.S.
94. Barbie	1.94	2.04	−5	U.S.
95. Polo/Ralph Lauren	1.93	1.91	+1	U.S.
96. FedEx	1.92	1.89	+2	U.S.
97. Johnnie Walker	1.65	1.65	0	Britain
98. Jack Daniels	1.58	1.58	0	U.S.
99. 3M	1.58	N/A	N/A	U.S.
100. Armani	1.51	1.49	+1	Italy

Note: Brands listed must derive 20 percent or more of sales from outside their home country, and there must be publicly available marketing and financial data on which to base the valuation.

Source: Interbrand, Citigroup; *Business Week,* August 5, 2002: 95–99.

Table 10.3 *Top Global Brand Portfolios*

COMPANY	2001 BRAND ($ BILLIONS)	2000 BRAND ($ BILLIONS)	PERCENT CHANGE	COUNTRY
1. Johnson & Johnson	68.21	NA	NA	U.S.
2. P&G	45.44	48.35	−6	U.S.
3. Nestlé	41.69	40.25	4	Switzerland
4. Unilever	37.85	37.10	2	Brit./Neth.
5. L'oréal	17.80	NA	NA	France
6. Diageo	15.00	14.56	3	Brit./Neth.
7. Colgate-Palmolive	14.36	13.64	5	U.S.
8. Danone	13.58	NA	NA	France

Source: Interbrand, Citigroup; *Business Week,* August 6, 2000: 64.

Selecting Brand Names

Selecting appropriate brand names on an international basis is substantially more complex than deciding on a brand name for just one country. Typically, a brand name is rooted in a given language and, if used elsewhere, may have either a different meaning or none at all. Ideally, marketers look for brand names that evoke similar emotions or images around the world.

Brand name and symbol selection is critical. International marketers must carefully evaluate the meanings and word references in the languages of their target audiences. Can the name be pronounced easily, or will it be distorted in the local language? A good example of brand adaptation is the name choice for Coca-Cola, which means "tasty and happy" in Chinese. Mercedes-Benz's Chinese name means "striving forward fast," and Sharp's means "the treasure of sound." However, branding in Asia, and especially in China, may rely even more on the visual appeal of logos than on brand names. The simple graphical logos of Volkswagen, Mercedes-Benz, and Lexus are rated high, whereas the icons of Cadillac, General Motors, and Fiat are less appealing.[29]

Single-Country versus Global Brand Names Global marketers are constantly confronted with the decision of whether the brand name needs to be universal. Brands such as Coca-Cola and Kodak have universal use and lend themselves to an integrated international marketing strategy. With worldwide travel so common, many companies do not think they should accept a brand name unless it can be used universally.

Of course, using the same name elsewhere is not always possible. In such instances, different names have to be found. Procter & Gamble had successfully marketed its household cleaner, Mr. Clean, in the United States for some time. This name, however, had no meaning except in countries using the English language. This prompted the company to arrive at several adaptations abroad, such as *Monsieur Propre* in France and *Meister Proper* in Germany. In all cases, however, the symbol of the genie with gleaming eyes was retained because it evoked similar responses abroad and in the United States.

Selecting a Global Name

Given the almost unlimited possibilities for names and the restricted opportunities to find and register a desirable one, international companies devote considerable effort to the selection procedure. One consulting company specializes in finding brand names with worldwide application. The company brings citizens of many countries together in Paris where, under the guidance of a specialist, they are asked to state names in their particular language that would combine well with the product to be named.[30] Speakers of other languages can immediately react if a name comes up that sounds unpleasant or has distasteful connotations in their language. After a few such sessions, the company may accumulate as many as 1,000 names that will later be reduced to 500 by a company linguist. The client company then is asked to select 50 to 100 names for further consideration. At this point, the names are subjected to a search procedure to determine which have not been registered in any of the countries under consideration. In the end, only about 10 names may survive this process. From these, the company will have to make the final selection. Although this process may be expensive, the cost is generally considered negligible compared with the advertising expenditures invested in the brand name over many years.

When confronted with the need to search for a brand name with global applications, a company can consider the following:

1. An arbitrary or invented word not to be found in any dictionary of standard English (or other language), such as Toyota's Lexus.
2. A recognizable English (or foreign-language) word, but one totally unrelated to the product in question, such as the detergent Cheer.
3. An English (or other language) word that merely suggests some characteristic or purpose of the product, such as Mr. Clean.
4. A word that is evidently descriptive of the product, although the word may have no meaning to persons unacquainted with English (or the other language), such as the diaper brand Pampers.
5. A geographic place or a common surname, such as Kentucky Fried Chicken.
6. A device, design, number, or some other element that is not a word or a combination of words, such as the 3M Company.[31]

Changing Brand Names

At times, firms may choose to change the name of a brand in local markets or even worldwide. This is not an easy choice. If a product has substantial market share in one or more markets, changing its name can confuse or even alienate consumers. Colgate-Palmolive, the large U.S.-based toiletries manufacturer, purchased the leading toothpaste brand in Southeast Asia, "Darkie." With a minstrel in blackface as its logo, the product had been marketed by a local company since 1920. After the acquisition in 1985, Colgate-Palmolive came under pressure from many groups in the United States to use a less offensive brand name. The company sponsored a large amount of research to find both a brand name and a logo that were racially inoffensive and yet close enough to the original to be recognized quickly by consumers. The company changed the name to "Darlie" after an exhaustive search. Still, in some markets where the "Darkie" brand had as much as 50 percent market share, it was a substantial marketing challenge to convert brand loyalty, intact, from the old to the new name.[32]

Today some multinational companies are reconsidering earlier decisions concerning brand names. Unilever launched Jif household cleaner in the U.K. in 1974. Twenty-five years later, the product held a 74 percent share of the market. Despite Jif's market dominance and name recognition, Unilever decided to change its name to correspond to the name under which it was sold in other major markets. When the product was first rolled out, it received different names based in part on ease of pronunciation in each local language. This resulted in Jif becoming Cif in France and 39 other countries. It was Viss in Germany and Vim in Canada. The product wasn't introduced in the United States, where the name was already associated with a peanut butter marketed by competitor Procter & Gamble. Unilever undertook extensive market research to ensure that consumers would not be upset by the change and also supported the new name with substantial promotion to reassure the customer that Cif was actually Jif.[33]

Federal Express launched its courier business in the United States in the 1970s. The Federal Express name reflected the U.S. overnight delivery service. As Federal Express opened its international operations, however, the name was a problem. In Latin America *federal* connoted corrupt police, and in Europe the name was linked to the former Federal Republic of Germany. In 1994, Federal Express changed its name to FedEx, which in some cases is used as a verb meaning "to ship overnight."[34] Because FedEx dealt with many multinational companies as clients, it wanted a single name to use globally.

Global Branding

The concept of global branding goes beyond simply establishing a global brand name. Yet experts disagree on what exactly makes a global brand. Is it global presence or global name recognition? There are certainly brand names such as Coca-Cola that are well known in most countries of the world. Does the name connote similar attributes worldwide? Is the product the same? Is the brand a powerful player in all major markets? Heineken qualifies on the first two conditions, but not on the third. It has positioned itself as a quality imported beer in its many export markets. The beer and the bottle remain the same across markets. However, its lack of adaptation has kept it a well-known but minor player in the various national markets.

As we have noted, Interbrand defines a global brand as one with sales of at least 20 percent outside the firm's domestic market. Other definitions are less encompassing, describing global brands as brands whose positioning, advertising strategy, personality, look, and feel are in most respects the same in all countries.[35] Firms that develop global brands with these characteristics are said to follow a **global brand strategy**.

There are several steps involved in developing and administering a global brand strategy:

▶ A firm must identify common customer needs worldwide and determine how the global brand can deliver both functional and emotional benefits to these customers.

▶ A process must be established to communicate the brand's identity to consumers, channels, and the firm's own employees.

▶ There should be a way to track the success of the global identity of the brand, such as the customer opinion surveys employed by Pepsi.

▶ The firm must determine whether it will follow a more centralized, top-down approach to global branding or a more gradual, bottom-up approach. Sony and Mobil take **top-down approaches** wherein a global management team determines the global brand strategy and then country strategies are derived from it. In a **bottom-up approach,** country strategies are grouped by similarities in such variables as the level of economic development and the competitive situation (whether or not the brand is dominant in the market). Common elements are first identified within these groupings. Over time, a more global strategy emerges as subsidiaries share experiences and best practices.[36]

World Beat 10.2 *How Belgium's Peasant Beer Became Premium*

At La Fleur en Papier D'ore, the oldest bar in Brussels, retired shopkeeper Jean-Paul De Boek can down five glasses of Stella Artois a day, because it is easy on his stomach and costs just $1.10 a pint. But in New York City, even if he could get past the bouncers at the hip bars where this Belgian beer is on tap, he would go broke keeping up the pace. A glass of Stella costs as much as $8 in Manhattan. "In Belgium Stella is a beer fit for an old peasant," Mr. De Boek says. To pay such prices, "Americans must be insane."

Interbrew NV, the Belgian brewer of Stella Artois, figures its financial future lies in snob appeal. By marketing a beer that is run-of-the-mill in Belgium as a premium label elsewhere, and insisting that foreigners pay dearly for it, Interbrew aims to boost profitability and finally reach its goal of unseating Heineken NV as the world's second largest beer maker. (Anheuser-Busch of the United States is number one.)

Interbrew, in many ways, is playing copycat to its archrival. Heineken, based about 125 miles away in Amsterdam, pioneered the global brand strategy, and its success has longed irked Interbrew and Belgium, which boasts more than 400 varieties of beer. Thus Interbrew came up with the Stella strategy. After a successful run in London—where the beer, the top import in the United Kingdom, is advertised as "reassuringly expensive"—Interbrew picked New York as the venue in which to test seriously the merits of going global.

The company hired a team of 30-something partygoers from the beer industry to draw up a list of the 20 most exclusive bars in the city. The list included such hip joints as Chez Estrada and Market, favorite haunts of Madonna and other celebrities. An Interbrew sales team flew over from Belgium to explain that distributors should limit the Stella supply to those 20 bars and charge about $100 for a keg, well above the $85 commanded by Heineken.

The timing was lucky. Stella hit New York during an explosion of interest in Belgian mussels, chocolate, and waffles. Stella's U.S. sales grew to 47.7 million quarts in 2001, up from 26.5 million in 2000. Even so, it has a long way to go to catch up with Heineken, which has annual U.S. sales of 530 million quarts. And the strategy is risky, depending as it does on adding luster to a brand so ordinary in Belgium that it is sold in plastic cups at fast-food restaurants. "Ever since I found out Stella is the Budweiser of beers in Belgium, I'm somewhat embarrassed to drink it," says one New York lawyer.

Dan Bilefsky, "How Belgium's 'Peasant' Beer Became 'Premium' in U.S." *Wall Street Journal*, April 12, 2002, p. A13.

In any case, a **brand champion** should be given the responsibility for building and managing a global brand. This should include monitoring the brand across markets, as well as authorizing the use of the brand on other products and businesses (brand extensions). The brand champion can be a senior manager at corporate headquarters, a product development group, or the manager of a lead country or one with major market share for the brand. For example, Unilever gave its French subsidiary custody over its Lipton brand.[37]

Pan-regional Branding

Although there are few genuinely global brands, pan-regional branding is increasing in importance. For example, the Shangri-La Hotel chain, with thirty-four hotels, has built a strong regional brand across Asia. Shangri-La offers all the amenities of a luxury hotel, along with Asian hospitality. The staff uniforms reflect the local costumes. Shangri-La uses its advertising to appeal to executives in Asia, who are often judged by the hotels they choose. The tag line on Shangri-La ads is "It must be Shangri-La."[38] In Latin America, Brazil's Varig Airlines has undertaken a design and logo change to broaden its regional appeal. The revamped Varig logo is modern and warm-looking, which supports an advertising program that features well-rested passengers getting off their flights.[39]

In the case of Europe, regional brands are called **Eurobrands**. In a survey of more than 200 European brand managers in 13 countries, 81 percent indicated that they were aiming for standardization and homogenization of brands, whereas only 13 percent said they were leaving each country free to decide its own strategy.[40] The survey clearly indicates a strong preference for a Eurobrand strategy for most companies. Two European firms that adopted Eurobrand strategies early are Electrolux and Danone.

Electrolux, the Swedish white-goods (household appliances) company, made over a hundred acquisitions in about 10 years, which left the company with over twenty brands sold in 40 countries. Large markets such as the United Kingdom and Germany had as many as six major Electrolux brands. A study by Electrolux found a convergence of market segments across Europe, with the consumers' need for "localness" being primarily in terms of distribution channels, promotion in local media, and use of local names instead of product design and features. From this analysis, Electrolux developed a strategy with two pan-European brands and one or two local brands in each market. The Electrolux brand was targeted to the high-prestige, conservative consumers, and the Zanussi brand was targeted to the innovative, trendsetter consumers. The local brands were targeted to the young, aggressive urban professionals and to the warm and friendly, value-oriented consumers.[41]

As BSN, the third largest food group in Europe, has grown beyond its base in France to become a pan-European company with global aspirations, it has found its name to be a weakness. BSN, which stands for the two former companies Boussois and Souchon-Neuvesel that merged in 1966, was recognized by 93 percent of people in France, but only by 7 percent in Italy and 5 percent in Spain. To support its global image, BSN changed its name to Danone after its dairy and yogurt brand.[42] Danone developed into one of the world's top brand names.[43]

Other cases of Eurobrands—products marketed across Europe with the same brand name, formula, and packaging, as well as the same positioning and advertising strategy—include Procter & Gamble's Pampers and Head & Shoulders, Michelin tires, and Rolex watches. Purely national brands in Europe are expected to decline in share from more than 50 percent today to about one-third in the next decade.

Private Branding

The practice of private branding, or supplying products to another party for sale under the latter's brand name, has become quite common in many markets. Private branding offers particular advantages to a company with strong manufacturing skills but little access to foreign markets. Arranging for distribution of the firm's product through local distributors or companies with existing distribution networks reduces the risk of failure and provides for rapid volume growth via instant market access.

Some Japanese companies used private branding to gain market access in Europe and the United States. Ricoh of Japan, originally known as a manufacturer of cameras, entered the market for small plain paper copiers (PPCs) via private-branding contracts with several U.S. and European firms. Ricoh used this strategy to enter markets when it was relatively unknown. Once established, the firm switched to selling its products under its own brand name. The company is now a global leader for both small personal copiers and fax machines.[44]

Private-branding contracts are not without drawbacks for the manufacturer. With control over marketing in the hands of another manufacturer or distributor, the firm remains dependent and can only indirectly influence marketing. For long-term profitability, companies often find that they need to create brand equity, which requires selling products under their own brands. Partnerships often end because of conflicting interests and can be costly to terminate.

▶ *Trademarks and Brand Protection*

Violations of **trademarks**—the names, words, and symbols that enable customers to distinguish among brands—have been an inescapable problem for global marketers. These violations can involve the legal hijacking or local **preemption of a brand name.** For example, someone could register the Gucci brand name in a country where Gucci had yet to register its brands. If Gucci wanted to enter that market, it would have to buy back its brand name or sell under another. Trademark preemption is especially easy in countries that do not require that the brand be sold in the market after registration.

International treaties to protect well-known international brands from being preempted in local markets go back to the Paris Convention of 1883. However, problems can arise even in signatory countries. Claiming its rights under the Paris Convention, Gucci fought two cases in Mexico against infringing firms. It won one case but lost the other. In the latter case, the Mexican judge was not convinced that the Mexican government had even ratified the Paris Convention more than 100 years before.

Today, the Paris Convention has been superseded by trademark protection rules under the World Trade Organization. Countries that join the WTO must establish national laws that protect global brands. These laws must encompass a procedure by which the owners of famous international brands can successfully oppose the registration of their brands by local preemptors. Local laws must be adequate to deter counterfeiters, and countries must not discriminate between local and foreign firms who apply for trademark protection. Depending on a country's level of economic development, it may be allowed up to 11 years to bring its local laws into compliance.

Holding countries to these requirements is somewhat ambitious, however, given the fact that the signatory countries of the WTO exhibited very different levels of trademark protection at the time they joined. A study of national trademark protection in the years prior to establishment of the WTO shows distinct patterns across country categories. Developed countries provided the best overall protection. Less developed countries and the transition economies of Russia and Eastern Europe exhibited much weaker local laws, and processing times for foreign trademark applications were exceptionally slow in the transition economies. Many newly industrialized countries, including Taiwan and South Korea, had already established local laws on a par with those of developed countries. However, a lack of resources undermined the ability of such countries to enforce these laws adequately.[45]

The norms established by the WTO are no doubt a step in the right direction, but problems still persist. Although the countries of the former Soviet bloc have adopted trademark protection laws in accordance with WTO guidelines, the enforcement of these laws remains problematic. There have been concerns that Russian judges and prosecutors don't understand the nature of Russia's newly adopted trademark laws—although the laws look good on paper. The U.S.-based tobacco company Philip Morris lost a case it brought in an effort to stop a Russian company from producing cigarettes whose packaging closely resembled that of two of Philip Morris's best-selling brands. Grupo Modelo, the Mexican beer company that makes Corona, also lost a trademark dispute with a Russian brewery that Modelo accused of stealing its brand name.[46]

Counterfeits and Piracy

Today, the biggest problem international marketers face in trying to protect their brands is counterfeiting. **Counterfeiting** is the illegal use of a registered trademark. A counterfeiter copies a branded product, cashing in on its brand equity. Counterfeiting injures both businesses and consumers. Counterfeit products are estimated to account for 3 percent of world trade according to the International Chamber of Commerce. The U.S. Department of Commerce estimated that some 750,000 U.S. jobs were lost as a consequence of foreign forgeries of U.S. products.[47] Some sources estimate the annual trade in counterfeit products at $250 billion on a global scale.[48]

U.K. sources estimate that the world pharmaceutical industry loses about 6 percent of total sales to counterfeit products.[49] In India, counterfeit pharmaceutical drugs have appeared on the market that are made of different chemical compounds and pose serious threats to patients.[50] Other sectors affected by counterfeiting include toys and sporting goods, which may lose as much as 13 percent of sales to this practice. Similarly, counterfeits of perfumes and toiletries account for 10 percent of global sales. Counterfeits of clothing and footwear account for 4 percent of total global sales.[51]

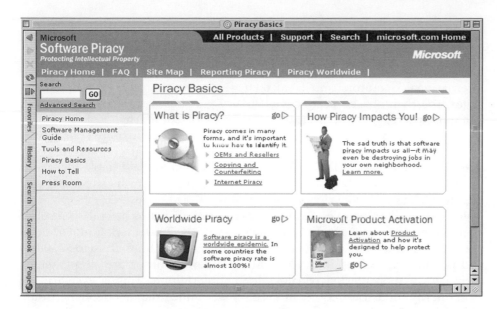

For Microsoft, fighting piracy is a global effort.

The term **piracy** is often applied to the counterfeit production of copyrighted material such as books, recorded music, and software. Because illegal production—or more aptly, reproduction—of these products is relatively simple and inexpensive, they become easy targets. Recorded music has long suffered from piracy, with global sales of counterfeits estimated at $4.5 billion worldwide. Counterfeit music is believed to outsell legitimate music in 20 countries, including Hong Kong, Malaysia, the Ukraine, Israel, Estonia, and Latvia, up from 14 countries a year earlier. The Ukraine has assumed the position of music counterfeit capital of Europe; legislation is inadequate, and the Ukrainian authorities lack commitment to clamp down on the perpetrators.[52]

Computer software firms are also battling pirates. Surveys indicate that about 40 percent of all new business software applications are pirated, resulting in a revenue loss of $11 billion a year. The biggest reported offenders were Vietnam, China, and Indonesia, each with over 90 percent of all installed new software pirated. Even in the United States, the piracy rate is estimated at 25 percent, resulting in some $2.9 billion in lost revenues each year. The problem is estimated to be even greater for consumer applications produced by Microsoft or Norton Utilities, where illegal copies have outsold legal copies.[53]

Counterfeiting of trademark-protected products flourishes in countries where legal protection of such trademarks is weak. In Vietnam the nature of copyright infringement is open to interpretation. Enforcement is weak because the government has few resources to enforce existing laws effectively or control the borders. Some international consumer goods companies doing business in Vietnam claim their sales are reduced by as much as 50 percent by the ready availability of illegal, and cheaper, products. Procter & Gamble is believed to have lost sales of up to 25 percent as illegal operators collected its containers and refilled them with counterfeit products. The same happened to brand-name cognac and whiskies. Reused bottles were filled with sugar rum.[54]

The emergence of e-business has contributed to the further growth of counterfeit global trade. Total online counterfeit business volume is estimated at $25 billion, a tenth of the total counterfeit volume. Internet counterfeiters are scattered across an estimated 5,000 websites. They include both international operators and local teenagers operating out of a basement. Rolex, the Swiss-based producer of luxury watches, regularly checks eBay auctions where, on any given day, hundreds of counterfeit Rolex watches may be up for bids. The manufacturers of many other luxury items do the same. Louis Vuitton regularly checks eBay and acts on counterfeit products.[55] By early 2001, eBay, concerned that it could be held liable for frauds or other illegal sales, began screening and removing from its site items that clearly infringed on copyrights.[56]

International companies have gone on the offensive to defend themselves against counterfeiting. The United States passed the Trademark Counterfeiting Act of 1984, which makes counterfeiting punishable by fines of up to $250,000 and prison terms of up to 5 years. Many other countries are strengthening their laws and increasing penalties for counterfeiting. This is even true of many newly industrialized countries that were once major offenders. Countries such as Brazil, Korea, and Taiwan now realize that their own domestic brands are being counterfeited in nearby countries. This has motivated local governments to become more serious about addressing the problem.

International firms are increasingly devising methods of their own to stop illegal counterfeiting. Many companies find that subcontractors, who know manufacturing processes, are becoming a problem. These companies may fulfill their regular contracts to an international company while selling extra volume on the black market. To stop such practices, new marketing systems are being developed both to allow companies to monitor abuses and to help customers spot counterfeit products. Polaproof by Polaroid provides a tamper-proof label. Other approaches include holograms and invisible marking devices or inks. Glaxo Wellcome, a leading UK pharmaceutical company, worked on making products and packaging unique so that they could not be copied by counterfeiters. Zantac, its leading ulcer drug, was designed as a five-sided, peach-colored pill. Prescribing doctors could look the drug up in the *Physician's Desk Reference* to verify its design.[57] When the Harry Potter series was launched in China, the publisher arranged for the books to be printed on a light green paper and planned a media blitz to explain to consumers how to tell the real thing from the counterfeit.[58] However, given the difficulty of tracking counterfeiters and the obvious opportunities for making quick profits, counterfeiting is a problem that international companies will have to deal with for some time to come.

Check out our website for anticounterfeiting links.

READ MORE ABOUT IT:
Check out "Harry Potter, Meet 'Ha-li Bo-te'" under *Supplemental Readings* on our website.

▶ *Packaging and Labeling for Global Markets*

Differences in the marketing environment may require special adaptations in product packaging. Different climatic conditions often demand a change in the package to ensure sufficient protection or shelf life. The role a package assumes in promotion also depends on the market retailing structure. In countries with a substantial degree of self-service merchandising, firms should choose a package with strong promotional appeal for consumer products. In addition, distribution handling requirements are not identical the world over. In the high-wage countries of the developed world, products tend to be packaged in such a way as to reduce further handling by retail employees. For consumer products, all mass merchandisers have to do is place products on shelves. In countries with lower wages and less elaborate retailing structures, individual orders may be filled from larger packaged units, a process that entails extra labor on the part of the retailer.

Specific packaging decisions that may be affected include size, shape, materials, color, and text. Size may differ by custom or in terms of existing standards, such as metric and nonmetric requirements. Higher-income countries tend to require larger unit sizes; these populations shop less frequently and can afford to buy larger quantities each time. In countries with lower income levels, consumers buy in smaller quantities and more often. Gillette sells razor blades in packages of five or ten in the United States and Europe, whereas singles are sold in some emerging markets.

Packages can assume almost any shape, largely depending on the customs and traditions prevailing in each market. Materials used for packaging can also differ widely. Whereas Americans prefer to buy mayonnaise and mustard in clear plastic containers, consumers in Germany and Switzerland buy these same products in tubes. Cans are the customary material in which to package beer in the United States, whereas most European consumers prefer glass bottles.

The package color and text have to be integrated into a company's promotional strategy and therefore may be subject to specific tailoring that differs from one country to another. The promotional effect is of great importance for consumer goods and has led some companies to attempt to standardize their packaging in color and layout. In areas such as Europe and Latin America, where consumers frequently travel to other countries, standardized colors help them identify a product quickly. This strategy depends on devising a set of colors or a layout with an appeal beyond one single culture or market. An example of a product with a standardized package color is Procter & Gamble's leading detergent, Tide. The orange and white box familiar to millions of U.S. consumers can be found in many foreign markets, even though the package text may appear in the language of the given country.

Cultural implications of packaging and labeling can sometimes create problems in unexpected ways. One exporter of software to Saudi Arabia identified its CD-ROMs for the Saudi market by putting the Saudi flag on the box. The flag bears the word *Allah*, the Arabic word for "God." For many devout Muslims, to discard the box would imply disrespect for God. As a result, the local distributor was left with lots of boxes that both customers and employees declined to throw away.[59]

In 1998 a new British law cut the number of pills that could be sold in packages of aspirin and acetaminophen to reduce overdoses leading to death and liver failure caused by impulsive self-poisoning. Tablets were also required to be blister-wrapped to make swallowing large quantities impulsively even more difficult. Three years later, in 2001, deaths by overdoses of these pills had decreased dramatically in the U.K.[60]

As consumers and governments become more concerned about the environmental consequences of excess or inappropriate packaging, companies are expected to develop packaging that is environmentally friendly. Responding to consumer concern, the U.K. retailer Sainsbury examines every product it sells to ensure each uses only the minimum packaging necessary.[61]

Labeling is another concern for international marketers. Labeling helps consumers understand better the products they are buying and can convey rudimentary instructions for their use. What languages must the labels be in? What government requirements are involved?

Increasingly, packaged-foods companies must adhere to government requirements concerning labeling, but many other products are affected as well. China is home to two-thirds of the world's cashmere goats. When the country began exporting cashmere sweaters and other garments, many manufacturers exaggerated the amount of cashmere in their products. This brought them into collision with the United States' 60-year-old Wool Products Labeling Act, which requires that fabrics and garments made out of wool and other fine animal hairs be accurately labeled to reflect their true content. The Federal Trade Commission can seek penalties in federal court as high as $11,000 for each violation.[62]

▶ *Marketing Services Globally*

International trade in services represents about 25 percent of total world trade. Services include business services, travel, transportation, and government services. One of the largest categories of service exports is business services. These services include communications, financial services, software development, database management, construction, computer support, accounting, advertising, consulting, and legal services. Trade in business services has traditionally taken place primarily among developed economies such as the United States, the Netherlands, France, Japan, the United Kingdom, Germany, and Italy.[63] Many services are now aimed at multinational companies themselves. IBM's Global Services is IBM's most rapidly growing division and is currently driving company growth while the hardware divisions struggle. Global Services supplies multinational firms with a variety of information technology services, from running a customer's information technology department to consulting on system upgrades and building global supply-chain management applications.[64]

Services differ from physical products in four key ways. They are **intangible**. They cannot be stored or readily displayed or communicated. Production and consumption of services are **simultaneous**. Services cannot be inventoried, and production lines do not exist to deliver standardized products of consistent quality. Therefore, delivered services are **heterogeneous** in nature. Finally, because services cannot be stored, they assume a **perishable** nature.[65]

These unique qualities of services affect their international marketing. There are fewer opportunities to realize economies of scale with services than with physical products. Guaranteeing product quality worldwide is more difficult, as is shifting product from one part of the world to another.

Business Services

Services aimed at business buyers that are most likely to be exported are those that have already met with success domestically. The experience of U.S.-based service companies can be used as an example. Some of the services that have been most successfully marketed abroad are financial services. Commercial banks such as Citibank, Chase, and BankAmerica have built such extensive branch networks around the world that foreign deposits and profits make up nearly half of business volume. Advertising agencies have also expanded overseas either by building branch networks or by merging with local agencies. More recently, many U.S.-based marketing research firms have expanded into foreign countries.

International accounting services have experienced tremendous growth as well. Overseas expansion is important to U.S.-based accounting firms for several reasons. Among the leading accounting firms, international revenue typically exceeds domestic revenue. Revenue is growing more rapidly abroad, and margins are also better for international operations. Many of the firms' accounting clients have gone through globalization themselves and demand different services. Also, the liberalization of trade in Europe and elsewhere has boosted cross-national business, increasing demand for international accountants.

Big British and U.S. law firms are also finding numerous opportunities overseas. The unification of Europe has accelerated cross-border mergers and acquisitions. Even though France and Japan have established local requirements to slow down the growth of foreign firms in their countries, the legal profession has become another global service industry. Many U.S. law firms are opening up overseas branch locations, primarily in London, to capture business from investment banks and other financial services firms that must have a presence in both New York and London, major capital market centers.[66]

Services for Consumers and Individual Households

Marketing services to consumers abroad turns out to be more difficult than selling to businesses. Because consumer behavior and usage patterns differ more between countries than industry usage patterns do, many services have to be adapted even more to local conditions to make them successful. Still, opportunities abound even in seemingly difficult markets. Insurance companies have achieved success in a number of emerging markets. For example, in Shanghai, China, the American International Group (AIG) sold more than 12,000 policies in 8 months. Although it took AIG more than 10 years to get licensed in China, the company believes the opportunities are tremendous.[67] AIG was one of only six foreign insurance firms licensed in China and was the first foreign firm to gain a license there.[68]

Culture and the Service Experience

Culture affects a number of aspects of the service experience, including customer expectations, the waiting experience, and the recruitment and behavior of service personnel.

Customer Expectations Customers may exhibit different expectations concerning service levels. Department stores in Japan still employ women in kimonos to bow and greet customers as they arrive at the store. Service personnel are available and solicitous. In the United States, consumers tend to be willing to forgo high levels of service in favor of low prices. They are more accustomed to self-service and may even feel nervous in the presence of hovering salespeople. Consumers in Switzerland are delighted when their local grocer chooses the best produce for them. As regular customers from the neighborhood, they deserve the best. Of course, this means that new customers are given the poorer produce. This would seem discriminatory and unfair to American customers. If residing in Switzerland, they would prefer to drive to a hypermarket where produce is prepackaged and the service encounter can be avoided altogether.

In many cultures, service does vary by the customer's group membership, in-groups enjoying better service than out-groups. Ironically, even in the highly individualistic United States, new technology may be allowing firms to vary their service among groups—at least between good customers and bad customers. When consumers call a credit card company with a problem, they are often asked to provide some basic information about themselves, such as their credit card number. This immediately alerts the company as to the caller's customer quality. Callers whose accounts are valuable and who are never in arrears can be quickly channeled to a very sympathetic service person. Callers whose accounts are often overdue may wait a very long time for someone to answer the phone. It is important to note, however, that these groupings are based on an individual's behavior, not on his or her social group.

The Waiting Experience Time is always an aspect of services, and attitudes toward the time it takes to be served vary across cultures. For example, waiters in European restaurants take care not to hurry patrons. Eating a meal is supposed to be an enjoyable experience most often shared with friends. Servers also wait to be asked to deliver the bill for the meal. Diners may wish to sit for hours. Americans would wonder what had happened to their waiter. Americans expect fast service at restaurants and like the bill to be dropped promptly on the table. What would be a good service experience for a European diner would be a bad one for an American.

In Russia, long lines are a tradition.

Attitudes toward waiting in line vary as well. The English are famous for their orderly and patient waits in lines, or queues. In the French-speaking part of Switzerland, members of this otherwise polite population are likely to become a jostling mob when caused to wait at an entrance. Americans introduced the idea of establishing a single line leading to multiple service points instead of having separate lines for each point. This invention addressed the common American complaint that one inevitably ended up standing in the slowest-moving line. Americans have difficulty understanding why the rest of the world hasn't adopted this idea.

In certain parts of the world, social norms may require that men and women stand in different lines. This can be observed at metro stops in Mexico City during rush hours. In Egypt the imported design of having an "in" line leading to a service point and an exit leading away from it was reinterpreted as one line for men and one for women, with each line alternately taking its turn at the service point.

Service Personnel When the local manager of a U.S.-based hotel chain was preparing to open a new hotel in Egypt, he was faced with a dilemma. American tourists would expect waitresses who could take their order in English. Egyptian women who spoke English almost invariably came from the upper classes. No young lady from those classes would be caught in public serving food to strangers. In a panic, the manager called friends and family and finally borrowed enough sisters, daughters, and nieces to staff the restaurant in time for opening day. Within a week, one waitress met and married a Saudi multimillionaire who came to eat at the restaurant. Whether apocryphal or not, the story spread like wildfire, and the manager never again had trouble recruiting waitresses!

In many cultures, such as the Middle East, working in a service occupation is often considered akin to being a servant. This social stigma can make it hard to recruit qualified personnel for some positions, especially those that require higher levels of education as well as technical and interpersonal skills. Until relatively recently, stewardesses for many airlines from the Middle East had to be imported from Europe, and nursing has never achieved the status in the Middle East as in the West. Men as well as women feel the stigma. It is not uncommon for well-paid technical repairmen, such as those in work in air conditioning, to dress in a suit and tie and carry their tools in a briefcase.

▶ *Global Warranty and Service Policies*

Buyers around the world purchase products with certain performance expectations and consider company policies for backing promises. As a result, warranties and service policies can become an integral aspect of a company's international product strategy. Companies interested in doing business abroad frequently find themselves at a disadvantage, relative to local competitors, in the area of warranties and service. With the supplier's plant often thousands of miles away, foreign buyers sometimes want extra assurance that the supplier will back the product. Thus a comprehensive warranty and service policy can become a very important marketing tool for international companies.

Product Warranties

A company must address its warranty policy for international markets either by declaring its domestic warranty valid worldwide or by tailoring warranties to specific countries or markets. Although declaring a worldwide warranty with uniform performance standards would be administratively simple, local market conditions often dictate a differentiated approach. In the United States, most computer manufacturers sell their equipment with a 30- or 60-day warranty, whereas 12 months is more typical in Europe and Japan.

Companies are well advised to consider actual product use. If buyers in a foreign market subject the product to more stress or abuse, some shortening of the warranty period may become necessary. In developing countries, where technical sophistication is below North American and European standards, maintenance may not be adequate, causing more frequent equipment breakdowns. Another important factor is local competition. Because an attractive warranty policy can be helpful in obtaining sales, a firm's warranty policy should be in line with those of other firms competing in the local market.

Still, failure to maintain quality, service, or performance in one country can rapidly have a negative impact in other countries.[69] In February 1990, Perrier, the French bottled-water company, had to withdraw its Perrier water from U.S. retail stores after the product was found to contain benzene in concentrations above the legal limit. This U.S. test result triggered similar tests by health authorities in other countries. Soon Perrier had to withdraw its products in other countries, eventually resulting in a worldwide brand recall. Nearly 10 years later, Coca-Cola experienced a similar problem with bottling plants in Belgium, leading to a recall of many products not only in Belgium but also in France and Poland. Some 200 consumers complained of illness after drinking Coca-Cola products. This prompted Coca-Cola's largest product recall in the firm's history.[70]

Global Product Service

For some products, no warranty will be believable unless backed with an effective service organization. Although service is important to the consumer, it is even more crucial to the industrial buyer, because any breakdown of equipment or product is apt to cause substantial economic loss. This risk has led industrial buyers to be conservative in their choice of products, always carefully analyzing the supplier's ability to provide service in the event of need.

To provide the required level of service outside the company's home base poses special problems for global marketers. The selection of an organization to perform the service is an important decision. Ideally, company personnel are preferable because they tend to be better trained. However, this approach can be organized economically only if the installed base of the market is large enough to justify such an investment. In cases where a company does not maintain its own sales subsidiary, it is generally more efficient to turn to an independent service company or a local distributor. To provide adequate service via independent distributors requires extra training for the service technicians, usually at the manufacturer's expense. In any case, the selection of an appropriate service organization should be made in such a way that fully trained service personnel are readily available within the customary time frame for the particular market.

Closely related to any satisfactory service policy is an adequate inventory for spare parts. Because service often means replacing some parts, the company must store sufficient inventory of spare parts within reach of its markets. Whether this inventory is maintained in regional warehouses or through sales subsidiaries and distributors depends on the volume and the required reaction time for service calls. Industrial buyers will generally want to know, before placing substantial orders, how the manufacturer plans to organize service.

Firms that demonstrate serious interest in a market by committing themselves to setting up their own sales subsidiaries are often at an advantage over firms that use distributors. One German truck manufacturer that entered the U.S. market advertised the fact that "97 percent of all spare parts are kept in local inventory," thus assuring prospective buyers that they could get spares readily. Difficulty in establishing service outlets may even influence a company's market entry strategy. This was the case with Fujitsu, a Japanese manufacturer of electronic office equipment. By combining forces with TRW, a U.S.-based company, Fujitsu was able to sell its office equipment in the U.S. market backed by the extensive service organization of TRW.

Because the guarantee of reliable and efficient service can be such an important aspect of a firm's entire product strategy, investment in service centers sometimes must be made before any sales can take place. In this case, service costs must be viewed as an investment in future volume rather than merely as a recurring expense.

▶ *Managing a Global Product Line*

In early sections of this chapter, we discussed issues concerning individual products. Most companies, however, manufacture or sell a multitude of products. Some firms, such as General Electric, produce as many as 200,000 different items. To facilitate marketing operations, companies group these items into product groups consisting of several product lines. Each product line is made up of several individual items that are quite similar. For example, Quaker Oats organized its European operation into four pan-European business groups: pet food, cereals, Gatorade, and corn oil.

A company with several product lines must decide which are most appropriate for international marketing. As with each individual product decision, the firm can either offer exactly the same line in its home market and abroad or, if circumstances demand, make appropriate changes. In some cases, product lines abroad may be broader than those at home. About 90 percent of Coca-Cola's global sales are in traditional brands such as Coke and Sprite. In Japan, however, these account for only one-third of sales as a consequence of 25 years of successful product innovation in the Japanese subsidiary.[71] However, the product lines abroad are frequently characterized by a narrower width than those found in a company's domestic market.

The circumstances that can lead to deletions from product lines vary, but some reasons dominate. Lack of sufficient market size is a frequently mentioned reason. Companies with their home base in large markets such as the United States, Japan, or Germany will find sufficient demand in their home markets for even the smallest market segments, justifying additional product variations and greater depth in their lines. Abroad, opportunities for such segmentation strategies may not exist, because the individual segments may be too small to warrant commercial exploitation. Lack of market sophistication is another factor in product line variation. Aside from the top twenty developed markets, many markets are less sophisticated and their stage of development may not demand some of the most advanced items in a product line. Finally, new-product introduction strategies can affect product lines abroad. For most companies, new products are first introduced in their home markets and are introduced abroad only after the product has been successful at home. As a result, the lag in extending new products to foreign markets also contributes to a product line configuration that differs from that of the firm's domestic market.

Firms confronted with deletions in their product lines sometimes add specialized offerings to fill the gap in the line, either by producing a more suitable product or by developing an entirely new product that may not have any application outside a specific market. However, such a strategy can be pursued only by a firm with adequate research and development strength in its foreign subsidiaries.

Exploiting Product Life Cycles

Experience has shown that products do not always occupy the same position on the product life cycle curve in different countries. As Figure 10.1 shows, it is possible for a product to be in different stages of the product life cycle in different countries. A firm can extend product growth by expanding into new markets to compensate for declining growth rates in mature markets. On the other hand, a company can enter new national markets too rapidly, before the local market is ready to absorb the new product. To avoid such pitfalls and to take advantage of long-term opportunities, international companies may pursue the following strategies.

During the introductory phase in a product's life cycle, the product may have to be debugged and refined. This job can best be handled in the original

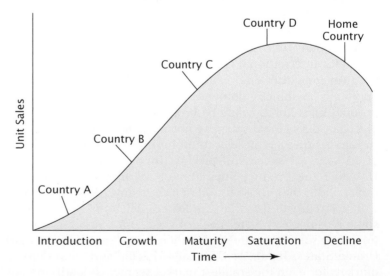

Figure 10.1 *Possible Product Life Cycle for a Product in Different Countries*

market or in a country close to company research and development centers. Also, the marketing approach will have to be refined. At this stage, the market in even the more advanced countries is relatively small, and demand in countries with lower levels of economic development will hardly be commercially exploitable. Therefore, the introductory stage is usually limited to the advanced markets, often the company's domestic market.

When a product faces life cycle maturity or decline in one market, it may still be marketed successfully in others. Volkswagen originally introduced its famous Beetle car in the 1930s but later withdrew it from production everywhere except Mexico. There the Beetle remains the best-selling car and helps make VW a leading car producer. The model has been adapted for modern environmental requirements but comes only in a simple version without extras or options. The car is priced at $5,300, and the company has pledged to keep the price pegged to increases in the minimum wage.[72] More recently, VW began to export a totally redesigned beetle car from Mexico into the U.S. market.

It should be remembered that for some high-technology products, life cycles are very short. In these cases, products are likely to be sold worldwide—or at least in all viable markets—soon after their introduction in the domestic market.

▶ *Conclusions*

To be successful in global markets, companies often need to be flexible in product and service offerings. Although a given product may be very successful in a firm's home market, environmental differences between markets can often force a company to make unexpected or costly changes. A small group of products may be marketed worldwide without significant changes, but most companies will find that global success depends on a willingness to adapt to local market requirements. For many firms, additional efforts are required if the company wishes to develop global brands, to police counterfeits, and to assure foreign clients that the company will stand behind its products. For companies that successfully master these additional international difficulties while showing a commitment to foreign customers, global success can lead to increased profits and to more secure market positions both domestically and globally.

Do you need to adapt your product for your target country? How would you register and protect your brand? Continue with your *Country Market Report* on our website.

Review Questions

1. What are the advantages of standardizing products worldwide?

2. What are the major reasons for a company to choose a global brand name for its product? Under what circumstances would using different names in different countries be advisable?

3. Why is it difficult to decide whether to change a local brand name to a global brand name?

4. What is ISO 9000? What is ISO 14000?

5. Why are books, recorded music, and software so susceptible to product piracy?

6. Why is it more difficult to pursue product standardization when marketing services?

7. Why do a firm's product lines often vary across national markets?

Questions for Discussion

1. Compare probable product adaptations for consumer products versus high-technology industrial products. What differences exist? Why?
2. American fast food, music, and movies have become popular around the world with little product adaptation, whereas U.S. retailers, banks, and beer companies have had to adapt their products more to global markets. Why?
3. Why do you think Poles already recognized the Coke name and logo when the product was first introduced in Poland?
4. What are the pros and cons of a top-down approach to global branding? What are the pros and cons of a bottom-up approach?

For Further Reading

Aaker, David, and Erich Joachimsthaler. "The Lure of Global Branding." *Harvard Business Review*, November-December 1999: 137–144.

Berthon, Pierre, Leyland Pitt, Constantine S. Katsikeas, and Jean Paul Berthon. "Virtual Services Go International: International Services in the Marketspace." *Journal of International Marketing* 7, 3 (1999): 84–105.

Douglas, Susan, C. Samuel Craig, and Edwin J. Nijssen. "Integrating Branding Strategy Across Markets: Building International Brand Architecture." *Journal of International Marketing* 9, 2 (2001): 97–114.

Gillespie, Kate. "Protecting Global Brands: Toward a Global Norm." *Journal of International Marketing* 10, 2 (2002): 99–112.

Kelz, Andreas, and Brian Block. "Global Branding: Why and How?" *Industrial Management & Data Systems* 93, 4 (1993): 11–17.

Wilson, Steven R. "The Impact of Standards on Industrial Development and Trade." *Quality Progress* 32, 7 (July 1, 1999): 71.

Case 10.1	*"Ethical" Products*

As global competition increases, consumers demand quality products at cheap prices. In order to lower costs, many international firms have moved production to developing countries. Much of this manufacturing is outsourced to local contractors. Increasingly, however, many consumers are factoring ethical, as well as economic, concerns into their buying decisions. To meet these new concerns of consumers, firms must now ensure that no products are produced in sweatshops where workers are underage, overworked, or beaten.

Consumer concern over products made in sweatshops exploded in the late 1990s. Activists embarrassed famous brands with exposés of working conditions abroad. Key targets were Wal-Mart Stores and Nike shoes. Student protests ensued, and consumer boycotts proved costly to the firms. In 1997 a White House task force was established, including consumer activists and industry representatives, to suggest codes of conduct for overseas production. The task force even considered allowing complying firms to label their products "not made in sweatshops."

Mattel and Disney are two companies that have adopted codes of conduct and attempt to enforce them. Mattel hired an independent panel to monitor its factories and is considered by many to be a model for others. Social auditors visit Mattel factories three times a year. Disney had completed 10,000 overseas inspections by 2001 and had cut off subcontractors that failed to make improvements.

In fact, a new industry of social auditing appears to have emerged overnight. Companies have hurried to become certified under the new global standard in ethical production—Social Accountability 8000. Both nongovernment agencies in developing countries and major international auditing firms have become involved in overseeing firm compliance to the new standard. During 2000, Pricewaterhouse Cooper conducted 15,000 inspections related to SA 8000 in the Chinese province of Guangdong alone.

Nike has formed a labor practices department and has supplied Global Alliance, a Baltimore-based activist group, with a $7.9 million grant to study social problems in its contracted factories. Still, a report released in 2001 identified widespread problems among Nike's Indonesian subcontractors. Major concerns dealt with limited medical care and forced overtime. Sexual molestation was widespread in a workplace environment where female workers accounted for over 84 percent of the workforce. Nearly 14 percent of interviewed workers reported witnessing physical abuse, especially when managers were under pressure to meet production goals. Nike, with six full-time staff in Indonesia for labor practices alone, was poised to respond to the findings. However, the company noted that it had far more leverage over its shoe subcontractors, who often worked exclusively for Nike. Its clothing subcontractors were a different story. Those local firms often worked for a dozen different companies.

In the meantime, Italian apparel manufacturers were taking advantage of sweatshop concerns. The Italian Trade Commission spent $25 million on a 5-year promotional campaign to convince U.S. consumers to buy Italian. The advertisements presented Italy as a country where skilled artisans produced high-quality garments. The campaign was deemed a success, and the Italian share of the U.S. apparel-import market climbed from 4.5 percent to 5.9 percent.

Discussion Questions

1. What can global firms do to make their products more socially acceptable?
2. What do you think they should do? Why?
3. What are the costs to global firms of keeping their products sweatshop-free?
4. What are the possible costs of not complying with SA 8000?

Sources: Shu Shin Luh, "Report Claims Abuses by Nike Contractors," *Wall Street Journal*, February 22, 2001, p. A16; "Business Ethics: Sweatshop Wars," *The Economist*, February 27, 1999: 62; and Wendy Bounds and Deborah Ball, "Italy Knits Promotional Support in U.S.," *Wall Street Journal*, December 15, 1997, p. B2.

Case 10.2 | *Chasing Pirates*

Pirated software is a major challenge to Microsoft, which loses hundreds of millions of dollars a year to the practice. Piracy also costs governments in lost tax revenues. Mexico, for instance, is estimated to lose $200 million a year to pirated software. Piracy rates vary by country, the rates in developing countries being significantly higher than those in developed countries:

England	20%	Philippines	92%
India	80%	Thailand	82%
Indonesia	97%	Vietnam	97%
Mexico	40%	United States	30%
Pakistan	90%		

To combat piracy, Microsoft added an edge-to-edge hologram on its CD-ROMs to ensure buyers of the product's authenticity. Still, an estimated two million websites sell pirated software. As a result, the company aggressively monitors the Internet to uncover sites for illegal downloading.

Closing down pirates overseas has taken several forms. In Bulgaria, Microsoft launched a campaign to eradicate pirated software by offering full packages discounted 60 percent off their previous price. Buyers were also entitled to the next version at no extra charge. In Pakistan, Microsoft offered to provide a training program for software instructors and to install laboratories in the top 50 universities and colleges in the country. This $150 million package would be in exchange for better government enforcement of antipiracy laws. In Malaysia, Microsoft installed a toll-free phone number and offered substantial rewards for evidence against companies using pirated software.

Bill Gates, chairman and CEO of Microsoft, himself traveled to China to sign an agreement with the government there to promote the authentic use of software. Under the agreement, several key government entities pledged to buy Microsoft and to avoid pirated products. In exchange, Microsoft agreed to provide technical training and consulting. Later the same year, Microsoft brought its first piracy case to the Chinese courts. Engineers were found to be using pirated Microsoft products in the office building of the Yadu Group. The Yadu Group argued that they were innocent because the engineers worked not directly for them but for a sister company. The Chinese court found in favor of Yadu and ordered Microsoft to pay $60 in court costs.

In Singapore, a country of 4 million people, Microsoft loses over $3 million a year to pirates. Microsoft began a campaign in the Singapore schools to educate students concerning the illegality of piracy. Despite Singapore's excellent reputation for law enforcement in general, U.S. officials put it on their list of 32 countries to watch for poor enforcement of copyrights. Under similar pressure from the United States, Taiwan has been cracking down more on piracy. A firm caught exporting pirated software was fined $7.9 million, and its owner was sentenced to 2 years in jail.

Discussion Questions

1. What do you think accounts for the different piracy rates across countries?
2. Identify the different strategies Microsoft uses to combat counterfeits.
3. Why does Microsoft expect each of these efforts to be useful? What is your opinion?

Sources: Dow Jones Business News, May 5, 2000, March 6, 2000, August 24, 1999, and March 28, 1999; "Mexico," *Reuters English News Service*, May 19, 2000; Ridzuan A. Ghani, "Microsoft in New Campaign to Curb Software Piracy," *New Straits Times*, May 1, 2000, p. 6; "Microsoft Incorporates New Anti-Piracy Technologies," *PR Newswires*, February 10, 2000; "Microsoft Loses Piracy Suit," *Asian Wall Street Journal*, December 20, 1999, p. 3; and *BBC Worldwide Monitoring*, March 10, 1999.

Notes

[1] Pierre Berthon, Leyland Pitt, Constantine S. Katsikeas, and Jean Paul Berthon, "Virtual Services Go International: International Services in the Marketspace," *Journal of International Marketing* 7, 3 (1999): 96.

[2] Chen May Yee, "E-Business in Asia, It's Not a Wide-Open Web," *Wall Street Journal*, July 9, 2001, p. B1.

[3] Mylene Mangalindan and Kevin Delaney, "Yahoo! Ordered to Bar the French from Nazi Items," *Wall Street Journal*, November 21, 2000, p. B1.

[4] Peter Ford, "Need Software in, Say, Icelandic? Call the Irish," *Christian Science Monitor*, February 6, 2001, p.1.

[5] "After Early Stumbles, P&G Is Making Inroads Overseas," *Wall Street Journal*, February 6, 1989, p. B1.

[6] Rick Yan, "To Reach China's Consumers, Adapt to Guo Qing," *Harvard Business Review*, September–October 1994: 9.

[7] Elisabeth Malkin, "Mexico Goes Top-Flight," *Business Week*, June 26, 2000.

[8] Claudia Puig, "'Hannibal' Ignites Worldwide Controversy," *USA Today*, March 7, 2001, p. D06.

[9] Charles Batchelor, "International Standards," *Financial Times*, October 14, 1993: 23–25.

[10] Tom Reilly, "The Harmonization of Standards in the European Union and the Impact on U.S. Businesses," *Business Horizons*, March/April 1995: 28–34.

[11] For more details, see Raymond G. Krammer, "Technical Barriers to Free Trade," Congressional Testimony by Federal Document Clearing House, April 28, 1998 (testimony by R.G. Krammer, Director of National Institute of Standards and Technology, before the House Committee on Science Subcommittee on Technology).

[12] Robert A. Guth and Almar Latour, "Japanese Makers Hope to Export Web-Ready Cellphones Worldwide," *Wall Street Journal*, April 19, 2001, p. B1.

[13] www.iso.ch.

[14] Michael R. Czinkota and Ilkka A. Ronkainen, "European Product Standards: Headache or Headache Relief?" in *International Marketing*, 4th ed. (Fort Worth, TX: Harcourt, 1995), p. 261.

[15] Brandon Mitchener, "Increasingly, Rules of Global Economy Are Set in Brussels," *Wall Street Journal Europe*, April 23, 2002. p. A1.

[16] Michael J. Thomas, ed., *International Marketing Management* (Boston: Houghton Mifflin, 1969), p. 35.

[17] Vernon R. Alden, "Who Says You Can't Crack Japanese Markets?" *Harvard Business Review*, January–February 1987: 52–56.

[18] Ford, "Need Software in, Say, Icelandic?"

[19] "Pizza in Japan Is Adapted to Local Tastes," *Wall Street Journal*, June 4, 1993, p. B1.

[20] "Foreign Fast Food Firms Flourish in Pakistan," *AFP*, March 22, 1999.

[21] Ford, "Need Software in, Say, Icelandic?"

[22] "Think Globally, Bake Locally," *Fortune*, October 14, 1996: 205.

[23] "Three Scientists Seek U.S. Data on Genetic Engineering," *New York Times*, March 8, 1978, p. A-19.

[24] "The Man Who's Selling Japan on Jeeps," *Business Week*, July 19, 1993: 56–57.

[25] "Coke Sells Water by the Cup in India," Daily News for May 14, 2002, AdAge Global at www.adageglobal.com.

[26] "The Brand's the Thing," *Fortune*, March 4, 1996: 75.

[27] "The Brand's the Thing."

[28]"Gaining Recognition for Asian Brands," *Ad Age International*, June 1996, p. I-36.

[29]Bernd Schmitt, "Language and Visual Imagery: Issues of Corporate Identity in East Asia," *Columbia Journal of World Business*, Winter 1995: 2–36.

[30]"Trademarks Are a Global Business These Days, But Finding Registrable Ones Is a Big Problem," *Wall Street Journal*, September 1, 1975, p. 28.

[31]George W. Cooper, "On Your 'Mark,'" *Columbia Journal of World Business*, March–April 1970: 67–76.

[32]"Darkie no, Darlie yes," *South China Morning Post*, May 16, 1999, p. 2.

[33]Ernest Beck, "Unilever Renames Cleanser," *Wall Street Journal*, December 27, 2000, p. B8.

[34]"Landor: Experts on Identity Crisis," *Ad Age International*, March 1997, p. I-44.

[35]David A. Aaker and Erich Joachimsthaler, "The Lure of Global Branding," *Harvard Business Review*, November–December 1999: 137–144.

[36]Aaker and Joachimsthaler, "The Lure of Global Branding."

[37]Susan P. Douglas, C. Samuel Craig, and Edwin J. Nijssen, "Integrating Branding Strategy Across Markets: Building International Brand Architecture," *Journal of International Marketing* 9, 2 (2001): 110.

[38]"Shangri-La on Earth," *Advertising Age International*, March 1997, p. I-24.

[39]"Regional Brands: Varig Eyes the Skies Outside of Brazil," *Advertising Age International*, March 1997, p. I-19.

[40]"Who Favors Branding with Euro Approach?" *Advertising Age International*, May 25, 1992, p. I-16.

[41]Christopher A. Bartlett and Sumantra Ghosal, "What Is a Global Manager?" *Harvard Business Review*, September–October 1992: 125.

[42]"BSN Puts New Name on the Table," *Financial Times*, May 11, 1994: 18.

[43]"Danone Hits Its Stride," *Business Week International*, February 1, 1999: 18

[44]"Ricoh Distributes Whistle Communications' Award-Winning Internet Solutions in Japan," *PR Newswire*, March 23, 1998.

[45]Kate Gillespie, Kishore Krishma, and Susan Jarvis, "Protecting Global Brands: Toward a Global Norm," *Journal of International Marketing* 10, 2 (2002): 99–112.

[46]Guy Chazan, "Philip Morris Suffers a Setback in Russian Suit on Trademarks," *Wall Street Journal*, October 13, 1999, p. A26.

[47]"Stop, Thief," *International Management*, September 1990: 48.

[48]"Sleaze E-Commerce," *Wall Street Journal*, May 14, 1999, p. W1.

[49]"Counterfeit Costs Pounds 8 Billion a Year," *Times of London*, June 14, 1999, p. 48.

[50]"Fake Drugs Numb Profits of Indian Pharmaceutical Industry," *Agence France-Presse*, July 16, 1999.

[51]"Counterfeit Costs Pounds 8 Billion a Year."

[52]"Music Piracy Remains Headache for Big Labels," *Wall Street Journal Europe*, June 11, 1999, p. UK16.

[53]"Software Piracy Costs Billions in Revenue," *Baltimore Sun*, June 13, 1999, p. 2D.

[54]"Vietnam's Prolific Counterfeiters Take a Walk on 'LaVile' Side," *Asian Wall Street Journal*, June 4, 1998, p. 1.

[55]"Sleaze E-Commerce," *Wall Street Journal*, May 14, 1999, p. W1.

[56]Glenn R. Simpson, "E-Bay to Police Site for Sales of Pirated Items," *Wall Street Journal*, February 28, 2000, p. A3.

[57]"Businesses Battle Bogus Products," *AP Online*, January 26, 1999.

[58]Matt Forney, "Harry Potter, Meet 'Ha-li Bo-te,'" *Wall Street Journal*, September 21, 2000, p. B1.

[59]Ford, "Need Software in, Say, Icelandic?"

[60]John O'Neil, "Reducing Drug Overdoses, by Packaging," *New York Times*, May 29, 2001, p. 8.

[61]"Keeping It to a Minimum," *Financial Times*, May 28, 1992. Special section: Packaging and the Environment, p. 5.

[62]Kathy Chen, "Cashmere Clothes to Undergo More FTC Monitoring," *Wall Street Journal*, May 4, 2001, p. B1.

[63]"World Trade in Commercial Services by Selected Region and Economy," *World Trade Organization*, Trade in Services section of the Statistics division, March 1999.

[64]Suzanne Koudsi, "Sam's Big Blue Challenge," *Fortune*, August 13, 2001: 144.

[65]Berthon et. al., "Virtual Services Go International," pp. 85–86.

[66]"US Law Firms Are on the Prowl in London," *Wall Street Journal Europe*, June 1, 1999, p. 4.

[67]"AIG Sells Insurance in Shanghai, Testing Service Firms' Role," *Wall Street Journal*, July 21, 1993, pp. 1, A-9.

[68]"China Shows Promise for Foreign Entrants," *Life Insurance International*, November 1, 1998: 14.

[69]"Brit Helps Perrier Move Beyond the Recall Crisis," *Advertising Age*, November 12, 1990.

[70]"Coca-Cola Poland Details Scope of Product Recalls," *Wall Street Journal*, July 14, 1999, p. A17.

[71]Michael Flagg, "Coca-Cola Adopts Local-Drinks Strategy in Asia," *Wall Street Journal*, July 30, 2001.

[72]"Miss the VW Bug? It Lives Beyond the Rio Grande," *New York Times*, October 20, 1990, p. 2.

11 Developing New Products for Global Markets

Betty Boop was an American icon for the World War II generation. She appeared in one of the first cartoons with sound and has danced the hula with Popeye the sailor. In June 2001, an advertisement in the *Wall Street Journal* proclaimed a limited edition of Betty Boop commemorative stamps. Though clearly designed with the U.S. public in mind, the stamps weren't issued by the U.S. Post Office. Instead they were legal postage of the African country of Chad.

Today more than ever before, product ideas for global markets are not limited to the domestic product line but arise from a variety of sources. In Chapter 10, we focused on decisions concerning product adaptation and product line management. Here we concentrate on the strategic issue of product design and development for

Chapter Outline

global markets (see Figure 11.1). The first part of this chapter covers a series of alternatives involving product extension, adaptation, and innovation strategies. We then address the complexities of designing products for many markets simultaneously. The next part of the chapter is devoted to product development strategies for international companies. The emphasis is on organizational issues and approaches that will enhance a firm's ability to innovate in a changing marketplace. We conclude the chapter with a discussion of issues related to new product launches.

Learning Objectives

After studying this chapter, you should be able to:

► Differentiate among five strategic options for introducing products into foreign markets.

► Define modularity and explain its impact on global product development.

► Compare and contrast the product development roles played by a multinational firm's headquarters and the roles played by its subsidiaries.

► Explain the importance of lead markets and note their importance to product development.

► Describe how companies may access new products by purchasing research and development or by importing products from other firms.

► Discuss the use of acquisitions, joint ventures, and alliances for the purpose of product development.

► Explain the process of introducing new products to global markets, including concept testing, test marketing, and the timing of new product introduction.

Figure 11.1 *Selecting Opportunities for Global Products*

▶ *Introducing Products into Foreign Markets*

Traditionally, a company follows one of three basic strategies when introducing products into a foreign market. A company can pursue an **extension strategy,** which means adopting the same approach as in the home market. Alternatively, the firm can choose an **adaptation policy,** wherein the company makes some changes to fit the new market requirements. When an entirely new approach is required, the company can adopt an **invention strategy**. These three basic strategies can be further refined into the five options that are shown in Table 11.1 and explained in the following sections.

Option One: Product Extension–Communications Extension One extension strategy calls for marketing a standardized product with the same communications strategy across the globe. Although this strategy has considerable attraction because of its cost-effectiveness, it is rarely feasible for consumer products. The few exceptions include companies in the soft-drink industry and some luxury-goods firms. Industrial products, with a greater homogeneity of buyers internationally, offer a somewhat greater opportunity for this strategy, but here again, the extension strategy is far from the norm.

The cost-effectiveness of this strategy should not be underestimated, however. Product adaptations entail additional research and development expenses and tooling costs. They do not allow economies of scale to the extent possible under an extension strategy. Savings can also be realized from the creation of a single communications strategy. However, international marketers should consider the anticipated impact on demand in the foreign mar-

Table 11.1 *Global Product Strategies*

STRATEGY	PRODUCT FUNCTION OR NEED SATISFIED	CONDITIONS OF PRODUCT USE	ABILITY TO BUY PRODUCT	RECOMMENDED PRODUCT STRATEGY	RECOMMENDED COMMUNICATIONS STRATEGY	RANK ORDER FROM LEAST TO MOST EXPENSIVE	PRODUCT EXAMPLES
1	Same	Same	Yes	Extension	Extension	1	Soft drinks
2	Different	Same	Yes	Extension	Adaptation	2	Bicycles, motorscooters
3	Same	Different	Yes	Adaptation	Extension	3	Gasoline, detergents
4	Different	Different	Yes	Adaptation	Adaptation	4	Clothing, greeting cards
5	Same	—	No	Invention	Develop new communications	5	Hand-powered washing machines

Source: From Warren J. Keegan, "Multinational Product Planning: Strategic Alternatives." Reprinted from *Journal of Marketing*, 33 (January 1969): 58–62, published by the American Marketing Association. Reprinted by permission.

ket if the product is not fully suited to local tastes or preferences. Past experience shows that rigidly enforcing a product and communications extension policy can lead to disaster and that such a policy should be adopted only if all requirements with respect to product function, consumer needs, use conditions, and ability to buy are met.

Option Two: Product Extension–Communications Adaptation When reasons for buying a product differ from country to country, but the use conditions and standards remain identical, the same product can be marketed but with a change in the communications strategy. Examples can be found among bicycle and motorcycle manufacturers. In developing countries, a bicycle or motorcycle is primarily a means of transportation, whereas the same products are used for recreation purposes in developed countries.

This strategy is still quite cost-effective, because communications adaptation is less expensive than tailoring a product to a local market. In Eastern Europe, tobacco companies have had great success developing local brands that appeal to national pride. The product is basically the same, but the brand and communications are adapted to each local market. British American Tobacco (BAT) captured a significant share of the Polish market with its brand Jan III Sobieski, named for a popular Polish figure.[1] R.J. Reynolds was equally successful in Russia with its new Peter I brand, which captured 18 percent of the local market.[2]

Option Three: Product Adaptation–Communications Extension This strategy is appropriate when the physical event surrounding product use varies but the sociocultural event is the same as in the company's home market. Although changes in a product are substantially more costly than changes in the communications approach, a company will follow this course when the product otherwise may not sell in a foreign market. In some cases, product formulations are changed without consumers knowing it, as with detergents and gasoline, so that the product can function under different environmental circumstances.

Option Four: Product Adaptation–Communications Adaptation A strategy of dual adaptation is generally favored for a product when both use conditions and sociocultural concerns vary among markets. A manufacturer of processed soup may vary its product on the basis of cultural tastes as well as market norms. It might sell condensed soups in some markets and powdered soups in others. This manufacturer's communications strategies are also likely to vary with the role soup plays in each culture. In one market the communications strategy might emphasize families eating together. In another it might emphasize soup as a way for busy people to eat on the run. To make this option profitable, however, the foreign market or markets need to be of sufficient volume to justify the costs of dual adaptation.

Option Five: Product Invention When the ability to purchase a product is generally wanting, some companies have elected to reinvent the product, usually by redesigning the original product to a lower level of complexity. Making the resulting, substantially cheaper product available leads to more purchases. In response to the desire of many developing countries to own their own television-manufacturing plants, the Dutch multinational Philips redesigned its equipment and tools to suit the volume requirements of some of the world's poorest countries. Companies also can develop or invent entirely new products. For example, trumpet players in Japan had difficulty practicing, because most Japanese houses have thin walls and brass playing is banned in most parks. Yamaha seized the opportunity and developed an electronic mute that deadened the sound to the outside world, while allowing the player to listen through headphones. In the first 4 months, Yamaha sold 13,000 units.[3]

▶ *Developing a Global Product*

Firms increasingly experience pressure for cost reduction in order to remain competitive. Yet there are relatively few opportunities for producing completely standardized products. As a result, many firms now employ a new strategy, global product development. In **global products,** a portion of the final design is standardized. However, the design retains some flexibility so that the end product can be tailored to the needs of individual markets. This represents a move to standardize as much as possible those areas involving common components or parts.

One of the most significant changes in product development strategy in the 1990s was **modularity**. This process involves the development of standard modules that can easily be connected with other standard modules to increase the variety of products. For example, General Motors has established a modular product architecture for all its global automobile projects. Future GM cars will be designed using combinations of components from seventy different body modules and about a hundred major mechanical components such as engines, power trains, and suspension systems.

This modularized approach has become especially important in the automobile industry, where both U.S. and European manufacturers are increasingly creating world components to combat growing Japanese competitiveness. Ford introduced one of the first world cars during the 1981 model year. Ford's Escort model was simultaneously assembled in the United States,

World Beat 11.1 *Can the Grinch Steal Christmas Abroad?*

For U.S. audiences, the mean, green title character in Universal's film *Dr. Seuss' How the Grinch Stole Christmas* needs no introduction. But outside the United States, mention of the Grinch elicits a "Who?"—and they're not talking about the residents of Whoville.

When U.S. movie studios make film versions of popular American properties like the Grinch, they often find themselves with a presold domestic hit—and a lot of work to do everywhere else in the world. Indeed, the Grinch's ubiquity in the United States is matched only by his low profile abroad. Moreover, the movie was scheduled to open in most overseas markets shortly after its American debut, meaning there wasn't time for word-of-mouth from its U.S. release to stoke interest abroad.

Book publishers have already found that Dr. Seuss presents peculiar problems because of the tricky language that makes it difficult to translate. This problem was mitigated somewhat in the film by a decision to minimize the trademark Seuss nonsense even in the movie's English-language version. The Seussian metered narration is absent in long stretches of the movie, replaced by new dialogue among the characters.

Nonetheless, Universal and its overseas distributor, United International Pictures, took unusual care to make certain that the linguistic nuances got across in as many tongues as possible. Most U.S. films are translated into just four non-English languages—French, Spanish, Italian, and German—with the rest of the world getting subtitles. But Grinch was translated into about 30 languages. Local narrators were given leeway to adjust the translated verse if they thought it didn't make sense. In some cases, the translators were able to preserve rhymes partly by making up their own words to go with Dr. Seuss' made-up words. In Spanish, the "Pontoos" mountains where the Grinch lives were replaced by the "Pontienes" range—a word concocted to rhyme with "los quienes," meaning "the Whos" in Spanish.

Source: Bruce Orwall, "Can Grinch Steal Christmas Abroad?" Wall Street Journal, November 16, 2000, p. B1.

Great Britain, and Germany from parts produced in ten countries. The U.S.-assembled Escort contained parts made in Japan, Spain, Brazil, Britain, Italy, France, Mexico, Taiwan, and West Germany. The European assembly plants, in return, bought automatic transmissions from a U.S. plant. Ford was estimated to have saved engineering and development costs amounting to hundreds of millions of dollars, because the design standardized engines, transmissions, and ancillary systems for heating, air conditioning, wheels, and seats. Still, the U.S. and European Escorts were two distinctly different cars.

Ford's global car, the Mondeo (called Contour in the United States), was launched in 1993 in Europe and in 1994 in the United States. Ford expected to gain significant economies of scale by selling 700,000 cars a year. Although sales in Europe were strong, the Mondeo-derived U.S. models did not do very well. These models turned out to be too expensive for their segments in the U.S. market.[4]

For its latest version of world cars, Ford has modified its strategy. Instead of trying to build like-models in multiple markets, the company has moved toward building and launching different versions of cars on exactly the same chassis (underpinning), thus allowing a greater variety of car models while still saving on critical components such as drive trains and transmissions. In accordance with this new strategy, Ford launched a new Escort as part of its 1999 model range with distinct European and U.S. versions.

Ironically, just as Ford was seeking common designs for markets, some Japanese car companies were moving in the opposite direction. Honda has steadily added to its development and design function in North America. Toyota launched its popular Camry in 1991. Three inches wider than its Japanese version, the Camry was intended to be better able to challenge the standard North American sedans of Ford and General Motors. Toyota also developed a new large pickup truck that was unsuitable for Japan's much narrower roads.

The challenge faced by Ford and other automobile manufacturers is similar to that faced by manufacturers and marketers of both industrial and consumer products all over the world. Cost pressures force them to standardize, while market pressures require more customization of products. Conceptually, these companies can gain from increasing the standardized components in their products while maintaining the ability to customize the product "at the end" for each market segment.

Most international firms must take advantage of economies of scale on the standardized portion, or core, of their products. Different firms achieve different levels of standardization, but rarely is a firm able to standardize its product 100 percent. For one company, even moving from a global core representing 15 percent of the total product to 20 percent of the total product may result in a considerable cost improvement and represent the maximum level of standardization desirable. For another firm, the core may have to represent 80 percent of the total product to achieve the same effect. These levels depend on the characteristics of the market that the company or industry faces.

Many firms now develop new products with global markets in mind. These global products are based on cores and derivatives. The product core might be the same for all products in all regions. An extended core might apply for each region but differ across regions. Each region might launch product derivatives specific to the regional conditions. This core strategy allows for maximizing the appeal of different configurations, while maintaining a stable product base and thus reducing basic development costs.

The shift from local to global development requires that the company consider the unique or special concerns for major markets from the outset, rather than later attempting to make various adaptations to the initial model or prototype. The early introduction of global considerations not only ensures that the product will achieve wide acceptance but also makes it possible to maximize the commonality of models to achieve economies in component manufacturing. A global product, then, is not identical in all countries. Instead, a global product is engineered from the outset with the goal of maximizing the percentage of identical components, design, and parts to the point where local needs can be met with a minimum of additional costs in tooling, engineering, and development.

▶ New Product Development Processes for Global Markets

Developing new products or services for global markets poses unique challenges to a firm. In contrast to the strictly domestic company, international firms can assign development responsibilities to any one of their often numerous international subsidiaries. Aside from the question of who should perform development work, there are organizational problems to overcome that pertain to participation by experts in many subsidiaries. No doubt, the future success of international firms will depend to a substantial degree on how well they marshal their resources on a global scale to develop new products for foreign markets.

The Organization of Head-Office Sponsored Research and Development

Most companies that currently engage in research and development on a global scale originally conducted their development efforts strictly in centralized facilities in the firm's domestic market. Even today, the largest portion of research and development (R&D) monies spent by international firms goes to support efforts in domestically located facilities. As a result, most new product ideas are first developed in the context of the domestic market. Initial introduction at home is followed by a phase-in introduction to the company's foreign markets.

There are several reasons for this traditional approach. First, research and development must be integrated into a firm's overall marketing strategy. This requires frequent contacts and interfacing between R&D facilities and the company's main offices. Such contacts are maintained more easily with close proximity. Many companies centralize research and development because they are concerned that duplication of efforts will result if this responsibility is spread over several subsidiaries. Centralized R&D is thought to maximize results from scarce research funds. A final important reason for centralization is the company's experience in its domestic market. Typically, the domestic market is very important to the company, and in the case of international companies based in the United States, Germany, and Japan, it is often the largest market as well. As a result, new products are developed with special emphasis on the domestic market, and R&D facilities, therefore, should be close by. Traditionally, the level of R&D in a company or country has been considered one of the best indicators of long-term growth. For example, Gillette's global success is unquestionably the result of a hefty R&D investment. According to its CEO, "Good products come out of market research. Great products come out of R&D."[5] Gillette introduces about twenty new products per year, most of which are successful. One recent major new product introduction, the Mach 3 shaving system, cost $750 million to research and develop.[6]

Still, an OECD study found that although investments in science and engineering were important, equally important was the diffusion of the new technology.[7] There are many good reasons for centralizing product development at the company's head office, but it remains a challenge for a centralized engineering and development staff of the firm to keep all relevant product modifications in mind before the design is frozen. Experience shows that later changes or modifications can be expensive. To keep a product acceptable in many or all relevant markets from the outset requires the product development staff to become globalized early in the creation process. Only a "globally thinking" product development staff will ensure the global acceptability of a product by incorporating the maximum possible number of variations in the original product.

International Lead Markets and Research and Development

As we noted in Chapter 8, participation in lead markets can be an important part of global strategy. In general, a **lead market** is a market whose level of development exceeds that of the markets in other countries worldwide and whose developments tend to set a pattern for other countries. Lead markets are not restricted to technological developments as embodied in product hardware. The concept covers developments in design, production processes, patterns in consumer demand, and methods of marketing. Therefore, virtually every phase of a company's operation is subject to lead market influences, although those focusing on technological developments are of special importance.

In the middle of the twentieth century, the United States achieved a position of virtual dominance as a lead market. Not only were U.S. products the most advanced with respect to features, function, and quality, but they also tended to be marketed to the most sophisticated and advanced consumers and industrial buyers. This U.S. advantage was partially based on superior production methods, especially the pioneering of mass production in the form of the assembly line. The U.S. advantage extended to management methods in general, and particularly to access to new consumers. The rapid development of U.S.-based multinational firms was to a considerable degree based on the exploitation of these advantages in applying new U.S. developments abroad and in creating extensive networks of subsidiaries across a large number of countries.

But the overwhelming lead of the United States over other countries did not last. Foreign competitors from Europe and Japan eroded the U.S. firms' advantages. As a result, no single country or market now unilaterally dominates the world economy. Although the United States may have lost its lead in steel, television, radios, shoes, textiles, and automobiles, it still leads the world in electronics, biosciences, and aerospace.

The general-purpose computer industry remains dominated largely by U.S. companies, with the United States serving as the lead market. However, there are many signs that this position is being challenged. In 1989, U.S. companies held a 61 percent share of computer sales, down from 81 percent in 1983. Over the same period, the share of Japanese companies rose from 8 percent to 22 percent. The United States once dominated the Japanese personal computer (PC) market, but U.S. manufacturers in 1992 only held 15 percent of that market, whereas Japan-based NEC held 53 percent. U.S. manufacturers such as Apple, IBM, Compaq, and Dell have rebounded with high-quality graphics, software specifically modified for Japan, and low prices. As a result, the leading Japanese suppliers, NEC and Fujitsu, fell to 30 percent and 24 percent, respectively, in 1998.[8]

Still, the fragmentation of lead markets has led to a proliferation of product development centers, substantially complicating the task of keeping abreast of the latest developments in market demands, product design, and production techniques. Even formerly developing countries, such as South Korea, have achieved lead-market status in some categories. It was the Korean company Samsung that announced the creation of the world's first next-generation 1-gigabyte computer chip, a major development that is bound to change the nature of the industry.[9]

To prosper in today's increasingly internationalized business climate, corporations must keep track of evolving lead markets as major sources for new product ideas and production techniques. New product ideas can stem from influences in buyer demand, manufacturing processes, and scientific discoveries. No single country may play a lead role in all facets of a firm's business. This means that any corporate research and development effort must look for new developments abroad rather than solely in the domestic market.

Should any part of a company's market become subject to foreign lead-market influences, the organization of a firm's research and development function will have to be adjusted. Steel companies in the United States and manufacturers of automobiles, shoes, and textiles cannot disregard developments elsewhere in the world, because the United States is no longer the lead market for these industries.

To expose itself to lead-market developments, Kodak invested in a research and development center in Japan. The company hired about one hundred professional researchers and directed the lab to concentrate on electronic-imaging technology.[10] Japanese and European firms have also seen the need to locate research and development facilities in lead markets. Nissan set up an R&D center in Detroit. Recognizing that Detroit is an important bastion of the automotive industry, Nissan wanted to be there to maintain a solid global position.[11] In 2002, Swiss drug giant Novartis AG announced that it would move its worldwide research headquarters to Cambridge, Massachusetts. The new center would seek to develop drugs for diabetes, cardiovascular diseases, and infectious diseases.[12]

The Role of Foreign Subsidiaries in Research and Development

Each year General Motors gives what it calls Kettering Awards to employees whose ideas help GM retain technology leadership, improve customer service, or save production time and costs. In 2001, thirteen Kettering Awards recognized researchers and engineers not only from the United States, Canada, and Germany but from Brazil and India as well.[13]

Subsidiaries may assume certain R&D functions if products require some adaptation to the local market. For example, Microsoft sponsored a nationwide contest in Russia to develop a Russian version of Microsoft Windows in hopes of generating an attractive product for the Russian market.[14] The ensuing research and development capability is often extended to other applications unique to the local market. In many instances, however, new products may prove to have potential in other markets, and as a result they get transferred to other subsidiaries.

Foreign subsidiaries of international firms rarely play an active role in research and development unless they have manufacturing responsibilities. Sales subsidiaries may provide the central organization with feedback on product adjustments or adaptation, but generally their participation does not go beyond the generation of ideas.

International subsidiaries assume special positions when lead markets change from one country to another. Countries that assume lead-market status tend to be among the most advanced industrial nations of North America, Europe, and Asia. Larger international firms quite often have subsidiaries in all these markets. A subsidiary located in a lead market is usually in a better position to observe developments and to accommodate new demands. Consequently, international firms with subsidiaries in lead markets have an opportunity to turn such units into effective "listening posts." Unilever found that some countries of the world were very good at innovation in research and marketing, so it set up a global network of innovation centers. These centers were directed to expand their in-depth experience in research and marketing for Unilever's four categories of personal-care products: dental, hair, deodorant, and skin. This expertise was then shared around the world.[15]

Increasingly, multinational firms are investing in research facilities abroad in order to obtain input from key markets. To globalize their own research, Japanese companies have made heavy investments in U.S.-based research facilities. Hundreds of Japanese scientists already work side by side with Americans in research laboratories on exchange programs. This investment aims at accessing scientific talent in other countries. Companies chasing such talent around the world are opening development centers wherever talent can be found. In China many Western firms have opened development facilities to obtain access to Chinese scientific talent and to understand the Chinese market better. Among those firms are Intel and Microsoft, which have opened research centers near Beijing, where many of China's leading universities are clustered.[16] Microsoft indicated that it planned to spend $80 million over 6 years to expand its new research center in China, which is to house 100 employees. One of the main tasks of the lab is to find ways to make software more useful to Chinese computer users.[17]

To develop a global product also requires a different organizational set-up. Changes instituted by General Motors are indicative of actions taken by other international firms. With the advent of world cars, GM realized that the company needed closer coordination between its domestic units and its overseas subsidiaries. GM moved its international staff from New York to Detroit

Students on the campus of Beijing University. An increasing number of global firms are opening research facilities in China in order to take advantage of Chinese scientific talent.

in order to speed up communication between domestic and international staffs. GM adopted the "project center" concept to manage its engineering effort. Each division or foreign subsidiary involved in a new car design lends engineers to a centrally organized project center, which designs, develops, and introduces the new model. Upon introduction of the model, the project center is disbanded. Of course, not every firm will find a project center approach feasible. Other alternatives include assigning primary responsibility to a subsidiary that has special capability in the new product field.

In the future, international companies will have to make better use of the talents of local subsidiaries in the development of new products. Increasingly, the role of the subsidiary as simply a selling or production arm of the company will have to be abandoned, and companies will have to find innovative ways to involve their foreign affiliates in the product development process. This involvement can be patterned after several role models. The **strategic leader** role, with responsibility for developing a new range of products to be used by the entire company, may be assigned to a highly competent subsidiary in a market of strategic importance. Another subsidiary with competence in a distinct area may be assigned the role of **contributor**, adapting some products in smaller but nevertheless important markets. Most subsidiaries, being smaller and located in less strategic markets, will be expected to be **implementers** of the overall strategy, without making a major contribution either technologically or strategically.[18]

Purchasing Research and Development from Foreign Countries

Instead of developing new products through its own research and development personnel, a company may acquire such material or information from independent outside sources. These sources are usually located in foreign countries that have acquired lead-market status. Managers commonly read literature published in lead markets. Also, through regular visits to foreign countries and trade fairs, managers maintain close contact with lead markets. Increasingly, however, these ad hoc measures are becoming insufficient for maintaining the necessary flow of information in rapidly changing markets.

For companies without immediate access to new technology embodied in new products, the licensing avenue has been the traditional approach to gaining access to new developments from lead markets. U.S. technology has been tapped through many independent licensing arrangements. Japanese companies have made extensive use of the licensing alternative to acquire technologies developed in countries that were lead markets from Japan's point of view.

Licensing can be a boon to entrepreneurs who have little funds for research and development. One Spanish entrepreneur who originally organized study-abroad programs for Spanish university students decided to bring U.S. universities to Spain via the Internet. Building on his relationships with three prestigious American universities—Columbia University, the University of Chicago, and the University of California at Berkeley—he secured the Spanish-language rights to their online courses. The company translates courses and contracts with banks and with small and medium-sized businesses interested in outsourcing corporate education. His company, Off Campus Internet SL, plans to offer 500 courses online by 2005. The company is investigating expansion in Mexico, Chile, and Argentina as well.[19]

Importing as a Source of New Products

Some corporations decide to forgo internally sponsored research and development, instead importing finished products directly from a foreign firm to supplement their product lines. Such a strategy of importing new products should be pursued with great care and perhaps only in areas that do not represent the core of the firm's business and technology.

A number of U.S. bedding and towel manufacturers use imports to extend their product offerings. Thomaston Mills announced it would import Austrian-made luxury towels and bathrobes in order to move its product line more upscale. According to the company's president, "Where we can come up with a real good product by importing it and adding it, we'll be doing it."[20]

Acquisitions as a Route to New Products

Acquiring a company for its new technology or products is a strategy many firms have followed in domestic markets. To make international acquisitions for the purpose of gaining a window on emerging technologies or products is becoming an acceptable strategy for many firms. Robert Bosch, a German firm, acquired an interest in American Microsystems, and Philips of Holland purchased Signetics. In both cases, the foreign firms had to pay substantial premiums over the market value of the stock as a price for an inside look at new product development.

Japanese companies illustrate how the acquisition strategy can be used to gain access to new products and technologies. Japanese firms are reported to have invested about $350 million in some sixty deals for a wide range of minority positions in U.S.-based high-technology firms. In 1989 Chugai Pharmaceutical acquired Gen-Probe of San Diego to get access to the firm's products, including test kits for the detection of cancer and viral infections. Gen-Probe later became a recognized world leader in the development, manufacture, and commercialization of diagnostic products based on its patented genetic-probe technologies.[21]

Even companies from developing countries are beginning to follow this route. Piramal Enterprises, an Indian company, has successfully acquired the Indian operations of foreign pharmaceutical companies, such as Aspro Nicholas, Hoffman-LaRoche, and Boehringer Mannheim. These multinationals, hampered in their operations by government price controls, weak patent protection, and restrictions on foreign companies' activities, were happy to sell off their Indian subsidiaries. Piramal slimmed down management, increased sales, raised prices, and entered licensing agreements in order to get a steady stream of new technologies.[22] Recently, Indian software companies have been acquiring software companies in the United States. These acquisitions are partially motivated by a desire to access more value-added products.

Joint Ventures for New Product Development

Forming a joint venture with a technologically advanced foreign company can also lead to new product development, often at lower costs. In the 1960s and 1970s, it was largely Japanese companies that sought to attract foreign technology for the manufacture of advanced products in Japan. Today, many of these Japanese companies can be found in the forefront of their industries. Typically, these joint ventures were set up as separate entities with their own manufacturing and marketing functions.

Today, firms from many different countries participate in joint ventures. General Motors operates a joint venture in Japan with Suzuki, a company where it has a 10 percent share participation, and with Isuzu, a truck producer of which General Motors owns 49 percent. GM jointly develops cars with those firms for local markets.[23] Ford used a joint venture in Taiwan to build a new development center to develop products specifically for the Taiwanese market.[24] Even e-business calls for joint ventures. Softbank of Japan established joint ventures in Europe with Vivendi of France to provide services for e-business firms.[25]

Alliances for New Product Development

Many companies are finding alliances an effective way to share technology and research and development for competitive advantage. For example, Electrolux, the Swedish appliance manufacturer, has concluded a broad-based alliance with Toshiba of Japan. The two firms plan to cooperate in producing household appliances through the exchange of technology, product sourcing, and purchasing. Some fifteen projects are being undertaken, which span technology development, procurement, environmental issues, and sales in the Japanese market.[26]

To share the huge cost of developing new products, some companies have established or joined consortia to share in new product development. Under the **consortium approach**, member firms join in a working relationship without forming a new entity. On completion of the assigned task, member firms are free to seek other relationships with different firms.

Because the development of new aircraft is particularly expensive, the aircraft industry offers several examples of the consortium approach to product development. The high development costs require that large passenger aircraft be built and sold in series of two hundred or three hundred units to break even. Under these circumstances, several companies form a consortium to share the risk. One of the first highly successful efforts was the European Airbus, developed and produced by French, British, and German manufacturers.

Similarly, the major jet engine companies engage in a number of consortia. U.S.-based General Electric has had a long-term agreement with Snecma of France. The alliance has been highly successful, capturing a majority of large aircraft engine orders and producing its 10,000th engine in 1999.[27] Pratt & Whitney, the other leading U.S. firm, entered into a partnership with MTU, a subsidiary of the German firm Daimler-Benz. GE, Snecma, United Technologies (Pratt & Whitney), and Rolls Royce were invited by three Japanese engine producers—Mitsubishi Heavy Industries, Ishikawajima-Harima, and Kawasaki Heavy Industries—to help build new engines for supersonic planes. The four European and U.S. companies could provide technology assistance to the Japanese partners, saving development costs and time.[28]

▶ *Introducing New Products to Global Markets*

Once a product has been developed for commercial introduction, a number of complex decisions still need to be made. Aside from the question of whether to introduce the product abroad, the firm has to decide on a desirable test-marketing procedure, select target countries for product introduction, and determine the timing or sequence of the introduction. Given the large number of possible markets, decisions surrounding new product introduction often have strategic significance.

Determining which product to introduce abroad depends, of course, on sales potential. Following a careful analysis, a marketer develops a list of target countries. The company then can choose from among several paths leading to actual introduction in the target countries.

Concept Tests

Once a prototype or sample product has been developed, a company may decide to subject its new creation to a series of tests to determine its commercial feasibility. It is particularly important to subject a new product to actual use conditions. When the development process takes place outside the country of actual use, a practical field test can be crucial. The test must include all necessary usage steps to provide complete information. In a classic case, CPC International tested the U.S. market for dehydrated soups made by its newly acquired Knorr subsidiary. The company concentrated primarily on taste tests to ensure that the final product suited U.S. consumers. Extensive testing led to different soup formulations from those sold in Europe. CPC, however, had neglected to have consumers actually try out the product at home as part of their regular cooking activities. Such a test would have revealed consumers' discontent with the Knorr dehydrated soups' relatively long cooking time—up to 20 minutes, compared to 3 minutes for comparable canned soups. The company recognized these difficulties only after a national introduction had been completed and sales fell short of expectations.

The concept-testing stage would be incomplete if the products were tested only in the company's domestic market. A full test in several major markets is essential so that any shortcomings can be addressed at an early stage before costly adaptations for individual countries are made. Such an approach is particularly important in cases where product development occurs on a multinational basis with simultaneous inputs from several foreign subsidiaries. When Volkswagen tested its original Rabbit models, test vehicles were made available to all principal subsidiaries in order to ensure that each market's requirements were met by the otherwise standardized car.

Test Marketing

Just as there are good reasons to test-market a product in a domestic market, an international test can give the firm valuable insights. A key question is where the market test should be held. Companies in the United States have largely pioneered test-marketing procedures, because it has been reasonably simple to isolate a given market in terms of media and distribution. This may not always be possible in smaller countries and even less so in countries

World Beat 11.2 *On a Roll*

Polaroid's general manager of new product development, Clifford Hall, was strolling through Tokyo when he noticed teenage girls cramming into photo booths that took instant minipictures. He mentioned it to a Polaroid customer, Tomy Company, a Japanese toy manufacturer. Tomy executives promptly came back to Polaroid with a small instant-camera model. Their plan: Polaroid would design it, and Tomy would sell it.

Sandra Lawrence, Polaroid's vice-president of new products and product planning, immediately took to the idea. A mother of three, she knew from her own dinner table conversations that kids didn't use her company's cameras. Tomy's version, she thought, would be "a cool idea." Philip Norris, a veteran Polaroid inventor, went to work right away. Within weeks, he had fashioned several models, which Polaroid took to Tomy officials in their offices outside Tokyo. The Pocket camera was set in motion.

But in a meeting back at Polaroid's headquarters in Cambridge, Massachusetts, the vice-president of technology listened with grave doubts as Ms. Lawrence and Mr. Hall explained the Pocket concept. He wondered about the impact of a product with "very marginal" image quality. The marketing staff told him the camera was being launched in Japan, which would limit the potential damage. And they made another concession: The camera would prominently display the Tomy name and play down Polaroid's. If it did well overseas, the company would introduce a different version in the United States with better optics. When the camera hit Japan, the Tomy name was emblazoned in red letters on the face of the product; the Polaroid name appeared in the lower left corner, blended into the black molding.

The internal debate fizzled, though, as skyrocketing sales figures came in from Japan. Encouraged, Polaroid hit the U.S. market with an aggressive marketing campaign. The company advertised heavily on teenage TV shows. Polaroid also advertised on popular teen websites, including chickclick.com. And it proudly put the Polaroid name on the camera's front, in clear white lettering. After only a few months, the company had already sold more than a half-million Pocket cameras.

Source: Alec Klein, "On a Roll," Wall Street Journal, May 2, 2000, p. A1.

---

where most of the media are national rather than local. As a result, the opportunities for small local market tests are substantially reduced outside the United States.

To overcome the shortage of test-market possibilities, international firms often substitute the experience in one country for a market test in another. Special attention should be given to the lead market as a potential test market. Any new product that succeeds in its lead market may be judged to have good potential elsewhere as other markets mature. Although market tests are commonly conducted by U.S.-based firms before full-scale introduction in the U.S. market, subsidiaries tend to use these early U.S. results as a basis for analysis. However, use of the U.S. market as a test market depends on the market situation and on the degree to which results can be extrapolated to other countries. Circumstances are never exactly the same, and early U.S. results must be regarded with caution.

Another approach to test marketing is to use a foreign country as a proving ground before other markets are entered. In Europe, smaller markets such as the Netherlands, Belgium, Austria, and Switzerland may be used to launch a new product. Because of these countries' small size, a test would

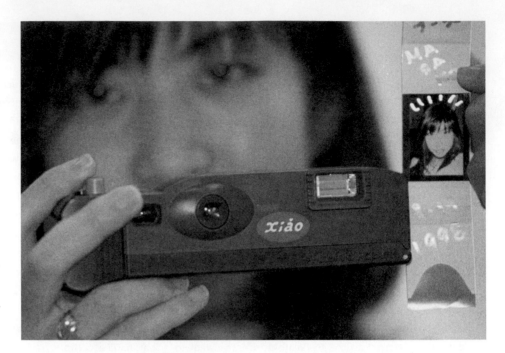

Polaroid's Pocket Camera is displayed at the Tokyo Toy Show. The camera was launched first in Japan. Only later was it introduced to Polaroid's home market, the United States.

include national introduction, and the results would be assumed to be applicable in other countries. Sometimes the test market may not even be the place of initial launch. IBM tested a new branding campaign for its Global Services line in Canada but launched it in the United States. Testing overseas prior to U.S. launch may even be cheaper, but it requires a better understanding of how to translate foreign results into probable outcomes in the U.S. market.

The selection of countries for new product launches is increasingly based on test marketing in perhaps one or two countries, with a rapid move toward a global roll-out. Heinz tested its new teenager-oriented ketchup campaign in Canada and then rolled it out worldwide with minor modifications. Clearly, global marketing is moving rapidly toward the time when testing and test interpretation will be done on the basis of data from different—and sometimes distant—markets, and the time when each local market was tested locally before launch is rapidly passing.[29]

Timing of New Product Introductions

Eventually, a company will be faced with establishing the timing and sequence of its introduction of a new product in its home market and foreign markets. When should the product be introduced in each market? Should the firm use a phased-entry or a simultaneous-entry approach? As we have noted, firms usually introduce new products first in their domestic markets to gain experience in production, marketing, and service. Foreign market introductions are usually attempted only after a product has proved itself in the domestic market.

Although international firms have subsidiaries in numerous countries, initial product introductions were traditionally limited to the industrialized nations, and new product introductions in overseas markets lagged consider-

For Further Reading

Cheng, Joseph L. C., and Douglas J. Bolon. "The Management of Multinational R&D: A Neglected Topic in International Business Research." *Journal of International Business Studies*, First Quarter 1993: 1–18.

Fedows, Kasra. "Making the Most of Foreign Factories." *Harvard Business Review*, March–April 1997: 73–88.

Kuemmerle, Walter. "Building Effective R&D Capabilities Abroad." *Harvard Business Review*, March–April 1997: 61–70.

Mabert, Vincent A., John F. Muth, and Robert W. Schmennor. "Collapsing New Product Development Time." *Journal of Product Innovation Management*, September 1992: 200–212.

Shaoming Zou and Aysegul Ozsomer. "Global Product R&D and the Firm's Strategic Position." *Journal of International Marketing* 7, 1 (1999): 57–76.

Case 11.1 Rethinking World Cars

With automobile markets maturing in the triad, both Ford and General Motors must look for growth elsewhere. Two large emerging markets, India and Russia, promise sales growth but present challenges as well.

India is the world's second most populous country and one of its poorest, with a per-capita income of only $425 a year. For 40 years the Indian car market was protected from foreign competition and was dominated by only two models of cars. When the government liberalized the automobile market in the mid-1990s, global competitors flocked to India. By 2001 there were fifteen automobile firms with production in India, a phenomenon that led to considerable overcapacity in the market.

Ford was among the firms that had been attracted to India. However, the Ford Escort fared poorly in this market. The company found out first-hand that the Indian consumer wanted the best but would not spend much money for it. Ford responded by designing the Ikon, their first car built for consumers in the developing world. More than four hundred engineers and development personnel were assigned the task, at a cost of $500 million.

Essentially, Ford remade its Fiesta model. More headroom was added to accommodate men who wore turbans. Doors opened wider for women who wore saris. The air conditioning was adjusted to India's heat, and air-intake valves were fitted in such a way as not to be vulnerable to the flooding that accompanied India's monsoon season. Shock absorbers were toughened to withstand potholed streets. Ford even convinced certain of its suppliers to set up plants near the Ford plant in India in order to meet India's local-content requirements. Extensive product testing was done under India's harsh driving conditions. The Ikon was priced between $9,500 and $16,000, and its sales in India quickly surpassed those of the Escort.

About the time the Ikon was enjoying its first sales in India, General Motors decided to take quite a different route to market in Russia. GM identified Russia as one of eight countries that would account for two-thirds of global growth in car sales in the coming decade. Unfortunately, in 2001 Russia was plagued with both political and economic risk. Furthermore, GM was concerned that a stripped-down model of a Western car—GM's traditional approach to markets in developing countries—would not be cheap enough for the Russian market. Although such a car could be assembled inexpensively in Russia, the engineering to create the adapted model would be extremely expensive. Also, market research showed that Russians thought little of cars assembled in Russia, even if they included foreign-made parts and bore a prestigious brand name. If a car were assembled in Russia, it would be attractive only if it sold at an extremely low price.

GM decided, therefore, to put its Chevrolet brand on a product developed by Avtovaz, a struggling automobile producer from the Soviet era. As the Soviet car producer, Avtovaz had dominated not only the Russian market but also the Soviet bloc market until the fall of communism, when it lost its captive export markets and the Russian market became deluged with imported cars. Avtovaz's cheapest car, priced at $3,000, was the boxy four-door "classic." Most of its models included no automatic transmission, no emission controls, and no power steering. The company developed only one new model in the 1990s. With Russia's political uncertainty and collapsed economy, Avtovaz lacked the funds to bring the model to production.

After considerable negotiations, GM and Avtovaz agreed to enter a $333 million joint venture to produce the Niva. GM would contribute much-needed cash, as well as designing and supervising the production facilities. Avtovaz would contribute the Niva design and would also save GM the costs of developing a parts and distribution system, because the car would be sold and serviced through the Avtovaz system. Still concerned about political risk in Russia, GM convinced the European Bank for Reconstruction and Development to lend the venture $93 million and to invest another $40 million in exchange for a 17 percent equity stake.

The new Niva was noisy, delivered a rough ride, and had a low-power engine, but it passed basic safety testing, carried a GM logo, and could be sold for $7,500. The premium model would get Opel transmissions. Surveyed consumers liked the Niva better than other Russian models. In addition, GM identified, among its international operations, potential export markets for up to 25,000 of the 75,000 cars to be produced each year.

Discussion Questions

1. What are the similarities and differences between the car markets in India and Russia?
2. Which market do you think is the most difficult? Why?
3. Compare the pros and cons of Ford's model invention strategy and GM's joint venture strategy.

Sources: Gregory L. White, "Off Road," *Wall Street Journal*, February 20, 20001, p.A1; and Jon E. Hilsenath, "A Car to Suit India's Taste," *Wall Street Journal*, August 8, 2000, p. A17.

Case 11.2 *Launching Intuition*

In the first year of the new millennium, Estee Lauder launched Intuition, its biggest new fragrance in 5 years. The new fragrance was allotted a record-breaking $30 million advertising budget. Lauder aimed for $100 million in sales in the first year, more than double the sales of most other new fragrances.

A typical launch of a Lauder fragrance began with its introduction in the United States. The product would then be introduced to overseas markets in 6 months to a year. In an unprecedented move, the launch of Intuition bypassed the United States. Instead, it was introduced in France and Britain in September 2000, with a roll-out to the rest of Europe, Asia, and Latin America in October. About 40 percent of sales of prestige fragrances take place in November and December.

Estee Lauder owned five of the top ten women's fragrances sold at department stores across the United States. However, only one Lauder perfume made the top ten in Europe. It was Pleasures, launched in 1996. The United States fragrance market, especially for the premier lines sold in department stores, remained in a slump. For the past 5 years, sales had been flat or down each year. In Europe the market had grown about 8 percent the previous year.

By the late 1990s, Lauder's overseas sales had reached 50 percent. At that time, creative divisions were set up in Paris and Tokyo to develop products for local consumer needs. Intuition was the first collaborative effort between Lauder's U.S. and European development centers. Intuition's formula was lighter than the traditionally heavy European fragrances and was targeted at the younger woman (starting in her mid-twenties). It was marketed as Lauder's first fragrance with a European sensibility, although the company wanted Intuition eventually to be seen as a global fragrance. At an unspecified date, Intuition was to be introduced in the United States. Some managers believed that U.S. sales might even be improved if Intuition could be billed as previously "available only in Europe."

Discussion Questions

1. What are possible reasons for the unconventional development and launch of Intuition?
2. What difficulties might the company face with such a launch?

Sources: "Estee Lauder Follows Its Intuition with European Fragrance Debut," *The Rose Sheet*, September 3, 2000; Emily Nelson, "Nosing Abroad," *Wall Street Journal*, September 30, 2000, p. B1; and "Will Europe Take to Intuition?" *Straits Times*, November 1, 2000.

Notes

[1] "BAT–Rothmans Merger to Affect Polish Operations," *Polish News Bulletin*, June 16, 1999.

[2] "Japan Tobacco Wins RJR's Russia Unit," *Moscow Times*, March 11, 1999, p. 11.

[3] "Yamaha: Perfect Pitch?" *The Economist*, February 17, 1996: 62.

[4] "The Revolution at Ford," *The Economist*, August 7, 1999: 51.

[5] "Gillette Knows Shaving—How to Turn Out Hot New Products," *Fortune*, October 14, 1996: 207–210.

[6] "New Razor Hype Boosts Gillette's Shares" (A Barron's Feature), *Dow Jones News Service*, July 11, 1998.

[7] "Playing Godmother to Invention," *The Economist*, May 24, 1997: 76.

[8] "Japan's PC Shipments Seen to Rise 7.3 Percent in 1998," *Agence France-Presse*, March 6, 1998.

[9] "South Korea's Samsung Announces Next-Generation Computer Chip," *Agence France-Presse*, June 28, 1999.

[10] "When the Corporate Lab Goes to Japan," *New York Times*, April 28, 1991, sec. 3.

[11] "Companies Set Up Overseas R&D Bases," *Nikkei Weekly*, November 9, 1992, p. 13.

[12] Jeffrey Krasner, "Drug Research Giant Heads to Cambridge," *Boston Globe*, May 7, 2002, p. A1.

[13] "GM Innovations Recognized," *PR Newswire*, April 25, 2001.

[14] "Microsoft Urges Russian Software Bootleggers: Join Us," *Wall Street Journal*, May 18, 1993, p. B4.

[15] "Fanning Unilever's Flame of Innovation," *Advertising Age International*, November 23, 1992: I-3.

[16] "China: Back to the Future," *Far Eastern Economic Review*, March 11, 1999: 10.

[17] "Microsoft Lab in China," *Wall Street Journal*, November 6, 1998.

[18] Kasra Ferdows, "Making the Most of Foreign Factories," *Harvard Business Review*, March–April 1997: 73–88.

[19] Keith Johnson, "The Business-Spanish Lessons: An Entrepreneur Wants to Bring U.S. Universities to Spaniards," *Wall Street Journal*, March 12, 2001, p. R18.

[20] Mary Ellen Lloyd, "Textile Firms Boosting Sales Overseas," *Wall Street Journal*, July 3, 2000.

[21] "Gen-Probe Expands with a New State of the Art Manufacturing Facility," *Chemical Business NewsBase*: Press Release, May 17, 1999.

[22] "Pharmaceuticals in India: Best of Both Worlds," *The Economist*, December 7, 1996: 6.

[23] "GM Says Auto Plant in Japan Is Part of Long-term Strategy," *Agence France-Presse*, August 6, 1999.

[24] "Ford Joint Venture in Taiwan to Invest in New Product Development," *AFX News*, May 5, 1999.

[25] "Softbank to Set Up Joint Ventures in Britain, France," *Japan Computer Industry Scan*, July 5, 1999.

[26] "Toshiba, Electrolux in Alliance," *National Post*, May 27, 1999, p. C12.

[27] "GE French Alliance Pays Off; CFMI Will Build Its 10,000th Engine," *Cincinnati Post*, March 10, 1999, p. 5C.

[28] "GE, Rolls Royce, Snecma Reportedly Join Japan Jet Engine Project," *AFX News*, April 19, 1999.

[29] "Test It in Paris, France, Launch It in Paris, Texas," *Advertising Age*, May 31, 1999: p. 28.

[30] "P&G Puts Two Cleaning Products on Its New Marketing Fast Track," *Wall Street Journal*, May 18, 1999, p. B6.

[31] Bruce Orwall and Evan Ramstad, "Fast Forward," *Wall Street Journal*, June 12, 2000, p. A1.

[32] "DHL and EXE Begin Global Roll-Out," *Business Wire*, February 13, 2002.

[33] Nanette Byrnes, "Panning for Gold in Local Markets," *Business Week*, September 18, 2000: 54.

12 Pricing for International and Global Markets

In Recent Years the Justice Department has brought some of America's largest criminal cases to trial. The defendants are global managers from Belgium, Britain, Canada, France, Germany, Italy, Japan, Mexico, the Netherlands, South Korea, and Switzerland as well as from the United States. The charge is collusion with competitors to fix global prices. The penalty is a hefty fine for the company and a jail sentence for the manager. One price-fixing case involved vitamins. Multinational pharmaceutical firms reached produc-

tion and price agreements that raised prices to packaged-foods companies such as General Mills, Kellogg's, Coca-Cola, and Procter & Gamble. These higher prices were of course passed on to consumers who took vitamins, drank milk, or ate cereal. Similarly, investigators uncovered a 17-year price-fixing conspiracy among American, German, and Japanese producers of sorbates, a food preservative. This cartel is estimated to have affected over a billion dollars in sales in the United States alone. Global cartels have raised

prices on such diverse products as soft drinks, dynamite, and offshore oil and gas drilling platforms. Increasingly, governments in Europe and Asia are joining the United States in investigating the pricing policies of global firms.[1]

What would make a manager risk a jail sentence to fix a global price? The globalization of markets offers several possible explanations. Competition has intensified. Firms not only compete in foreign markets but also face foreign competition in their home markets. Consolida-

Chapter Outline

Learning Objectives

After studying this chapter, you should be able to:

▶ Differentiate between full-cost pricing and marginal-cost pricing and explain the implications of both to global marketers.

▶ Note how international transportation costs, tariffs, taxes, local production costs, and channel costs all affect pricing decisions.

▶ Explain how different income levels, buyer power, and competitive situations in national markets can require different pricing strategies across these markets.

▶ Compare and contrast the ways in which exchange rate fluctuations and inflation rates complicate global pricing.

▶ List various examples of government price controls that global marketers might encounter.

▶ Define dumping and describe how it can constrain pricing strategies.

▶ Describe how global marketers can manage export price escalation, determine transfer prices, and effectively quote prices in foreign currencies.

▶ Define parallel imports, explain their causes, and list ways in which they may be controlled.

▶ Differentiate among various forms of countertrade and balance the risk and opportunities of dealing with noncash exchanges.

tion in many industries has created fewer but bigger competitors. Demanding consumers want better products at lower prices. Pressures to lower prices abound. But pricing is the part of the marketing mix that delivers potential profits to the firm. For some companies, the temptation to bring order and certainty to a global market must seem overwhelming.

Managing global pricing is indeed more complex than establishing national pricing strategies. This chapter provides an overview of the key factors that affect pricing policies in an international environment (see Figure 12.1). We assume that you understand the basic pricing decisions that companies must make in a single-country or domestic environment. In this chapter, we focus on the unique aspects of international pricing. First we look at how cost considerations affect international pricing decisions. We next explore the impact of market and environmental factors. Then we examine managerial pricing issues such as transfer pricing, global pricing, and countertrade.

Figure 12.1 *Global Pricing Strategies*

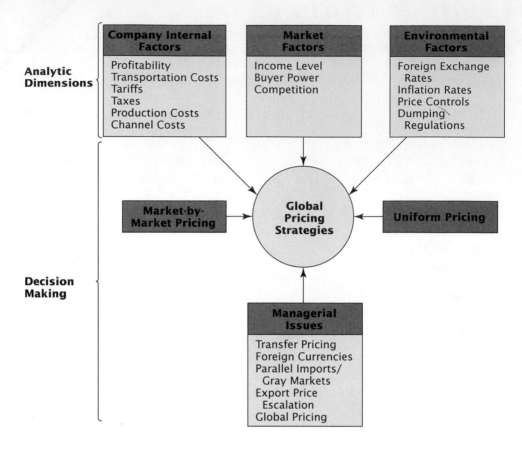

▶ *Profit and Cost Factors That Affect Pricing*

Most companies begin pricing deliberations on the basis of their own internal cost structure and their profit targets. Any effective pricing policy starts with a clear understanding of these cost and profit variables. Therefore, understanding the various cost elements can be considered a prerequisite for a successful international pricing strategy.

According to standard accounting practice, costs are divided into two categories: fixed costs and variable costs. **Fixed costs** do not change over a given range of output, whereas **variable costs** vary directly with output. The relationship of these variables is shown in Table 12.1 for a fictitious company, Western Machine Tool, Inc., a manufacturer of machine tools that sell for $60,000 per unit in the U.S. market.

The total cost of a machine tool is $54,000. Selling it at $60,000, the company will make a profit of $6,000 before taxes from the sale of each unit. However, if 1 additional unit is sold (or not sold), the marginal impact amounts to more than an additional profit (or loss) of $6,000, because the extra cost of an additional unit will be limited to its variable costs only, or $26,000, as shown in Table 12.2. For any additional units sold, the **marginal profit** is $34,000, the amount in excess of the variable costs.

Let's say Western Machine Tool has a chance to export a unit to a foreign country, but the maximum price the foreign buyer is willing to pay is $50,000. Machine Tool, using full-cost pricing, argues that the company will

Table 12.1 *Profit and Cost Calculation for Western Machine Tool, Inc.*

Selling price (per unit)			$60,000
Direct manufacturing costs			
Labor	$10,000		
Materials	15,000		
Energy	1,000	$26,000	
Indirect manufacturing costs			
Supervision	5,000		
Research and development	3,000		
Factory overhead	5,000	13,000	
General administrative cost			
Sales and marketing overhead	10,000		
Full costs	5,000		54,000
Net profit before tax		15,000	$ 6,000

incur a loss of $4,000 if the deal is accepted. However, only $26,000 of additional variable cost will be incurred for a new machine, because all fixed costs are incurred anyway and are covered by all prior units sold. The company can in fact go ahead with the sale and claim a marginal profit of $24,000. In such a situation, a profitable sale may easily be turned down unless a company is fully informed about its cost composition.

Cost components are subject to change. For example, if growing export volume adds new output to a plant, a company may achieve economies of scale that result in overall reductions in unit cost.[2] This consideration further supports the use of a marginal-pricing strategy. Marketers should beware, however, if marginal pricing significantly hurts domestic competition in the export markets. As we will see later in the chapter, this can lead to charges of dumping and consequent legal action against the exporters.

Transportation Costs

International marketing often requires the shipment of products over long distances. The cost of shipping can become an important part of the international pricing policy of some firms. A study of how U.S. and Korean companies set

Table 12.2 *Marginal Profit Calculation for Western Machine Tool, Inc.*

Selling price (per unit)			$60,000
Variable costs			
Direct manufacturing costs			
Labor	$10,000		
Materials	15,000		
Energy	1,000	$26,000	
Total variable costs			26,000
Contribution margin (selling price minus variable costs)			$34,000

overseas prices suggests that companies that charge higher prices in foreign markets than in domestic markets do so because of transportation costs. In other words, these companies, both American and Korean, appear to use a cost-plus model for setting prices overseas, consciously adding in transportation costs to establish the price they eventually charge in foreign markets.[3]

For commodities in particular, low transportation costs can determine who gets an order. For more expensive and differentiated products, such as computers or sophisticated electronic instruments, transportation costs usually represent only a small fraction of total costs and rarely influence pricing decisions. For products between the two extremes, companies can substantially affect unit transportation costs by selecting appropriate transportation methods. For example, the introduction of container ocean vessels has made cost-effective shipment of many products possible. Roll-on, roll-off ships (ro-ro carriers) have reduced ocean freight costs for cars and trucks to very low levels, making exporters more competitive vis-à-vis local manufacturers. Still, because all modes of transportation, including rail, truck, air, and ocean, depend on a considerable amount of energy, the total cost is of growing concern to international companies and can be sensitive to the world price of oil.

Tariffs

When products are transported across national borders, tariffs may have to be paid. Tariffs are usually levied on the landed costs of a product, which include shipping costs to the importing country. Tariffs are normally assessed as a percentage of the landed value. The WTO, like its predecessor GATT, has gone a long way in bringing tariffs down. However, they can still prove significant for certain products in certain markets, and even low tariffs can prove problematic in competitive environments.

Tariff costs can have a ripple effect and increase prices considerably for the end user. Intermediaries, whether they are sales subsidiaries or independent distributors, tend to include any tariff costs in their costs of goods sold and to calculate operating margins on the basis of this amount. As a result, the impact on the final end-user price can be substantial whenever tariff rates are high.

Sometimes international firms attempt to avoid or lessen the cost effects of tariffs by having their products reclassified. The British company Land Rover has marketed its Range Rover four-wheel-drive (4WD) utility vehicle in the United States since 1987. When the U.S. tariffs for trucks were temporarily increased from 2.5 to 25 percent in an effort to stem imports, 4WD vehicles were subject to the higher tariff. Land Rover complained that its $40,000 vehicle should not be classified as a truck, pointing out that the utility vehicle had four doors, not just two like the typical light truck. The vehicle was reclassified, and the higher duty was avoided. In 1991, however, the United States began to charge a 10 percent surtax on luxury vehicles above $30,000, potentially affecting the sales of the Range Rover again. This time the U.S. tax authorities agreed to classify four-wheel-drive vehicles as trucks, and the Range Rover again avoided the tax. Range Rovers are shipped to the United States as cars to avoid the truck surcharge, but they have an increased weight of 6,019 pounds (up from 5,997 pounds) because the tax authorities' truck definition starts at vehicles of 6,000 pounds.[4]

Check out our website for links to information on national tariffs.

Taxes

Local taxes also affect the final cost of products. A variety of taxes may be imposed. One of the most common is the value added-tax (VAT) used by member countries of the European Union. This tax is similar to the sales tax collected by state governments in the United States but involves more complicated assessment and collection procedures based on the value added to the product at any given stage.

Each EU country sets its own value-added tax structure. However, common to all is a zero tax rate (or exemption) on exported goods. A company exporting from the Netherlands to Belgium does not have to pay any tax on the value added in the Netherlands. However, Belgian authorities do collect a tax, at the Belgium rate, on products shipped from the Netherlands. Merchandise shipped to any EU member country from a nonmember country, such as the United States or Japan, is assessed the VAT rate on landed costs, in addition to any customs duties that may be applied to those products.

In 2002 the European Union approved a controversial tax requiring all Internet companies to pay tax on sales of digitally downloadable goods, such as software, music, and other virtual products, purchased in Europe. The U.S. government had opposed the new tax. However, European e-commerce companies already paid a nationally levied tax on every Internet-based sale they made—putting them at a competitive disadvantage compared to U.S.- and Asia-based Internet companies. Under the new system, non-European-based Internet companies doing business in the European Union must register in one of the EU member countries and pay taxes on all Internet sales—downloadable or delivered by mail. Subsequently, the taxes are to be distributed on the basis of the location of the buyers. Observers believe that the EU system could become the model for taxing digitally downloadable product everywhere.[5]

Different countries also assess different "sin taxes." These are taxes assessed on products that are legal but are discouraged by the society. Cigarettes and alcoholic beverages commonly fall into this category. For example, Sweden countered a history of massive alcohol abuse in the nineteenth century by enacting Europe's highest taxes on alcoholic beverages in the twentieth century. These taxes increased prices to consumers, who in turn reduced their consumption. Sweden's alcohol-related deaths and illnesses fell to among the lowest in the developed world. However, Sweden's having joined the European Union threatens to undermine these gains. Swedes in the southern part of the country can now drive across a bridge to buy alcohol in Denmark at a far lower price and bring it back into Sweden. Researchers at Sweden's National Institute of Public Health predict a 10 percent rise in consumption as a result of the relaxed import allowance.[6]

Local Production Costs

Up to this point, we have assumed that a company has only one producing location, from which it exports to all other markets. However, most international firms manufacture products in several countries. In such cases, operating costs for raw materials, wages, energy, and/or financing may differ widely from country to country, allowing a firm to ship from a particularly advantageous location in order to reduce prices by taking advantage of lower costs. Companies increasingly choose production locations that give them

World Beat 12.1 *Poaching Foreign Patients*

In a global recruitment campaign, German hospitals are positioning themselves as significant players in the international health care field by luring foreign patients to Germany for treatment. The campaign follows 2 years of research by the German government and a consortium of hospitals. On the basis of the findings, policymakers decided to focus on the international market.

The Kuratorium, a nonprofit organization set up for this effort, distributes glossy brochures that tout package stays including marble baths, Internet connections, and high-tech examination rooms. Brochures are distributed to German embassies and hospital associations worldwide.

Although the concept of luring foreign patients isn't new, this is the first time the German government has driven such a marketing effort. State officials are confident they will succeed. Unlike many European countries, Germany has a surplus of doctors—at any given time, between 10,000 and 15,000 doctors remain unemployed in Germany. The upshot: Many of the doctors are highly specialized, delivering top treatment at low prices. Some operations cost 50 percent less than in the United States.

Treatments range from heart surgery and eye operations to hip replacement. Hospitals offer travel arrangements, hotel reservations, translation services, and ambulatory transport. German health care executives hope to take advantage of what they see as frustrated and untapped markets in other countries: patients on long waiting lists in Scandinavia, rich private health care customers in the Middle East and Africa, and the growing number of affluent citizens in Russia and Central and Eastern Europe. The Kuratorium recently signed its first contract with Skandia Lifeline Ltd., a Swedish insurance company and has entered negotiations with insurance companies in Italy, Spain, France, Russia, and the United States.

Source: Meera Louis, "Germans Lure Foreign Patients to Hospitals," *Wall Street Journal*, December 6, 2000, p. B12.

READ MORE ABOUT IT:
Check out "Visions of Sugar Plums" under *Supplemental Readings* on our website.

advantages in production costs as well as freight, tariffs, or other transfer costs. Consequently, judicious management of sourcing points may reduce product costs and result in added pricing flexibility.

Recently, Mexico has attracted many U.S. candy manufacturers. Part of the attraction is the youthful Mexican market known for its sweet tooth. However, Mexico is also being used as a platform to export candy back to the U.S. market. Mexican workers earn as little as one-tenth the pay of U.S. factory workers. Even more important is the lower cost of sugar in Mexico—about half the federally supported U.S. cost.[7]

Channel Costs

Channel costs are a function of channel length, distribution margins, and logistics. Many countries operate with longer distribution channels than those in the United States, causing higher total costs and end-user prices because of additional layers of intermediaries. Also, gross margins at the retail level tend to be higher outside the United States. Because the logistics system in a large number of countries is also less developed than that in the United States, logistics costs, too, are higher on a per-unit basis. All of these factors add extra costs to a product that is marketed internationally.

Campbell Soup Company, a U.S.-based firm, found that its retailers in the United Kingdom purchased soup in small quantities of twenty-four cans per case of assorted soups, requiring each can to be handpicked for shipment. In the United States, the company could sell one variety of soup to retailers in cases of forty-eight cans per case. To handle the smaller purchase lots in England, the company had to add another level of distribution and new facilities. As a result, distribution costs were 30 percent higher in England than in the United States.[8]

▶ *Market Factors That Affect Pricing*

Companies cannot establish pricing policies in a vacuum. Although cost information is essential, prices must also reflect the realities of the marketplace. International markets are particularly challenging because of the large number of local economic situations to be considered. Three factors in particular stand out and must be analyzed in greater detail: income level, buyer power, and competition.

Income Level

As we have discussed in previous chapters, the income level of a country's population determines the amount and type of goods and services bought, especially in consumer markets. When detailed income data are not available, incomes are expressed by gross domestic product (GDP) or gross national product (GNP) divided by the total population. GDP is the total value of goods and services produced in a country. GNP includes this plus any income that residents receive from abroad. The new measures, GNP per capita and GDP per capita, are surrogate measures for personal income and are used to compare income levels among countries. To do so, all GNPs and GDPs have to be converted into the same currency. As we also noted earlier, converting GNP or GDP per capita converted into dollars on the basis of market exchange rates may understate the true purchasing power of a country's consumers. It is more accurate to look at developing countries' GNP or GDP per capita converted into dollars on the basis of relative purchasing power.

Furthermore, **disposable income**—the amount left after the basic necessities of food, shelter, and clothing have been acquired—can vary from country to country. In much of Southeast Asia, children in their twenties still live with their parents. Virtually all the income they earn is disposable, which makes them an attractive target market. In China, employees of state organizations often receive lucrative housing benefits, a practice that markedly increases their disposable income.

As a result of widely differing income and price levels, elasticity of demand for any given product can be expected to vary greatly. Countries with high income levels often display lower price elasticities for necessities such as food, shelter, and medical care. These lower elasticities in part reflect a lack of alternatives such as "doing it yourself" that forces buyers in these countries to purchase such goods even at higher prices. By contrast, in many countries with lower income levels, a considerable part of the population has the additional alternatives of providing their own food or building their own shelters should they not have enough money to purchase products or services on a cash basis. The availability of such options increases price elasticity, because these consumers can more easily opt out of the cash economy than can consumers in developed economies.

Many multinational firms can realistically target only a select segment of the population in poorer countries, even when they adjust their prices downward. To accommodate a lower income level in China, McDonald's has typically resorted to introductory pricing that sometimes fails to cover the full cost of the burger. Lower prices attract more customers. As volume increases, costs are covered, and a restaurant becomes profitable despite its lower prices.[9] Still, a McDonald's meal remains expensive in the Chinese context. A Chinese family of three can pay about 100 yuan, or about 10 percent of a typical monthly urban salary, to eat one meal out.[10]

Firms should regularly reassess their pricing policy in developing countries, especially if they are charging relatively high prices and targeting the

Automobile prices in China are dropping fast. As a result, automobile sales in China may reach 5 million cars per year by 2010.

elite. The growing middle classes in these countries can become a more attractive segment to target than a small upper class. In 2001 General Motors announced its development of a Farmers Car for China's 800 million rural inhabitants, whose incomes are even lower than those of city dwellers, in an attempt to tap a market segment hitherto ignored by multinational car manufacturers. The proposed price of the car was $7,000, down from the $40,000 charged for Buicks then sold to Chinese city dwellers.[11] Soon cars sold in the city were becoming more affordable, as many manufacturers began to lower automobile prices. In 2002 a Chinese consumer could buy a Buick Sail for under $14,000. As a result of lower car prices, China's middle classes are expected to buy 5 million cars a year by 2010.[12]

READ MORE ABOUT IT:
Check out "Motor Nation" under *Supplemental Readings* on our website.

Buyer Power

Just as disposable income is an important consideration in consumer markets, buyer power is crucial in business-to-business markets. Large buyers can become important to supplier firms, and in turn these buyers can demand lower prices from suppliers. If there are only a few buyers in a national industry, prices may be lower than in markets where there are many smaller buyers. In some global industries in particular, marketers face the challenge of increasing buyer power at the international level. Aircraft component suppliers are increasingly responding to demands from big aerospace companies such as Honeywell and Pratt & Whitney to cut prices, even if it means moving production from the United States to Mexico to realize cost savings that can be passed on to the powerful buyers.[13]

Competition

The intensity and power of competition can also significantly affect price levels in any given market. A firm acting as the sole supplier of a product in a given market enjoys greater pricing flexibility. The opposite is true if that same company has to compete against several other local or international firms. Therefore, the number and type of competitors greatly influence pricing strategy in any market. The public postal, telephone, and telegraph (PTT) services of most countries were until recently public monopolies, which could charge high rates with no threat of competition. As the Japanese telecommunications market liberalized, U.S. and other suppliers have been quick to respond. AT&T World Access offered international calling opportunities at approximately half the standard rate offered by Japanese providers.[14] After the German telecom market was opened in 1998, fifty-one new companies entered the market. They have captured one-third of the market from Deutsche Telekom, and long-distance rates have dropped 90 percent.[15]

Occasionally, price levels are manipulated by cartels or other agreements among local competitors. Cartels in the United States are forbidden by law. Furthermore, U.S. companies may find themselves in violation of U.S. laws if they actively participate in any foreign cartel. Although many other foreign governments allow cartels provided that they do not injure the consumer, the European Union is becoming stricter toward cartels. Following a 5-year investigation, the EU fined twenty-three Western European chemical companies $80 million for the price fixing of two plastic products. The companies were found guilty of forming secret pricing cartels to keep up the price of PVC and low-density polyethylene.[16]

The U.S. government has a very strict approach to cartels, and any cartel such as those just described would clearly be against existing U.S. laws. The U.S. Justice Department found four graphite electrode manufacturers guilty of conspiring to suppress and eliminate competition. As a result, the one German, one U.S., and two Japanese companies paid fines totaling $284 million.[17]

► Environmental Factors That Affect Price

We have thus far treated pricing as a matter of cost and market factors. A number of environmental factors also influence pricing at the international level. These external variables, which are not subject to control by any individual company, include foreign exchange rates, inflation, and government price controls. These factors restrict company decision-making authority and can become major concerns for country managers.

Exchange Rate Fluctuations

One of the most unpredictable factors affecting prices is the movement of foreign exchange rates. As the exchange rate moves up and down, it affects all producers. When a company's costs are in their domestic currency, as this currency weakens, the firm's costs appear lower in another currency. For example, when the euro was launched in January 1999, each euro was valued at $1.20. By July 1999, the euro had dropped to $1.00. As a result, products manufactured in Europe were cheaper in dollar terms and more attractive in the U.S. market, as well as in other national markets where governments pegged their currencies to the U.S. dollar.[18]

Foreign exchange fluctuations can also present difficulties for companies that export from countries with appreciating currencies. These firms are forced to accept decreased margins on sales denominated in foreign currencies or else raise prices in order to maintain their prior margins. The latter option could, of course, cause a drop in export demand. This was clear when the Russian ruble fell 22 percent over a period of a few months. Exports to Russia fell 50 percent. Faced with the option of buying a tube of locally produced toothpaste for 7 rubles or a tube of imported Colgate for 24 rubles, fewer Russian consumers chose the Colgate.[19]

Check out our website for links to national currency information.

Inflation Rates

The rate of inflation can affect product costs and may force a company to take specific action. Inflation rates have traditionally fluctuated over time and, more important, have differed from country to country. The United States and Europe have successfully managed inflation by raising interest rates whenever the economy starts to heat up, keeping inflation at 0–2 percent. Historically, inflation has been a problem in developing countries. In some cases, inflation rates have risen to several hundred percent. Argentina, Bolivia, Brazil, and Nicaragua have all experienced 4-digit hyperinflation in the past. A company can usually protect itself from rapid inflation if it maintains constant operating margins and makes constant price adjustments, sometimes on a monthly basis.

In countries with extremely high inflation, companies may price in a stable currency, such as the U.S. dollar, and translate prices into local currencies on a daily basis. Vision Express, which has been very successful in Russia, charges customers in dollars to avoid the inflation that lifts ruble prices rapidly. Most of the customers, largely entrepreneurs and businesspeople, seem to be able to get dollars. In fact, one study by the Russian central bank found that 20 percent of transactions in the Russian economy were in dollars.[20]

Price Controls

In some countries, government and regulatory agencies control the prices of products and services. Price controls may be applied to an entire economy to combat inflation. Alternatively, regulations may be applied selectively to specific industries. As a result of market liberalization, across-the-board price controls are now uncommon, although such controls remain in a few countries, such as the former Soviet republic of Belarus.[21] Industry-specific controls are more common. In response to rising prices in 2002, the Thai government threatened cement producers with price controls if they failed to cap their prices voluntarily through the end of the year. Furthermore, the cement producers agreed to cut off distributors who attracted complaints of overcharging.[22]

Pharmaceuticals are subject to price controls in many countries, including Canada, Japan, and European states. In the European Union, where many aspects of the countries' economies are coordinated, methods of controlling prices for drugs can vary considerably. In the United Kingdom, drug prices are established through the Pharmaceutical Price Regulation Scheme (PPRS). Although companies are allowed to set prices for most individual drugs, the government limits their overall profitability. As a result of the common government policy of limiting prices of drugs in many countries, consumers often pay less than in the United States. The same $100 worth of drugs in the United States would cost $76 in Canada, $67 in the U.K., $47 in Sweden, and $32 in Australia.[23]

Dumping Regulations

The practice of selling a product at a price below full costs is referred to as dumping. Because of potential injuries to domestic manufacturers, most governments have adopted regulations against dumping. Antidumping actions are allowed under provisions of the World Trade Organization (WTO) as long as two criteria are met: "sales at less than fair value" and causing "material injury" to a domestic industry. The first criterion is usually interpreted to mean selling abroad at prices below those in the country of origin. The WTO rules prohibit assessment of retroactive punitive duties and require all procedures to be open.

In the 1980s and early 1990s, 80 percent of antidumping charges were brought by the United States, Canada, the EU, and Australia—often against Asian countries. However, many of the new antidumping cases have been brought to the WTO by developing countries such as South Africa, India, Brazil, Indonesia, and Mexico. The United States, the EU, Canada, and Australia have brought less than one-third of the cases. Forty-three of the cases were brought against the EU and its members.[24] International marketers have to be aware of antidumping legislation that sets a floor under export prices, limiting pricing flexibility even in the event of overcapacity or an industry slowdown. On the other hand, antidumping legislation can work to a company's advantage, protecting it from foreign competition.

▶ *Managerial Issues in Global Pricing*

Now that we have given you a general overview of the context of international pricing, we turn to managerial issues—matters that require constant management attention and are never really resolved. These issues include export price escalation, transfer pricing, quoting prices in foreign currencies, parallel markets, uniform pricing strategies, and managing countertrade.

Managing Export Price Escalation

The additional costs described earlier may raise the end-user price of an exported product substantially above its domestic price. This phenomenon, which is called export price escalation, may force a company to adopt either of two strategies. First, a company may accept its price disadvantage and adjust the marketing mix to promote a luxury status. By adopting such a strategy, the company sacrifices volume to keep a high unit price. For example, in Guangzhou, China, Pizza Hut found that its typical price per person for a restaurant meal was 40–50 RMB, whereas a value meal at McDonald's cost 16–25 RMB. Pizza Hut decided it was desirable to position itself as a casual dining restaurant with table service rather than counter service to differentiate its offering from the fast-food restaurants and thereby command a higher price.[25] Alternatively, a company may reengineer its products to be less costly or grant a discount on the standard domestic price to bring the end-user price more in line with prices paid by domestic customers. Such discounts may be justified under a strategy of marginal-cost pricing. Also, export sales may generate greater economies of scale in production, thus covering the lower export price. Because of reduced marketing costs at the manufacturer's level, particularly when a foreign distributor is used, an export price equal to the domestic price is often not justified. However, legal limits related to antidumping regulations may prevent price reductions below a certain point.

Determining Transfer Prices

A substantial amount of international business takes place between subsidiaries of the same company. It is estimated that in-house trading between subsidiaries accounts for one-third of the volume among the world's 800 largest multinationals. An **international transfer price** is the price paid by the importing or buying unit of a firm to the exporting unit of the same firm. For example, the U.S. marketing subsidiary of a Taiwanese manufacturer of personal computers will pay a transfer price for the machines it receives from Taiwan. The actual transfer price may be negotiated by the units involved or may be set centrally by the international firm. How these prices are set continues to be a major issue for international companies and governments alike.

Because negotiations of transfer prices do not represent arm's-length negotiations between independent participants, the resulting prices frequently differ from free-market prices. Companies may deviate from arm's-length prices to maximize profits or to minimize risk and uncertainty.[26] To pursue a strategy of profit maximization, a company may lower transfer prices for products shipped from some subsidiaries, while increasing prices for products shipped to others, in order to accumulate profits in countries where it is advantageous, while keeping profits low elsewhere.

Different tax, tariff, or subsidy structures among countries frequently invite such practices. By accumulating more profits in a low-tax country, a company lowers its overall tax bill and thus increases profit. Likewise, tariff duties can be reduced by quoting low transfer prices to countries with high tariffs. In cases where countries use a different exchange rate for the transfer of goods from that used for the transfer of capital or profits, a firm may attempt to use transfer prices to remove money from the country, rather than transferring profits at less advantageous rates. The same is true for countries with limits on profit repatriation. Furthermore, a company may want to accumulate profits in a wholly owned subsidiary rather than in one in which it has minority ownership. By using the transfer price mechanism, it can avoid sharing profits with local partners.

Companies may also use the transfer price mechanism to minimize risk or uncertainty by moving profits or assets out of a country with chronic balance-of-payment problems and frequent devaluations. Because regular profit remittances may be strictly controlled in such countries, many firms see high transfer prices as the only way to repatriate funds and thereby reduce the amount of assets at risk. The same practice may be employed if a company anticipates political or social disturbances or a direct threat to profits through government intervention.

In actual practice, companies choose a number of approaches to transfer pricing. Market-based prices are equal to those negotiated by independent companies or at arm's length. Of thirty U.S.-based firms, 46 percent were reported to use market-based systems.[27] Another 35 percent used cost-based systems to determine the transfer price. Costs were based on a predetermined formula that could include a standard markup for profits.

Internal Considerations Rigorous use of the transfer pricing mechanism to reduce a company's income taxes and duties or to maximize profits in strong currency areas can create difficulties for subsidiary managers whose profits are artificially reduced. It may be hard to motivate managers when the direct profit incentive is removed. Furthermore, company resource allocation may become inefficient, because funds are appropriated to units whose profits are artificially increased. Conversely, resources may be denied to subsidiaries whose income statements were subject to transfer-price-induced reductions. It is generally agreed that a transfer pricing mechanism should not be used for resource allocations; the gains incurred through tax savings may easily be lost through other inefficiencies.

External Problems Governments do not look favorably on transfer pricing mechanisms aimed at reducing their tax revenues. U.S. government policy on transfer pricing is governed by tax law, particularly Section 482 of the Revenue Act of 1962. The act is designed to provide an accurate allocation of costs, income, and capital among related enterprises to protect U.S. tax revenue. Market prices are generally preferred by the Internal Revenue Service (IRS). The IRS will accept cost-plus markups if market prices are not available and economic circumstances warrant such use. Not acceptable, however, are transfer prices that attribute no profit to the U.S. unit. Other methods, such as negotiated prices, are acceptable as long as the transfer price is comparable to a price charged to an unrelated party.

In addition, the IRS requires all companies to maintain detailed explanations of the rationale and analysis supporting their transfer pricing policy. The IRS developed the Advanced Pricing Agreement Program (APA), which became effective on December 31, 1993. Under this program, a company can obtain approval from the IRS for their transfer pricing procedures.

According to a study by the General Accounting Office, 67 percent of all the foreign-controlled companies doing business in the United States, some 40,195 companies, do not pay any U.S. taxes. The largest 15,363 U.S. companies pay an average of $8.1 million per year in taxes, whereas the 2,767 largest foreign companies pay an average of only $4.2 million per year. Senator Dorgan estimates that foreign-controlled companies doing business in the United States are failing to pay $45 billion owed in U.S. taxes. Transfer pricing is the primary method they use to avoid paying taxes.[28] As a result of U.S. tax regulations, the countries of the OECD have agreed to a new set of transfer pricing guidelines closely modeled on the U.S. rules.[29]

Australia, Japan, and Korea all have formal transfer pricing arrangements, and China, India, and New Zealand all have informal programs.[30] However, the strengthening of government regulations all around the world makes it necessary for global businesses to document and defend their transfer pricing methods. According to a study of 280 multinational companies operating in Europe, 85 percent had been audited on transfer pricing over a 3-year period.[31]

Quoting Prices in a Foreign Currency

For many international marketing transactions, it is not always feasible to quote in a company's domestic currency when selling or purchasing merchandise. Although the majority of U.S. exporters quote prices in dollars, there are situations in which customers may prefer quotes in their own national currency. When two currencies are involved, there is the risk that a change in exchange rates may occur between the invoicing date and the settlement date for the transaction. This **transaction risk** is an inherent factor in international marketing and clearly separates domestic from international business.

Astro-Med Inc., a small manufacturer of high-quality printers that is based in Warwick, Rhode Island, experienced firsthand the reaction of a customer when the export price list was quoted in U.S. dollars. During the negotiations for a printer quoted at $200,000, its German customer balked at being presented with a price list, sales manual, and brochures all produced for the U.S. market.[32] A research study of 671 companies in the United States, Finland, and Sweden found that companies that respond to customers' requests for prices quoted in their local currencies benefit from a larger volume of export business.[33]

In such circumstances, alternatives are available to protect the seller from transaction risk. These alternatives are available because of the nature of foreign exchange. For most major currencies, international foreign exchange dealers located at major banks quote a spot price and a forward price. The **spot price** determines the number of dollars to be paid for a particular foreign currency purchased or sold today. The **forward price** quotes the number of dollars to be paid for a foreign currency bought or sold 30, 90, or 180 days from today. The forward price, however, is not necessarily speculation about what the spot price will be in the future. Instead, the forward price reflects interest rate differentials between two currencies for maturities of 30, 90, or 180 days. Consequently, there are no firm indications of what the spot price will be for any given currency in the future.

A company quoting in foreign currency for purchase or sale can simply leave settlement until the due date and pay whatever spot price prevails at the time. Such an **uncovered position** may be chosen when exchange rates are not expected to shift or when any shift in the near future will result in a gain for the company. With exchange rates fluctuating widely on a daily basis, even among major trading nations such as the United States, Japan, Germany, and the United Kingdom, a company can expose itself to substantial foreign exchange risks. Because many international firms are in business to make a profit from the sale of goods rather than from speculation in the foreign exchange markets, managers generally protect themselves from unexpected fluctuations.

One such protection lies in **hedging.** Instead of accepting whatever spot market rate exists on the settlement in 30 or 90 days, a company can opt to contract through financial intermediaries for future delivery of foreign currency at a set price, regardless of the spot price at that time. This allows the seller to incorporate a firm exchange rate into the price determination. Of course, if a company wishes to predict the spot price in 90 days and is reasonably certain about the accuracy of its prediction, it may attempt to choose the more advantageous of the two: the expected spot or the present forward rate. However, such predictions should only be made under the guidance of experts familiar with foreign exchange rates.

To illustrate the selection of a hedging procedure, assume that a U.S. exporter of computer workstations sells two machines valued at $24,000 to a client in the United Kingdom (see Table 12.3). The client will pay in British pounds quoted at the current (spot) rate on July 16 of $1.5650, or £15,335.46. This amount will be paid in 2 months (60 days). As a result, the U.S. exporter will have to determine how to protect such an incoming amount against foreign exchange risk. Although uncertain about the outcome, the exporter's bank indicates that there is equal chance for the British pound spot rate to remain at $1.5650 (scenario C), to devalue to $1.45 (scenario A), or to appreciate to $1.65 (scenario B). As a result, the exporter has the option of selling the amount forward in the 60-days forward market, at $1.5684.[34]

Table 12.3 *Hedging Scenarios*

	A	B	C
Spot rate as of July 16	$1.5650	$1.5650	$1.5650
Spot rate as of September 16 (estimate)	1.45	1.65	$1.5650
U.S. dollar equivalent of £15,335.46 at spot rates on July 16	24,000.00	22,236.42	25,303.51
Exchange gain (loss)	0	(1,763.58)	1,303.51

The alternative available to the exporter to sell forward the invoice amount of £15,335.46 at $1.5684 will obtain a sure $23,947.98 at a cost of $52.02 on the transaction. In anticipation of a devaluation of the pound, such a hedging strategy would be advisable. Consequently, the $52.02 represents a premium to ensure against any larger loss such as the one predicted under scenario B. However, a company would also forgo any gain as indicated under scenario C.

Sometimes hedging is not an option when a firm is dealing with soft currencies or currencies undergoing upheaval. In 1998, prior to an expected devaluation of the ruble, nearly all exporters to Russia were seeking hedging contracts. Hedging contracts for rubles became increasingly hard to find and then disappeared from the market altogether. When the Turkish government allowed the pegged lira to float in 2001, the lira collapsed nearly 40 percent over a few days. In the immediate disarray that ensued, hedging opportunities for the lira were similarly difficult to locate.

An alternative to hedging is **covering through the money market**. This involves borrowing funds in the currency at risk for the time until settlement. For example, a U.S. exporter that is holding accounts receivable in euros and is unwilling to absorb the related currency risk may borrow euros and exchange them for dollars for working-capital purposes. When the customer eventually pays in euros, the U.S. exporter uses these euros to pay off the loan. Any currency fluctuations will be canceled, resulting in neither loss nor gain.

Dealing with Parallel Imports, or Gray Markets

As a result of different market and competitive factors, international marketers often choose to sell the same product at different prices in different national markets. When such price differences become large, individual buyers or independent entrepreneurs step in and buy products in low-price countries to re-export to high-price countries, profiting from the price differential. This arbitrage behavior creates what experts call the **gray market** or **parallel imports**, because these imports take place outside of the regular channels controlled by authorized distributors or company-owned sales subsidiaries. For the United States alone, parallel-market annual volume is estimated to be $130 billion.

World Beat 12.2   *Just Say "No" to Europe?*

As pressure on drug prices rises on all fronts, pharmaceutical makers are pushing back in price-controlled Europe with warnings of serious repercussions if changes aren't made.

The industry has long chafed under European government efforts to cap drug prices and keep health care budgets in check. Five markets—the United Kingdom, Germany, France, Italy and Spain—account for roughly 80 percent of European profits for drug makers. For these firms, the toughest problem is accepting a low price in one country that could be used by the others either as a negotiating lever or as a source of low-price drugs imported directly. Also, differences in prices lead to parallel markets, where wholesalers buy drugs in bulk in countries with low prices and then ship them for sale in countries where higher prices are allowed. Prices in Germany, the U.K., the Netherlands, and Nordic countries are usually higher than those in the southern tier of the continent.

Although they stop short of making direct threats for the moment, drug companies hint that they might be forced to make investment and product decisions that will hurt Europe if they don't get some relief. In a speech to the Swiss Chamber of Commerce, the chairman of Novartis AG cautioned that drug companies will funnel more research investment out of Europe and send it to the United States if the environment becomes more unfavorable. Withholding products when it can't get an adequate price is a drug company's ultimate weapon. "That's a last and hopefully never-to-be-used alternative," says the executive vice-president of Pfizer.

Source: Vanessa Fuhrmans and Scott Hensley, "Price Controls in Europe Draw Drug Makers' Criticism," *Wall Street Journal*, December 13, 2001, p. B4.

A woman purchases prescription medicine at a pharmacy in Juarez, Mexico. The same medicine sells for a much higher price just across the border in the United States. Such discrepancies in prices encourage gray markets.

Companies deplore parallel imports because they hurt relationships with their authorized dealers. Parallel imports are also credited with adding to Coca-Cola's public relations difficulties subsequent to a product-harm crisis in Europe. The company began a product recall after hundreds of Coke drinkers complained of getting sick. Unfortunately, tracking down the questionable Belgium-produced Coke was complicated; it began showing up in places it shouldn't have been, such as Spain, Germany, and the United Kingdom. But this should have come as no surprise. The gray market for soft drinks in the U.K. is estimated at 20 percent share of market.[35]

Most important, gray markets undermine a company's ability to charge different prices in different markets in order to maximize global profits. But legal attempts to stop parallel imports have been stymied by the fact that governments around the world have proved ambivalent—and even somewhat positive—toward parallel imports. When Quality King International purchased shampoo in Malta made by Lanza Research Company and reimported it into the United States, Lanza sued Quality King on the basis of violation of trademark law but lost its case in the U.S. Supreme Court.[36]

Parallel importing has become a big problem within the European pharmaceutical industry, where prices of prescription medicines are usually set by national governments. Wholesalers buy truckloads of branded ulcer and cancer drugs at bargain prices in Spain and Portugal and resell them in Britain and Germany, where prices are higher. Sanofi-Synthelabo estimates that 80 percent of the British sales of its blood pressure treatment Avapro go through parallel importers who buy it in countries such as Spain.[37] Drug companies have sought protection from the European Court of Justice, but this court ruled that wholesalers have the right to trade goods freely throughout Europe, regardless of different fixed prices among the various states.[38]

During the 1990s, the Bayer Group attempted to stop the parallel import into the U.K. of a Bayer cardiovascular medicine, Adalat, from France and Spain, where the price of the drug was 40 percent lower. Bayer limited the amount wholesalers in these two countries could receive to the estimated demand of their own markets. The wholesalers complained, and in 1996 the European Commission fined Bayer for what it considered anticompetitive agreements to limit parallel imports. In fact there was no agreement between Bayer and its wholesalers—far from it. In 2000 a European court of appeal annulled the 1996 decision, exonerating Bayer.[39]

Although current EU legislation allows for parallel trading between countries within the EU, it supports the firm's right to stop parallel imports of branded products from outside the EU. Brand owners have argued that such imports hurt the consumer because the goods can be old, damaged, manufactured to different specifications, or even fakes. Consequently, they can undermine the value of brands. Levi Strauss sold its 501 Jeans in Paris at twice the price paid in the United States, inspiring many EU retailers to buy much of their Levi's inventory from unauthorized sources outside the EU. Levi Strauss sued twenty-four European retailers, including Tesco, the British supermarket giant, for parallel importing from outside the EU.[40] The company argued that such practices were in violation of European trademark law. In April 2001, the European Court of Justice ruled in favor of Levi Strauss, and in 2002 the company won its case against Tesco. The rulings confirmed that retailers could not sell trademarked goods from outside the European Economic Area (the EU plus Ireland, Liechtenstein, and Norway) without explicit permission from the trademark holder.

Parallel imports *within* the European Union have been further encouraged by the introduction of the euro, which allows easy price comparisons from country to country. A study by French L'Express found that prices within Europe could vary by up to 500 percent. For example, a 1.5-liter container of Coca-Cola costs 0.7 euro in Portugal and 1.9 euros in Finland, and a Sony Premium 180-minute video-cassette costs 1.98 euros in Portugal and 10.52 euros in France. Some experts recommend that international marketers adopt a proactive strategy and develop a pan-European pricing strategy. This strategy should take into account the price elasticities of different markets and should maximize the potential European profit margin rather than gravitating to the lowest price in Europe.[41]

Gray markets are also encouraged by the Internet, which enables buyers to compare prices easily across countries. In some cases, intermediaries are not even necessary to fuel parallel imports. Many older Americans click on to Canadian-based Internet pharmacies to order cheaper prescription drugs.[42] This importation is technically illegal in the United States, where pharmaceutical companies have successfully argued that product quality could be diminished and consumers hurt by unregulated access to overseas drugs. However, consumer groups continue to lobby against this law, and its repeal is a commonly recurring political debate.

Fluctuating currency values are sometimes credited with creating temporary opportunities for parallel imports. Even if prices are similar in two national markets, a change in the relative values of their currencies results in different prices and a consequent opportunity for arbitrage. However, research involving U.S. exporters has shown that changes in currency rates have had a relatively insignificant impact on parallel trading overall. Instead, the study identified three factors that significantly discouraged parallel imports. Firms that customized products more for local markets experienced fewer problems, as did firms that maintained greater control over their distribution systems, including owning them. Parallel imports were also less likely to occur if an international firm maintained greater centralized control than if it allowed national subsidiaries greater autonomy.[43] This last finding is all the more poignant in that intrafirm competition has been known to fuel gray markets. Forced to meet inflated sales quotas, many U.S., Asian, and Latin American managers at Bausch & Lomb knowingly sold contact lenses and sunglasses to gray-market distributors in order to boost their own sales figures, thus creating a massive problem with parallel imports for the company at large.[44]

Once the problem of parallel imports arises, a firm may use a number of strategies in a reactive way. These include cutting prices in higher-price markets, limiting supplies to wholesalers in lower-priced markets, and even acquiring the diverter involved. A firm can also promote to consumers any product differences that exist between the authorized products and the parallel imports. However, a number of proactive strategies may be implemented to prevent the practice from occurring at all. A company may provide product differentiation between markets solely to try to stop gray markets. Strategic pricing may be used to keep prices within the range of each other, thus destroying opportunities for arbitrage. Companies may also use strict legal enforcement of restrictive contracts with wholesalers where these are allowed by law or may even resort to lobbying governments to enact regulations designed to prevent further parallel imports. For example, international drug companies argued in hearings before the Israel Knesset (parliament) that parallel imports endangered public health because of fake and fraudulent medicines.[45] However, as we have seen, the courts have not been unilaterally sympathetic toward shutting down parallel markets. Companies are on the defensive and bear the burden of explaining why some consumers must pay more than others for the same product.

Setting Global Prices

To maximize a company's revenues, it would appear logical to set prices on a market-by-market basis, seeking in each market the best combination of price and expected volume to yield the maximum profit. This strategy was common for many firms in the early part of their international development. For many consumer products, there are still significant price differences across many countries. For example, Figure 12.2 depicts price differences for a movie ticket in different European cities, and Table 12.4 illustrates how McDonald's Big Mac prices can vary by country.

With the advent of global branding, international firms have become more concerned about issues of global pricing. They rarely dictate uniform prices in every country but do establish a particular pricing policy across countries—relatively higher prices for premium brands and relatively lower prices for value brands. In a study of global pricing policies among multinational companies from developed countries, the likelihood that a subsidiary would follow a pricing policy similar to that of the parent company in the home market was found to be influenced by market similarity in economic conditions, legal environment, customer characteristics, and stage in the product life cycle.[46]

Figure 12.2 *Price of a Movie Ticket*

Source: "Price of a Movie Ticket in Major Metropolitan Areas" from "Prices at the Europlex," *The Economist*, March 27, 1999, p. 110. Copyright © 1999 The Economist Newspaper Group, Inc. Reprinted with permission. Further reproduction prohibited.

Table 12.4 *Big Mac Prices*

	PRICE	
	IN LOCAL CURRENCY	**IN U.S. DOLLARS**
United States	$2.49	2.49
Argentina	Peso2.50	0.78
Australia	A$3.00	1.62
Brazil	Real 3.60	1.55
Britain	£1.99	2.88
Canada	C$3.33	2.12
Chile	Peso1400	2.16
China	Yuan10.50	1.27
Denmark	DKr24.75	2.96
Euro Area	Euro 2.67	2.37
Hong Kong	HK$11.20	1.40
Hungary	Forint 459	1692
Indonesia	Rupiah16,000	1.71
Japan	¥292	2.01
Malaysia	M$5.04	1.33
Mexico	Peso 21.9	2.37
New Zealand	NZ$3.95	1.77
Poland	Zloty 5.90	1.46
Russia	Rouble 39.00	1.25
Singapore	S$3.30	1.81
South Africa	Rand 9.70	.87
South Korea	Won3,100	2.36
Sweden	SKr26.0	2.52
Switzerland	SFr 6.30	3.81
Taiwan	NT$70.0	2.01
Thailand	Baht 55.0	1.27

Source: "The Hamburger Standard," *The Economist*, April 27, 2002, p. 27. 2002 The Economist Newspaper Group. Reprinted with permission. Further reproduction prohibited.

However, for products that are similar in many markets and for which transportation costs are not significant, substantial price differences quickly result in the emergence of the gray market. This has led some firms to consider a policy of more uniform pricing worldwide. Employing a **uniform pricing strategy** on a global scale requires that a company charge the same price everywhere when that price is translated into a base currency. In reality, this becomes very difficult to achieve whenever different taxes, trade margins, and customs duties are involved. Furthermore, firms that start out with identical prices in various countries soon find that prices have to change to stay in line with often substantial currency fluctuations.

Although it is becoming increasingly clear that market-by-market pricing strategies will cause difficulties, many firms have found that changing to a uniform pricing policy is rather like pursuing a moving target. However, a company can employ **modified uniform pricing** by carefully monitoring price levels in each country and avoiding large gaps that encourage gray marketers to move in and take advantage of large price differentials.

Noncash Pricing: Countertrade

International marketers are likely to find many situations in which an interested customer will not be able to arrange hard-currency financing. In such circumstances, the customer might offer a product or commodity in return. The supplier must then turn the product offered into hard currency. Such transactions, known as **countertrade**, were estimated at 15–25 percent of world trade in the mid-1980s.[47] Although countertrade was originally associated with communist regimes, political changes in the former Soviet bloc have not eliminated the need for countertrade. Russia and many Eastern European countries remain plagued by a scarcity of foreign exchange. For example, when the leading department store in the Czech Republic could not get access to sufficient Western goods even after market liberalization, the store traded paper for Lego toys and Czech cheese for Italian vermouth.[48]

Over 100 countries have some form of countertrade requirement as part of their public procurement program. Malcolm Taylor, president of the Australian Countertrade Association, reports that in 1998, 2 percent of Southeast Asia's trade was countertrade, and it was expected to grow to 20 percent by 2001.[49] To respond to this challenge, international marketers have developed several forms of countertrade. The following sections explain each one and then examine the problems associated with countertrade transactions.

Barter Barter, one of the most basic types of countertrade, consists of a direct exchange of goods between two parties. Barter involves no currency and is concluded without the help of intermediaries. One of the largest barter deals ever, valued at about $3 billion, was signed by PepsiCo and Russia. Since 1974 PepsiCo has engaged in business with Russia, shipping soft-drink syrup, bottling it into Pepsi-Cola, and marketing it within Russia. To gain access to the Russian market so early, PepsiCo entered an agreement to export Stolichnaya vodka to the United States, where it was sold through an independent liquor company.

Compensation Arrangements One usually speaks of a compensation transaction when the value of an export delivery is at least partially offset by an import transaction, or vice versa. Compensation transactions are typical for large government purchases, such as for defense projects, when a country wants to obtain some additional exports in exchange for the awarding of a contract.[50] For the past 20 years, the government of Indonesia has required winners of major government contracts to take part of their payment in Indonesian commodities apart from oil and gas. Compensation transactions fall into several categories, as described below.

Full versus Partial Compensation Full compensation is similar to barter in that a 100 percent mutual transfer of goods takes place. However, deliveries are made and paid for separately. By signing the sales agreement, the exporter commits itself to purchasing products or services at an amount equal to that specified in the export contract. An option exists to sell such a commitment to a third party who may take over the commitment from the exporter for a fee. For example, Vietnam agreed to provide the Philippine Phosphate Corporation with 50,000 tons of rice for an equivalent value of fertilizer.[51]

Under partial compensation, the exporter receives a portion of the purchase price in hard currency and the remainder in merchandise. The exporter will not be able to convert such merchandise into cash until a buyer can be found, and even then must usually do so at a discount. A partial-compensation transaction was concluded in 1998 between Thailand and an Italian company building electric services there, which agreed to take 30 percent of the value of the contract, or 218 million baht, in agricultural products, including rubber, rice, and tapioca.[52]

Triangular Compensation   Triangular compensation arrangements, also called **switch trades**, involve three countries. The exporter delivers hard goods (salable merchandise) to an importer. As payment, the importer transfers **hard goods** (easily salable merchandise) or **soft goods** (heavily discounted merchandise that may prove more difficult to resell) to a specialist firm, or switch trader. The switch trader then reimburses the exporter for the goods received and arranges to resell the merchandise. Such negotiations may become complex and time-consuming and are best left to firms that specialize in such trades.

Marc Rich & Co., a Swiss commodities firm, has been very successful in the republics of the former Soviet Union with complicated triangular arrangements. For example, in one deal the company bought 70,000 tons of raw sugar in Brazil and shipped it to Ukraine to be processed. It paid for the processing with some of the sugar and then shipped 30,000 tons of the refined sugar 6,000 miles to several huge Siberian oil refineries, which needed the sugar for their workforce. Strapped for hard currency, the oil refineries paid with 130,000 tons of low-grade A-76 gasoline, which was shipped to Mongolia. The Mongolians paid for the gasoline with 35,000 tons of copper concentrate, which was shipped across the border to Kazakhstan, where it was refined to copper metal and shipped to a Baltic port. Marc Rich then sold the copper on the world market for hard currency—and a profit.[53]

Offset Deals   One of the most rapidly growing types of countertrade is the offset transaction. In an offset transaction, the selling company guarantees to use some products or services from the buying country in the final product. These transactions are particularly common when large government purchases are involved, such as purchases of public utilities or defense-related equipment. The South African government has used offset deals very effectively to stimulate local industrial development in exchange for purchasing military equipment. Saab and British Aerospace landed the sale of twenty-eight Gripen fighter planes by agreeing to input sourcing and investment in South Africa valued at 480 percent of the contract value.[54]

Cooperation Agreements   Cooperation agreements, or **buybacks**, are special types of countertrade deals extending over longer periods of time. Cooperation agreements usually involve related goods, such as payment for new textile machinery by the output produced by these machines.

Although the sale of large equipment or of a whole factory can sometimes be clinched only by a cooperation agreement involving buyback of plant output, long-term negative effects must be considered before any deal is concluded. In industries such as steel or chemicals, the effect of high-volume buyback arrangements between Western exporters of manufacturing technology and Eastern European importers has sometimes been devastating. Western countries, especially Europe, have been flooded with surplus products, and the EU has established a general policy on cooperation arrangements to avoid further disruption of its domestic industries.

Dangers of Countertrade Countertrade agreements can be complex and time-consuming. Thus they can be surprisingly demanding of corporate resources. Another danger of countertrade arrangements is the difficulty in finding a buyer for the merchandise accepted as part of the transaction. Sometimes such transactions are concluded with organizations in countries where industry is protected. The merchandise, not easily salable on its own merits, may be of low quality. As a result, the exporter may have to sell the merchandise at a discount. The size of these discounts can vary considerably and can even run as high as a third of product value.

At the conclusion of the sales agreement, the exporter should obtain a very clear understanding of the merchandise offered for countertrade. The origin, quality, quantity, and delivery schedules for the merchandise should all be spelled out. Given such a detailed description, a specialized trader can provide an estimate of the appropriate discount. The astute exporter will raise the price of the export contract to cover such potential discounts on the compensating transaction. Therefore, it is paramount that the exporter not agree on any price before this other information is in hand. Maintaining flexibility in negotiation requires skill and patience but can spell the difference between making a profit or a loss on a countertrade transaction.

Organizing for Countertrade International companies are moving toward organizing countertrade for higher leverage. Many larger firms have established specialized units whose single purpose is to engage in countertrade. Many independent trading companies offer countertrading services, and several large U.S. banks have formed their own countertrade units. Smaller companies can also take advantage of countertrade by utilizing specialist brokers or joining barter networks. Companies such as the Australia-based International Barter Network appeal to small and medium-sized firms by facilitating cash flow and reducing cash expenses. A member company accumulates barter credit when it transfers products to another company within the network. In turn, this credit can be used to purchase goods from other members worldwide.[55]

Check out our website for countertrade links.

▶ *Conclusions*

Managing pricing policies for an international firm is an especially challenging task. The international marketer is confronted with a number of uncontrollable factors deriving from the economic, legal, and regulatory environment, all of which have an impact on how prices are established in various countries. Although these influences are usually quite manageable in any given country, pricing across many markets means coping with price differentials that evolve out of environmental factors working in various combinations in different countries. Managing these price differentials and keeping them within tolerable limits are major tasks in international pricing.

One of the most critical factors affecting price levels is foreign exchange fluctuation. Today, managers find currencies moving both up and down, and the swings have assumed magnitudes that may substantially affect the competitiveness of a company. Understanding the factors that influence the foreign exchange market and mastering the technical tools that protect firms against large swings have become required skills for the international marketer. To the extent that a company can make itself less vulnerable to exchange rate movements than its competitors are, it stands to gain additional competitive advantage.

Because the factors that affect price levels on an international scale are always fluctuating, the international pricing task is a never-ending process in which each day may bring new problems to be resolved. Whenever a company is slow to adapt or makes a wrong judgment, the market is very quick to exploit any weaknesses. As long as uncontrollable factors such as currency rates and inflation are subject to considerable fluctuations, the pricing strategies of international companies will have to remain under constant review.

What should you consider when setting prices in your target country? Continue with *Country Market Report* on our website.

Review Questions

1. What is the advantage of marginal-cost pricing over full-cost pricing?

2. What factors can decrease transportation costs?

3. What factors can affect disposable income across countries?

4. Under what conditions can a firm be charged with dumping?

5. Why are governments interested in transfer prices within multinational firms?

6. What is transaction risk?

7. Why is hedging attractive to international marketers?

8. List actions by which a firm might control parallel imports. Are there any limitations to these actions?

9. What is a cooperation agreement? How does it differ from other forms of countertrade?

10. List the possible dangers to the firm of countertrade.

Questions for Discussion

1. Discuss the difficulties involved in having a standardized price for a company's products across all countries. What advantages does charging a standardized price offer?

2. You are an exporter of industrial installations and have received a $100,000 order from a Japanese customer. The job will take 6 months to complete and will be paid in full at that time. Now your Japanese customer has called you to request a price quote in yen. What will you quote in yen? Why?

3. What factors may influence McDonald's to price their Big Mac differently throughout Latin America?

4. What should be the government's position on the issue of parallel imports? Should the government take any particular actions?

For Further Reading

Assmus, Gert, and Carsten Wiese. "How to Address the Gray Market Threat Using Price Coordination." *Sloan Management Review* 36, 3 (1995): 31–42.

Cavusgil, S. Tamer. "Pricing for Global Markets." *Columbia Journal of World Business*, Winter 1996: 66–78.

Davis, H. Thomas Jr. "Transfer Prices in the Real World—10 Steps Companies Should Take Before It Is Too Late." *CPA Journal* 64, 10 (October 1994): 82–83.

Dolan, Robert J., and Hermann Simon. *Power Pricing*. New York: The Free Press, 1996.

Samiee, Saeed, Patrick Anckar, and Abo Akademi. "Currency Choice in Industrial Pricing: A Cross-national Evaluation." *Journal of Marketing* 62, 3 (July 1998): 112–127.

Case 12.1	*The Price of Coffee in China*

When Starbucks, the Seattle-based coffee shop chain, entered China in 1999, it faced a country of tea drinkers. Still, Japan too had been a country of tea drinkers but had evolved into a major coffee market. Starbucks itself had recently entered Japan and was already the top-ranked restaurant chain in 2000, according to a prestigious industry study. In fact, top management at Starbucks was astounded at the firm's brand recognition across Asia, an awareness that had come about with virtually no investment in advertising.

In considering China, Starbucks noted that coffee consumption in a country is directly related to income. The firm sought to take advantage of growing disposable income in China, where per-capita income had reached $750 a year. In particular, Starbucks believed there would be substantial demand among younger urbanites in China. Confident in their decision, the firm entered the Chinese market in 1999 with plans to open ten shops in Beijing in 18 months. The first Starbucks in Beijing was located in a shopping center across the street from a five-star hotel.

Nevertheless, some were skeptical about the Starbucks move. In the 1990s, coffee sales had grown between 5 and 8 percent a year in China, but when the economy slumped in the late 1990s, many foreign expatriates left the country. Consequently, coffee sales growth had tapered off. However, Starbucks's stated strategy was to set prices lower than those of comparable coffee shops al-ready opened in China. These other coffee shops targeted expatriates, tourists, and elite Chinese. Starbucks hoped to target a larger segment of Chinese society.

Starbucks imported all its coffee beans into China, despite the fact that China was attempting to improve both the quality and the size of its own coffee harvests. Other nations, such as Vietnam, had expanded coffee production in the late 1990s. This had resulted in a world supply of coffee beans that exceeded demand by 10 percent. In 1999 a devaluation of Brazil's currency provided this major coffee exporter with an increased competitive edge over new entrants into the coffee market.

When Starbucks opened in Beijing, the store offered the same coffee products and other merchandise available in its U.S. shops. Prices were similar to those charged in New York City, with a grande latte priced at $4.50. A local coffee shop in the same complex that charged prices even higher than those at Starbucks announced that it would lower prices to below those of the new U.S. competitor.

Discussion Questions

1. What are the possible arguments for pricing a grande latte at $4.50 in Beijing?
2. What are the possible arguments for pricing lower? For pricing higher?

3. Could purchasing Chinese coffee beans in the future affect Starbucks's pricing strategy in China? Explain.

Sources: Associated Press, "Starbucks Tries to Tempt Tea-Loving Chinese," January 12, 1999; Ian Johnson, "Reading the Tea Leaves, China Sees a Future in Coffee," *Wall Street Journal*, February 5, 1999; and "Trouble Brewing," *The Economist*, March 10, 2001.

Case 12.2 *The Price of Life*

In March 2001, Merck announced that it would cut prices 40–55 percent in African markets on two of its recent AIDS-fighting drugs. Merck's powerful three-drug cocktail would be available in Africa for $1,330 a year, compared to approximately $11,000 in the United States. The company noted that it would be realizing no profits at this new price. Merck also pledged to extend these discounts to poor countries elsewhere in the world. Bristol-Myers followed suit, promising to slice the price of its AIDS drug Zerit to only $54 a year in Africa. At this price, Bristol-Myers claimed to be selling below costs. The company called on donor governments in Europe, Japan, and the United States to join in a vigorous international response to the AIDS crisis in Africa, where 25 million people are estimated to be infected with the HIV virus that eventually causes AIDS.

These announcements were somewhat surprising, because thirty-nine major pharmaceutical companies had begun litigation the week before to stop Indian pharmaceutical firms from selling generic versions of their patented drugs, including AIDS drugs, in the South African market. Since the 1970s, India had refused to recognize pharmaceutical patents in order to supply its vast poor population with recent pharmaceutical products at much cheaper prices. Indian firms had become adept at reverse-engineering

drugs, and had become efficient producers of high-quality generics. (When it joined the World Trade Organization, India agreed to return to honoring international pharmaceutical patents on January 1, 2005.)

In February 2001, two Indian generic drug firms, Cipla and Hetero, had entered a price war in Africa. The effect of this war on the annual cost in U.S. dollars to users for several AIDS drugs is shown in Table 1.

While pharmaceutical companies faced decreasing prices in Africa, they were under attack in the United States as well. Drug prices were higher in the United States than in Europe, where governments paid for most prescription drugs. Consequently, European governments negotiated prices with pharmaceutical firms. For example, the antipsychotic drug Clozaril could cost $51.94 in Spain, $89.55 in Germany, $271.08 in Canada, and $317.03 in the United States. Ironically, over-the-counter drugs and generic versions of prescription drugs whose patents had expired were cheaper in the United States than in Europe because of greater competition in the U.S. market.

In 2000 both the U.S. House of Representatives and the Senate approved measures permitting pharmacists and wholesalers to import cheaper drugs from other countries. This practice had long

Table 1 *Annual Cost in U.S. Dollars to Users for AIDS Drugs*

DRUG	U.S. PRICE	AFRICAN PRICE	CIPLA	HETERO
Crixivan (Merck)	$6,016	$600	N.A.	$2,300
Stocrin (Merck)	$4,730	$500	N.A.	$1,179
Zerit (Bristol-Myers)	$3,589	$252	$70	$47
3TC (Glaxco)	$3,271	$232	$190	$98
Combovir (Glaxco)	$7,093	$730	$635	$293

Source: Adapted from "New Regime," *Wall Street Journal*, March 7, 2001.

been prohibited in response to alleged safety concerns. In December of that year, the Clinton administration refused to act on the legislation, again stating concerns about safety.

Discussion Questions

1. What factors contribute to the large disparities in drug prices found among various countries?
2. What could be the motivations for Merck and Bristol-Myers to discount prices further on their AIDS drugs in Africa?
3. Should U.S. consumers pay higher prices than Europeans for pharmaceuticals? Why or why not?

4. Should U.S. consumers pay higher prices than Africans? Why or why not?

Sources: Mark Schoofs and Michael Waldhoz, "New Regime," *Wall Street Journal*, March 7, 2001, p. A1; Michael Waldholz and Rachel Zimmerman, "Bristol-Myers Offers to Sell Two AIDS Drugs in Africa at Below Cost," *Wall Street Journal*, March 15, 2001, p. B1; Jesse Pesta, "India Braces for Brave New Drug World," *Wall Street Journal*, March 7, 2001, p. A17; Laurie McGinley and Rachel Zimmerman, "High U.S. Drug Prices May Give Pharmaceutical Makers a Headache," *Wall Street Journal*, July 21, 2000, p. B1; and "Wrong Move on Drug Imports," *Hartford Courant*, December 28, 2000.

Notes

[1] Stephen Labaton, "The World Gets Tough on Fixing Prices," *New York Times*, June 3, 2001, p. 1.

[2] For a detailed discussion of the experience curve concept, see Derek F. Abell, *Managing with Dual Strategies*. (New York: The Free Press, 1993), chap. 9.1.

[3] Mary Anne Raymond, John F. Tanner Jr., and Jonghoo Kim, "Cost Complexity in Pricing Decisions for Exporters in Developed and Emerging Markets," *Journal of International Marketing* 9, 3 (2001): 19–40.

[4] "What's In a Name?" *The Economist*, February 2, 1991: 60.

[5] "EU to Tax Downloadable Goods to Blunt U.S.'s Competitive Edge," *Dow Jones Business News*, May 7, 2002.

[6] Carol J. Williams, "EU Complicates Sweden's Relationship with Liquor," *Washington Post*, March 11, 2001, p. A17.

[7] Joel Millman, "Visions of Sugar Plums South of the Border," *Wall Street Journal*, February 13, 2002, p. A15.

[8] Philip R. Cateora and John L. Graham, *International Marketing*, 10th ed. (Boston: Irwin McGraw-Hill, 1999), p. 562.

[9] "Macworld," *The Economist*, June 29, 1996: 61.

[10] "Houses, Cars Become All-Consuming Passion," *Nikkei Weekly*, January 20, 1997: 18.

[11] Karby Leggett, "In Rural China, GM Sees a Frugal But Huge Market," *Wall Street Journal*, January 16, 2001, p. A19.

[12] Dexter Roberts and Alysha Webb, "Motor Nation," *Business Week*, June 17, 2002: 44–45.

[13] Joel Millman, "Aerospace Suppliers Gravitate to Mexico," *Wall Street Journal*, January 23, 2002, p. A17.

[14] Joshua Ogawa, "AT&T Adds Corporate Call Back Service," *Nikkei Weekly*, November 4, 1996: 9.

[15] Gautam Naik and William Boston, "Deregulation Dismays Deutsche Telekom," *Wall Street Journal*, January 14,1999.

[16] "Don't Save the Yen," *The Economist*, February 8, 1997, p. 18.

[17] "Bruce Ingersoll, "Germany's SGL to Pay $135 Million Fine," *Wall Street Journal*, May 5, 1999, p. B12.

[18] David Woodruff, "Weakened Euro May Enliven Economies," *Wall Street Journal*, April 15, 1999, p. A17.

[19] Betsy McKay, "Ruble's Decline Energizes Firms Who Manage to Win Back Consumers," *Wall Street Journal*, April 23, 1999, p. B7.

[20] George Melloan, "Another Russian Crisis," *Wall Street Journal*, June 2, 1998, p. A23.

[21] "Putin Takes Cautious Approach to Union with Belarus," *Associated Press Newswires*, June 11, 2002.

[22] Phusadee Arunmas, "Cement Producers Agree to Ceiling on Prices," *Bangkok Post*, April 26, 2002, p. P1.

[23] Carol Gentry, "Bay State May Negotiate Price of Pharmaceuticals," *Wall Street Journal*, December 9, 1998, p. NE1.

[24] "World Trade: Poorer Nations Starting More Dumping Cases," *Financial Times*, May 6, 1999, p. 21.

[25] Stephan A. Butscher, "Maximizing Profits in Euro-Land," *Journal of Commerce*, May 5, 1999: A5.

[26] Digital Equipment Corporation, 1996 Annual Report, p. 40.

[27] For a conceptual treatment, see *Transfer Pricing* (Washington, DC: Tax Management, Inc., 1995).

[28] William Glanz, "Foreign Firms Skirt U.S. Tax Laws," *Washington Times*, April 15, 1999, p. 14.

[29] Michael C. Durst, "United States: Transfer Pricing," *International Tax Review* (London), February 1999: 56–60.

[30] Michael Happell, "Asia: An Overview," *International Tax Review*, February 1999: 7–9.

[31] Foo Eu Jin, "Transfer Pricing Poses Threat to Firms," *Business Times* (Malaysia), March 10, 1999: 3.

[32] "Learning the Language of EC Trade," *Providence Journal-Bulletin*, March 1, 1989, p. C1.

33 Saeed Samiee, Patrick Anckar, and Abo Akademi, "Currency Choice in Industrial Pricing: A Cross-national Evaluation," *Journal of Marketing* 62, 3 (July 1998): 25–27.

34 "Foreign Exchange," *Wall Street Journal*, July 16, 1999, p. C15.

35 Matthew Rose and Ernest Beck, "Coke's Public-Relations Trouble Was Worsened by Gray Trade," *Wall Street Journal*, July 6, 1999, p. A12.

36 "Gray Goods Cleared by Court," *Chain Store Age (New York)*, April 1998: 34.

37 Vanessa Fuhrmans and Gautam Naik, "Drug Makers Fight a Desperate Battle for Pricing Power," *Wall Street Journal Europe*, June 7, 2002, p. A1.

38 "Pharmaceuticals Drug Trafficking," *The Economist*, December 17, 1996: 65.

39 "Chemicals/Competition: EU Court Overturns Bayer's Euro 3 Million Fine in Parallel Import Case," *Europe Information Service European Report*, October 28, 2000.

40 "Parallel Imports: Hardly the Full," *The Economist*, February 27, 1999: 72.

41 Stephan A. Butscher, "Maximizing Profits in Euro-Land," *Journal of Commerce*, May 5, 1999: A5.

42 Laura Johannes, "Canadian Web Drugstores Offer Deep Discounts and Legal Quandaries," *Wall Street Journal*, January 18, 2001, p. B1.

43 Mathew B. Myers, "Incidents of Gray Market Activity Among U.S. Exporters: Occurrences, Characteristics, and Consequences," *Journal of International Business Studies* 30, 1 (First Quarter 1999): 105–126.

44 Mark Maremont, "Blind Ambition," *Business Week*, October 23, 1995: 78–92.

45 "Israel Adopts Dutch Drug Import Pricing System," Marketletter (London), February 23, 1998: 1.

46 Marios Theodosiou and Constantine S. Katsikeas, "Factors Influencing the Degree of International Pricing Strategy Standardization of Multinational Corporations," *Journal of International Marketing* 9, 3 (2001): 1–18.

47 "Beleaguered Third World Leads the Barter Boom," *Financial Times*, February 28, 1984: 6.

48 "Czech Retailer Leads in Effort for Western Goods," *New York Times*, November 26, 1990, p. D7.

49 "Czech Retailer Leads in Effort for Western Goods."

50 "Philippines to Swap Fertilizer for Rice with Vietnam," *World Reporter*, May 9, 1999: 1.

51 "Philippines To Swap Fertilizer for Rice With Vietnam."

52 "Countertrade: Farm Goods Swapped for Italian Electricity," *Bangkok Post*, July 23, 1998, p. 1.

53 "Commodity Grant: Marc Rich & Co. Does Big Deals at Big Risk in the Former USSR," *Wall Street Journal*, May 13, 1993, pp. 1 and A6.

54 Robert Koch, "Saab-British Aerospace Take Big Step Ahead of Competitors," *Agence France-Presse*, November 18, 1998, p.1.

55 "Bartercard Plans Expansion in Thailand," *Bangkok Post*, October 3, 2000, p. 3.

13 Managing Global Distribution Channels

Shoppers in Caracas habitually patronize the small corner store. Venezuela's retail sector essentially consists of family-owned shops, modest-size supermarkets, and a few specialty chains. Even the modern malls are amalgams of boutiques. In summer 2001, however, the hypermarket Tiendas Exito opened in an eastern suburb of Caracas. The new joint venture of French, Colombian, and Venezuelan partners met with some skepticism in the press. Would Venezuelans really abandon the social ritual of shopping at the small local store?

Undaunted, the new hypermarket presented itself as resolved to help its customers curtail their expenses by undercutting competitors' prices by 8 percent. Volume purchasing, centralized warehousing and shipping, and computerized inventory control—all revolutionary in the local context—would be employed to deliver on this promise. And such a promise could be appealing to the Caracas public. An international study placed Caracas as the world's eighth most expensive city to live in, more expensive than Paris, Los Angeles, or Geneva. Yet for salaries, it rated thirteenth lowest of the fifty-eight cities studied. One month after Tiendas Exito opened, sales were running 35 percent above expectations.[1]

Distribution systems have traditionally been shaped by a variety of factors—level of economic development, disposable income of consumers, the qual-

Chapter Outline

Learning Objectives

After studying this chapter, you should be able to:

▶ List and describe the key players within both home-market channels and foreign-market channels.

▶ Explain the impact on national channel strategy of distribution density, channel length, and channel alignment.

▶ Describe how costs, product line, control, coverage, and synergy all influence the proper choice of channel members.

▶ Suggest ways to locate foreign distributors.

▶ List ways to motivate and control foreign distributors.

▶ Suggest alternative entry strategies for markets where competitors already control distribution channels.

▶ List and explain the five key areas of global logistics management.

▶ Explain the growing global importance of large-scale retailers, international retailing, direct marketing, online retailing, information technology, and smuggling.

ity of infrastructure such as roads and telecommunications, as well as culture, physical environment, and the legal/political system. Global marketers need to understand how environmental influences may affect distribution policies and options. Using this knowledge, they must establish efficient channels for products on a country-by-country basis. They must also consider how the emergence of regional and global distributors and changes in global logistics can affect their operations at the transnational level.

In this chapter, we discuss the structure of global distribution systems and methods for selecting, locating, and managing channel members. We explore how the international firm gains access to local channels and manages international logistics. We conclude with a look at global trends in distribution.

▶ *The Structure of the Global Distribution System*

Marketers who develop distribution strategies must decide how to transport products from manufacturing locations to the consumer. Although distribution can be handled completely by the manufacturer, often products are moved through intermediaries, such as agents, wholesalers, distributors, and retailers. An understanding of the structure of available distribution systems is extremely important in the development of a strategy. There are two major categories of potential channel members: (1) those located in the home country and (2) those located abroad. The various channels available to a manufacturer are shown in Figure 13.1.

Home-Market Channel Members

From the home country, a manufacturer can utilize the services of an export management company or an export agent, or it can use company personnel to export products. We discussed these channel members in Chapter 9. What follows is a brief review.

Export Management Company The export management company (EMC) is a firm that handles all aspects of export operations under a contractual agreement. The EMC normally takes responsibility for the promotion of products, marketing research, credit, physical handling or logistics, patents, and licensing. Arrangements between an EMC and a manufacturer will vary,

Figure 13.1 *International Marketing Channel Alternatives*

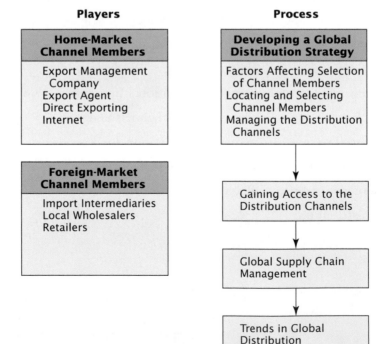

Players

Home-Market Channel Members
Export Management Company
Export Agent
Direct Exporting
Internet

Foreign-Market Channel Members
Import Intermediaries
Local Wholesalers
Retailers

Process

Developing a Global Distribution Strategy
Factors Affecting Selection of Channel Members
Locating and Selecting Channel Members
Managing the Distribution Channels

↓

Gaining Access to the Distribution Channels

↓

Global Supply Chain Management

↓

Trends in Global Distribution

depending on the services offered and the volume expected. The advantages of using an EMC are several: (1) little or no investment is necessary to enter the international marketplace, (2) no company personnel are required, and (3) the EMC will have an established network of sales offices, as well as international marketing and distribution knowledge.[2] The main disadvantage of using an EMC is that the manufacturer gives up direct control of the international sales and marketing effort. Also, if the product has a long purchase cycle and requires a large amount of market development and buyer education, the EMC may not expend the effort necessary to penetrate a new market.

Export Agents Export agents are individuals or firms that assist manufacturers in exporting goods. They are similar to EMCs, except that they tend to provide more limited services and to focus on one country or one part of the world. Export agents understand all the requirements for moving goods through the customs process, but they do not provide the marketing skills that an EMC provides. These agents focus more on the sale and handling of goods. The advantage of using an export agent is that the manufacturer does not need to have an export manager to handle all the documentation and shipping tasks. The main disadvantage is the export agent's limited market coverage. To cover different parts of the world, a firm would need the services of numerous export agents.

Direct Exporting Instead of using an EMC or export agent, a firm can export its goods directly, through in-house company personnel or an export department. Because of the complexity of trade regulations, customs documentation, insurance requirements, and worldwide transportation alternatives, people with special training and experience must be hired to handle these tasks. Also, the current or expected overseas sales volume must be sufficient to support the in-house staff.

Internet Many smaller manufacturers have been establishing their own web presence. This approach gives foreign clients easier access to smaller firms and tends to mitigate the need to use some form of agent. For the web presence to pay off, the site needs to be constructed in such a way that a foreign buyer can easily access information, obtain forms for ordering, and deliver e-mail questions. Experts also point out that a website needs to be marketed appropriately to the relevant search engines so that it shows up well placed under certain key search names. Although the web presence goes a long way toward reaching and communicating with foreign markets, the manufacturer that sets its sights on exporting still needs to deal with the areas of logistics and credit information. For logistics, companies such as Federal Express, UPS, and Emery provide considerable online help, something of great use to smaller companies that have had no opportunity to acquire that particular expertise.[3]

Foreign-Market Channel Members

As shown in Figure 13.1, once products have left the home market, there are a variety of channel alternatives in the global marketplace: import intermediaries, local wholesalers or agents, and retailers. Even with local manufacturing, the company will still need to get its products from the factory to the consumers.

Import Intermediaries Import intermediaries identify consumer needs in their local market and search the world to satisfy those needs. They normally purchase goods in their own name and act independently of manufacturers. As independents, these channel members use their own marketing strategies and keep in close contact with the markets they serve. A manufacturer that wants to distribute in an independent intermediary's market area should investigate this channel partner as one way to reach wholesalers and retailers in that area.

Local Wholesalers or Agents In each country, there will be a series of possible channel members who move manufacturers' products to retailers, to industrial firms, or in some cases to other wholesalers. Local wholesalers will take title to the products, whereas local agents will not take title. Local wholesalers are also called distributors or dealers. In many cases, a local wholesaler receives exclusive distribution rights for a specific geographic area or country.

The structure of wholesale distribution varies greatly from country to country. For example, although Denmark and Portugal have approximately the same number of wholesalers, the Danish wholesaler will serve an average of 1.3 retailers, whereas in Portugal a wholesaler will serve an average of 5.5 retailers.[4] The functions of wholesalers can also vary by country. In some countries, wholesalers provide a warehousing function, taking orders from retailers and shipping them appropriate quantities of merchandise. Wholesalers in Japan perform basic wholesale functions but also share risk with retailers by providing them with financing, product development, and even occasional managerial and marketing skills.

Retailers Retailers, the final members of the consumer distribution channel, purchase products for resale to consumers. The size and accessibility of retail channels vary greatly by country. The population per retailer in Europe varies from a low of only 48 people in Poland to 564 people in Russia.[5] Japan has a large number of retailers, with 13 per 1,000 inhabitants, compared with 6 in Europe and the United States. For example, Shiseido, a maker of cosmetics, has 25,000 outlets that sell only its products, and Matsushita has 19,000 electrical appliance stores.[6] Until recently, all retailing in China was conducted through state-owned stores. Since the economic liberalization, the number of retail outlets in China has grown from 1.4 million in 1980 to 10 million in 1996. The percentage of state-owned stores has fallen from 92 percent to 40 percent.[7] The global marketer must evaluate the available retailers in a country and develop a strategy around the existing structure.

Business-to-Business Channels When the firm is selling to businesses instead of consumers, channels may still resemble those we have described. Small businesses in particular may purchase supplies from retail outlets that have been supplied by wholesalers. Many business-to-business sales go through shorter channels, however. Export agents, import intermediaries, or the manufacturer itself often contacts business customers directly without the use of further intermediaries.

▶ *Analyzing National Channels*

A distribution strategy is one part of the marketing mix, and it needs to be consistent with other aspects of the marketing strategy: product policies, pricing strategy, and communication strategy. Figure 13.2 depicts important factors to consider when developing a distribution strategy. Before deciding on distribution strategies, global marketers must understand the nature of channels in their various markets. Of particular interest are the following variables:

1. ***Distribution density.*** Density is the amount of exposure or coverage desired for a product, particularly the number of sales outlets necessary to provide for adequate coverage of the entire market.
2. ***Channel length.*** The concept of channel length involves the number of intermediaries involved in bringing a given product from the firm to the consumer.
3. ***Channel alignment and leadership.*** Alignment is the structure of the chosen channel members to achieve a unified strategy.
4. ***Distribution logistics.*** Logistics involves the physical flow of products as they move through the channel.

The decisions involved in the first three of these areas cannot be approached independently. The decisions are interrelated, and they need to be consistent with other aspects of the marketing strategy. Although it is important to evaluate the distribution strategy logically, marketing managers often

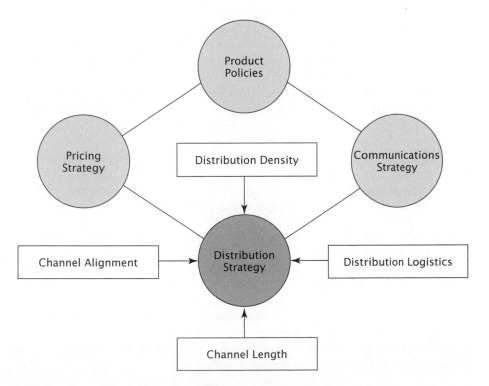

Figure 13.2 *Distribution Policies*

must work with an international distribution structure established under previous managers. That existing system may limit a company's flexibility to change and grow. Nevertheless, a creative marketer can usually find opportunities for circumventing the current arrangement. For example, Nordica of Italy had been selling in Japan for 25 years when the company decided it wanted more direct control over distribution. Nordica reached a financial agreement with its exclusive distributor, Daiwa Sports, and hired the eighty-five employees who had been handling its line. This allowed Nordica to take control without losing the experience and contacts developed by its distributor.[8] The following sections illustrate how company policies must adapt to distribution density, channel length, and channel alignment.

Distribution Density

The number of sales outlets or distribution points required for the efficient marketing of a firm's products is referred to as the **density of distribution**. The density is dependent on the shopping or buying habits of the average customer. Choosing the optimum distribution network requires the marketer to examine how customers select dealers and retail outlets by product category. For many consumer goods, an **extensive**, or wide, distribution is required if the consumer is not likely to exert much shopping effort. Such products, which are called convenience goods, are bought frequently and in nearby outlets. For other products, such as appliances or clothing, consumers may visit two or more stores. These products require a more limited, or **selective,** distribution, with fewer outlets per market area. For specialty goods, products that inspire consumer loyalty to specific brands, a very limited, or **exclusive,** distribution is required. It is assumed that the customer will search for the desired product and will not accept substitutes.

The key to distribution density, then, is the consumer's shopping behavior, in particular the effort expended to locate a desired item. This behavior, however, may vary greatly from country to country. In the United States, for example, where per-capita income is high, consumers shop for many regular-use items in supermarkets and other widely accessible outlets, such as drugstores. In other countries, particularly some with a much lower per-capita income, the purchase of such items is likely to be a less routine affair, and consumers may be willing to exert more effort to locate such items. This makes possible a less extensive distribution of products.

Where consumers buy certain products also varies a great deal from country to country. In Germany, contact lens solution is found only in stores that sell eyeglasses, but in France, it is also found in most drugstores. Whereas many magazines are sold in grocery stores in the United States, in the United Kingdom they are sold mainly through news agents. It is important to find out, early in your distribution analysis, where consumers buy the types of products you plan to market.

In the business-to-business sector as well, differences in buyer behavior or in the use of a particular product may require changes in distribution outlets and density. In the United States, for instance, radiology supply products are sold directly to hospitals and radiology departments through hospital supply distributors. In France, however, patients must pick up radiology supplies by prescription from a pharmacy before visiting the radiology department at the hospital. In this latter case, radiology supplies have to be promoted to physicians and then stocked at pharmacies to be successful. The distribution necessary in France is much more extensive than in the United States, where only hospitals are channel members.[9]

Channel Length

The number of intermediaries directly involved in the physical or ownership path of a product from the manufacturer to the customer is indicative of the **channel length**. Long channels have several intermediaries. Short or direct channels have few or no intermediaries. Channel length is usually influenced by three factors: (1) a product's distribution density, (2) the average order quantity, and (3) the availability of channel members. Products with extensive distribution, or large numbers of final sales points, tend to have longer channels of distribution. Similarly, as the average order quantity decreases, products move through longer channels to enhance the efficiency of distribution.

Because distribution density affects channel length, it is clear that the same factors that influence distribution density influence channel length; foremost among these is the shopping behaviors of consumers. The average order quantity often depends on the purchasing power or income level of a given customer group. In countries with lower income levels, people often buy food on a daily basis at nearby small stores. This contrasts sharply with more affluent consumers, who can afford to buy enough food or staples for a week or even a month and who don't mind traveling some distance to do more infrequent shopping.

Wholesale channels in Japan are the longest in the developed world, with most products moving through as many as six intermediaries. This lengthy distribution channel is more reminiscent of distribution systems in developing countries than of those in developed countries. High distribution costs inherent in this inefficient system cause Japan to have elevated prices—$20 for a bottle of aspirin and $72 for a package of golf balls that cost $26.80 in U.S. stores.[10]

However, the Japanese distribution system is under pressure to change. For example, Seiko Epson bypassed traditional Japanese channel members and began a direct-sales effort to sell its NEC and IBM-compatible PCs. Following the lead of Dell Computer, Seiko Epson chose to attract consumers by offering significant savings through its direct-marketing effort.[11]

Channel Alignment

One of the most difficult tasks of marketing is to ensure that various channel members coordinate their actions so that a unified approach can be achieved. The longer the channel, the more difficult it becomes to maintain a coordinated and integrated approach. On an international level, the coordinating task is made all the more difficult because the company organizing the channel may be far away from the distribution system, with little influence over the local scene. The international company will find it much easier to control the distribution channel if a local subsidiary with a strong sales force exists. In countries where the company has no local presence and depends on independent distributors, control is likely to slip to the independent distributor. This loss of control may be further aggravated if the international company's sales volume represents only a small fraction of the local distributor's business. Of course, the opposite will be true when a high percentage of the volume consists of the international corporation's products.

Often one participant emerges as the **channel captain** or dominant member. The channel captain frequently dictates terms of pricing, delivery, and sometimes even product design that affect other channel members. Countries differ in what sort of firm typically emerges as this dominant member. In the United States, for example, the once-strong wholesalers have become less influential, and manufacturers now play the dominant role in some channels. More and more in the United States, large retailers (such as Home Depot and Wal-Mart) have become channel captains. In Japan, on the other hand, wholesalers continue to dominate the channel structure. In many developing countries, independent distributors are very strong because they are the only authorized importers. Global marketers must be aware of these national differences that can significantly affect a firm's bargaining power in channel negotiations.

Distribution Logistics

Distribution logistics focuses on the physical movement of goods through the channels. An extremely important part of the distribution system, logistics is discussed in detail later in the chapter.

▶ Factors Influencing the Selection of Channel Members

A marketer needs to identify and select appropriate distribution partners in various national markets. This selection of distribution partners is an extremely important decision, because the partner often will assume a portion of the marketing responsibility, or even all of it. Also, the distribution partner usually is involved in the physical movement (logistics) of products to the customers. A poor decision can lead to lackluster performance. Changing a distribution partner can be expensive or sometimes impossible because of local laws. PepsiCo went through a year-long court battle to terminate its 22-year contract with Perrier to bottle and distribute Pepsi in France. PepsiCo contended that Perrier had underperformed, allowing Pepsi-Cola's share to decline from 17 percent to 7 percent over the previous 10 years.[12] The very success of a firm's international efforts depends on the partners it selects. A number of factors influence the selection of distribution partners. These include costs, the nature of the product and product line, the desired level of control and coverage, and the potential synergy between the international firm and its channels.

Costs

Channel costs fall into three categories: initial costs, maintenance costs, and logistics costs. The **initial costs** include all the costs of locating and setting up the channel, such as executive time and travel to locate and select channel members, the costs of negotiating an agreement with channel members, and the capital costs of setting up the channel. Capital costs include the costs for inventories, goods in transit, accounts receivable, and inventories on consignment. The establishment of a direct-sales channel often requires the maximum investment, whereas use of distributors generally reduces the investment required. The **maintenance costs** of the channel include the costs of the company's salespeople, sales managers, and travel expenses. They also include the costs of auditing and controlling channel operations and the profit margin given to channel intermediaries. The **logistics costs** comprise the transportation expenses, storage costs, the cost of breaking bulk shipments into smaller lot sizes, and the cost for customs paperwork.

Predicting all of these various costs when selecting different channel members is often difficult, but it is necessary in order to estimate the cost of various alternatives. High distribution costs usually result in higher prices at the consumer level, which may hamper entry into a new market. Companies often establish direct channels, hoping to reduce distribution costs. Unfortunately, however, most of the functions of the channel cannot be eliminated, so these costs eventually show up anyway.

Product and Product Line

The nature of a product can affect channel selection. If the product is perishable or has a short shelf life, then the manufacturer is forced to use shorter channels to get the product to the consumer more rapidly. Delta Dairy, a Greek producer of dairy products and chilled fruit juices, was faced with increased transportation costs of shipping from Greece to France when the United Nations banned transit across the former Yugoslavia. In addition, Delta lost 5 days of product shelf life. As a result, the firm set up production in Switzerland to shorten the distance to the French market.[13]

A technical product often requires direct sales or highly technical channel partners. For example, Index Technology of Cambridge, Massachusetts, sold a sophisticated software product to automate the development of software systems called computer-aided systems engineering. The company entered the United Kingdom and Australia with a direct-sales effort, but to limit initial costs, it decided on distributors for France, Germany, and Scandinavia. However, insufficient revenues from these distributors led the company to set up its own sales efforts in France and Germany and to purchase its distributor in Scandinavia. The highly technical nature of the product required Index to invest more time and money in distribution than would be necessary if the firm sold a generic or unsophisticated product.

The size of the product line also affects the selection of channel members. A broader product line is more desirable for channel members. A distributor or dealer is more likely to stock a broad product line than a single item. Similarly, if a manufacturer has a very broad, complete line, it is easier to justify the cost of a more direct channel. With more products to sell, it is easier to generate a high average order on each sales call. With a limited product line, an agent or distributor will group a firm's product together with products from other companies to increase the average order size.

Control, Coverage, and Synergy

Each type of channel arrangement offers the manufacturer a different level of control. With direct sales, a manufacturer can control price, promotion, amount of effort, and type of retail outlet used. If these are important, then the increased level of control may offset the increased cost of a direct-sales force. Longer channels, particularly with distributors who take title to goods, often result in little or no control. In many cases, a company may not know who is ultimately buying the product.

Coverage is reaching the geographic area that a manufacturer wants to cover. Although coverage is usually easy to get in major metropolitan areas, gaining adequate coverage of smaller cities or sparsely populated areas can be difficult. Selection of one channel member over another may be influenced by the market coverage that the respective agents or distributors offer. To assess an agent's or distributor's coverage, the following must be determined: (1) location of sales offices, (2) salespersons' home base, and (3) previous year's sales by geographic location. The location of sales offices indicates where efforts are focused. Salespeople generally have the best penetration near their homes, and past sales clearly indicate the level of the channel member's success in each geographic area.

The choice of channel members or partners can sometimes be influenced by the existence of complementary skills that can increase the total output of the distribution system. This synergy normally occurs when a potential distributor has some skill or expertise that will allow quicker access to the market. For example, when Compaq entered the international personal computer market, it decided to sell only through a network of strong authorized dealers. While Compaq focused on developing market applications such as sales force automation, computer-aided design, and office productivity, it used the dealers to penetrate the marketplace. By the time of its merger with Hewlett-Packard in 2001, Compaq held market shares outside its domestic market of 3.7 percent in Japan, 6 percent in other Asian markets, 17.3 percent in Western Europe, and 14.6 percent in the rest of the world—compared to 13.8 percent in the United States.

▶ *Locating and Selecting Channel Partners*

Building an international distribution system normally takes 1 to 3 years. The process involves the series of steps shown in Table 13.1. The critical aspect of developing a successful system is locating and selecting channel partners.

The development of an international distribution strategy in terms of distribution density, channel length, and channel alignment will establish a framework for the "ideal" distribution partners. The company's preference regarding key factors that influence selection of channel partners (costs,

Table 13.1 *Process of Establishing an International Distribution System*

1. Develop a distribution strategy.
2. Establish criteria for selecting distribution partners.
3. Locate potential distribution partners.
4. Solicit the interest of distributors.
5. Screen and select distribution partners.
6. Negotiate agreements.

products, control, coverage, and synergy) will be used with the distribution strategy to establish criteria for the selection of partners. Selection criteria include geographic coverage, managerial ability, financial stability, annual volume, and reputation. Several sources are useful in locating possible distribution partners. They include:

1. *U.S. Department of Commerce.* The Agent Distributor Service is a customized service of the Department of Commerce that locates distributors and agents interested in a certain product line. Also, the department's Export Marketing Service can be used to locate distribution partners.
2. *Banks.* If the firm's bank has foreign branches, they may be happy to help locate distributors.
3. *Directories.* Country directories of distributors or specialized directories, such as those listing computer distributors, can be helpful.
4. *Trade shows.* Exhibiting at an international trade show, or just attending one, exposes managers to a large number of distributors and their salespeople.
5. *Competitors' distribution partners.* Sometimes a competitor's distributor may be interested in switching product lines.
6. *Consultants.* Some international marketing consultants specialize in locating distributors.
7. *Associations.* There are associations of international intermediaries or country associations of intermediaries; for example, Japan has numerous industry associations.
8. *Foreign consulates.* Most countries post commercial attachés at their embassies or at separate consulates. These individuals can be helpful in locating agents or distributors in their country.

After compiling a list of possible distribution partners, the firm may contact each, providing product literature and distribution requirements. Prospective distributors with an interest in the firm's product line can be asked to supply such information as lines currently carried, annual volume, number of salespeople, geographic territory covered, credit and bank references, physical facilities, relationship with local government, and knowledge of English or other relevant languages. Firms that respond should be checked against the selection criteria. Before making a final decision, a manufacturer's representative should go to the country and talk to retailers or the industrial end users to narrow the field to the strongest two or three contenders. While in the country, the manufacturer's representative should meet and evaluate the distribution partner candidates.

Check out our website for links to distributor information.

▶ *Managing Global Distribution*

Selecting the most suitable channel participants and gaining access to the market are extremely important steps in achieving an integrated and responsive distribution channel. However, without proper motivation of and control over that channel, sales may remain unsatisfactory. This section discusses the steps that must be taken to ensure the flow of the firm's products through the channel by gaining the full cooperation of all channel members.

Motivating Channel Participants

Keeping channel participants motivated is an important aspect of international distribution policies. Financial incentives in the form of higher-than-average gross margins can be a very powerful inducement, particularly for the management of independent distributors, wholesalers, and retailers. The expected gross margins are influenced by the cultural history of that channel. For example, if a certain type of retailer usually gets a 50 percent margin and the firm offers 40 percent, the effort the retailer makes may be less than desired. Inviting channel members to annual conferences and introductions of new products is also effective. By extending help to the management of distributorships in areas such as inventory control, accounts collection, and advertising, the international firm can cultivate goodwill that will later stand it in good stead. Special programs may also be instituted to train or motivate the channel members' sales forces.

Programs to motivate foreign independent intermediaries are likely to succeed if monetary incentives are considered along with efforts that help make the channel members more efficient and competitive. To have prosperous intermediaries is, of course, also in the interest of the international firm. These programs or policies are particularly important in the case of independents that distribute products of other manufacturers as well. Often they are beleaguered by the principals of the other products they carry. Each is attempting to get the greatest possible attention and service from the distributor. Therefore, the international firm must find ways to ensure that the channel members devote sufficient effort to its products.

The motivation of channel partners and the amount of effort devoted to the firm's product line can be enhanced by a continuous flow of two-way information between manufacturer and distributor. The amount of effort an international firm needs to expend depends on the marketing strategy for that market. For example, if the firm is using extensive advertising to pull products through a channel, the intermediary may be expected only to take orders and deliver the product; there is no need for it to contribute to the sales effort. If, on the other hand, the marketing strategy depends on the channel members' developing the market or pushing the product through the channel, then a significant sales effort will be required. As much as possible, the manufacturer should send product news and public relations releases to encourage attention to its product line and to support its distributors' efforts in its behalf.

More intense contact between the export manufacturer and the distributor will usually result in better performance by the distributor. Caterpillar found that dealer training could develop a strong competitive advantage that was difficult for Japanese competitor Komatsu to counter in the market for earth-moving equipment. In fact, during the pilot of Caterpillar's training program, participating dealers increased revenue by 102 percent.[14]

Periodic visits to distribution partners can have a positive effect on their motivation and control. Often it is helpful to travel with a channel member salesperson to gain knowledge of the marketplace and to evaluate the skills of the salesperson. The most important benefit of a visit to the channel member is that it gives a clear message that the member's performance is important to the firm. Visits strengthen the personal relationship between the manufacturer and the channel member.

Changing channel strategies can be costly but necessary, especially as national markets evolve. However, until an international firm decides to eliminate a channel member, it should beware of strategies that cause conflict between manufacturers and channel members. The most common causes of channel conflict are (1) bypassing channels to sell directly to large customers, (2) oversaturating a market with too many distributors, and (3) opening new discount channels that offer the same goods at lower prices.[15]

Controlling Channel Participants

An international company will want to exert enough control over channel members to help guarantee that they accurately interpret and appropriately execute the company's marketing strategies. The firm wants to be sure that the local intermediaries price the products according to the company's policies. The same could be said for sales, advertising, and service policies. Because the company's reputation in a local market can be tarnished when independent intermediaries handle local distribution ineffectively or inefficiently, international companies closely monitor the performance of local channel members. One way to exert influence over the international channel members is to spell out the specific responsibilities of each, such as minimum annual sales, in the distribution agreement. Attainment of the sales goal can be required for renewal of the contract.

In fact, many international companies grant distribution rights only for short time periods, with regular renewal. Caution is advised, however, because cancellation of distribution rights is frequently subject to both social norms and local laws that prohibit sudden termination. Although termination of a distributor or agent for nonperformance is a relatively simple action in the United States, termination of international channel members can be very costly in many parts of the world. In Japan, foreign firms must be especially careful in their selection of a local distributor, because firms are expected to commit themselves to a long-term relationship. When a firm terminates a distributor, it reflects poorly on that firm.[16] Finding another distributor could prove difficult under those circumstances.

In some countries, the international firm may have to pay a multiple of its local agent's annual gross profits in order to terminate the agent. In other countries, termination compensation for agents and distributors can include the value of any goodwill that the agent or distributor has built up for the brand, in addition to expenses incurred in developing the business. The international firm may also be liable for any compensation claimed by discharged employees who worked on the product line. As a result, termination of a channel member can be a costly, painful process governed in nearly all cases by local laws that may tend to protect and compensate the local channel member.

Nonetheless, research suggests that multinational corporations operating in developing countries commonly buy or fire their local distributors or develop their own marketing and sales subsidiaries. These firms complain that distributors in emerging markets often fail to invest in business growth and aren't ambitious enough.[17]

World Beat 13.1 *Reviving Fading Handicrafts*

For generations, the blacksmith caste of the Himalayan foothills of Nepal eked out a living hammering copper into pots, jugs, and tools. Then mass-produced aluminum and plastic vessels undercut their wares, and many of these landless artisans were forced to seek work in nearby towns or across the border in India.

Now, even though their village doesn't yet have a telephone, the Internet is helping to bring blacksmiths home. Their copper items are appearing on World2Market.com, a website that sells handicrafts made by artisans in developing countries. Membership in the local blacksmith cooperative is ballooning, and incomes are rising. At least one family now cooks on a gas stove instead of firewood.

The ancient and modern worlds are converging in cyberspace. A bevy of new Internet sites are selling home furnishings, accessories, and toys made by traditional craftspeople. By giving artisans direct access to a global marketplace, the Internet has the potential to improve the lot of poor families from Asia to the Americas. The benefits to Mexican mask makers and Indian quilt weavers are just beginning to show.

One recent morning, the patio of a clay and stone hut is a hive of activity as dozens of men and women sit beating, burnishing, and decorating copper vases, bowls, and teapots. The goods are bound first for the Association of Craft Producers, a nongovernmental association in Katmandu that supplies World2Market.com. The craft association helps Nepalese artisans bolster their traditional skills, while design and marketing staff at World2Market.com keeps the association abreast of U.S. consumer tastes. Products made by the association's 850 members have been sold in the West for 14 years, but the Internet is giving them access to a wider market and dreams of an e-commerce bonanza.

Source: Miriam Jordan, "Web Sites Revive Fading Handicrafts," *Wall Street Journal*, June 12, 2000, p. B1.

▶ *Gaining Access to Distribution Channels*

Entry into a market can be accomplished through a variety of channel members. However, the channel member whom it seems most logical to approach may already have a relationship with one of the firm's competitors. This poses some special challenges to international marketers. This section is aimed at illustrating alternatives that companies may employ when they encounter difficulties in convincing channel members to carry their products.

The "Locked-Up" Channel

A channel is considered locked up when a newcomer cannot easily convince any channel member to participate, despite the fact that both market and economic considerations suggest otherwise. Channel members customarily decide on a case-by-case basis what products they should add to or drop from their lines. Retailers typically select products that they expect to sell easily and in volume, and they can be expected to switch sources when better opportunities arise. Similarly, wholesalers and distributors compete for retail accounts or industrial users on economic terms. They can entice a prospective client to switch by buying from a new source that can offer a better deal. Likewise, manufacturers compete for wholesale accounts with the expectation that channel members can be convinced to purchase from any given manufacturer if the offer improves on the offers made by competitors.

Yet there are barriers that limit a wholesaler's flexibility to add or drop a particular line. The distributor may have an agreement not to sell competitive products, or its business may include a significant volume from one manufacturer that it does not want to risk upsetting. In Japan, relationships among manufacturers, wholesalers, and retailers are long-standing in nature and do not allow channel participants to shift their allegiance quickly to another source even when offered a superior product or price. Japanese channel members develop strong personal ties that make it very difficult for any participant to break a long-standing relationship. When Kodak entered the Japanese market, it had difficulty gaining access to the smaller retail outlets because Japan's Fujifilm dominated the four major wholesalers. A former president of Kodak Japan played golf for 3 years with the president of one of the wholesaling companies—but to no avail.[18]

Cultural forces may not be the only impediments blocking access to a channel of distribution. The members of a channel may not be willing to take any risks by pioneering unknown products. Competitors, domestic or foreign, may try to obstruct the entry of a new company. When American Standard, the world's largest supplier of plumbing fixtures, tried to enter the Korean market, it found itself locked out of the normal plumbing distributors, which were controlled by local manufacturers. American Standard looked for an alternative distribution channel that served the building trade. It found Home Center, one of the largest suppliers of homebuilding materials and appliances, and thus successfully circumvented the locked channels.[19]

Alternative Entry Approaches

International marketers have developed several approaches to the difficult task of gaining access to locked-up distribution channels. These include piggybacking, joint ventures, and acquisitions.

Piggybacking When a company does not find any channel partners interested in pioneering new products, the practice of piggybacking may offer a way out of the situation. **Piggybacking** is an arrangement whereby another company that sells to the same customer segment takes on the new products. The products retain the name of the true manufacturer, and both partners normally sign a multiyear contract to provide for continuity. The new company is, in essence, "piggybacking" its products on the shoulders of the established company's sales force.

Under a piggyback arrangement, the manufacturer retains control over marketing strategy, particularly pricing, positioning, and advertising. The partner acts as a rented sales force only. Of course, this is quite different from the private-label strategy, whereby the manufacturer supplies a marketer which then places its own brand name on the product. The piggybacking approach has become quite common in the pharmaceutical industry, where companies involve competitor firms in the launch of a particular new drug. Warner-Lambert, a major pharmaceutical company, launched its leading cholesterol-lowering drug Lipitor in the United States with the help of Pfizer. The drug was one of the most successful introductions ever.[20]

Coca-Cola initiated a new twist on the piggyback arrangement when it offered its extensive distribution system across Africa to assist Unaids, a United Nations agency fighting AIDS. Coke's distribution reaches every country in Africa except Sudan and Libya, and its products find their way even to the poorest villages. The company will be contributing warehouse and truck space, as well as logistics assistance to help charities find the best routes for their literature and testing kits. However, Coca-Cola can't help distribute AIDS drugs that have to be kept cool, because its trucks are not refrigerated.[21]

Joint Ventures As we noted in Chapter 9, when two companies agree to form a new legal entity, it is called a joint venture. Such operations have been quite common in the area of joint production. Our interest here is restricted to joint ventures in which distribution is the primary objective. Normally, such companies are formed between a local firm with existing market access and a foreign firm that would like to market its products in a country where it has no existing market access. For example, two domestic beer producers had tied up retail outlets in Mexico with exclusivity contracts. As a result, Anheuser-Busch decided to enter Mexico through a joint venture with Mexican beer giant Modelo rather than trying to build a distribution system from scratch. Many distribution joint ventures have been signed between Japanese firms and foreign companies eager to enter the Japanese market. Kodak formed a joint venture with Nagase Sangyo, an Osaka-based trading company specializing in chemicals, to attack global competitor Fuji in its home market. To enter the Brazilian appliance market, Whirlpool formed a partnership with Brasmotor, a local manufacturer in Sao Paulo, purchasing 31 percent of that company. The partnership paid off. Whirlpool had attained a 39 percent share of the white-goods market in Brazil by 1996.[22]

Acquisitions Acquiring an existing company can give a foreign entrant immediate access to a distribution system. Although it requires a substantial amount of capital, operating results tend to be better than those of new ventures, which usually entail initial losses. It is often less important to find an acquisition candidate with a healthy financial outlook or top products than to find one that has good relationships with wholesale and retail outlets. A good example of using the acquisition strategy to gain access to distribution channels was Merck's purchase of 51 percent of Japan's Banyu pharmaceutical company. [23]

▶ *Global Logistics*

The logistics system, including the physical distribution of manufactured products, is also an important part of international distribution. It involves planning, implementing, and controlling the physical flow of materials and finished products from points of origin to points of use. On a global scale, the task becomes more complex, because so many external variables have an impact on the flow of materials or products. As geographic distances to foreign markets grow, competitive advantages are often derived from a more effective structuring of the logistics system either to save time or costs or to increase a firm's reliability. The emergence of logistics as a means of achieving competitive advantage is leading companies to focus increased attention on

this vital area. Many manufacturers and retailers are restructuring their logistics efforts and divesting themselves of their in-house distribution divisions in favor of outside logistics specialists.

A capital- and labor-intensive function outside of the core business of
most companies, logistics has become increasingly complex. For many concerns, it represents 16 to 35 percent of total revenues. Marks & Spencer, a
U.K. retailer that operates in eight countries, found it could increase its sales
per square foot and eliminate the need for most stockrooms by increasing
the frequency of delivery. To guarantee delivery reliability, the company used
outside contractors. The company spun off its entire logistics system into a
partnership with a logistics firm, expecting to save a substantial part of its
UK£300 million annual distribution bill.[24]

Logistics Decision Areas

In this section, we describe the objectives of an international logistics system
and the various operations that have to be managed and integrated into an
efficient system. The total task of logistics management consists of five separate though interrelated jobs: (1) traffic or transportation management, (2)
inventory control, (3) order processing, (4) materials handling and warehousing, and (5) fixed-facilities location management. In what follows, we
examine each of these decision areas in more detail.

Traffic or Transportation Management Traffic management deals primarily with the modes of transportation for delivering products. Principal
choices are air, sea, rail, and truck, or some combination thereof. Transportation expenses contribute substantially to the costs of marketing products internationally, so special attention must be paid to selecting the transportation mode. Such choices are made by considering three principal factors:
lead time, transit time, and cost. Companies operating with long lead times
tend to use slower and therefore lower-cost transportation modes such as sea
and freight. When a short lead time is called for, faster modes of transportation such as air and truck are used. Long transit times require higher financial costs, because payments arrive later and because higher average inventories are stocked at either the point of origin or the destination. Here again,
the modes of transportation appropriate for long transit times are sea and
rail, whereas air and truck transportation can result in much shorter transit
times. Transportation costs are the third factor to consider when selecting a
mode of transport. Typically, air or truck transportation is more expensive
than either sea or rail for any given distance.

Local laws and restrictions can have a significant impact on transport
costs. For example, France restricted foreign truck drivers from traveling on
Sundays. The Dutch Transport Association reports that such bans cost firms
$60 million in Holland alone and billions across Europe. The Dutch have
asked the EU to investigate the forty-seven different bans in Europe that restrict transport on holidays, Sundays, and summer holidays.[25] Under NAFTA,
the United States was required in 2001 to open its borders to Mexican trucking, whose costs are substantially below those of the U.S. trucking industry.
The cost of trucking products from Mexico to the United States is expected
to fall as a result of this ruling.

Inventory Control The level of inventory on hand significantly affects the service level of a firm's logistics system. In international operations, adequate inventories are needed as insurance against unexpected breakdowns in the logistics system. However, to avoid the substantial costs of tied-up capital, inventory is ideally reduced to the minimum needed. To reduce inventory levels, a number of companies have adopted the Japanese system of just-in-time (JIT) deliveries of parts and components. For example, Rank Xerox produces its models for the entire world market (except the U.S. market) in four European plants. Prior to adopting a just-in-time system, the firm kept buffer stocks of 10 to 40 days and an inventory of finished goods of 90 days. Now there is no stock for just-in-time parts and components and an inventory of finished goods of only 15 days. The improvements are the result of a just-in-time strategy: a reduced number of suppliers, improved quality control, and a more efficient logistics system.[26]

Order Processing Because rapid processing of orders shortens the order cycle and allows for lower safety stocks on the part of the client, this area becomes a central concern for logistics management. The available communications technology greatly influences the time it takes to process an order, and the Internet has vastly improved our ability in this regard. Still, to offer an efficient order-processing system worldwide represents a considerable challenge to any company today. Doing this can be turned to competitive advantage; customers reap added benefits from such a system, and satisfied customers mean repeat business.

Toshiba Semiconductors, a major chip supplier based in Japan with global operations, revamped its global supply chain network to obtain faster deliveries and to ship its products on the shortest possible notice from any supply point in the world. Its customers required this level of service for just-in-time delivery. To obtain these benefits, the company is also employing a third-party logistics provider in Europe.[27]

Materials Handling and Warehousing Throughout the logistics cycle, materials and products will have to be stored and prepared for moving or transportation. How products are stored or moved is the principal concern of materials handling management. For international shipments, the shipping technology or quantities may be different, requiring firms to adjust domestic policies to these new circumstances. Warehousing in foreign countries involves dealing with different climatic conditions. Longer average storage periods may make it necessary to change warehousing practices. In general, international shipments move through different transportation modes than domestic shipments. Substantial logistics costs can be saved if the firm adjusts its shipping arrangements to the prevalent handling procedures abroad.

Automated warehousing is a relatively new concept for the handling, storage, and shipping of goods. Warehouses are often adjacent to the factory, and all goods are stored automatically in bins up to twelve stories high. The delivery and retrieval of all goods are controlled by a computer system. Even though automated warehouses require significant up-front capital and technology, they ultimately reduce warehousing costs significantly.

Fixed-Facilities Location Management The facilities crucial to the logistics flow are production facilities and warehouses. To serve customers worldwide and to maximize the efficiency of the total logistics system, production facilities may have to be placed in several countries. This often entails a tradeoff between economies of scale and savings in logistics costs.

The location of warehousing facilities can greatly affect the company's ability to respond to orders once they are received or processed. It can also support the company's warranty policy, particularly its ability to deliver replacement products and parts on a timely basis. A company with warehouses in every country where it does business would have a natural advantage in delivery, but such a system increases the costs of warehousing and, most likely, the required level of inventory systemwide. Therefore, the international firm should seek a balance that satisfies the customer's requirements for timely delivery and also reduces overall logistics costs. Microsoft opened a single warehouse and distribution center in Dublin, Ireland, to serve Europe. The new distribution center both made it possible to serve all European markets effectively and made it unnecessary for Microsoft to keep a warehouse and inventory in each country.[28]

Managing the Global Logistics System

National Semiconductor supplies customers in Asia, Europe, and North America from its plant in Malaysia—all within 2 or 3 days. The company originally used forty-two different freight forwarders and fifteen different airlines. When FedEx took over as exclusive contractor in 1992, distribution costs fell from 3.3 percent to 1.3 percent of total revenues. But National Semiconductor felt that it still took too long for the chips to reach the customers. In 2001 the contract was given to UPS Logistics Group of United Parcel Service Inc. Utilizing custom software, UPS's warehouse in Singapore can process the incoming chips—including bar-coding, repackaging, and putting them on ships and planes—in less than an hour.[29]

The objective of a firm's international logistics system is to meet the company's commitments at the lowest cost. High-quality logistics does pay off. With 50 percent of all customer complaints to manufacturers resulting from poor logistics, there are substantial rewards for well-managed logistics that results in better service. Research by the Strategic Planning Institute revealed that companies with superior service received 7 percent higher prices and grew 8 percent more rapidly than low-service companies. Also, on average they were 12 times more profitable.[30]

With markets becoming more scattered and dispersed over numerous countries, the opportunities to glean competitive advantages in international logistics grow. Firms that are able to coordinate the various logistics areas can achieve both substantial cost savings and enhanced market positions by increasing service levels at minimum costs.

▶ *Global Trends in Distribution*

Distribution systems throughout the world are continually evolving in response to economic and social changes. A manager developing a worldwide distribution strategy must consider not only the state of distribution today but also the expected state of distribution systems in the future. Five major trends are currently prevailing throughout the world: (1) the growth of larger-scale retailers, (2) an increased number of international retailers, (3) the proliferation of direct marketing, (4) the dominant role of information technology to support a distribution strategy, and (5) the emergence of organized smuggling.

Larger-Scale Retailers

There is a trend toward fewer but larger-scale retailers. As countries become more economically developed, the retail scene comes to be dominated by fewer, larger stores. Three factors contribute to this trend: an increase in car ownership, an increase in the number of households with refrigerators and freezers, and an increase in the number of working wives. Whereas the European housewife of 20 years ago may have shopped two or three times a day in local stores, the increase in transportation capacity, refrigerator capacity, and family cash flow, along with the reduction in available shopping time, has increased the practice of one-stop shopping in supermarkets.

In the U.K., the most striking change in the retail marketplace was the opening of warehouse clubs. With six clubs opening in 1993 and 1994, U.K. consumers were able to buy merchandise at 25 to 30 percent less than at the typical retailer.[31] This trend, along with the growth of superstores or hypermarkets, has significantly reduced the number of medium-sized and small stores in many countries. For example, the number of food stores in the Netherlands fell by 22.1 percent from 1982 to 1992, while the number of superstores increased 33.3 percent.[32]

IKEA, the Scandinavian retailer, has been very successful in Europe, Asia, and the United States in luring customers into its 200,000-square-foot stores. The IKEA strategy of offering a narrow range of low-cost furniture that the customers themselves select, deliver, and assemble results in a lower price to the consumer.[33] Once in the store, customers are given tape measures, cata-

Small retailers are a tradition in France and other European countries, but they increasingly compete with much larger hypermarkets.

logs, paper, and pencils. Child care strollers are available, as well as free diapers. Each store has a restaurant with Scandinavian delicacies such as smoked salmon and Swedish meatballs. Customers can also borrow roof racks to help them bring furniture home. IKEA has created a fun shopping experience that encourages people to enjoy themselves and make purchases. Sales per square foot are three times higher than in traditional furniture stores. Its most recent stores were opened in Shanghai and Beijing, and the company has plans to expand in Russia and other Asian countries.[34]

International Retailers

As the IKEA case suggests, the number of international retailers is rising.[35] Most originate in advanced industrial countries and spread to both the developed and the developing countries of the world. For example, Sears is now in Mexico, South America, Spain, and Japan; Walgreen's is in Mexico; and Tandy is in Belgium, the Netherlands, Germany, the United Kingdom, and France. The trend was started by a number of large retailers in mature domestic markets that saw limited growth opportunities at home compared to the potential opportunities overseas. Among the most successful have been franchises and discount retailers. The path toward an international presence has been made smoother by a number of facilitating factors, such as enhanced data communications, new forms of international financing, and lower governmental barriers to entry. The single European market has also motivated European retailers to expand abroad as they see a number of new international retailers entering their domestic markets.[36]

Overall, American retailers have entered foreign markets later than European and Japanese retailers. However, Wal-Mart's entry into its first foreign market, Mexico, met with phenomenal success. Ten years after first entering

A smiling employee at Wal-Mart's store in Wisner, Germany. Surprisingly, many German shoppers dislike Wal-Mart's friendly style.

World Beat 13.2 *Culture Shock in Germany*

Entrenched and conservative, German shoppers are used to things the way they are. To them, friendliness smells like a sales pitch. Helpfulness should not be intrusive. And, as a rule, they don't like it when people touch their things. So when Wal-Mart, the world's number-one retailer, started unrolling its supersized plans across Germany, it ran into a little culture shock. Grumpy Teutonic shoppers recoiled when employees greeted them in the aisles. Customers, used to fending for themselves, resisted when cashiers tried to pack their purchases in free plastic bags. For a company that prides itself on service, Germany has been a challenge.

The marriage of American hominess and German frostiness has been rocky so far for Wal-Mart. Expansion plans have been scaled back, and downsizing has been ordered. Much of the challenge in Germany lies in coaxing attitudinal changes in a country where the customer traditionally comes last.

As founder of the Cologne-based Agency for Friendliness, Tanja Baum has coached thousands of German workers who are trying to break sour habits. "We have a societal problem, not a service problem," she said. She attributes the trouble to the social revolution of the late 1960s, when politeness was deemed a "bourgeois relic." Germans sometimes hesitate to be too friendly because that demeanor could be perceived as hypocrisy or as currying favor. "That's why they look down on American 'synthetic friendliness.' They accuse the United States of doing everything for a purpose—'They want to sell me something, that's why they are so friendly,'" says friendliness coach Baum.

Source: Daniel Rubin, "Wal-Mart Runs into Culture Shock in Germany," *KRTBN Knight-Ridder Tribune Business News*, December 27, 2001.

the Mexican market in 1991, Wal-Mart dominated the country's retail sector. The U.S. retailer joint-ventured with Cifra, the leading Mexican retailer and pioneer of discount stores in Mexico. In the early 1990s, the venture faced several problems. Tariffs inflated the prices of products imported from the United States, and Wal-Mart faced considerable red tape in obtaining import permits. Delivery schedules were unreliable because of poor road systems. With the inauguration of NAFTA, tariffs tumbled, paperwork diminished, and road construction and improvement soared. Wal-Mart buys directly from U.S. suppliers and consolidates orders in its own distribution center in Laredo, Texas. Trucks hired from Wal-Mart deliver products to its Mexican stores the next day. As a large-volume buyer, Wal-Mart can require suppliers to label in Spanish. Most important, it can demand lower prices. The company passes these cost savings on to the Mexican customer, offering prices that the traditional small retailers can't match.[37]

Despite its success in Mexico, other markets have proved more difficult. Wal-Mart remains only sixth in Brazil, where it faces stiff local competition as well as French competitor Carrefour. When first entering the market, Wal-Mart failed to note that most target families owned only one car and did all their shopping on weekends. Car parks and store aisles at their superstores were unable to accommodate the weekend rush.[38] However, the company is experimenting with a new concept—smaller outlets in working-class neighborhoods. These outlets have concrete floors, no air conditioning, and less merchandise selection than Wal-Mart's original stores. But they deliver products at prices 5 percent below those charged in the surrounding smaller stores. Credit is even available for qualified customers.[39]

Wal-Mart has also faced problems since it entered the highly regulated German market in 1997. In September 2000, German authorities ordered Wal-Mart and two German competitors to raise prices on a number of products. The stores were accused of selling below costs, on a regular basis, products such as milk, sugar, and flour. This endangered small and medium-sized retailers and violated German antitrust law.[40]

The Asian markets have been particularly attractive to global retailers since the late 1990s. Unfortunately, some have found the Asian market problematic. Lane Crawford (a Hong Kong retailer), U.S.-based Kmart, and the French group Galeries Lafayette have withdrawn from Singapore. Wal-Mart also experienced difficulty in Asia. The two discount stores that Wal-Mart opened in Hong Kong, with the Thai conglomerate Charoen Pokphand, failed, and the partnership was dissolved. However, Wal-Mart's second attempt, opening two stores in Schezhen with a pair of Chinese partners, is performing better.

J.C. Penney, a U.S.-based department store chain, is another retailer that discovered the advantages of local partners. After unsuccessful forays into Indonesia, Chile, and the Philippines, Penney bought control of Lojas Renner, a regional Brazilian chain with twenty-one stores. Unlike its earlier attempts at internationalization, here Penney kept the Brazilian management and store name. The joint venture has blended Penney's knowledge of merchandising and its access to capital with Renner's local-market know-how. For example, Renner issues charge cards to customers whose family income may only be $150 a month and offers interest-free installment plans. Customers can ring a bell in the dressing room to call a sales attendant if they want to try a different size—an amenity Penney doesn't offer at home. Two years later, the venture had doubled its number of stores. With sales per square foot in Renner above those in their stores in the United States, Penney is examining how it might learn some lessons from Renner.[41]

A recent study reveals competence in retail logistics to be a major determinant of success for large retailers that move abroad. This competence allows these retailers to contain costs, shorten procurement times, and respond more quickly to customer needs.[42] Still, a retailer's size within a national market remains critical to gaining many economies and sustaining competitive advantage. In turn, size remains a function of the population and its spending power, as well as of the number of competitors a retailer encounters. Not all attempts to internationalize have been successful for retailers. In 2002, British retailer Marks & Spencer announced that it would be refocusing operations on the company's core U.K. business, selling and closing stores in the United States and continental Europe.[43]

Direct Marketing

Although the United States is the global leader in direct marketing, the market is also growing elsewhere. Whereas in the United States the direct-marketing segment is dominated by specialty catalogs, in France as in other European countries the market is dominated by general-merchandise catalogs. But U.S. direct-marketing companies can do well in foreign markets such as France. U.S. mail-order firms account for 25 percent of French foreign direct-marketing sales, second behind German companies, who took the largest share with 50 percent.[44]

The complex, multilayered Japanese distribution system encouraged some foreign companies to go directly to consumers. The growth in direct marketing in Japan is supported by a number of demographic and technical factors. The dramatic increase in employed women from 50 percent to 75 percent has resulted in fewer available shopping hours. The introduction of toll-free telephone and cable has also made it easier to shop at home. One of the most successful direct-marketing companies in Japan is Amway. With sales of $1.5 billion in 1999, the company employs approximately 1.1 million independent distributors, using a direct-sales model.[45]

Direct marketing plays a role in emerging markets as well but faces a number of challenges. In Russia, direct marketing tends to be viewed negatively as one of those new-fangled Western business concepts. Bertelsmann, the German-based media company, put its planned Book Club India project on hold after realizing that a segmentation exercise on India's twenty-three largest urban markets yielded a total of only 297,000 potential club members, too small to pursue the opportunity. [46] The infrastructure in most developing countries in terms of delivery and telecommunications lags behind markets in the developed world. Still, urban consumers in Brazil receive an average of ten direct-mail pieces a month. Telemarketing is hampered by a lack of phones (only one in ten Brazilians has a phone), but Brazil is nevertheless a large market and tends to be ahead of the rest of Latin America in direct marketing.

In the late 1990s, direct-sales firms such as Amway, Avon, and Mary Kay proved highly successful in many emerging markets. The success of these companies was due in large part to their ability to recruit independent sales persons to promote their products. Many people in developing countries saw this as an opportunity to supplement meager incomes. Many local clones emerged, and in China, these companies often proved fraudulent, defrauding their salespeople of their investment. Overnight, in April 1998, the Chinese authorities denied the right to sell door-to-door. The only way for Amway, Avon, and Mary Kay to salvage their investments was to agree to market their products through regular retail stores.[47] However, under pressure from the U.S. government, China agreed to lift sanctions on direct selling by January 1, 2003.

Online Retailing

The Internet has opened an entirely new channel for retailers and manufacturers to sell their products. The United States is the undisputed leader in online retailing or e-commerce. It still leads the world in low-cost Internet connections, and phone service in the United States can be unmeasured for local calls. In many other countries, this is not the case. A lengthy Internet connection can turn into an expensive shopping foray, particularly if nothing is purchased. U.S.-based online retailers, such as Amazon.com, have expanded abroad with specific "stores" in the U.K. and Germany. Most online retailing, however, crosses borders; consumers can reach any store anywhere with a legitimate Internet address.

In other countries, online retailing continues to expand. In Germany, surveys found that some 27 percent of all Internet users had ordered or purchased a product online by 1999.[48] However, Japan's estimated online revenue for 2000 was US$1.8 billion, only 6 percent of U.S. revenues. Sales in Japan continue to be crippled by consumers' security-conscious fears of purchasing by credit card online. E-tailers are further hit by exorbitant charges and cumbersome paperwork required of them by credit card companies. The Japanese also avoid credit cards because of the 10 to 14 percent charges on balances unpaid for more than 2 months. These charges appear outrageous compared to the 0.05 percent that the Japanese earn on savings accounts.[49]

Not deterred by these problems, start-up company Thinkamerican.com signed up several boutique brands in its bid to launch a cultural portal linking shoppers in Japan to American brands. One advantage of cyberspace sales in Japan is the opportunity to avoid having to buy or rent any of the country's prohibitively expensive real estate, while still tapping into the world's second largest economy.[50]

Online retailing requires a large connected population. As many e-commerce executives know, online retailing also depends on a solid fulfillment cycle that delivers the ordered merchandise quickly into the hands of the consumer. When this is to take place across borders, issues of taxation and tariffs may still remain, slowing down delivery systems. Many foreign markets do not yet offer reliable fulfillment centers for use by small online retailers. However, the trend is clearly in the direction of resolving this problem. Once this has occurred, many more consumers will reach into online stores in faraway places, potentially turning every online marketer into an international retailer.

READ MORE ABOUT IT: Check out "Cultural Portal" under *Supplementary Readings* on our website.

Information Technology

The worldwide retail industry is moving rapidly toward the use of electronic checkouts that scan the bar codes on products, speeding up checkout, reducing errors, and eliminating the need to put a price label on each item. Electronic checkout also improves a store's ability to keep track of inventory and of purchase behavior. Some stores are experimenting with self-scanning as a way to speed up checkout and reduce costs. Royal Ahold of Holland, the parent company of Stop & Shop in the United States, introduced this practice in Europe and is now experimenting with it in the U.S. market. The same applies to Shaw's, another U.S.-based supermarket chain with a European parent, J. Sainsbury of the U.K.[51] Modern retailing systems are clearly emerging in many parts of the world, and their diffusion takes place very rapidly. This pushes the retailing environment in many countries toward a world standard that is best in class wherever it evolves.

Smuggling

Smuggling has recently emerged as a serious challenge to many international marketers.[52] Polish customs estimated that in 1993, consumer products smuggled into Poland were equal to 20 percent of legal imports. In the same year, Indian customs credited the smuggling of gold, silver, and consumer durables into India with supporting a black-market economy equivalent to 20 percent of the national GDP. In 1995 about half of all computer sales in Brazil involved smuggled computers. Today, smuggling accounts for an estimated one-third of all cigarettes sold worldwide.

Smuggling is the illegal transport of products across national borders. Smuggling may involve the distribution of illicit products such as illegal drugs and arms. It also encompasses the illegal distribution of products that are legal to sell and use, such as computers, cosmetics, and VCRs. In the 1990s the products most commonly smuggled into Mexico were consumer electronics, food and alcohol, clothing, automobiles and auto parts, and toys and games. It is the smuggling of legal products that concerns us here.

Smuggling is most prevalent in developing countries and in the transitional economies of the former Soviet bloc. It arose in response to traditionally high tariffs and low quotas placed on imported goods. For example, a smuggled VCR in Mexico could sell for US$200, whereas its legally imported equivalent would sell for US$600. With the move toward trade liberalization in the emerging world, we would expect smuggling to fade as tariffs and quotas decline.

Although smuggling has decreased in some countries, it hasn't been eradicated. There are two main reasons for this. First, trade liberalization is not universal or complete. The tariff levels on many products in many countries still promote smuggling. Second, tariffs are not the only taxes that smugglers can avoid. They can also avoid sales taxes and value-added taxes. If smugglers are to become legitimate importers, they must declare themselves to customs. This enables governments to identify them and demand income taxes from them. Therefore, the lowering of tariffs decreases the cost advantage that smugglers previously enjoyed but doesn't completely remove it.

For many years, international marketers viewed smuggling as a benign and even positive phenomenon. In some cases, smugglers distributed products to otherwise inaccessible markets. In other cases, smugglers delivered products to consumers at a considerably lower price, supporting greater sales and mar-

Serbia's prime minister watches as police destroy crates of contraband cigarettes. The street value of the confiscated cigarettes was estimated at US$60 million.

ket growth. In either case, the international firm stood to gain by realizing greater sales revenue as the result of the smuggling of its products.

In fact, a recent analysis of the records of major international cigarette companies reveals that many executives in these firms knew that certain international distributors were involved in large-scale smuggling operations and cooperated in some ways to assist them. Between 1997 and 2001, three managers of British American Tobacco pleaded guilty or were convicted of smuggling.[53] Several countries in Europe and the developing world have initiated lawsuits against cigarette companies to recover taxes lost as a result of the smuggling of cigarettes. The behavior of the international cigarette industry is likely to make governments all the more skeptical of other international firms that claim ignorance of smuggling operations.

Furthermore, the darker side of smuggling is becoming apparent. In the past 10 years, smuggling has evolved along lines of traditional organized crime. It has become more centralized and violent. As margins are squeezed by trade liberalization, smugglers have sought ways to protect their cost advantage, such as counterfeiting the products they previously bought. Some smugglers who transport consumer goods into developing countries have allied themselves with drug cartels to launder drug money. This phenomenon has caused firms such as Hewlett-Packard, Ford, General Motors, Sony, Westinghouse, Whirlpool, and General Electric to be invited by the U.S. Attorney General to answer questions about how the distribution of their products may have become involved in the laundering of drug money.[54] In the future, both host and home governments may require international marketers to take more precautions to ensure that their products are not distributed through these illegal channels.

READ MORE ABOUT IT: Check out "U.S. Companies Tangled in Web of Drug Dollars" under *Supplemental Readings* on our website.

▶ *Conclusions*

To be successful in the global marketplace, a company needs market acceptance among buyers and market access via distribution channels. To achieve access, the firm must select the most suitable channel members, keeping in mind that substantial differences exist among countries on both the wholesale and the retail levels. There are major differences among countries in distribution. Local habits and cultures, legal restrictions, and infrastructure can all affect the success of distribution in a new country.

Proper distribution policies have to allow for the local market's buying and shopping habits. A company should not expect the same distribution density, channel alignment, or channel length in all its markets. The logistics system must reflect both local market situations and the difficulties inherent in moving products longer distances. Finding willing and suitable channel members may prove extremely difficult. Access may be achieved only by forging special alliances with present channel members or local companies that have access to them. Once the distribution system has been designed, participants still need to be motivated and controlled to ensure that the firm's marketing strategy is properly executed. Increasingly, governments may hold international firms liable for smuggled products, forcing marketers to control their channels better.

There is a major technological revolution taking place with online retailing and the widespread use of the Internet by consumers. These trends are

To assess distribution strategies for your product and explore local channels, continue with the *Country Market Report* on our website.

likely to reshape the global distribution system and the way companies tap into markets all over the world. Access to the Internet makes it easier for business or household customers to tap into foreign suppliers. This has far-reaching consequences for all global marketers and needs to be taken into consideration as the new world economy adapts to the Internet challenge over the next few years.

Review Questions

1. Your firm is just beginning to export industrial paints. What factors would you consider in deciding whether to use either an export management company or an export agent rather than direct exporting?

2. Define distribution density, channel length, and channel alignment. Give at least one example of how each can differ between countries.

3. Define piggybacking. When would this distribution strategy be attractive?

4. List and explain the five "jobs" related to global logistics management.

5. What factors support—and what factors discourage—direct marketing in different countries?

Questions for Discussion

1. You have been assigned the task of selecting distributors in Malaysia to handle your firm's line of car batteries. What criteria will you use to select among the twelve possible distributors?

2. The performance of your agents and distributors in South America has been poor over the past 3 years. List possible ways in which to improve the management of these agents and distributors.

3. Given the trends in global retailing, what distribution strategies should a worldwide manufacturer of women's clothing consider?

4. Your firm has just entered the Polish market for bottled water. The major distributor is owned by a competitive producer of bottled water. What strategies can you use to gain access to this market?

5. Compare and contrast, from the manufacturer's point of view, the problems that parallel imports cause (Chapter 12) with those caused by smuggling. If governments increasingly restrict international marketers from stopping parallel imports, can these same marketers be held responsible for products' being smuggled? Explain your reasoning.

For Further Reading

Arnold, David. "Seven Rules of International Distribution," *Harvard Business Review*, November–December 2000: 131–137.

Gillespie, Kate, and J. Brad McBride. "Smuggling in Emerging Markets." *Columbia Journal of World Business*, Winter 1996: 40–54.

Kim, Keysuk, and Changho Oh. "On Distributor Commitment in Marketing Channels for Industrial Products: Contrast Between the United States and Japan." *Journal of International Marketing* 10, 1 (2002): 72–97.

McDonald, William J. "International Direct Marketing in a Rapidly Changing World." *Direct Marketing*, March 1, 1999: 44

Case 13.1 | *Giants in Asia*

The world's two largest retailers have targeted Asia with varying results. U.S.-based Wal-Mart and France's Carrefour both offer large stores stocked with groceries and general merchandise. Their entry into new national markets is invariably a shock to local retailers, who suddenly see the status quo of decades upset by these international competitors.

Government officials in China have credited Wal-Mart with revitalizing the retail sector. For years, government-owned retailers offered the same limited products, while employees took naps on the counters. When Wal-Mart opened its new store underneath the soccer stadium in the city of Dalian, the store was soon packed to capacity. Still Wal-Mart chose to enter China slowly in order to learn as it went along. When it opened its first stores, customers arrived on bicycles and made only small purchases. Wal-Mart also discovered that it couldn't sell a year's supply of soy sauce to customers who lived in small apartments. Furthermore, the firm faced a variety of government restrictions. Foreign retailers needed government-backed partners, and cities often restricted the size of stores. In response to these challenges, Wal-Mart invited government officials to visit its headquarters in the United States, donated to local charities, and even built a school. Wal-Mart sourced nearly all its products locally, and nearly all employees were Chinese. To understand Chinese consumption patterns better, Wal-Mart's American manager walked the streets to see what the Chinese were buying.

Carrefour, which had 9,000 stores in 27 countries, began its Asian operation in Taiwan in 1989. Twelve years later it had opened 96 hypermarkets in Asia, including stores in China and Korea. Carrefour entered Indonesia at the height of the Asian financial crisis in 1998, opening 6 stores in the capital city of Jakarta in just 2 years. The new stores compete on selection and low prices and challenge both open-air markets and the city's small, Chinese-owned neighborhood grocers. The 280-member Indonesian Retail Merchant Association has urged Jakarta to impose zoning restrictions on hypermarkets. Carrefour is also a threat the larger, locally established grocery chains. One such chain, Hero supermarkets, admitted it couldn't compete with Carrefour on overall prices and chose instead to discount high-visibility products such as rice and to offer a variety of promotional specials. Hero also competes on freshness and has an excellent reputation among consumers for its produce.

In 2001 Carrefour entered the Japanese market, investing $150 million to set up its first three stores. Carrefour had avoided Japan previously because of its high land prices. Although a depressed Japanese economy had lowered land prices, it meant the stores were opening in a climate of slow retail sales. Like Wal-Mart in China, Carrefour found itself making adaptations to local culture. Within days of opening in Japan, the stores began selling more vegetables in packages of two or three, as other Japanese grocers do, instead of by weight. To provide competitive prices, Carrefour plans to buy 54 percent of its products directly from Japanese suppliers. This would circumvent the cumbersome wholesaling system of Japan, but it would require convincing Japanese producers to abandon long-standing relationships with their distributors—something that other foreign retailers have had difficulty doing. In the meantime, Japanese grocery chains are restructuring and moving more to direct sourcing themselves.

Both Indonesian and Japanese competitors can take some hope in the fact that Carrefour had to retreat from the Hong Kong market in September 2000. The company cited stiff competition and restrictive development laws. Analysts suggested that the hypermarkets were unable to attract enough customers, who were unwilling to go out of their way to do their daily shopping.

Discussion Questions

1. What competitive advantages do foreign retailers such as Wal-Mart and Carrefour enjoy when they enter Asian markets?
2. What are some possible competitive advantages of local retailers?
3. Why do you think governments regulate retailing practices?

Sources: David Kruger, "Retailing—Challenge at the Checkout," *Far Eastern Economic Review*, January 18, 2001: 38; Peter Wonacott, "Wal-Mart Finds Market Footing in China," *Wall Street Journal*, July 17, 2000, p. A31; and Warren Caragata, "Attack of the Hypermarkets," *Business Week*, May 22, 2000: 104.

| Case 13.2 | *Who's to Blame?* |

In 2000 and 2001, several European countries, including Germany, Italy, France, Belgium, and Finland, filed suits against U.S. tobacco giants Philip Morris and R.J. Reynolds alleging that the two firms had cooperated with smugglers of cigarettes. The countries sought compensation for unpaid custom duties as well as unpaid value-added taxes. The European Union estimated that these losses came to billions of dollars. European governments weren't the only losers. An estimated third of all cigarettes sold in the world are smuggled. Malaysia has estimated that its losses in taxes due to smuggled cigarettes amounted to US$1.3 billion in 2000 alone. These cigarettes arrived mainly from Indonesia and Thailand and were brought in under the aegis of crime syndicates. Malaysia, like most other countries, taxed cigarettes heavily not only as a source of revenue but also as a proven method for discouraging smoking.

At the same time in India, British American Tobacco (BAT) was facing an exposé resulting from the public examination of its internal communiqués. In 1993, BAT products were legally restricted in India to duty-free shops and hotels but were in fact smuggled into India on an extensive scale from the United Arab Emirates. A memorandum issued by a top BAT executive discussed how the firm could advertise its brands without calling attention to the fact that most of the cigarettes were smuggled into the country. The memorandum went on to discuss contingency plans if any of the normal smuggling channels were shut down. When the *Business Standard* called BAT for comment, the company sent the following reply:

> . . . where governments are not prepared to address the underlying causes of the smuggling problem (excessive tax on tobacco), businesses such as ours are faced with a dilemma. If the demand for our products [is] not met, consumers will either switch to our competitor brands or there will be the kind of dramatic growth in counterfeit products that we have seen in Asian markets. . . . [W]here any government is unwilling to act or their efforts are unsuccessful, we act, completely within the law, on the basis that our brands will be available alongside those of our competitors in the smuggled as well as the legitimate market.

Fuji and Kodak, on the other hand, were dis-mayed at the smuggling of their film into China, where it sold for far less than it did through the firms' official channels. Photosensitive products were among the goods most commonly smuggled into China. Retailers carried the smuggled products to increase their margins and boost sales. The smuggled film was easily identifiable. No Chinese language, required by law, appeared on the package. Instead, the packages of film were labeled in English, Russian, Indonesian, Vietnamese, Korean, or Arabic. The Chinese government assured Fuji and Kodak that they were taking the situation seriously and were beginning to stem the tide of smuggling.

China recently introduced severe penalties for smuggling, including life sentences and even the death penalty. China's smuggling law not only targets smugglers but also encompasses anyone who buys from smugglers. They too can be charged with smuggling. Vietnam is another country that has taken serious steps against smugglers. In 1999 the head of a private company and the chief of the smuggling investigation bureau of Ho Chi Minh City's customs department were sentenced to death for smuggling. The case involved seventy-four people who were charged with smuggling $71.3 million worth of electrical goods and home appliances into Vietnam.

Discussion Questions

1. Why would BAT cooperate with smugglers?
2. How could smuggling hurt Fuji and Kodak?
3. Why do you think some countries are introducing stiff penalties for smuggling?
4. Whom do you think should be held responsible for smuggling—the manufacturer, the smugglers themselves, the retailers, or the final consumer?

Sources: "Belgium, Finland Join EU Lawsuit Against U.S. Tobacco Companies," *Associated Press Newswires*, February 21, 2001; "Government Cracks Down on Smuggling Channels," *South China Morning Post*, October 16, 2000, p. 6; Surajeet Das Gupta, "Did BAT Organize Cigarette Smuggling into India?" *Business Standard*, December 4, 2000, p. 1; "Cigarette Smuggling Costs Malaysia $1.3 B a Year," *Times of India*, November 26, 2000; and "Vietnam Official to Stand Trial for Car Smuggling," *Dow Jones International News*, September 11, 2000.

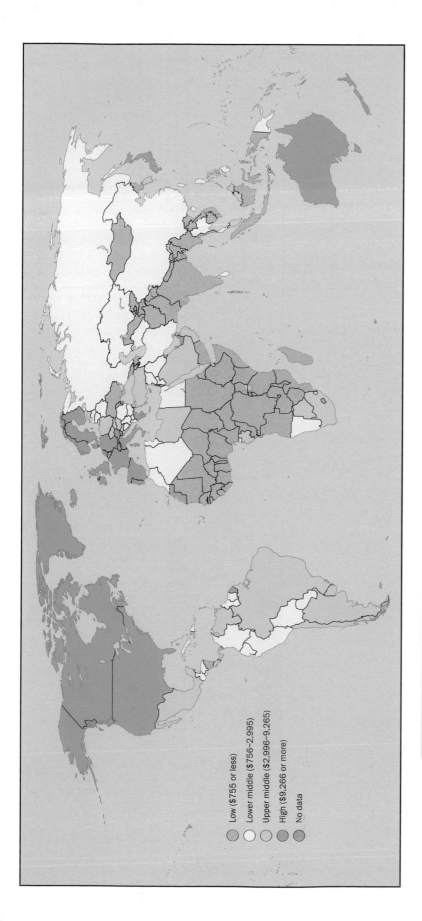

Income per person

GNI per capita, 2000

Gross national income (formerly referred to as GNP)—the sum of gross value added by resident producers (plus taxes less subsidies) and net primary income from nonresident sources—divided by midyear population.

Map legend:
- Low ($755 or less)
- Lower middle ($756–2,995)
- Upper middle ($2,996–9,265)
- High ($9,266 or more)
- No data

Distribution of world population among economies grouped by GNI per capita
- 15% — Low ($755 or less)
- 11% — Lower middle ($756–2,995)
- 34% — Upper middle ($2,996–9,265)
- 41% — High ($9,266 or more)

GNI per capita, 2000, $
- East Asia & Pacific: 1,060
- Europe & Central Asia: 2,010
- Latin America & Caribbean: 3,670
- Middle East & North Africa: 2,090
- South Asia: 440
- Sub-Saharan Africa: 470
- High income: 27,680

(scale: 0 10,000 20,000 30,000)

GNI per capita, 2000, $

	Economies	GNI $ billions 2000	Population millions 2000	GNI per capita $ 2000
Low ($755 or less)	63	997	2,460	410
Lower middle ($756–2,995)	54	2,324	2,048	1,130
Upper middle ($2,996–9,265)	38	3,001	647	4,640
High ($9,266 or more)	52	24,994	903	27,680
World	207	31,315	6,057	5,170

Source: Adapted from the *2002 World Bank Atlas.* Reprinted by the permission of the World Bank.

Income growth

GDP per capita growth, 1990–2000

The average annual percentage change in a country's real GDP per capita. To exclude the effects of inflation, constant price GDP is used in calculating the growth rate.

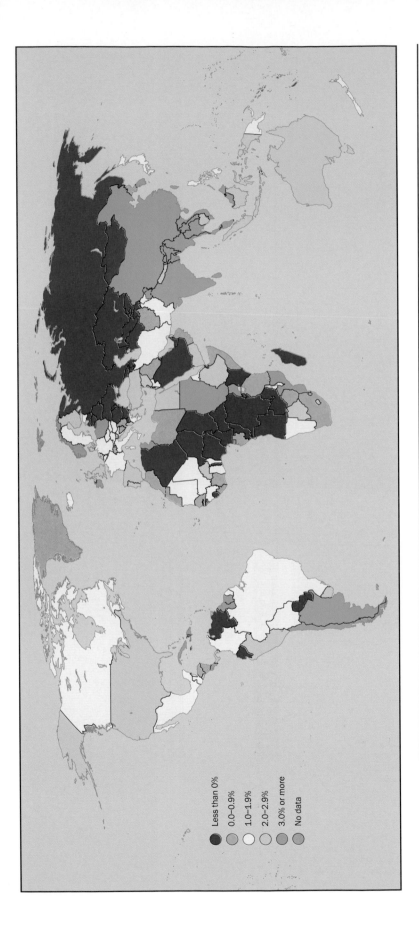

Less than 0%
0.0–0.9%
1.0–1.9%
2.0–2.9%
3.0% or more
No data

GDP per capita annual growth rate, 1990–2000, percent

	Economies	GNI $ billions 2000	Population millions 2000	GNI per capita $ 2000
Less than 0%	53	943	752	1,250
0.0–0.9%	17	496	166	2,980
1.0–1.9%	41	12,578	1,122	11,210
2.0–2.9%	31	13,550	975	13,890
3.0% or more	36	3,618	2,933	1,230
No data	29	129	108	1,190

Index of GDP per capita, 1980–2000, 1980 = 100

350
250
150
50
0

1980   1990   2000

East Asia & Pacific
Latin America & Caribbean
Middle East & North Africa
South Asia
Sub-Saharan Africa

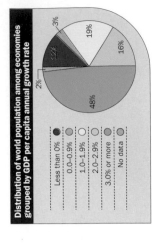

Distribution of world population among economies grouped by GDP per capita annual growth rate

2%
3%
12%
19%
48%
16%

Less than 0%
0.0–0.9%
1.0–1.9%
2.0–2.9%
3.0% or more
No data

Source: Adapted from the *2002 World Bank Atlas.* Reprinted by the permission of the World Bank.

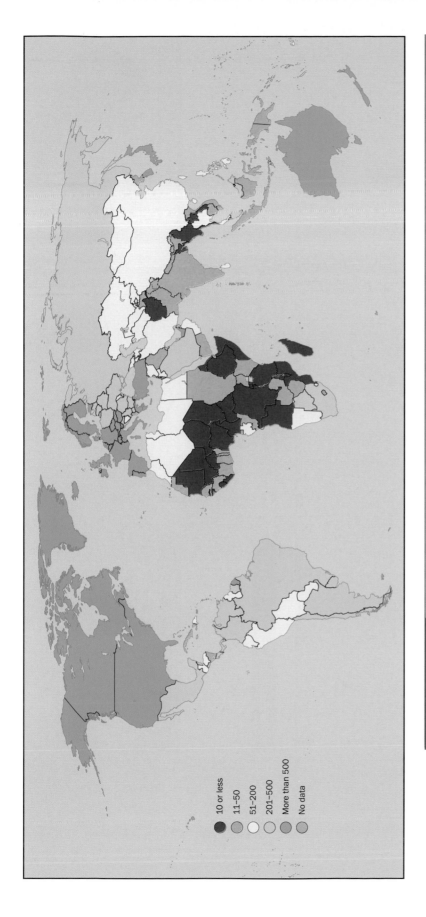

Telephones

Telephone lines and mobile phones per 1,000 people, 2000

Telephone lines connecting a customer's equipment to the public switched telephone network and mobile phones, per 1,000 people.

Distribution of world population among economies grouped by telephones per 1,000 people

- 10 or less
- 11–50
- 51–200
- 201–500
- More than 500
- No data

11%
17%
29%
13%
30%

Fixed lines and mobile telephones per 1,000 people, 2000

East Asia & Pacific	171
Europe & Central Asia	314
Latin America & Caribbean	271
Middle East & North Africa	122
South Asia	31
Sub-Saharan Africa	32
High income	1,136

0   400   800   1200

Fixed lines and mobile telephones per 1,000 people, 2000

	Economies	GNI $ billions 2000	Population millions 2000	GNI per capita $ 2000
10 or less	27	162	643	250
11–50	36	810	1,758	460
51–200	42	1,845	1,806	1,020
201–500	42	2,727	803	3,390
More than 500	55	25,763	1,044	24,690
No data	5	9	3	2,640

Map legend:
- 10 or less
- 11–50
- 51–200
- 201–500
- More than 500
- No data

Source: Adapted from the *2002 World Bank Atlas*. Reprinted by the permission of the World Bank.

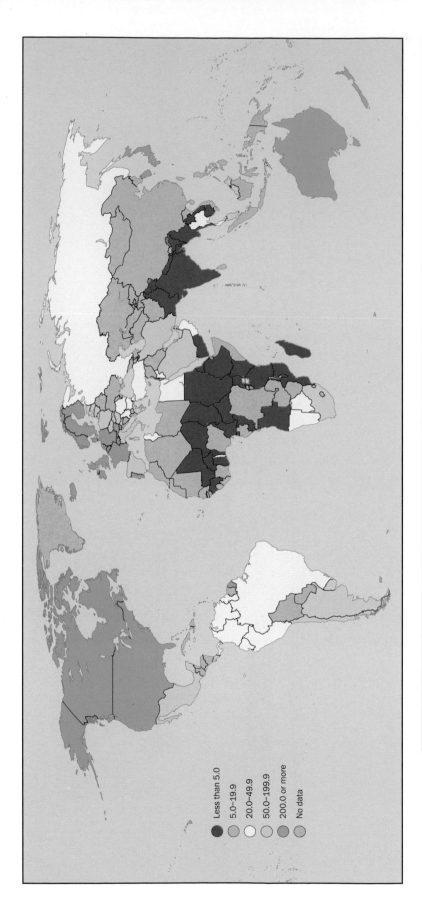

Less than 5.0
5.0–19.9
20.0–49.9
50.0–199.9
200.0 or more
No data

Personal computers

Personal computers per 1,000 people, 2000

The estimated number of self-contained computers designed to be used by a single individual, per 1,000 people.

Personal computers per 1,000 people, 2000	Economies	GNI $ billions 2000	Population millions 2000	GNI per capita $ 2000
Less than 5.0	30	684	1,729	400
5.0–19.9	32	1,583	2,021	780
20.0–49.9	24	1,660	684	2,430
50.0–199.9	38	3,704	507	7,300
200.0 or more	29	23,430	834	28,090
No data	54	254	282	900

Personal computers per 1,000 people, 2000

East Asia & Pacific	21.7
Europe & Central Asia	45.4
Latin America & Caribbean	43.6
Middle East & North Africa	31.2
South Asia	4.2
Sub-Saharan Africa	9.2
High income	392.7

0   100   200   300   400   500

Distribution of world population among economies grouped by personal computers per 1,000 people

5%
14%
8%
11%
33%
29%

- Less than 5.0
- 5.0–19.9
- 20.0–49.9
- 50.0–199.9
- 200.0 or more
- No data

Source: Adapted from the *2002 World Bank Atlas.* Reprinted by the permission of the World Bank.

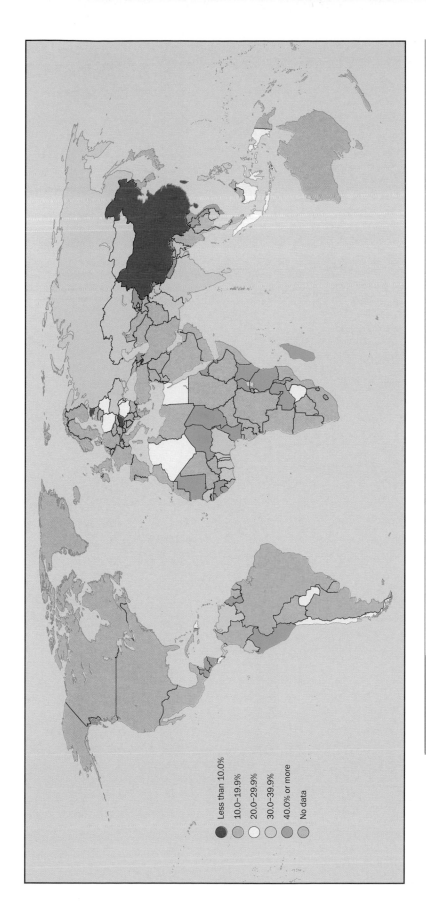

Poverty

Population below the national poverty line, 1984–2000

The percentage of the population living below the national poverty line.

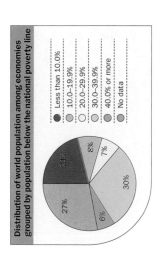

Distribution of world population among economies grouped by population below the national poverty line

- Less than 10.0%
- 10.0–19.9%
- 20.0–29.9%
- 30.0–39.9%
- 40.0% or more
- No data

Percentage of the population below the national poverty line in selected developing economies, 1984–2000

Economy	Percentage
Azerbaijan	68.1
Brazil	17.4
China	4.6
Egypt, Arab Rep.	22.9
India	35.0
Vietnam	50.9
Zambia	86.0

Percentage of the population below the national poverty line, 1984–2000

Economies		GNI $ billions 2000	Population millions 2000	GNI per capita $ 2000
Less than 10.0%	3	1,115	1,274	880
10.0–19.9%	12	1,745	499	3,500
20.0–29.9%	13	615	427	1,440
30.0–39.9%	21	1,151	1,836	630
40.0% or more	31	200	373	540
No data	127	26,489	1,649	16,060

Population below the national poverty line, 1984–2000

Map legend:
- Less than 10.0%
- 10.0–19.9%
- 20.0–29.9%
- 30.0–39.9%
- 40.0% or more
- No data

Source: Adapted from the *2002 World Bank Atlas.* Reprinted by the permission of the World Bank.

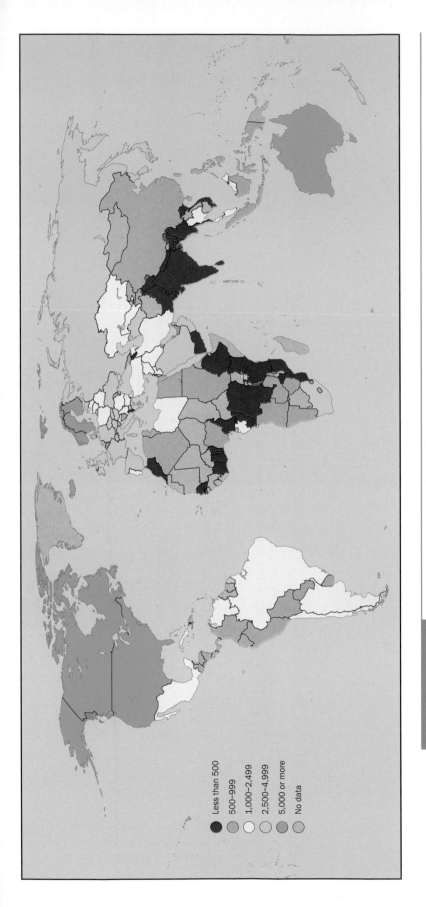

Energy use

Energy use per capita, 1999

Annual consumption of commercial energy divided by the population, expressed in kilograms of oil equivalent.

Energy use per capita, 1999, kilograms of oil equivalent

	Economies	GNI $ billions 2000	Population millions 2000	GNI per capita $ 2000
Less than 500	24	750	1,785	420
500–999	30	1,767	2,014	880
1,000–2,499	29	2,621	785	3,340
2,500–4,999	33	14,373	883	16,280
5,000 or more	15	11,651	372	31,280
No data	76	152	218	700

Energy use per capita, 1999, kilograms of oil equivalent

	GNI per capita ($)
East Asia & Pacific	920
Europe & Central Asia	2,628
Latin America & Caribbean	1,171
Middle East & North Africa	1,279
South Asia	441
Sub-Saharan Africa	671
High income	5,448

0   2,000   4,000   6,000

Distribution of world population among economies grouped by energy use per capita

- ● Less than 500
- ● 500–999
- ○ 1,000–2,499
- ● 2,500–4,999
- ● 5,000 or more
- ● No data

29%
4%
6%
15%
13%
33%

Map legend:
- ● Less than 500
- ● 500–999
- ○ 1,000–2,499
- ○ 2,500–4,999
- ● 5,000 or more
- ● No data

Source: Adapted from the *2002 World Bank Atlas.* Reprinted by the permission of the World Bank.

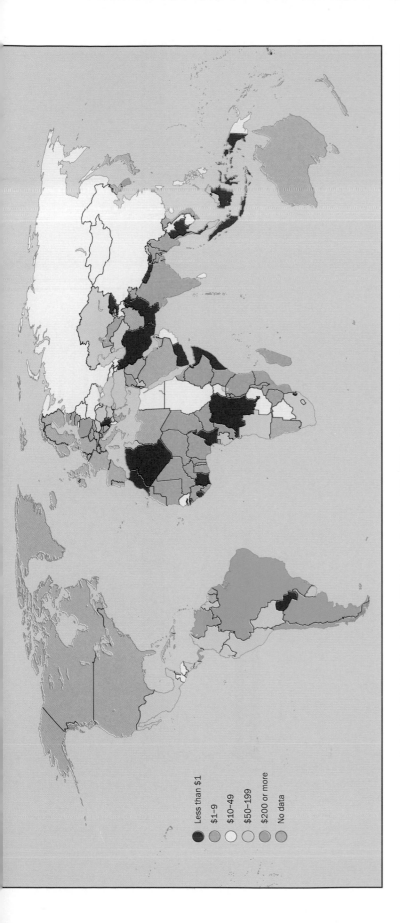

Private capital flows

Net private capital flows per capita, 2000

Net private debt and nondebt flows to developing economies, including commercial bank lending, bonds, other private credits, foreign direct investment, and portfolio equity investment, divided by population.

Net private capital flows per capita, 2000 and 2001, $ billions

● 2000 ○ 2001

Region	2000	2001
East Asia & Pacific		65.7
Europe & Central Asia	45.0 / 45.4	
Latin America & Caribbean	22.5	
	69.4	97.3
Middle East & North Africa	1.1 / 4.3	
South Asia	9.3 / 4.3	
Sub-Saharan Africa	7.1 / 14.5	

Scale: 0   40   80   120

Distribution of world population among economies grouped by net private capital flows per capita

● Less than $1 — 11%
● $1–9 — 29%
○ $10–49 — 29%
○ $50–199 — 7%
● $200 or more — 6%
● No data — 17%

Net private capital flows per capita, 2000, $

Economies		GNI $ billions 2000	Population millions 2000	GNI per capita $ 2000
Less than $1	25	560	696	810
$1–9	32	684	1,747	390
$10–49	28	1,655	1,779	930
$50–199	29	1,299	440	2,950
$200 or more	23	1,803	373	4,840
No data	70	25,314	1,022	24,770

Map legend:
● Less than $1
● $1–9
○ $10–49
○ $50–199
● $200 or more
● No data

Source: Adapted from the *2002 World Bank Atlas.* Reprinted by the permission of the World Bank.

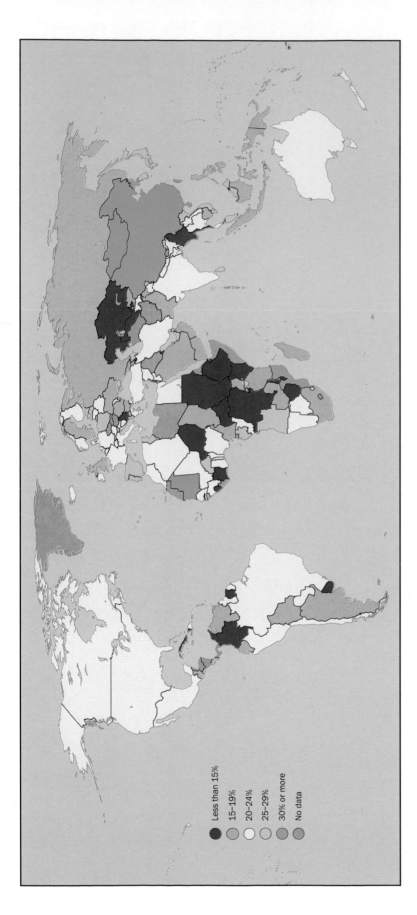

Investment

Gross capital formation as a share of GDP, 2000

Outlays on additions to the fixed assets of an economy plus net changes in the level of inventories, as a percentage of gross domestic product.

Map legend:
- Less than 15%
- 15–19%
- 20–24%
- 25–29%
- 30% or more
- No data

Gross capital formation as a share of GDP, 2000, percent

Economies	GNI $ billions 2000	Population millions 2000	GNI per capita $ 2000
Less than 15%	25	277	409	680
15–19%	43	3,239	1,071	3,020
20–24%	55	20,083	2,687	7,470
25–29%	26	6,246	447	13,970
30% or more	24	1,328	1,346	990
No data	34	142	97	1,470

Gross capital formation as a share of GDP in selected developing economies, 2000, percent

Argentina	16
Brazil	21
China	37
India	24
Korea, Rep.	29
Mexico	23
Russian Federation	17

(scale: 0 10 20 30 40)

Distribution of world population among economies grouped by gross capital formation as a share of GDP

- Less than 15% — 2%
- 15–19% — 44%
- 20–24% — 7%
- 25–29% — 22%
- 30% or more — 18%
- No data — 7%

Source: Adapted from the *2002 World Bank Atlas.* Reprinted by the permission of the World Bank.

Notes

[1]Marc Lifsher, "Will Venezuelans Shun Mom and Pop for the Hypermarket?" *Wall Street Journal*, June 28, 2001: A13.

[2]"Get Ready, Export Intermediaries Use Internet to Prepare for 21st Century," *Journal of Commerce*, August 19, 1998: 5.

[3]Ibid.

[4]*Retailing in the European Single Market 1993*, Table EUR1a.

[5]*European Marketing Data and Statistics*, 32nd ed. (Euromonitor Publications, 1997), Table 1203.

[6]"Marketing in Japan—Taking Aim," *The Economist*, April 24, 1993: 74.

[7]*International Marketing Data & Statistics* (Euromonitor Publications, 1996), Table 1201.

[8]"Nordica and Salomon Put the Boots In," *Financial Times*, August 30, 1990: 12.

[9]Warren J. Keegan, *Multinational Marketing Management* (Englewood Cliffs, NJ: Prentice-Hall, 1989), p. 175.

[10]"Revolution in Japanese Retailing," *Fortune*, February 7, 1994: 143, 146.

[11]"Seiko Epson Clones Strategy of U.S. Rival," *Nikkei Weekly*, January 17, 1994: 8.

[12]"Pepsi Wins Its Battle with Perrier over Marketing," *Financial Times*, December 18, 1992: 18.

[13]"Delta Dairy Streamlined Food Producer," *Financial Times*, July 8, 1993: 11.

[14]S. Tamer Cavusgil, "The Importance of Distributor Training at Caterpillar," *Industrial Marketing Management* 19 (1990): 5.

[15]Allan J. Magrath and Kenneth G. Hardy, "Avoiding the Pitfalls in Managing Distribution Channels," *Business Horizons*, September–October 1987: 31.

[16]Keysuk Kim and Changho Oh, "On Distributor Commitment in Marketing Channels for Industrial Products: Contrast Between the United States and Japan," *Journal of International Marketing* 10, 1 (2002): 89.

[17]David Arnold, "Seven Rules of International Distribution," *Harvard Business Review*, November–December 2000: 132–133.

[18]David P. Baron, "Integrated Strategy, Trade Policy, and Global Competition," *California Management Review* 39, 2 (Winter 1997): 169.

[19]"American Standard Succeeds in Korea by Outflanking Local Firms' Lockout," *Financial Times*, August 26, 1993: A6.

[20]"Two Drug Giants Are Expected to Set $70 Billion Merger," *New York Times*, November 4, 1999, p. C10.

[21]Donald G. McNeil Jr., "Coca-Cola Joins AIDS Fight in Africa," *New York Times*, June 21, 2001, p. 8.

[22]"Brasmotor's Success Draws Competitors," *Wall Street Journal*, July 11, 1997, p. A10.

[23]"You Can Make Money in Japan," *Fortune*, February 12, 1990: 45.

[24]"M&S Distribution Deal Could Cut Costs by 20 Percent," *Supply Management*, June 24, 1999: 12.

[25]"Haulers Urge Brussels to Curb Lorry Bans," *Financial Times*, July 16, 1997: 4.

[26]Ibid.

[27]"Toshiba Sets Fast-forward System," *Electronic Buyer's News*, August 2, 1999: 10.

[28]"Microsoft Alters Distribution Chain for Europe," *Financial Times*, November 12, 1993: 20.

[29]Ilan Greenberg, "UPS Targets Logistics Business in Asia," *Wall Street Journal*, April 26, 2001, p. A17.

[30]Neil S. Novich, "Leading-Edge Distribution Strategies," *Journal of Business Strategy*, November–December 1990: 49.

[31]"Silent Enemy Stalks the Aisles," *Financial Times*, November 30, 1993: 15.

[32]"Europe's Smaller Shops Face Finis," *Wall Street Journal*, May 12, 1993, p. B1.

[33]Michael Porter, "What Is Strategy?" *Harvard Business Review*, November/December 1996: 65.

[34]"ІКЕА," *Times of London*, January 14, 1999, p. 26.

[35]"Shopping All Over the World," *The Economist*, June 19, 1999: 59.

[36]Alan D. Treadgold, "The Developing Internationalization of Retailing," *International Journal of Retail and Distribution Management* 18, 2 (1990): 5.

[37]David Luhnow, "Crossover Success," *Wall Street Journal*, August 31, 2001, p. A1.

[38]"Shopping All Over the World."

[39]Miriam Jordan, "Wal-Mart Gets Aggressive About Brazil," *Wall Street Journal*, May 25, 2001, p. A8.

[40]Ernest Beck, "Stores Told to Lift Prices in Germany," *Wall Street Journal*, September 11, 2000, p. A27.

[41]Miriam Jordan, "Penney Blends Two Business Cultures," *Wall Street Journal*, April 5, 2001, p. A15.

[42]Irena Vida, James Reardon, and Ann Fairhurst, "Determinants of International Retail Involvement: The Case of Large U.S. Retail Chains," *Journal of International Marketing* 8, 4 (2000): 37-60.

[43]Erin White, "Marks & Spencer Swung to Profit in Latest Year," *Wall Street Journal*, May 22, 2002.

[44]"France: Catalog Sales Market," U.S. Department of State, U.S. and Foreign Commercial Service, April 1998.

[45]"Amway Japan Announces Fiscal 1999 First Quarter," *PR Newswire*, July 14, 1999.

[46]"International Direct Marketing in a Rapidly Changing World," *Direct Marketing*, March 1, 1999: 44.

[47]"Amway Gets Okay to Operate in China," *Grand Rapids Press*, July 21, 1998, p. A1.

[48]"Germany: Europe's On-line Front Runner," *Communications Week International*, March 15, 199: 6.

[49]Ken Belson, "Net Shopping," *Business Week*, July 31, 2001: 64.

[50]Lisa Vickery, "E-Business: 'Cultural Portal' Could Translate Way to Profit," *Wall Street Journal*, February 12, 2001.

[51]"New Concepts Check Out: Self-scanning Reduces Lines, Personal Scanning Checks Out," *Boston Herald*, January 25, 1999, p. O27.

[52]This section is largely taken from Kate Gillespie and J. Brad McBride, "Smuggling in Emerging Markets: Global Implications," *Columbia Journal of World Business*, Winter 1996: 40–54.

[53]Maud S. Beelman, Duncan Campbell, Maria Teresa Ronderos, and Erik J. Schelzig, "Major Tobacco Multinational Implicated in Cigarette Smuggling, Tax Evasion, Documents Show," Investigative Report, The Center for Public Integrity, www.public-i.org/story_01_013100.htm.

[54]Lowell Bergman, "U.S. Companies Tangled in Web of Drug Dollars," *New York Times*, October 10, 2000, p. 1.

14 Global Promotion Strategies

Each Year the Goliaths of the civil aircraft industry face off at the Paris Air Show. America's Boeing Company and Europe's Airbus Industrie attempt not only to make sales but also to capture the imaginations of potential clients. Company representatives meet with major customers to discuss current products and establish the leads that will eventually result in sales of these big-ticket items. But promoting current products is not enough. The Paris Air Show is a time to unveil new ideas and present the company's vision of the future of flight. This vision, as well as actual products, will help establish the image of each company. In this global industry, corporate image is very important. Can the firm deliver on its promises of speed, economy in-cabin amenities, and innovative ideas?[1] International marketers in civil aircraft must communicate to potential customers that the answer is yes.

Global promotion strategies encompass a firm's marketing communications and include personal selling, sales promotion, public relations, and advertising. Managing the communications process for a single market is no easy task. And the task is even more difficult for global marketers, who must communicate to prospective customers in many national

Chapter Outline

Learning Objectives

*After studying this chapter, you
should be able to:*

▶ List the major factors that determine a firm's ability to use a
push or a pull promotion strategy
in different national markets.

▶ Contrast the benefits to the international marketer of using an
international sales force with those
of using local sales forces.

▶ Describe the impact that different purchasing behaviors, buying
criteria, languages, and negotiation styles can have on international selling.

▶ Explain the importance of
global account management.

▶ Describe how global marketers
can successfully utilize international trade fairs and consortia as
well as manage the international
bidding process.

▶ Cite examples of how sales promotions vary across cultures, and
suggest reasons for these differences.

▶ Note recent international trends
in sales promotions, sports sponsorships, telemarketing, and managing word-of-mouth.

▶ Give examples of international
public relations disasters, and suggest ways in which global marketers can promote the goodwill of
their firms.

markets. In the process, they struggle with different cultures, habits, and languages.

We begin this chapter by examining the cross-cultural implications of push strategies and pull strategies. We proceed to the challenge of developing a personal-selling effort on both the international and the local level, discussing differing sales practices as well as issues of recruitment and compensation of sales forces. Other promotion issues involving business-to-business and government sales are then discussed. We continue by exploring the global aspects of sales promotions, sports sponsorships, telemarketing, managing word-of-mouth, and public relations. (Advertising, a key element of the promotion mix, will be covered in detail in Chapter 15.)

▶ *Global Promotion Strategies*

How to manage the promotion mix globally is a critical question for many companies. Some firms do business in a certain way and do not rethink their promotion decisions when they internationalize. However, many companies find themselves in countries or situations that require an adjustment or a substantial change in their promotion mix. This section and the ones that follow are devoted to understanding how different international environments affect promotion mix decisions.

Pull versus Push Strategies

A **pull strategy** is characterized by a relatively greater dependence on promotion, including sales promotions and advertising, directed at the final buyer or end user for a product or service. Pull campaigns are typical for consumer-goods firms that target a large number of consumers. Pull campaigns are usually advisable when the product is widely used by consumers, when the channel is long, when the product is not very complex, and when self-service is the predominant shopping behavior. Increased or decreased reliance on pull campaigns for global markets depends on a number of factors. Most important are access to advertising media, channel length, and the leverage the company has with the distribution channel.

Marketers accustomed to having a large number of media available may find the choices limited in overseas markets. For many products, pull campaigns that rely heavily on advertising work only if access to electronic media, particularly television, is available. In some other countries, access to those media is restricted through time limits imposed by governments. Consequently, companies find it difficult to duplicate their promotional strategies when moving from an unregulated environment to more restricted environments.

Channel length is another major determinant of the feasibility of a pull campaign. Companies in consumer markets often face long channels. As a result, they try to overcome channel inertia by aiming their promotion directly at end users. When a company markets overseas, it may face an even longer channel because local distribution arrangements are different. Such is the case in Japan, where channels tend to be much longer than those in the United States. As a result, a greater reliance on a pull strategy may be advisable or necessary.

Distribution leverage is also different for each company from market to market. Gaining cooperation from local selling points, particularly in the retail sector, may be more difficult than in the domestic market. The fight for shelf space can be very intensive; shelf space in most markets is limited. Under these more competitive situations, reliance on a pull campaign becomes more important. If consumers are demanding the company's product, retailers will make every effort to carry it.

In contrast to a pull strategy, a **push strategy** focuses on the distributors of a product rather than on the end user or ultimate buyer. Incentives are offered to wholesalers or retailers to carry and promote a product. A company may have to resort to a push strategy when lack of access to advertising media makes a pull strategy less effective. Limited ability to transfer a pull strategy from a company's home market has other effects on the company's perfor-

---

World Beat 14.1 *Hindu Festival Attracts U.S. Marketers*

As millions of Hindu pilgrims mass at the confluence of the Ganges and Yamuna rivers for a festival of ritual cleansing, many are grabbing a Coke or a Pepsi to quench their thirst. Those are just two of the companies moving beyond their traditional marketing venues of sporting events and movies in search of fresh ways to reach India's rural masses. Their latest venue is the Kumbh Mela—a Hindu festival that comes every 12 years and draws 30 million participants over a period of a month.

Better yet for marketers, many of the people come from remote villages and small towns. About 80 percent of India's one billion people live in rural areas, far from the reach of most modern media. Getting them to try a product while at the festival could be the start of potentially extensive word-of-mouth advertising.

The latest festival was particularly awash with marketers pushing bottled soft drinks. The industry expects consumption to rise rapidly as more Indians indulge in Western-style food and beverages amid a growing afflu-

ence. PepsiCo's Indian unit tied up with the state tourism department to sell Pepsi at stalls and restaurants in addition to its own 20 exclusive vendors. Rival Coca-Cola was selling at 115 stalls. Coke also had 15,000 posters, as well as billboards, banners, and police assistance booths painted red with the famous logo.

Some criticize the commercialization of an ancient religious tradition. Still smarting from its colonial past, India is frequently suspicious of foreign products and ideas. Many nationalist Hindus frown upon foreign products and see Coke and Pepsi as symbols of economic imperialism.

Still, the marketers' strategy may be working among some. One medical-store owner from India's eastern state of Orissa swaggered up to a makeshift tent shop to treat himself to his fifth bottle of Pepsi in three days. So, what does he think? "I like it," he says.

Source: Rasul Bailay, "A Hindu Festival Attracts the Faithful and U.S. Marketers," *Wall Street Journal*, February 12, 2001.

---

mance in foreign markets. Reduced advertising tends to slow the product adoption process in new markets, forcing the firm to accept slower growth. In markets crowded with existing competitors, newcomers may find it difficult to establish themselves when avenues for pull campaigns are blocked.

Consequently, a company entering a new market may want to consider such situations in its planning and to adjust its expected results accordingly. A company accustomed to a given type of communications mix usually develops an expertise or a distinctive competence in the media commonly used. When the firm is suddenly faced with a situation in which that competence cannot be fully applied, the risk of failure or underachievement multiplies. Such constraints can even affect entry strategies and the market selection process.

▶ *Personal Selling*

Personal selling takes place whenever a customer is met in person by a representative of the marketing company. When doing business globally, companies must meet customers from different countries. These individuals may be used to different business customs and will often speak a different language. That is why personal selling is extremely complex and demands some very special skills on the part of the salesperson.

The complexity of a product usually influences how extensively personal selling is used. The level of complexity has to be compared with the product knowledge of the clients. A company selling the same products abroad as those sold domestically may find that more personal selling is necessary abroad if foreign clients are less sophisticated than domestic clients. A U.S. company may use the same amount of personal selling in Europe as it does in the United States but may need to put forth a greater personal-selling effort in developing countries if the product is new to those markets.

Although very effective as a promotion tool, personal selling requires the intensive use of a sales force and can be costly. Costs vary across countries. In the United States, a typical sales call is estimated to cost in excess of $300. This has motivated some companies to investigate other forms of promotion. Dell Computer considered sales calls too expensive in Brazil and instead mailed brochures to potential small-business clients. It took the company over a year to put together a list of names and addresses, because these were not readily available in Brazil. However, the mail campaign was a success in the end.

In this section, we differentiate between international selling and local selling. When a company's sales force travels across countries and meets directly with clients abroad, it is practicing **international selling**. This type of selling requires the special skill of being able to manage within several cultures. Much more often, however, companies engage in **local selling**: they organize and staff a local sales force made up of local nationals to do the selling in only one country. Different problems arise in managing and operating a local sales force than in managing multicountry salespersons.

International Selling (Multicountry Sales Force)

The job of the international salesperson seems glamorous. One imagines a professional who frequently travels abroad, visiting a large number of countries and meeting with businesspeople of various backgrounds. However, this type of work is quite demanding and requires a special set of skills.

International salespersons are needed only when companies deal directly with their clients abroad. This is usually the case for industrial equipment or business services but is rarely required for consumer products or services. Consequently, for our purposes, international sales will be described in the context of industrial selling.

Purchasing Behavior In business-to-business selling, one of the most important parts of the job consists of identifying the buying unit in the client company. The buying unit consists of all persons who have input into the buying decision. The seller must locate and access the actual decision makers, who may hold different positions from company to company or from country to country. In different countries, the purchasing manager may have different responsibilities, and engineers may play a greater or a lesser role. Buying decisions are often more centralized in many Asian and Latin American firms. In many cases the owner of the firm will make the final buying decision. Gaining access to top management may not be easy and may cause delays. Even in Europe, the time between a first sales call and a purchase can be 50 percent longer than in the United States. Sales times in Japan can also be longer because of the Japanese emphasis on consensus in the buying unit.

The members of the buying unit will want to explore and debate alternatives, while striving for a sense of unity and collegiality among themselves.[2]

Buying Criteria In addition to different purchasing patterns, the international salesperson may have to deal with different decision criteria or objectives on the part of the purchaser. Buyers or users of industrial products in different countries may expect to maximize different goals. For example, Sealed Air had difficulty convincing businesses in Taiwan to purchase more expensive packaging systems to protect their products during shipping, even though these systems had proved cost-effective in avoiding breakage. Unlike buyers in other markets, Taiwanese manufacturers focused almost exclusively on the purchase price of the packaging.[3]

Language Overcoming the language barrier is an especially difficult task for the international salesperson. In Chapter 3 we discussed several issues related to culture and language that can affect international marketing in general and personal selling in particular. Different societies apply different forms of address, use or avoid certain body language, and feel differently about the appropriateness of showing emotion. Certain societies are low-context cultures wherein the meanings of words are explicit. Other societies are high-context cultures wherein the meanings of words are implicit and change according to who speaks them as well as when and where they are spoken. It is very difficult for a non-native speaker to become fluent in the language of a high-context culture.

Of course, the personal-selling effort is markedly enhanced if the salesperson speaks the language of the customer, but for many industries, dependence on the local language is not so strong today as it was just one or two decades ago. For many new and highly sophisticated products, such as electronics and aerospace, English is the language spoken by most customers. Consequently, with more and more executives speaking English in many countries, many firms can market their products directly without local intermediaries.

English is widely spoken in Europe and is the leading second language in Asia and Latin America. Consequently, the ability to speak a number of foreign languages is less of a necessity. Still, learning a foreign language can be an excellent way to understand a foreign culture, and language proficiency continues to have a very favorable impact on the sales process. Local customers often appreciate a sales representative who speaks their language; it indicates the company's commitment to their market as well as its appreciation of their people and culture.

In industries where knowledge of the local language is important, companies tend to assign sales territories to salespersons on the basis of language skills. A European multinational manufacturer of textile equipment assigns countries to its sales staff according to the languages they speak. This is more important in traditional industries such as textile manufacturing, where businesses are more local in orientation and where managers may not speak English well.

Even executives who speak fairly good English may not understand all the details of product descriptions or specifications. As a result, a company can make an excellent impression by having its sales brochures translated into some of the key languages. European companies routinely produce company publications in several languages. Translations from English may not be needed for Scandinavia, where English proficiency is common. However, they may be valuable for other parts of the world, where the level of English-language skills is not high.

Business Etiquette Global marketers selling to many markets are likely to encounter a diverse set of business practices as they move from one country to another. Because interpersonal behavior is intensely culture-bound, this part of the salesperson's job will vary by country. Many differences exist in how an appointment is made, how (and whether) an introduction is made, and in how much lead time is needed for making appointments. The salesperson must also know whether or not gifts are expected or desired. Exchanging business gifts is popular in Taiwan but less common in Saudi Arabia. In Switzerland it is better to wait until the sale is finalized before offering a gift to a client. Even then the gift should not be too expensive, or it may be construed as a bribe and thus give offense. When a salesperson travels to the same area repeatedly, familiarity with local customs can be expected. For newcomers and even experienced executives traveling to a new area, getting accurate information about local customs is crucial.

For example, visiting businesspeople must attend long banquets when engaging in sales negotiations with the Chinese. These banquets may start in the late morning or early in the evening. The diners usually sit at a round table, and the visitors are normally seated next to the host, who is expected to fill their plates at regular intervals. Foreigners are cautioned that frequent toasts are the norm and that many Chinese business hosts expect the guest to become drunk. Otherwise, the guest is believed not to have had a good time.[4] Also, what is expected or tolerated in some markets may be taboo in others. Whereas it is acceptable for visitors to arrive late in China, India, or Indonesia, arriving late in Hong Kong is not acceptable. Lateness causes the visitor to "lose face," which is an extremely serious matter among Hong Kong businesspeople.[5] In Switzerland, where punctuality is also highly valued, clients may be favorably impressed if the salesperson arrives 10 or 15 minutes early for an appointment.

No manager can be expected to know the business customs of every country, so important information must be obtained from special sources. A company's own foreign market representatives or sales subsidiary can provide key information or suggestions. Also, governments tend to collect data on business practices through their commercial officers posted abroad. Some business service companies, such as global accounting firms or global banks, also provide customers with profiles of business practices in foreign countries.

Foreign businesspersons receiving visitors from the United States or any other foreign country rarely expect the foreign visitor to be familiar with all local customs. However, it is always appreciated when the visitor can exhibit familiarity with the most common practices and some willingness to try to conform. Learning some foreign customs helps to generate goodwill toward the company and can increase the chances of making a sale.

Check out our website for links to business etiquette sources.

International Sales Negotiations

It is the ultimate job of most sales forces to make a sale. As we mentioned in Chapter 5, negotiations can play an important role in selling, especially to businesses and governments. The terms of a sale—price, delivery terms, and financing options—can all be negotiable. Negotiations in the global arena are complicated because the negotiating partners frequently come from different cultural backgrounds. As a result, misunderstandings or misjudgments can occur. To maximize their effectiveness in these often difficult and protracted negotiations, international sales personnel must be attuned to cultural differences.

Careful background preparation on the cultural norms prevalent in the foreign country is the starting point in successful negotiations and selling. A 15-year study of negotiation styles in seventeen cultures found significant differences from culture to culture. For example, the Japanese were the least aggressive, using few threats or warnings, whereas the French and Brazilians were considerably more aggressive, frequently employing threats and interruptions.[6] In some cultures, such as Russia, negotiations tend to be regarded as zero-sum games where there are only winners and losers. Other cultures consider negotiations more a tool for establishing mutually beneficial business relationships.

Time orientation is an important aspect for negotiating abroad. In some countries, such as China, negotiations tend to take much more time than in the United States or some other Western countries. One European company that operated a joint venture in China observed that during one meeting, 2 weeks were spent in a discussion that elsewhere might have taken only a few hours. In this situation, however, much of the time was used for interdepartmental negotiations among various Chinese agencies rather than for face-to-face negotiations with the European company.

Another difference between cultures is their attitude toward the final negotiated contract. Managers from the United States like to "get it all in writing." Contracts often spell out many contingencies and establish the position of both sides in light of these contingencies. Americans believe that the business relationship will proceed more smoothly if this is all worked out ahead of time. Other cultures consider this insistence on elaborate written contracts a sign of inflexibility or even lack of trust on the part of Americans. In Brazil even a written contract may not be regarded as binding but, rather, as open for continued renegotiation. In any case, an understanding of the prevailing cultural attitudes is necessary to successfully negotiate the final sale.

Local Selling (Single-Country Sales Force)

When a company is able to maintain a local sales force in the countries where it does business, many of the difficulties of bridging the cultural gap with clients are minimized. The local sales force can be expected to understand local customs, and the global company typically gains additional acceptance in the market. This is primarily because local sales forces are usually staffed with local nationals. However, many challenges remain, and managing a local sales force often requires different strategies from those used in running a sales force in the company's domestic market.

Role of Local Sales Force For firms that still use distributor sales forces to a large extent, a missionary sales force with limited responsibilities may suffice. A **missionary sales force** concentrates on visiting clients together with the local distributor's sales force. Its focus is on promoting the product rather than distributing the product or even finalizing the sale. If the global company's sales force needs to do the entire job, a much larger sales force will be necessary. The size of the local sales force depends to a large extent on the number of clients and the desired frequency of visits. This frequency may differ from country to country, which means that the size of the sales force will differ accordingly.

Control over a firm's sales activities is a frequently cited advantage of operating a **company-owned local sales force**. With its own sales force, the company can emphasize the products it wants to market at any time and can maintain better control over the way it is represented. In many cases, price negotiations, in the form of discounts or rebates, are handled uniformly rather than leaving these decisions to an independent distributor with different interests. Having a company sales force helps ensure that the personnel have the necessary training and qualifications. Control over all of these parameters usually means higher sales than those achieved with a distributor sales force.

Also, the local sales force can represent an important bridge to the local business community. For industries in which the buying process is local rather than global, the sales force speaks the language of the local customer. It can be expected to understand the local business customs and to bring the international firm closer to its end users. In many instances, local customers, although they may not object to buying from a foreign firm, may prefer to deal with local representatives of that firm.

The role of the local sales force needs to be coordinated with the promotion mix selected for each market. As many companies have learned, advertising and other forms of promotion can be used to make the function of the sales force more efficient. In many consumer-goods industries, companies prefer a pull strategy, concentrating their promotion budget on the final consumer. In such cases, the role of the sales force is restricted to gaining distribution access. However, as we have noted before, there are countries in which access to communications media is severely restricted. As a result, companies may place greater emphasis on a push strategy, relying heavily on the local sales force. This will affect both the role and the size of the firm's sales force.

Foreign Sales Practices Although sales forces are employed virtually everywhere, the nature of their interaction with the local customer is unique to each market and may affect local sales operations. For most Westerners, Japanese practices seem substantially different. Here is an example reported by Masaaki Imai, president of Cambridge Corporation, a Tokyo management consulting and recruiting firm.

When Bausch & Lomb first introduced its then-new soft-lens line into Japan, the company targeted influential eye doctors in each sales territory for its introductory launch. The firm assumed that once these leading practitioners signed up for the new product, marketing to the majority of eye doctors would be easier. However, a key customer quickly dismissed one salesperson. The doctor said that he thought very highly of Bausch & Lomb equipment but preferred regular lenses for his patients. The salesperson did not even have a chance to respond. He decided, because it was his first visit to this clinic, to wait around for a while. He talked to several assistants at the clinic and to the doctor's wife, who was handling the administration of the practice.

The next morning, the salesperson returned to the clinic and observed that the doctor was very busy. He talked again with the assistants and joined the doctor's wife when she was cooking and talked with her about food. When the couple's young son returned from kindergarten, the salesperson played with him and even went out to buy him a toy. The wife was very pleased with the well-intentioned babysitter. She later explained to the salesperson that her husband had very little time to listen to any sales presentations during the day, so she invited him to come to their home in the evening. The doctor, obviously primed by his wife, received the man very warmly, and they enjoyed *sake* together. The doctor listened patiently to the sales presentation and responded that he did not want to use the soft lenses on his patients right away. However, he suggested that the salesperson try them on his assistants the next day. Therefore, on the third day, the salesperson returned to the clinic and fitted several of the clinic's assistants to soft lenses. The reaction was very favorable, and the doctor placed an order on the third day of the sales call.[7]

Japanese customers often judge whether a company really wants to do business by the frequency of the sales calls they receive. Salespeople who make more frequent calls to a potential customer than the competition makes may be regarded as more sincere. This means that companies doing business in Japan have to make frequent sales calls to their top customers, even if only for courtesy reasons. Although this contact may occasionally be just a telephone call, the need to make frequent visits significantly affects the staffing levels of the company-owned sales force.

Recruiting Companies have often found recruiting sales professionals quite challenging in many global markets. Although the availability of qualified sales personnel is a problem even in developed countries, the scarcity of skilled personnel is even more acute in developing countries. Global companies, accustomed to having sales staff with certain standard qualifications, may not find it easy to locate the necessary salespeople in a short period of time. One factor that limits their availability in many countries is the local economic situation. A good economic climate will limit the number of people a company can expect to hire away from existing firms unless a substantial increase over their present compensation is offered.

Furthermore, sales positions don't enjoy uniformly high esteem from country to country. Typically, sales as an occupation or career has generally positive associations in the United States. This allows companies to recruit excellent talent, usually fresh from universities, for sales careers. These university recruits often regard sales as a relatively high-paying career or as a path to middle management. Such an image of selling is rare elsewhere in the world. In Europe, many companies continue to find it difficult to recruit university graduates into their sales forces, except in such highly technical fields as computers, where the recruits are typically engineers. When selling is a less desirable occupation, the quality of the sales force may suffer. The time it takes to fill sales positions can be expected to increase dramatically if the company wants to insist on top-quality recruits.

Compensation In their home markets where they usually employ large sales forces, global companies become accustomed to handling and motivating their sales forces in a given way. In the United States, typical motivation programs include some form of commission or bonus for meeting volume or budget projections, as well as vacation prizes for top performers. When a global company manages local sales forces in various countries, the company must determine the best way to motivate them. Salespersons from different cultures may not all respond the same way. Motivating practices may need to differ from country to country.

Jorge Vergara joined U.S.-based Herbalife when it first entered the Mexican market, and he soon became a star salesman. Then he left to start his own nutritional supplements company, Omnilife. Breaking with Herbalife's sales practices, Mr. Vergara modified his compensation system. Instead of rewarding on the basis of sales volume, he rewarded salespersons who sold consistently. He also paid them every 2 weeks, which is customary in Latin America, instead of monthly. After only 8 years, Omnilife became one of Latin America's largest sellers of nutritional supplements, ahead of both Herbalife and Amway Corporation.[8]

One of the frequently discussed topics in the area of motivating salespeople is the value of the commission or bonus structure. In countries that rate high on uncertainty avoidance, sales representatives may prefer to receive guaranteed salaries. U.S. companies, on the other hand, have tended to use some form of commission structure for their sales forces. Although this may fluctuate from industry to industry, U.S. firms tend to use a more flexible and volume-dependent compensation structure than European firms do. Japanese firms more often use a straight-salary type of compensation. To motivate the sales force to achieve superior performance, the global company may be faced with using different compensation practices depending on local customs.

READ MORE ABOUT IT:
Check out "Sweet Solution"
under *Supplemental Readings*
on our website.

► *Global Account Management*

Traditionally, account management has been performed on a country-by-country basis. This practice invariably leads, even in large global firms, to a country-specific sales force. However, as we noted in Chapter 5, some companies organize their sales force into global account teams. The **global account team** services an entire customer globally, or in all countries where a customer relationship exists. Global account teams may comprise members in different parts of the world, all serving segments of a global account and coordinated through a global account management structure.

Global accounts arose in response to more centralized purchasing within global firms. Companies that purchase similar components, raw materials, or services in many parts of the world realized that by combining the purchasing function and managing it centrally, they could demand better prices and service from suppliers. Today, many companies search the globe for the best buy.

Siemens's Automotive Systems Division has tailored its sales structure to these new realities. The company maintains global account teams for key customers such as Volkswagen and Ford. The teams are in charge of the firm's entire business, regardless of where the components are sourced or used. From the customer's perspective, the advantage stems from the clear designation of a counterpart who will handle all aspects of their business relationship.[9] The system of global account management is also practiced widely in the professional-service sectors. Globally active banks such as Citibank have maintained global account structures for years. Likewise, advertising agencies offer global clients global account management with seamless coordination across many countries. The world's leading account-ing firms, such as Deloitte Touche Tohmatsu International, have long-standing traditions of managing international clients from a single unit.[10]

Global account management is greatly enhanced by sophisticated infor-mation technology. With members of the team dispersed around the globe, it becomes essential to coordinate all actions meticulously. The development and rapid spread of such tools as videoconferencing and e-mail have greatly extended the reach of a management team beyond the typical one-location office. Many customers who are eager to do business across the world but who prefer to deal with fewer suppliers will increasingly demand this new sales approach. Many of the national selling organizations now maintained by international firms will inevitably be transformed into smaller but glob-ally acting units of account teams.

Nonetheless, global account management can present challenges to global marketers. A study of sixteen large multinational companies revealed that prices quoted to global accounts were more likely to fall than to rise. In 27 percent of cases, prices were assessed as becoming much lower within 3 years. In order to implement global account management, vendor compa-nies should be as global and as coordinated as their customers—or problems can arise. One firm was surprised to receive a call from a global customer de-manding service for a plant in Indonesia. The vendor had no sales or service operation in Indonesia but felt obliged to respond. Someone was flown out from a neighboring country at considerable expense.[11]

▸ *Selling to Businesses and Governments*

Promotion methods that are oriented largely toward business or government markets can be important to international firms operating in those markets. In particular, the use of international trade fairs, bidding procedures for in-ternational projects, and consortium selling all need to be understood in their international context.

International Trade Fairs

Participation in international trade fairs has become an important aspect of business-to-business marketing abroad. Trade fairs are ideal for exposing new customers and potential distributors to a company's product range and have been used extensively by both newcomers and established firms. In the United States, business customers can be reached through a wide range of media, such as specialized magazines with a particular industry focus. In many overseas countries, the markets are too small to allow for the publica-tion of such trade magazines for only one country. As a result, prospective customers usually attend these trade fairs on a regular basis. Trade fairs also offer companies a chance to meet with prospective customers in a less for-mal atmosphere. For a company that is new to a certain market and does not yet have any established contacts, participating in a trade fair may be the only way to reach potential customers.

There are an estimated 600 trade shows in 70 countries every year. For ex-ample, the Cologne Trade Fair brings together 28,000 exhibitors from 100 countries and 1.8 million buyers from 150 countries. The Hanover Fair is

Three chefs evaluate Cuban dishes made with American rice. After the United States relaxed its embargo of Cuba to allow the sale of foodstuffs, the USA Rice Federation sponsored this event in conjunction with an agribusiness expo in Havana.

considered the largest industrial fair in the world. With over 7,100 exhibitors in engineering and technology from over 70 countries, the fair attracts 330,000 visitors.[12] Other large general fairs include the Canton Fair in China and the Milan Fair in Italy.

Specialized trade fairs concentrate on a certain segment of an industry or user group. Such fairs usually attract limited participation in terms of both exhibitors and visitors. Typically, they are more technical in nature. Some of the specialized trade fairs do not take place every year. One of the leading specialized fairs for the chemical industry is the Achema, which is held in Germany every 3 years. The annual fairs that enjoy an international reputation include the air shows of Farnborough, England, and of Paris, where aerospace products are displayed. The Comdex computer trade show (held in Las Vegas in 2001) has run annually since 1979 and attracts 2,400 exhibitors and 220,000 visitors each year. This show has become so big that some exhibitors, such as Intel, IBM, and Compaq, have decided not to participate.[13]

Participation in trade fairs can save both time and effort for a company that wants to break into a new market and does not yet have any contacts. For new product announcements or demonstrations, the trade fair offers an ideal showcase. Trade fairs are also used by competitors to check out one another's most recent developments. They can give a newcomer an idea of the potential competition in some foreign markets. Consequently, trade fairs are a means of both selling products and gathering important and useful market intelligence. Therefore, marketers with global aspirations will do well to seek out the trade fairs directed at their industry or customer segment and to schedule regular attendance.

International exhibiting may require more planning than domestic shows. First, begin planning 12 to 18 months in advance, taking into account the fact that international shipping may involve delays. Second, check show attendance. Many shows allow the general public to attend, in which case you may want to arrange for a private area for meeting with viable prospects. Third, in the United States a show may be staffed by salespeople and middle managers. At many international shows, however, customers expect to see the CEO and senior management. Finally, use a local distributor, consultant, or sales representative to help with the local logistics and acquaint you with the local culture.[14]

A number of virtual trade shows have recently appeared on the Internet. For example, in 2000, WholesaleTradeshow.com launched the first online, global trade show for wholesale and off-price apparel, footwear, and team sports merchandise. Merchandise can be viewed and bought online. Buyers and sellers can transact business 24 hours a day, 7 days a week via the site, supported by a multilingual customer service team and optional export management services.[15]

Check out our website for trade fair links.

Selling Through a Bidding Process

Global marketers of industrial products may become involved in a bidding process, particularly when major capital equipment is involved. Companies competing for such major projects must take a number of steps before negotiations for a specific purchase can begin. Typically, companies actively seek new projects and then move on to prequalify for the particular project(s) they locate before a formal project bid or tender is submitted. Each phase requires careful management and the appropriate allocation of resources.

During the **search phase**, companies want to make sure that they are informed of any project meriting their interest that is related to their product lines. For particularly large projects that are government-sponsored, full-page advertisements may appear in leading international newspapers or may be posted on government websites. Companies can also utilize their networks of agents, contacts, or former customers to inform them of any project being considered.

In the **prequalifying phase**, the purchaser frequently asks for documentation from interested companies that wish to make a formal tender. No formal bidding or tender documents are submitted. Instead, the buyer is more interested in general company background and is likely to ask the firm to describe similar projects it has completed in the past. At this stage, the company will have to sell itself and its capabilities. A large number of companies may be expected to pursue prequalification.

In the next phase, the customer selects the companies—usually only three or four—to be invited to submit a formal bid. **Formal bids** consist of a written proposal of how to solve the specific client problem and the price the firm would charge for the project. For industrial equipment, this usually requires personal visits on location, special design of some components, and the preparation of full documentation, including engineering drawings, for the client. The bid preparation costs can be enormous, running as high as several million dollars for some very large projects. The customer will select the winner from among those submitting formal proposals. Rarely is it simply the lowest bidder who obtains the order. Technology, the type of solution proposed, the financing arrangements, and the reputation and experience of the firm all play a role.

Once an order is obtained, the supplier company may be expected to insure its own performance. For that purpose, the company may be asked to post a **performance bond**, which is a guarantee that the company will pay certain specified damages to the customer if the job is not completed in accordance with the agreed-upon specifications. Performance bonds are usually issued by banks on behalf of the supplier. The entire process, from finding out about a new prospect until the order is actually in hand, may take from several months to several years, depending on the project size or industry.

Consortium Selling

Because of the high stakes involved in marketing equipment or large projects, companies frequently band together to form a consortium. A **consortium** is a group of firms that share in a certain contract or project on a pre-agreed basis but act as one company toward the customer. Joining together in a consortium can help companies share the risk in some very large projects. A consortium can also enhance the competitiveness of the members if they are involved in turnkey projects. A **turnkey project** is one in which the supplier offers the buyer a complete solution so that the entire operation can commence "at the turn of a key."

Most consortia are formed on an ad hoc basis. For the job of creating a major steel mill, for example, companies supplying individual components might combine into a group and offer a single tender to the customer. The consortium members have agreed to share all marketing costs and can help one another with design and engineering questions. Similarly, a consortium could form to deliver a turnkey hospital to the Saudi Arabian government. This would involve building the physical facilities, installing medical equipment, recruiting doctors, and training staff—among other things. In either case, the customer gets a chance to deal with one supplier only, which substantially simplifies the process. Ad hoc consortia can be formed for very large projects that require unique skills from their members. In situations where the same set of skills or products is in frequent demand, companies may form a permanent consortium. Whenever an appropriate opportunity arises, the consortium members will immediately prepare to qualify for the bidding.

Consortium members frequently come from the same country. However, telecommunications consortia often combine a local firm, whose local connections are of great value, with one or two international telephone operating companies, which offer expertise in running a network. On occasion, these consortia include equipment suppliers that join to ensure that their equipment will be included in any eventual contract.

▶ *Other Forms of Promotion*

So far, our discussion has focused on personal and industrial selling as key elements of a promotion mix. However, forms of promotion other than selling and advertising can play a key role in marketing. As we discussed in Chapter 13, direct sales is not only a distribution strategy but a promotion strategy as well, because it involves communicating directly with the consumer. Another form of global promotion is sales promotion, which can include such elements as in-store retail promotions and coupons. Many of these tools are consumer-goods-oriented and are used less often in marketing industrial goods. In this section, we look at sales promotion activities, sports sponsorships, telemarketing, management of word-of-mouth, and public relations.

Sales Promotion

Sales promotion encompasses marketing activities that generate sales by adding value to products in order to stimulate consumer purchasing and/or channel cooperation. Sales promotions such as coupons, gifts, and various types of reduced-priced labels are used in most countries. In some countries, free goods, double-pack promotions, and in-store displays are also important. Government regulations and different retailing practices, however, tend to limit the options for global firms.

The area of sales promotion is largely local in focus. For example, in Mexico 85 percent of cement sales are to individuals. Millions of do-it-yourselfers buy bags of cement to build their own homes. Cemex, the market leader in cement sales, sometimes buys food for a block party when a house is finished. And the company's 5,000 distributors can earn point toward vacations by increasing sales.[16]

In the United States, coupons are the leading form of sales promotion. Consumers bring product coupons to the retail store and obtain a reduced price for the product. Companies such as A.C. Nielsen specialize in managing coupon redemption centers centrally so that consumer-goods firms can outsource the physical handling of these promotions. Second in importance are refund offers. Consumers who send a proof of purchase to the manufacturer receive a refund in the form of a check. Less frequently used are cents-off labels and factory bonus packs, which induce customers to buy large quantities via a price incentive.

Couponing varies significantly from country to country. Coupon distribution is popular and growing in Italy. Couponing is also now available on the Internet. For example, in South Africa, electronic coupons were posted at coupons.com.za.[17] In the United Kingdom and Spain, couponing is declining. Couponing is relatively new in Japan, where restrictions on newspaper coupons were lifted only in 1991.

An example of a sales promotion aimed at distributors is the slotting allowance. This is a payment made to retailers in return for their agreeing to take a new product. A slotting allowance helps compensate them for the time and effort expended in finding a space for the new product on their shelves. As products proliferate, finding shelf space is increasingly difficult, and firms must compete for access to that space. Slotting allowances in Europe's increasingly concentrated supermarket industry have become quite costly.

Although most sales promotions are relatively short-term, some may continue indefinitely. Promotions that encourage customer loyalty and repeat purchases are being used increasingly worldwide. Loyalty programs, such as frequent-flyer awards, have proliferated in the former Soviet bloc since the 1990s. Not all frequent-flyer programs were well managed. Polish Airlines established three levels of awards and service for frequent flyers (blue, silver, and gold) but actually treated all customers the same. This resulted in customer dissatisfaction with the program and in a large defection of frequent flyers to competitor British Airways.[18]

Most countries impose restrictions on some forms of promotions. Games of chance are frequently regulated. When reductions are made available, they often are not allowed to exceed a certain percentage of the product's purchase price. Japan, for instance, limits the value of a promotional gift attached to a product to a maximum of 10 percent of the product's price. In addition, the value of free merchandise cannot exceed 50,000 yen, or about $425. Even the value of prizes awarded through lotteries is restricted to a maximum of ¥1 million for an open lottery available to everyone and to ¥50,000 for lotteries attached to the purchase of specific products. For global firms such as American Express, these limits cause difficulties. In the United States, American Express offers free trips from New York to London as prizes to qualifying customers. The company would like to offer similar promotions to its Japanese customers, but the limitation of ¥50,000 allows for only a 3-day package tour from Tokyo to Seoul.[19]

Historically, Germany has been among the most restrictive countries as far as most sales promotions are concerned. Laws enacted in the 1930s drastically restricted the use of discounts, rebates, and free offers that the Nazi government regarded as products of Marxist consumer cooperatives. Only a few years ago, a German court stopped a drugstore from giving away free shopping bags to celebrate the store's birthday. A large retailer was blocked from donating a small sum to AIDS research for each customer transaction using a Visa card. A court declared that this promotion unfairly exploited the emotions of customers.

In 2001 Germany decided to repeal its 70-year-old laws against promotions. A European directive on e-commerce necessitated this change. The directive required that the rules of the country in which the vendor was based be applied to promotions within Europe. Fewer than one in ten Germans had ever made a purchase over the Internet. Still, the German government feared that this directive would eventually put German competitors at a disadvantage by preventing them from offering promotions similar to those allowed in neighboring countries. Despite the repeal of the antipromotion laws, a broad law against unfair competition remains on the books in Germany. Some fear that certain competitors could still attempt to use it to block the promotions of others.[20]

Because global firms will encounter a series of regulations and restrictions on promotions that differ among countries, there is little opportunity to standardize sales promotion techniques across many markets. Sales promotion can also be influenced by local culture, as well as by the competitiveness of the marketplace. A study of consumer attitudes regarding sales promotions found significant differences even among Taiwan, Thailand, and Malaysia. The Taiwanese consumer preferred coupons to sweepstakes. The Malaysians and Thais both preferred sweepstakes to coupons.[21] In Europe, McDonald's discovered that children were content with a simple word puzzle on a menu tray or a small stuffed animal and did not require the more expensive Happy Meal promotions that the company used in the United States.[22] This variation among markets has caused most companies to make sales promotions the responsibility of local managers, who are expected to understand the local preferences and restrictions.

Nonetheless, a firm should make certain that there is adequate communication among its subsidiaries to ensure that the best practices and new promotion ideas are disseminated throughout the firm. Sometimes it is even critical to communicate problems associated with promotions so that they will not be repeated in other national markets. In 1992 Pepsi began an under-the-bottle-cap promotion in Chile, where a preselected number of customers were to win a significant prize. A garbled fax led to a wrong number being announced for the promotion on Chilean television. Public anger turned to vandalism against the company and severely damaged Pepsi's brand equity in Chile. Unfortunately, the lesson from the Chilean case—the need to administer award promotions very carefully—was not communicated well to Pepsi's other operations. A few months later, a promotion in the Philippines that was intended to award $37,000 to one lucky winner fell victim to a computer error that produced thousands of winners. When Pepsi refused to honor the claims of all these winners, thirty Pepsi delivery trucks were burned, and company officials were threatened. Tragically, a woman and child were killed when a grenade tossed at a Pepsi truck rolled into a nearby store.[23]

Sports Promotions and Sponsorships

Major sports events are increasingly being covered by the mass media worldwide. The commercial value of these events has soared over the last decade. Today, large sports events, such as the Olympics and world championships in specific sports, cannot exist in their present form without funding by companies.

For some events, companies can purchase space for signs along the stadiums or arenas where sports events take place. When the event is covered on television, the cameras automatically take in the signs as part of the regular coverage. Aside from purchasing advertising spots or signage space in broadcast programs, individual companies can also engage in sponsorship. Main sponsors for the Olympic games pay a fee of $40 million to the International Olympic Committee.

To take advantage of global sports events, a company should have a logo or brand name that is worth exposing to a global audience. It is not surprising to find that the most common sponsors are companies that produce consumer goods with global appeal, such as soft-drink manufacturers, makers of consumer electronics products, and film companies.

To purchase sign space, a firm must take into consideration the popularity of certain sports. Few sports have global appeal. Baseball and American football have little appeal in Europe or parts of Asia and Africa. However, football (soccer) is the number-one spectator sport in much of the world. Between 1999 and 2002, MasterCard planned sponsorships of 400 championship matches with a projected cumulative television audience of 50 billion people.[24] Nike spends an estimated 40 percent of its global sports advertising budget on soccer. In August 2002, the company entered into a 13-year, $429 million contract to outfit England's Manchester United football club. Nike also sponsors the national soccer teams of six countries, including Brazil and the United States.[25]

Korean international firms have used sports sponsorship abroad extensively. Typically, Korean firms have underwritten individual teams overseas. Samsung has sponsored ten sports teams or events in Eastern Europe, eight in Latin America, and two each in Asia and the Middle East. Other Korean firms are active too. Hyundai supports Eastern European and African football teams, and the LG group has been very active in sponsoring local sports

World Beat 14.2 *The Olympics versus the World Cup*

Although many more countries are represented at the Olympics (some 200, compared with 32 qualifying World Cup teams) and although the World Cup marks don't have the cachet of the Olympic rings, in most corners of the world people are more fervent about soccer and their soccer team than about their Olympic team—and more likely to tune in to matches. Furthermore, World Cup sponsors have rights to on-field signage at the stadiums, and they enjoy nearly a year-long run-up to the event, thanks to the qualifying matches and draw.

The World Cup hasn't captured the American marketer's imagination beyond the heavyweights such as Coca-Cola, McDonald's, and MasterCard. A major reason is that interest in soccer as a spectator sport in the United States is low compared with interest in other major-league sports, such as football and basketball. But the United States isn't a good litmus test. Soccer reigns as the favorite TV sport in 24 out of 34 countries surveyed in a study by British Columbia–based Ipsos-Reid Corporation.

The sixteen official World Cup sponsors pay between $20 million and $50 million in cash and services, which buys them marketing rights to World Cup marks as well as behind-the-scenes access during the 2002 and 2006 World Cups and the 2003 women's World Cup. Unlike the Olympics, which doesn't allow signage at events, World Cup sponsors get two on-field advertising boards in all twenty stadiums. MasterCard, which tracks its exposure, receives 10 minutes to 13 minutes of visibility per 90-minute World Cup match. With 250 million registered soccer players and a billion spectators worldwide, companies can reach consumers through other soccer activities, such as local leagues and tournaments.

Source: Dana James, "World Cup Scores," *Marketing News*, February 18, 2002: 1, 15, and 18.

Soccer's FIFA is increasingly alarmed by "ambushers" such as Chinese fans who showed up at the World Cup in South Korea wearing Samsung caps. Samsung was not an official sponsor of the games, but thanks to the caps, the company enjoyed free publicity from the television coverage of the games.

teams. These Korean firms consider sports sponsorship a cost-effective way to boost their brand or company recognition in emerging markets.[26]

Through the intensive coverage of sports in the news media all over the world, many companies continue to use the sponsorship of sporting events as an important element in their global communications programs. Successful companies must exhibit both flexibility and ingenuity in the selection of available events or participants. In some parts of the world, sports sponsorship may continue to be the only available way to reach large numbers of prospective customers.

Telemarketing

Telemarketing can be used both to solicit sales and to offer enhanced customer service to current and potential customers. To make telemarketing effective, however, an efficient telephone system is required. Telephone sales for individual households may become practical when many subscribers exist and when their telephone numbers can be easily obtained. Because of the language problems involved, companies must make sure their telemarketing sales forces not only speak the language of the local customer but also do so fluently and with the correct local or regional accent.

However, not all countries accept the practice of soliciting business directly at home. A telemarketing directive in the European Union allows consumers to place their names on a telephone preference list to eliminate telemarketing calls to their homes. Any firm that continues to call potential customers can be fined.[27] Even so, telemarketing is already big business in Europe, where total full-time employment in the field is estimated at 1.5 million. In the United Kingdom, telemarketing volume was believed to have reached $16.2 billion in 1995.[28] Lands' End, the U.S.-based catalogue house, opened its European call center at the junction of the French, German, and Luxembourg borders. Employing fifty people, the call center operates 24 hours a day and was established to offer support to shoppers and answer questions.

Telemarketing has been intensifying elsewhere as well. In Latin America, growth has been substantial; thirty-six telemarketing firms have been reported to be active in Brazil, twenty-five in Argentina, and fifteen in Chile. Call centers have grown very rapidly in Brazil, where the market for telemarketing center software and hardware exceeds $500 million per year.[29] Still, many Brazilians can be more effectively reached by loudspeaker than by telephone. Wal-Mart successfully sent out green vans to roam modest neighborhoods in Sao Paulo inviting people, via loudspeaker, to apply for credit cards at the company's Todo Dia stores.[30]

On a global level, telephone sales may also be helpful for business-to-business marketing. Because costs for overseas travel are considerable, telemarketing across countries or on a global basis may prove very cost-effective. Similarly, the Internet can further decrease customer service costs by allowing firms to respond to customers' requests via e-mail.

Managing Word-of-Mouth

When importer Piaggio USA wanted to revive stagnant sales of Vespa scooters, it hired extremely attractive young women to pose as motorbike riders and frequent trendy cafes in Los Angeles. The scooter-riding models would then strike up conversations with other patrons at the cafes. When anyone complimented their bikes, they would pull out a notepad and write down the name and phone number of the local Vespa dealer. In Canada, Procter & Gamble promoted Cheer detergent by having brightly outfitted shoppers break into impromptu fashion shows in supermarkets, mentioning to onlookers that their clothes were washed in Cheer. In both cases, the marketers were attempting to catch the attention of potential customers not only to promote a sale but also to get people talking about their product to their friends. This managed word-of-mouth is called **buzz marketing**.[31]

Buzz can be cheap; there are no national media to buy and no costly price promotions. Instead, product recommendations appear to come from a customer's coolest friends. Still experts suggest that buzz marketing can backfire if consumers feel it is subversive or if too many companies are trying to do it. Then buzz can become merely annoying.[32] In an individualistic culture such as that which prevails in the United States and Canada, one's "coolest friend" can conceivably be a person one has just met. In more collectivist cultures, where people are more wary of outsiders, marketers may need to recruit members from each target in-group very carefully to play this role. An unknown actor may not do.

Word-of-mouth can also be important in business-to-business marketing, where referrals are often crucial. However, there appear to be cultural differences in how managers seek advice concerning potential purchases. A study of U.S. and Japanese corporate buyers of financial services revealed that the Japanese used referral sources—both business and personal—almost twice as often as did U.S. corporate buyers. This supported prior research that suggested that Japanese corporate buyers use a greater variety of referral sources than their American counterparts.[33]

Public Relations

A company's public relations function consists of marketing activities that enhance brand equity by promoting goodwill toward the organization. In turn, this goodwill can encourage consumers to trust a company and predispose them to buy its products. Tim Horton's is a chain of doughnut and coffee stores across Canada that has successfully fought off the world's largest doughnut chain, Dunkin Donuts Inc. After 30 years in Canada, Dunkin Donuts only holds a 6 percent share of the Canadian market. Among the things that Canadian customers like about Tim Horton's is its charity work operating camps for underprivileged children.[34]

Often international marketers find that public relations activities are necessary to defend the reputation of a brand against bad publicity. With millions of Europeans afraid of contracting mad-cow disease by eating beef, McDonald's Corporation began an unusual public relations campaign. Customers were invited to visit the McDonald's meatpacking plant in France, which supplies its 860 restaurants in that country. Touring visitors learned that ground meat was made of 100 percent muscle, not of the nerve tissue that caused the risk of disease.[35]

Public relations campaigns themselves can go wrong. Instead of neutralizing bad publicity, such campaigns can sometimes increase it. In our global society, such gaffes can be heard around the world. In 2001 Philip Morris's subsidiary in the Czech Republic—in an attempt to bolster goodwill with the

Benetton, the Italian clothing company, is one of many global firms that associate themselves with charitable causes.

Czech government—commissioned a study to show that cigarettes have positive financial benefits to the state. In addition to benefiting from the taxes assessed on cigarette sales, the Philip Morris subsidiary maintained, the state saves a great deal of pension money when a citizen dies prematurely from diseases attributed to smoking. When the press heard of this study, outraged editorials appeared in newspapers around the world.

One of the best-known public relations crises arose from the promotion strategy for baby formula that Nestlé employed in developing countries in the 1970s. Thirty years later, the crisis still haunts the firm and its industry. In the 1970s Nestlé and other producers of baby formula flooded maternity wards in less developed countries with free samples of their products. When new mothers ran out of the samples, they often discovered that their own breast milk had dried up. Few could afford the expensive formula. Some diluted it in an effort to make it last longer, and this sometimes resulted in the death of the baby. Activists organized a global boycott of Nestlé products, and UNICEF, the United Nations agency charged with protecting children, refused to accept cash contributions from the company.[36]

Major formula producers agreed to comply with a voluntary marketing code devised by UNICEF and the World Health Organization in 1981 that practically forbids any distribution of free formula. But the controversy hasn't stopped there. The companies have always understood this code to apply to less developed countries only, whereas UNICEF has stated that it understands the code to apply to developed countries as well. Recently, the controversy has heated up in the shadow of the AIDS epidemic in Africa. Studies show that about 15 percent of women with HIV in Africa will transmit it to their children through breastfeeding. Nestlé claims it has received desperate pleas from African hospitals for free formula but is afraid to violate the code. Both Nestlé and Wyeth-Ayerst Laboratories Inc. have offered to donate tons of free formula to HIV-infected women in Africa. UNICEF refuses to lend its approval because it doesn't want to appear to endorse an industry it has long accused of abusive practices.[37]

International marketers often are accused of promoting products that change consumption patterns to the detriment of local cultures. Proactive public relations campaigns can often help to offset this xenophobia. After the United States began bombing raids into Afghanistan in the fall of 2001, Muslim radicals in Indonesia bombed a Kentucky Fried Chicken store. No ill feeling was expressed at a McDonald's franchise in Indonesia that had established goodwill over the years in its surrounding Muslim community by donating food and dining facilities to Islamic institutions.[38] Many international firms become involved in charitable donations involving both money and employees' time. Others offer corporate-sponsored scholarships. Whatever the chosen venue, fostering goodwill for the corporation in local communities plays an increasing role in international promotion strategy.

► Conclusions

Promotion in an international context is particularly challenging because managers are constantly faced with communicating to customers with different cultural backgrounds. This tends to add to the complexity of the communications task, which demands a particular sensitivity to culture, habits, manners, and ethics.

Aside from the cultural differences that affect the content and form of communications, international firms also encounter a different set of cost constraints for the principal elements of the promotion mix, such as selling and advertising. Given such diversity from country to country, international firms have to design their communications carefully to fit each individual market. Furthermore, the availability of any one element cannot be taken for granted. The absence of any one element of the promotion mix, as a consequence of either legal considerations or level of economic development, may force the international firm to compensate with a greater reliance on other promotion tools.

When designing effective sales forces, international marketers need to compare the challenges involved in international selling with those inherent in local selling. International sales efforts can usually be maintained for companies selling highly differentiated and complex products to a clearly defined target market. In most other situations, wherein products are targeted at a broader type of business or at end users, international firms will typically have to engage a local sales force for each market. Local sales forces are usually very effective in reaching their own market or country. Establishing a local sales force and managing it are challenging tasks in most foreign markets and require managers with a special sensitivity to local laws, regulations, and trade practices.

As we saw in Chapter 13, as well as in this chapter, all forms of direct and interactive marketing apply to the international market as well. Many firms have succeeded by adopting U.S.-based or U.S.-originated direct-marketing ideas and using them skillfully abroad. With the international telecommunications infrastructure developing rapidly, the applications for telemarketing as well as Internet-based interactive marketing will expand. These will undoubtedly become important elements of the communications mix for globally active firms large and small.

What aspects of promotion should you consider for your product overseas? Continue with *Country-Market Report* on our website.

Review Questions

1. What factors appear to affect the extension of push strategies in international markets? What factors affect the extension of pull strategies?

2. Under what circumstances should a company pursue an international selling effort, and when is a local selling effort more appropriate?

3. What factors make local selling different from country to country?

4. Describe the typical requirements of the international bidding process.

5. What is a consortium and when is forming a consortium useful in making a sale?

6. Explain why the use of sales promotions can vary among countries.

7. How might the effectiveness of "buzz" marketing vary between individualist and collectivist cultures?

Questions for Discussion

1. What difficulties could arise if a U.S. salesperson expected to make a sale of industrial equipment during a 2-week visit in China?

2. Why do you think many countries restrict the promotional use of sweepstakes and other games of chance?

3. What types of companies would you suggest sponsor the next Olympic games? How would such firms profit from their association with the Olympic games?

4. What are the advantages and disadvantages of a virtual trade show compared to an actual one?

5. Do you support UNICEF's decision to oppose the donation of baby formula to African hospitals? Why or why not?

For Further Reading

Arnold, David, Julian Birkinshaw, and Omar Toulan. "Can Selling Be Globalized?: The Pitfalls of Global Account Management." *California Management Review* 44, 1 (Fall 2001): 8–20.

Griffith, David A., and John K. Ryans, Jr. "Organizing Global Communication to Minimize Private Spill-over Damage to Brand Equity." *Journal of World Business* 32, 3 (1997): 189–202.

Money, R. Bruce, and Deborah Colton. "The Response of the 'New Consumer' to Promotion in the Transition Economies of the Former Soviet Bloc." *Journal of World Business* 35, 2 (2000): 189–205.

Miller, Russell R. *Selling to Newly Emerging Markets*. Westport, CT: Quorum Books, 1998.

Simintiras, Antonis C., and Andrew H. Thomas. "Cross-cultural Sales Negotiations: A Literature Review and Research Propositions." *International Marketing Review* 15, 1 (1998): 10–28.

Case 14.1 *The South American Sales Dilemma*

Shortly after his thirty-fourth birthday, Jay Bishop was promoted from director of North American sales to director of global sales at Intelicon, a worldwide provider of digital marketing services. Among the services Intelicon provided were customized e-mail campaigns, online surveys and online customer loyalty and incentive programs. Jay moved into his new position in January. One of his first tasks was to review all global sales numbers in order to identify areas for growth and improvement. During this exercise, he noticed a number of discrepancies between the Latin American sales numbers and numbers for the rest of world. In particular, he noted that 420 sales calls in the United States had resulted in 180 actual sales, whereas in Latin America, only 40 sales had resulted from 200 such sales calls. Eager to make a good start in his new job (and under pressure from his superiors to fix the situation), Jay immediately scheduled a trip to visit offices in Brazil and Argentina in February. He was surprised, however, to receive calls from the country managers in both Sao Paulo and Buenos Aires telling him to put the trip off until March. Recognizing that he knew little about Latin American culture and not wanting to ignore the advice of his new subordinates early on, Jay followed their advice and rescheduled his trip for mid-March.

As often happens when one is busy, Jay's Latin American trip arrived quickly. Stepping off the plane in Sao Paulo after the 10-hour trip, he was exhausted but ready to work. Passing through customs and into the passenger arrival area, he looked furtively for Rivaldo Pessoa, the Brazilian country manager. Mr. Pessoa, however, was nowhere in sight and did not arrive for 30 minutes. Jay was quite frustrated, not to mention jetlagged. Moreover, Mr. Pessoa did not seem very apologetic when he blamed his tardiness on traffic and rain.

Rather than stopping at the hotel so he could drop off his luggage, Jay insisted that they go straight to the office and start analyzing why sales were down in Brazil. He kept trying to bring the topic up on the long drive into the city, but Mr. Pessoa insisted on asking him questions about his family and pointing out landmarks in the city, this being Jay's first visit to Brazil. "Why does this guy want to know my life story? Doesn't he know his job is at stake?" thought Jay. Eventually resigning himself to the fact that nothing would get done until they got to the office, Jay tried to sit back and enjoy the ride.

When they arrived at the office, Mr. Pessoa ushered Jay into the small conference room and then left for 10 minutes before returning with coffee and his two salespeople, Renata Pinheiro and Joao Prestes. Both spoke English well and seemed eager to make a good impression. Jay felt that neither had any idea why he was in Brazil, other than that it might be a goodwill tour. He wanted to get to the point, so he came out and said, "The reason I'm here is that we are not meeting our sales numbers for Latin America, and we need to change that." Mr. Pessoa looked a bit surprised, as did Renata and Joao. Jay pressed on, "I need to run through a few analytical questions to determine the root causes of the challenges in the Brazilian market so that we can fix them and take some of the pressure off of you guys." All three seemed to relax at that.

"Okay, let's begin," said Jay. "First, I want to learn more about your backgrounds, what brought you to Intelicon." Mr. Pessoa began: "Well, before I joined Intelicom 3 years ago, I worked over 20 years in the banking sector, most recently in investment banking at BNP Paribas. I helped take a number of Brazilian companies public and worked on numerous bond issues." Impressed, Jay turned to Joao, who said, "I started in professional services at IBM and worked there for 6 years. As the Internet took off, I wanted to get involved in a smaller, more web-based business, which is when I came to Intelicon." Renata finished: "I graduated from the Fundacao Getulio Vargas a year ago," she said, "and took a degree in marketing. My parents pressed me to go into the family business, but I wanted to make a name for myself and felt that consultative sales would be a great place to start. My parents, however, were shocked that I wanted to sell things rather than doing something they considered more respectable, like marketing or finance. I'm out to prove myself."

Needless to say, Jay was very impressed with his new staff and was even more confused about why they were having so much trouble selling Intelicon's services. He decided to move on to more probing questions. Looking to Mr. Pessoa, he asked, "How do you get your sales prospects? Do you cold-call? Is that successful?" Mr. Pessoa looked a bit perplexed. "I suppose," he said, "that we could probably cold-call more. Mostly we rely on personal contacts within the different organizations." Jay was puzzled. He had heard that this was a common practice in Latin America, but felt that it could be contributing to the long sales cycles that were causing the closing rates in Latin America to be so much lower than in the rest of the world.

Jay believed he was starting to fill in the picture. However, in order to understand thoroughly the challenges he was facing in Latin America, he knew he would have to attend some sales calls. Mr. Pessoa mentioned that he had two meetings scheduled later in the afternoon, one with Abril, a large media conglomerate in Sao Paulo, and the other with CVRD, a powerful mining concern. Jay said he would like to attend, and although Pessoa looked wary for an instant, he readily agreed.

The meeting with Abril started well. Mr. Pessoa clearly had a lot of experience presenting to an audience, and he seemed to know two of the four executives in the room as they caught up on family and friends for the first few minutes of the meeting. At the end of the presentation, Mr. Pessoa and Jay asked a number of probing questions and generally felt the meeting was going well. However, the executives kept raising objections. Eventually Mr. Pessoa folded, thanking them for their time and leaving. Once again, Jay was puzzled. He made a point of mentioning to Mr. Pessoa that sometimes getting a "no" was part of sales and that to be successful he needed to find ways to turn a "no" into a "yes." Mr. Pessoa looked a bit embarrassed but said that he did need to do more of this.

The traffic on the way to the meeting with CVRD was horrible, and much to Jay's chagrin, they arrived nearly an hour late. This did not seem to be a problem, however, because the vice-president they were slated to meet was also running late. Once again, Pessoa did an excellent job in the presentation of products and services, and there was clear interest on the part of the vice-president. Jay thought for sure they would close him on the spot and was getting that tingly feeling. Both sides went through the motions, discussing timelines and pric-

ing structures, but just when Jay was ready to go in for the kill, Pessoa thanked the gentleman for his time, said he would send him a proposal, and scheduled lunch together the following week. Jay did not know what to say. He guessed that the sale would eventually happen, but he also knew he needed to get revenue as soon as possible.

Exhausted, Jay headed back to his hotel and fell fast asleep. He had learned a lot in one day but realized that he still had a long way to go if he wanted to succeed. Tomorrow, he would fly to Argentina and do it all over again.

Discussion Questions

1. What might explain the lower ratio of sales to sales calls in Latin America compared to the United States?
2. In what ways might cultural differences explain differences in personal selling between Brazil and the United States?
3. What advice would you give Jay?

Source: Case prepared by Michael Magers. Used by permission.

Case 14.2 *Flying to Armenia*

British Airways (BA) is the world's biggest international airline, flying passengers to 535 destinations in 160 countries. One such destination is the Republic of Armenia, a small country at the crossroads of Europe and Asia. The whole territory of Armenia is only 11,506 square miles with a population of 3 million. However, an additional 7 million ethnic Armenians live outside Armenia. This Armenian diaspora remains intimately tied to its homeland across generations. Armenian communities around the world attend Armenian churches, teach their children the Armenian language, and celebrate Armenian national and cultural days with great passion. Many Armenians live in various countries of the Middle East and Europe, and one of the largest Armenian communities resides in the United States.

Recently, Armenia has been undergoing a rapid but difficult transition from a Soviet, centrally planned economy to a democratic society with a market economy. The 1990s were particularly diffi-

cult for the country. Armenia shared all the economic problems that resulted from the break-up of established economic relations among what had been the Soviet republics. In addition, Armenia faced an electricity crisis combined with a military territorial conflict with neighboring Azerbaijan. These problems led to a marked lowering of the standard of living of the population in the country and to overall economic difficulties.

However, with foreign aid from the IMF, the World Bank, the European Union, and the U.S. government, as well as substantial assistance from the diaspora, the economy began to stabilize in 1994, when Armenia registered a GDP growth rate of 5.4 percent. By the end of the decade, a legal and regulatory framework for the private sector was being created, and an increasing number of multinational corporations, including Coca-Cola, Adidas, Samsung Electronics, Mercedes-Benz, and Kodak, had established a presence in the country.

Armenia had attracted several international airlines that competed alongside its national carrier, Armenian Airlines. These carriers included British Airways, Swiss Air, Austrian Air, Russian Aeroflot, and Syrian Air. Although traveling was not something many Armenians could afford, it remained the only viable way to travel in and out of the country. Armenia was landlocked, and traveling through neighboring countries was not practical because of poor transportation infrastructure and intermittent political tensions. Most air travelers were employees of international aid organizations operating in Armenia, business travelers, or diaspora Armenians visiting their homeland.

British Airways first entered the Armenian market in December 1997 with twice-weekly service from London to Yerevan, the capital of Armenia. BA, along with Swiss Air and Austrian Air, charged higher prices than Armenian Airlines, Aeroflot, or Syrian Air. BA embarked on several successful promotions to attract customers, to establish brand recognition in the market, and to enhance its international reputation as a caring company. To mark the second anniversary of its instituting flights between London and Yerevan, British Airways put together a program of events designed to support cultural and humanitarian programs in Armenia. BA supported the Third International Chamber Music Festival, which took place in Yerevan from September to November 1999, by bringing two leading Armenian musicians—cellist Alexander Chaoshian and pianist Seda Danyel—from London to Yerevan to participate in the event.

The company also announced a special discount rate to about a dozen destinations, substantially increasing the number of tickets sold. During this campaign, BA contributed $10 from the price of each economy-class ticket and $50 from the price of each business-class ticket to one of Armenia's largest orphanages. (For comparison, per-capita spending for a child in such institutions was around $700 per year.) A special ceremony was held to bestow the funds on the orphanage. For that ceremony, the British Airways hot-air balloon, a familiar ambassador around the world, was brought to Armenia for the first time. The balloon was set to spend a day in Opera Square, the foremost center for cultural activities in Yerevan. Prior to that, British Airways ran a competition in which questions about BA were posed in the local media. People who phoned in with the right answers could meet the crew of the balloon and go for a short ride. This event was widely covered in the Armenian press and on the television news.

British Airways also introduced the Executive Club, BA's frequent-flyer program, to the Armenian market. As with other frequent-flyer programs, members of the Executive Club could earn free flight miles by traveling via British Airways as well as using certain hotels and car rentals. Club membership also offered a variety of other benefits, such as priority on flight waiting lists and a special agent to handle inquiries. British Airways ran a special promotion of the Executive Club at the elite Wheel Club, a favorite dining place of expatriates working in Armenia, especially English speakers. Any member of the Executive Club who ate at the Wheel received an entry into a prize drawing. Anyone who was not a member of the Executive Club could join at the Wheel. The top prize was a pair of tickets to any destination.

British Airways also ran a "Where in the World?" competition. People were invited to write in and say where in the world they dreamed of spending Valentine's Day with the person they loved and why they wanted to go there. The three most creative, funny, or touching entries won a pair of tickets to the dream destination. The event was announced on Hay FM, one of Armenia's most popular radio channels among young people. The event enjoyed a high response rate and engendered considerable word-of-mouth among Hay FM listeners, as well as publicity in the local press.

Discussion Questions

1. For each of the five promotions discussed in the case, identify the target market, explain the motivation behind the promotion, and suggest ways in which to measure the success of the promotion.
2. Why do you think each of these promotions worked well in the Armenian market?
3. Would these promotions be as successful in your country? Why or why not?

Source: Case prepared by Anna V. Andriasova. Used by permission.

Notes

[1] J. Lynn Lunsford, Daniel Michaels, and Andy Pasztor, "At the Paris Air Show, Boeing–Airbus Duel Has New Twist," *Wall Street Journal*, June 15, 2001, p. B4.

[2] Paul Romani, "Selling in the Global Community: The Japanese Model," *American Salesman*, October 1998: 21–25.

[3] Sealed Air Taiwan (A). Harvard Business School, Case No. 9 399-058.

[4] "Chemicals in China: Capacity for Enjoyment," *Financial Times*, September 30, 1986: VI.

[5] "Hong Kong: Executive Guide to the Territory," *Financial Times*, June 27, 1986: XV.

[6] William Briggs, "Next for Communicators: Global Negotiation," *Communication World*, December 1, 1998: 1–3.

[7] "Salesmen Need to Make More Calls Than Competitors to Be Accepted," *Japan Economic Journal*, June 26, 1979: 30.

[8] Jonathan Friedland, "Sweet Solution," *Wall Street Journal*, March 2, 1999.

[9] Jean-Pierre Jeannet, "Siemens Automotive Systems: Brazil Strategy, Case" (Lausanne: IMD, 1993).

[10] Jean-Pierre Jeannet and Robert Collins, "Deloitte Touche Tohmatsu International Europe, Case" (Lausanne: IMD, 1993).

[11] David Arnold, Julian Birkinshaw, and Omar Toulan, "Can Selling Be Globalized?: The Pitfalls of Global Account Management," *California Management Review* 44, 1 (Fall 2001): 8–20.

[12] "Welcome to Europe's Biggest Industrial Fair: Hannover Messe 1998," *Modern Materials Handling*, March 1998: E3.

[13] Jim Carlton, "Comdex Loses Appeal to Industry Players," *Wall Street Journal*, November 16, 1998. p. B6.

[14] Iris Kapustein, "Selling and Exhibiting Across the Globe," *Doors and Hardware*, September 1, 1998: 34.

[15] "WholesaleTradeshow.com Launches First Online Tradeshow for Wholesale and Offprice Merchandise," *PR Newswire*, March 14, 2000.

[16] Peter Fritsch, "Hard Profits," *Wall Street Journal*, April 22, 2002: A1.

[17] Anne Stephens and Andy Rice, "Digital Discounting Arrives," *Finance Week*, July 23, 1998: 33.

[18] R. Bruce Money and Deborah Colton, "The Response of the 'New Consumer' to Promotion in the Transition Economies of the Former Soviet Bloc," *Journal of World Business* 35, 2 (2000): 189–205.

[19] "U.S. Urges Easing of Product-Promotion Rules," *Nikkei Weekly*, November 6, 1995: 3.

[20] David Wessel, "Capital: German Shoppers Get Coupons," *Wall Street Journal*, April 5, 2001, p. A1.

[21] Lenard C. Huff and Dana L. Alden, "An Investigation of Consumer Response to Sales Promotion in Developing Markets," *Journal of Advertising Research*, May/June 1998: 47–57.

[22] Lisa Bertagnoli, "Continental Spendthrifts," *Marketing News*, October 22, 2001: 15.

[23] David A. Griffith and John K. Ryans, Jr., "Organizing Global Communications to Minimize Private Spill-over Damage to Brand Equity," *Journal of World Business* 32, 3 (1997): 189–202.

[24] "MasterCard Renews Commitments with FIFA World Cup Through 2002," *Comline Pacific Research Consulting*, March 19, 1999: 1–2.

[25] Maureen Tkacik, "Is Soccer the New Basketball for Nike?" *Wall Street Journal*, May 6, 2002, p. B1.

[26] "Chaebol Take a Sporting Chance, Raise Spending on Advertising," *Nikkei Weekly*, January 27, 1997: 26.

[27] Melinda Ligos, "Direct Sales Dies in China," *Sales and Marketing Management*, August 1, 1998: 14.

[28] "Eurotelemarketing in Trouble," *Advertising Age*, November 27, 1995: 4.

[29] "Brazil: Boom in the Call Centers Market," *Gazeta Mercantil*, May 31, 1999: 1.

[30] Miriam Jordan, "Wal-Mart Gets Aggressive About Brazil," *Wall Street Journal*, May 25, 2001, p. A8.

[31] Gerry Khermouch and Jeff Green, "Buzz Marketing," *Business Week*, July 30, 2001: 50–56.

[32] Ibid.

[33] R. Bruce Money, "Word-of-Mouth Referral Sources for Buyers of International Corporate Financial Services," *Journal of World Business* 35, 3 (Fall 2000): 314–329.

[34] Joel Baglole, "War of the Doughnuts," *Wall Street Journal*, August 23, 2001, p. B1.

[35] John Carreyrou and Geoff Winestock, "In France, McDonald's Takes Mad-Cow Fears by the Horns," *Wall Street Journal*, April 5, 2001, p. A17.

[36] Alix M. Freedman and Steve Stocklow, "Bottled Up," *Wall Street Journal*, December 5, 2000, p. A1.

[37] Ibid.

[38] Jay Solomon, "How Mr. Bambang Markets Big Macs in Muslim Indonesia," *Wall Street Journal*, October 26, 2001, p. A1.

15 Managing Global Advertising

Shortly After the Exxon Mobil Merger, the new company, based in Irving, Texas, announced plans to promote its four key brands—Exxon, Mobil, Esso, and General—with a global television advertising campaign.[1]

Global campaigns were not new to the company. Exxon's 1965 Esso tiger campaign, "Put a tiger in your tank," was launched in the United States, Europe, and the Far East.[2]

However, the new campaign was aimed at a hundred countries at a cost of $150 million. Five hours of film footage were developed centrally to be accessed by the company's various national subsidiaries. Up to six different casts stood by to act out essentially the same story line—with a few variations. The same scene could be shot with a Japanese man, a sub-Saharan African, a Northern European or a Southern European. Actors varied the hand they used in a scene depicting eating. (In some cultures, food is customarily eaten only with the right hand.) A voice-over told the same story in twenty-five different languages. Centralized production saved considerable production costs for ExxonMobil and helped ensure that television spots would be consistent and of similar quality around the world. It also meant substantial business for the agency—in this

Chapter Outline

case, Omnicon Group's DDB Worldwide—that landed the job. Not everyone agreed that centralization of advertising was a good idea. The CEO of a rival agency, Bcom3 Group's Leo Burnett Worldwide, noted that brands at different stages around the world require different messages and advertising campaigns.[3]

Two important questions must be answered in global advertising: (1) What should be the nature and content of the advertising itself? (2) How much of a local, and how much of a global emphasis should there be when advertising campaigns are developed? The first part of this chapter is organized around the explanation of key external factors and their influence on global advertising. The rest of the chapter focuses on major advertising decisions and helps explain how external factors affect these decisions.

Learning Objectives

After studying this chapter, you should be able to:

▶ Cite ways to avoid faulty translations and ways to minimize the need to translate.

▶ List examples of cultural limitations on the advertising message or on its execution.

▶ Identify key issues related to advertising that tend to be regulated by national governments.

▶ Define the global theme approach to advertising, and explain how it differs from a totally standardized campaign.

▶ List both the advantages and the special requirements of standardized campaigns.

▶ Explain how media availability, media habits, and scheduling international advertising all affect the advertising campaign.

▶ Differentiate among the three options of utilizing domestic advertising agencies, using local advertising agencies, and using international advertising networks.

▶ List the external and internal factors that influence a firm's decision whether to centralize or localize its advertising efforts.

► *Challenges in Global Advertising*

Probably no other aspect of global marketing has received as much attention as advertising. Many mistakes have been made in translating advertising copy from one language into another. Most occurred in the 1960s, when global advertising was in its infancy. Today, most companies and advertising agencies have reached a level of sophistication that reduces the chance of translation error.

Even when the translation hurdle is cleared, however, firms still need to consider the cultural and social background of the target market. Mistakes based on a misinterpretation of cultural habits are more difficult to avoid. And merely avoiding translation or cultural errors does not guarantee an effective advertising campaign. International marketers must also organize effective global campaigns.

Overcoming Language and Cultural Barriers

The proper translation of advertisements remains a challenge to global marketers. Even among English-speaking peoples, common words can vary, as Table 15.1 illustrates. Most translation blunders that plagued global advertising in the past were the result of literal translations performed outside the target country. Today, faulty translations can be avoided by enlisting local nationals or language experts. Global marketers typically have translations checked by a local advertising agency, by their own local subsidiary, or by an independent distributor located in the target country.

These same rules apply when translations are needed within a single country or regional market in order to reach consumers who speak different languages. When the California Milk Processor Board decided to translate its

Table 15.1 *English versus English*

AMERICAN DIALECT	BRITISH DIALECT
Apartment	Flat
Appetizer	Starter
Attic	Loft
Baby carriage	Pram
Car trunk	Boot
College	University
Commercial	Advert
Cookie	Biscuit
Doctor's office	Surgery
Make a decision	Take a decision
Pantyhose	Tights
Paper towel	Kitchen towel
To rent	To let
Realtor	Estate agent
Stove	Cooker
Sweater	Jumper
Washcloth	Flannel
Yard	Garden

World Beat 15.1 *The Center of the World*

On a recent visit to the Shanghai offices of a major toothpaste company, Linda Kovarik, associate director for strategic planning at ad agency Leo Burnett, noticed that many of the female employees kept framed glamour shots on their desk. The most frequent subject: themselves. "I'm not talking about a group hug with mom, dad, and grandpa; it's just themselves," says Ms. Kovarik. It was a telling portrait of the changing mindset of female consumers in China. "We are seeing a rise in materialism and ego. Women are expressing themselves in a way their mothers couldn't," she says. "Brands need to offer them room to be vain and to explain who they are."

Ms. Kovarik got a chance to gauge the mindset of Chinese women in a study of sixty-four consumers in Chengdu and Shanghai in May 2002. She recruited consumers to survey both men and women in their thirties and fifties about their perceptions of young Chinese women today. The myriad stereotypes of Chinese women—the exotic ingénue of the East, the filial traditionalist, the party stalwart—were entirely absent. Instead, one young woman wrote, "I am the center of the world, I am the focal point."

To understand how much the economic clout of Chinese women has changed, consider the following figures. The proportion of the female workforce in managerial positions rose from 2.9 percent in 1990 to 6.1 percent in 2000, while the proportion in professional or technical jobs rose to 22.8 percent, according to the National Bureau of Statistics.

Companies are taking note. In 1998, for example, Procter & Gamble's marketing strategy for Rejoice shampoo, one of the country's top-selling brands, pulled an ad that featured an airline hostess and replaced it with one that featured a woman working as an airline mechanical engineer. The change was driven by consumer surveys that showed women had become more career-focused. Since then, women have again raised the bar, and Rejoice has tried to keep pace. The latest ad for Rejoice Refresh shampoo features a girl playing beach volleyball. "You find a lot of these girls in China," says Rejoice's brand manager. "They're very demanding. They want to be better, but they also want to fulfill other aspirations. Previously, that was career fulfillment, but these days it's also about 'I would like to become a more beautiful lady.'"

Source: Cris Prystay, "As China's Women Change, Marketers Notice," *Wall Street Journal*, May 30, 2002, p. A11.

popular "Got milk?" campaign into Spanish, an adwoman who had moved to Los Angeles from Caracas, Venezuela, warned them that the slogan took on the meaning "Are you lactating?" in Spanish. The board wisely decided to adapt the campaign to ask, "And you, have you given them milk today?"[4]

In the European Union, nine official languages are spoken. As a result, many advertisers emphasize visual communication rather than attempting to communicate their message through the various languages. Visual ads that incorporate pictures rather than words can be more universally understood. Visuals have the advantage of being less culture-specific. For example, Cartier, the French luxury-products firm, launched a global campaign in 123 countries with multinational positioning. The campaign featured minimal copy (words) and emphasized dramatic photography so that the same message could be conveyed in Brazil, Japan, Russia, and dozens of other countries. The campaign used magazines only. Although the campaign was designed and executed centrally, the campaign budgets were dispersed among Cartier's twenty-five subsidiaries.[5]

When Federal Express Corporation launched its first pan-regional campaign for Latin America and the Caribbean, the benefits of express shipping were not well known to consumers in the region. But soccer was. FedEx launched an ad depicting naked soccer players whose uniforms had been lost because FedEx wasn't used to ship them. To save money, the company sought to develop a single advertisement to use in English-, Spanish-, and Portuguese-speaking markets. So that the ad didn't look dubbed, camera angles were employed to appear close to the characters without ever showing their mouths.[6]

Still, some managers of global brands are rethinking the power of local language. The Welsh Language Board encourages the use of the traditional language of Wales in advertisements. Although in decline through most of

Starwood Hotel's Free Weekends Worldwide campaign is an example of the global theme approach. Some features are standard across markets. Other features vary slightly. Destinations in Canada, Mexico, and the United States are depicted in the advertisement targeted to members of Starwood's preferred guest program in Latin America. Different locations, including one in Tokyo, are included in a similar advertisement targeted to the Japanese market.

the twentieth century, Welsh is enjoying a renaissance. Today it is spoken by half a million people in Britain. Coke recently agreed to use Welsh in bilingual posters.[7]

A second contributor to global advertising mistakes has been failure to take into account the cultural attitudes of consumers in foreign countries. Benetton, the Italian clothing manufacturer, launched a campaign under the theme "United Colors of Benetton." One of its ads portrayed a black woman breast-feeding a white baby. Another featured a black and a white man locked together in handcuffs. The ads won awards in France, but they came

under protest from civil rights groups in the United States and had to be withdrawn in that market.

Although FedEx's campaign depicting naked soccer players was very successful in raising brand awareness across Latin America, in other countries and for other products, using nudity can be far more controversial. Sara Lee, the U.S.-based firm that owns such lingerie brands as Playtex, Cacharel, and Wonderbra, faced intense opposition to a series of billboards in Mexico. The company launched its global Wonderbra campaign, which, as part of its outdoor advertising, featured a Czech model posing in the bra. In several Mexican cities, citizens protested the ads as offensive. The company redesigned its billboards for Mexico, clothing the model in a suit.[8]

Sometimes global firms take a proactive approach to cultural differences. In a major re-branding campaign for the Mars candy bar, outdoor billboards ran phrases aimed to trigger feelings of pleasure in local audiences. In Britain the slogan ran "Saturday 3 p.m.," referring to the much-anticipated soccer kick-off time. In France the word "August" evoked the month when the whole country traditionally goes on vacation. In Germany the words "the last parking space" were chosen for their particular national appeal.[9]

To ensure that a message is in line with the existing cultural beliefs of the target market, companies can use resources similar to those used to overcome translation barriers. Local subsidiary personnel or local distributors can judge the cultural content and acceptability of the message. Advertising agencies with local offices can be helpful as well. It is the responsibility of the international marketer to make sure that knowledgeable local nationals have enough input so that the mistake of using an inappropriate appeal in any given market can be avoided.

The Impact of Regulations on International Advertising

In many instances, the particular regulations of a country prevent firms from using standardized approaches to advertising even when these would appear desirable. Malaysia, a country with a large Muslim population, has prohibited ads showing women in sleeveless dresses and pictures showing underarms.[10] China forbids the use of superlative adjectives, as in "best quality" and "finest ingredients." Some European countries require that candy advertising show a toothbrush symbol.

Similarly, differing national rules govern the advertising of pharmaceuticals, alcohol, tobacco, and financial services. Advertising for cigarettes and tobacco products is strictly regulated in many countries. The European Union banned all advertising of tobacco on billboards as of August 2001 and in print advertising as of May 2000.[11] The 191 members of the World Health Organization are negotiating a treaty to establish global regulations on cigarette advertising, as well as designating where smoking would be allowed. This treaty, which will be the first binding treaty on social behavior, should be in effect in 2003.[12]

One of the few areas where cigarette and tobacco advertising is still relatively restriction-free is Central Asia and the Caucasus, formerly part of the Soviet Union. Most of these countries permit cigarette advertising on radio and television, although some relegate it to late-night slots. Such freedoms, however, are rare, and global marketers are well advised to check the local regulations carefully before launching any type of advertising campaign.[13] A stunt pilot was arrested in Lithuania for illegally advertising cigarettes during his maneuvers. The national parliament had just recently banned tobacco ads.[14]

Advertising directed at children is also subject to considerable regulation. Any toy company intending to launch a pan-European advertising campaign could run into a wide variety of differing rules and regulations even within the European Union. In Sweden all advertising aimed at children under the age of twelve is forbidden. In Greece, TV advertising of toys is banned between 7:00 in the morning and 10:00 in the evening.[15]

The European Union is debating a series of rulings that could have great impact on advertising in Europe. The discussions involve efforts toward greater consistency of regulations. Such consistency is generally viewed as desirable throughout Europe and might eventually result in uniform regulations for advertising. This would greatly enhance the potential for pan-European marketing campaigns and make global advertising more efficient. Many expect Sweden's assuming the EU presidency will result in more consistent advertising regulations but may also mean more restrictive national regulations on pharmaceuticals, food, and advertising to children.[16]

▶ *Selecting an Advertising Theme*

Marketers that have products sold in many countries must decide what level of standardization is appropriate for each advertising theme and its creative execution. Early failures by inexperienced companies that employed a totally standardized approach inspired some firms to shift to the other extreme. For a while, most international companies allowed each market to design its own campaigns. In the mid-1960s, European-based advertising executives began to discuss the possibility of greater standardization. Erik Elinder was among the first to extol the benefits of a more standardized approach. Elinder argued that European consumers were increasingly "living under similar conditions although they read and speak different languages."[17]

Global versus Local Advertising

Global advertising—standardizing advertising across all markets—has received a considerable amount of attention and is considered the most controversial topic in international advertising. Saatchi & Saatchi, a British advertising agency, rose to prominence on the basis of its global advertising campaigns. This company claimed that worldwide brands with global campaigns would become the norm.[18]

One of the best examples of a successful standardized campaign was Philip Morris's Marlboro campaign in Europe. Marlboro's success as a leading brand began in the 1950s when the brand was repositioned to ensure smokers that the flavor would be unchanged by the effect of the filter. The theme "Come to where the flavor is. Come to Marlboro country" became an immediate success in the United States and abroad.[19]

Patek Philippe, maker of prestige watches, supported its brand with a standardized television campaign utilizing the theme "You never actually own a Patek Philippe. You merely look after it for the next generation." The campaign has been successful in the United States, Europe, China, Japan, Singapore, and Taiwan.[20]

Standardized campaigns have increased over the years. Most studies of international advertising standardization in the 1970s and 1980s concluded that very little standardization was being used. However, a study of thirty-eight multinationals in the 1990s noted that about half of these companies employed extensive or total standardization when developing and executing their global advertising. Only a quarter stated that standardization was very limited or nonexistent.[21] Still, many marketing executives remain skeptical of the value of global advertising campaigns. A study of European consumers revealed a strong preference for local advertisements, even when consumers preferred global products. In many cases, the most memorable ads proved to be those promoting local brands.[22]

Global campaigns do appear to work, however, if the target market is relatively narrowly defined. For example, Procter & Gamble doubled the sales of Pringles potato chips in 4 years to $1 billion. Now one of P&G's top three global brands, Pringles is sold in over forty countries. P&G attributes the global success of Pringles to a uniform advertising message aimed at young children and teens. The message used around the world is "Once you pop you can't stop." Although P&G allows some local differences in product market-to-market, such as flavor variations, the bulk of the advertising is standardized.[23]

Levi Strauss, on the other hand, a company that admits to being a global company and having a global brand, has been cautious about global advertising. Essentially, the company believes that advertising should remain in the country where it is developed. In Europe the brand is positioned more as a 1950s-era Americana item, whereas the U.S. strategy takes more of a youthful approach.[24]

Still Levi's has been moving cautiously toward more global advertising. Recently, Levi's brought some of the European commercials created by its U.K. agency into the United States. Its latest step was to appoint its first vice-president for global marketing and assign a global advertising budget of $350 million, of which $250 million is allocated to the United States. The company is also attempting to get more advertising mileage by moving its best practices around the world.[25]

A number of other companies have begun the process of developing regional or global brands supported by standardized campaigns:

▶ L'Oréal, the French cosmetics company, has increased its sales to $12.4 billion through its global campaigns for Maybelline, Ralph Lauren perfumes, Helena Rubinstein cosmetics, and Redken hair care products.[26]

▶ H.J. Heinz developed a global campaign for Heinz ketchup to develop consistency in the brand image and advertising across its various national markets.[27]

▶ Volvo launched a $98 million campaign to add styling and design to the automobile's long-standing safety image worldwide.[28]

▶ Jaguar found that its new S-type model appealed to similar customers around the world, so it launched the same campaign from "Chicago to Riyadh, Tokyo and Berlin." This allowed Jaguar to enjoy a consistent image worldwide and save money by not having to develop a different theme for each market.[29]

▶ Sony developed a massive global effort dubbed the Millennium Project to position its electronics, music, and software empire as the leading lifestyle and technology brand for the twenty-first century.[30]

Many firms adopt a **modularized approach** to global advertising. A company may select some features as standard for all its advertisements, while localizing others features. Most common is the **global theme** approach, wherein the same advertising theme is used around the world but is varied slightly with each local execution. Coke's recent global campaign featuring "Coke Moments" is developed and shot in a number of the brand's top markets, including Brazil, Germany, Italy, France, and South Africa as well as the United States. In "Spanish Wedding," a demure young woman enjoys a Coke while dressing for the big day.[31]

Advantages of Global Advertising One advantage of a more standardized approach to advertising involves the economics of a global campaign. To develop individual campaigns in many countries is to incur duplicate costs, such as those for photographs, layouts, and the production of television commercials. In a standardized approach, these production costs can be reduced, and more funds can be spent on purchasing media space. For example, Unilever paid $700,000 for one series of TV commercials to be used in eighteen Asian and European countries. By reusing its commercials in many countries, the company saved on production costs. Furthermore, the company was able to spend more on the original version and therefore produce a better advertisement.[32] Another reason for using a standardized approach is related to global brand names. Many companies market products under a single brand name in several countries within the same region. With the substantial amount of international travel occurring today and the considerable overlap in media across national borders, companies are increasingly interested in creating a single brand image. This image can become confused if local campaigns are in conflict with each other.

Requirements for Global Campaigns For a company to launch a worldwide standardized campaign, some requirements must first be met with regard to the global brand, customer awareness, and consumer attitudes.

Many companies view a standardized brand name or trademark as a prerequisite to a standardized campaign. Not only should the name always be written in identical format, but it should also be pronounced identically. Trademarks or corporate logos can also help in achieving greater standardization of corporate campaigns. Such well-known logos as those of Kodak, Sony, and General Electric are used the world over. The power of a company's brand name has considerable influence on whether the company can use a standardized campaign. Few brand names are universally known.

Because products may be at different stages of their product life cycles in different countries, different types of advertising may be necessary to take into account various levels of customer awareness. Typically, a campaign during the earlier stages of the product life cycle concentrates on familiarizing people with the product category, because many prospective customers may not have heard about it. In later stages, with more intensive competition, campaigns tend to shift toward emphasizing the product's advantages over competitive products. Consider the experience of Procter & Gamble when advertising first became available in what was formerly East Germany. Instead of using the typical ads for West German consumers, which portrayed lifestyle situations, P&G developed a series of local television advertisements that featured specific information on a product's function. The company had found that consumer products such as fabric softeners, liquid detergents, and household cleaners were misunderstood in East Germany. P&G expected that in time, it would be able to air the same television commercials throughout reunited Germany.[33]

READ MORE ABOUT IT:
Check out "From Trash to Treasure" under *Supplemental Readings* on our website.

Products may also face unique challenges in certain markets requiring nationally tailored advertising campaigns. For example, Skoda automobiles are sold throughout Europe and in parts of Asia and Latin America. But in Britain they acquired a deplorable reputation. In a consumer survey, 60 percent of respondents said they would never consider buying a Skoda—even after Volkswagen AG bought the Czech car company and vastly improved the models. The solution was an ad campaign exploiting British humor and Skoda's position as the butt of many jokes. Each self-deprecating advertisement ended with "It's a Skoda. Honest." This very successful campaign improved the acceptance of the car in the British market.[34]

As we noted earlier, cultural differences can also restrict the use of standardized advertising. Taco Bell, a U.S.-based chain with 7,000 restaurants, found that Gidget the talking Chihuahua dog used in advertisements in the United States could not be used in Asia, where many consider dogs a food delicacy, or in Muslim countries, where many consider it taboo to even touch a dog.[35] If standardized advertising is to be used, the needs and restrictions of all relevant markets must be considered early in the development of the advertising campaign.

Land of the Soft Sell: Advertising in the Japanese Market

Japan is the world's second-largest advertising market, after the United States.[36] Many Western firms face special challenges when developing advertising themes for this important market. The dominant style of advertising in Japan is an image-oriented approach, or "soft sell." This contrasts sharply with the more factual approach, or "hard sell," typical in the United States and with the use of humor prevalent in the United Kingdom.[37]

Because different cultural backgrounds yield varying consumer attitudes, it is quite reasonable to expect differences in advertising appeals. In Japan, consumers tend to be moved more by emotion than by logic, in contrast to North Americans or Europeans, and Japanese advertisements often have a strong nonverbal content. Consequently, consumers need to be emotionally convinced about a product. This leads to advertising that rarely mentions price, shies away from comparative advertising aimed at discrediting the products of competing firms, and occasionally even omits the distinctive features or qualities of a product. According to some experts, Western advertising is designed to make the product look superior, whereas Japanese advertising is designed to make it look desirable. The Japanese language even has a verb (*kawasarern*) to describe the process of being convinced to buy a product contrary to one's own rational judgment.

Nonetheless, the Japanese are interested in foreign countries and words, particularly those of the English language. Research conducted for the Nikkei Advertising Research Institute in Japan compared the number of foreign words appearing in advertising headlines. Japan, with 39.2 percent, used the highest number of foreign words, followed by Taiwan with 32.1 percent, Korea with 15.7 percent, and France with 9.1 percent. The United States used foreign words in only 1.8 percent of the headlines investigated.[38]

Japanese television commercials are full of U.S. themes. They often employ U.S. stars or heroes and frequently incorporate U.S. landscapes or back-

World Beat 15.2 *Bad Beer Ads?*

Is this any way to sell beer to the British? New poster ads for Japan's Asahi beer, appearing on billboards and in tube stations throughout London, feature third-rate celebrities in tacky settings, with text that is a mix of Japanese ideograms and stilted English translations. One poster depicts a fur-draped Dickie Davies, former host of a British daytime television sports show, nuzzled by a leering blonde in a casino. The tagline: "Remarkable and Finesse. So good."

The idea is to gently mock Japanese advertising with a sophisticated parody. But to many British eyes, the ads look like they came straight from Tokyo on the cheap. "The campaign isn't even adapted properly for the U.K.," says one real estate agent. "I mean, the English makes no sense." That, of course, is the point, as the campaign's fans well understand. "It's hysterical. I see people all the time who don't understand them," says a London banker. "It's so kitsch it's cool."

The cheeky ads stem from a trip by a WCRS agency team to Tokyo, where they toured the city with representatives from Asahi's U.K. distributor. During the visit, they noticed how uniform advertising in Tokyo appeared to be. Everywhere they went, across TV, posters, and points of sale, they saw beaming celebrities alongside an enormous product shot and logo, over-enthusiastically endorsing all sorts of products.

The advertising efforts have helped double the volume of Asahi sold in Britain. Asahi also has distributors in Germany and France but doesn't plan to export the U.K. ads. The company aims to tailor its marketing efforts to individual countries.

Source: Sarah Ellison, "Bad Beer Ads," *Wall Street Journal Europe*, May 15, 2000.

grounds. By using American actors in their commercials, Japanese companies give the impression that these products are very popular in the United States. Thanks to the Japanese interest in and positive attitudes toward many U.S. cultural themes, such strategies have worked out well for Japanese advertisers. When Mitsubishi Electric paid rock singer Madonna a reported $650,000 for the right to use fragments of a rock tour, the company's VCR sales doubled in 3 months, during which time Mitsubishi's competitors experienced only a 15 percent increase.[39]

Advertising in Japan has also differed from Western practice in its management and structure. In Japan, firms have been less concerned with conflicts of interest within agencies. As a result, competing brands have been handled by the same agency. Dentsu, Japan's largest advertising agency, dominates the market, and the agency accounts for about 30 percent of all media billings in Japan, including 50 percent of prime-time television. Thus Dentsu usually commands the best price and the best space in the press.[40] No other major advertising market in the world is so dominated by a single local agency.

The Impact of Recent Changes in Eastern Europe

Eastern Europe is another part of the world that offers both opportunities and challenges to international marketers. With the political reforms in Eastern Europe, the opportunity to advertise suddenly became available to foreign companies, and advertising has since developed into an acceptable economic activity. A survey of Ukrainian consumers revealed that 98 percent of Ukrainians are now more aware of advertising, especially advertising on

A successful advertising campaign made candy bar Snickers a well-known name in Russia.

television and billboards.[41] In Russia, outside posters and neon signs were among the first types of advertising to appear; Samsung and Goldstar, both of South Korea, were among the first firms to pay the $200,000 in annual fees for two spots in Moscow or St. Petersburg.[42]

As Eastern European markets make the transition to market economies, Western firms have had significant opportunities to build brand awareness quickly. For example, only 5 percent of Russians could identify Snickers as the name of a candy bar in 1992. One year later, after a campaign featuring the Rolling Stones's "(I Can't Get No) Satisfaction," 82 percent were familiar with the name.[43]

Czech consumers and Western consumers are said to differ relatively little, but significant differences persist elsewhere. When an international soft-drink company wanted to introduce its brand to Bulgaria with ads emphasizing health-minded young people, the local agency recommended instead a focus on glitzy nightclubs and bars, because many young Bulgarian consumers were starved for such images after decades of communist rule.

In most Eastern European nations, advertising is still in the early phases of development. According to one expert, "The last hundred years of western advertising [experience] have been compressed into just four years for us."[44] The present infrastructure is radically different from what international firms are used to. Few full-service advertising agencies exist, although many Western agencies are now establishing local offices. Cultural differences also stymie Western advertisers. One Western food company wanted to introduce bouillon cubes to Romania via ads featuring a happy family gathered around the dinner table. The campaign had to be changed because Romanian consumers were not familiar with the family dinner concept.[45]

Credibility of Advertising

Countries view the value of advertising in very different ways. A recent survey conducted by the marketing research company Roper Starch investigated advertising credibility in forty countries.[46] In the United States, 86 percent of consumers were eager to criticize advertising practices, particularly those aimed at children, whereas 75 percent of consumers praised advertising's creativity. In Asia, consumers were more positive. Forty-seven percent indicated that advertisements provided good product information, and 40 percent said that advertisers respected consumers' intelligence. Globally, the results were 38 percent and 30 percent, respectively. Consumers in the former Soviet Union were among the most skeptical. Only 9 percent of consumers there believed that advertising provided good information, and only 10 percent said it respected consumers' intelligence. Globally, 61 percent of consumers appreciated advertising for both its creativity and its entertainment value, but only 23 percent of consumers living in the former Soviet Union agreed.

Differences in the credibility of advertising in general, and in that of some media in particular, must be taken into consideration by the international firm. Companies may want to place greater reliance on advertising in countries where its credibility is very high. In other countries, the marketer should think seriously about using alternative forms of communication.

▶ Global Media Strategy

Global marketers today account for major purchases of media space. Table 15.2 lists the top one hundred global marketers in media spending outside the United States. A variety of media are available across the world. Difficulties arise because not all media are available in all countries. And if they are available, their technical capability to deliver a message to the required audience may be limited. Therefore, global marketers must consider the availability of various media for advertisers as well as the media habits of the target country.

Media Availability

Advertisers in the United States and many European countries have become accustomed to the availability of a full range of media for advertising purposes. Aside from the traditional print media, consisting of newspapers and magazines, the U.S. advertiser has access to radio, television, billboards, cinemas, and the Internet. In addition, direct mail can be used with most prospective client groups. This wide choice among media is not available in every country. Therefore, a company marketing its products in several countries may find itself unable to apply the same media mix in all markets. Even when certain media are available, access may be partially restricted. For example, in Poland the public and private channels may devote no more than 10 percent of their airtime to advertising.[47]

Marketers can also employ global media. Global television includes news networks, such as BBC World and CNN, and consumer channels, such as Animal Planet, Discovery, ESPN, and MTV. However, the global print media consist largely of magazines targeted at business executives, such as *Business*

Table 15.2 *Top 100 Global Marketers by Media Ad Spending Outside the United States*

RANK IN 2000	RANK IN 1999	ADVERTISER	HEADQUARTERS	SPENDING OUTSIDE THE U.S. 2000	% CHANGE FROM 1999	COUNTRY COUNT
1	1	Unilever	London/Rotterdam	$2,967	0.7	56
2	2	Procter & Gamble Co.	Cincinnati	2,610	−8.8	66
3	3	Nestlé	Vevey, Switzerland	1,560	9.8	53
4	9	Toyota Motor Corp.	Toyota City, Japan	1,345	31.2	43
5	4	Volkswagen	Wolfsburg, Germany	1,290	0.5	26
6	5	Coca-Cola Co.	Atlanta	1,176	−0.7	64
7	7	Ford Motor Co.	Dearborn, Mich.	1,127	3.5	39
8	6	General Motors Corp.	Detroit	1,028	−13.1	39
9	10	PSA Peugeot Citroen	Paris	1,004	4.1	25
10	12	Fiat	Turin, Italy	988	19.4	23
11	11	Renault	Paris	914	−2.9	29
12	8	L'Oréal	Paris	913	−11.8	38
13	28	Kao Corp.	Tokyo	715	96.1	4
14	19	McDonald's Corp.	Oak Brook, Ill.	694	26.5	48
15	13	Mars Inc.	McLean, Va.	692	0.4	27
16	22	Vodafone Group	Newbury, Berkshire, U.K.	673	33.7	9
17	14	Nissan Motor Co.	Tokyo	665	0.4	34
18	17	Henkel	Duesseldorf	654	3.0	32
19	18	Ferrero	Perugia, Italy	633	0.8	26
20	15	Sony Corp.	Tokyo	556	−13.1	35
21	16	Philip Morris Cos.	New York	541	−14.9	36
22	20	Danone Group	Levallois-Perret, France	539	1.0	18
23	21	France Telecom	Paris	527	2.5	11
24	26	DaimlerChrysler	Auburn Hills, Mich./Stuttgart	424	10.3	18
25	25	Telefonica	Madrid	419	8.3	4
26	27	Beiersdorf	Hamburg, Germany	407	11.3	35
27	44	AOL Time Warner	New York	372	80.5	22
28	24	Colgate-Palmolive Co.	New York	370	−16.1	47
29	29	Honda Motor Co.	Tokyo	367	9.8	17
30	35	British Telecommunications	London	344	32.8	4
31	37	Reckitt Benckiser	Windsor, Berkshire, U.K.	341	39.7	18
32	54	Lion Nathan	Sydney	326	116.3	4
33	30	Daewoo Corp.	Seoul	314	9.2	24
34	34	IBM Corp.	Armonk, N.Y.	284	5.9	15
35	23	Vivendi Universal	Paris	268	−44.0	18
36	47	LG Group	Seoul	262	38.5	21
37	31	Carrefour Group	Paris	257	−9.9	11
38	63	Tele2	Stockholm	253	100.0	11
39	41	GlaxoSmithKline	Greenford, Middlesex, U.K.	251	11.6	33
40	32	PepsiCo	Purchase, N.Y.	243	−13.1	33
41	33	Matsushita Electric Industries	Osaka	243	−10.4	14
42	46	Samsung Electronics	Seoul	243	25.2	25

Table 15.2 *Top 100 Global Marketers by Media Ad Spending Outside the United States* (Continued)

RANK IN 2000	RANK IN 1999	ADVERTISER	HEADQUARTERS	SPENDING OUTSIDE THE U.S. 2000	% CHANGE FROM 1999	COUNTRY COUNT
43	39	Mazda Motor Corp.	Hiroshima, Japan	240	5.8	16
44	40	Mitsubishi Motors Corp.	Tokyo	226	0.5	17
45	45	Hyundai Motor Co.	Seoul	225	13.6	20
46	36	Bertelsmann	Guetersloh, Germany	223	−10.0	10
47	48	Royal KPN	The Hague, The Netherlands	223	24.7	5
48	66	Siemens	Munich	221	100.2	27
49	51	Wm. Wrigley Jr. Co.	Chicago	219	32.6	28
50	60	Nokia	Helsinki	203	57.5	28
51	38	Kellogg Co.	Battle Creek, Mich.	203	−15.8	18
52	42	Johnson & Johnson	New Brunswick, N.J.	202	−8.8	33
53	49	Diageo	London	201	13.5	22
54	55	EMI Group	London	196	32.4	12
55	50	BMW	Munich, Germany	192	10.3	15
56	58	News Corp.	Sydney	164	23.3	4
57	59	B.A.T Industries	London	151	15.4	24
58	53	Ajinomoto Co.	Tokyo	148	−5.1	4
59	43	Joh. A. Benckiser	Ludwigshafen, Germany	143	−32.6	21
60	56	Interbrew	Leuven, Belgium	140	−2.5	6
61	62	Coop	Basel, Switzerland	139	9.6	5
62	61	Heineken	Amsterdam	134	5.1	12
63	52	Bacardi	Hamilton, Bermuda	129	−18.0	11
64	82	Canon	Tokyo	122	72.0	14
65	73	Suzuki Motor Co.	Hamamatsu, Japan	122	39.6	9
66	67	Toshiba Corp.	Tokyo	120	9.9	4
67	64	MG Rover Group	Bickenhill, U.K.	120	2.7	7
68	65	Kimberly-Clark Corp.	Irving, Texas	112	0.6	17
69	57	Philips Electronics	Eindhoven, The Netherlands	111	−20.0	21
70	76	Fuji Heavy Industries	Cherry Hill, N.J.	110	36.8	5
71	69	Cadbury Schweppes	London	108	4.3	13
72	71	Sharp Corp.	Osaka, Japan	103	12.9	7
73	68	Hitachi	Tokyo	101	−7.5	4
74	74	Tricon Global Restaurants	Louisville, Ky.	98	18.1	16
75	86	Motorola	Schaumburg, Ill.	93	40.2	8
76	70	Bayer	Leverkusen, Germany	91	−9.1	12
77	72	Woolworth Group	Rochdale, Lancashire, U.K.	87	−3.6	5
78	80	United International Pictures	Amsterdam	86	20.2	7
79	75	BellSouth Corp.	Atlanta	81	−3.0	4
80	85	Kia Motors Co.	Seoul	79	15.2	10
81	81	Gillette Co.	Boston	76	6.6	23
82	94	Compaq Computer Corp.	Houston	73	31.5	16

Table 15.2 *Top 100 Global Marketers by Media Ad Spending Outside the United States* (Continued)

RANK IN 2000	RANK IN 1999	ADVERTISER	HEADQUARTERS	SPENDING OUTSIDE THE U.S. 2000	% CHANGE FROM 1999	COUNTRY COUNT
83	96	Microsoft Corp.	Redmond, Wash.	72	44.7	13
84	79	Ingka Holdings	Humlebaek, Denmark	72	–0.5	8
85	83	Tchibo Holding	Hamburg, Germany	71	0.0	15
86	89	Ericsson	Stockholm	71	13.0	22
87	77	Telia	Farsta, Sweden	71	–8.3	4
88	91	Virgin	London	68	12.5	5
89	84	Hewlett-Packard Co.	Palo Alto, Calif.	66	–4.5	16
90	97	HSBC Holdings	London	66	35.3	7
91	98	Allianz	Munich	64	33.6	8
92	78	Hasbro	Pawtucket, R.I.	63	–17.8	5
93	95	Oetker Group	Bielefeld, Germany	61	11.4	6
94	93	Boots Co.	Nottingham, U.K.	60	7.8	8
95	92	Novartis	Basel, Switzerland	56	0.4	11
96	88	Agrolimen	Barcelona	56	–12.0	5
97	90	Mattel	El Segundo, Calif.	56	–10.8	5
98	100	Sara Lee Corp.	Chicago	51	15.8	12
99	87	Electrolux	Stockholm	50	–21.7	15
100	99	Walt Disney Co.	Burbank, Calif.	6.2	8	1,054

Note: Figures are in millions of U.S. dollars. The 1999 rankings reflect data collected in 2001. Country count is the number of countries where spending was reported for 2000. Primary non-U.S. data from ACNielsen; U.S. measured media data from Taylor Nelson Sofres' CMR. *Source: Advertising Age.*

Week, The Economist, Fortune, and *Time,* along with only a few consumer magazines such as *Reader's Digest* and *Elle.*[48]

The regional distribution of the media spending of top global marketers is shown in Table 15.3. These differences in global advertising spending partially reflect different media availability. In Latin America, television advertising has reached a higher percent of GDP than in any other region of the world.[49] Already the demand for television slots in Mexico has caused a surge in prices there. Televisa's flagship Channel 2 announced price increases of up to 265 percent for key time slots.[50] As a consequence of the limited accessibility of commercial television in Europe, TV advertising has been less important there than in North America and Asia.[51] Billboard advertising, however, is growing in Europe. Outdoor advertising accounted for 6 percent of overall advertising expenditures in 2001, not counting classified ads. And in Belgium, France, and Switzerland, its contribution was nearly double that figure. New technology and higher-quality images are credited with spurring this growth.[52]

In light of media differences, as well as market differences, global managers must remain flexible in crafting their media plans. A company cannot expect to use its preferred medium to the fullest extent everywhere. Consequently, global advertising campaigns must be flexible enough to adapt to local situations. For example, when international insurers recently entered

Table 15.3 *Top 25 Global Marketers' Regional Distribution of Media Spending*

RANK IN 2000	ADVERTISER	U.S. MEDIA AD SPENDING IN 2000	AFRICAN AD SPENDING	ASIAN AD SPENDING*	EUROPEAN AD SPENDING	LATIN AMERICAN AD SPENDING	MIDDLE EASTERN AD SPENDING
1	Unilever	$698	$24	$931	$1,713	$291	$7
2	Procter & Gamble Co.	1,542	7	589	1,513	397	41
3	Nestlé	327	7	404	985	163	1
4	Toyota Motor Corp.	790	6	905	365	0	13
5	Volkswagen	424	4	14	1,101	150	0
6	Coca-Cola Co.	403	15	399	515	226	8
7	Ford Motor Co.	1,196	0	49	800	153	6
8	General Motors Corp.	2,951	0	52	579	154	16
9	PSA Peugeot Citroen	0	0	0	987	17	0
10	Fiat	2.0	3	0	896	90	0
11	Renault	0	2	0	851	62	0
12	L'Oréal	494	3	21	826	36	0
13	Kao Corp.	42.1	0	715	0	0	0
14	McDonald's Corp.	710	4	298	352	1	5
15	Mars Inc.	288	0	36	656	0	0
16	Vodafone Group	41.8	0	11	662	0	0
17	Nissan Motor Co.	619	2	346	264	22	10
18	Henkel	8.4	0	10	644	0	0
19	Ferrero	34.5	0	0	633	0	0
20	Sony Corp.	659	0	306	228	2	2
21	Philip Morris Cos.	1,770	0	56	443	18	2
22	Danone Group	54.5	0	0	525	15	0
23	France Telecom	1.5	0	18	471	0	38
24	DaimlerChrysler	1,686	2	2	236	51	2
25	Telefonica	43.6	0	0	293	126	0

Note: Figures are millions of U.S. dollars. Rank based on non-U.S. spending. Country count is the number of countries where spending was reported for 2000. Primary non-U.S. data from ACNielsen; U.S. measured media data from Taylor Nelson Sofres' CMR.
*Asia includes Australia and New Zealand.
Source: Advertising Age.

India's life insurance market, they estimated that only a quarter of the market had been tapped. As a result, advertisements explaining the benefits of life insurance proliferated. The ubiquitous ads appeared on billboards, in newspapers, on colorful websites, and on posters decorating kiosks.[53]

Satellite Television

Satellite television channels, which are not subject to government regulations, have revolutionized television in many parts of the world. One of the most successful global satellite ventures is MTV. This music channel, which was launched in 1981 in the United States, now reaches 250 million homes in more than 60 countries.[54] Even such a specialized channel as the Discovery Channel already reaches some 87 million subscribers in 90 countries.[55]

The leader in this field of privately owned channels is Sky Channel, owned by Rupert Murdoch, who controls vast media interests in many countries. Murdoch purchased the Star Satellite System in 1993. It serves 45 million people from Egypt to Mongolia.[56] By 2005, Murdoch expects to see 178 million cable or satellite homes in Asia, about 150 million of those being in China, India, and Japan.[57] With its transnational reach, the Star System relies heavily on advertising revenue from such advertisers as Nike and Coca-Cola.[58]

For satellite-shown commercials to be effective, companies must be able to exploit a global brand name and a uniform logo. Also, language remains a problem. English is the common language of the majority of satellite channels. However, there is a trend toward local-language satellite broadcasts. Satellite channels are now available in several European languages, such as German, French, and Swedish.

Most observers admit that the availability of satellite commercial networks has already had an impact on the national regulatory boards of countries that tended to restrict or limit commercial airtime. Most predict that less restricted commercial television will become the norm. Overall, satellite television is likely to enlarge the television advertising market substantially in Europe and in developing countries.

A satellite dish sits on a rooftop in Damascus, Syria. In many developing countries advertisers can now take advantage of increased media availability.

Media Habits

Besides being concerned with media availability, international marketers must also consider media habits in different national markets. Substantial differences in media habits exist worldwide. As we have already seen, the penetration of various media can differ substantially from one country to another. In addition, advertisers encounter radically different literacy rates in many parts of the world. Different cultural traits may also favor one medium over another, regardless of media penetration ratios and literacy rates.

Both the ownership or usage of television and radio, and the readership of print media (newspapers and magazines) vary considerably from one country to another. The developed industrial nations show high penetration ratios for all three major media carriers. Developing countries have fewer radio and television receivers per capita and lower newspaper circulation. In general, the penetration of all of these media increases with the average income of a country. In most countries, the higher-income classes avail themselves first of the electronic media and newspapers. International marketers have to be aware that some media, though generally accessible to the advertiser, may be of only limited use because they reach only a small part of the country's population.

The literacy of a country's population can strongly influence a firm's media decisions. Although this is less of a concern for companies in the industrial-products market, it is a crucial factor in consumer-goods advertising. In countries where large portions of the population are illiterate, the use of print media is of limited value. Both radio and television have been used by companies to circumvent the literacy problem.

Television and radio can be used to overcome this problem, but they cannot be used in areas where the penetration of such receivers is limited. This applies particularly to developing countries that have low electronic-media penetration and low literacy rates. However, over the past 20 years, the diffusion of electronic media in developing countries has spurred a surge in television advertising. In 2000, 38 percent of India's total advertising expenditures went to television, and television advertising is expected to overtake print advertising by 2005.[59] In Egypt, the second-largest advertising market in the Middle East, after Saudi Arabia, television accounts for 50 percent of advertising expenditures.[60]

Banner advertising on the Internet is a more recently devised way to try to reach literate, online consumers. But media habits vary here as well. Hong Kong's Internet surfers' average click rate for advertising banners at the top of the page is 0.78 percent, compared to 0.45 in Britain and 0.31 percent in the United States.[61]

Scheduling International Advertising

Media expenditures tend to peak before sales peak. How long before depends on the complexity of the consumers' buying decision and the length of their deliberation. This principle, though somewhat generalized here, applies to international markets as well as to domestic ones. Differences exist, however, because of varying sales peaks, national vacations, and religious holidays and because of differences in the deliberation time with regard to purchases.

Sales peaks are influenced both by climatic seasons and by customs and traditions. Winter months in North America and Europe are summer months in countries of the Southern Hemisphere, such as Australia, New Zealand, South Africa, Argentina, and Brazil. Of course, the season influences the purchase and consumption of many consumer goods, such as clothing, vacation services, travel, and soft drinks. Vacations are particularly important for some European countries. Religious holidays may also affect the placement or timing of advertising. During the Islamic Ramadan, many Muslim countries do not allow any advertising to be placed.

For industrial products, the timing of advertising in support of sales efforts may be affected by the budgetary cycles that prevail in a given country. For countries with large state-controlled sectors, heavy emphasis needs to be placed on the period before a new national or sector plan is developed. Private-sector companies tend to be more heavily influenced by their own budgetary cycles, which usually coincide with their fiscal years. In Japan, many companies begin their fiscal year in June rather than in January. To the extent that capital budgets are completed before the new fiscal year commences, products that require budgetary approval will need advertising support in advance of budget completion.

The time needed to think about a purchase has been cited as a primary consideration in deciding how long it is appropriate for the advertising peak to precede the sales peak. In its domestic market, a company may be accustomed to a given deliberation time on the part of its customers. But because deliberation times may be determined by income level or other environmental factors, other markets may exhibit different patterns. The purchase or replacement of a small electrical household appliance may be a routine decision for a North American household, and the purchase may occur whenever the need arises. In a country with lower income levels, such a purchase may be planned several weeks or even months ahead. Consequently, a company engaged in international advertising needs to evaluate carefully the underlying assumptions of its domestic advertising policies and not just automatically assume that they apply elsewhere.

► *Organizing the Global Advertising Effort*

A major concern for global marketing executives revolves around the organization of the company's global advertising effort. Key concerns include the role of the head office versus the roles that subsidiaries and the advertising agency should play. Marketers are aware that a more harmonious approach to the international advertising effort may enhance both the quality and the efficiency of the total effort. Organizing the effort deserves as much time as individual advertising decisions about individual products or campaigns. In this section, we look in greater detail at the selection of an advertising agency and at the managerial issues that arise in running a global advertising effort in a multinational corporation.

Selection of an Advertising Agency

Global companies have a number of options with respect to working with advertising agencies. Many companies develop an agency relationship domestically and must decide whether they expect their domestic agency to handle their global advertising business as well. In some foreign markets, companies need to select foreign agencies to work with them—a decision that may be made by the head office alone or left to the local subsidiaries. Recently, some agencies have banded together to form international networks to attract more global business.

Working with Domestic Agencies When a company starts to grow internationally, it is not unusual for the domestic advertising agency to handle the international business as well. However, this is possible only when the domestic agency has global experience and capability. Many smaller domestic agencies do not have international experience. Companies are then forced to make other arrangements. Frequently, the global company begins by appointing individual agencies in each of the various foreign markets where it is operating. This may be done with the help of the local subsidiaries or through the staff at the company's head office. Before long, however, the company will end up with a series of agency relationships that may make global coordination very difficult.

Working with Local Agencies The local advertising agency is expected to understand the local environment fully and is in a position to create advertisements targeted to the local market. Although it markets one of the world's best-known brands, Mercedes-Benz has a strategy of utilizing many local agencies. Its $400 million worldwide advertising budget is spread across 200 local agencies. The company follows a policy of enlisting the most creative shop in each country. Prior to 1980, the company did engage heavily in global advertising, using the Ogilvy & Mather Worldwide agency. When Ogilvy & Mather pursued the business of competitor Ford Motor Company, Mercedes fired the agency. Mercedes has since adopted a policy of varying its brand image from country to country. As a result, it is not in a position to use global advertising campaigns at this time. Instead, the company's versatile advertising effort is supervised by a small staff of six at the head office in Germany.[62]

Working with International Advertising Networks Many companies with extensive international operations find it too difficult and cumbersome to deal simultaneously with a large number of agencies, both domestic and international. For this reason, multinational firms have tended to concentrate their accounts with some large advertising agencies that operate their own global networks. Table 15.4 lists the world's top ten advertising agency brands. Among the leaders are Dentsu, McCann-Erickson Worldwide, BBDO Worldwide, J. Walter Thompson, and Ogilvy & Mather Worldwide. These networks may include media-buying operations that help global firms consolidate their global media buying, often resulting in better deals.

The first generation of international networks was created by U.S.-based advertising agencies in the 1950s and 1960s when clients encouraged their U.S. agencies to move into local markets where the advertising agencies were weak. Leaders in this process were J. Walter Thompson, Ogilvy & Mather, BBDO, and Young & Rubicam. British entrepreneurs Saatchi & Saatchi and WPP dominated the second wave of international networks. Other networks were developed by French and Japanese agencies.[63] The 1980s saw many mergers of medium-sized agencies around the world. In the 1990s, mergers and acquisitions occurred among even the largest global

Table 15.4 *World's Top 10 Core Agency Brands (ranked by worldwide gross income in 2001)*

RANK IN 2001	RANK IN 2000	AGENCY	HEADQUARTERS	GROSS INCOME IN 2001	% CHANGE FROM 2000	BILLINGS IN 2001
1	1	Dentsu	Tokyo	$2,078.1	−11.6	$14,120.3
2	2	McCann-Erickson Worldwide	New York	1,857.9	2.1	17,725.8
3	3	BBDO Worldwide	New York	1,611.7	1.3	14,582.1
4	4	J. Walter Thompson Co.	New York	1,536.1	3.2	10,465.4
5	5	Euro RSCG Worldwide	New York	1,441.2	−2.2	10,123.7
6	6	Grey Worldwide	New York	1,321.0	−2.1	8,487.7
7	7	DDB Worldwide Communications	New York	1,214.6	−2.5	9,796.8
8	9	Ogilvy & Mather Worldwide	New York	1,135.4	3.8	10,688.0
9	12	Leo Burnett Worldwide	Chicago	1,072.3	8.1	9,458.9
10	10	Publicis Worldwide	New York	1,066.0	3.5	7,940.0

Note: Figures are millions of U.S. dollars.
Source: Advertising Age.

agencies. Some of these mergers utilized the umbrella of a holding company that allowed each agency to retain its brand identity while enjoying the advantages of greater size and the ability to access the full global reach of all alliance partners.[64] The world's largest advertising organizations are listed in Table 15.5.

Utilizing global advertising agencies or networks can be desirable in countries where advertising is not as developed as in the major markets of North America and Europe. For example, global agencies are favored in Eastern Europe, where up to 90 percent of the advertising in some markets is handled by affiliates of global agencies. They can leverage a vast knowledge within the agency network and transfer much-needed skills in order to attract business from such leading firms as Coca-Cola, Nestlé, and Unilever.[65] In 2000, communist Vietnam opened to foreign advertising agencies—albeit those operating with a local, Vietnamese partner. Nearly two dozen international agencies flooded into Vietnam, the world's thirteenth most populous country.[66]

International advertising networks are especially sought after because of their ability to handle global campaigns. Usually, one set of advertisements will be created and then circulated among the local affiliates. Working within the same agency or network guarantees consistency and a certain willingness among affiliate offices to accept direction from a central location. Therefore, as companies develop their global business and coordinate their global campaigns, they are likely to consolidate agencies. Colgate-Palmolive became the first packaged-goods company to consolidate its entire worldwide $500 million advertising budget in the hands of a single agency. In a similar vein, IBM selected Ogilvy & Mather to control its $450 million in billings, which had previously been scattered among forty different agencies. Procter & Gamble used nine core agencies for its U.S. business but placed its international advertising with only three global networks. Kraft Foods also moved to three networks to handle its advertising in more than thirty countries.[67]

Table 15.5 *World's Top 50 Advertising Organizations (ranked by worldwide gross income from all marketing-related activities)*

RANK 2001	RANK 2000	ADVERTISING ORGANIZATION	HEADQUARTERS	WORLDWIDE GROSS INCOME 2001	WORLDWIDE GROSS INCOME % CHANGE FROM 2000	WORLDWIDE BILLINGS IN 2001
1	2	WPP Group	London	$8,165.0	2.5	$75,711.0
2	1	Interpublic Group of Cos.	New York	7,981.4	−1.9	66,689.1
3	3	Omnicom Group	New York	7,404.2	6	58,080.1
4	4	Publicis Groupe (includes Bcom3 Group)	Paris	4,769.9	2	52,892.2
5	5	Dentsu	Tokyo	2,795.5	−8.9	20,847.8
6	6	Havas Advertising	Levallois-Perret, France	2,733.1	−2.1	26,268.5
7	7	Grey Global Group	New York	1,863.6	1.7	12,105.7
8	8	Cordiant Communications Group*	London	1,174.5	−7	13,388.0
9	9	Hakuhodo	Tokyo	874.3	−13	6,862.2
10	10	Asatsu-DK	Tokyo	394.6	−8.7	3,500.6
11	11	TMP Worldwide	New York	358.5	−13.8	1,705.6
12	12	Carlson Marketing Group	Minneapolis	356.1	−8.7	2,611.1
13	17	Incepta Group	London	248.4	13.6	695.0
14	13	DigitasA	Boston	235.5	−18.3	NA
15	15	Tokyu Agency	Tokyo	203.9	−11.3	1,782.6
16	16	Daiko Advertising	Tokyo	203.0	−10.2	1,585.0
17	14	Aspen Marketing Group	Los Angeles	189.2	−24	1,262.2
18	18	Maxxcom	Toronto	177.1	−0.1	386.7
19	20	Cheil Communications	Seoul	142.0	−5.6	796.0
20	23	Doner	Southfield, Mich.	114.2	4	1,070.8
21	19	Ha-Lo Industries	Niles, Ill.	105.0	−33.3	NA
22	22	Yomiko Advertising*	Tokyo	102.2	−7.7	1,022.2
23	21	SPAR Group	Tarrytown, N.Y.	101.8	−8.3	678.8
24	30	Cossette Communication Group	Quebec City	95.2	12.1	488.2
25	28	DVC Worldwide	Morristown, N.J.	92.6	4.4	680.9
26	25	Clemenger Group	Melbourne, Australia	91.0	−10.7	606.9
27	29	Rubin Postaer & Associates	Santa Monica, Calif.	90.3	3.7	851.4
28	27	Hawkeye Communications	New York	87.8	−2.9	585.4
29	24	Panoramic Communications	New York	86.2	−16.7	1,194.1
30	31	Richards Group	Dallas	84.5	1.2	570.5
31	26	Asahi Advertising	Tokyo	84.3	−14	572.0
32	45	inChord Communications (Gerbig Snell/Weishemer)	Westerville, Ohio	76.1	26.9	630.1
33	35	Bartle Bogle Hegarty	London	73.9	−5	581.3
34	32	Wieden & Kennedy*	Portland, Ore.	73.8	−9.9	777.2
35	38	Cramer-Krasselt	Chicago	72.7	2.9	478.2
36	37	M&C Saatchi Worldwide	London	71.7	−0.3	577.1
37	34	LG Ad	Seoul	67.6	−13.6	492.4
38	33	Nikkeisha	Tokyo	66.5	−17.7	440.1
39	36	AKQA	San Francisco	66.0	−12	264.0
40	40	Armando Testa Group	Turin, Italy	62.9	−6.1	698.4
41	43	Sogei	Tokyo			

Table 15.5 *World's Top 50 Advertising Organizations (ranked by worldwide gross income from all marketing-related activities)* (Continued)

RANK		ADVERTISING ORGANIZATION	HEADQUARTERS	WORLDWIDE GROSS INCOME		WORLDWIDE BILLINGS
2001	2000			2001	% CHANGE FROM 2000	IN 2001
42	48	Springer & Jacoby	Hamburg, Germany	61.3	−0.8	437.2
43	47	ChoicePoint Direct	Peoria, Ill.	60.6	2.9	404.4
44	44	Gage	Minneapolis	59.4	0.3	396.3
45	39	Harte-Hanks Direct & Interactive	Langhorne, Pa.	58.6	−4.7	391.1
				57.0	−15.9	353.8
46	59	360 Youth	Cranberry, N.J.			
47	51	Ryan Partnership	Westport, Conn.	56.7	29.5	407.2
48	46	Envoy Communications Group	Toronto	56.3	1.8	319.9
49	54	MARC USA	Pittsburgh	54.8	−8.3	NA
50	64	Data Marketing	Santa Clara, Calif.	53.2	1.6	586.0

Note: Totals are in millions of U.S. dollars and by equity. The 2000 column is based on figures reported in 2002. Minority-held agencies qualify as advertising organizations.
*Ad Age estimate.
Source: Advertising Age.

Coordinating International Advertising

The role the international marketing executive plays in a company's international advertising effort may differ from firm to firm and depends on several factors. Outside factors, such as the nature of the market or of the competition, as well as internal factors, such as company culture or philosophy, may lead some firms to adopt a more centralized approach in international advertising. Other firms may prefer to delegate more authority to local subsidiaries and local agencies. Key factors that can cause a firm to either centralize or decentralize decision making for international advertising are reviewed in the sections that follow.

External Factors Affecting Advertising Coordination One of the most important factors influencing how companies allocate decision making for international advertising is market diversity. For products or services where customer needs and interests are homogeneous across many countries, greater opportunities for standardization exist, and companies are more likely to centralize decision making. Companies operating in markets with very different customer needs or market systems are more likely to decentralize their international-advertising decision making. Local knowledge is more important to the success of these firms.

The nature of the competition can also affect the way an international firm plans for decision making related to advertising. Firms that essentially face local competition or different sets of competitors from country to country may find it more logical to delegate international advertising to local subsidiaries. On the other hand, if a company is competing everywhere against a small set of international firms, the company is more apt to centralize key marketing decisions in an attempt to coordinate its actions against its global competitors. In such cases, advertising decision making may be centralized as well.

Internal Factors Affecting Advertising Coordination A company's own internal structure and organization can also greatly influence its options in terms of centralizing or decentralizing decision making about international advertising. The opportunities for centralizing are few when a company's approach is to customize advertising for each local market. However, when a company adheres to a standardized advertising format, a more centralized approach will be possible and probably even desirable.

Skill levels and efficiency concerns can also affect the level of centralization. Decentralization is possible only when the advertising skills of local subsidiaries and local agencies are sufficient for them to perform successfully. Decentralization is often believed to result in inefficiencies or decreased quality because a firm's budget may be spread over too many individual agencies. Instead of having a large budget in one agency, the firm has created minibudgets that may not be adequate to attract the best creative talent to work on its products. Centralization often gives the firm access to better talent, though knowledge of the local markets may be sacrificed. On the other hand, international advertising cannot be centralized successfully in companies where the head-office staff does not possess a full appreciation of the international dimension of the firm's business.

The managerial style of the international company may also affect the centralization decision on advertising. Some companies pride themselves on giving considerable freedom to managers at their local subsidiaries. Under such circumstances, centralizing advertising decisions may be counterproductive. The general approach taken by the company's top management toward international markets is closely related to its desire to centralize or decentralize international advertising.

However, because the internal and external factors that characterize the company are subject to change over time, the decision to centralize or decentralize will never be a permanent one. In 2000, Coca-Cola shifted more advertising decision making to its subsidiaries. In 2002, advertising oversight shifted back to headquarters in Atlanta. Lackluster sales and some embarrassing ads—an angry grandmother streaking down a beach in Italy—proved fatal to Coke's "think local" strategy.[68]

READ MORE ABOUT IT: Check out "Local Strategy Fizzles" under *Supplemental Readings* on our website.

▶ *Conclusions*

The complexity of dealing simultaneously with a large number of different customers in many countries, all speaking their own languages and subject to their own cultural heritage, presents a real challenge to the international marketer. Proponents of global advertising point to the convergence of customer needs and the emergence of "world consumers," customers who are becoming ever more homogeneous whether they live in Paris, London, New York, or Tokyo. However, many aspects of the advertising environment remain considerably diverse. Although English is rapidly becoming a global language, most messages still have to be translated into local languages. Widely differing regulations in many countries on the execution, content, and format of advertisements still make it very difficult to apply

Should advertising for your product be standardized, customized or modularized? What adaptations might be necessary for your target market? Continue with *Country Market Report* on our web site.

standardized solutions to advertising problems. Media availability to advertisers differs substantially in different parts of the world, so global companies still need to adapt their media mix to the local situation.

Most marketers realize that total customization is not desirable because it would require that each market create and implement its own advertising strategies. Top creative talent is scarce everywhere, and better creative solutions tend to be costlier ones. As a result, companies appear to be moving toward modularization, in which some elements of the advertising message are common to all advertisements whereas other elements are tailored to local requirements. Successful modularization requires that companies plan such an integration of responsibilities from the very outset, considering the full range of possibilities and the requirements that will need to be satisfied across their major markets. This is a considerable challenge to international marketing executives and their advertising partners.

Review Questions

1. What major factors affect the extension of an international advertising campaign into several countries?

2. Give an example of global theme advertising.

3. Explain how media availability, media habits, and scheduling international advertising affect the advertising campaign.

4. What are the advantages of using global agency networks?

5. List the external and internal factors that influence a firm's decision whether to centralize or localize advertising decisions.

Questions for Discussion

1. What has motivated the apparent increase in the use of standardized advertising across national markets?

2. What do you think causes attitudes about the credibility of advertising to vary among countries?

3. What advice would you give to a U.S. firm interested in advertising in Japan?

4. How will the advertising industry have to react to evolving conditions in developing countries and the former Soviet bloc?

5. How will increased Internet access affect international advertising?

For Further Reading

De Pelsmacker, Patrick, and M. Geuens. "Reactions to Different Types of Ads in Belgium and Poland." *International Marketing Review* 15, 4 (1998): 277–290.

Harker, Debra. "Achieving Acceptable Advertising: An Analysis of Advertising Regulation in Five Countries." *International Marketing Review* 5, 2 (1998): 101–118.

Keillor, Bruce D., Stephen Parker, and T. Bettina Cornwell. "Using Advertising to Manage Consumer Satisfaction in an International Market." *Journal of Global Marketing* 12, 1 (1998): 27–46.

Tharp, Marye, and Jaeseok Jeong. "The Global Network Communications Agency." *Journal of International Marketing* 9, 4 (2001): 111–131.

Whitelock, Jeryl, and Jean-Christophe Rey. "Cross-cultural Advertising in Europe: An Empirical Survey of Television Advertising in France and the UK." *International Marketing Review* 15, 4 (1998): 257–276.

| Case 15.1 | *Advertising to Kids* |

Children in the United States see an estimated 20,000 commercials a year. Marketers spend $5 billion a year directly targeting children. And much more advertising reaches children when they are not even the target audience.

In 2000 the U.S. Federal Trade Commission (FTC) discovered internal memos detailing how companies commonly target their marketing of violent games, music, and movies to children. This prompted lawmakers to reconsider tightening laws on advertising to children. In a follow-up study in 2001, the FTC discovered that the movie and videogame industries had improved their practices but that the recording industry continued to show total disdain for public concerns about marketing violent and sexually explicit products to underage children. This encouraged the call for laws that would restrict advertisements—whether targeted directly to children or not—that reached large audiences under the age of seventeen.

A number of industries already set their own standards for advertising to children. The beer industry discourages placing ads on programs where half or more of the audience is under the age of eighteen. Several movie studios set their cut-off standard at 35 percent. Still, the Association of National Advertisers continues to lobby against any legislation that would restrict advertising for violent movies, videogames, or music; it contends that such restrictions would curtail free speech, a fundamental American freedom enshrined in the American Bill of Rights. Ironically, a study conducted by the National Institute on Media and the Family discovered that 99 percent of students in grades 7 through 12 could identify Budweiser as a brand of beer—significantly more students than could identify the purpose of the Bill of Rights. Nonetheless, advertisers won a legal victory when the Supreme Court struck down the state of Massachusetts's restrictions on billboard advertising of cigars and smokeless tobacco products. The law, aimed at protecting children, was deemed to violate the advertisers' freedom of speech.

The controversy over advertising to children is not restricted to the United States. In Britain, advertisements that provoke children to behave improperly are taboo. Regulators have no direct authority to ban advertisements, but they enjoy powerful influence with the nation's media. A television ad created by the Publicus Group for Hewlett-Packard featured children throwing snowballs at a passing train. Regulators considered this an incitement to antisocial behavior, and the spot was removed.

In Belgium, state broadcasters are forbidden to air advertisements aimed at children for 5 minutes on either side of a children's show. Greece bans toy advertising on television between seven a.m. and ten p.m. In Sweden, television advertising aimed at children has been illegal since 1991. Critics of the Swedish advertising ban are quick to point out that Swedish children have access to international channels that allow them to see ads from other countries. TV3, a Swedish channel that broadcasts from the United Kingdom, is free to advertise to children because of its British location. Even so, a number of European countries, including Greece, Belgium, Italy, and Poland, are debating tightening their restrictions. Advertisers argue that increased regulation across Europe could greatly curtail children's programming on the many private channels not subsidized by governments.

Across the world in Indonesia, a recent cigarette-advertising campaign came under attack by educators and politicians. The campaign featured animated characters, including ants, roosters, and snails, dancing to music. Critics believed that the ad encouraged children, who make up the majority of cartoon lovers, to think that smoking was a good thing. The company quickly removed the offending ad. In Indonesia, the penalty for marketers who target children is a hefty fine and a jail sentence of up to 5 years.

Discussion Questions

1. Why is advertising directed at children regulated in so many cultures? Why is there so much variation in these regulations?
2. Should the European Union develop a common policy toward advertising that targets children? Why or why not? What barriers to such a policy might exist?
3. What restrictions on advertising directed at children would you favor? Why?

Sources: Suzanne Kapner, "Agencies Say British Regulators Are Too Quick to Ban Ads," *New York Times*, January 4, 2002, p. 4; Ronald Brownstein, "Targeting Kids," *Dallas Morning News*, May 6, 2001, p. 4J; Vanessa O'Connell, "Advertising Marketers to Attack Bills Restricting Ads," *Wall Street Journal*, July 25, 2001, p. B5; Sarah Ellison, "Marketing to Children Sparks Criticism in Europe," W*all Street Journal*, December 18, 2000; "Kid Gloves: Banning Advertising to Children," *The Economist*, January 6, 2001; and "Cigarette Maker Pulls Ad Cartoon," *Jakarta Post*, December 14, 2001.

Case 15.2   *The Alliance*

In 1999 Dentsu, Japan's largest advertising agency, joined Leo Burnett and the MacManus Group, both headquartered in the United States, in an agreement to create one holding company, Bcom3, for the three agency networks. Although the three remained legally distinct companies, certain benefits were expected to arise from this new alliance. Leo Burnett and the MacManus Group hoped to cut costs by exploring ways to reduce redundant divisions and subsidiaries. Dentsu expected Bcom3 to expand its access to worldwide advertising networks for their clients, mainly Japanese companies. With a relatively small international presence, Dentsu could not currently serve a Japanese client in a foreign market as well as Leo Burnett or the MacManus Group could. By gaining the ability to tap into the international subsidiaries of Leo Burnett and the MacManus Group, Dentsu significantly enhanced its global presence virtually overnight.

But would this new alliance really be good for Dentsu? Dentsu Inc. was the largest independent advertising agency in the world. Founded in 1901 as a combination news and advertising agency, Dentsu evolved into a propaganda service known as Domei News Service during World War II. Dentsu is still 48 percent owned by Kyodo and Jiji, Japan's two major wire services. In the early postwar years, Dentsu helped launch Japanese commercial television and viewership rating services. Dentsu retains equity stakes in several television stations and helps conceive and market some programming. For the fiscal year ending March 30, 2000, Dentsu reported worldwide billings of about ¥1,600 billion, or US$15,100 million. Of these billings, ¥84.3 billion came from Dentsu's own overseas subsidiaries: ¥16.4 billion from North America, ¥10.7 billion from Europe, and ¥57.2 billion from Asia.

Dentsu dominates the Japanese advertising industry. Unlike the European and the American advertising industries, the industry in Japan has no taboo against an advertising agency representing competitors. Japanese clients are generally comfortable with different divisions or teams within the same ad agency handling competitor accounts. This is one reason why the biggest advertising agencies in Japan have become disproportionately large compared to agencies in Western markets. Dentsu itself handles ads for about 3,000 firms, including nearly all of Japan's major corporations. According to industry estimates, Dentsu books on average 31 percent of all television commercials and 20 percent of newspaper ads in Japan.

However, the 1990s had been problematic for Dentsu. A recession in Japan in the early 1990s hurt profit margins, and growth had fallen to a 25-year low. The late 1990s were also slow in Japan. In 1992 Nissan Motor Company, Dentsu's long-term client, shocked management at Dentsu when it announced it was leaving to start a new relationship with Hakuhodo Inc. Hakuhodo, the second-largest advertising agency in Japan, was half Dentsu's size. Hakuhodo had previously formed an alliance with the U.S.-based multinational advertising agency TBWA, and in 1991 Hakuhodo had bought 15 percent of TBWA's equity. Management at Nissan Motor explained that Nissan wanted to consolidate its marketing activities worldwide in cooperation with Hakuhodo and TBWA. Nissan Motor recognized that Dentsu was the number-one agency in Japan, but the Japanese market alone was not big enough for Nissan Motor's profit objectives. The Nissan experience was a watershed. From then on, Dentsu was concerned that other "old friends" might defect.

Bcom3 also included two major media-buying firms, Starcom Worldwide and Mediavest. Media-buying firms exercise more power in negotiating with media companies, such as newspapers, television, and radio, because of their large purchases of media space and consequent market power. Dentsu performed media buying within its own organization but had never developed the size or market power of international firms such as Starcom or Mediavest.

Therefore, Dentsu could profit from discounted media prices by working through these Bcom3 companies. In addition, these media-buying firms possessed advanced media-planning tools to help clients develop efficient and effective media portfolios, such as means of determining what percentages of a campaign budget should go to national radio, newspaper, regional television, and so on.

Dentsu already was involved in a 50/50 joint venture with Young and Rubicam in Asian markets. It was the oldest surviving alliance between a Japanese and a U.S. advertising agency. Nonetheless, Dentsu's own subsidiaries in Asia competed with the joint venture. The relationship between the two partners was further strained when the WPP Group bought Young and Rubicam in 2000. Dentsu considered WPP a major competitor. WPP held a 20 percent stake in Japan's third-largest agency.

For Dentsu, an alliance with such firms as Leo Burnett and the MacManus Group offered a channel to service its clients better internationally, augmenting the business of its own overseas subsidiaries. After 2 years, however, management at Dentsu was reviewing the situation. The biggest advantage for Dentsu to date had been the cost savings associated with buying $100 million worth of advertising space each year in the United States for Japanese copier maker Canon. But Bcom3 was not yet capturing the many new global accounts that the partners had envisaged. Unlike Nissan Motor, most Japanese corporations had not consolidated their global advertising business within a few agencies. Most managers of Japanese subsidiaries in international markets were not Japanese. They often preferred to choose their own agencies, in spite of the relationship between headquarters in Japan and Dentsu. Furthermore, most Japanese multinational corporations had already built long-term relationships with Western advertising agencies.

Discussion Questions

1. Why was Dentsu interested in the Bcom3 alliance?
2. Why would Leo Burnett and the MacManus Group be interested in an alliance with Dentsu?
3. What problems can arise when two or more advertising agencies form an alliance? How might these problems be exacerbated if the agencies are from different cultures?
4. What recommendations would you give Dentsu?

Source: Case prepared by Jaeseok Jeong. Used by permission.

Notes

[1] "ExxonMobil Launches Advertising Campaign to Announce New Company," *PR Newswire*, December 3, 1999.

[2] Bill Chase, "Letters to the Editor," *Wall Street Journal Europe*, July 24, 2001, p. 9.

[3] Vanessa O'Connell, "Exxon 'Centralizes' New Global Campaign," July 7, 2001, *Wall Street Journal*, p. B6.

[4] Christopher Woodward, "Got Spanish? Anita Santiago Helps Advertisers Bridge the Gap Between Anglo and Latino Cultures," *Business Week*, August 14, 2000.

[5] "Cartier Softens French Accent in International Campaign," *Advertising Age*, October 7, 1996: 12.

[6] Paula Lyon Andruss, "FedEx Kicks Up Brand Through Humor," *Marketing News*, July 30, 2001: 4

[7] Jim Pickard, "Coca-Cola to Use Welsh in Adverts," *Financial Times (London)*, July 6, 2000.

[8] "Mexico Forces a Wonderbra Cover-Up," *Financial Times*, August 19, 1996: 4.

[9] Dagmar Mussey, "Mars Goes Local," *Ad Age Global*, May 10, 2002.

[10] Eirmalasare Bani, "Lipton Shoots Its Latest Commercial in Malaysia," *Business Times (Malaysia)*, June 9, 1999: 15.

[11] Vincent Moss, "Blair Speeds Up Total Ban on Tobacco Adverts," *Mail on Sunday*, May 23, 1999, p. 7.

[12] Frances Williams, "Curbs on Tobacco: WHO to Launch Talks on Treaty," *Financial Times*, October 26, 1999: 6.

[13] Melissa Akin, "Duma Smoking Bill Proves Nothing Is Sacred," *Moscow Times*, June 11, 1999, p. 1.

[14] "Cigarette Stunt Pilot Fined for Airborne Cigarette Advertising," *Associated Press Newswires*, September 20, 2000.

[15] "Campaigns sans Frontieres," *Financial Times*, May 31, 1996: 10.

[16] Harriet Green, "Cam Campaign International: Issue Marketing to Children," *Campaign*, May 7, 1999: 34.

[17] Erik Elinder, "How International Can European Advertising Be?" *Journal of Marketing*, April 1965, p. 9.

[18] "Saatchi & Saatchi Will Keep Gobbling," *Fortune*, June 23, 1986: 36.

[19] "Defending the Rights of Marlboro Man," *The Economist*, April 21, 1990: 84

[20] "Patek Philippe: Tradition Anyone?" *Ad Age International*, January 11, 1999: 9.

[21]Greg Harris, "International Advertising Standardization: What Do Multinationals Actually Standardize?" *Journal of International Marketing* 12, 4 (1994): 13–30.

[22]Nancy Giges, "Europeans Buy Outside Goods, But Like Local Ads," *Advertising Age International*, April 27, 1992: I–1.

[23]Judann Pollack, "Pringles Wins Worldwide with One Message," *Ad Age International*, January 11, 1999: 14.

[24]"Levi's Ads Have London Flair," *Advertising Age*, August 7, 1995: 33.

[25]"Levi's Global Guru Shakes Up Culture," *Advertising Age International*, November 1996: I-20.

[26]Gail Edmondson et al., "The Beauty of Global Branding," *Business Week*, June 28, 1999: 70.

[27]Patricia Sabatini, "Heinz Re-enlists Leo Burnett for Global Campaign," *Pittsburgh Post-Gazette*, March 27, 1999, p. C1.

[28]Jean Haliday, "European Automakers Plan Global Advertising Campaigns," *Automotive News Europe*, September 28, 1998: 6.

[29]Bradford Wernie, "Jaguar Goes Global," *Automotive News Europe*, April 12, 1999: v.

[30]Andrew McMains and Tobi Elkin, "Sony Eyes Massive 2000 Image Effort," *Adweek*, July 27, 1998: 3.

[31]Hillary Chura and Richard Linnett, "Coca-Cola Readies Global Assault," *Advertising Age*, April 2001: 1.

[32]"Ads Astride the World," *Financial Times*, April 13, 1989: 16.

[33]"Lifestyle Ads Irk East Europeans," *Advertising Age*, October 8, 1990: 56.

[34]Dana James, "Skoda Taken from Trash to Treasure," *Marketing News*, February 18, 2002: 4–5.

[35]Normandy Madden and Andrew Hornery, "As Taco Bell Enters Singapore, Gidget Avoids the Ad Limelight," *Ad Age International*, January 11, 1999: 13.

[36]Alexandra Harney, "Interest in Japan Surges as Agencies Begin to Think Globally," *Campaign*, September 11, 1998: 23.

[37]Gregory M. Rose, Victoria D. Bush, and Lynn Kahle, "The Influence of Family Communication Patterns on Parental Reactions Toward Advertising: A Cross-national Examination," *Journal of Advertising*, January 1, 1998: 71.

[38]Jae W. Hong, Aydin Muderrisoglu, and George M. Zinkhan, "Cultural Differences and Advertising Expression: A Comparative Content Analysis of Japanese and U.S. Magazine Advertising," *Journal of Advertising* 16, 1 (1987): 55–62.

[39]"Madonna in Japan," *Fortune*, September 15, 1986: 9.

[40]Alexandra Harney, "The Dentsu Story," *Campaign*, April 9, 1999: 38.

[41]Jean Grow vonDorn and Irina Akimova, "Advertising in the Ukraine: Cultural Perspectives," *International Journal of Advertising*, May 1, 1998: 189.

[42]"UK Helps to Make Advertising and Promotion a Priority." *Financial Times*, December 8, 1988, p. 12.

[43]"In Moscow, the Attack of the Killer Brands," *Business Week*, January 10, 1994: 40.

[44]"Full of Eastern Promise," *Financial Times*, June 8, 1995: 13.

[45]Ibid.

[46]"Ex-Soviet States Lead World in Ad Cynicism," *Advertising Age*, June 5, 1995: 3.

[47]"Czech Government Targets Public Television Network," *Advertising Age International*, January 1997: I-6.

[48]Juliana Koranteng, "Global Media," *Ad Age International*, February 8, 1999: 23.

[49]"Advertising," *The Economist*, January 18, 1997: 104.

[50]Elliot Spagat, "Mexican TV Networks' Ad Rates Surge," *Wall Street Journal*, October 28, 1998: B12.

[51]"Advertising," p. 104.

[52]Alessandra Galloni, "Look Up," *Wall Street Journal Europe*, April 4, 2001.

[53]Beverly Matthews, "Foreign Life Insurers Eye India," *Reuters English News Service*, April 3, 2001.

[54]"MTV Makes the Big Record Groups Dance to Its Tune," *Financial Times*, July 4, 1995: 17.

[55]"Programming Globally—With Care," *Advertising Age International*, September 18, 1995: I-14.

[56]"Wired Planet." *The Economist*, February 12, 1994, p. 12.

[57]"Rival Media Scions Plot Growth in Asia-Pacific," *Advertising Age*, September 19, 1996: 46.

[58]"A Minefield of Uncertainty," *Financial Times—Cable and Satellite Broadcasting*, October 6, 1992: v (special section).

[59]"Advertisers Need to Move in a Rapidly Changing Market," *Economic Times*, June 15, 2000.

[60]"Egyptian Spending on Advertising Growing 30% a Year," *Middle East Executive Reports*, August 1998: 10.

[61]*Reuters English News Service*, April 4, 2001.

[62]"Luxury Loves Company," *Advertising Age International*, March 1997: I-34.

[63]Andreas Grein and Robert Ducoffe, "Strategic Responses to Market Globalisation Among Advertising Agencies," *International Journal of Advertising*, August 1, 1998: 301.

[64]Marye Tharp and Jaeseok Jeong, "The Global Network Communications Agency," *Journal of International Marketing* 9, 4 (2001): 113.

[65]"Agencies Expanding E. European Penetration," *Advertising Age International*, October 1996: I-8.

[66]Michael Flagg, "Vietnam Opens Industry to Foreigners," *Wall Street Journal*, August 28, 2000, p. B8.

[67]"$500 Million in Colgate Eggs in One Y&R Basket," *Advertising Age*, December 4, 1995: 1.

[68]Betsy McKay, "Coke Hunts for Talent to Re-Establish Its Marketing Might," *Wall Street Journal*, March 6, 2002, p. B4.

Part 5 *Managing the Global Marketing Effort*

COMPETENCE LEVEL	DECISION AREAS
Environmental Competence	**Understanding the Global Marketing Environment** **CH 2** *The Global Economy* **CH 3** *Cultural and Social Forces* **CH 4** *Political and Regulatory Climate*
Analytic Competence	**Analyzing Global Opportunities** **CH 5** *Global Buyer Behavior* **CH 6** *Global Competitors* **CH 7** *Global Marketing Research*
Strategic Competence	**Developing Global Marketing Strategies** **CH 8** *Global Marketing Strategies* **CH 9** *Global Market Entry Strategies*
Functional Competence	**Designing Global Marketing Programs** **CH 10** *Global Product and Service Strategies* **CH 11** *Developing New Products for Global Markets* **CH 12** *Pricing for International and Global Markets* **CH 13** *Managing Global Channels* **CH 14** *Global Promotion Strategies* **CH 15** *Managing Global Advertising*
Managerial Competence	**Managing the Global Marketing Effort** **CH 16** *Organizing for Global Marketing*

16 Organizing for Global Marketing

3M Created Its International operations group in 1951, launching subsidiaries in Australia, Canada, France, Germany, Mexico, and the United Kingdom. In 1984 it became the first foreign firm to have a wholly owned subsidiary in China. Today, half of the company's sales are outside the United States, and three-quarters of its managers have worked in a foreign country. Yet despite its long history as an international firm, 3M still grapples with the question of how best to organize itself.

Over the years, 3M developed an organizational matrix—several structures superimposed on each other. Managers of country subsidiaries share responsibility with division managers located at headquarters in St. Paul, Minnesota. Disagreements over strategy sometimes arise. Subsidiary managers seek to maximize total sales and profits in their countries. Division managers seek to maximize the global sales and profits of their product lines. Despite the matrix, most concede that the

country managers often exercise the greater power. In this respect, some are concerned that 3M has been left behind; most other global firms have centralized power over the past 20 years. However, 3M's vice-president of international operations disagrees. Running 3M's international business from St. Paul would be too burdensome. The matrix allows the company to react quickly to local markets. Who better than the local manager to decide whether and how to raise prices in Ger-

Chapter Outline

many? Thus the debate continues. Who is better qualified to decide how to market a product abroad—the person who best knows the product or the person who best knows the country?[1]

An important aspect of global marketing is the establishment of an appropriate organization. The organization must be able to formulate and implement strategies for each local market and for the global market as well. The objective is to develop a structure and control system that will enable the firm to respond to distinct variations in each market while applying the relevant experience that the company has gained in other markets and with other products. To be successful, companies need to find a proper balance between these two needs. A number of organizational structures are suitable for different internal and external environments. No one structure is best for all situations.

Learning Objectives

After studying this chapter, you should be able to:

▶ List and explain the internal and external factors that affect how global organizations are structured and managed.

▶ Note the advantages and disadvantages of the different ways of structuring a firm with international sales.

▶ Discuss global mandates, and note how global mandates can affect a firm's organization.

▶ Explain why organizational issues for born-global firms differ from those for traditional multinational companies.

▶ Give examples of how technology can be utilized to support internal global communications systems.

▶ List and explain the elements of an effective global control strategy.

▶ Discuss the conflicts that can arise between international headquarters and national subsidiaries.

▶ Consider a career in global marketing.

▶ *Elements That Affect a Global Marketing Organization*

The success of a global strategy will be acutely influenced by the selection of an appropriate organization to implement that strategy. The structure of an international organization should be congruent with the tasks to be performed, the need for product knowledge, and the need for market knowledge. The ideal structure of such an organization should be a function of the products or services to be sold in the marketplace, as well as of the external and internal environments. Theoretically, the way to develop a global marketing organization is to analyze the specific tasks to be accomplished within an environment and then to design a structure that will support these tasks most effectively. A number of other factors complicate the selection of an appropriate organization, however. In most cases, a company already has an existing organizational structure. As the internal and external environments change, companies will need to reevaluate that structure. The search for an appropriate organizational structure must balance local responsiveness against global integration.[2] It is important to understand the strengths and weaknesses of different organizational structures as well as the factors that usually lead to change in the structure.

Corporate Goals

Every company needs a mission. The mission is the business's framework—the values that drive the company and the vision it has for itself. The mission statement is the glue that holds the company together. It asks four questions: (1) Why do we exist? (2) Where are we going? (3) What do we believe in? (4) What is our distinctive competence?[3]

After declaring its mission, no company should begin establishing an international organization until it has reviewed and established its strategies and objectives. Some global firms even include strategy statements in their missions. Corporate leaders develop strategic visions with slogans such as "Encircle Caterpillar" for Komatsu and "Beat Xerox" for Canon. If the head of a company can instill this sense of winning throughout the firm, it will inspire the organization to excel and achieve far greater goals.[4]

Corporate World View

Corporate management can adopt one of several world views concerning global markets. These world views, or orientations, will significantly affect the choice of organizational structure. Some firms adopt an **ethnocentric** orientation. Management is centered on the home market. Ideas that emanate from there are considered superior to those that arise from the foreign subsidiaries. Headquarters tells its subsidiaries what to do and solicits little or no input from the subsidiaries themselves. Top managers in the foreign subsidiaries are most often managers sent from headquarters on relatively short-term assignments. Alternatively, corporate management can take a **polycentric** orientation, wherein each market is considered unique. This is at the heart of the multidomestic strategies discussed in Chapter 1. Local subsidiaries are given great leeway to develop and implement their own strategies. Little or no interdependencies arise among subsidiaries. Management positions in local subsidiaries are usually filled by local nationals. Some polycentric firms evolve a focus that is regional rather than national. Geographic regions such as Europe and Latin America, rather than single national markets, are seen as possessing unique features that require separate marketing strategies. Decision making becomes centralized at the regional level, but regions still remain relatively independent of headquarters and of each other. A **geocentric orientation** returns power to global headquarters, but this orientation is very distinct from an ethnocentric orientation. A geocentric firm focuses on global markets as a whole rather than on its domestic market. Good ideas can come from any country, and the firm strives to keep communication lines open among its various units. Even top management at corporate headquarters is likely to come from many nations. Most important, all national units, including the domestic one, must consider what is best for the whole organization and act accordingly.

Other Internal Forces

Other internal factors often affect the international organization as well. These factors include the volume and diversity of the firm's international business, its economic commitment to international business, the available human resources, and flexibility within the company.

Importance of International Sales The size and importance of a firm's international business affect its organizational structure. If only a small percentage of sales (1 to 10 percent) is international, a company will tend to have a simple organization such as an export department. As the proportion of international sales increases relative to total sales, a company is likely to evolve from having an export department to having an international division and then to having a worldwide organization. Companies may even consider moving global headquarters out of the home country when overseas sales become dominant. Japan's Sony Corporation, Nintendo Company, and Sega Enterprises have all considered moving their headquarters to the United States.[5]

Diversity of International Markets Served As the number and diversity of international markets increase, it becomes necessary to have a more complex organization to manage the marketing effort, and it requires a larger number of people to understand the markets and implement the strategies.

Level of Economic Commitment A company that is unwilling or unable to allocate adequate financial resources to its international efforts will not be able to sustain a complex or costly international structure. The less expensive organizational approaches to international marketing usually result in less control by the company at the local level. It is extremely important to build an organization that will provide the flexibility and resources to achieve the corporation's long-term goals for international markets.

Human Resources Available and capable personnel are just as vital to a firm as financial resources. Some companies send top domestic executives to foreign operations only to find that these expatriates do not understand the nation's culture. The hiring of local executives is also difficult, because

World Beat 16.1 *Everyone Wants to Win*

When more than four hundred managers from around the world gathered in the summer of 2000 at an executive-training seminar at IMD, the business school in Lausanne, Switzerland, a central topic was the booming American economy. Among Europeans, who made up the bulk of participants, the reaction was a mixture of admiration and disdain. Many expressed envy of American technology, entrepreneurial spirit, and productivity and of everything to do with the Internet revolution, but they also spoke disparagingly of American managers. Among their chief put-downs: Americans are provincial, ignorant of world affairs, uncouth, and too materialistic.

One sales manager at a German manufacturer who travels to Illinois half a dozen times a year to do business with a big customer says it has taken him a long time to understand U.S. culture. He enjoys the friendliness and openness of his customers in Illinois and their ability to make quick decisions. Yet the manager, who was born and raised in France and speaks five languages fluently, was surprised to learn how few of them had traveled abroad and how personally nonglobal they were. He was also taken aback when employees of his U.S. client called him by his first name. "In Germany you don't do that until you know someone for 10 years—and

never if you are at a lower rank," says the manager. But he has learned to live with the informality.

U.S. executives who have run businesses on the Continent say Americans also have to meet their foreign colleagues halfway—by educating themselves about European culture and by not assuming the American way is always the best. A manager who formerly ran General Electric's medical-equipment business in Europe said the first thing he did on arriving at his headquarters in Paris was to take a 4-week immersion course in French. He also studied European history and culture and, with his wife, made friends with many French people.

GE's biggest European rival in medical equipment is Munich-based Siemens, so the manager began holding staff meetings in Germany for 2 to 3 days each month, which also gave his international team a chance to visit hospitals there, learn the health care system, and get close to customers. In his work, he built up a diverse staff of 2,000 employees from 38 countries. "The biggest problem, I learned, was seeing how diversity yields better discussions and decisions," he says. Regardless of nationality, "everyone wants to win."

Source: Carol Hymowitz, "In the Lead," *Wall Street Journal*, August 15, 2000, p. B1.

READ MORE ABOUT IT:
Check out "Your Career Matters" under *Supplemental Readings* on our website.

competition for such people can be extremely intense. When Panasonic began to build up its U.K. organization, the company recruited graduates from British universities. The graduate trainees were then sent to Japan for a year to absorb Japanese culture and discipline. With a long-term approach to developing local talent, Panasonic preferred "to grow its own."[6] Archrival Sony used executive search firms extensively to recruit local managers.[7] Motorola puts hundreds of executives through workplace simulation exercises to try to identify the best candidates with the necessary international management skills to run a global business.[8] Because people are such an important resource in international organizations, a lack of appropriate personnel can constrain a firm's organizational growth.

Flexibility When a company devises an organizational structure, it must build in some flexibility, especially to be prepared in case reorganization becomes necessary in the future. A study of the implementation of a global strategy for seventeen products found that organizational flexibility was one of the keys to success. The structure must be flexible enough to respond to the needs of consumers and the challenges of global competitors. Even companies that establish a perfect design for the present find themselves in trouble later on when the firm grows or declines.

External Forces

A number of external factors can affect how global organizations are structured and managed. The most important of these are geographic distance, time zone differences, types of customers, and government regulations. In the international environment, each issue should be examined to determine its effect on the organization.

Geographic Distance Technological innovations have somewhat eased the problems associated with physical distance. Companies, primarily in the United States and other developed countries, enjoy such conveniences as next-day mail and e-mail, facsimile machines, videoconferencing, mobile phones, mobile data transmissions, and rapid transportation. However, these benefits cannot be taken for granted in international operations. Distance becomes a distinct barrier when operations are established in less developed countries, where the telecommunications infrastructure may be more primitive. Moreover, companies invariably find it necessary to have key personnel make trips to engage in face-to-face conversations. Organizations in the same region are often grouped together to help minimize travel costs and the travel time of senior executives. Technology has shortened, but not eliminated, the distance gap.

Time Zones One problem even high technology cannot solve is time differences (see Figure 16.1). Managers in New York who reach an agreement over lunch will have a hard time finalizing the deal with their headquarters in London until the following day, because by that time, most executives in England will be on their way home for the evening. The 5-hour time difference results in lost communication time and impedes rapid results. Electronic mail has contributed substantially to the interaction among far-flung units, but adaptations still need to be made. Brady Corporation of Milwaukee produces industrial sign and printing equipment. About 45 percent of its sales are outside the United States. Managers in Milwaukee commonly take conference calls at 6 a.m. and place calls late at night to catch the company's Asian managers during their workdays.[9]

Types of Customers Companies may need to take their "customer profiles" into account in structuring their global marketing organizations. Companies that serve a very few, geographically concentrated global customers will organize their global marketing efforts differently from firms that serve a large number of small customers in country after country. For example, if a firm has key global customers, it may adjust its organization and select its office locations according to where its customers are located. Many companies that sell equipment or parts to automotive firms maintain marketing units near major concentrations of automotive activity, such as Detroit and Stuttgart, Germany. Supplier parks sit adjacent to Ford manufacturing sites in Spain,

Figure 16.1 *Time Zones of the World*

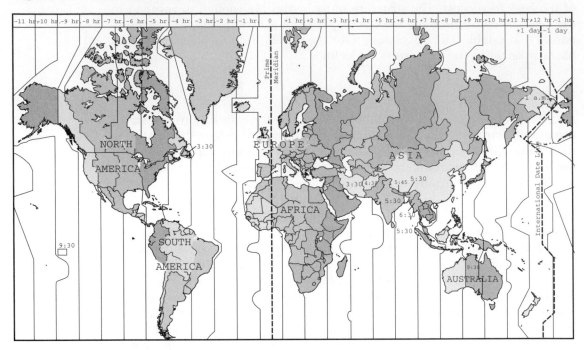

Germany, and Brazil, and are increasingly planned for U.S. locations.[10] On the other hand, companies that sell to large numbers of customers tend to maintain more regional, or even country-specific, organizations, with relatively less centralization. Similarly, if customer needs or competition varies greatly from country to country, there is less impetus to centralize.

Government Regulations How various countries attract or discourage foreign operations can affect the structure of the global organization. Laws involving imports, exports, taxes, and hiring differ from country to country. Local taxes, statutory holidays, and political risk can deter a company from establishing a subsidiary or management center in a country. Some countries require a firm that establishes plants on their territory to hire, train, and develop local employees and to share ownership with the government or local citizens. These requirements for local investment and ownership may dictate an organization that allows greater local decision making.

▶ *Types of Organizational Structures*

The global marketplace offers many opportunities. To take advantage of these opportunities, a company must evaluate its options, develop a strategy, and establish an organization to implement the strategy. The organization should take into account all the factors affecting organizational design (see the preceding section) in determining which structure is best suited to its current strategic needs. In this section, we review the various types of international and global organizational structures.

Companies Without International Specialists

Many companies, when they begin selling products to foreign markets, operate without an international organization or even an international specialist. A domestically oriented company may receive inquiries from foreign buyers who saw an advertisement in a trade magazine or attended a domestic trade show. The domestic staff will respond to the inquiry in the same way they respond to any other. Product brochures will be sent to the potential buyer for review. If sufficient interest exists on the part of both buyer and seller, then more communication (e-mails, faxes, telephone calls, personal visits) may transpire. With no specific individual designated to handle international business, it may be directed to a sales manager, an inside salesperson, a product manager, or an outside salesperson.

Companies without an international organization incur limited costs, but on the other hand, with no one responsible for international business, that business will probably provide little sales and profit. When the firm attempts to respond to the occasional inquiry, no one will understand the difficulties of translation into another language, the particular needs of the foreign customer, the transfer of funds, fluctuating exchange rates, shipping, legal liabilities, or the other many differences between domestic and international business. As the number of international inquiries grows or management recognizes the potential in international markets, international specialists will have to be added to the domestic organization.

International Specialists and Export Departments

The complexities of selling a product to a variety of different countries prompt most domestically oriented firms to establish some international expertise. This can vary from retaining a part-time international specialist to having a full complement of specialists organized into an export department. Figure 16.2 is a sample organization chart for an organization operating with an international specialist.

International specialists and export departments primarily perform a sales function. They respond to inquiries, manage exhibits at international trade shows, and handle export documentation, shipping, insurance, and financial matters. International specialists may also maintain contact with embassies, export financing agencies, and various departments of commerce. The international specialist or export department may use an export agent, an export management company, or import intermediaries to assist in the process.

Hiring international specialists gives firms the ability to respond to and process foreign business. The size of this type of organization will be directly related to the amount of international business handled. The costs should be minor when compared to the potential.

However, international specialists and export departments are often reactive rather than proactive in nature. They usually respond to inquiries. Few evaluate the worldwide demand for a product or service, identify opportunities, or develop a global strategy. Also, because international sales are so

Figure 16.2 *Organization with an International Specialist*

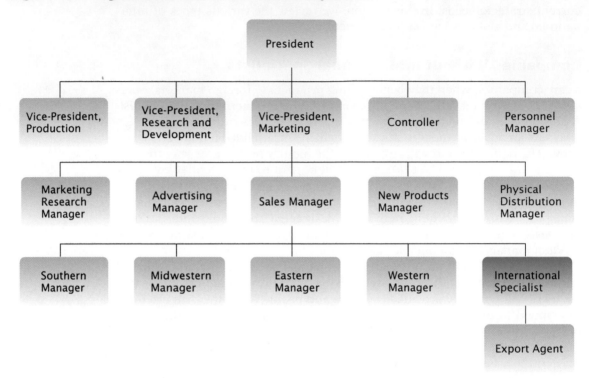

small, the international specialist may have little opportunity to modify current products or services to meet international market needs. In most cases, products are sold as is, with no modification.

International Divisions

As sales to foreign markets become more important to the company, and the complexity of coordinating the international effort extends beyond the capacity of a specialist or an export department, the firm may establish an international division. The international division normally reports to the president. This gives it equal status with other functions such as marketing, finance, and production. Figure 16.3 illustrates the organizational design of a firm using an international division.

International divisions are directly involved in the development and implementation of global strategy. Heads of international divisions have marketing managers, sales managers, and perhaps even production managers reporting to them. These divisions focus all their efforts on international markets. As a result, they are often successful at increasing international sales.

The international division actively seeks out market opportunities in foreign countries. The sales and marketing efforts in each country are supported through regional or local offices. These offices understand the local environments, including legal requirements, customer needs, and competition. This close contact with the market improves the organization's ability to perform successfully.

Figure 16.3 *Organization with an International Division*

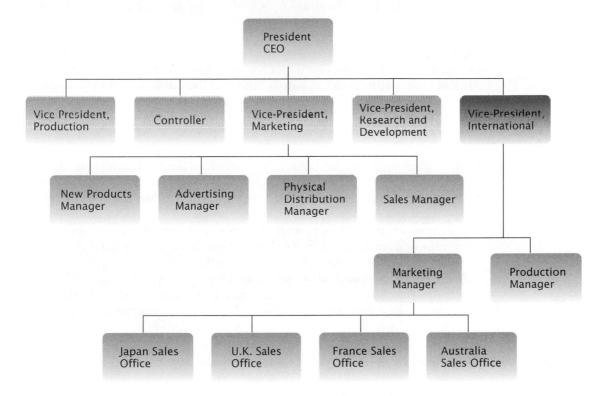

The use of international divisions is most common among large international firms with many different product lines or businesses. When none of the divisions has extensive international experience, all international business may be combined into the international division. For example, Alcon is a $1.5 billion U.S.-based company active in the ophthalmic area. Alcon's domestic business was organized along four product lines—equipment, pharmaceuticals, professional materials for surgeons, and over-the-counter eye-care products. Its international business, however, combined all products under an international division.

Worldwide or Global Organizations

As a firm recognizes the potential size of the global market, it begins to change from a domestic company with some business overseas to a worldwide company pursuing a global strategy. At this point, international divisions are superseded by new global structures. A company can choose to organize in terms of one of three dimensions: geography, function, or product. The matrix organization, another possible type of worldwide organization, combines two or more of these dimensions.

Geographic Organizational Structures The geographic organizational design is appropriate when the company needs an intimate knowledge of its customers and their environments. Such a design gives the company an opportunity to understand the local culture, economy, politics, laws, and competitive situation. Geographic organizational structures can be either regionally focused or country-based structures.

Regional Management Centers Regional management centers enable an organization to focus on particular regions of the world, such as Europe, the Middle East, Latin America, North America, the Caribbean, or the Far East. Figure 16.4 illustrates the regional structure of a worldwide geographic organization.

The reasons for using a regional geographic approach to organizational design are related to market similarity and size. A group of countries that are located close together and have similar social and cultural histories, climates, resources, and (sometimes) languages may have many similar needs for products. Often these regional country groups have unified themselves for political and economic reasons. The European Union (EU) and Mercosur are such regional groupings. Also, once a market reaches a certain size, the firm must employ a staff dedicated to maximizing revenues from that area of the world and to protecting the firm's assets there.

The regional approach to a worldwide organization has a number of benefits. It allows a company to locate marketing and manufacturing efforts in such a way as to take advantage of regional agreements such as the North American

Figure 16.4 *Geographic Organization by Regional Management Centers*

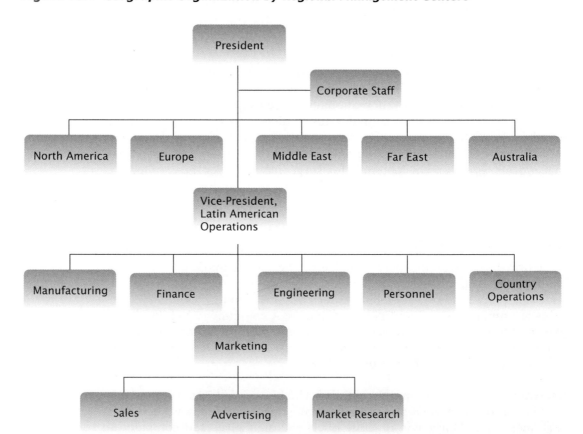

World Beat 16.2 *Hong Kong Headquarters*

Hong Kong has shrugged off concerns over high costs and worsening pollution and is pulling ahead of rivals such as Singapore as a center for regional headquarters, according to a study of more than 1,100 companies. Hong Kong's government, which has increasingly fretted as expatriate managers have grumbled about smog and the cost of rent and labor, has already drawn cheer from the report. The study found that Hong Kong scores high in what companies see as most important when choosing a location for regional headquarters: political and legal stability, good infrastructure, professional services, and quality local managers. Cost and quality-of-life issues came farther down companies' lists of priorities.

Respondents indicated that the city on the southern Chinese coastline will benefit from foreign investors' interest in nearby China, Japan, and South Korea. Singapore, Hong Kong's nearest rival in terms of numbers of regional headquarters, is much farther from these countries. The survey indicated that companies may increasingly use Singapore as a base only for operations in Southeast Asia, where investment flows are smaller. Singapore also suffers because of perceived instability in neighboring Indonesia. Tokyo came in a distant third in the survey. Many respondents said that managers based there found themselves overwhelmed with managing their Japanese operations and unable to coordinate work effectively elsewhere in the region.

Source: Gren Manuel, "Hong Kong Tops the List in Asia for Business Location, Study Says," *Wall Street Journal*, January 10, 2001, p. A19.

Free Trade Agreement (NAFTA). Also, the regional approach puts the company in closer contact with distributors, customers, and subsidiaries. Regional management can respond to local conditions and react faster than a totally centralized organization wherein all decisions are made at the headquarters.

In Europe many large international companies were originally organized on a national basis. The national organizations, including those in France, Germany, Italy, and the United Kingdom, often were coordinated loosely through European headquarters. The development of a single European market caused companies to rethink their European organizations often to reduce the role of the national organization in favor of a stronger pan-European management. A study of twenty multinational companies found that a major benefit of a regional or pan-European structure was reduced operational costs. The study showed that by consolidating accounting services such as accounts payable, billings, and accounts receivable, firms could save 35–45 percent on these costs.[11] Another study of Western European and U.S.-based firms with significant operations in Central and Eastern Europe revealed that regional management centers were an attractive organizational device to exploit market similarities and supply local offices with support and expertise.[12]

Restructuring of manufacturing and logistics in Europe is proceeding at a rapid pace as companies centralize production to lower costs and increase flexibility. For example, Anglo-Dutch Unilever, one of the world's largest manufacturers of consumer products, set up a new organization called Lever Europe. Previously, Unilever had been decentralized, each national organization having full autonomy to modify and market products as dictated by

Beirut's Mediterranean climate and Western lifestyle long made it a favorite choice for multinational corporations seeking a location for their Middle East regional headquarters. But the Lebanese civil war in the 1980s forced multinationals to move out of Beirut. Many relocated their Middle East headquarters to European cities such as Athens, London, or Paris.

local conditions. This decentralization led to a hodgepodge of brands, resulting in the same liquid abrasive cleaner being called Cif, Jif, Vif, or Viss, depending on the country. By choosing a regionally based organization, Unilever centralized both marketing and manufacturing and reduced the decision-making authority of its country managers.[13] By doing so, Unilever attempted to balance the need for centralized research, finance, and packaging with the need to stay close to its markets.[14]

Regional organizations have their disadvantages, however. First, regional organization implies that many functions are duplicated, either at regional head offices or in the countries. Such duplication, together with the need to rent offices in different locations, tends to add significantly to costs. A second, more serious disadvantage is that regional organizations inherently divide global authority. In a purely regionally organized company, only the CEO has true global responsibility. Developing global marketing strategies for products or services is difficult, because regional managers tend to focus on a limited regional perspective.

Country-Based Organizations The second type of geographic organization is the country-based organization, which utilizes a separate unit for each country. Figure 16.5 illustrates a simple country-based geographic organization.

A country-based organization resembles a regional structure, except that the focus is on single countries rather than on a group of countries. For example, instead of having a regional management center in Brussels overseeing all European sales and operations, the company has an organizational unit in each country. The country-based organization can be extremely sensitive to local customs, laws, and needs, all of which may differ considerably even though the countries participate in a regional organization such as the EU or NAFTA.

Figure 16.5 *Country-Based Geographic Organization*

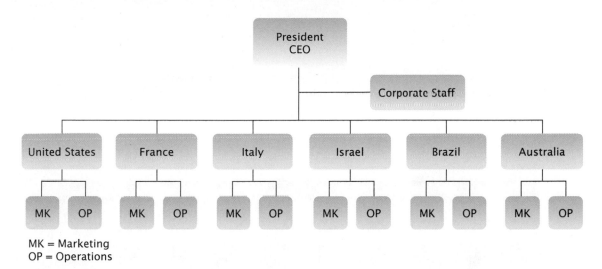

MK = Marketing
OP = Operations

One difficulty that plagues a country-based organization is its higher costs. Therefore, it is important to ensure that the benefits of a local organization offset its cost. Coordination with headquarters can also prove difficult. If a company is involved in forty countries, it can be cumbersome to have all forty country-based organizational units reporting to one or a few people in the company's headquarters. A final problem is that a country-based unit cannot take advantage effectively of regional groupings of countries, such as rationalizing production.

Country organizations are being phased out or reduced as regional organizations emerge. For example, in response to the signing of NAFTA, many firms began to integrate their separate organizations for Canada, the United States, and Mexico. Among these was Lego, the Danish toy maker. Lego reduced the responsibility of its Canadian operation and combined some executive positions at its Enfield, Connecticut, operation. At the same time, it decided to develop its Mexican market from the U.S. location as well. Other firms have chosen the same path, integrating their Canadian subsidiaries with their U.S. companies and developing their Mexican markets from the U.S. base.

To deal with the shortcomings of a country-based structure, many firms combine the concepts of regional and country-based organizations, as shown in Figure 16.6. Combining regional and country-based approaches minimizes many of the limitations of both designs, but it also adds an additional layer of management. Some executives think that superimposing a regional headquarters makes the country-level implementation of strategy more cumbersome rather than improving it. In order for the company to benefit from a regional center in such a combined approach, there must be some value in a regional strategy. Each company must reach its own decision regarding the proper geographic organization design, its cost, and its benefits.

Figure 16.6 *Organization Using Both Country-Based Units and Regionally Based Structure*

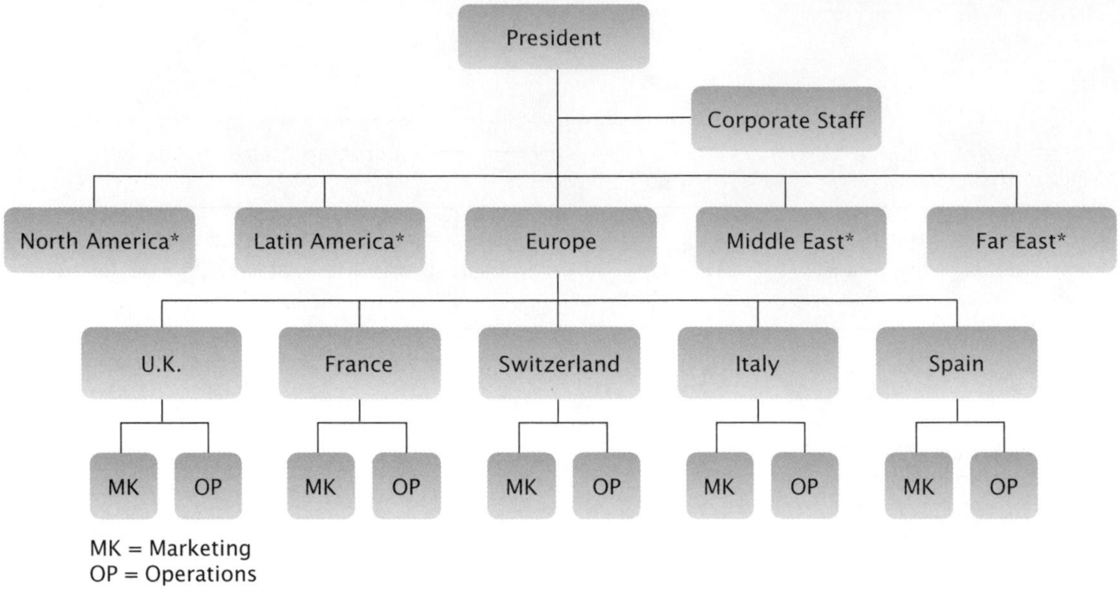

MK = Marketing
OP = Operations

*Under these regional offices would be country organizations similar to those shown for the European center.

Functional Organizational Structures A second way of organizing a worldwide firm is by function. In such an organization, the top executives in marketing, finance, production, accounting, and research and development all have worldwide responsibilities. For international companies, this type of organization is best for narrow or homogeneous product lines, with little variation between products or geographic markets. As shown in Figure 16.7, the functional organization has a simple structure. Each functional manager has worldwide responsibility for that function. Usually, the manager supervises people responsible for the function in regions or countries around the world.

Ford Motor Company recently moved in the direction of a functional organizational structure. Operating on a more or less regional structure, Ford had created major operating units in North America, Europe, Latin America, Africa, and Asia. Each regional unit was responsible for its own operations, developing and producing cars for its regional markets. Faced with strong competition from its bigger rival, General Motors, and from the more efficient Japanese companies such as Toyota, Ford realized that under its regional set-up it incurred a massive penalty for unnecessary duplication of key functions and efforts. Even though Ford served almost identical customer needs in many countries, the company was developing separate power trains and engines. It was purchasing different component parts at a cost of $3 billion, an astronomical figure compared to what an integrated operation would cost.[15]

Ford had tried global integration before, but usually on a project basis, not by integrating the entire organization. In the late 1970s, Ford created a subcompact car (Fiesta) that it hoped would be marketed in Europe and the United States. The resulting infighting prevented a true world car from being developed. Instead, the company ended up with two similar cars developed separately in Europe and North America. Again in the 1990s, Ford spent

Figure 16.7 *Functional Global Organization*

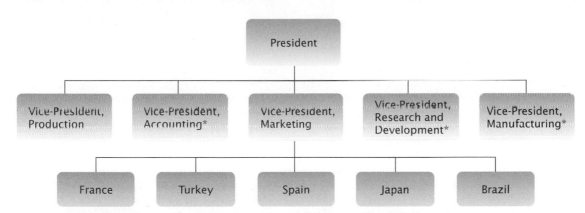

*Each functional vice-president has managers of that function in the countries served reporting to him or her, as illustrated with the vice-president, marketing.

about $6 billion to develop midsize cars for both Europe and North America. Successful in Europe, the cars did not fare well in the United States, where they were launched too late.[16]

Ford began its reorganization in the mid-1990s by merging its North American organization with its European car operation, creating an integrated firm under the "Ford 2000" banner.[17] The new organization of Ford Automotive called for four major functions, each to be headed by one executive with global responsibility. The most important function was vehicle development, structured around five centers in the United States and in Europe. The other global functions were marketing and sales, manufacturing, and purchasing.[18]

The development center for small cars was located in Europe with locations in both Germany and the United Kingdom. The United States received the development centers for rear-wheel-drive cars and commercial trucks, all with global development responsibility.[19] Some 25,000 Ford managers either moved from one location to another or were reassigned to report to new supervisors. The company expected to cut development costs by using fewer components, fewer engines, and fewer power trains, as well as by speeding up development cycles. As a result of this reorganization, Ford projected savings of $2–$3 billion per year.[20]

Still, "Ford 2000" was undergoing modifications even before the arrival of the millennium. In late 1999, Ford's chairman, Jacques Nasser, decided to return some power to Ford's regional business units. The move was made to enable Ford to respond more quickly to consumer trends. It would allow managers on the ground to respond quickly without waiting for direction from headquarters.[21]

Product Organizational Structures A third type of worldwide marketing organization is based on product line rather than on function or geographic area (see Figure 16.8.) Under this structure, each product group is responsible for marketing, sales, planning, and (in some cases) production and research and development. Other functions, such as legal, accounting, and finance, can be included in the product group or performed by the corporate staff.

Figure 16.8 *Global Product Organization*

Structuring by product line is common for companies with several unrelated product lines. A product focus is appropriate when the differences involved with marketing the various product lines are greater than the perceived differences between the geographic markets. During the 1990s, a number of companies, such as Philips and ICI, established strong product divisions.[22] Typically, the end users for a product organization vary by product line, so there is no advantage in having the same group handle marketing for the different product lines.

A product organization concentrates management on the product line, which is an advantage when the product line constantly changes with advancements in technology. Headquarters can develop global products and arrange global roll-outs. A product organization is effective in monitoring competition that is globalized rather than localized. Also, the firm can add new product groups as it adds new, unrelated products through acquisition.

The product organization has limitations as well. Knowledge of specific geographic areas can be limited, because each product group may not be able to afford to maintain a large local presence in each market. Because decision making becomes more centrally located under a product structure, sensitivity to local market conditions can be diminished. This lack of knowledge and sensitivity may cause the company to miss local market opportunities. The top managers of international product divisions can themselves present a problem, particularly if they are promoted from the domestic side of the business. They can be ethnocentric and relatively uninterested in or uneasy with international markets.

Also, if each product group goes its own way, the company's international development may result in inefficiencies. For example, two product divisions may be purchasing advertising space independently in the same magazine. This will prove more expensive than combining the purchases. To offset the inefficiencies of a worldwide product organization, some companies provide for global coordination of activities such as advertising, customer service, and government relations.

Matrix Organizational Structures As the Ford example suggests, some companies have grown frustrated with the limitations of a one-dimensional geographic, functional, or product organization structures. To overcome these drawbacks, the matrix organization was developed. As shown in Figure 16.9, the matrix organization allows for two or more dimensions of theoretically equal weight (here, geographic and product dimensions) in the organizational structure and in decision-making responsibility. A matrix organization often includes both product and geographic management components. Product management has worldwide responsibility for a specific product line, whereas geographic management is responsible for all product lines in a specific geographic area. These management structures overlap at the national product/market level. A matrix organization structure has a dual rather than a single chain of command, which means that many individuals will have two superiors.

One of the most extensive global matrix organizations is that of ABB, a Swedish-Swiss company with several major businesses in electric power generation, railways, industry automation, and environmental equipment. Created as the result of a merger between Swedish-based Asea and Swiss-based Brown Boveri, the company operates worldwide in nearly sixty product areas. Each product division has global responsibility for strategy and is measured on the basis of its own profit-and-loss account. On the other side of the matrix are numerous country organizations responsible for implementing the global strategy in their assigned territories. Each local manager reports to a regional manager as well as to the assigned global product manager. For the matrix to work, both the regional manager and the product manager must jointly agree on the local strategy, budget, and business approach. The company has been structured into more than 3,000 units with dual reporting. ABB has also promoted cooperation among its management to make the best of the matrix organization.[23]

Firms tend to adopt matrix organizations when they need to be highly responsive to two dimensions (such as product and geography.) For example, Procter & Gamble discovered that its matrix organization enabled it to keep in touch with local markets but also provided the centralized control that allowed a much quicker roll-out of products worldwide than was possible under its prior, country-based organization.[24]

Matrix organizations are not without their challenges. Some critics of Unilever's matrix structure complained that its complexity—with some managers in charge of product categories, others in charge of brands, and still

Figure 16.9 *Matrix Organization*

Under this organizational structure, the brand managers for brands X, Y, and Z in any European country would report directly to two different bosses—vice-president product line E and the director of marketing for Europe.

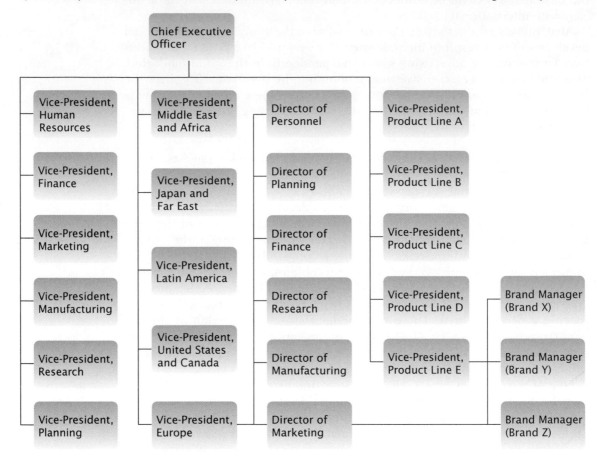

*Each regional vice-president has functional managers reporting to him or her, as illustrated with the vice president, Europe.

others in charge of geographic areas—resulted in duplication of authority and confusion of responsibility.[25] Power struggles are a common problem, especially when a matrix organization is first established. Relationships are tested as each side of the matrix attempts to "find its place" in the organization. In fact, the key to successful matrix management is the degree to which managers in an organization can resolve conflict and achieve the successful implementation of plans and programs. The matrix organization requires a change in management behavior from traditional authority to an influence system based on technical competence, interpersonal sensitivity, and leadership.

The matrix organization also requires a substantial investment in dual budgeting, accounting, transfer pricing, and personnel evaluation systems. The additional complexity and cost of a matrix organization can be offset, however, by the benefits of the dual focus. Overall, the matrix structure can permit an organization to function better in an uncertain and changing environment.

▶ *New Trends in Global Organizations*

Global companies must continually adapt their organizations to the needs of the marketplace. Bartlett and Ghoshal interviewed 236 managers in diverse groups of nine companies—Procter & Gamble, Kao, Unilever, ITT, Ericsson, NEC, General Electric, Philips, and Matsushita. On the basis of these companies' responses, they suggest that the challenges of global efficiency, local responsiveness, and global learning have become so pervasive that the global organization of the future will have to contend with all of them simultaneously.[26]

As companies compete on a worldwide basis, they must develop global economies of scale. Instead of supporting manufacturing plants in each major market, they need to standardize products or components. Electrolux, Black & Decker, Unilever, and many other firms have rationalized their manufacturing to yield economies of scale. Although the washing machine or power tool may vary from country to country, the motors can be standardized and manufactured in large volume to reduce costs. The organizational structure needs in some way to encourage this trend toward efficiency.

The increased cost of R&D, shortened product life cycles, and consumer demand for the latest technology have increased the need for development and diffusion of worldwide learning. This learning is often related to R&D but can also include marketing or manufacturing learning. ITT's strategy of individually developing its telecommunication switch technology for each country, without gaining any global expertise, was one of the factors leading to the company's exit from that business. On the other hand, the culmination of P&G's 7 years of research to develop a heavy-duty, liquid laundry detergent in Europe was quickly and successfully transferred to the United States in the form of Liquid Tide.

Global Mandates

As companies globalize their marketing organizations, the question of who should receive global mandates becomes an important concern. A **global mandate** is the expressed assignment to carry out a task on a global scale. Global mandates may be assigned to individual managers or to company teams. In either case, responsibility extends across all geographic locations, and the teams or marketing managers often make decisions that can affect all national subsidiaries. We have already discussed two types of global mandates—global account management (Chapter 5) and global brand management (Chapter 10). Global mandates can also be of a temporary nature. Executives may be named to a task force or **global team** to deal with a particular global marketing issue, such as how to respond to a major change in product technology. Who should receive a global mandate is an important decision for all globally active firms. It would be difficult to implement a global marketing strategy if the company did not endow key marketing executives with global mandates.[27]

Organization of the Born-Global Firm

In Chapter 8 we introduced the concept of born-global firms. From their inception or very shortly thereafter, these new firms target global markets. Almost immediately, international sales account for a large proportion of their total sales. There are several explanations for this phenomenon. Entrepre-

A customer outside a computer store in Bangalore, India. Bangalore-based firms play an increasing role in information technology worldwide. Most of these firms are "born global."

neurs are increasingly exposed to global opportunities as a result of the communications revolution. Many global entrepreneurs have themselves worked or studied in foreign countries. Many realize that their customers and competition are global. A large number of global start-ups can be found in Silicon Valley, where rapidly changing technologies encounter worldwide demand.[28]

Born globals can benefit from the fact that they have no organizational history. Other firms have traditionally passed through several structural reorganizations as they evolved into global firms. Born-global firms can adopt global organizations from the start. This is enviable in that structural change can entail heavy costs and business disruptions. However, there is something to be said for the more traditional, gradual evolution of a global organization. Firms that move into international markets more slowly can build up market and cultural knowledge over time. They cultivate and support ever more extensive worldwide organizations by recruiting and training knowledgeable and experienced managers and staff. Born globals attempt to do this practically overnight and can find their managerial resources stretched to the limit. As in other entrepreneurial ventures, they can find themselves with fewer assets than opportunities.

▶ *Controlling the Global Organization*

As an international company becomes larger and more globally focused, maintaining control of international operations becomes increasingly important. Establishing a system to control marketing activities in numerous markets is not an easy job. However, if companies expect to implement their global strategies, they must establish a control system to regulate the many activities within their organizations.

Communication Systems

Effective communication systems facilitate control. Global strategies that require standardization and coordination across borders will need an effective communication system to support them. Headquarters staff will need to receive timely and accurate local input from national subsidiaries. Then decisions can be made quickly and transmitted back to the local management for rapid implementation.

As physical distances separating headquarters and national subsidiaries increase, the time and expense involved in communications increase, and so does the potential for error. Nonetheless, global communications are vastly improved over what they were only a few years ago. The quality of telecommunications has soared while its costs have plummeted. Today most countries have sufficient communications infrastructures. Still, communications infrastructures vary among countries, and problems can continue to arise in less developed countries.

Global information networks are now available that allow improved communication around the world. For example, the Internet links millions of computer users and gives them access to information, research, and services. These information superhighways are reducing many of the constraints imposed by geography. Increasingly, global businesses are harnessing the Internet for purposes of internal communications. Over the long term, these relatively inexpensive global networks will allow for better control. For example, Siemens operates in 190 countries and has instituted an internal system, or "sharenet," for posting knowledge throughout the global company. The sharenet came in handy when Siemens Malaysia wanted to bid on a high-speed data network linking Kuala Lumpur and its new airport. Lacking the know-how necessary for such a project, the subsidiary turned to the sharenet and discovered that Siemens was already working on a similar project in Denmark.[29]

Elements of a Control Strategy

Control is a cornerstone of organization. Control provides the means to direct, regulate, and manage business operations. The implementation of a global marketing program requires a significant amount of interaction not only among various national subsidiaries but also among the individual areas of marketing, such as product development and advertising, and among the other functional areas, such as production and research and development. The control system is used to measure these business activities along with competitive and market reactions. Deviations from the planned activities and results are analyzed and reported so that corrective action can be taken.

A control system has three basic elements: (1) the establishment of standards, (2) the measurement of performance against those standards, and (3) the analysis and correction of any deviations from the standards. Although control is a conceptually simple aspect of the organization process, a wide variety of problems arise in international situations, resulting in inefficiencies and intracompany conflict.

Developing Standards Corporate goals are achieved through the effective implementation of a marketing strategy in the international firm's many national markets. Standard setting is driven by these corporate goals.

Standards must be clearly defined, universally accepted, and understood by managers throughout the global organization. The standards should be set through joint deliberations involving corporate headquarters personnel and each local marketing organization. Normally, the standard setting is done annually when the operational business plan is established.

Firms can employ both behavioral and performance standards. **Behavioral standards** refer to actions taken within the firm. They can include the type and amount of advertising to be developed and utilized, the market research to be performed, and the prices to be charged for a product. **Performance standards** refer to market outcomes. They might include trial rates by customers or sales by product line. Recently, there has been a trend toward broadening the measures of business performance beyond financial data. More and more companies are measuring quality, customer satisfaction, innovation, and market share.[30]

Measuring and Evaluating Performance After standards are set, performance must be monitored. In order to monitor performance against standards, management must be able to observe current performance. Much of the numerical information, such as sales and expenses, will be reported through the accounting system. Other items, such as the implementation of an advertising program, will be communicated through a report. At times, personal visits and meetings may be advisable when management is attempting to evaluate more complex issues, such as the success or failure of coordinated national actions against a global competitor.

Analyzing and Correcting Deviations from the Standards The purpose of establishing standards and reporting performance is to ensure achievement of corporate goals. To achieve these goals, management must evaluate how well performance is living up to the standards the company has set and must initiate corrective action when performance is below those standards. As a consequence of distance, communication issues, and cultural differences, the control process can be difficult in the international setting.

Control strategy can be related to the principle of the carrot and the stick: using both positive and negative incentives. On the positive side, outstanding performance can be rewarded with increased independence, more marketing dollars, and salary increases or bonuses for the managers. On the negative side, unsatisfactory performance can mean reduction in all those items, as well as the threat that the managers responsible will lose their jobs. The key to correcting deviations is to get managers to understand and agree with the standards and then ensure that they have the means to correct the deficiencies. Hence the managers are often given some flexibility with resources. For example, if sales are down 10 percent, managers may need the authority to increase advertising or reduce prices to offset the sales decline.

Corporate Culture as Control

In addition to the processes we have described, many international firms attempt to establish cultural control. If an international firm can establish a strong corporate culture across its subsidiaries, then managers from its various units share a single vision and values. Some believe that this corporate socialization enables global firms to operate with less burdensome hierarchical structures and fewer time-consuming procedures.

Matsushita (Panasonic) provides managers with 6 months of cultural training, and Unilever's new hires go through corporate socialization as well. Such initiation programs help to build the vision and shared values of a strong corporate culture. Managers also receive ongoing training. For example, Unilever brings 400 to 500 international managers from around the world to its international management-training center. Unilever spends as much on training as it does on R&D, not only to upgrade skills but also to indoctrinate managers into the Unilever family. This helps build personal relationships and informal contacts that can be more powerful than any formal systems or structures.

However, we must remember that the corporate culture of a firm mirrors to a large extent the national culture of its homeland. When a U.S. multinational socializes its local managers to "think and act American," this can make communication and control within the multinational easier. However, local managers must still operate within many national cultures that are different from the American culture. It is equally important that they maintain their local culture and remain capable of relating to local customers, competitors, and governments.

▶ *Conflict Between Headquarters and Subsidiaries*

Despite attempts to build a transnational corporate culture within multinational firms, a universal problem facing international marketing managers is the internal conflict that arises between headquarters and subsidiaries. Table 16.1 summarizes several significant differences in perceptions of marketing issues between subsidiaries and home offices that emerged from a recent study of U.S. companies with operations in Hong Kong. The study also identified four areas in which subsidiaries perceived their autonomy as significantly less than did headquarters—pricing, logo and name, and the choice of an advertising agency.[31] This is probably not surprising, given our prior discussion of the impact of global branding, increased price coordination worldwide, and the trend among multinationals to consolidate advertising within one or a few agency networks.

Conflicts between headquarters and subsidiaries are inevitable because of the natural differences in orientation and perception between the two groups. The subsidiary manager usually wants more authority and more local differentiation, whereas headquarters wants more detailed reporting and greater unification of geographically dispersed operations. The parent is usually the more powerful in the relationship, but sometimes a subsidiary can take over a parent company. Trendy U.S. retailer Esprit watched its sales in the United States decline while sales in Asia and Europe soared to over $1 billion a year. In 2002, its Hong Kong office bought full rights to the Esprit brand around the world for $150 million. Its first goal: Revamp strategy in the U.S. market.[32]

Conflict is not all bad. Conflict generates constant dialogue between different organizational levels during the planning and implementation of strategies. This dialogue can result in a balance between headquarters and subsidiary authority, global and local perspective, and standardization and differentiation of the global marketing mix. And it can allow new and better ideas to surface from any part of the global organization.

READ MORE ABOUT IT: Check out "Can Esprit Be Hip Again?" under *Supplemental Readings* on our website.

Table 16.1 *Perceptions of Issues Related to Marketing in Home Office and Subsidiaries*

MARKETING ISSUE	HOME OFFICE	SUBSIDIARY
1. Visits from home office managers to subsidiaries are usually productive.	Agrees more	Agrees less
2. Problems come up frequently because the home office doesn't understand the variety of opinions that can exist at a subsidiary as a consequence of the more widely differing backgrounds there than at the home office.	Agrees less	Agrees more
3. Problems come up frequently because the home office doesn't understand that a subsidiary's culture can be different from that of the home office.	Agrees less	Agrees more
4. There is not enough emphasis at the subsidiaries on strategic thinking and long-term planning.	Agrees more	Agrees less
5. Subsidiaries are encouraged to suggest innovations to the home office.	Agrees more	Agrees less
6. The home office generally tries to change subsidiaries, rather than trying to understand and perhaps adapt to them.	Agrees less	Agrees more
7. Subsidiaries have enough flexibility to cope effectively with changing local conditions.	Agrees more	Agrees less
8. Knowledge is transmitted freely from the home office to subsidiaries.	Agrees more	Agrees less
9. There is a lack of carryover of marketing knowledge from one subsidiary to another.	Agrees more	Agrees less
10. The home office tries to involve subsidiaries' marketing managers meaningfully in decision making.	Agrees more	Agrees less

Source: Adapted from Chi-Fai Chan and Neil Bruce Holbert, "Marketing Home and Away," *Journal of World Business*, 36, 2 (Summer 2001): 207.

▶ *Considering a Global Marketing Career*

A viable organizational structure, a unifying corporate culture, and effective control systems all enable a firm to compete in the global arena. Equally important are the individuals who manage the firm. Throughout this book, we have presented the argument that virtually all firms are affected by increased global competition. In turn, most firms not only will deal with competitors from other countries but also will depend on sales that are increasingly multinational. Many will need to adapt to buyers who are becoming increasingly global themselves. Because of this, firms will need managers who understand the issues we have discussed here: the impact of the global environment on marketing, global strategic planning, managing a marketing mix across cultures, and effectively managing relations between headquarters and subsidiaries to ensure that global strategy is well implemented. Any marketer who eventually reaches the upper echelons of management will need an understanding of the concepts we have covered in this book.

In many companies, global marketing is not always an entry-level job, especially for recent university graduates. Firms often choose to fill globally oriented positions with marketers who have first had domestic experience. A good career strategy is to join a company that has global operations and whose culture you admire. After proving yourself in the home market, you should be eligible for a global position in only a few years. This is especially true if you are assigned to the firm's headquarters. Informal networking with international executives can be a good way to broadcast your interest in international markets and global strategy—and companies are always in need of such motivated managers.

Besides this traditional route to a career in global marketing, there are other ways to go international—even at an entry level. Consider smaller companies that need help with international markets immediately. Export management companies are one option. For these types of firms, skills in the local language of a key target market can make you stand out. If you are an American citizen, you might join the Peace Corps. The Peace Corps offers positions that are business-oriented, and you receive language and cultural training. Look for a job with a foreign multinational that operates in your country. Even if you don't work with foreign markets right away, you will gain the experience of working with different cultures within your organization. Or consider positions in purchasing with a company that deals extensively with foreign suppliers. Knowing about global marketing can make you a more sophisticated buyer. Many U.S. managers in entry-level positions in purchasing find themselves flying to Mexico or the Far East to help manage the buyer-supplier relationship. Finally, government positions such as those with local or national commerce departments can provide excellent experience and can put you in touch with many corporate executives working in international markets.

Whether you choose a more traditional route to a career in global marketing or find a particular niche that is right for you, the need for a global mindset and the numbers of challenging and exciting positions for global marketers will only increase in the future.

▶ *Conclusions*

Organizing the marketing efforts of a company across a number of countries is a difficult process. As the scope of a company's international business changes, its organizational structure must be modified in accordance with the internal and external environments. In this chapter, we have reviewed the various types of organizations commonly used, showing the benefits of each. The dynamic nature of business requires that a company constantly reevaluate its organizational structure and processes and make any modifications necessary to meet the objectives of the firm.

The task of molding an organization to respond to the needs of a global marketplace also involves building a shared vision and developing human resources. A clear vision of the purpose of the company that is shared by everyone gives focus and direction to each manager. Managers can be a company's scarcest resource. A commitment to recruiting and developing managers who understand the complexities of the global marketplace and the importance of cross-cultural sensitivity should help the international firm build a common vision and values, which in turn facilitate the implementation of a global strategy.

Review Questions

1. Explain how a firm's customers help determine the proper global structure for the firm.

2. List and explain the three different corporate world views. How do they affect the global organization?

3. How does an international division differ from an export department?

4. Compare the pros and cons of a geographically based organization with those of a product-based organization.

▶ Matrix organizations can be very costly and complex. What advantages do they offer to offset these problems?

▶ What are the organizational challenges faced by firms that are born global?

▶ How can corporate culture serve as a means of control within a multinational organization?

Questions for Discussion

1. How does a domestic organization evolve into an international organization? What type of international organization is likely to develop first? What type is likely to develop second? Why?

2. In order to achieve better international sales (which currently account for about 30 percent of total revenues), the U.S.-based toy manufacturer Mattel decided to put U.S. division heads in charge of international sales. Discuss the pros and cons of such a move in general and for a firm in the toy industry in particular.

3. Apart from its formal organizational structure, how can the global company ensure that it is responding to the market and achieving efficiency, local responsiveness, and global learning?

4. What are the advantages and limitations of using the Internet as a means of internal communication within a global organization?

5. What suggestions would you propose to bridge the gaps between headquarters and subsidiaries that are noted in Table 16.1?

For Further Reading

Chan, Chi-fai, and Neil Bruce Holbert. "Marketing Home and Away: Perception of Managers in Headquarters and Subsidiaries." *Journal of World Business* 36, 2 (Summer 2001): 205–221.

Greiner, Larry E. "Revolution as Organizations Grow." *Harvard Business Review*, May–June 1998: 55–67.

Kedia, Ben L., and Ananda Mulcherji. "Global Managers: Developing a Mindset for Global Competitiveness." *Journal of World Business* 34, 3 (1999): 230–251.

Kets de Vries, Manfred F.R.. "Charisma in Action: The Transformation Abilities of Virgin's Richard Branson and ABB's Percy Barnevik." *Organizational Dynamics* 26, 3 (January 1, 1998).

Lei, David, John W. Slocum, and Robert A. Pitts. "Designing Organizations for Competitive Advantage: The Power of Unlearning and Learning." *Organizational Dynamics* 27, 3 (January 1, 1999): 24–28.

Case 16.1	*How Local Should Coke Be?*

During the 1970s and 1980s, Coke had expanded its soft-drinks business rapidly overseas. It had consolidated its bottling networks to cover increasingly large territories in response to an increasingly centralized retail trade. Many decisions about advertising and packaging were dictated from Atlanta. With the purchase of Minute Maid orange juice in the late 1990s, Coke was hoping to gain economies of scale for global dominance in the juice business in addition to its presence in soft drinks.

By 2000, however, Coke was rethinking its U.S.-based centralized approach to running its global business. For the first time in its 114-year history, Coke's top executives met together outside Atlanta headquarters. It was a harbinger of things to come. From now on, the Coke board would meet outside the United States once a year. This change was one of many instigated by Coke's new CEO, Douglas Daft, who was attempting to turn the company around after 2 years of poor profits. Daft himself was an Australian who had attracted attention with his successful management of Coke's Japanese subsidiary, where his localization approach had built a successful tea and coffee business. Under Daft, Atlanta was envisioned as a support to Coke's national subsidiaries, rather than as the traditional central headquarters that would mandate and direct the company's worldwide operations. Coke would cease to be big, slow, and out of touch and would instead be light on its feet and sensitive to local markets. One immediate effect of Daft's more localized strategy was the cutting of 2,500 jobs at Atlanta headquarters. Asian and Middle East operations, previously managed out of Atlanta, would be transferred to Hong Kong and London, respectively.

The backlash against Coke's centralized approach first emerged in Europe. Europe represented 20 percent of worldwide volume and 28 percent of worldwide profits. Two incidents caused Coke's new management to reconsider its European policy. In 1999, as a result of various court rulings across Europe, Coke had to scale back significantly its attempt to buy Cadbury Schweppes's beverage brands. A contamination scare also forced Coke to destroy 17 million cases of Coke at a cost of $200 million. Amid the bad publicity arising from this incident, Coke was accused of being evasive and arrogant and of delaying too long in its response while waiting for direction from Atlanta.

Daft decided to break up responsibility for Europe, which had long been handled by a single division that oversaw 49 markets. Ten new geographic groups were formed on the basis of culturally and economically clustered markets. After all, what did Finland and Italy have in common? In another break with the past, nine of the new groups were to be run by non-Americans. Previously, half of the top executives in Europe had been sent over from the United States. Europe would be the test case to see whether Coke could get closer to its consumers by altering its organization. The new European groups were still under orders to push Coke's four core brands—Coca-Cola, Fanta, Sprite, and Diet Coke—but they were encouraged to explore new products and develop flavors with local appeal. Germany responded with a berry-flavored Fanta, and Turkey developed a pear-flavored beverage.

Soon other changes were evident. The formal suits seen at headquarters in Atlanta were replaced by more informal dress codes. Local lawyers were employed instead of lawyers sent from the United States. Reporters seeking a Coke spokesperson could contact expanded communications offices in European countries instead of having to contact Atlanta. Previously, only a single global website had been allowed; now local subsidiaries could run their own websites. Coke's Belgian site—in Dutch, French, and English—received 3 million hits in its first month. One manager noted that developing the website took only a few weeks, whereas it would have taken 8 months under the old centralized system. Belgium was also the site for a new localized promotion idea. Coke hostesses were sent to discos at night to hand out bottles of Coke and promote the idea of a "Coke pause" in a night of otherwise hard drinking. A local spokesman supported the new promotional idea, noting that Belgians were party animals—something Atlanta headquarters might have been slow to appreciate.

Although a euphoric freedom appeared to spread across Europe, the success of the new organizational structure was less clear when it came to the bottom line. Sales slipped slightly in Europe just as localization was being put in place. Some believed that Coke's restructuring of Europe was an overreaction to some bad publicity. They argued that Coke would always be a foreign target. McDonald's had tried to assuage French farmers with a local purchasing campaign, only to meet with indifference. Was Coke doomed to face similar indifference as it attempted to localize? As for the contaminated-bottles crisis, a year later in Belgium, sales had returned to normal levels, and schools where students had reported getting sick had renewed their contracts with Coke. And Atlanta was sending further messages that there would be limits to localization. One top executive at the German operations was fired for running television advertisements aimed at the radical youth movement.

Another early challenge to localization would likely be Coke's launch of its sports drink Powerade in Europe. The sports-drink market in Europe was only $1 billion, compared to $61 billion in the United States, but it was growing fast. Competition in Europe was fragmented but included Powerade's archrival Gatorade, owned by Coke's archrival PepsiCo. Gatorade held 78 percent of the U.S. market and was strong in Europe as well. Powerade would essentially retain its American formula but would taste slightly different because of ingredient regulations of the European Union. The new launch might possibly cannibalize Aquarius, Coke's other recent launch into the sports-drink market in Europe. However, a company spokesperson noted that

Aquarius was meant to be drunk after exercising, whereas Powerade was to be drunk while exercising as well. At headquarters, managers envisioned the target market for their new introduction as European males age thirteen to twenty-nine. Powerade was scheduled to debut in Europe in nine national markets—France, Germany, Greece, Hungary, Italy, Poland, Spain, Sweden, and Turkey.

Discussion Questions

1. What are the pros and cons of changing Coke's single European structure into ten different regional groups?
2. Do you agree with Coke's firing of the executive in Germany? Why or why not? How should Coke avoid incidents like this in the future?
3. If you were the manager of Coke in Germany or Turkey, where would you invest your greatest effort, behind the launch of Powerade or behind the launch of your locally developed fruit-flavored drinks? What factors would guide your decision?
4. What suggestions would you offer to Coke about its global organizational structure and control?

Sources: William Echikson and Dean Foust, "For Coke: Local Is It," *Business Week*, July 3, 2000: 122; Dean Foust and Gerry Khermouch, "Repairing the Coke Machine," *Business Week*, March 19, 2001: 86–88; Bert Roughton Jr., "Independence Adds Marketing Oomph to Coke Abroad," *Atlanta Constitution*, June 11, 2000, p. 1G; Christopher Seward, "View from Top; Coke Wandered Off Its Path," *Atlanta Constitution*, March 28, 2000, p. 5D; Jabulani Sikhakhane, "Going Local in the Face of Globalization," *Financial Mail*, May 26, 2000: 28; Betsy McKay, "Coke Surprisingly Makes Minute Maid Its Unit of the Hour," *Wall Street Journal*, November 16, 2001, p. B3.; and Alessandra Galloni, "Coke to Launch Powerade Across Europe," *Wall Street Journal*, October 16, 2001, p. B11.

Case 16.2 *The Globalization of Indian IT*

Wipro Ltd. originated as an Indian firm operating in the vegetable oils trade about half a century ago. By the beginning of the twenty-first century, it had evolved into one of India's largest software services companies, employing 6,700 software engineers. Located in India's high-tech city of Bangalore, Wipro began in the software business by writing code on contract, handling multimillion-dollar contracts with international companies such as General Electric, Nokia, and Home Depot. In 2001, however, its president, Vivek Paul, aspired to bring the company up the value-added chain to become one of the top ten information technology (IT) companies in the world. Instead of simply writing code, Wipro would expand into the more lucrative area of business process consulting, offering supply chain management and deciphering customer trends from sales data—and competing with the likes of IBM Global Services and Electronic Data Services. But was this vision viable? Could Wipro go from an Indian firm with overseas clients to a truly global corporation virtually overnight? One estimate suggested that Wipro would need to hire an additional 30,000 employees worldwide in order to accomplish this goal.

In the early 1990s, key Indian software development companies such as Wipro Ltd. and Infosys Technologies Ltd. had already captured a lucrative market by handling code-writing jobs from larger international companies. Working from sites such as a high-technology industrial park in Bangalore, Indian software companies could take advantage of both lower-paid Indian talent and the telecommunications revolution in order to service overseas markets quickly and effectively. Programmers in Bangalore earned only $800 a month in 2001, although salaries were rising at a rate of 15 percent a year. Western consulting companies, however, were beginning to challenge the competitive advantage of Indian firms by opening Asian software centers. Furthermore, India as a site for code writing was being challenged by such other low-cost countries as China, the Philippines, and Vietnam.

Moving into more sophisticated and higher-margin IT products meant both converting current clients and attracting new ones. Wipro convinced Thomas Cook Financial Services not only to use them for designing a system for automating Thomas Cook's foreign currency transactions but also to hire them to install the system within the

British multinational. But new, smaller accounts would also be necessary if Indian firms were to carve out a significant global market share. Videos-DotCom sent some work to Wipro when its Texas-based staff was too busy. Subsequently, it switched most of its development work to Bangalore, citing Wipro's extensive e-commerce experience, development skills, pricing, and overall quality. Infosys won a contract from EveryD.com, a Japanese online shopping and banking service for housewives. Its job encompassed developing the business plan, designing the portal, and writing the operational software. The Japanese customer noted that Infosys wasn't the cheapest of alternatives but that it had the necessary expertise and delivered the product on time.

In addition to these more established companies, Indian start-up software companies were developing their own products and taking them directly to the largest national market—the United States. Some executives of these Indian start-up companies found themselves moving overseas almost immediately. The chairman of Bombay-based I-Flex Solutions, a financial services software developer, moved to New Jersey in order to be able to call on potential clients personally. Over a period of just a few years, the company had posted 25 percent of its 1,425 employees to 4 continents. Despite being an Indian start-up, Talisma Corporation, a customer relations management software developer, was established and based in Seattle, where it could employ U.S. salespeople to promote its made-in-India product. One year later, Talisma had 19 offices in 7 countries.

Such IT start-ups contributed to the fact that by 2000, India had become one of Asia's major destinations for venture capital. Much of this investment came from Indians who had made their fortunes in the 1990s. Still, Indian capital markets were generally noted for their conservatism. Firms were expected to post profits consistently. A loss of money, even in the short term, was considered unacceptable. Laying out large sums of money, such as those needed for the acquisition of other firms, was often judged to be very risky.

Some of the venture capital flowing into India came from expatriate Indians. Many Indian IT engineers worked or had worked in the United States. Silicon Valley's Indian high-tech population numbered around 200,000 and was considered to be the area's most successful immigrant community. Many Indians working in the IT industry in the United States believed that despite their technical expertise—or possibly because of it—they were being overlooked for management positions. Ironically, American companies considered their technical skills too valuable to lose by transferring them to management. Partially as a reaction to this, many Indians working in the United States considered starting their own businesses either in India or in the United States. Indians living in the United States often invested in each other's start-up companies, sat on each other's boards, and hired each other for key jobs. In fact, companies with Indian founders could often hire teams of developers more rapidly than the average U.S. company without the benefit of ethnic ties to the Indian community. IndUs Entrepreneurs (TIE) of Santa Clara emerged as one of the preeminent networking groups for Indian entrepreneurs. It hosted monthly Angel Forums at which entrepreneurs could pitch plans to potential investors. The IndUS Entrepreneurs website states as the group's goal the duplication of the Silicon Valley success story in India.

Discussion Questions

1. Why will Indian IT firms have to transform themselves into more global corporations in the future?
2. How will their internationalization experience differ from the experience of U.S.-based firms in the latter half of the twentieth century?
3. What unique advantages and disadvantages do these firms possess?
4. Which organizational structure do you think would be appropriate for a more global Wipro? Why?

Sources: Bruce Einhorn and Manjeet Kripalani, "India 3.0," *Business Week,* February 26, 2001: 44–46; Rasul Bailay, "Angels in India," *Wall Street Journal,* March 15, 2001, p. A15; Melanie Warner, "The Indians of Silicon Valley," *Fortune,* May 15, 2000: 356–372; Julelcha Dash, "Indian Entrepreneurs Take Charge," *Computer World,* April 3, 2000: 39; and Mark Clifford, Manjeet Kripalani, and Heidi Dawley, "The 21st Century Corporation," *Business Week Online,* August 28, 2000.

Notes

[1]Kevin Maler, "3M Looks to Expand Global Sales," *Knight-Ridder Tribune Business News*, June 17, 2001.

[2]Sumantra Ghoshal and Nitin Nohria, "Horses for Courses: Organizational Forms for Multinational Corporations," *Sloan Management Review*, Winter 1993: 27.

[3]Andrew Campbell, Marion Devine, and David Young, *A Sense of Mission* (London: Economist Books, 1990), pp. 19–41.

[4]Gary Hamel and C. K. Prahalad, "Strategic Intent," *Harvard Business Review*, May–June 1989: 63–68.

[5]David P. Hamilton and Robert Steiner, "Sony's Idei Tightens Reins Again on Freewheeling U.S. Operations," *Wall Street Journal*, January 24, 1997, p. A10.

[6]"A Tortoise That Stays Within Its Shell," *Financial Times*, October 30, 1989: 13.

[7]Ibid.

[8]David Woodruff, "Your Career Matters," *Wall Street Journal*, November 11, 2000, p. B1.

[9]Jason Gertzen, "Milwaukee-Based Manufacturer Seeks Overseas Expansion," *Knight-Ridder Tribune Business News*, June 11, 2001.

[10]Will Pinkston, "Ford Mulls Suppliers Park Near Atlanta," *Wall Street Journal*, July 12, 2000, p. S1.

[11]"European Study Finds Companies Can Save 35–45% by Moving to Financial Shared Services," *A. T. Kearney (News Release)*, December 16, 1993, p. 1.

[12]Arnold Schuh, "Global Standardization as a Success Formula for Marketing in Central Eastern Europe?" *Journal of World Business* 35, 2 (Summer 2000): 133–148.

[13]Ian Fraser, "Now Only the Name's Not the Same," *Eurobusiness*, April 1990: 22–25.

[14]Floris A. Maljers, "Inside Unilever: The Evolving Transnational Company," *Harvard Business Review*, September-October 1992: 48.

[15]"Ford Maps Out a Global Ambition," *Financial Times*, April 3, 1995: 9.

[16]"Ford's Really Big Leap at the Future," *Fortune*, September 18, 1995: 134.

[17]"Ford: Alex Trotman's Daring Global Strategy," *Business Week*, April 3, 1995: 94.

[18]"The World That Changed the Machine," *The Economist*, March 30, 1996: 63.

[19]"Ford: Alex Trotman's Daring Global Strategy."

[20]"A Global Tune-up for Ford," *Business Week*, May 2, 1994: 38.

[21]Joseph B. White, "Ford's CEO Nasser Considers Giving More Authority to Firm's Regional Units," *Wall Street Journal*, September 17, 1999, p. A16.

[22]"ICI Proffers More Corporate Clout to Its Customers," *Financial Times*, September 7, 1990: 12.

[23]Christopher A. Bartlett, "ABB's Relays Business: Building and Managing a Global Matrix," Harvard Business School Case, 1993.

[24]"Behind the Tumult at P&G," *Fortune*, March 7, 1994: 82.

[25]Ernest Beck, "Familiar Cry to Unilever: Split It Up!" *Wall Street Journal*, August 4, 2000, p. A7.

[26]Christopher Bartlett and Sumantra Ghoshal, *Managing Across Borders* (London: Hutchinson Business Books, 1989), pp. 16–17.

[27]Jean-Pierre Jeannet, *Managing with a Global Mindset* (London: Financial Times Pitman, 2000), p. 171.

[28]Benjamin M. Oriatt and Patricia Phillips McDougall, "Global Startups," *Academy of Management Executive* 9, 2 (May 1995): 43.

[29]"Electric Glue," *The Economist*, June 2, 2001.

[30]Michael Goold, *Strategic Control* (London: Economist Books, 1990), p. 120.

[31]Chi-fai Chan and Neil Bruce Holbert, "Marketing Home and Away: Perceptions of Managers in Headquarters and Subsidiaries," *Journal of World Business* 36, 2 (Summer 2001): 205–221.

[32]Sarah McBride, "Can Esprit Be Hip Again?" *Wall Street Journal*, June 17, 2002, p. B1.

Appendix *Cases*

Case 1	*Frank Davis Comes to Madagascar*

Antananarivo, Madagascar Frank Davis entered the cocktail lounge at the Madagascar Hilton Hotel, located in the nation's capital city of Antananarivo, and quickly scanned the room. Behind a cloud of cigarette smoke in the corner there was a table of boisterous French businessmen. A few other tables of two or three people were scattered throughout the lounge. Frank chose a seat at the bar next to a well-dressed white man who looked like he might be American. This was Frank's first visit to Madagascar and he wanted to get the impressions of other Americans doing business there.

"What would you like?" asked the bartender in slightly accented English.

"A beer, please. What kind do you have?" Frank asked.

"Actually the THB isn't bad. It's the local beer," offered the well-dressed gentleman next to Frank.

"Thanks. I'll try a THB," Frank told the bartender.

"Is this your first time in Madagascar?" asked the man after introducing himself as Jean-Paul, an American of French descent.

"Yes. I'm here evaluating the local business climate. I work for a U.S. food processing company, Summit Foods, that is interested in the local spice market. How about you?"

"I head up the operations of a textile company in Madagascar's free trade zone, Zone Franche. I've been here since right after the presidential election in 1993."

Frank was somewhat familiar with the recent political history based on background material he had received from the U.S. State Department. Madagascar was a former French colony that had gained independence in 1960. Since independence, there have been four presidents: Tsiranana, from 1960–1972, and Ratsimandrava, assassinated in 1975, were both in power during the First Republic. Then came Ratsiraka, who introduced the country to the Second Republic and socialism, but he was forced to yield to a transitional government in 1991 after a six-month strike. In February 1993 the current president, Zafy, was elected after a popular referendum which adopted a new constitution establishing a mixed presidential-parliamentary regime. Since the late 1980s and particularly under Zafy's Third Republic, the country was attempting to shift to a free-market economy from a centrally planned one.

"A textile company?" said Frank. "Then you must be pretty familiar with the general investment climate here. My boss is convinced there's a lot happening in this country because he has a distant relative who made a fortune here. But I haven't had a chance to look around yet, except for the ride from the airport to the hotel, and that was pretty depressing. The poverty seems to be so pervasive, and yet we passed several Mercedes and sport utility vehicles that didn't seem to be driven by foreigners. I don't get it."

Jean-Paul laughed and shrugged his shoulders. Although he was smiling, his eyes seemed to be sad. "Investment climate? Investment climate . . . Well, I guess it depends on how you define it, and how badly you want to invest. It also depends on who you know and who you are willing to pay to get things done." Frank's eyebrows shot up. "Pay to 'get things done'? Like what things?" he thought to himself. He let Jean-Paul continue.

"The Third Republic is about two years old. The present administration was elected after a general strike that brought the government and the economy to a standstill. Conditions were bad, wages were low and people got sick of socialism because it seemed to be benefiting only those in power, not the country. The new administration claims to support free-market capitalism, but according to many of my Malagasy business associates, this crew is almost as bad as the crew they voted out."

"But your company is still here. Obviously you are making money if you're still here, right?"

"Believe it or not, we're making money despite the local business climate and the Malagasy government, not because of it. Thanks to the Zone Franche, we pay no taxes on our export receipts and we can hold our profits in U.S. or French currency. Otherwise all the foreign exchange we earn would have to be directly deposited into local banks and then would be automatically converted and held in Malagasy currency. If we were not in the Zone Franche, each time we needed foreign exchange to do business outside the country, we would have to apply for it and, of course, pay a fee! Our firm is doing okay here due to the low barriers

Exhibit 1 *Spices of Madagascar*

ENGLISH NAME	FRENCH NAME	MALAGASY NAME	LATIN NAME
SPICES CURRENTLY EXPORTED			
Cinnamon	Cannelle	Kanela	Cinnamonum zeylanicum
Tumeric	Curcuma	Tamotamo	Cucuma longa
Ginger	Gingembre	SakamalaJirofoo	Zinngiber officinale Roscoe
Clove	Girofle	Jirofo	
Hot or Chili pepper	Piment capsicum	Sakay	Capsicum frutescens
Black peppercorn	Poivre noir	Kipoavatra mainty	Piper nigrum
Green peppercorn	Poivre vert	Dioavatra maitso	Piper nigrum
Vanilla	Vanille	Lavanila	Vanilla fragrans
SPICES WITH EXPORT POTENTIAL			
Pink Peppercorn	Baie rose	Voatsiperifery	Schirus terebenthifolius
Mace	Macis		Myristica fragrans
Nutmeg	Noix de muscade		Myristica fragrans

Source: May 1994 Study of Madagascar Exports for Horticultural Products, ATW Consultants for USAID

to entry in the textile industry, low labor costs and the ability of the Malagasy work force to master new skills quickly. But you would not believe all we've gone through to get where we are now." Jean-Paul fell silent and took a long drink of his beer.

Frank was thoughtful. "This guy doesn't seem too optimistic, but he himself said he's making money. I wonder what kinds of problems he ran into."

"Don't get me wrong. This is a beautiful country and the people work incredibly hard. When I first came here after President Zafy took office, I was full of optimism and could see lots of possibilities. I've been in operations management for 20 years. I've dealt with unions, weathered the effects of the energy crisis and foreign competition on the textile industry, as well as the relocation of our company to the southeastern United States from Massachusetts, my home state. I've even helped my company locate a facility in Taiwan. But it hasn't prepared me for some of the things I've dealt with here." He smiled ruefully and pushed back his chair. "Oh, and one more thing," Jean-Paul added.

"What's that?" Frank asked, eager for more information

"Do you have an umbrella?"

"An umbrella? No. Why?" Frank asked, puzzled by the amused expression on Jean-Paul's face.

"Buy one, you'll need it. We're getting into the rainy season here, complete with cyclones. You'll see what I mean soon enough. I wish you luck."

"Cyclones!" Frank thought to himself. "Thanks," he said to Jean-Paul's back as he headed towards the door. Frank wasn't sure whether Jean-Paul was wishing him luck with his assignment or in weathering the rainy season in Madagascar. He felt a bit discouraged, but at the same time his interest was piqued. He smelled a challenge and envisioned himself as an investment pioneer in rugged territory.

Frank's Assignment

Frank Davis had been sent to Madagascar on an exploratory mission by his supervisor, Martin Herlihy, a regional vice president of a multinational food processing company, Summit Foods, based in the United States. Frank had been asked to identify potential opportunities for the company to either import agricultural products or set up a food processing operation in Madagascar. He was also asked to assess the country's general investment climate. Even if opportunities could be found, Frank's boss knew there could be several nonqualifiable costs of doing business in a developing country that could render an otherwise profitable project infeasible.

Exhibit 2 *Exports of Non-Traditional Spices from Madagascar*

CUSTOMS CODE	SPICES	QUANTITY IN KG	VALUE FOB (1000 FMG)*	PRICE/KG OB (1000 FMG)*
1993				
090411100	Green peppercorns in brine	371,559	1,616,136	4,350
090411900	Other peppercorns, not ground	1,470,148	2,506,289	1,705
090412000	Peppercorns, ground or crushed	4,824	37,064	7,683
090420000	Chili peppers, dried or ground	20,022	96,635	4,826
090610000	Cinnamon, whole	1,169,319	1,704,081	1,457
090620000	Cinnamon, ground or crushed	46,724	86,310	1,847
090810000	Nutmeg	143	1,725	12,063
090930000	Cumin seeds	150	99	660
090950000	Fennel seeds	245	36	147
091010000	Ginger	17,461	8,682	497
091020000	Saffron	146	194	1,329
091030000	Tumeric	2,256	15,402	6,827
091040000	Thyme	48	81	1,688
091050000	Curry	232	1,518	6,543
0910099000	Other spices	476	6,619	13,905
	TOTAL	**3,103,753**	**6,080,871**	

Source: State Data Bank (BDE) Antananarivo
*Average rate of exchange in 1993: 1 US$ = 1,900 FMG
1FF = 330 FMG

Frank's foresight and good judgment had saved the company money in past expansion projects, and Martin knew Frank would be thorough in considering the many factors that could influence a potential investment. Martin was eagerly awaiting Frank's assessment of the situation.

Martin Herlihy was interested in expanding Summit Foods' product offerings to include spices. Due to the heightened health consciousness of U.S. and European consumers, spices were quickly replacing oils and heavy sauces as a natural flavor enhancer in both commercially processed and prepared-at-home foods. Given the increased numbers of dual-income families, consumers cooked at home less often than they did twenty years ago. However, they were using more volume and a greater variety of spices when they did cook at home. Ethnic cooking and ethnic restaurants were extremely popular, and that preparation required many nontraditional spices.

Madagascar was known for its spices, particularly vanilla and cloves. Martin asked Frank to find out about other types of spices grown in Madagascar and their current production levels. He felt

strongly that the Malagasy government would encourage export of spices because he knew that cloves and vanilla were historically the main sources of foreign currency earnings in the country.

The restaurant at the Hilton did not serve dinner for another hour and a half. Frank decided to take a walk around the neighborhood of the hotel. Although he had researched Madagascar as thoroughly as possible before he left the States, he had not found much information beyond the official reports put out by government agencies such as the State Department and the Commerce Department. He had learned that Madagascar was the world's fourth largest island with a population of 12.5 million, 1 million of whom lived in the capital, Antananarivo, where he was staying. The annual population growth rate was estimated to be 3.19%, with a fertility rate of 6.68 children per woman. In economic terms, this could mean a largely untapped consumer market if the people had disposable income to spend. But Frank was not sure how to assess that yet. The annual per capita income was about $230 but he did not know what the median income was, or what the cost of living was.

He knew Madagascar was approximately the size of Texas and rich in natural resources such as graphite, chromite, coal, bauxite, titanium, salt, quartz and tar sands, as well as semiprecious stones. His environmentally-conscious friends in the States knew that the country was home to many species and even genuses of flora and fauna that were indigenous nowhere else in the world. He also knew that there was widespread soil erosion caused by deforestation and overgrazing, and that this was contributing to desertification of the island. Several species of plant and animal life were endangered.

Frank also knew a little about the Malagasy people. Their ethnic origin was a combination of Malay-Indonesian, African, Arab, French, Indian and Creole. The religious composition of the population was 7% Muslim, 41% Christian and 52% indigenous beliefs. A strong emphasis on ancestor veneration characterized most spiritual belief in the country. Over 90% of the Malagasy work force was employed in the agricultural sector, including fishing and forestry, and the major exports included coffee, vanilla, cloves, shellfish, sugar and petroleum products. The chief industries were largely agricultural product processing (such as meat canneries, soap factories, breweries, tanneries and sugar refining plants) and textile factories, like the company Jean-Paul represented.

The first thing that struck Frank after leaving the grounds of the Hilton Hotel was the poor condition of the infrastructure—streets, sidewalks, and the storm drainage or sewer system (he was not quite sure what the purpose was of the little streams that ran alongside the streets)—and the absence of traffic signals. Come to think of it, he did not remember stopping at a single red light on the way from the airport. An extensive and well-maintained transportation network certainly would contribute to the success of any agriculturally-based economy where the producers were geographically dispersed throughout the country.

Frank also recalled that the Madagascar airport was served almost exclusively by Air Madagascar, a state-owned enterprise. The lack of competition would likely keep the cost of freight and passenger travel high, with little incentive to improve service efficiency. Despite the poor roads and lack of traffic signals, there was certainly no shortage of cars in the capital, and almost every third car seemed to be a taxi. The air was hot and hazy, thick with car exhaust. Frank noticed several buses so full of people that the back doors remained open and two or three people clung to the outside.

As he continued down the street, Frank was approached by several people selling a variety of items which they pushed at him: handicrafts, Ray Ban sunglasses, brooms, tire irons, a basketball and some fruits or vegetables he did not recognize.

"Non, merci," he said over and over again, but they continued to walk alongside him displaying their wares.

"Bon marché! Combien, Monsieur?" They were ready to bargain but Frank had no money and no need for a tire iron in Madagascar. He began to feel annoyed and a bit overwhelmed by the entourage of

Exhibit 3
SCENES OF MADAGASCAR

Buildings fill the hillsides around downtown Antananarivo

A street vendor displays local produce in the market

vendors. He decided to turn back after another several minutes of sales pitches in French and another language which he assumed was Malagasy. It occurred to him that he needed to change his money at the hotel before dinner anyway. As he came closer to the hotel, he was approached by a bare-footed little boy in dirty rags carrying a baby on his back. "That boy can't be any more than 5 years old," Frank thought, shocked by the sight. "And the baby isn't even old enough to walk. Where are the parents?"

"Monsieur, donnez-moi la monnaie? Donnez-moi la monnaie?" the boy begged, thrusting his little hand forward. His big brown eyes implored Frank to give him some spare change. His face was dirty and his nose runny. Frank was torn inside but looked away and walked quickly back to the hotel, just as the sky was turning dark and threatening rain. Frank reminded himself to buy an umbrella as he took refuge in the air-conditioned lobby from both the rain and the pitiful scene he had confronted outside. He headed for the cashier to change his money.

The Flottement

The exchange rate was just under 4000 Malagasy francs (FMG) to a dollar. Frank recalled that when he left the United States two days before, the rate was about 3600 FMGs. "Could the rate have changed that much in three days?" Frank asked himself. Then he recalled what he had read about the monetary system. In May 1994 the FMG moved from a fixed exchange rate system to a floating exchange rate. The FMG was untied from the French franc to fluctuate on its own against hard currencies, but the French franc (FF) remained the main currency of reference. This step to liberalize the Malagasy currency was referred to as the flottement, and was required by the International Monetary Fund (IMF) in fulfillment of a planned structural adjustment program. As a result of the flottement, the FMG lost about half of its value almost overnight, setting off wide-scale price increases. Because of the weak economy, Madagascar's currency was weak. It had consistently lost value relative to hard currencies since the flottement was instituted.

"Do you need to stamp this?" Frank pushed a small currency declaration form across the counter to the cashier. He had been given the form by the stewardess on his flight in to Madagascar and told to declare all his currency, traveler's checks, credit card account numbers and personal checks. The paper was barely large enough to contain all the information requested, but Frank complied. He did not want to be unnecessarily detained for not following procedures when he left the country. His tour book had warned him that airport officials would ask him how much he spent in the country and whether he was taking any Malagasy money outside the country with him.

"I'm sorry sir, we don't have a stamp. Only the banks stamp the form if you change money there," the cashier informed him.

"But aren't I required by law to have a stamp? How can the hotel exchange money for me but not stamp my form? I'm not sure I understand." Frank was genuinely puzzled.

"If you want your form stamped, you must go to a bank. But the banks are closed until Monday. If you want to exchange your money here, I'll give you a receipt, but I don't have a stamp. Do you want to change it here?"

Frank hesitated. He wanted to follow the rules but he did not quite understand them, and the cashier did not really clarify it for him. He needed the money now and the banks were closed. Was he expected to wait two days to exchange his money, or would he have to explain his predicament to the airport officials and risk being detained at the airport? He finally decided to exchange only as much money as he thought he would need for the weekend, and hope it would not be an issue later. He did not see any other option.

"For a country that is badly in need of foreign exchange, they certainly make it difficult to convert your money," he thought to himself as he left the counter.

Government Approvals

Frank entered the dining room and was seated promptly at a corner table set for one. A short time later Jean-Paul poked his head inside the restaurant and, seeing Frank, waved and approached his table.

"Mind if I join you?" he asked.

"Not at all." Frank gestured towards a chair, "Please, have a seat."

"How are you doing? I barely missed getting caught in the torrential downpour. It's coming down pretty hard out there."

Both men stared out the window at the pouring rain. The sky was dark and ominous. It was hard to believe that just 45 minutes ago the sun had been shining brightly with barely a cloud in the sky.

After giving their dinner orders to the waiter, Frank decided to broach the topic of Madagascar's investment climate again with Jean-Paul. He felt that although Jean-Paul seemed a bit cynical, there was probably a lot he could learn from his experiences. He planned to try to schedule appointments at the Ministry of Commerce, Ministry of Industry, Energy and Mining, and Ministry of Transport, Meteorology and Tourism during his one month visit. He felt that an initial discussion with Jean-Paul would help him put things into a context and develop some meaningful questions for his interviews with the various Ministers.

"So Jean-Paul, I'm interested in hearing more about your experiences in Madagascar, if you don't mind sharing them with me. Tell me about some of the obstacles or problems your company encountered when trying to set up a facility," Frank asked.

"Well, the first thing any company interested in setting up business in Madagascar needs is an agreement, or official approval of the government. The hard part is deciding who to approach to obtain this approval, and how to present your business proposal. You need some type of approval from every ministry which has jurisdiction over any part of your business. For example, in our case, we needed the okay of seven ministries, and each ministry has a set of questions that must be answered and documents that must be filed. Some ministries asked for the same information, others asked for information which seemed irrelevant or outside their jurisdiction. One ministry lost our dossier, but didn't bother to inform us—and maybe they didn't realize themselves—until we called to inquire about the status of the approval two months after submitting everything. The amount of red tape here is mind-boggling."

"Is there some sort of checklist or description of the type of documentation required? I mean, do they want a full blown business plan? A letter from your financial institution? What do they base approval on?" Frank asked, trying to get a clearer picture of what the Malagasy government would request.

"That's just the problem. No one seems to know. It changes from ministry to ministry, day to day. To the first ministry we approached we gave every piece of documentation we thought they could possibly use. I figured that if I was forthcoming with information and demonstrated a serious willingness to do business in Madagascar, the review process would be shorter because they didn't have to keep asking for additional information. I even gave them the names and resumes of the managers we intended to bring in to manage the new facility," explained Jean-Paul.

"That seems like a reasonable approach. Did it help expedite things?" Frank asked.

"Expedite? That's not quite the word I would use. Try *mora mora*," responded Jean-Paul. "It means slowly, slowly in Malagasy—and is often used to describe the 'Malagasy way,'" he grinned. "That first ministry was the ministry that lost it all. Or at least that's what they told us after two months."

Jean-Paul went on to explain that there seemed to be a great deal of overlap between the ministries, and even conflicting information about what types of business activities are encouraged. The laws of one ministry were often superseded by proclamations, decrees and statutes of that ministry or a different one. There was also a lack of communication between ministries, and Jean-Paul got the feeling there were little rivalries and power plays among the ministries.

"Reasons for denial or disapproval are not given, so it's difficult to address their concerns and try again. I heard from a friend that he knew someone who was denied an agreement because they wouldn't offer an interest in their project to people high up in the ministry."

"It sounds like there's a problem with administrative efficiency and consistency. But you could probably find that sort of problem in any large organization in any country, really," Frank remarked.

"That may be true. But if you want to do business in this country and save yourself a lot of time and trouble, I'd suggest you find yourself an influential partner who is highly-placed in the government."

The waiter arrived with their dinner. As he laid the plate down in front of Frank, the lights went out and music stopped. The waiter immediately lit the candle on the table as other waiters circulated around the dining room to light those at other tables.

"*Bon appetit!*" the waiter said to the two men, as he walked back towards the dark kitchen. Dumbstruck, Frank watched the hotel employees for a few minutes waiting to see if someone would take control of the situation and explain to the customers what was going on. Jean-Paul and many of the other diners began eating as if nothing was awry.

"If you're waiting until the lights come back on to eat your dinner, it'll probably be cold. You might as well eat. The power will come back on eventually. It goes out just about every time there's a big rain. During rainy season, that could mean at least once a day."

Frank was surprised. Frequent power outages could obviously cause problems with production schedules and delivery dates. And what about information management? Companies which were highly dependent on data must have to take special precautions to safeguard it. Frank made a mental note to find out what provisions were made for back-up power sources, if any.

"What other types of problems have you dealt with?" Frank asked.

"The property rights laws," Jean-Paul answered. "It's been the policy of our company to purchase land and do the construction ourselves, to very exacting specifications. We have built two factories in other countries in the recent past and have found the best layout and configuration for our machinery and assembly lines. So we prefer to build from scratch rather than lease. But, as you may know, foreigners cannot own land in Madagascar. This posed a problem for us, and frankly our CEO took this to be a signal of distrust by the government."

Frank was not aware of this prohibition against foreign ownership of land. Jean-Paul went on to explain that the Malagasy culture considered the land to be sacred. He had even heard a man once say that to the Malagasy, the land is like their body. It was passed down through the generations from the ancestors, and the fact that Madagascar was an island nation probably contributed to their beliefs. Jean-Paul explained that many people get around this law by using Malagasy partners, but that this arrangement can be extremely costly and risky because the foreigner is beholden to the Malagasy. If there is ever a dispute or the relationship deteriorates, the foreigner has questionable legal recourse.

Jean-Paul's company solved the problem by leasing the land under a 99-year lease and constructing a building that would revert to the property owner at the end of the lease term. The rent was paid in foreign currency because of the high inflation rate. This eliminated the need to have the rents adjusted monthly as the value of the Malagasy franc declined.

"Is that legal? It seems like the government keeps very close tabs on the exchange of foreign currency," Frank remarked. Jean-Paul shrugged.

Visits to Assess the Potential for Exporting Spices

Over the next several days, Frank tried to make appointments to speak with government officials, agricultural membership organizations, food processors, exporters and anyone else who he thought would have valuable information about the export potential for non-traditional spices. At the Ministry of Agriculture he hoped to obtain national production statistics but soon learned that the information available was inaccurate, outdated and incomplete. He also found out that the centralized or geographically concentrated cultivation of spices was declining in Madagascar, as the plantations once run by the French were either abandoned or extremely run down. Some spices were grown wild and harvested by independent peasants, so yields varied from year to year. Many plants from the large plantations had succumbed to disease, and those that grew wild often were damaged by severe weather and by the rampant deforestation taking place on the island, because they were not grown in a self-contained and protected area. The wide dispersion of spices also could pose a problem for processors, as the roads and communication infrastructure were almost nonexistent in many rural areas.

On the positive side, Frank was heartened to find out that spices were not restricted export products. Initially, he feared that they might be classified as protected flora, and therefore could not be exported except by special permit due to environmental regulations. Frank did have some concerns about the quality grade of the spices and whether it was comparable to those on the world market. He found out that there were government standards, set by the Ministry of Commerce, for most types of spices. However, these standards pertained to physical characteristics, such as the length and width of the vanilla bean, rather than the quality, growing and harvesting conditions. The majority of spices grown in Madagascar were exported, with 80% going to Europe. Frank hoped that boded well for the U.S. market, and that the Malagasy spices would meet U.S. standards, which are typically the highest on the world market.

Exhibit 4 *Countries of Destination for Exports of Nontraditional Spices from Madagascar*

COUNTRY	QUANTITY (KG)	%	VALUE FOB (1000 FMG)	%
Ranked by Value of Freight on Board (FOB), 1993				
France	1,096,803	35	1,971,797	32
Germany	469,833	15	1,088,027	18
Great Britain	471,346	15	721,459	12
Belgium	149,473	5	583,252	10
Netherlands	367,213	12	568,748	9
Reunion	68,557	2	171,382	3
Spain	87,221	3	162,850	3
South Africa	73,036	2	146,562	2
Poland	83,515	3	130,993	2
Italy	32,268	1	114,219	2
Soviet Union	12,500	0	97,170	2
Singapore	53,850	2	79,017	1
Tunisia	36,050	1	53,921	1
Nigeria	25,000	1	51,447	1
Niger	24,000	1	33,557	1
Denmark	3,730	0	28,963	0
Egypt	18,000	1	25,366	0
Comoros	22,627	1	17,536	0
Ghana	6,462	0	15,386	0
Sweden	1,259	0	7,804	0
Switzerland	300	0	4,899	0
USA	297	0	3,448	0
Austria	360	0	3,047	0
Mauritius	50	0	16	0
Malta	2	0	4	0
Monaco	1	0	1	0
TOTAL	**3,103,753**	**100**	**6,080,871**	**100**

Source: State Data Bank (BDE) Antananarivo

Average rates of exchange in 1993:
1 FF   =   330 FMG
1 US$ = 1,900 FMG
1 ECU = 2,200 FMG

Meeting a Malagasy Businessman

Frank set up a meeting with the proprietor of a Malagasy spice processing company to learn more about the organization of spice production in Madagascar, and to gauge preliminary receptivity to the idea of forming a partnership with Summit Foods. He hoped to gain a better understanding of how the agricultural sector functioned, and what types of concerns Malagasy operators may have about working with an American importer.

Frank was early for his 2:00 p.m. appointment despite the traffic jam caused by market day in Antananarivo. He was offered a seat in a crowded office where five employees appeared to share one telephone and one typewriter. He noticed the office workers used and reused sheets of carbon paper to make copies of their work. At 2:15 p.m., Frank asked if Mr. Rakotomanana knew he was here. The workers exchanged glances and one of them told him he should be back shortly. Frank figured he may be tied up in traffic somewhere. All of the meetings he had attended so far had begun at least 20 minutes late. The Malagasy took lunch from noon until 2:00 p.m., and many returned home for the noon meal with their family.

At 2:55 p.m., Mr. Rakotomanana arrived. Frank was slightly annoyed because he realized he would probably miss his next meeting, scheduled for 3:30 p.m. He asked if he could use the phone briefly to call his next appointment. On his first few tries, there was no dial tone. One of the office workers volunteered to try calling for him so the meeting could begin.

After explaining who he was and Summit Foods' interest in spices, Frank spoke about his stay so far in Madagascar and asked for some recommendations about what tourist destinations he should visit. They discussed the weather, the local street market and the traffic, and Frank complimented Mr. Rakotomanana on his efficient staff. Frank was interested in touring Mr. Rakotomanana's processing plant but he did not yet feel comfortable asking to do so. Mr. Rakotomanana's manner was friendly, but still quite formal. Frank finally described in detail the techniques and processes used by Summit Foods, and asked Mr. Rakotomanana some basic questions about his operations. It was about 4:00 p.m. when Mr. Rakotomanana offered to take Frank on a tour.

The tour was brief, but Frank was impressed by how much they were able to produce in such small space with the unsophisticated equipment they used. He almost felt as though he were in a time warp. Many of the processes they used had been used in the United States in the 1940s and 1950s. Frank then asked some questions about the company's current customers and processing capacity: "You mentioned that your customers are all domestic. What is your current production capacity?"

"Yes. We like to produce for the Malagasy market. I cannot say for certain because our capacity depends on our customers. During harvest season, we hire temporary workers and they work longer hours until the work is finished," Mr. Rakotomanana explained.

"Are you interested in possibly producing for export as well?"

"Yes."

"Do you have the capacity to produce large quantities over a sustained period of time, for a large export customer such as Summit Foods, for example?"

"Yes. Of course." Mr. Rakotomanana seemed very definitive about that.

"Or would it be necessary to expand your operations, perhaps with the assistance of a partner like my company, through some sort of partnership agreement, to ensure you could meet demand?" Frank offered.

"Yes. I think that would be interesting," Mr. Rakotomanana eagerly replied.

"And your company would be willing to share in the capital expenses of such an expansion, if it were needed?"

Mr. Rakotomanana hesitated, and did not look back up at Frank. "I cannot say. This must be discussed with my family."

"Of course. I understand. I am only exploring the possibilities at this point. Do you think you might be interested in discussing this further at a later date?" Frank asked hopefully. He did not want to push too hard, but wanted to get a clearer indication of what this processor could do for Summit Foods, and on what terms.

"Yes. I think it would be interesting."

"I am leaving in about three weeks. Would you like to set up a meeting next week, after you have a chance to discuss things with your family?"

"Oh, yes."

"When would be convenient for us to get together again?" Frank inquired. He was beginning to feel his approach may be too aggressive.

"I must talk with my family."

"Can you call me at the hotel, or should I phone you later to set up a meeting?" Frank at least wanted a definitive next step, since setting up the meeting had been so difficult to begin with.

"Yes."

Frank wasn't sure which question Mr. Rakotomanana was responding to.

"You can call me at the Madagascar Hilton?"

"Oh, yes."

"Or would you prefer that I call you?" Frank felt he might have a better chance of solidifying plans if he called Mr. Rakotomanana because he had already scheduled several meetings outside the hotel the next week.

"Oh, yes. I think that would be very interesting." The men shook hands and Frank departed.

As he left the building Frank thought to himself, "He certainly was an amiable guy, but a bit hard to read. Was he being realistic about his company's capabilities? He almost seemed too accommo-

Exhibit 5 *Alternative Sources of Supply for Spices*

Sales Prices Include Cost, Insurance and Freight			
Spices	**Origin**	**Unit**	**Price**
Cinnamon			
sticks	Madagascar	kg	
pieces	Madagascar	kg	5.75–6 FF
ground	Madagascar	kg	11–12 FF
Mace	Indonesia	ton	2,375 US$
	Nouvelle Guinée		
Chili pepper	Togo	kg	18–25 FF
	Central Africa		
	Republic of China		
	Madagascar		35–60 FF
	Martinique		35–100 FF
	Morocco		8–10 FF
Peppercorn			
I. white	Sarawak	ton	1,525–3,750 US$
	Sarawak DW		1,525–3,750 US$
	Muntok		1,525–3,750 US$
	Brazil		1,900–3,300 US$
II. black	Lampong	ton	1,050–1,895 US$
	Sarawak		1,000–1,835 US$
	Brazil		1,000–1,700 US$
	Madagascar		1,050–1,700 US$
Ginger	Brazil	kg	9–22 FF
	Thailand		12–19 FF
Chili pepper, green	Morocco	kg	6–10 FF
	Madagascar		30–60 FF
	Martinique		30–100 FF

Source: Marchés Tropicaux et Mediterranéens, 1993

dating." Frank was not sure how well the meeting had gone.

Assessing the Credit Market

Frank ran into Jean-Paul at the Hilton on his way into the dining room, so they decided to have a drink together before dinner. Frank wanted to know about the commercial loans market in Madagascar. If he were able to set up a partnership agreement or close a long-term deal with a Malagasy processor, the processor would most certainly need to expand in order to handle Summit Foods' business. Frank

preferred to deal with one or two large suppliers rather than dozens of smaller ones, and he was fairly certain there were few, if any, with enough production capacity to take on a customer such as Summit Foods while continuing to serve their current customer base.

"What can you tell me about the credit situation here?" Frank asked. "I know the national government is far outspending its receipts and I'm sure that affects the availability of credit here. Did your company finance anything locally?"

"The banks here are extremely risk averse. Even so, they still have many nonperforming loans in their portfolio. We didn't need to use any local banks for financing but we use a Mauritian-owned bank for our accounts payable and our payroll because we don't have a lot of faith in the local banking institutions. Two of the five banks are still partially owned by the Malagasy government, although they're in the process of privatizing. Until that happens, we'll stick with Union Commercial Bank."

Jean-Paul went on to explain that the prime rate was set by the Banque Centrale, which serves much the same purpose as the Federal Reserve Bank in the United States. The five commercial banks then set their rates accordingly.

"Just out of curiosity, what is the current rate to commercial borrowers?" Frank asked.

"Twenty-three percent," Jean-Paul answered, grinning.

"No, really." Frank laughed.

"I'm dead serious, Frank. And they require a 50% guarantee."

"A guarantee? What do you mean? How does that work?"

Jean-Paul explained that a borrower must deposit 50% of the total amount of the loan in the bank, or commit some other type of collateral that is acceptable to the bank.

Frank was incredulous. "That's crazy. If you had the money to begin with, you obviously wouldn't need the loan."

Jean-Paul shrugged. He went on to explain that banks and other funding institutions depended a great deal on a borrower's reputation through word of mouth. There are no formal credit bureaus in Madagascar. Knowing the "right" people was essential.

Frank now understood the capital constraints firms like Mr. Rakotomanana's were facing. After Frank described his earlier conversation with Mr.

Rakotomanana, Jean-Paul explained the concept of *fihavanana,* or family harmony, which was central to Malagasy culture. "It is a critical decision-making factor in all family decisions. Preserving the *fihavanana* is of great importance in this culture, and if often leads to 'uneconomic' business decisions. You are not dealing with what economic theory traditionally refers to as 'rational actors.' What makes perfect business sense to you may not even be a consideration to your Malagasy colleague."

Jean-Paul had another appointment, so Frank ate alone that night. Over dinner he considered what he had learned about doing business in Madagascar during his first week, and what additional information he would need before he left the country in three weeks. He was scheduled to receive a call from Martin Herlihy tomorrow morning to give him a progress report.

Madagascar was eight hours ahead of the United States, so Martin would likely be calling around 6:00 a.m. local time. Frank wanted to think through the pros and cons tonight so he would be clear-headed tomorrow morning when the call came through. He knew Martin would be interested in "the numbers," but there were so many other nonquantifiable factors that warranted as much if not more consideration than the numbers. He was not even at the stage where he could discuss production volume, profit margins and freight costs. Frank was not sure how to present what he learned thus far because, since Martin had not visited the country, he would not easily grasp the business environment nor see both the potential opportunities and obstacles to doing business in a developing country such as Madagascar.

This case was written by Valerie VinCola of Emory University. It is intended as a basis for class discussion rather than to illustrate either effective or ineffective handling of an administrative situation.

From *Portraits of Business Practices in Emerging Markets, Volume 2, Cases for Management Education,* Richard G. Linowes, Editor, Institute of International Education, and U.S. Agency for International Development.

Case 2	*AGT, Inc.*

AGT, Inc. is a marketing research company located in the city of Karachi, Pakistan. Jeff Sons Trading Company (JST) has approached it to look at the potential market for an amusement park in Karachi. Because the city is crowded and real estate costs are high, it will be difficult to find a large enough piece of land on which to locate such a facility. Even if land is available, it will be expensive and that will have a detrimental effect on the overall costs of the project. JST needs to know the potential of this type of investment. They want the market research to identify if a need for the amusement park exists and, if it does, what the public's attitude toward that type of recreational facility might be. If a need is found and support is sufficient, then they want to know the type of amusement park required by potential customers. JST will make its investment decision based on the results of this study.

Background

Pakistan is a typical less developed country (LDC) of the Third World faced with the usual problems of rapidly increasing population, sizable government deficit, and heavy dependence on foreign aid. The country's economy has grown rapidly in the last decade, with GDP expanding at 6.7 percent annually, more than twice the population growth. Like any other LDC, it displays dualism in its economic system: the cities have modern facilities, the smaller towns have some or none. The same holds true for income distribution patterns. Real per capita GDP is Rupees 10,000, or US $400 annually. There is a small wealthy class (1 to 3%), a middle class consisting of another 20 percent, and the remainder of the population is poor. Half of the population lives below the poverty line. Most of the middle class is an urban working class.

Karachi, as the country's largest city and boasting a dense population of over 6 million, has been chosen as the site of the first large-scale amusement park in Pakistan. Current recreational facilities in Karachi, including a poorly maintained zoo, are modest, and people with families avoid visiting most facilities because of the crowds. There are other small parks, but they are not sufficient to cater to such a large population. The main place people go for recreation is the beach. The beaches near Karachi are not well developed and are regularly polluted by oil slicks from the port.

Our working hypothesis is that Karachi citizens have a growing need to spend their leisure time in recreational activities. (Indeed, many middle class and wealthy citizens already take vacations with their families and spend money on recreational activities abroad.) To determine whether there is a true need for this type of recreational facility, we propose to conduct a market research feasibility study.

Potential problems facing the construction of an amusement park in Karachi include:

- The communications infrastructure is poor.
- Only a small percentage of the people own their own transportation.
- Public and private transportation systems are not efficient.
- Maintaining law and order is a problem, said to be similar in scope to the crime problem in Los Angeles.

Research Objectives

To make an investment decision, JST outlined the research objectives necessary to design a marketing strategy that would accomplish the desired return on investment goals. These objectives were the following:
1. Identify the potential demand for this project.
2. Identify the primary target market and what they expect of an amusement park.

Information Needs

To fulfill their objectives, JST determined that they would need the following information:

Market

a. Is there a need for this project in this market?
b. How large is the potential market?
c. Is this market large enough to be profitable?

Consumers

a. Are the potential customers satisfied with the existing facilities in the city?

b. Will these potential consumers utilize an amusement park?
c. Which segment of the population is most interested in this type of facility?
d. Is the population ready to support this type of project?
e. What media could be used to promote the park successfully to potential customers?

Location

a. Where should this project be built to attract the most visitors?
b. How will consumers' existing attitudes on location influence the viability and cost of this project?
c. Will the company have to arrange for transportation to and from the facility if it is located outside the city area?
d. Is security a factor in determining the location of the facility?

Recreation Facilities

a. What type of attractions should the company provide at the park to attract customers?
b. Should there be overnight accommodations within the park?
c. Should the facility be available only to certain segments of the population or should it be open to all?

Proposal

With the objectives just outlined in mind, AGT, Inc. presented the following proposal:

The city of Karachi's population has its different economic clusters scattered haphazardly throughout the city. To conduct market research under these conditions and obtain accurate results will consequently be difficult. We recommend an extensive study to make sure we have an adequate sampling of opinion from the target market. Given these parameters, we recommend that the target market be defined as follows:

Desired Respondent Characteristics

- Upper Class: 1% (around 60,000)
- Middle Class: 15 to 20% (around 900,000 to 1,200,000)

- Male and female
- Age: 15 to 50 years (for survey; market includes all age groups)
- Income level: Rs 25,000 and above per year (Rs: 2000 per month)
- Household size: families will be better for the purposes of the sample
- Involved in entertainment activities
- Involved in recreational activities
- Actively participates in social activities
- Member of different clubs
- Involved in outdoor activities

To obtain accurate information regarding respondents' characteristics, we have to approach the market very carefully because of prevailing circumstances and existing cultural practices. People have little or no knowledge of market surveys. Obtaining their cooperation, even without cultural barriers, via a phone or mail survey will be difficult. In the following paragraphs we will discuss the negative and positive points of all types of surveys and select the appropriate form for our study.

The first, and possibly best, method for conducting the survey under these circumstances will be through the mail, which will not only be cheaper than other methods but can also cover all the population clusters easily. We cannot rely on a mail survey alone, however, because the mail system in Pakistan is unreliable and inefficient. We can go through courier services or registered mail, but doing so will cause the cost to skyrocket.

The other option is to conduct a survey by telephone. In this city of 6 million there are about 200,000 working telephones (one per 152 persons). Most of the telephones are in businesses or government offices. The problem is not that the citizens of Karachi cannot afford a telephone, but that they cannot get one because of the short supply. Another problem with a telephone survey is cultural; it is not considered polite in Pakistani society to call a stranger and start asking questions. It would be even more of a breach of etiquette if a male survey member were to reach a female household member. Because people are not familiar with marketing surveys, they would not be willing to volunteer the information we require on the telephone. The positive feature of a telephone survey is that most upper class women do not work and can be reached easily. To contact them, however, we would need to use a survey staff composed of females only. Overall, the chances of cooperation with a telephone survey are very low.

A mall/bazaar intercept could also be used. Again, however, we will face some cultural problems. It's not considered ethical for a male to approach a female in the mall. The only people willing to talk in public are likely to be men and we will thus miss female opinion.

To gather respondent data by survey in a country such as Pakistan, we will have to tailor our existing data collecting methods and make them fit the circumstances and cultural practices of that marketplace. As a company based in Pakistan with experience in living under these cultural practices, we propose the following design for the study and the questionnaire.

Design of the Study

Our study will contain a mixture of three types of survey, with each survey making use of a different method. We recommend the following types of surveys, tailored to fit the prevailing circumstances:

1. Mail Survey

We plan to modify this type of survey to fit the existing situation and to be maximally efficient. Specific changes have been made to counter the inefficient postal system and to generate a better percentage of response. We plan to deliver the surveys to respondents by the newspaper deliverymen rather than by mail. The average circulation of the various newspapers in Karachi ranges from 50,000 to 200,000 per day. The two dailies chosen have the largest circulation in the city.

A questionnaire will be placed in each newspaper delivered to respondents. This questionnaire will introduce us to the respondent and will ask for his cooperation, and it will include return postage and the firm's address. Identification of the firm will give respondents some confidence that they are not volunteering information to unknown parties. A small promotional gift will be promised for returning the completed survey. Since respondents who intend to claim the gift will give us their address, this will help us maintain a list of respondents for future surveys. Delivery with the daily newspaper will also allow us to focus easily on specific clusters.

We expect some loss in return mail because there is no acceptable way to get the questionnaires back except through the government postal system. Accordingly, we plan to deliver 5,000 questionnaires to counter the anticipated loss in return mail. The cost of this survey will be less than it would be if we mailed the questionnaires. Because this will be the first exposure for many respondents that allows them to give their views about an as yet nonexistent product, we do not have any return percentage on which to base our survey response expectations. In fact, this information may well provide the basis for future studies.

2. Door-to-Door Interviews
We will have to tailor the mall/bazaar intercept, as we did the mail survey, to get the highest possible response percentage. Instead of intercepting at malls, we believe it will be better to send surveyors door to door. This method can generate a better percentage of responses and also allows us to identify the respondents accurately. To conduct this survey, we will solicit the cooperation of the local business schools in providing us with students who will act as our surveyors. By using these young students we stand a better chance of generating a higher response than we would using older staff. We also plan to hire some additional personnel, mostly females, and train them to conduct this survey.

3. Additional Mail Survey
We plan to conduct this part of the survey to identify different groups of people already involved in similar types of recreational activity. There are eight to ten exclusive clubs in the city of Karachi. A few focus solely on some outdoor activity such as yachting and boating, golf, and the like. Their membership numbers vary from three to five thousand. The high cost of membership and monthly fees have restricted these clubs to the upper middle class and the wealthy. We can safely say that the people using these clubs belong to the 90th percentile of income level.

We propose to visit these clubs and personally ask for members' cooperation in participating in our survey. We also plan to obtain the clubs' membership list and have the questionnaire delivered to them. They will be asked to return the completed questionnaire to the club office or to mail it in the postage-paid reply envelope. We believe that this group will cooperate and give us high-quality feedback.

The second delivered survey will be to local schools. With the schools' cooperation, we will ask that this questionnaire be delivered by pupils to their parents. The cover letter will ask parents to fill out the questionnaire and return it to the school. This survey will provide a good sample of people who want outdoor activities for their children. We hope to generate a substantial response through this method.

Questionnaire Design

The type of questions asked should help our client make the decision about whether to invest in the project. (See proposed questionnaire.) Through the survey questionnaires we should be able to answer the question "Is the population ready for this project and are they willing to support it?" The questionnaire, a mixture of open-ended and close-ended questions, should also help to answer the following questions:

- Is there a market for this type of project?
- Is the market substantial?
- Is the market profitable?
- Will this project fill a real need?
- Will this project be only a momentary fad?
- Is the market evenly distributed in all segments/clusters, or is there a high demand in some segments?
- Is the population geared toward and willing to spend money on this type of entertainment facility? If so, how much?
- What is the best location for this project?
- Are people willing to travel some distance to reach this type of facility? Or do they want it within city limits?
- What types of entertainment/rides do people want in an amusement park?
- Through what type of media or promotion can prospective customers best be reached?

Discussion Questions

1. What are the objectives of the research project? Does the survey satisfy these objectives?
2. How do elements of culture affect the research design, collection of data, and analysis? Contrast this case with the design, collection of data, and analysis of a similar survey project in a more developed country such as the United States.
3. What alternative data collection methods might be useful to pursue? What are the strengths and weaknesses of these alternative methods?

Case prepared by William J. Carner. Used by permission.

QUESTIONNAIRE

1. Are there adequate recreational facilities in the city?
   Yes ☐   No ☐

2. How satisfied are you with the present recreational facilities?
   (Please rate from 0–10 degrees)

   0—1—2—3—4—5—6—7—8—9—10
   Poor   Excellent

3. How often do you visit the present recreational facilities?(Please check)
   Weekly   ☐
   Fortnightly   ☐
   Monthly   ☐
   Once in two months   ☐
   Yearly   ☐
   More (indicate number)____   ☐
   Not at all   ☐

4. Do you visit recreational areas with your family?
   Yes ☐   No ☐
   If no, why not?
   Security   ☐
   Distance   ☐
   Expense   ☐
   Crowd (not family oriented)   ☐
   Poor service   ☐
   Other (Please specify)   ☐
   _____

4a. Do you stay overnight?
   Yes ☐   No ☐
   If yes, how long? _____
   (Please indicate number of days)

4b. If no, would you have stayed if provided the right circumstances or facilities?
   Yes ☐   No ☐

5. Have you ever visited an amusement park?
   (Here in Pakistan ☐   Abroad ☐)
   Yes ☐ (Please go to question 5b)
   No ☐ (Please go to question 5a)

5a. If no, why not?
   Security   ☐
   Distance   ☐
   Expense   ☐
   Crowd (not family oriented)   ☐
   Poor service   ☐
   Other (Please specify) _____   ☐
   _____

5b. If yes, when did you last visit an amusement park?
   Last month   ☐
   Last six months   ☐
   Within a year   ☐
   More (specify number)   ☐
   WHERE? _____

6. What did you enjoy most in that park?
   Roller coasters   ☐
   Water slides   ☐
   Children's play areas   ☐
   Shows   ☐
   Games   ☐
   Simulators   ☐
   Other_____   ☐

6a. How much did you spend in that park? (approximately)
   Rs 50 or less   ☐
   51 to 100   ☐
   101 to 150   ☐
   151 to 200   ☐
   More than 200   ☐
   WHERE? _____

6b. How would you rate the value received?
   (Please rate from 0–10 degrees)

   0—1—2—3—4—5—6—7—8—9—10
   Poor   Excellent

7. Would you utilize an amusement park if one were built locally?
   Yes ☐   No ☐

8. What would you like to see in an amusement park? (Please give us your six best choices.)
   a._____   d._____
   b._____   e._____
   c._____   f._____

9. Where would you like its location to be?
   Within city area   ☐
   Beach area   ☐
   Suburbs   ☐
   Outskirts of city   ☐
   Indifferent   ☐

10. How many kilometers will you be willing to travel to the park?
   Under 10 K   ☐
   11 to 20   ☐

21 to 35	☐
36 to 55	☐
56 to 65	☐
More than 65	☐

11. How often do you take vacations for recreational purposes?

Never	☐
Once a year	☐
Twice a year	☐
More (please specify) _____	☐

Please Tell Us About Yourself:

12. Please indicate your age.

Under 15	☐
16 to 21	☐
22 to 29	☐
30 to 49	☐
50 to 60	☐
Over 60	☐

13. Please indicate your gender:
    Male ☐   Female ☐

14. Are you married?
    Yes ☐   No ☐

15. How many children do you have?
    Please indicate number_____

16. Please indicate your total family income. (Yearly)

Under 12,000	☐
Over 12,000 to 15,000	☐

Over 15,000 to 20,000	☐
Over 20,000 to 25,000	☐
Over 25,000 to 40,000	☐
Over 40,000 to 60,000	☐
Over 60,000 to 80,000	☐
Over 80,000	☐

17. Do you own your own means of transport?
    Yes ☐   No ☐

18. Any other comments?
    (If you need more space, please attach an additional sheet.)

    _____
    _____
    _____
    _____
    _____
    _____

Thank you, we appreciate your time!

Important:
If you want us to contact you again in the later stages of this project, or if you are interested in its results, give us your name and address and we will be glad to keep you informed. Thank you.

_____
_____
_____
_____
_____
_____

Case 3	*tonernow.com: A Dotcom Goes Global*

Introduction

It was the second week in April 2000. Dotcom euphoria gripped the U.S. economy and venture capital was flowing everywhere. Henry Kasindorf and Rich Katz, young founders of a New Jersey-based brick-and-mortar company recently turned dotcom, had received communications from all over the world soliciting their participation in licensing agreements, partnerships, and other similar relationships. Serious offers had come from Australia, Brazil, South Africa, Central America, and Europe. Their company, tonernow.com, was hot.

This case was written by Martha Lanning, Research Associate, William F. Glavin Center for Global Entrepreneurial Leadership, under the direction of Jean-Pierre Jeannet, F.W. Olin Distinguished Professor of Global Business. This case was written as a basis for class discussion rather than to illustrate either effective or ineffective handling of a business situation. Copyright © 2000 by Babson College, William F. Glavin Center for Global Entrepreneurial Leadership. Not to be used or reproduced without written permission.

William F. Glavin Center for Global Entrepreneurial Leadership
Distributed by The European Case Clearing House, England and USA.
North America, phone: +1 781 239 5884, fax: +1 781 239 5885, e-mail: ECCHBabson@aol.com.
Rest of the World, phone: +44 (0)1234 750903, fax: +44 (0)1234 751125, e-mail: ECCH@cranfield.ac.uk.
All rights reserved. Printed in UK and USA. Web Site: http://www.ecch.cranfield.ac.uk.

Kasindorf and Katz were facing a big question: should operations remain focused on the U.S. or should the company go global? The business was expanding and many issues required immediate attention. Globalization would inject even greater urgency into the situation.

tonernow.com was the e-commerce arm of IQ Computer Products, a company Kasindorf and Katz had founded in 1993. The brick-and-mortar segment of the business, not counting the website, was now selling approximately $5 million. Some two-thirds of this volume went to individual retail clients and one-third to wholesalers and distributors.

The tonernow.com website launched in beta format on September 15, 1999, now carried over 3,000 products at discounts of 30% to 70% off manufacturer list prices. The site also offered a proprietary line of compatible toner products.

Toner was a black, powdered, plastic substance contained in cartridges used in printers, copiers, and fax machines. Toner powder adhered to parts of a drum that had been properly charged for toner coverage. A fuser assembly within the printer or copier machine melted the toner to fuse it to the page, resulting in a sharp text that could not be smudged. When toner ran out, the machines could not function. Toner was critical for office productivity.

Company History

Kasindorf and Katz had met as freshmen undergraduates at Babson College in 1987, the year Kasindorf achieved recognition for his successful launch of a condom vending machine business. Kasindorf described his rocky beginning as an entrepreneur:

"I used all my professors. One in law helped me with the contracts, marketing helped me with the brochures. I was fascinated by all the resources that were available, some of the best in the world! I attended a student government meeting and brought the project up for approval, but the Assistant Dean shot me down. I stormed into the Dean's office and got it OK'd. That business was fun, it got my feet wet. There were a lot of legal issues, such as liability if one of the condoms broke. Also, I was a freshman and in the middle of finals I got 12 voice mails from reporters!"

Within months, Kasindorf had set up condom dispensers in college bathrooms throughout the Boston area. Two years later he sold the business for $25,000 and used the proceeds to start another

venture. The partners laughed as they recalled their early collaboration:

Kasindorf: "We didn't take much of a liking to each other."

Katz: "We didn't hit it off."

Kasindorf: "I needed a ride, I told him it would take five minutes, it took 40, and he liked me even less! Then we had a Human Communications class together. My only memory is that Rich got a 37 on the midterm and I got a 16.[1] We sort of bonded after that."

The T-Shirt Business

Kasindorf and Katz soon founded a screen-printed T-shirt company operating on campus. The shirts featured creative graphics using well-known consumer goods logos and sold like hotcakes. Kasindorf explained:

"The copyright hounds had their bounty hunters looking for us. You do have to change 20% of the design so you're not infringing on someone else's mark. We had friends at other schools who started selling the T-shirts for us. Then *U.S. News & World Report* came out with the Babson ranking, and we launched a new T-shirt highlighting the No. 1 ranking during homecoming weekend.[2] In 1988–1989, our picture ran in the Babson College publication with the *U.S. News & World Report* ranking."

IQ Computer Products

After graduating from Babson College, Kasindorf and Katz briefly went their separate ways, each working elsewhere. However, in May 1993, they teamed up again, this time purchasing two small manufacturing companies with combined revenues under $300,000. According to Katz, "One was a sole proprietorship, a guy was making toner products out of his garage."

Based on this purchase, Kasindorf and Katz opened business activity in Spring Valley, NY, some 45 miles from New York City. The new enterprise produced toner and employed four people in addition to Kasindorf and Katz: one in customer service, one to perform accounting and clerical tasks, and two in manufacturing. Operations included manufacturing, customer service, accounting, warehousing, and sales.

---

1. Out of a possible score of 100 on the midterm exam.
2. *U.S. News & World Report* ranked Babson College the No. 1 business school in the U.S. for entrepreneurial studies.

Recycling toner cartridges was encouraged on an industry-wide basis. The two partners saw this as an advantage, an aspect of the business that would aid in cost control and make the product "recession-proof."

Funding came entirely from cash flow, profits, and a small bank loan. In 1993, the partners held notes to the two original owners. Within two years the notes were paid off.

By 1994, business was exploding out of the 900 square feet facility in Spring Valley. The young entrepreneurs consolidated the two original firms, named the new entity IQ Computer Products (IQCP), and moved the company to its present site in Englewood, NJ. Kasindorf discussed the decision to locate in Englewood:

> "We wanted to stay in New York, and so did the employees. We took it to the State to inquire regarding subsidies and incentives, but they laughed at us because we were under one million dollars in sales. The next week I went to Trenton[3] to talk to the same department, but in New Jersey. They had a team of people assembled in a conference room. They offered training and incentives, and each one made a proposal to us on why we should locate in New Jersey. They welcomed us with open arms."

Growing the Business

During the period 1994–1998, the company added products and diversified as Kasindorf and Katz grew the business. They brought the repair division, previously subcontracted, in-house and hired their own technicians.

In 1994, IQCP sold in three states: New York, New Jersey, and Connecticut. IQCP also serviced a small number of other states by UPS.[4] In 1997, the company began using Federal Express to offer three-day delivery to California with standard ground rates. That same year, business expanded into Canada. By 1998, IQCP was selling in 14 states, mainly in the Northeast but also in California and Colorado.

The partners elaborated on the importance of building customer relationships.

> Katz: "We felt we could sell products other than those we manufactured. Our customers told us they wanted other products. Our customers asked <u>us</u> because the level of service we offered was so far above what other companies offered."

3. Capital of the state of New Jersey.
4. United Parcel Service, a delivery service.

Kasindorf: "We hand-delivered the product, no matter how large or small the order. Our rep showed up with a nice shirt and our IQCP logo, offered to clean the printer and install the customer's cartridge so it would achieve optimal performance. People started to see the attention we gave."

Katz: "When we started, quality was a major issue in the industry."

Kasindorf: "People are leery of this industry. Therefore, it's important for us to appear as legitimate as possible. We advertise in the *New York Times*, we bring large customers here to tour our facility."

Katz: "We encourage people to call our reference list. We've had long-standing relationships with our customers, and they rave about us. We are very, very careful here. It's a 'razor blade' product, people come back and buy it again and again. We want people to have an experience second to none. If there's a problem, we replace it with no charge and we handle it quickly."

Kasindorf: "We sell to some of the largest law firms in New York City. We are right there when their laser printers need repair. They rely on us."

Website Launch

In 1998, Kasindorf and Katz made the decision to go dotcom. They looked at what was necessary for their company to remain successful and determined that it would be essential to develop an e-commerce strategy and get online. As Kasindorf put it, "We knew we had to now or we'd be left behind."

Kasindorf and Katz knew what was successful *offline*, and they wanted to translate that to *online*. They also wanted to avoid cannibalizing their existing business. The primary options were either to create online ordering for existing clients or to create an entirely new entity as the e-commerce solution.

Kasindorf and Katz decided to create a new entity. They would develop it as an e-commerce arm of the IQCP business. They needed to launch a website, and they would require it to be:

- Serious and straight forward
- User-friendly
- Easy to navigate
- Fun with a couple of unique twists

The partners hired a full-service PR firm. In addition, they hired a freelance media consultant to do media planning.

Kasindorf: "We knew we did not want to do this in-house. We met with a lot of big communications companies and realized the budget we had to develop the site was low. We also realized we'd probably get lost in some of these companies. So we decided to look for more of a boutique-type web developer. We found a great little company in Silicon Alley."

Katz: "Henry really oversaw the process. We trust our vendors, but we really wanted to have a heavy hand in terms of how the site was developed. We knew how our customers wanted the experience to <u>feel</u>."

Kasindorf: "For eight months, it was all I did. It was tremendously stressful! Even as good as the developers were."

Katz: "We had to develop all the relational links. It was 3,000 products!"

The staff in-house set about developing a large relational database that would allow prospective customers to shop four ways: by key word, brand, product type, or product number. The project took six months and thousands of "man-hours" with five people dedicated full-time. The complete project cost approximately $200,000, half of which went to development alone.

The team designed the database to cross-sell and up-sell each product so that when a prospective customer input a product specification, the website would automatically offer helpful suggestions. The up-sell offered suggestions such as "this printer also takes product so-and-so, we have these products at different prices, do you want to buy it/these also?" The cross-sell offered tonernow.com's own branded products once the customer had input a selection, for example a compatible or related product version, some manufactured on a private label basis and others by tonernow.com.[5] The cross-sell also offered incentives such as double points for a rewards program.

Kasindorf described the complexity of the project:

"We had fantastic developers, but they did not know anything about product. It was up to us to develop the back-end issues. We learned through focus groups that most people really don't know what they need. Also, product numbers are long, and there's no apparent connection between the number and the product. We wanted to make the site user-friendly, for people to get what they wanted in two clicks or less. Most competitor sites require five clicks or more. There is nothing out there like our proprietary database, it's unique to the industry. We have people who want to license use of the database because of how powerful it is."

The Ambush Campaign

The next task was to develop a budget for the first three months after launch. An important part of this step was to look at the different vehicles for advertising. The budget would allocate money for various types of advertising such as banner ads, email marketing, radio, TV, and billboard.

The partners examined many names for the new entity and finally found one they liked. It was owned by a cyber-squatter, so they bought it. The new name would be *tonernow.com*.

The original plan was to launch the website in June, but it quickly became apparent that June would be impossible.

Kasindorf: "There was no way for June to work. September 15 was Internet World at the Javits Center.[6] We decided on an ambush campaign. No display at the expo. We had men dressed in white jumpsuits with the tonernow.com logo, in front of a giant tonernow.com billboard, handing out shopping bags with T-shirts to each person."

Katz (laughing): "We really used our T-shirt expertise!"

Dotcom Results

Once the website launched, resulting activity was entirely new business. No activity migrated from the brick-and-mortar operation to the website. Kasindorf and Katz had decided to maintain two separate profit centers and market to two separate databases. They would possibly migrate individual customers, two-thirds of the brick-and-mortar segment of the business, to the website at a later time. They had not publicized the website to their traditional customers in order to avoid cannibalization. Moreover, the website sold at lower margins, and significant customer migration would have reduced margins overall.

Gross sales rocketed upward. From initial sales volume of a few thousand dollars in December

---

5. As an input example, product EPS-SO2-0089.

6. The Jacob K. Javits Convention Center, New York's premier trade show and convention venue with more than 814,400 square feet of exhibit space.

1999, by January 2000 business had jumped 115%, by February 209%, and by March 118%.

Going for Venture Capital

The partners soon turned their attention to crafting a business plan.

> Katz: "Toward the end of the year was when we started to focus on VC. It had always been understood that at some point, we'd get venture capital and take the company public."

> Kasindorf: "We had first-mover advantage, we were more a 'click-and-mortar' rather than e-commerce. Very appealing to the VC people. We'd shown we could grow in a brick-and-mortar way. It was more a question of how much equity we'd have to give up and who we'd go with, not if we'd go."

The partners expected to get exactly what they sought in the first round, but they were in for a few surprises. The first surprise was that profitability was not required.

> Kasindorf: "In our projections we were showing profitability after two years. Investment bankers, consultants, and VC people told us we were *not showing a loss!*"

> Katz: "It just made sense to us, that we were in business to make a profit."

> Kasindorf: "Another thing! We'd walk into a VC meeting wearing business suits, not ripped jeans, wearing tattoos and carrying our skateboards. The first meeting we ever had, we walked out of there with a $37 million valuation."

> Katz: "We began to get offers on the table. Then in spring the NASDAQ got hit hard."

The Toner Supplies Industry

The toner supplies industry was a highly fragmented segment within the larger office supplies industry. In 1999, the market for toner supplies was estimated at $30 billion. Players in the market included OEMs, office superstores, dealers of equipment such as copiers, printers and fax machines, catalog distributors, and re-manufacturers.

Customers were extremely sensitive to price and convenience. When toner ran out, the productivity of an office machine was placed on hold until new toner could be supplied. Thus, same day delivery was a key to success.

Laser copying and printing had dramatically changed the industry in recent years. Developments such as color printing had placed new demands on paper quality. Paper needed to be able to handle black and white toner printing as well as printing that used the newer four-color toner technology. Color toner particles had recently been made smaller in order to improve print quality.

Competition

Toner cartridges and inkjet cartridges formed a highly specialized niche segment of the office supplies industry. Toner and other supplies carried a much higher margin than hardware. Within this segment there was no single dominant player. Several large companies held a major share of the toner supplies market: Hewlett-Packard (H-P), Lexmark, Xerox, IBM, Canon, and Ricoh, among other OEMs.

In early 2000, Konica Corp. and Minolta Co. both of Japan announced an agreement in the areas of information technology equipment and printer toner production. The agreement involved a joint venture to manufacture toner.

In 1999, H-P had launched a new line of toner supplies, eliptica, to compete with Xerox. Two years earlier Xerox had begun to offer H-P compatible laser printer cartridges, and the eliptica line was H-P's counterstrike response. After only eight months of operation, H-P surprised the industry in spring 2000 by announcing the end of the eliptica venture in order to re-focus on other strategic growth opportunities.

H-P was the world's largest maker of printers, and China was the world's fastest growing market. Printer sales in China totaled some $900 million in 1999. H-P had been selling printers in China since the mid-1980's and now controlled almost one quarter of the market.

Cartridge Recycling

The resale of toner and related products was highly profitable with gross margins ranging from 20% to 70%. Empty toner cartridges that had been used could be returned to be recycled. The process ideally involved cleaning and refitting the cartridge, as well as filling it with new toner. However, many "re-manufacturers" used shortcuts and provided recycled cartridges of poor quality.

Industry Fraud

Fraud was a serious problem for the industry. Customers using counterfeit supplies risked poor equipment performance, low supply yields, inferior print quality, toner leakage, high cartridge failure rates, and increased equipment downtime.

Illegal operations typically contacted potential victims by telephone, misrepresenting themselves as having taken over the previous toner supplier's operation, or as a firm that worked in tandem with the legitimate supplier. These "telemarketers" sold low quality goods to unsuspecting customers. Advances in communications technology had increased the opportunity for this type of fraud.

Xerox had been working with federal authorities to crack down on counterfeit toner distributors. In 1999, federal agents raided a warehouse in Milwaukee seizing 47,000 counterfeit supplies boxes estimated at a market value of $8 million.

Building a Strategy for the Future

In spring 2000, Kasindorf and Katz had been shopping their company to venture capital people with the expectation of increasingly lucrative offers. However, the valuation of tonernow.com had tanked when the NASDAQ plummeted.

The deals now on the table were lower than the partners had previously considered desirable. Moreover, taking one of the deals would force them to relinquish at least some measure of control to their funding source.

Overview of the Current Business

Since 1994, tonernow.com had grown significantly. The firm employed 30 people and sold in all 50 states. Over 3,000 different products were offered with approximately 40 manufactured in-house. Some 10% of the products covered 80% to 90% of the market. tonernow.com sourced OEM products from vendors and also provided 300 compatible products that were not OEM-branded. Compatibles were manufactured either by tonernow.com or by another firm and sold under the tonernow.com name.

The mission of tonernow.com was to become the best known brand in the imaging supplies industry. The objective was to deliver high-end value through e-commerce while offering the following service elements:

- The Web's largest selection of toner products

- A superior website with built-in guidance tools and support designed for cross-selling and up-selling to products with superior margins
- Discounts from 30% to 70% lower than manufacturer's prices
- Service and maintenance programs for business equipment
- A rewards program with incentives for return customers
- Free next-day shipping with Federal Express
- Email reminders and an auto-ship program
- Online and offline ordering options
- National advertising

Customer Service: A Key to Success

The company had retained many of its original customers as a result of superior customer service.

Kasindorf: "When we were just 23 and starting out, people saw the commitment we had to serving them. Among our customers we have very low attrition rates. Companies we were doing business with in 1993 are still our customers."

Katz: "We definitely benchmark other companies. We look at them to see if they're doing something right. And we learn from our customers."

Kasindorf: "As we've grown, there have been a lot of internal pressures. The ability to have two partners running the business is unique in that we're able to feed off each other in certain ways. We're able to do that in a way that has really contributed to our growth. Our roles are not completely pigeonholed, we have insight into each other's areas, and that's beneficial."

Katz: "When we first started, we were both into selling, selling, selling. We had no idea how things would develop. As you grow, there's always the issue of costs getting out of control. As a result, I am now more involved with the operations. Henry is more the outside guy who handles sales and marketing. He instituted the procedures of how we deal with customer relations. I've kinda stayed inside and developed cost-cutting measures. We run a manufacturing operation, and neither of us had any manufacturing or engineering background. Also, we have some very big competitors. They've put obstacles in our way, and we've had to figure out how to get around them."

Changing Realities

By spring 2000, tonernow.com had attracted attention from outside the U.S. Katz remarked that the attention had been entirely unsolicited:

"We got noticed through trade shows. But as soon as we became a dotcom, it added instant credibility. When people saw the functionality of the site, they were just wowed by it. International contacts were also wowed by it. Once they got into our site, they saw we had a great deal to offer."

A number of deals had been proposed, and the partners were now considering options for international expansion. They would need to examine every aspect of the business: from legal to operational, from inquiry handling to delivery process, including customer relationships and confirmation of shipping dates. The move from small domestic player to globalization posed many challenges, among which might be any or all of the following:

- Licensing the technology
- Setting up licensing agreements
- Dealing with royalties
- Collecting payment via credit card
- Translating foreign currency into U.S. dollars
- Access to tonernow.com's proprietary database
- Restrictions to impose on website use run through other countries
- How to maintain control of the technology
- Cross-cultural revisions of the website to make it readily understandable
- Legal requirements of setting up business activity
- Same day delivery

Options on the Table

tonernow.com had received communications from Europe, Australia, Brazil, Central America, and South Africa. (**Exhibits 1–3**) In some cases, a concrete business proposal had been offered. Suggestions included the following:

Gateway page: This element would enable a customer in a foreign country to log on to the tonernow.com website and then be directed to the specific site for his/her geographic region.

Localization: Making cultural and linguistic changes in the website or gateway page in order to give the look and feel of the local country.

Licensing: Making the website structure and content available in a non-U.S. setting, including templates, shipping, data base, product information, and costing data, among other elements. Specifically, licensing would provide website content, brand relationships, and alternative revenue though co-op funds available with the brands. In addition, a licensing agreement would include:

- International contacts for global contracts
- Comprehensive collateral materials
- Outbound marketing material (bulk email copy, promotions, online coupons)
- Launch support
- Development of local media affiliations
- Proprietary strategic information

The structure that would be required to handle business differed for each geography, and the partners did not want to undertake a different strategy for each region. Kasindorf saw this as a "monumental chore." He was also concerned about the level of service:

"Who would send the second confirmation that confirms the ship date? C.O.D. orders and credit card orders online are an issue, because some people don't want to input their credit cards online. Who will handle customer service inquiries? Certainly you want someone local to do this."

Brazil: The contact company had connections with all the major players including the government. They had come to CEBIT, the major industry trade show in Hanover, Germany, looking for opportunities. For tonernow.com to go into Brazil as an after-market supplier might make sense because entry barriers were high. Katz stated:

"We found there was only one licensee there for each manufacturer. To bring us in on a gray market basis would kill our margins. We would have to come in selling our own branded product because the distribution channels are so tight."

Australia: tonernow.com had exhibited at a large print industry show in California where they met an Australian distributor of toner supplies. The partners recalled his offer:

"He told us 'we want to use your site in Australia, how can we do this?' Licensing the technology would result in people getting access to our proprietary database. The alternative would be to set them up as licensees of the technology to use the site in their restricted geographic territory. We did the analysis, to look into running the site for them, and also collecting payment with credit cards in Australian dollars."

Conclusion

Conducting business internationally would require playing the game with more than one set of rules. (**Exhibit 4**) Whether to globalize or remain domestic was the big question. tonernow.com was a small, new company. It shared little in common with firms running large global operations. The partners considered the ramifications of setting up business on an international scale:

Katz: "In the U.S. when you shake on it, it's a done deal, but in other countries you're not sure. Also in some countries, to get a domain name is very expensive. Fraud overseas is a lot harder to combat than fraud in the U.S."

Kasindorf: "We've started to question everything. Sales are very strong, site revenues are growing, but we're bleeding because of the costs associated with doing business in this manner: advertising, overhead, promotions 'buy one get one free' to gain market share. We are about eight months late with what we were trying to do because the landscape has changed so much. We've gotten into a difficult financial situation thinking we did not <u>need</u> to be as profitable as we had planned."

Katz: "A lot of dotcom casualties have already happened. We want to be very careful."

Exhibit 1 *Europe*

EMAIL FROM HENRY TO EUROPE
••• *I enjoyed meeting you and discussing our mutual e-commerce interests. At this point we are in discussions with firms in various regions who are interested in forming alliances to build the tonernow.com brand on a global level.*

It would be helpful if you could provide me with an understanding of your interest in working with tonernow.com and whether you are interested in pursuing further discussions. Many synergies exist between our firms, and a well thought out strategy of how we could work together would be mutually beneficial.

EMAIL FROM EUROPE BACK TO HENRY
••• *Further to our recent telephone conversations and meetings, I have thought long and hard about how we could take this opportunity forward. The opportunities I see are as follows:*

1. *We could fulfill tonernow.com orders to customers within their countries and also fulfill a manufacturing role for tonernow.com.*
2. *We could bring on other companies in Europe who can also fulfill customer requirements in both.*
3. *We could introduce various OEMs to the tonernow.com distribution model.*

I will call you tomorrow to discuss the above in more detail. I would like to work with you on these options but need to know whether they fit in with your plans. Other considerations are: languages for Europe, software compatibility (i.e. order processing and stock system reconciliation), and dealer blind shipping timescales.

Exhibit 2 *Brazil*

EMAIL FROM BRAZIL TO HENRY
••• *As we talked about in Germany, one of the product lines we have interest to work with, and have been talking about, is the ink jet cartridges. So far it looks to us like it would not be good in Brazil to work with remanufactured cartridges, and we are*

evaluating the possibilities for importing compatible ones. We have received several proposals for that, mainly from European and Asian companies. One has a strong capability to give huge discounts on their lines, and we are about to receive some samples from them in order to test quality matters.

EMAIL FROM HENRY BACK TO BRAZIL

●●● In terms of your market analysis for Brazil, I believe that a strategy with compatible products would be very effective for you. Please understand that there are many companies in the market producing and distributing "compatible" toner cartridges that are "remanufactured." Our firm produces and distributes both types of products.

I realize this may be a bit confusing, but packaging requirements enable us to use the term "compatible" if a certain amount of internal components are replaced during our production process. I realize that there are many companies throughout the world that would like to earn your business for the Brazil market, and I recommend that you proceed slowly and cautiously as this can be very complex.

We can develop a comprehensive user-friendly website for you specifically for your market. The website can be a useful marketing tool for your sales reps, and your customers will appreciate the fact that they can access the information online, order product or simply get product reference information. We can negotiate with the various suppliers on your behalf to produce products for your market under the brand name on a private label basis, therefore you will not be tied to any one manufacturer's brand except your own.

Exhibit 3 *Central America*

EMAIL FROM HENRY TO CENTRAL AMERICA

●●● We are currently undergoing our first round of venture capital financing. I have recruited some senior members for our senior management team and one of the first steps we are taking is to partner with a major distributor in the European market. I am currently analyzing the possibilities for Latin America and the Caribbean in this market.

Currently the U.S. and European markets are highly fragmented and lack a dominant player. Our focus is to become the world leader in these markets via the Internet. We have relationships with many of the OEMs in each of the markets that we are targeting, and they will be working closely with us to achieve our objectives.

Please let me know if you have an interest in working with us, in what territories you can provide distribution, with which manufacturers you currently have relationships, and whether you have or are planning to implement an e-commerce strategy.

EMAIL FROM CENTRAL AMERICA BACK TO HENRY

●●● Thanks for your continued interest. The opportunity to distribute the recycled toners is not as clear-cut for us as it would be for other companies. Let me explain. We have been approved to distribute (product xyz) in several countries of Central America. We will be investing a lot to open operations in each of these countries.

I know that some non-original supplies are being imported into these countries, and we certainly do not have 100% share of the original toner market, so there is room for growth. My main concern is that we may only substitute the (product xyz) toners for yours, thereby lowering our sales volumes and possibly the margin. The margin is the clincher.

I have no idea what your toners sell for and how much I can earn on each one. I'm sure you will have good news for me in this department. Please send me your price list and the credit terms we could work on. I'm sure we will be able to do something together.

Exhibit 4 *Legal Advice*

(Excerpt from an entity in Europe)

As you are aware, in many jurisdictions it is necessary to have some sort of local presence before a local domain name can be obtained. We can assist in helping you satisfy these local presence requirements, whether it be by setting up a branch office or a limited company, registering a trademark or in some cases just providing a local address. We hope to be able to provide a seamless service.

As you will appreciate, setting up said alliance will involve a lot of work on our part and although we are some way down the line, it will inevitably take some time, possibly another couple of months, to put in place all the necessary arrangements and set up the technology. However, in the meantime, we have been approached by a number of clients of (company name) who wish to proceed more quickly.

We have already gathered a substantial amount of information and made contacts in most jurisdictions. In many we are in a position to begin offering our services. If you provide us with a list of the jurisdictions in which you are interested, we will forward to you further information regarding whether there is a local presence requirement in those jurisdictions, and if there is, the easiest option for satisfying this requirement.

In setting up this project, one of the most difficult issues to date has been ascertaining the costs of setting up local entities in each jurisdiction. Where it is possible to determine the actual costs, it is apparent that there are significant differences in costs. Therefore to simplify matters to date we have been suggesting a fixed fee per country. This gives you as the client a greater degree of certainty and makes it easier for us to manage the process and achieve consistency in the services we are offering.

However, if there is a relatively small number of countries, you may prefer to work individual fees for each country. We can discuss this with you in more detail when your exact requirements are known.

Case 4	*Alcon Laboratories*

In the spring of 1997, Ed Schollmaier, president and CEO of Alcon Laboratories, Inc. returned from a major meeting with senior management of Nestlé S.A., Alcon's shareholder. At Alcon's headquarters in Fort Worth, Texas, Schollmaier provided the executive management team with a recap of his discussion with Peter Brabeck, Nestlé's recently appointed CEO.

Peter has made it clear that he wants to intensify growth from within the Nestlé company, rather than just through acquisition. He realizes that much of Nestlé's brand portfolio is concentrated on mature products. For increasing growth, Nestlé will have to spend much more than in the past on market development and research. This will cost money and requires a higher profitability for the company. As a result, Alcon has a chance to remain a major strategic element for Nestlé, returning superior profits and thus helping the food company to achieve its overall growth objectives. To make this strategic contribution to Nestlé's corporate growth, we will have to continue to grow at 8% annually over the next decade, turning Alcon from the $2.0 billion business it will be in 1997 into a $5.0 billion company by 2010. And all of this against a world market that cannot be expected to grow more than 4% annually.

Alcon Laboratories was the global leader in a $7.3 billion ophthalmic industry with strong market positions in ophthalmic pharmaceuticals, surgical supplies, and vision care products. A member of Nestlé's corporate family since 1977, Alcon had been a strong contributor to its parent's growth and profitability over the years, an especially noteworthy feat given the competitive environment of the 1990s.

Health care reform in the United States had brought particular challenges to the industry and, in 1994, Schollmaier had considered revising Alcon's growth targets to adjust for expected negative impacts. With a sharply defined strategy and good execution, however, Alcon had thrived, growing from $1.2 billion in sales to nearly $2 billion over the past six years. In contrast, Allergan, Alcon's closest competitor in all three segments, had fallen from being a company of nearly equal size to Alcon in the late 1980s to only 60 percent, and it had reported a 1 percent decline in sales for the first quarter of 1997. Far from abating, however, the storm clouds of health care reform persisted, and it remained unclear what the alphabet of managed care—HMOs (Health Maintenance Organizations), PBMs (Pharmacy Benefits Management Companies), PPMCs (Physician Practice Management Companies)[1]—would eventually spell. Who would wield the most bargaining power and what would be the impact on companies that supplied products to the market?

In addition to managing the impacts of health care reform on the ophthalmic industry, Alcon also had to confront potential new competitive threats, both from established pharmaceutical companies and from innovative technologies. In response to the growing promise of the global ophthalmic market, several multinational drug companies were in the process of developing dedicated sales infrastructures to compete more effectively against the industry leaders. Although Alcon had excellent access to new technologies, such as laser surgery, through its industry relationships, the path of eventual commercialization and impact on existing markets and products was unknown.

The challenges of dynamic marketplace reform and competitor initiatives, coupled with the projection of lackluster overall industry growth, promised to severely test Alcon's ability to achieve the targeted levels of both growth and profitability that Nestlé required. Looking back on his long career as CEO, Schollmaier was proud of what Alcon had accomplished and was eager to ensure that his company would play a critical role in Nestlé's strategy for the twenty-first century.

Company Background

Founding and Early Growth

Robert D. Alexander and William C. Conner combined the first syllables of their last names to found Alcon Prescription Laboratories, a pharmacy in Fort Worth, Texas. The two pharmacists, who made and sold their own sterile injectable vitamins, saw an opportunity to manufacture ophthalmic pharmaceuticals on a mass production basis employing sterile and consistent techniques. Ophthalmology as a medical specialty was in a period of transition, moving from a demesne that included eye, ear, nose, and throat, to a concentration solely on the eyes. At the time, no major pharmaceutical company was significantly engaged in ophthalmic compounds, which were usually prepared as individual orders in local shops, often leading to contamination that could cause eye infections. Within several years of Alcon's founding, however, at least ten other small firms recognized and pursued the market potential of ophthalmic drugs. Of those early entrants, only Alcon and Allergan remained as identifiable companies by the 1990s, the rest having long since either been bought out and consumed or withered away.

Alexander and Conner incorporated in 1947 to raise funds and started actively marketing their products to pediatricians, selected GPs (General Practitioners), ENTs (ear, nose, throat) and ophthalmologists. Ten years later a thirty-person salesforce was promoting Alcon eye-care products throughout the United States, and revenues reached the $1 million mark. Ed Schollmaier joined the Alcon sales division straight out of Harvard Business School in 1958 and quickly started his ascent up the management ranks. At the request of Bill Conner, Schollmaier undertook a two-week special assignment in 1960 to define Alcon's mission, determine its future business potential, and develop a strategic plan for the company. Schollmaier's research convinced him that Alcon's pharmaceutical business had the potential to grow to $25 million within a reasonable period, a projection

---

[1]Please refer to the "Ophthalmic Industry Note" (GM 717) for more information on these organizations.

that Conner thought somewhat optimistic, given existing sales of $2 million.

Schollmaier articulated what were to be the five key components of Alcon's strategy over the next decade.

1. *Fill in the blanks.* Concentrate on the needs of ophthalmologists. Develop and sell products for every identified segment of the ophthalmic pharmaceutical market, the initial target market.
2. *Enlarge the market.* Increase market size by developing new products for new segments and actively pursue the acquisition of compounds from other companies.
3. *Pursue nonpharmaceutical ophthalmic needs.* Identify ophthalmic opportunities outside the pharmaceuticals, such as lenses and surgical products.
4. *Explore nonophthalmic medical specialties.* Explore opportunities in other subspecialties which share technology or market similarities with Alcon's basic ophthalmic business.
5. *Initiate international expansion.* Start selling in foreign markets.

Alcon undertook all elements of the articulated strategy, increasing its own research and development efforts, securing drug compounds with ophthalmic potential from other pharmaceutical firms, and opening sales offices abroad, first in Latin America and then in Europe. The company made numerous small acquisitions to obtain technology, enter new fields, and especially to expand internationally. Within a few years Alcon had launched operating divisions focused on the specialties of urology, allergy, dermatology, radiology, and pediatrics. By 1967, sales reached $10 million, and the strategic initiatives laid out by Schollmaier, with the exception of the move outside ophthalmology, were well established. The effort to expand into new specialties placed significant demands on the company that threatened to derail the success of the core ophthalmic business, which was growing more rapidly and showed more potential than the other specialties. The separate divisions required too much organization-building and consumed more management time than was justified by their prospects. It was also not feasible for Alcon to provide the technology support required to keep all the segments on the leading edge in innovation. By 1970, Alcon abandoned the effort to build the nonophthalmic business and gradually sold

them all off except for its dermatological skin-care products.

Ed Schollmaier was promoted to president in 1972, assuming leadership of Alcon from its founders. Investment in research and development, small acquisitions, and international expansion all continued to provide the basis for strong growth, and by 1977 Alcon had 22 manufacturing facilities in the United States and overseas, and sales from 100 countries neared $100 million. Alcon had been a public company since the late 1940s, but had not received much investor notice until the late 1960s when its growth and profitability attracted attention. In 1972, the company was listed on the New York Stock Exchange and enjoyed favorable recommendations, but Schollmaier also vividly recalled the downside to Wall Street exposure.

> *One time Morgan Guaranty dropped us from their list of recommended stocks because they wanted to shift their allocation away from mid-cap companies, and they decided simply to cut out five or six names. Alcon was one. It had nothing to do with how we were doing or with any particular problem, and all of a sudden the price of Alcon stock dropped from the low 30s to 18. Then everybody started to worry about how we were going to get the stock price back up. We were consumed with the need for quarterly performance.*

Nestlé's Acquisition and Management of Alcon

Nestlé, a multinational food company based in Switzerland, acquired Alcon in 1977 after an extensive investigation of investment opportunities in the United States. Nestlé had excess cash at the time and had set a goal of having 60 percent of its excess cash invested in the stable U.S. economy. The Nestlé acquisitions of U.S. food companies Libby and Stouffer had led to a consent agreement with the FTC, barring it from further immediate food industry purchases, and it redirected its interest toward other sectors. The cosmetics business was appealing, but Nestlé's investment in L'Oréal, a large international French cosmetics firm, reduced the value of making other U.S. cosmetics acquisitions. The growth prospects in health care, and the possibility of marketing synergy with its existing infant formula business, also attracted the Swiss firm.

Nestlé avoided the first-tier pharmaceutical firms, deeming them too expensive, and found most of the second-tier firms lacking management talent and R&D competence. Then, according to Schollmaier, Nestlé "stumbled on to Alcon. We were the right size, had good R&D and marketing, and they liked the management." Part of the rationale for a pharmaceutical acquisition was related to Nestlé's partial ownership of L'Oréal. The CEO of L'Oréal at the time suggested to Nestlé: "You buy your own pharma company, and we at L'Oréal will buy ours. If we eventually merge our firms, we will combine the businesses."

Alcon had a somewhat different perspective on the acquisition. According to Schollmaier:

We at Alcon were looking for a safe haven. With our founders interested in liquidating their investment, we wanted to avoid becoming subject to the tyranny of quarterly profit pressures. We also had no interest in getting acquired by a large pharmaceutical company. For us, Nestlé was the perfect match despite the fact that there was no technology or market synergy between our businesses. We saw them as providing us with management stability and investment funds to grow the business.

Characteristic of most of the then Nestlé-owned companies, Alcon management retained substantial autonomy for developing and implementing strategy yet benefited substantially from its parent's strong financial resources. Nestlé helped fund the building of new plants in the United States and other countries, including a facility in Puerto Rico, and enabled Alcon to expand its research program to a scale that Alcon's size as an independent company could not have supported. More important than providing actual cash, Nestlé enabled Alcon to adopt a long-term approach (Schollmaier banished the word "quarter" from Alcon's corporate lexicon) and to undertake initiatives sooner than it otherwise could have justified. Shortly after Nestlé's acquisition, Alcon purchased Burton Parsons and constructed a $26 million R&D building expansion. In 1989, the support of Nestlé also permitted Alcon to acquire Coopervision Surgical, a promising but problem-plagued company that Allergan considered too risky to buy.

The purchase of Coopervision for roughly $350 million provided major benefits, expanding Alcon's presence in surgical instrumentation and intraocular lenses and enabling it to offer a complete, leading-edge surgical product line. Alcon had traditionally been a pharmaceutical company, and, although it offered surgical products, it trailed Cooper, which pioneered foldable lenses and technologically advanced ophthalmic surgical equipment. Alcon was able to resolve Cooper's production difficulties and improve its operations, and the Cooper products contributed substantially to the development of Alcon's international surgical business, its fastest growing segment. Cooper had a good second-tier management and within a few years the company had been successfully merged into Alcon. According to Schollmaier:

For Alcon, the Cooper acquisition was a turning point. It represented quite a risk since their products were not really ready for the market and, although representing breakthrough ideas, they were below the required quality and reliability which we considered essential for success in this market. Without the support of top Nestlé management at that time, we might have stepped back from this opportunity.

Following its acquisition of Alcon, Nestlé never took the next step of acquiring additional pharmaceutical businesses. Under the leadership of its then newly appointed CEO, Helmut Maucher, Nestlé focused on a series of acquisitions in the food industry that led to substantial external growth. Schollmaier recalled:

Alcon continued to grow, however, with Nestlé's financial assistance, and we became Nestlé's most profitable business segment with average operating earnings of 24% compared to 10% for the food business.

Growth accelerated sharply in the late 1980s and early 1990s, propelled by the amply-funded R&D, well-defined focus on eye-care, and strategic acquisitions (refer to **Exhibit 1**). In spite of Alcon's growth, however, in the early 1990s Nestlé corporate management was increasingly confronted with questions at annual shareholder's meetings and from security analysts on the future of its eye-care subsidiary. Many observers felt that Nestlé could easily divest Alcon since the intended buildup of a pharmaceutical business and potential combination with L'Oréal had never materialized. As Schollmaier articulated, however, Alcon could easily justify its position in Nestlé's corporate family.

During the early 1990s, our own superior profitability was key. Nestlé top management could always point to our superior results. We had established a track record that we have come to call the 10-11-12-13% "magic" formula: We planned for a 10% sales growth, 11% growth in operating profit, a 12% growth in profit before tax, and a 13% growth in net profit. With this type of performance, we were looking forward with confidence towards continued success.

Exhibit 1 *Alcon Sales ($U.S. millions)*

YEAR	SALES
1947	Start
1957	1
1967	10
1977	100
1987	500
1991	1,050
1992	1,200
1993	1,300
1994	1,500
1995	1,700
1996	1,900
1997	2,000+ projected

Source: Alcon

Impact of U.S. Health Care Reform

As health care reform gathered momentum in the United States, there was widespread consensus that the twin forces of stricter government policies and growing leverage of managed care would have a detrimental impact on health care companies. Reflecting this concern, the share prices of many large pharmaceutical firms were sharply lower in 1993 and 1994. Schollmaier commented on the situation:

As a result of all this change, health care companies started merging and restructuring. Operations were streamlined and costs were cut. Everyone became used to the idea of providing more for less. Margins became reduced as companies had to pass discounts on to managed care firms.

It was at this time that Schollmaier and his management team thought about the need to possibly change Alcon's strategy and reduce the performance expectations of Nestlé.

With the changes in health care taking place, Nestlé management told us that they would understand if the magic formula would be reversed. For some time, we spoke of 10-9-8-7% sales and earnings growth. In early 1994, we at Alcon debated intensively whether we should lower the goals and Nestlé's expectations. In the end, we not only kept it, but we actually improved the performance through several strategic moves.

Strategic Response to U.S. Health Care Reform

Schollmaier understood that even though Nestlé might be willing to accept lower performance for a few years, if Alcon's profitability lagged it would be forced to reduce its commitment to R&D. Without sufficient investment in new product development to drive growth, Alcon would struggle to return to its former level of profitability and possibly jeopardize its position with its corporate parent. He also understood that with change came opportunity, and Alcon's response to the cost and competitive pressures of health care reform included new initiatives designed to address specific aspects of managed care as well as enhanced attention to existing elements of the company's strategy. The key features of the strategy and its implementation included:

- *Narrow focus.* Concentrate on what the company knows and does best and can support technologically. A core precept since the early 1970s when it discontinued its efforts in other medical specialty areas, Alcon tightened its focus further by divesting the dermatology business to the Nestlé L'Oréal joint venture, Galderma Laboratories.

- *Full line approach.* Develop comprehensive product lines to maximize sales and marketing efforts and overhead efficiencies. Alcon filled in gaps in its segment offerings through acquisition, and product development. It also created a generic drug business to respond to the growth in that market and to provide a defense against new entrants.

- *Low-cost producer.* Drive down manufacturing and other operating costs through continuous "noncrisis basis" evaluation of facilities and all functional activities. Alcon began to consolidate some of its manufacturing to achieve economies of scale and became the low-cost producer in the industry, a position that provided considerable flexibility when competitors sought to gain market share through price cutting.

- *Global presence.* Leverage U.S. experience internationally, seek to be first presence in new markets and to be in every country. Alcon sought to maximize the impact of every product by using its expertise in regulatory approval to introduce products into as many countries as possible. It also focused increased attention on the large and highly profitable Japanese market.

- *Organizational stability.* Promote management continuity, foster strong individual growth, and develop executive succession plan. In the mid-1990s Alcon achieved a workforce reduction through normal attrition and retirement, avoiding the layoffs that sapped management talent and energy from many health care industry participants. Turnover was very low among Alcon management, a limited number of whom had come from competitors.

- *Managed care division.* Alcon created a new division—Managed Care—to respond to the growth of managed care institutions and the emerging decision-making power of nonclinical customers in the United States.
- *R&D productivity.* Focus internal R&D for maximum result and leverage external resources: major pharmaceutical companies, industry relationships, and contacts.

Corporate Culture

Complementing Alcon's commercial strategies were a culture and philosophy that embodied a sense of corporate responsibility in the mission of preserving and restoring sight, as articulated by Tim Sear, executive vice president.

> We have a role to play. In Sub-Saharan Africa there are 500 ophthalmologists for 500 million people. There are 30 million people blind to the world from cataracts whose sight could be restored in 20–30 minutes. Some have been blind for 10 or 15 years. We have to reinvest in ophthalmology. We have been successful, and we have to give something back. That's part of our mission.

Alcon gave back through direct charitable activities and educational programs. Every year it donated $10s of millions of free medical supplies to ophthalmologists in developing countries who were willing to provide their services free of charge. Alcon's educational initiatives included associations with ophthalmic centers of excellence around the globe, distribution of instructional videos, and sponsorship of "web labs," where leading ophthalmologists demonstrated new surgical procedures and treatments, and students had the opportunity to use new instruments and practice techniques.

Alcon's leading position in the ophthalmic arena was emblemized by the Alcon Research Institute, started in 1982. Alcon initiated the program by appointing a committee of external academic and industry leaders. Five honorees, each awarded $10,000, presented their papers at the first symposium. After ten years, the grants had grown to $100,000, and the annual symposia drew hundreds of the leading academic and practicing ophthalmologists in the world. Alcon Labs funded the awards and hosted the two-day event, considered to be the premier academic ophthalmic meeting in the world, but the company did not participate in committee selection or deliberation, thereby preserving the Institute's independence.

The Institute, Alcon's reputation, and the longevity of its executive team enabled the company to develop relationships with many of the leading ophthalmologists in the world. Many at Alcon considered the extent and quality of those relationships to be "unique . . . when senior Alcon people travel they typically visit the top ophthalmologists in whatever country they happen to be in." These relationships, coupled with the recognition Alcon received from its association with the Institute and from its charitable and educational programs, as well as from its own research efforts and position as the largest dedicated ophthalmic company, provided significant benefits, according to Allen Baker, executive vice president:

> Because of Alcon's reputation, people with new ideas, new inventions, new techniques, tend to come to us to get help in commercializing them. Thus Alcon gains a significantly greater amount of research knowledge than it actually has to fund.

Divisions

In 1997, Alcon had four operating divisions: **Ophthalmic, Surgical,** and **Vision Care,** all reporting to Tim Sear, and **International,** headed by Allen Baker.

Ophthalmics

Ophthalmics accounted for just under a third of Alcon's 1997 sales, equally split between the United States and international markets, and represented 15 percent of the global ophthalmic drug industry (refer to **Exhibit 2**). Revenue growth had stagnated in the early 1990s but had been on an upward track over the past four years, rising from 4 percent in 1993 to 8 percent growth in 1995. Division plans projected 5 to 7 percent growth through the rest of the decade but were historically conservative. Approximately 60 percent of U.S. sales were under some form of managed care contract, with discounts ranging from 1 percent to 15 percent.

Marketing and Sales

The impacts of managed care and the newfound prescribing authority of the optometrists in the United States required changes in Alcon's sales structure and methodology to address changes in purchase patterns and the geometric growth of potential customers. A salesforce of 90 in the United States, overseen by 10 regional and national managers, called on the traditional clinical customer

Exhibit 2 *Alcon Pharmaceutical Market Shares (1997)*

	NORTH AMERICA	EUROPE	LATIN AMERICA	JAPAN	REST OF WORLD	TOTALS
Glaucoma Products (roughly half of market)	21%	15%	28%	4%	12%	**15%**
Other Products* (roughly half of market)	29%	27%	40%	1%	18%	**22%**
Totals	**24%**	**21%**	**34%**	**2%**	**15%**	**18%**

Source: IMS/Management Estimates

*Other Products includes: steroids, antibiotics, steroid/antibiotic combinations, artificial tears, antiallergies, decongestants, and mydriatic/cycloplegies. Alcon has product entries in all these categories.

group, 12,000 practicing ophthalmologists. (There was relatively minor overlap between this group and the surgical ophthalmologists who were customers of the other segments.) While the educational aspects of the sales mission were unchanged, the salesforce increasingly did not engage in negotiations regarding price or order taking. These tasks were handled by the business side of the managed care organizations and were the focus of Alcon's new Managed Care division. Alcon developed a separate, fifty-person sales organization to call on the large numbers of managed care gatekeepers (primary care physicians and pediatricians). Additionally the pharmaceutical division cross-trained the sixty Vision Care salespeople to sell pharmaceuticals to optometrists, although the top prescribers were also the responsibility of the regular drug sales group.

Generics—Falcon

The U.S. market for generic versions of drugs had grown into a major business over the past fifteen years, facilitated by FDA approval procedures and the elimination of antisubstitution laws, and propelled by pressures to reduce costs. By the mid-1990s generics accounted for 33 percent of the U.S. ophthalmic pharmaceutical market units, although growth had leveled off due to the pace of new product introductions. Internationally, generic markets were at various stages of development but tended to be much smaller than the United States. Alcon entered the generics arena in 1994 primarily as a defensive move to protect itself against competition on the low end. It created a dedicated subsidiary, Falcon, which offered products only in the United States. Within two years Falcon had captured 29 percent of the generics market, largely on the basis of a single product.

Surgical

In spite of Alcon's roots as a pharmaceutical company, by the mid-1990s, its surgical division had become its largest business, contributing 45 percent of sales and boasting the highest growth rate. Acquisition of Coopervision in 1989, the leading manufacturer of ophthalmic instrumentation and intraocular lenses, augmented Alcon's position as the industry leader in surgical solutions and supplies. In almost every product line Alcon held the number one market share position in the United States and globally (refer to **Exhibit 3**), and held about 50 percent of the total $800 million U.S. market in cataract procedures.

Products: Differentiation, Trends, Opportunities Alcon's surgical products conformed to its broadline strategy, offering a one-stop shop that provided everything needed (including equipment financing) for a surgical procedure from instrumentation to disposable supplies to surgical pharmaceuticals and solutions.

- *Custom Packs.* Alcon developed the concept of the custom pack which provided in one sterile package all of the supplies needed for a surgical procedure. Alcon had attained a 60 percent share of the market. Advances in information technology had simplified the selling process and reduced the order cycle time from several weeks to three days. During an interview with a surgical nurse, a salesperson could develop a prototype on a laptop, display the contents and packing order textually and graphically, and then download the specifications to the facility in Houston, Texas, that assembled all the components. Alcon was willing to include the offerings of any other suppliers but offered better pricing based on a higher percentage of its own products in the pack.

Exhibit 3 *Surgical Instrumentation and Supplies Segment Market Share (1997)*

SEGMENT	UNITED STATES	JAPAN	OTHERS*
IOLs	31%	38%	36%
Disposables	62%	47%	48%
Irrigating Sol	90%	56%	69%
Viscoelastics	44%	0%	34%
Cataract Equip	60%	65%	50%
Cataract Paks	52%	65%	50%
Vitrectomy Equip	40%	53%	20%
Vitrectomy Paks	50%	78%	61%
Refractive	2%	0%	19%
Access/Stand Alone	54%	4%	6%
% of Total	**50%**	**37%**	**27%**
Total Sales	**440**	**114**	**214**

Source: Management Estimates
*Others in this instance encompasses Europe, Latin America, and Rest of World. No significant market share differences exist in these sectors.

- *Instrumentation.* At the former Coopervision plant in Irvine, California, Alcon manufactured instrumentation for surgical procedures, such as the phacoemulsification system used in cataract operations; vitrectomy equipment, used for surgery on the retina; and eye-testing equipment. In response to customer dissatisfaction with the need to replace equipment every two or three years to keep pace with technological innovation, Alcon implemented the concept of upgradable technology platforms for its instrumentation products in 1993. A worldwide field technical services group of over 300 factory-trained technicians maintained machines and installed hardware and software upgrades every few years or as required.

- *Intraocular lenses.* In 1995 Alcon introduced the first acrylic foldable IOL (intraocular lens), the **AcrySof,** a new technology that provided improved performance over silicone lenses. Alcon adopted a policy of not discounting its **AcrySof** lens, in spite of considerable pressure from large hospital groups. In the absence of enactment of the Medicare regulation specifying multiple reimbursement rates based on IOL technology, Alcon attempted to make its own market-driven, performance-based case for receiving its asking price. Sear saw a direct analogy to the pharmaceutical model: "New drugs that are superior and provide better outcomes command premiums. There's no reason that same logic shouldn't apply with IOLs." Some executives carried the pharmaceutical model further, suggesting the possibility of going directly to the end-user pa-

tient, as drug companies had increasingly done to promote their new offerings.

- *Office computer system.* Also housed in the surgical division was an office computer product that enabled large, geographically disperse networks of providers to manage their patient scheduling, financial records/billing, and electronic medical records. It also enabled the capability to streamline their supply ordering and track surgical and therapeutic clinical outcomes. The product was a losing cost center but was considered to have strategic value.

Marketing and Sales

Alcon responded to changes wrought by health care reform by segmenting the market and by understanding where best to focus its sales effort. Before managed care, Alcon's strategy was to supply superior quality merchandise and charge premium prices. To accommodate cost pressures and to protect its high-end business, the surgical division planned to introduce new versions of products that were targeted at and priced for lower-end market tiers. For example, in addition to **Viscoat** and **Duo-Visc,** its top-line viscoelastics, which were priced at $55 and $75, Alcon was going to offer **Cellugel** at $25–$30. The **Hydrosof** IOL, which would sell for $50–$100, offered a less expensive alternative to the $150 **AcrySof** lens.

In the United States, Alcon's 50 percent share of the cataract market was slanted toward the higher-margin hospital segment. Surgicenters (ASCs) tended to be more cost-conscious than hospitals and also to demand more value, such as help with marketing and other services. On the plus side, ASCs usually gave all the business for procedures to one supplier and were a much higher user of custom packs, whereas hospitals preferred to maintain their ability to mix and match different brands. Alcon lost some ASC business to competitors who were willing to win market share on price reductions. It was overwhelmingly successful in competing for hospital-based business, however, where physicians tended to have greater influence in the purchase decision. As Caldwell remarked: "When a physician controls product selection we win many more times than we lose." Moreover, Alcon was usually able to retain that business when it transitioned to an ASC. Thus, surgical division focused its resources on increasing its share of the hospital segment, with a goal of moving from 40–50 percent to 70–80 percent.

Alcon's U.S. surgical salesforce consisted of 100 people dedicated to surgical disposables, 50 to equipment, and 20 focused on the office computer product, all overseen by 20 managers. The 170 front-line salespeople generated over $500 million in sales, nearly three times the per capita industry average. The group focused on the 6,000 to 8,000 surgical ophthalmologists and also interacted with Alcon's Managed Care group who dealt with the managed care customers on the business side.

Vision Care

Alcon sold off several small European contact lens companies in the mid-1980s, citing unfavorable competitive conditions, but it kept and grew the lens care business. In 1995 Alcon carved out its U.S. Vision Care business from Ophthalmics and created a separate division with a dedicated sales force and management structure, and by 1996 the division represented 23 percent of sales. The evolution of contact lens technology had presented significant challenges to Alcon over the years, as it saw its 33 percent share of the U.S. market in the late 1980s dissolve under the onslaught of disposables and multipurpose solutions. Margins for products to care for conventional and planned replacement lenses, especially enzymes, carried much higher margins than multipurpose solutions. In spite of the differences between Vision Care and the other divisions, Alcon followed the same basic

strategy, as articulated by Orlando Rodriguez, director of marketing:

As with the other segments, it's technology first, then marketing. We are a technology-driven company and we can use that to build competitive advantage in vision care as well as in surgical or ophthalmics. The aim is to provide both convenience and cost benefits.

Several new products in the mid-1990s sought to challenge the market leaders and offer novel methods for lens cleaning and care. To differentiate its multipurpose solution from Bausch & Lomb's Renu, which contained a surfactant (detergent), Alcon introduced **Optifree Express,** a surfactant-free cleaning solution that provided effective cleaning but didn't impair the quality of the lens. **SupraClens,** launched in 1996, offered a new approach to lens care. A drop on each lens in the case, following a cleaning with a multipurpose solution, enhanced lens performance, providing immediate gratification. A survey indicated that two-thirds of participants reported that using SupraClens was as easy or easier than using a multipurpose solution.

SupraClens is our attack on disposables. It makes planned replacement and conventional lenses achieve a level of comfort and vision quality that is closer to what disposables are designed to provide. It also makes disposables perform better and last their entire expected two-week lifetime.

Marketing Initiatives

Complementing its technology development, Vision Care was pursuing two marketing initiatives to gain market share in its core product lines and to push into new areas. Although Alcon no longer had its own lens business around which to build brand synergy, it was attempting to form alliances with other lens manufacturers to develop brand relationships. In late 1996, Alcon entered into an agreement to remunerate Wesley Jessen, a contact lens manufacturer, for its endorsement of Alcon's vision care products and was close to a similar deal with other lens manufacturers. The other initiative, recently underway, involved Vision Care's access to the retail channel. As the Over-the-Counter (OTC) arm of Alcon, Vision Care saw potential opportunities to introduce products from the pharmaceutical side into the OTC market, moving more extensively beyond lens care into other eye-care products.

International Division

Alcon entered markets outside the United States in the 1950s and by 1996 international sales accounted for just under half of total revenues (refer to **Exhibit 4**). Increasing Medicare reimbursement pressures within the United States and less regulation on surgical costs in international markets led to a significant shift toward surgical sales within the International Division (refer to **Exhibit 5**). According to Schollmaier:

> For the past decade, a major technology wave swept the ophthalmology industry, such as how cataract surgery is performed, and the use of phaco, smaller flexible IOLs. This wave had its beginning in the United States and then moved to Europe, Latin America, and eventually Japan. We followed that wave with the best equipment and IOLs, teaching the surgeons everywhere how to use them.

Country organizations ranged from large manufacturing facilities to two-person sales offices and included wholly-owned subsidiaries, distributor arrangements, and scientific offices. The size and type of organization depended upon the size of the market, macroeconomic conditions, the developmental status, system of health care delivery, state of ophthalmic practice, and the manner in which Alcon's position had evolved.

Exhibit 5
International Business Segment Mix

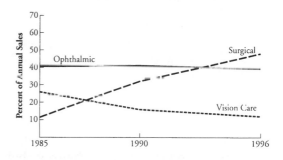

	1985	1990	1996
Total International Sales (Millions)	**126.5**	**325.6**	**825.6**
• Ophthalmic	50.8	133.4	326.3
• Vision Care	32.9	53.0	101.9
• Surgical	14.6	105.3	396.1
• Other*	28.2	33.9	1.3

*Mostly Galderma and Webcon in 1985 and 1990. Subsequently divested.
Source: Alcon

Exhibit 4
International vs. Domestic Product Mix

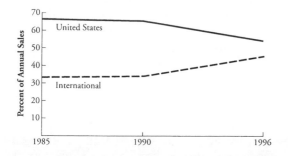

	1985	1990	1996
Total Sales (Millions)	**377.2**	**940.0**	**1,805.1**
• Domestic	250.7	614.4	979.5
• International	126.5	325.6	825.6

Source: Alcon

In a typical scenario, Alcon initially filled mail orders from an ophthalmologist who had heard of the company, then arranged for a local distributor to handle its offerings and eventually moved to a direct or indirect sales force. When sales reached a sufficient level, Alcon formed a legal entity—branch office or subsidiary—depending upon local conditions, and legal/regulatory requirements. Continued growth then dictated support staff, accounting, and other functions.

Alcon also made numerous small acquisitions to gain entry to new international markets, and it inherited a diverse array of products over the course of its early global expansion. Initially Alcon kept many of the local products and gave country managers responsibility for new product registrations. To streamline the regulatory approval process and to optimize the profitability of its product portfolio in the 1980s, Alcon centralized all product registration activity at headquarters. It adopted a global product strategy aimed at introducing the same products into as many markets as possible.

Pricing in foreign markets varied significantly, depending upon the degree of governmental cost control and the extent to which private health care systems had developed. In many countries the prices of pharmaceuticals was substantially lower than in the United States, though surgical supplies were less impacted and vision care products, not covered by national health plans, were entirely market-driven. Alcon's international strategy was to be everywhere with every product, regardless of pricing pressure and short-term obstacles to market development. The company invested considerably during the 1970s and 1980s in building a global infrastructure that, by 1997, it considered second to none. Sear commented:

> You can't pick and choose which products you sell or which markets you're in. We have to be everywhere. As soon as a market opens up, we're there. When Latvia, Estonia, and Lithuania opened up in 1990 we had people there within a matter of weeks with a suitcase full of products to hand out. Our man went to see the Minister of Health. Tell them we're Alcon and we'll be back. They'll always remember Alcon was first.

Exhibit 6 shows a comprehensive picture of Alcon's global market share by region.

Managed Care Division

In April 1996, Alcon created a separate division in response to the growing importance and bargaining power of large managed care organizations in the United States. Except for one outside person from a large pharma company who was brought in to develop the organization, the Managed Care group was built internally and comprised sixteen up and coming and/or experienced salespeople drawn from sales management and national account positions in the other divisions. In late 1996, Cary Rayment,

formerly comanager of the surgical division, was put in charge. Reflecting the differences in types of managed care institutions, account responsibility was grouped by customer segment, with HMOs and PBMs separate from PPMCs.

The mission of the organization was to establish Alcon as the preferred ophthalmic supplier by creating innovative contracting arrangements, providing services and developing relationships. Managed Care's goals were to ensure that Alcon sales representatives had access to decision makers, negotiate deals that maximized price consistent with optimal formulary inclusion, and to provide a single contact point representing Alcon to the business customer. Blaise McGoey, vice president U.S. Ophthalmics, offered a more pithy articulation of the objectives: "Managed Care gets us the hunting license to go sell our products. Excellent clinical selling is worthless today without good relationships with the business customers and the right formulary positions."

Ensuring inclusion in formularies involved both defensive and offensive strategies. A defensive measure was simply making sure that products were not excluded from a particular formulary through an NDC lock-out. Though sometimes forced into a defensive posture, Alcon preferred to develop offensive approaches that sought exclusive positions, preferred status in a formulary or a guaranteed market share. The levels of discount on drugs in a contract were tied to their status in the formulary and to a measure of market share performance.

Rayment attributed a good measure of Alcon's recent success to the resources the company had invested in Managed Care and to the division's role in helping to integrate the efforts of the other divisions. With some of its customers, the group was trying to develop comprehensive contracts that incorporated products from all three of Alcon's prod-

Exhibit 6 *Alcon Share of Market 1990 and 1996*

	NORTH AMERICA		EUROPE		LATIN AMERICA		REST OF WORLD		JAPAN	
	1990	1996	1990	1996	1990	1996	1990	1996	1990	1996
PHARMACEUTICALS	23%	24%	12%	18%	30%	34%	12%	15%	0%	1.6%
SURGICAL	37%	54%	10%	25%	8%	30%	15%	30%	12%	37%
VISION CARE*	18%	31%	6%	12%	25%	37%	5%	13%	0%	1.4%
LENSES		n/a		n/a		n/a		n/a		n/a

Source: Alcon
*Soft Contact Lens Care

uct areas. In its role as the single contact point, Managed Care had the opportunity to cross-sell different products and create comprehensive performance incentive packages. The benefits of this contributed to a new attitude and perspective within Alcon, as Rayment described:

> We used to have very much a stovepipe mentality here. I saw Blaise (McGoey) in the elevator but didn't really know or bother much about what he had going on. Now there is much more cross-functional communication than there used to be. I think it helps us as we deal with the needs and opportunities of integrated health care organizations.

Research and Development

New products and new technology were the lifeblood of pharmaceutical and health care companies, and Alcon had always devoted substantial resources to its research and development efforts, emblemized by the Alcon Research Center. Spending on research and development rose steadily as a percent of sales, reaching nearly 9 percent by the mid-1990s, equaling a total outlay of $160 million in 1997 (refer to **Exhibit 7**). R&D was projected to decrease to about 8 percent of sales by the year 2000, though there was a clear understanding that if emerging projects required additional funding, the money would be available. Nearly half of Alcon's 1996 sales came from products developed in the previous ten years.

Managed care stimulated the drive to develop new products whose value was augmented by an understanding of health economics. The clearest path to secure inclusion on formularies and premium pricing was to offer novel treatments that provided the best value in the context of integrated care. As McGoey succinctly stated about Alcon's strategy:

> Technology drives the day. If I have the best product, I don't care what obstacles you put in front of me, I can win.

Exhibit 7   R&D Spending—1997

	$ MIL	% SALES
PHARMACEUTICAL	100	13
SURGICAL	40	5
VISION CARE	20	4

Source: Alcon

Alcon's R&D strategy combined narrowly focused internal efforts with external partnerships and alliances. As a niche pharmaceutical supplier, Alcon had fostered expertise in product development rather than in basic research. Historically it had licensed many of the compounds in its drugs from the major pharmaceutical companies and then fine-tuned the application and delivery vehicle. As big players grew reluctant to license compounds with substantial market potential and started to demand higher fees, Alcon moved more into basic research, which was closely targeted to areas where it had demonstrated competence. In the mid-1990s Alcon started to introduce products created completely in-house, such as Iopidine, a treatment for serious glaucoma cases.

A major goal of Alcon's R&D effort was to reduce the time it took to develop products, obtain regulatory approval, and get new products into the marketplace, especially in cases where a competitor had gained first mover advantages with an innovative treatment and was capturing market share. In addition to its technological expertise, Alcon developed strong competitor intelligence capability to understand what markets other industry participants were pursuing. It also recognized that it could create a competitive advantage by honing its ability to move quickly through the regulatory approval process.

Growth Opportunities

According to Schollmaier, Alcon needed to review its strategy of selective growth and determine whether this strategy was still appropriate in light of the changed corporate goals of Nestlé. Reviewing international opportunities, Schollmaier was careful to point out that the profitability of the various international markets had changed over time. Traditionally, the pharma business in the United States was significantly more profitable than elsewhere due to the fact that per unit prices outside the United States were only about one-third of the level in the United States. The profitability of the surgical division is about the same both internationally and in the United States, although the United States had traditionally had higher prices, and thus profits, than internationally. This was assumed to have been the impact of the U.S. health care reform. The surgical business, although very profitable, was lagging behind the U.S. pharmaceutical business profitability.

The questions that are being posed to us are quite simple: Can we grow in our accustomed markets, or segments, or do we have to broaden our range or even diversify out of ophthalmology? Which business segments should we emphasize? Which geographies should we emphasize? To what extent should we rely on growth from industrialized countries vs. emerging economies? But we cannot play our strategic role within the Nestlé family if we stay still, thus the need to grow to maintain our importance.

Growth Options

Faced with Nestlé's challenge, Alcon's management team began to review and evaluate immediate and longer-term options for achieving the growth and profitability goals. In addition to the areas that Alcon currently targeted, the team considered paths that deviated somewhat from the narrow focus that had been one of the hallmarks of Alcon's strategy. Potential options included:

- *Market share growth.* Alcon held leading positions in most of the surgical segments, but had lost ground in some of the pharmaceutical product lines, notably antiglaucoma drugs.

- *Geographical expansion.* Demographic and economic trends dictated that significant future growth in ophthalmic markets lay outside the United States. Alcon's global product strategy and centralized regulatory approval process enabled it to introduce its product lines in most geographic areas. There were markets, however, such as Japanese pharmaceuticals, where Alcon was underrepresented. Emerging markets, such as China, also offered substantial opportunity (refer to **Exhibits 8, 9, and 10**).

- *Market growth.* Technological advances and novel therapeutic treatments offered the potential to expand existing markets and create new ones. For example, the dramatic improvements in cataract removal and IOLs had spurred growth in a market projected at one point to decline. Similar possibilities in other areas invite continued research. New drugs or surgical procedures to treat ARMD (Age Related Macular Degeneration), CMV retinitis and diabetic retinopathy promised to generate significant sales where no markets currently existed. Additionally, there was potential for Alcon to increase its share of surgical markets it currently served by filling out remaining gaps in its product lines and thereby increasing its revenues per procedure.

- *Refractive market.* Alcon did not currently offer a line of refractive surgical products. The surgical technique was expected to evolve toward intraocular implants where Alcon's technological lead in the use of acrylic materials for IOLs gave it a possible long-term advantage. The procedure was expected to be commonplace, though expensive, in five years, with the lenses being a large portion of the cost.

- *Ear, Nose and Throat (ENT).* Concerned about the distraction of organization building and the challenge of providing R&D support, Alcon had discontinued its planned diversification into other medical specialties in the early 1970s. There were competencies, however, that Alcon possessed in 1997 that argued for reexamining that strategy. Several of Alcon's ophthalmic pharmaceutical compounds had potential applications in the treatment of ENT afflictions. Alcon had developed the ability to successfully market to clinical specialists and the reputation of the Alcon brand was widely recognized

Exhibit 8 *New Market Segments and Geographic Opportunities*

	POTENTIAL PRODUCT MARKETS	GEOGRAPHIC MARKETS
PHARMACEUTICAL	CMV Retinitis Diabetic Retinopathy Age-Related Macular Degeneracy	Japan, China, India, Indonesia, Russia
SURGICAL	Refractive Office-Based Equipment	Indonesia, Russia, Mexico, Middle East, Africa
VISION CARE	Contact Lenses Diagnostic Equipment OTC Products Spectacles and Frames	China, India, Middle East, Africa, Eastern Europe

Source: Alcon

Exhibit 9 *Alcon Sales in China and India ($U.S. thousands)*

	1995	1996	1997	PROJECTED 1998 (2 X 6 M)
China				
Pharmaceuticals	500	1,000	1,650	2,000
Surgical	1,900	3,200	5,700	7,400
Vision Care	—	50	100	125
Total	**2,400**	**4,250**	**7,450**	**9,525**
India				
Pharmaceuticals	—	—	—	—
Surgical	1,000	1,500	1,825	2,650
Vision Care	—	—	—	—
Total	**1,000**	**1,500**	**1,825**	**2,650**

Source: Alcon Internal Financials

among physicians. Additionally, in some countries ophthalmology was not a separate specialty from ENT, and therefore EENT (Eye, Ear, Nose and Throat) physicians represented one clinical customer.

As Alcon's management team examined these options, one executive, acting as the devil's advocate, challenged the premise of what the company was attempting to do.

Exhibit 10 *Worldwide Eye Care Market—Present and Projected ($U.S. factory sales in millions)*

	NORTH AMERICA	EUROPE	LATIN AMERICA	JAPAN	REST OF WORLD	TOTAL
PHARMACEUTICALS						
Market Size 1996	1150	950	300	1150	300	3850
Market Estimate 2005	2300	1250	450	1800	450	6250
Growth 1990–1996	9%	2%	5%	5%	8%	5%
Growth 1997–2005	8%	3%	4%	5%	4%	5%
SURGICAL						
Market Size 1996	800	700	100	400	200	2200
Market Estimate 2005	1200	950	150	650	250	3200
Growth 1990–1996	2%	5%	8%	12%	9%	6%
Growth 1997–2005	4%	4%	4%	6%	4%	4%
VISION CARE						
Market Size 1996	600	450	140	350	160	1700
Market Estimate 2005	600	500	150	550	200	2000
Growth 1990–1996	2%	2%	2%	2%	2%	2%
Growth 1997–2005	NC	1%	1%	6%	2%	2%

(continued)

Exhibit 10 *Worldwide Eye Care Market—Present and Projected ($U.S. factory sales in millions) (Continued)*

	NORTH AMERICA	EUROPE	LATIN AMERICA	JAPAN	REST OF WORLD	TOTAL
SUB-TOTAL						
Market Size 1996	2550	2100	540	1900	660	7750
Market Estimate 2005	4100	2700	750	3000	900	11450
Growth 1990–1996	5%	4%	5%	6%	7%	5%
Growth 1997–2005	5%	3%	3%	5%	4%	4%
CONTACT LENSES						
Market Size 1996	1450	400	150	400	400	2800
Market Estimate 2005	1550	500	200	600	600	3450
Growth 1990–1996	4%	6%	7%	7%	7%	5%
Growth 1997–2005	1%	4%	4%	6%	6%	3%
TOTAL						
Market Size 1996	4000	2500	690	2300	1060	10550
Market Estimate 2005	5650	3200	950	3600	1500	14900
Growth 1990–1996	5%	4%	5%	6%	7%	5%
Growth 1997–2005	4%	3%	3%	5%	5%	4%

Source: IMS/Management Estimates

We've been very successful by remaining tightly focused on a narrow band of technologies and markets and doing really well at what we do. Are we going to risk the foundation of that success by trying to push for growth and profit levels at a rate that we can't sustain? Are we going to change our strategy and veer off course, possibility destroying the golden goose we've built?

Case 5	*Delissa in Japan (Revised)*

"We can maintain our presence in Japan or we can pull out ... "

In the autumn of 1997, Bjorn Robertson, who had recently been named Managing Director of Agria, Sweden's leading dairy products cooperative, met with his team to review the international side of the business. The four men sat around a table piled high with thick reports, Nielsen audits, film storyboards, yogurt cups, and a mass of promotional material in Japanese. Agria's "Delissa" line of fresh dairy products was sold all over the world through franchise agreements. Several of these agreements were up for review, but the most urgent one was the agreement with Nikko of Japan.

"In the light of these results, there are several things we can do in Japan. We can maintain our presence and stay with our present franchisee, we can change our franchisee, or we can pull out. But, let's look first at how badly we are really doing in Japan." Bjorn Robertson looked across the conference table at Peter Borg, Stefan Gustafsson and Lars Karlsson, each of whom had been involved with Agria's Japanese business over the past few years.

Robertson read aloud to the others a list of Agria's major foreign ventures featuring the Delissa yogurt brand: "U.S.A. launch date 1977, market share is 12.5 percent; Germany launch 1980, market share is 14 percent; U.K. launch 1982, market share is 13.8 percent; France launch 1983, market share is 9.5 percent; Japan launch 1987, market share today is 2–3 percent." Robertson circled the figure with his marker and turned to look around at his team. "Under 3% after 10 years in the market! What happened?" he asked.

History

Agria was founded in 1973 when a group of Swedish dairy cooperatives decided to create a united organization that would develop and sell a line of fresh dairy products. The principal engineers of the organization were Rolf Anderen and Bo Ekman, who had established the group's headquarters in Uppsala, near Stockholm. In 1980, after the individual cooperatives had been persuaded to drop their own trademarks, the Delissa line was launched. This was one of the few "national" lines of dairy products in Sweden. It comprised yogurts, desserts, fresh cheese, and fresh cream. In the two decades that followed, Agria's share rose from 3 percent to 25 percent of the Swedish fresh milk products market. Anderen's vision and the concerted efforts of 20,000 dairy farmer members of the cooperative had helped build Agria into a powerful national and international organization.

By 1997, more than 1.1 billion Delissa yogurts and desserts were being consumed per year worldwide. In fiscal year 1996, Delissa had sales of $2.1 billion and employed 4,400 people in and outside Sweden.

Industrial franchising was not very widespread in the 1980s, and few Swedish dairy products firms had invested money abroad. However, Ekman's idea of know-how transfer ventures, whereby a local license would manufacture yogurt using Swedish technology and then market and distribute the product using its own distribution network, had enabled Delissa to penetrate over thirteen foreign markets with considerable success and with a minimal capital outlay. In contrast, Delissa's biggest competitor worldwide, Danone—a French food conglomerate marketing a yogurt line under the "Danone" brand name—had gone into foreign markets, mainly by buying into or creating local companies, or by forming regular joint ventures.

By the time Bjorn Robertson took over as European marketing director in 1991, the Delissa trademark—with the white cow symbol so familiar in Sweden—was known in many different countries worldwide. Delissa was very active in sponsoring sports events, and Robertson—himself a keen cross-country skier and sailor—offered his personal support to Delissa's teams around the world.

When he reviewed the international business, Robertson had been surprised by the results of Agria's Japanese joint venture, which did not compare to those achieved in most foreign markets. Before calling together the international marketing team for a discussion, Robertson requested the files on Japan and spent some time studying the history of the alliance. He read:

Proposal for Entry into the Japanese Market

In early 1985, the decision was made to enter the Japanese market. Market feasibility research and a search for a suitable franchisee is underway, with an Agria team currently in Japan.

Objectives

The total yogurt market in Japan for 1986 is estimated at approximately 600 million cups (100mn ml). The market for yogurt is expected to grow at an average of at least 8% p.a. in volume for the next five years. Our launch strategy would be based on an expected growth rate of 10% or 15% for the total market. We have set ourselves the goal of developing a high quality range of yogurts in Japan, of becoming well known with the Japanese consumer. We aim to reach a 5% market share in the first year and 10% share of market within three years of launch. We plan to cover the three main metropolitan areas, Tokyo, Osaka, and Nagoya, within a two-year period, and the rest of the country within the next three years.

Robertson circled the 10 percent with a red pen. He understood that management would have hesitated to set too high a goal for market share compared to other countries since some executives felt that Japan was a difficult market to enter. But, in 1993, the Japanese operation had not reached its target. In 1997, Delissa's share of the total yogurt market had fallen to 2 percent, without ever reaching 3 percent. Robertson wrote a note to the Uppsala-based manager responsible for Far Eastern business stating that he felt Agria's record in Japan in no way reflected the type of success it had had elsewhere with Delissa. He began to wonder why Japan was so different.

The report continued with a brief overview of the Japanese yogurt market:

Consumption

Per capita consumption of yogurt in Japan is low compared to Scandinavian countries. It is estimated at around 5.3 cups per person per year in Japan, versus 110 in Sweden and 120 in Finland. Sales of yogurt in Japan are seasonal, with a peak period from March to July. The highest sales have been recorded in June, so the most ideal launch date would be at the end of February.

Types of yogurt available in Japan—1986

In Japan, yogurt sales may be loosely broken down into three major categories:

- Plain (39% of the market in volume): Called "plain" in Japan because the color is white, but it is really flavored with vanilla. Generally sold in 500 ml pure pack cups. Sugared or sometimes with a sugar bag attached.

- Flavored (45% of the market in volume): Differentiated from the above category by the presence of coloring and gelifiers.
  Not a wide range of varieties, mainly: vanilla, strawberry, almond, and citrus.

- Fruit (16% of the market in volume): Similar to the typical Swedish fruit yogurt but with more pulp than real fruit.
  Contains some coloring and flavoring.

Western-type yogurts also compete directly in the same price bracket with local desserts—like puddings and jellies—produced by Japanese competitors.

Competition

Three major Japanese manufacturers account for about half of the total real yogurt market:

Snow Brand Milk Products is the largest manufacturer of dairy products in Japan and produces drinking milk, cheeses, frozen foods, biochemicals and pharmaceuticals. Turnover in 1985 was 443.322 million yen ($1 = ¥234 in 1985).

Meiji Milk Products, Japan's second largest producer of dairy foods, particularly dried milk for babies, ice cream, cheese. Its alliance with the Bulgarian government helped start the yogurt boom in Japan. Turnover in 1985 was 410,674 million yen.

Morinaga Milk Industry, Japan's third largest milk products producer processes drinking milk, ice cream, instant coffee. It has a joint venture with Kraft U.S. for cheese. Turnover in 1985 was 301,783 million yen.

The share of these three producers has remained stable for years and is approximately: Yuki-jirushi (Snowbrand) 25%; Meiji 19%; Morinaga 10%.

The Japanese also consume a yogurt drink called "Yakult Honsha" which is often included in statistics on total yogurt consumption as it competes with normal yogurt. On a total market base for yogurts and yogurt drink, Yakult has 31%. Yakult drink is based on milk reconstituted from powder or fresh milk acidified with lactic acid and glucose. Yakult is not sold in shops, but through door-to-door sales and by groups of women who visit offices during the afternoon and sell the product directly to employees.

Along with some notes written in 1985 by Mr. Ole Bobek, Agria's Director of International Operations, Robertson found a report on meetings held in Uppsala at which two members of Agria's negotiating team presented their findings to management.

Selecting a Franchisee

We have just returned from our third visit to Japan where we once again held discussions with the agricultural cooperative, Nikko. Nikko is the country's second largest association of agricultural cooperatives; it is the Japanese equivalent of Agria. Nikko is a significant political force in Japan but not as strong as Zennoh, the National Federation of Agricultural Cooperatives which is negotiating with Sodima, one of our French competitors. Nikko is price leader for various food products in Japan (milk, fruit juice, rice) and is active in lobbying on behalf of agricultural producers. Nikko is divided into two parts: manufacturing and distribution. It processes and distributes milk and dairy products, and it also distributes raw rice and vegetables.

We have seen several other candidates, but Nikko is the first one that seems prepared to join us. We believe that Nikko is the most appropriate distributor for Agria in Japan. Nikko is big and its credentials seem perfect for Agria, particularly since its strong supermarket distribution system for milk in the three main metropolitan areas is also ideally suited for yogurt. In Japan, 80% of yogurt is sold through supermarkets. We are, however, frustrated that, after prolonged discussions and several trips to Japan, Nikko has not yet signed an agreement with Agria. We sense that the management does want to go ahead but that they want to be absolutely sure before signing. We are anxious to get this project underway before Danone, Sodima or Chambourcy[1] enter Japan.

The same report also contained some general information on the Japanese consumer, which Robertson found of interest:

Some Background Information on the Japanese Consumer

Traditionally, Japan is not a dairy products consumer, although locally produced brands of yogurt are sold along with other milk-based items such as puddings and coffee cream.

Many aspects of life in Japan are miniaturized due to lack of space: 60% of the total population of about 120 million is concentrated on 3% of the surface of the islands. The rest of the land mass is mountainous. In Japan, 85% of the population live in towns of which over one third have more than half a million people. This urban density naturally affects lifestyle, tastes, and habits. Restricted living space and lack of storage areas mean that most Japanese housewives must shop daily and consequently expect fresh milk products in the stores every day as they rarely purchase long-life foods or drinks. The country is fairly homogeneous as far as culture and the distribution of wealth is concerned. Disposable income is high. The Japanese spend over 30% of their total household budget on food, making it by far the greatest single item, with clothing in second place (10%).

The market is not comparable to Scandinavia or to the United States as far as the consumption of dairy products is concerned. There are young housewives purchasing yogurt today whose mothers barely knew of its existence and whose grandmothers would not even have kept milk in the house. At one time it was believed that the Japanese do not have the enzymes to digest milk and that, only a generation ago, when children were given milk, it was more

likely to be goat's milk than cow's milk. However, with the market evolving rapidly towards "Westernization," there is a general interest in American and European products, including yogurt.

Although consumption of yogurt per capita is still low in Japan at the moment, research shows that there is a high potential for growth. When we launch, correct positioning will be the key to Delissa's success as a new foreign brand. We will need to differentiate it from existing Japanese brands and go beyond the rather standardized "freshness" advertising theme.

Distribution

Traditionally, Japanese distribution methods have been complex; the chain tends to be many-layered, making distribution costs high. Distribution of refrigerated products is slightly simpler than the distribution of dry goods because it is more direct.

The Japanese daily-purchase habit means that the delivery system adopted for Delissa must be fast and efficient. Our basic distribution goal would be to secure mass sales retailer distribution. Initially, items would be sold through existing sales outlets that sell Nikko's drinking milk, "Nikkodo." The milk-related products and dessert foods would be sold based on distribution to mass sales retailers. The objective would be to make efficient use of existing channels of distribution with daily delivery schedules and enjoy lower distribution costs for new products.

The Japanese Retail Market

The retail market is extremely fragmented with independent outlets accounting for 57% of sales (vs. 3% in the U.S.). With 1,350 shops for every 100,000 people, Japan has twice as many outlets per capita as most European countries. Tradition, economics, government regulations, and service demands affect the retail system in Japan. Housewives shop once a day on the average and most select the smaller local stores, which keep longer hours, deliver orders, offer credit, and provide a meeting place for shoppers. Opening a Western-style supermarket is expensive and complicated, so most retailing remains in the hands of the small, independent, or family business.

Japan has three major metropolitan areas: Tokyo, Osaka, and Nogaya, with a respective population of 11, 3, and 2 million inhabitants. Nikko's Nikkodo, with a 15% share of total, is market leader ahead of the many other suppliers. Nikko feels the

[1]Chambourcy was a brand name for yogurt produced and distributed by Nestlé in various countries. Nestlé, with sales of $52 billion in 1996, was the world's largest food company; its headquarters are in Vevey (Switzerland).

distribution chain used for Nokkodo milk would be ideal for yogurt. Each metropolitan area has a separate distribution system, each one with several depots and branches. For instance, Kanto (Great Tokyo)—the largest area with over 40 million people—has five Nikko depots and five Nikko branches.

Most of the physical distribution (drivers and delivery vans) is carried out by a subsidiary of Nikko with support from the wholesalers. The refrigerated milk vans have to be fairly small (less than two tons) so that they can drive down the narrow streets. The same routes are used for milk delivery, puddings, and juices. Our initial strategy would be to accept Nikko's current milk distribution system as the basic system and, at the same time, adopt shifting distribution routes. Japan's complicated street identification system, whereby only numbers and no names are shown, makes great demands on the distribution system and the drivers.

The Franchise Contract

Robertson opened another report written by Ole Bobek, who had headed up the Japan project right from the start and had been responsible for the early years of the joint venture. He left the company in 1990. This report contained all the details concerning the contract between Agria and Nikko. In 1985, Nikko and Agria had signed an industrial franchise agreement permitting Nikko to manufacture and distribute Delissa products under license from Agria. The contract was Agria's standard Delissa franchisee agreement covering technology transfer associated with trademark exploitation. Agria was to provide manufacturing and product know-how, as well as marketing, technical, commercial, and sales support. Agria would receive a royalty for every pot of yogurt sold. The Nikko cooperative would form a separate company for the distribution, marketing, and promotion of Delissa products. During the pre-launch phase, Per Bergman, Senior Area Brand Manager, would train the sales and marketing team, and Agria's technicians would supply know-how to the Japanese.

By the end of 1986, a factory to produce Delissa yogurt, milk, and dairy products had been constructed in Mijima, 60 miles northwest of Tokyo. Agria provided Nikko with advice on technology, machinery, tanks, fermentation processes, and so forth. Equipment from the United States, Sweden, Germany, and Japan was selected. A European-style Erka filling machine was installed which would fill two, four, or six cups at a time, and was considered economical and fast.

Robertson opened another report by Bobek entitled "Delissa Japan—Pre-Launch Data." The report covered the market, positioning, advertising and media plan, minutes of the meetings with Nikko executives and the SRT International Advertising Agency that would handle the launch, analysis of market research findings, and competitive analysis. Robertson closed the file and thought about the Japanese market. During the planning phase before the launch, everything had looked so promising. In its usual methodical fashion, Agria had prepared its traditional launch campaign to ensure that the new Agria/Nikko venture guaranteed a successful entry into Japan for Delissa. "Why then," wondered Robertson, "were sales so low after nine years of business?" Robertson picked up the telephone and called Rolf Anderen, one of Agria's founders and former chairman of the company. Although retired, Anderen still took an active interest in the business he had created. The next day, Robertson and Anderen had lunch together.

The older man listened to the new managing director talking about his responsibilities, the Swedish headquarters, foreign licensees, new products in the pipeline, and so forth. Over coffee, Robertson broached the subject of the Japanese joint venture, expressing some surprise that Delissa was so slow in taking off. Anderen nodded his understanding and lit his pipe:

Yes, it has been disappointing. I remember those early meetings before we signed up with Nikko. Our team was very frustrated with the negotiations. Bobek made several trips, and had endless meetings with the Japanese, but things still dragged on. We had so much good foreign business by the time we decided to enter Japan, I guess we thought we could just walk in wherever we wanted. Our Taiwanese franchise business had really taken off, and I think we assumed that Japan would do likewise. Then, despite the fact that we knew the Japanese were different, Wisenborn—our international marketing manager—and Bobek still believed that they were doing something wrong. They had done a very conscientious job, yet they blamed themselves for the delays. I told them to be patient and to remember that Asians have different customs and are likely to need some time before making up their minds. Our guys went to enormous pains to collect data. I remember when they returned from a second or third trip to Japan with a mass of information, media costs, distribution data, socioeconomic breakdowns, a detailed assessment of the competitive situation, positioning statements, etc. But no signed contract. [Anderen chuckled as he spoke.] Of course, Nikko finally signed, but we never were sure what they really thought about us, or what they really expected from the deal.

Robertson was listening intently, so Anderen continued:

The whole story was interesting. When you enter a market like Japan, you are on your own. If you don't speak the language, you can't find your way around. So you become totally dependent on the locals and your partner. I must say that, in this respect, the Japanese are extremely helpful. But, let's face it, the cultural gap is wide. Another fascinating aspect was the rite of passage. In Japan, as in most Asian countries, you feel you are observing a kind of ritual, their ritual. This can destabilize the solid Viking manager. Of course, they were probably thinking that we have our rituals, too. On top of that, the Nikko people were particularly reserved and, of course, few of them spoke anything but Japanese.

There was a lot of tension during those first months, partly because France's two major brands of yogurt, "Yoplait" and "Danone" were actually in the process of entering the Japanese market, confirming a fear that had been on Bobek's mind during most of the negotiation period.

Anderen tapped his pipe on the ashtray and smiled at Robertson.

If it's any consolation to you, Bjorn, the other two international brands are not doing any better than we are in Japan today.

What About These Other European Competitors?

The discussion with Anderen had been stimulating and Robertson, anxious to get to the bottom of the story, decided to speak to Peter Borg, a young Danish manager who had replaced Bergman and had been supervising Agria's business in Japan for several years. Robertson asked Borg for his opinion on why "Danone" and "Yoplait" were apparently not doing any better than Delissa in Japan. Borg replied:

I can explain how these two brands were handled in Japan, but I don't know whether this will throw any light on the matter as far as their performance is con-

cerned. First, Sodima, the French dairy firm, whose Yoplait line is sold through franchise agreements all over the world, took a similar approach to ours. Yoplait is tied up with Zennoh, the National Federation of Agricultural Cooperative Association, the equivalent of Sodima in Japan. Zennoh is huge and politically very powerful. Its total sales are double those of Nikko. Yoplait probably has about 3% of the total Japanese yogurt market, which is of course a lot less than their usual 15–20% share in foreign markets. However, Zennoh had no previous experience in marketing yogurt.

Danone took a different approach. The company signed an agreement with a Japanese partner, Ajinomoto. Their joint venture, Ajinomoto-Danone Co. Ltd., is run by a French expatriate together with several Japanese directors. A prominent French banker based in Tokyo is also on the board. As you know, Ajinomoto is the largest integrated food processor in Japan, with sales of about $3 billion. About 45% of the company's business is in amino acids, 20% in fats, and 15% in oil. Ajinomoto has a very successful joint venture with General Foods for "Maxwell House," the instant coffee. However, Ajinomoto had had no experience at all in dealing with fresh dairy products before entering this joint venture with Danone. So, for both of the Japanese partners—Ajinomoto and Zennoh, this business was completely new and was probably part of a diversification move. I heard that the Danone joint venture had a tough time at the beginning. They had to build their dairy products distribution network from scratch. By the way, I also heard from several sources that it was distribution problems that discouraged Nestlé from pursuing a plan to reintroduce its Chambourcy yogurt line in Japan. Japanese distribution costs are very high compared to those in Western countries. I suspect that the Danone-Ajinomoto joint venture probably only just managed to break even last year.

"Thanks, Peter," Robertson said. "It's a fascinating story. By the way, I hear that you just got married to a Japanese girl. Congratulations, lucky chap!"

After his discussion with Borg, Robertson returned to his Delissa-Nikko files. Delissa's early Japanese history intrigued him.

Entry Strategy

The SRT International Advertising Agency helped develop Delissa's entry into what was called the "new milk-related products" market. Agria and

Nikko had approved a substantial advertising and sales promotion budget. The agency confirmed that, as Nikko was already big in the "drinking milk" market, it was a good idea to move into the processed milk or "eating milk" field, a rapidly growing segment where added value was high.

Bjorn Robertson studied the advertising agency's pre-launch rationale which emphasized the strategy suggested for Delissa. The campaign, which had been translated from Japanese into English, proposed:

> Agria will saturate the market with the Delissa brand and establish it as distinct from competitive products. The concept "natural dairy food is good to taste" is proposed as the basic message for product planning, distribution, and advertising. Nikko needs to distinguish its products from those of early-entry dairy producers and other competitors by stressing that its yogurt is "new and natural and quite different from any other yogurts."
>
> The core target group has been defined as families with babies. Housewives have been identified as the principal purchasers. However, the product will be consumed by a wider age bracket from young children to high school students.
>
> The advertising and point-of-sale message will address housewives, particularly younger ones. In Japan, the tendency is for younger housewives to shop in convenience stores (small supermarkets), while the older women prefer traditional supermarkets. Housewives are becoming more and more insistent that all types of food be absolutely fresh, which means that Delissa should be perceived as coming directly from the manufacturer that very day. We feel that the "freshness" concept, which has been the main selling point of the whole Nikko line, will capture the consumers' interest as well as clearly differentiate Delissa from other brands. It is essential that the ads be attractive and stand out strikingly from the others, because Nikko is a newcomer in this competitive market. Delissa should be positioned as a luxurious mass communication product.

The SRT also proposed that, as Japanese housewives were becoming more diet conscious, it might be advisable to mention the dietary value of Delissa in the launch rationale. Agria preferred to stress the idea that Delissa was a Swedish product being made in Japan under license from Agria Co., Uppsala. They felt that this idea would appeal to Japanese housewives, who associated Sweden with healthy food and "sophisticated" taste. The primary messages to be conveyed would, therefore, be: "healthy products direct from the farm" and "sophisticated taste from Sweden." Although, it was agreed that being good for health and beauty could be another argument in Delissa's favor, this approach would not help differentiate Delissa from other brands, all of which project a similar image.

In order to reinforce the product's image and increase brand awareness, the SRT proposed that specific visual and verbal messages be used throughout the promotional campaign. A Swedish girl in typical folk costume would be shown with a dairy farm in the background. In the words of the agency, "We feel that using this scene as an eye-catcher will successfully create a warm-hearted image of naturalness, simplicity, friendliness, and fanciful taste for the product coming from Sweden." This image would be accompanied by the text: "Refreshing nature of Delissa Swedish yogurt: it's so fresh when it's made at the farm."

Also included in the SRT proposal:

Advertising

To maximize the advertising effort with the budget available, the campaign should be run intensively over a short period of time rather than successively throughout the year. TV ads will be used as they have an immediate impact and make a strong impression through frequent repetition. The TV message will then be reinforced in the press. The budget will be comparable to the one used for launching Delissa in the United States.

Pricing

Pricing should follow the top brands (Yukijirushi, Meiji, and Morinaga) so as to reflect a high-class image, yet the price should be affordable to the housewife. The price sensitivity analysis conducted last month showed that the Delissa could be priced at 15% above competitive products.

Launch

In January 1987, Delissa's product line was presented to distributors prior to launch in Tokyo, Osaka, and Nagoya. Three different types of yogurt were selected for simultaneous launch:

- Plain (packs of 2 and 4)
- Plain with sugar (packs of 2 and 4)

- Flavored with vanilla, strawberry, and pineapple (packs of 2). (Fruit yogurt, Delissa's most successful offering at home and in other foreign markets, would be launched a year or two afterwards.)

All three types were to be sold in 120 ml cups. A major pre-launch promotional campaign was scheduled for the month before launch with strong TV, newspaper, and magazine support, as well as street shows, in-store promotions, and test trials in and outside retail stores. On March 1, 1987, Delissa was launched in Tokyo, and on May 1 in Osaka and Nagoya.

1990: Delissa After Three Years in Japan

Three years after its launch, Delissa—with 2 percent of the Japanese yogurt market—was at a fraction of target. Concerned by the product's slow progress in Japan, Agria formed a special task force to investigate Delissa's situation and to continue monitoring the Japanese market on a regular basis. The results of the team's research now lay on Robertson's desk. The task force from Uppsala included Stefan Gustafsson (responsible for marketing questions), Per Bergman (sales and distribution), and Peter Borg (who was studying the whole operation as well as training the Nikko salesforce). The team spent long periods in Tokyo carrying out regular audits of the Delissa-Nikko operations, analyzing and monitoring the Japanese market, and generating lengthy reports as they did so, most of which Robertson was in the process of studying.

Borg, eager to excel on his new assignment, sent back his first report to headquarters:

Distribution/Ordering System

I feel that the distribution of Delissa is not satisfactory and should be improved. The ordering system seems overcomplicated and slow, and may very well be the cause of serious delivery bottlenecks. Whereas stores order milk and juice by telephone, Delissa products are ordered on forms using following procedure:

Day 1 A.M.: Each salesman sent an order to his depot.

Day 1 P.M.: Each depot's orders went to the Yokohama depot.

Day 2 P.M.: The Yokohama depot transmitted the order to the factory.

Day 2 P.M.: Yogurt was produced at Nikko Milk Processing.

Day 3: Delivery to each depot.

Day 4: Delivery to stores.

Gustafsson agrees with me that the delivery procedure is too long for fresh food products, particularly as the date on the yogurt cup is so important to the Japanese customer. The way we operate now, the yogurt arrives in the sales outlet two or three days after production. Ideally, the time should be shortened to only one day. We realize that, traditionally, Japanese distribution is much more complex and multilayered than in the West. In addition, Tokyo and Osaka, which are among the largest cities in the world, have no street names. So, a whole system of primary, secondary, and sometimes tertiary wholesalers is used to serve supermarkets and retailers. And, since the smaller outlets have very little storage space, wholesalers often have to visit them more than once a day.

I wonder if Nikko is seriously behind Delissa. At present, there are 80 Nikko salesmen selling Delissa, but they only seem to devote about 5 percent of their time to the brand, preferring to push other products. Although this is apparently not an uncommon situation in many countries, in Japan it is typical—as the high costs there prohibit having a separate salesforce for each line.

Borg's report continued:

Advertising

Since we launched Delissa in 1987, the advertising has not been successful. I'm wondering how well we pretested our launch campaign and follow-up. The agency seems very keen on Delissa as a product, but I wonder if our advertising messages are not too cluttered. Results of recent consumer research surveys showed only 4% unaided awareness and only 16% of interviewees had any recall at all; 55% of respondents did not know what our TV commercials were trying to say.

A survey by the Oka Market Research Bureau on advertising effectiveness indicated that we should stress the fact that Delissa tastes good...delicious. Agria's position maintains that according to the Oka survey, the consumer believes that all brands taste good, which means the message will not differentiate Delissa. Research findings pointed out that Delissa has a strong "fashionable" image. Perhaps this advantage could be stressed to differentiate Delissa from other yogurts in the next TV commercial.

Delissa in Japan: Situation in and Leading Up to 1997

In spite of all the careful pre-launch preparation, ten years after its launch in Japan, Delissa had only 3 percent of the total yogurt market in 1997. Although Agria executives knew the importance of taking a long-term view of their business in Japan, Agria's management in Sweden agreed that these results had been far below expectations.

A serious setback for Agria had been the discovery of Nikko's limited distribution network outside the major metropolitan areas. When Agria proposed to start selling Delissa in small cities, towns, and rural areas, as had been agreed in the launch plan, it turned out that Nikko's coverage was very thin in many of these regions. In the heat of the planning for the regional launch, had there been a misunderstanding on Nikko's range?

Robertson continued to leaf through Agria's survey of Japanese business, reading extracts as he turned the pages. A despondent Borg had written:

1994: The Japanese market is very tough and competition very strong. Consumers' brand loyalty seems low. But the market is large with high potential—particularly amongst the younger population—if only we could reach it. Nikko has the size and manpower to meet the challenges and to increase its penetration substantially by 1996. However, Nikko's Delissa organization needs strengthening quickly. Lack of a real marketing function in Nikko is a great handicap in a market as competitive as Japan.

Distribution is one of our most serious problems. Distribution costs are extremely high in Japan, and Delissa's are excessive (27% of sales in 1994 vs. 19% for the competition). Comparing distribution costs to production costs and to the average unit selling price to distributors of 54.86 yen, it is obvious that we cannot make money on the whole Delissa range in Japan. Clearly, these costs in Japan must be reduced while improving coverage of existing stores.

Distribution levels of about 40% are still too low, which is certainly one of the major contributing factors for Delissa's poor performance. Nikko's weak distribution network outside the metropolitan areas is causing us serious problems.

1995: Delissa's strategy in Japan is being redefined (once more). The Swedish image will be dropped from the advertising since a consumer survey has shown that some consumers believed that "fresh from the farm" meant that the yogurt was directly imported from Sweden—which certainly put its freshness into question! Ads will now show happy blond children eating yogurt...

Over time, the product line has grown significantly and a line of puddings has recently been added. Nikko asks us for new products every three months and blames their unsatisfactory results on our limited line.

By 1997, plain yogurt should represent almost half of Delissa's Japanese sales and account for about 43% of the total Japanese market. The plain segment has grown by almost 50% in the past three years. However, we feel that our real strength should be in the fruit yogurt segment, which has increased by about 25% since 1994 and should have about 23% of the market by next year. So far, Delissa's results in fruit yogurt have been disappointing. On the other hand, a new segment—yogurt with jelly—has been selling well: 1.2 million cups three months after introduction. Custard and chocolate pudding sales have been disappointing, while plain yogurt drink sales have been very good.

Robertson came across a more recent memo written by Stefan Gustafsson:

Mid-Year Results

Sales as of mid-year 1996 are below forecast, and we are unlikely to meet our objective of 55 million 120 ml cups for 1998. At the present rate of sales, we should reach just over 42 million cups by year-end.

Stores Covered

In 1997, Delissa yogurt was sold mainly in what Nielsen defined as large and super large stores. Delissa products were sold in about 71% of the total stores selling Nikko dairy products. We think that about 7,000 stores are covered in the Greater Tokyo area, but we have found that Nikko has been somewhat unreliable on retailer information.

Product Returns

The number of Delissa products returned to us is very high compared to other countries. The average return rate from April 1996 to March 1997 was 5.06% vs. almost 0% in Scandinavia and the international standard of 2–3%. The average shelf life of yogurt in Japan is fourteen days. Does the high level of returns stem from the Japanese consumer's perception of when a product is too old to buy (i.e., five–six days)? The level of return varies greatly with the type of product: "healthy mix" and fruit yogurt have the highest rate, while plain and yogurt with jelly have the lowest return rate.

Media Planning

Oka's latest results suggest that Delissa's primary target should be young people between thirteen and twenty-four and its secondary target: children. Budget limitations demand that money be spent on advertising addressed to actual consumers (children), rather than in trying to reach the purchasers (mothers) as well.

However, during our recent visit to Japan, we found that Nikko and the agency were running TV spots—that were intended for young people and children—*from 11:15 to 12:15 at night*. We pointed out that far more consumers would be reached by showing the spots earlier in the evening. With our limited budget, careful media planning is essential. Nikko probably was trying to reach both the consumer and distributor with these late-night spots. Why else would they run spots at midnight when the real target group is children? Another question is whether TV spots are really what we need.

Looking at some figures on TV advertising rates in Japan, Robertson found that the price of a 15-second spot in the Tokyo area was between 1,250,000 and 2,300,000 yen in 1997 depending on the time it was run, which seemed expensive compared to European rates ($1 = ¥121 in 1997).

Robertson continued to peruse the report prepared by Stefan Gustafsson:

Positioning

I'm seriously wondering whom we are trying to reach in Japan and with what product. The Nielsen and Oka research findings show that plain yogurt makes up the largest segment in Japan, with flavored and fruit in second and third positions. It is therefore recommended that regular advertising should concentrate on plain yogurt, with periodic spots for the second two categories. However, according to Nikko, the company makes only a marginal profit on plain yogurt, thus they feel it would be preferable to advertise fruit yogurt.

In light of this particular situation and the results of the Oka studies, we suggest that plain yogurt be advertised using the existing "brand image" commercial (building up the cow on the screen) and to develop a new commercial for fruit yogurt based on the "fashion concept." We also believe that, if plain yogurt is clearly differentiated through its advertising, sales will improve, production costs will drop, and Nikko will start making money on the product.

Last year, to help us understand where we may have gone wrong with our positioning and promotional activities, which have certainly changed rather often, we requested the Oka agency to conduct a survey using in-home personal interviews with a structured questionnaire; 394 respondents in the Keihin (Tokyo-Yokohama) metropolitan area were interviewed between April 11 and April 27, 1997. Some of the key findings are as follows:

Brand Awareness

In terms of unaided brand awareness, Meiji Bulgaria yogurt had the highest level with 27% of all respondents recalling Bulgaria first and 47% mentioning the brand without any aid. Morinaga Bifidus was in second place. These two leading brands were followed by Yoplait and Danone with 4% unaided awareness and 14% and 16% recall at any time. For Delissa, the unaided awareness was 3% and 16% for recall. In a photo-aided test, Delissa plain yogurt was recognized by 71% of all respondents with a score closer to Bulgaria. In the case of fruit yogurt, 78% recognized Delissa, which had the same level as Bulgaria. Awareness of Delissa was higher than Bifidus and Danone but lower than Yoplait. In the case of yogurt drink, 99% of all respondents were aware of Yakult Joy and 44% recognized Delissa (close to Bulgaria).

Interestingly, the brand image of Meiji Bulgaria was the highest of the plain yogurt brands in terms of all attributes except for "fashionability." At the lower end of the scale (after Bulgaria, Bifidus, and Natulait), Delissa was close to Danone and Yoplait in brand image. Delissa was considered less desirable than the top three, especially as far as the following characteristics were concerned: taste, availability in stores for daily shoppers, frequency of price discounting, reliability of manufacturer, good for health. Delissa's image was "fashionable." ["Is this good or bad?" Gustafsson had scribbled on the report. "Should this be our new platform??? We've tried everything else!"]

Advertising Awareness

In the advertising awareness test, half of all respondents reported that they had not noticed advertising for any brand of yogurt during the past six months. Of those who had, top ranking went to Bifidus with 43%, Bulgaria 41% and Delissa in third place with 36%. Danone was fifth with 28% and Yoplait sixth with 26%. Respondents noticed ads for Delissa mainly on TV (94%), followed by in-store promotion (6%), newspapers (4%), and magazines (4%); 65% of the people who noticed Delissa ads could recall something about the contents of the current ads, and 9% recalled previous ads. However, when asked to describe the message of the Delissa ads, 55% of the respondents replied that they did not know what the company was trying to say.

Consumption

77% of all respondents had consumed plain yogurt within the past month: 28% Bulgaria, 15% Bifidus, 5% Yoplait, 4% Danone, and 3% Delissa. The number of respondents who had at least tried Delissa was low (22%) vs. 66% for Bulgaria, the best scoring brand. In the plain category, Delissa was third of the brands mainly consumed by respondents. Bulgaria was number 1 and Bifidus number 2. In the fruit segment (under yogurt consumed with the past month), Delissa was in third place (5%) after Yoplait (10%) and Bulgaria (8%). Danone was in fourth place with 3%. ["So where do we go from here?" Gustafsson had scrawled across the bottom of the page.]

Robertson closed the file on Gustafsson's question.

Where Do We Go From Here?

Robertson looked around the table at the other members of his team and asked, "What happened? We still haven't reached 3 percent after ten years in Japan!" Bjorn knew that Borg, Gustafsson, and Karlsson all had different opinions as to why Delissa had performed badly, and each manager had his own ideas on what kind of action should be taken.

Gustafsson had spent months at Nikko, visiting retailers with members of the sales force, instigating new market research surveys and supervising the whole Nikko-Delissa team. Language problems had made this experience a frustrating one for Gustafsson, who had felt cut off from the rest of the Nikko staff in the office. He had been given a small desk in a huge room along with over 100 people with whom he could barely communicate. The Japanese politeness grated on him after a while and, as no one spoke more than a few words of anything but Japanese, Gustafsson had felt lonely and isolated. He had come to believe that Nikko was not committed to the development of the Delissa brand in Japan. He also felt that the joint venture's market share expectations had been absurd and was convinced the franchise misrepresented the situation to Agria. He felt that Nikko was using the Delissa brand name as a public relations gimmick to build itself an international image. When he spoke, Gustafsson's tone was almost aggressive:

I don't know what to think, Bjorn. I know I don't understand our Japanese friends and I was never quite sure that I trusted them, either. They had a disconcerting way of taking control right from the start. It's that extreme politeness. You can't argue with them, and then suddenly they're in command. I remember when the Nikko managers visited us here in Sweden . . . a busload of them smiling and bowing their way around the plant, and we were bowing and smiling back. This is how they get their way and this is why we had such mediocre results in Japan. Agria never controlled the business. Our distribution set-up is a perfect example. We could never really know what was going on out there because language problems forced us to count on them. The same with our positioning and our advertising, "We're selling taste; no, we're selling health; no, we're selling fashion—to babies, to grandmas, to mothers." We thought we were in control but we weren't, and half the time we were doing the opposite of what we really wanted.

Bjorn, the Japanese will kill Delissa once they've mastered the Swedish technology. Then, they'll develop their own brand. Get out of the joint venture agreement with Nikko, Bjorn. I'd say, get out of Japan altogether.

Robertson next turned his attention toward Borg, who had a different view of the problem. He felt that the Nikko people, trained to sell the drinking milk line, lacked specific knowledge about the eating milk or yogurt business. Borg—who had also taken over sales training in Japan after replacing Bergman—had made several trips a year to train the Nikko people both in marketing the Delissa brand, and in improving distribution and sales. He had also trained a marketing manager. Borg had worked closely with the Japanese at the Tokyo headquarters.

Borg said, "I understand how Stefan feels . . . frustrated and let down, but have we given these people enough time?"

"Enough time!" said Gustafsson, laughing. "We've been there for over ten years and, if you look at our target, we have failed miserably. My question is 'have they given us enough support?'" Turning to Gustafsson, Borg continued:

I know how you feel, Stefan, but is ten years that long? When the Japanese go into business abroad, they stay there until they get a hold on the market, however long it takes. They persevere. They seem to do things at their own speed and so much more calmly than we do. I agree on the question of autonomy. It's their very lack of Western aggressiveness that enables them to get the upper hand. Their apparent humility is disarming. But, Bjorn, should we really leave the joint venture now? When I first went to Japan and found fault with everything we were doing, I blamed the whole thing on Nikko. After nearly six years of visits, I think I have learned something. We cannot approach these people on our terms or judge them as we would judge ourselves. We cannot understand them any more than they can understand us. To me, the whole point is not to even try and understand them. We have to accept them and then to trust. If we can't, then perhaps we should leave. But, Bjorn, I don't think we should give up the Japanese market so easily. As Stefan says, they can be excruciatingly polite. I wonder—beneath that politeness—what they think of us.

Lars Karlsson, the product manager, had been looking after the Japanese market only a short time, having been recruited by Agria from Procter & Gamble 18 months earlier.

Bjorn, for me, perhaps the most serious defect in our Japanese operation has been the poor communication between the partners and a mass of conflicting data. I came into the project late and was amazed at the quantity of research and reporting that had taken place over the last ten years by everyone concerned. Many of the reports I saw were contradictory and confusing. As well, the frequent turnover of managers responsible for Japan has interrupted the continuity of the project. And, after all the re-search we did, has anyone really used the findings constructively? How much is our fault? And another thing, have we been putting enough resources into Japan?

There are so many paradoxes. The Japanese seem to be so keen on the idea of having things Western, yet the successful yogurts in Japan have been the ones with that distinctive Japanese flavor. Have we disregarded what this means? Agria people believe that we have a superior product and that the type of yogurt made by our Japanese competitors does not really taste so good. How can this be true when we look at the market shares of the top Japanese producers? It obviously tastes good to the Japanese. Can we really change their preferences? Or should we perhaps look at our flavor?

It's interesting. Yoplait/Zennoh and Ajinomoto/Danone's joint ventures could be encountering similar problems to ours. Neither has more than 3% of the Japanese yogurt market and they have the same flavor that we do.

Robertson listened to the views and arguments of his team with interest. Soon, he would have to make a decision. Almost ten years after launching Delissa with Nikko, should Agria cancel its contract and find another distributor? Or should the company renew the arrangement with Nikko and continue trying to gain market share? Or should Agria admit defeat and withdraw from Japan completely? Or was it, in fact, defeat at all? Robertson was glad that he had gathered his team together to discuss Delissa's future; their thoughts had given him new insights on the Japanese venture.

Case 6 *Make Yourself Heard: Ericsson's Global Brand Campaign*

In February 1998, Ericsson launched a major global communication campaign for its brand of mobile phones. This was the first time a leading telecommunication company had launched a brand campaign on such a scale. Inspired by "the simple fact that personal contact is the most important and powerful element in mobile communication," the management of Ericsson's mobile phone and terminals division had decided to launch the massive advertising despite reservations expressed by others that the focus on brand building could take resources and attention away from the increasing number of new products

Ericsson was bringing into the mobile phone market. But in the words of Jan Ahrenbring, vice president of marketing communications:

The brand campaign is about Ericsson values, not just products. The brand platform is meant to convey a clear message about Ericsson's belief in the values of self-expression and ease of communication in relating to one another.

Company Background

Ericsson is a leading supplier of equipment and services for the telecommunications industry. The company produces advanced systems and products for wired and mobile telecommunications in both public and private networks, sold to customers in more than 130 countries.

In 1997 Ericsson had 100,774 employees and 168 billion Swedish krona (SKr) in sales.[1] Close to 90 percent of its turnover was generated out-

[1]In 1998: U.S. $1=SKr7.9

side of Sweden, where it was founded more than 120 years ago.

Since early 1997 Ericsson's vast operations in virtually the entire telecommunications field had been organized into three business areas:

Radio Systems. Mobile voice and data communication systems. 1997 sales: SKr78 billion.

Infocom Systems. Multimedia communications solutions for transmission of voice, data and images to network operators, service providers, and enterprises. 1997 sales: SKr48 billion.

Mobile Phones and Terminals. End-user mobile phones and terminals, such as pagers. 1997 sales: SKr42 billion.

(Refer to **Exhibit 1** for a partial organization of Ericsson.)

In 1996 a large strategy study was completed. Entitled "2005: Entering the 21st Century," it constituted the basis for Ericsson's future strategy:

Ericsson's mission is to understand our customers' opportunities and needs and to provide communications solutions better than any competitor. In doing this, Ericsson can offer its shareholders a competitive return on their investments.

In recent years Ericsson's R&D budget exceeded 20 percent of sales. More than 18,000 employees in 23 countries were active in research and development. The management estimated that with the fast pace of technological development, its entire product portfolio would be completely renewed within two years.

In 1997 Ericsson's mobile phone *systems* were estimated to have served 54 million subscribers in 92 countries. With 40 percent of the world market for such systems sold to network operators, the company was the leader in this area.

Ericsson entered the market for hand-held mobile *phones* only in 1987. This was the first time the company marketed its products to consumers. The 1997 reorganization of Ericsson, which made mobile phones a separate division, was motivated by a recognition that, as an end-user market, mobile phones had their own "different business logic." The market share for Ericsson's mobile phones had strengthened recently compared with its two global rivals—Nokia and Motorola. (Refer to market share data in **Exhibit 2.**)

Exhibit 1 *Partial Organization Chart, Ericsson Group and Mobile Phones and Terminals*

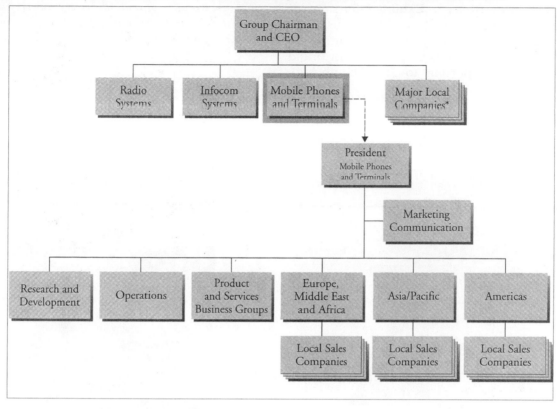

*Large local companies reported directly to group CEO
Source: Company Records

Exhibit 2 *Mobile Phones: Global Market Shares*

	1995	1996	1997
Nokia	23%	21%	21%
Motorola	31%	26%	22%
Ericsson	11%	12%	16%
All others* (Sony, Philips, Panasonic, etc.)	35%	41%	41%
Total	**100%**	**100%**	**100%**

*No single brand held a global share higher than 7%
Source: Company Records

Past Advertising

Ericsson's advertising had been limited before it entered the mobile phone business. As a company targeting a few large telecommunication customers, typically large PTT organizations or business organizations, the management saw little need for advertising. Even after the introduction of its first mobile phone, the company abstained from heavy advertising. In the words of a senior mobile phone manager:

> *In a hot market for mobile phones we sold whatever we produced, and the assumption at the time was simply that if we made good products, we didn't need advertising.*

Most early mobile phone ads were initiated by Ericsson's local sales companies around the world. In each ad, a phone product was introduced under a communication strategy that was decided by Ericsson's country management.

In 1995 Ericsson successfully implemented its first pan-European advertising campaign for a new phone line, GH337. Under headlines all starting with "It's about . . . ," the ads introduced the new product's features. (Refer to **Exhibit 3** for samples of press advertising.)

Reflecting on the first pan-regional campaign, Goran Andersson, the marketing director for brand communications (reporting to Jan Ahrenbring), recalled:

The local management were not used to supporting such an initiative and, naturally, they were not very happy with the idea at the beginning. But that campaign showed us all that together we can do very useful things.

Following the reorganization of the mobile phone into a separate division, the management embarked

Exhibit 3 *Pan-European Press Advertising 1995*

on its first global communication initiative. In 1997 Ericsson entered into an agreement with United Artists Pictures to place its mobile phones in the James Bond movie *Tomorrow Never Dies*. The division's management saw the product placement as an opportunity to show that "Ericsson is the leading technological and style innovator . . . and to demonstrate its phones as part of everyday life." For a period of twelve weeks the company used the James Bond film theme for tie-in tactical ads for new products around the world. (Refer to **Exhibit 4** for a copy of local James Bond advertising in Austria.)

It was estimated that in 1997 close to SKr2 billion was spent advertising Ericsson mobile phones worldwide. Of this total, 75 percent was spent by local organizations on product campaigns. The remainder was accounted for by pan-European or global product ads which appeared on such media as CNN, in-flight and business magazines.

Brand Building

The division management at mobile phone and terminals had closely monitored the forces that were fast changing the global mobile phone business. In the late 1990s the market was growing faster than ever, but becoming increasingly competitive. While in early 1997 there were 137 million mobile phone subscribers worldwide, this number was expected to grow to 590 million by 2002. The growth was expected to be fastest in Asia-Pacific, followed by Latin America, Europe, and North America. Meanwhile, there were an estimated twenty producers of mobile phones, a number that was expected to grow significantly in the near future.

Management had come to believe that future leadership in the mobile phone business was the privilege of those few companies that could build strong brands with the end-users. For division management the need for brands with differentiated consumer value was justified for a number of reasons:

1. Product differences among manufacturers were beginning to narrow down. Differentiation purely based on technology and features was becoming more difficult.

2. New products were witnessing ever-shrinking life cycles. While a new Ericsson mobile phone introduced in 1992 was in the market for three years before being replaced by more advanced, and lower cost, models, the recent launches were expected to have life cycles of twelve to eighteen months. A prolifera-

Exhibit 4 *James Bond Tie-In Advertising: Austria 1997*

tion of short-cycle models made product-specific communication expensive and possibly not effective.

3. The new generation of end-users was looking for different features in a phone than those who had entered the market early on. While the early adopters had been primarily business users who had looked for advanced features and small size, future growth was expected to come from nonbusiness consumers who looked for different values in a mobile phone.

Furthermore, the management believed that in its competitive market, Ericsson could enjoy its traditional price premium (ranging for some models from 5 percent up to 30 percent over Nokia and Motorola) only if its reputation for technological leadership could be backed up with a strong brand. Goran Andersson commented:

While the network operators have tried to commoditize mobile phones by nearly giving them away to attract subscribers, we want the consumer to ask not just for a phone, but Ericsson's mobile phone—even if it costs more. Like the business buyers before them, we like the newcomers to the market to think of our products as something special, worth a premium.

While local market conditions differed widely, it was estimated that close to 60% of all mobile phones sold around the world was brought directly by consumers through a retail outlet. The rest was sold by network operators through their own promotional schemes. The share of retail sales was expected to grow.

Market Studies

In 1997 mobile phone division management commissioned a couple of studies the conclusions of which reinforced their own analysis of the trends in the mobile phone market, and the growing importance of brands in consumer choice. The first study, entitled "Take Five," was a global segmentation effort aimed at better understanding the profiles of the mobile phone consumer. Researched in 24 countries in Europe, the Americas, and Asia, the study concluded that lifestyle and consumer values were better predictors of consumer behavior than traditional demographic factors. The study identified five global consumer segments, each with a different profile:

- *Pioneers.* Active individualists and explorers. Interested in and knowledgeable about technology. Motivated by innovation, they are impulsive

buyers, attracted by strong brands and will pay for quality. Their loyalty is to technology, not brands.

- *Achievers.* Hard-working, competitive individualists. Willing to take risks, they are motivated by productivity, comfort, success, and advance technology that is also useful, time-saving, and visible. Care about appearance, but have limited brand loyalty.

- *Materialists.* Status seekers, they are attracted by well-known brands. Main motivations are recognition, status, and sense of belonging. They want trendy products and are attracted to known brands.

- *Sociables.* Convivial and community-oriented, they are highly rational, well-informed and buy products that are easy to use and attractive. They are loyal to brands.

- *Traditionalists.* Attracted to social harmony rather than change, they are attracted to established products with basic features that offer ease and reliability. Low prices and well-known brands are important to them. They tend to be brand loyal.

The study proposed that the five segments are measurable by size, penetration, and inclination to purchase. While in the early stages of market development in each country the pioneers were by far the largest group of mobile phone buyers, over time other segments entered the market and grew in both absolute and relative terms. The management believed that the global segmentation had the capacity of guiding action along a wide range of activities, from strategic planning and product development to brand marketing and sales. Future products were to be conceived, designed, and marketed with the values of different segments in mind.

The second international study, done in parallel with the first, was aimed at assessing Ericsson's current brand perceptions and defining directions for the future. The corporate "soul searching," as some members of the management labeled the study, revealed that Ericsson was perceived differently in different countries and by different segments. Nevertheless, the brand was commonly perceived as "cold, distant, conservative, and technology oriented." The study also revealed that the brand awareness and recognition was low in most markets, especially among the growing numbers of nonbusiness customers. For example, in the United Kingdom, which was typical of the more developed markets, spontaneous awareness among mobile phone users, and those who might purchase in the next twelve months, was 36 percent. This figure was at par with Motorola, but significantly below Nokia at 45 percent. In the United States, on the other hand, Ericsson's brand awareness was nil.

Among the second study's final conclusions, partly aimed at educating the management regarding the need for brand building, were the following statements:

1. For many people working in fast-moving technological fields at Ericsson, branding may be a concept which is difficult to accept. They like things to be concrete, technologically different; branding, though, is a product of the "mind and heart." But it would be a mistake to believe that branding is unimportant because good brands outlive any passing technological breakthrough.

2. The ultimate goal in branding is to cement a relationship with our consumers. Capturing a share of his mind . . . his imagination . . . his emotions . . . . It will generate sentiments like "The Ericsson mobile phone brand really understands what I am about—my hopes, my dreams." By creating a strong emotional and psychological bond, the Ericsson brand will give the consumers a reason to buy beyond price, features, or rebates.

3. Ericsson must work on two fronts simultaneously: Build a strong brand based on a consistent brand platform and pursue its traditional product innovation, which can quickly meet the ever-changing needs of consumers.

The study proposed a *brand platform* that was "not about cold technology, but about human contact . . . the contact that comes through human conversation, through people talking and listening." It defined Ericsson's *brand ambition* as "to be recognized as the brand that makes personal contact the most important element in mobile telecommunication."

Competition

The growing mobile phone market was dominated by three players: Nokia, Motorola and Ericsson. Others with well-recognized brand names, such as Sony and Philips, were also present but held smaller market shares. Nokia was known for a constant stream of advanced new products. Its latest model, Nokia 9000 Communicator, combined voice, fax, e-mail and Internet functionality in a device that retailed at around $1000. Nokia's international

advertising, using the slogan "Connecting People," had stressed these advanced features. Motorola, a leader in the field, had lost market share for lack of new models and poor marketing. After a recent reorganization, Motorola seemed to be fighting back. Its newest product, StarTAC, weighing 95 grams and selling at approximately $700, was the world's smallest phone, a claim stressed in the company's recent advertising. Before StarTAC, Ericsson's GH337, which sold to consumers for less than $200, had held the title of the world's smallest mobile phone.

Mobile phone prices had generally declined in recent years. In the United States, for example, the average consumer prices had dropped from $182 to $111 since 1994.

Global Brand Campaign

In 1996, with a view to launching a global brand campaign, the mobile phone and terminals division hired Young & Rubicam, an advertising agency with an extensive international network. To maintain a degree of consistency in communication, local Ericsson organizations, long-accustomed to working with their own choice of agencies, were now required to work exclusively with Young & Rubicam.

In discussions that followed their appointment, the ad agency proposed two alternative platforms for a global brand campaign. Both platforms were seen by the agency as having the potential of fulfilling the brand ambition set out in the earlier study. The first proposal revolved around the slogan: "One Person, One Voice," but it was rejected for a number of reasons, including its political overtones, which limited its use in some countries.

The second platform was captured in the slogan: "Make yourself heard." The agency and the management both believed that this platform was true to the goal of projecting Ericsson as a human and compassionate company, thus setting it apart from all the other feature-oriented mobile phone brands. In the words of Ericsson's group chairman, Lars Ranqvist, "It is our belief that communication is between people—the rest is technology." The management also believed that the platform empowered people to communicate what is on their minds, and showed respect for individuals and what they had to say.

For press advertising the agency proposed a gallery of faces and a range of situations demon-

Exhibit 5 *Global Brand Campaign Billboard Advertising 1998*

strating shared thoughts, experiences, and ideas that would capture the spirit of communication between people around the world. The pictures were to be of ordinary people in everyday situations. Each ad would carry a statement in smaller print at the bottom giving Ericsson's credentials, including the fact that the company's products were used in "40 percent of all mobile communications around the world."[2] For TV, distinctive white-on-black TV commercials would feature a wordplay that would bring "Make yourself heard" to life. (Refer to **Exhibits 5 and 6** for samples of campaign billboards and TV commercial storyboards.[3])

Unlike all previous Ericsson campaigns, the proposed ads did not show any mobile phone products. This unusual omission was thought to be the right approach, and for good reasons. First, the agency wanted to deflect attention away from specific products and their features towards the umbrella brand. Second, different models were being sold in different parts of the world, thereby limiting what could be shown in a standardized global campaign. Third, both the management and the agency wanted to leave the door open for the future use of Ericsson brand on nonphone products or services. Finally, in the words of Jan Hedquist, Young & Rubicam account executive, "The inclusion of a product would destroy the sense of intimacy we are trying to establish with the consumer. We would be seen as hawking something."

To ensure that the company was betting on the right campaign, "Make yourself heard" and its accompanying visual communication were pretested in nineteen countries, representing 85 percent of total mobile phone sales. The key findings were:

---

[2]The full body copy of press ads read: *"Ericsson has been helping people share their thoughts for over 120 years. Today, Ericsson equipment is used in 40% of all mobile phone communications around the world. By mobile phone, data, pager or cordless phone—Ericsson gives you the power to be heard. Wherever you are, whenever you want."*

[3]In some markets, such as Sweden and the United Kingdom, the slogan "Make yourself heard" was to appear in English. In other markets it would be translated into the local language. The copy was in local language.

Exhibit 6 *Global Brand Campaign TV Commercial Storyboards 1998*

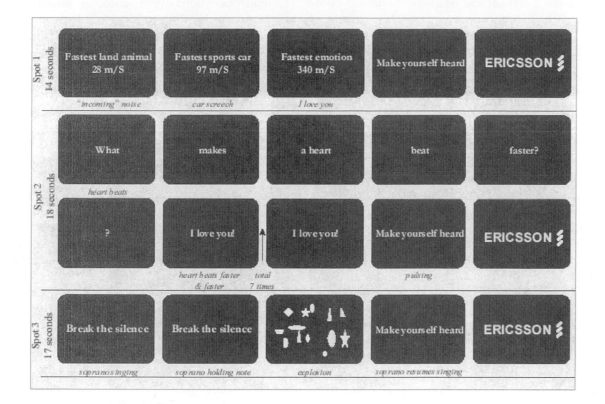

- Ads generated unusually consistent reactions across countries. The slogan "grew" on people, showing its long-term potential.

- The slogan was found to have a universal appeal. It was seen to be intelligent.

- Consumers found Ericsson as the brand that "will help you say what you need/want to say"; "cuts distance, mentally and physically, between people"; "knows about and is interested in people"; and "supports a global community."

The research agency conducting the pretest found the outcome so encouraging that it reported the following: "These are the most positive and consistent results we have seen in advertising research."

Early in 1998 a decision was made by the top management of the mobile phones and terminals to launch the proposed global brand campaign, starting in Europe. The Americas and Asia-Pacific markets were to follow later in the year. The budget for the first leg of the campaign was not publicly announced, but it was estimated to be in the SKr250–300 million range. Of this expenditure, 20 percent was to be financed by the head office, and the rest by the regions (25 percent) and local markets (55 percent). The media spread was different in different markets, but generally 70 percent was targeted for press, and the rest for TV and outdoors.

To assess the campaign's results, tracking studies measuring consumer awareness and brand image for Ericsson and its rivals were to be conducted weekly in twenty countries.

Future Decisions

Barely a few weeks after its launch in mid-February 1998, the "Make yourself heard" campaign was generating reactions and raising new issues. Some observers were wondering if the company was putting its resources in the right place. A commentary in the U.K.-based *Marketing Weekly* called the global campaign a "courageous" move, but wondered if it "detracts from product advertising and, even more pertinently, from sales."[4]

[4]O'Sullivan, Tom. "Ericsson strives to make itself heard." *Marketing Week*, February 5, 1998.

Within the organization the campaign was raising other issues. One was whether the brand campaign should be coordinated with the product-oriented advertising sponsored by the regions and local operations. Goran Andersson explained:

As a brand campaign "Make yourself heard" isn't designed for any particular product or segment. It is about Ericsson and its values as a brand. On the other hand, more targeted product and segment ads are currently being run by the regional and local sales operations. The questions are whether or not the brand and the product campaigns should be coordinated and, if so, how.

Exhibit 7 shows a copy of a recent product advertising run by the European region for Ericsson's new GH688 model. Targeted at a segment the earlier research had identified as "Achievers," the ad emphasized the product's features and carried the tag line "Made for business. Good for life." Product ads accounted for 80 percent of Ericsson's advertising budgeted for 1998; the rest was devoted to the brand campaign.

Andersson was aware of the fact that local and regional operations were jealously guarding their autonomy in deciding tactical product advertising. He also knew that the global campaign did not satisfy everyone in the local sales organizations. "Eighty percent of the complaints I get from the field is about why we don't show a mobile phone in these ads," he noted.

Nevertheless, Andersson believed that the next phase of Ericsson's brand communication should address the growing number of new models that were coming out of development and which were targeting specific lifestyle segments. Five such models were expected to be launched in 1998 alone. "The question is," Andersson commented, "how to connect and link your global brand campaign with hundreds of local advertising and promotions which are by their very nature tactical, product specific, and increasingly targeted at well-defined consumer segments." **Exhibit 8** shows a copy of the press ad for the launch of GF788, a product targeted at the "Sociables" segment.

Exhibit 7
European Region's Product Campaign
Press Advertising 1998

Exhibit 8
Local Product Campaign
Press Advertising 1997

Another related issue was the relationship between the mobile phone division's brand campaign and the communication strategies of other divisions. The recent publicity around the global campaign had made some members of the corporate management wonder if the message "Make yourself heard" was not equally appropriate for the other divisions of Ericsson. For Ahrenbring, vice president of marketing communication, a legitimate question was whether the brand campaign was an appropriate vehicle to promote a company dedicated to high technology.

Currently, Radio and Infocom Systems divisions were running limited press ads under different platforms. **Exhibit 9** shows a recent Radio Systems ad for a new line of base stations targeted at mobile phone network companies.

While flattered by the excitement the global brand campaign had generated in other business areas, Andersson was more concerned with the future of branding in his own division:

If "Make yourself heard" becomes a corporate brand platform, how can we in the mobile phone division communicate those values which are so intrinsic to

our way of doing business? Doesn't that mean we would be condemned back to product advertising?

Latest News

On April 21 Andersson was to meet with the three regional heads of mobile phone and terminals to discuss the future of the global campaign. The issues of brand vs. product advertising were very much on everybody's mind. Early campaign results from around Europe indicated increased awareness for the Ericsson brand among the general public: surveys also showed a trend towards positive and long lasting top-of-mind brand attributes. The first phase of the European campaign was supposed to wind down by the end of April.

Just a few days before the April meeting, Andersson came across a news item carried by the *Wall Street Journal Europe* under the banner "Motorola Launches New Image Campaign." The paper reported that Motorola was about to launch a $100 million-plus global advertising campaign, the largest in its history, to "beat back rivals and change its image from sturdy to contemporary."[5] The article explained that Motorola's new campaign, under the theme of "Wings," was based on a year-long research that showed "consumers were looking for an inspirational, uplifting, high-utility relationship with communication devices." Against a background of Mick Jagger's music, the paper reported, the voice in TV commercials reassured the viewers that "Motorola gives you wings. Wings sets you free." An account executive for Motorola's ad agency, McCann-Erickson, was quoted as saying "Motorola is known but not preferred . . . Consumers tend to say 'good quality, durable,' but there is no real affinity for who the company is, what the brand is. It lacks personality." According to the paper, Motorola was trying to correct a situation in recent years in which it had lost market shares to both Nokia and Ericsson.

Exhibit 9
Radio Systems Press Advertising 1998

This case was prepared by Professor Kamran Kashani as the basis for class discussion rather than to illustrate effective or ineffective handling of a business situation. "Make Yourself Heard: Ericcson's Global Brand Campaign" Copyright © 1998 by IMD–International Institute for Management Development, Lausanne, Switzerland. All rights reserved. Not to be used or reproduced without written permission directly from IMD, Lausanne, Switzerland.

[5]Beatty, Sally. "Motorola Launches New Image Campaign." *Wall Street Journal Europe*, April 17–18, 1998.

Credits

Page numbers are given in bold.

6 (Photo) Courtesy of Nestlé S.A.; **8** (Photo) © Erica Lansner/ Black Star Publishing/Picture-Quest; **19** (Photo) © Shepard Sherbell/CORBIS SABA; **20** (Figure 2.1) From *The Economist*, October 3, 1998. Copyright © 1998 The Economist Newspaper Ltd. All rights reserved. Reprinted with permission. Further reproduction prohibited. www.economist.com; **30** (Photo) AP/Wide World Photos; **37** (Photo) © AFP/CORBIS; **40** (World Beat 2.2) Reprinted from the April 1, 2002 issue of *Business Week* by special permission. Copyright © 2002 by The McGraw-Hill Companies, Inc.; **51** (Photo) © Craig J. Brown/ Index Stock Imagery/Picture-Quest; **52** (Table 3.1) Mushtaq Luqmani, Zahir A. Quraeshi, and Linda Delene, "Marketing in Islamic Countries: A Viewpoint," *MSU Business Topics*, Summer 1980, pp. 20-21. Reprinted with permission of the authors.; **57** (World Beat 3.1) *The Wall Street Journal Eastern Edition* by Yumiko Ono. Copyright © 2002 by Dow Jones & Co., Inc. Reproduced with permission of Dow Jones & Co., Inc. via Copyright Clearance Center.; **62** (Photo) Liesl Riddle; **63** (Figure 3.3) From *The Economist*, December 23, 1995. Copyright © 1995 The Economist Newspaper Ltd. All rights reserved. Reprinted with permission. Further reproduction prohibited. www.economist.com; **71** (Figure 3.4); **74** (Photo) Noboru Hashimoto; **89** (Photo) © Yvette Cardozo/ Words & Pictures/PictureQuest; **102** (Figure 4.1) Reprinted with the permission of The Free Press, a Division of Simon & Schuster Adult Publishing Group, from *Managing in Developing Countries: Strategic Analysis and Operations Techniques* by James E. Austin. Copyright © 1996 by James E. Austin; **104** (Photo) AP/Wide World Photos; **106** (World Beat 4.2) Reprinted from the September 17, 2001 issue of *Business Week* by special permission. Copyright © 2001 by The McGraw-Hill Companies, Inc.; **121** (Figure 5.1) From *The Economist*, November 28, 1998. Copyright © 1998 The Economist Newspaper Ltd. All rights reserved. Reprinted with permission. Further reproduction prohibited. www.economist.com; **123** (Table 5.1) World Development Indicators 2001 by World Bank. Copyright © 2001 by World Bank. Reproduced with permission of World Bank via Copyright Clearance Center.; **124** (World Beat 5.1) Copyright © 2001 *Los Angeles Times*. Reprinted by permission from the Los Angeles Times.; **124** (Photo) AP/Wide World Photos; **128** (Photo) © Sovfoto/ Eastfoto/Picture-Quest; **129** (Figure 5.3) U.S. Department of Labor, Bureau of Labor Statistics, September 2002; **132** (Photo) Courtesy Fluor Corporation; **135** (Figure 5.4) From Mushtaq Luqmani, Ghazi M. Habib, and Sami Kassem, "Marketing to LDC Governments," *International Marketing Review*, Spring 1998. Reprinted with permission.; **136** (World Beat 5.2) Reprinted from the January 14, 2002 issue of *Business Week* by special permission. Copyright © 2002 by The McGraw-Hill Companies, Inc.; **137** (Table 5.3) From Transparency International, www.transparency.org; **140** (Table 5.4) From Transparency International, www.transparency.org; **149** (Photo) © David Young-Wolff/PhotoEdit; **151** (Table 6.1) From *Fortune*, Global 500, July 22, 2002. Copyright © 2002 Time Inc. All rights reserved.; **157** (Table 6.2) Reprinted from the September 9, 2001 issue of *Business Week* by special permission. Copyright © 2001 by The

sion.; **451** (World Beat 16.2) *The Wall Street Journal Eastern Edition* by Gren Manuel. Copyright © 2001 by Dow Jones & Co., Inc. Reproduced with permission of Dow Jones & Co., Inc. via Copyright Clearance Center.; **452** (Photo) Guido Alberto Rossi/Getty Images; **460** (Photo) Jay Ullall/stockphoto.com; **464** (Table 16.1) Reprinted from *Journal of World Business*, Vol. 36, Chi-Fai Chan and Neil Bruce Holbert, "Marketing Home and Away," p.207. Copyright © 2001, with permission from Elsevier Science. **472** (Case 1) From *Portraits of Business Practices in Emerging Markets*, Volume 2, edited by Richard G. Linowes. This case is reprinted with the permission of the Institute of International Education. Any further reproduction is prohibited without the express written consent of IIE. IIE gratefully acknowledges support provided by the U.S. Agency for International Development through the Emerging Markets Development Advisors Program.; **482** (Case 2) Case written by William J. Carner. **487** (Case 3) Copyright © 2000 by Babson College, William F. Glavin Center for Global Entrepreneurial Leadership. Not to be used or reproduced without written permission.; **496** (Case 4) Copyright © 1998 by IMD – International Institute for Management Development, Lausanne, Switzerland. All rights reserved. Not to be used or reproduced without written permission directly from IMD, Lausanne, Switzerland.; **510** (Case 5) Copyright © 2002 by IMD – International Institute for Management Development, Lausanne, Switzerland. All rights reserved. Not to be used or reproduced without written permission directly from IMD, Lausanne, Switzerland.; **521** (Case 6) Copyright © 1998 by IMD – International Institute for Management Development, Lausanne, Switzerland. All rights reserved. Not to be used or reproduced without written permission directly from IMD, Lausanne, Switzerland.

Insert maps

Adapted from the *2002 World Bank Atlas*. Copyright © The International Bank for Reconstruction and Development/The World Bank. Used by permission.

Insert photos

1 AP/Wide World Photos; **2** (**2 photos**) AP/Wide World Photos; **3** (**2 photos**) AP/Wide World Photos; **4** AP/Wide World Photos; **5** AP/Wide World Photos; **6** AP/Wide World Photos; Jonathan Nourok / PhotoEdit; **7** Nicholas DeVore / Getty Images; AP/Wide World Photos; **8** AP/Wide World Photos. All flags provided by Worldatlas.com.

Company and Name Index

Subject Index